Adolescent Suicide

Adolescent Suicide
Assessment and Intervention
SECOND EDITION

Alan L. Berman, PhD
David A. Jobes, PhD
Morton M. Silverman, MD

AMERICAN PSYCHOLOGICAL ASSOCIATION
WASHINGTON, DC

Published by
American Psychological Association
750 First Street, NE
Washington, DC 20002
www.apa.org

To order   Tel: (800) 374-2721; Direct: (202) 336-5510
APA Order Department   Fax: (202) 336-5502; TDD/TTY: (202) 336-6123
P.O. Box 92984   Online: www.apa.org/books/
Washington, DC 20090-2984   E-mail: order@apa.org

In the U.K., Europe, Africa, and the Middle East, copies may be ordered from
American Psychological Association
3 Henrietta Street
Covent Garden, London
WC2E 8LU England

Typeset in Goudy by Argosy Publishing, Newton, MA

Printer: United Book Press, Inc., Baltimore, MD
Cover Designer: Berg Design, Albany, NY
Technical/Production Editor: Argosy Publishing, Newton, MA

The opinions and statements published are the responsibility of the authors, and such opinions and statements do not necessarily represent the policies of the American Psychological Association.

Library of Congress Cataloging-in-Publication Data
Berman, Alan L. (Alan Lee), 1943–
    Adolescent suicide: assessment and intervention / Alan L. Berman, David A. Jobes, Morton M. Silverman.—2nd ed.
        p. cm.
    Includes bibliographical references and index.
    ISBN 1-59147-193-1
    1. Teenagers—Suicidal behavior. 2. Suicide—Prevention. I. Jobes, David A. II. Silverman, Morton M. III. Title.

    HV6546.B46 2005
    362.28'0835—dc22

                                                                                2005006318

British Library Cataloguing-in-Publication Data
A CIP record is available from the British Library.

Printed in the United States of America
Second Edition

CONTENTS

Foreworde . . . . *vii*

Acknowledgments. . . . . *ix*

Introduction 3

I. Research and Clinical Practice 11

Chapter 1.   The Epidemiology of Adolescent Suicide 13

Chapter 2.   The Theoretical Context 43

Chapter 3.   The Empirical Context 77

Chapter 4.   Assessment 119

Chapter 5.   The Treatment of the Suicidal Adolescent 169

Chapter 6.   An Integrative–Eclectic Approach
to Treatment 207

Chapter 7.   Standards of Care and Malpractice in
Suicide Treatment 259

114859

II. Prevention and Postvention 287

Chapter 8.   Prevention 289

Chapter 9.   Survivors of Suicide and Postvention 335

Appendix A: Adolescent Suicide Resources 365

Appendix B: Recommended Readings 371

References 373

Author Index 427

Subject Index 439

About the Authors 455

FOREWORDE

I spell Foreworde with an olde-fashioned *e* to indicate that the title is a revised version of an earlier foreword.

It is not often that life gives one a clear shot at a second chance—an opportunity to improve on the first go-round and get things just right. I shall try to make clear the ways in which this book has grown in the last 13 years—time for a Bar Mitzvah—and let stand the changes, and, hopefully, maturation, in my own view of things.

The three authors of this revised volume are old friends of mine. Actually, I am the one who is old and they are midlife, in full stride, in the blush of full maturity. I see them as the Athos, Porthos, and Aramis of adolescent suicide. They are the Phi, the Beta, and the Kappa of teenage self-destruction. They have made adolescent suicide a special area in the total suicidological spectrum and have filled that sector with first-rate scholarship and accessibility. They bring zest and dedication to the American Association of Suicidology and the American Psychological Association. I am proud to be associated with them and their first-rate enterprise. There is much to be grateful for in this revision. It has the feel of a new book. A great deal of research on adolescent suicide has been published in the last decade; its quality is light years ahead of what was available to authors in the late 1980s. All that is reflected in this fresh content.

Some salutary changes can be noted. The first is the addition of Mort Silverman as the third partner, whose gifts have touched especially the prevention chapter and the treatment chapter with sensible emphasis on biological treatments that reflect the facts about the extent to which adolescents are being medicated. Other changes include a new chapter on forensic suicidology, mostly on malpractice issues relative to standards of care with adolescents; a separate chapter on postvention reflecting the need for clinical attention to survivors; an updating of the references so as to reflect the wealth of new research findings over the last decade; a number of mind-catching new case studies—always an interesting aspect in a volume of this sort; and, finally, an extensive list of national and international resources relating to adolescent suicide.

This book both falls into line and leads the parade in its emphases on the central role of the clinical practitioner in suicide prevention and on the core role of the individual patient in pain.

It is relevant to note that in the definitive assessment of the first edition in *The New England Journal of Medicine*, the reviewer wrote that [the authors] "have undertaken and masterfully accomplished the ambitious task of providing a careful, critical review of the current research on adolescent suicide [and produced] an excellent, easy-to-read compilation of everything that should be known about adolescent suicide…[providing] an outstanding and important contribution." A hard act to follow, but now we see that the first edition is actually surpassed by an even more comprehensive and brilliantly assembled second effort. It is the gold standard for its genre.

The encompassing body of contents includes sections on epidemiology, theory, research strategies, detection, treatment, postvention, national and international resources, research findings, and case studies.

This second edition is wise in a special way. It reflects the tensions within contemporary suicidology—between epidemiology and case studies, between observation and introspection, between (Windleband's and Allport's) nomothetic and idiographic, between the present decade of behavior and the forthcoming decade of the mind, between suicide as mental disease and suicide as a sociocultural reflection and a societal moral and ethical problem. It provides an all-seeing eye into self-destruction and inimical behaviors in general and relates these issues, by inference and by direction, to adolescence as an integral part of the human life process.

Everyone who owns and leans on the first edition and everyone who somehow missed using it will want to own this second edition as both a shield and a sword in relation to suicide prevention.

This book is not the last word. The issues and problems and torments of suicide will last through the 75th century, but this book is the best current book on adolescent suicide that there is—and, as an old-time suicidologist, I am enormously grateful to my three dear friends for having lent it to us.

Edwin S. Shneidman
University of California, Los Angeles

ACKNOWLEDGMENTS

We would not have undertaken a significant revision of the original text if it had not been for the ongoing inspiration and contributions from our colleagues and mentors, as well as from our patients whom we have endeavored to serve with the best of practice and science. They have taught us much about the suicidal process and how and when to intervene.

We are especially grateful to our wives and children who have supported us throughout this process and who understand well why we devoted so much time and energy to this revision: Joan, Jeff, and Greg (Alan L. Berman); Colleen, Connor, and Dillon (David A. Jobes); and Kineret, Ariana, Noah, and Ethan (Morton M. Silverman).

Adolescent Suicide

INTRODUCTION

Tom was 17, the younger of two sons of divorced parents, and a second-semester high school senior. In a matter of months, years of barely passing grades (the result of his and his mother's general lack of interest in academics) would have no more impact on Tom's life. Although not an exemplary student, Tom was an athlete of note, starring on both the school football team and wrestling squad—starring, that is, until early in the fall, when a knee injury and subsequent surgery ended his high school athletic career.

School rules prohibited him from using the available weight equipment for rehabilitating his knee and working out with his ex-teammates. With the source of his self-esteem shattered, Tom grew noticeably despondent. Over the next several months, his beer drinking escalated, and after he was caught drinking on school grounds, he was suspended for a week. Thereafter, he was prohibited from campus immediately at the end of each school day.

Friends acknowledged that Tom was depressed. To two of his buddies he talked about wanting to kill himself. One later stated that Tom spoke of "putting a gun to his head." Failing grades in two of his courses his first semester, although eliciting no observable response from Tom, surely did not help matters. He would have to complete summer school to graduate.

In February, Tom had a physical altercation with a fellow student over some relatively trivial issue. Fighting was not typical of Tom, whose size and strength tended to win over others through intimidation. Tom began to talk obsessively to his friends about some vague threat of harm and to speak of avenging some unspecified wrong. To each friend he told a different story, changing victims, dates, and circumstances. In addition, he asked at least two girls if they would miss him if he died. One girl astutely asked if he was thinking about suicide. He responded simply, "No."

But events were to show clearly that he had been. His obsession seemed to take on more urgency, and he spoke with some drama of planning retribution late in the week. When Tom rejected offers of friends to join him, they dismissed his story as just bravado. In school on Friday that week, Tom appeared agitated and "jumpy." That was the last anyone saw of him. On Friday afternoon, Tom smuggled out of his house the .22-caliber revolver his mother kept for "home protection" and went deep into the woods behind his home. His body was found early that evening by some hikers; Tom had died of a contact gunshot wound to the head. Later it was noticed that in one of his school notebooks, Tom had doodled "Friday Death Day—Happy Death Day." On another page he had drawn some rather primitive stick figures, the last in the series holding a gun to its head.

Until his death, Tom had lived, breathed, and experienced life as did any number of his cohort. He was an imperfect kid, perhaps with a fragile ego. His decompensation occurred in a relatively short period of time. His losses were profound: his consequent depression, evident to several of his friends, exacerbated his drinking, which, no doubt, in turn caused both more loss and more despair. In retrospect, Tom was too dependent on one source of self-esteem. In retrospect, the loss of his athleticism became the proximate case of his suicide; his life apparently had no other meaningful attachment. But retrospection is a gift of the future—the wisdom of hindsight. For the most part, the impact of this loss on Tom was denied or avoided by others in his life. What his friends knew and what one even questioned led not one of them to suggest that Tom seek or receive help. Neither his mother nor his coaches—the important adults in his life—encouraged him to seek help.

Tom probably colluded in keeping that attention and help at a distance. His behaviors were not direct appeals for help, so they were easy to minimize. Tragically, the legacy of that minimization, denial, and avoidance was the unnecessary and premature loss of Tom's life and the enduring pain of his survivors.

To those who did not know Tom, his death quickly translates into a mortality statistic. He becomes yet another adolescent suicide, one of roughly 2,000 (among 15- to 19-year-olds) in the United States in the year of his death, over half of whom died by the use of a firearm or explosive (National Center for Injury Prevention and Control, 2005).

In the 15 years since we began writing the first edition of this book, more than 60,000 American youth under the age of 25 have died by suicide (National Center for Injury Prevention and Control, 2005). 60,000! Almost half of these were younger than 20. Each and every one of these tragic deaths, like Tom's, leaves a wake of survivors—family, loved ones, friends, and colleagues—who must painfully bear the wounds of their loss.

As we drafted this revised introduction, ironically the last section of this book to be rewritten, there was published in a popular American magazine (Sager, 2003) a profile of a 17-year-old high school junior named Jesse Epstein from Orange County, California. The piece was dubbed "The Man of Tomorrow Goes to the Prom." In many respects, Epstein is described in the article as a typical, albeit intelligent, achieved, and striving, teenager from a loving and intact family. He glues himself to ESPN's SportsCenter, is into fantasy-league baseball with a passion, jokes around with his friends and girlfriend, instant-messaging them seemingly all day and night, leaves his clothes strewn about his bedroom floor impervious to his mother's requests to straighten up his room, and is readying himself for the ordeal of preparing for the SATs and college applications in his senior year. But one short paragraph distinguishes his life, not perhaps from others of his generation but surely from those of us born in earlier decades:

> He's known four kids who committed suicide, three in the last two years. One was his locker partner in middle school...[who]went into the garage one day and shot himself with his dad's shotgun. Every year, the mom of another suicide kid talks at an assembly. Every year she cries. (p. 145)

Whereas rates of death and illness among the young have declined over the past several decades in a context of increasingly advanced medical technology and care, it is discomforting, at the least, to witness both the high rates and the ubiquity of suicide and suicidal behaviors in today's generation of adolescents. To give but one snapshot of this, in just the last few weeks of completing this second edition and packaging it to our publisher, we received media reports of a third suicidal jump in just a few months from a library at New York University ("NYU Shaken," 2003), a Connecticut mother being successfully prosecuted for the suicide of her 12-year-old son ("Suicide," 2003), the discovery and thwarting of a planned suicide pact among nine teens in Iowa ("Iowa Cops," 2003), and an attempt in a Florida county to pass a city ordinance to prohibit a planned public-assisted suicide as part of a rock concert aimed at teens (Pinellas County Attorney's Office, personal communication, Clearwater, Florida, October 15, 2003).

Death is no doubt one of the most painful realities of life. The death of someone close leaves both a physical and emotional void that provokes profound feelings of grief, loss, and anger among those who survive. Yet for the most part, we are able to keep a relative emotional distance; we somehow find a way to mourn and continue.

Developmentally, we are most likely to first confront death through the loss of a grandparent or a pet, usually by natural causes of age or disease. Daily we are reminded by news reports of war and famine, of AIDS, or of drugs, crime, and homicide on our city streets. For most youth, however, death happens far away, or at some future time, or to others, especially those who lead lives of excessive risk. Thus in a predominantly youth-oriented culture, particularly among the youth of that culture, death is a topic easily avoided or denied. It is in this context that the death of a young person rapes our sensibilities, especially when that death is self-imposed (Berman & Carroll, 1984). It is in this context that the suicide of a young person rapes the lives of peers and loved ones.

Suicide among young people is indeed a difficult and painful reality that many, including mental health professionals, may be tempted to avoid and deny. Yet the clinical practitioner can ill afford such avoidance or denial. Some empirical data are relevant here. Surveys have determined that the average practicing psychologist who is directly involved in patient care has a 1 in 3 chance of losing a patient to suicide some time during the course of his or her professional career (Greany, 1995). Masters-level mental health professionals are 3 times more likely than those trained at the doctoral level to experience a patient suicide (McAdams & Foster, 2000). For psychiatrists, a patient suicide will be experienced by more than 1 out of 2 practicing clinicians (Chemtob, Hamada, Bauer, Kinney, & Torigoe, 1988). Other studies suggest that psychologists in training have between a 1 in 6 (Kleespies, Smith, & Becker, 1990) and a 1 in 7 (Brown, 1987) chance of losing a patient to suicide, with 40% of graduate students in clinical psychology likely experiencing either a completion or serious suicide attempt by a patient while still in training (Kleespies, Penk, & Forsyth, 1993). On a broader level, Schein (1976) has found that suicide is the most commonly encountered emergency situation for mental health professionals. Work with suicidal patients has consistently been found to be the most stressful of all clinical endeavors (Deurtch, 1984). To come full circle, Chemtob et al. (1988) report that psychologists who lose a patient to suicide experience that loss much as they would the death of a family member. And, as if this stress were not enough, one added consequence might be the threat or reality of a malpractice action brought against the clinician. Such are the grim realities of working with the suicidal patient.

In this context, it is therefore paradoxical that mental health professionals actually receive so little training in the handling of this common and difficult clinical problem. Formal and ongoing suicidology training in psychiatric residencies, clinical psychology training programs, and social work and nursing programs appears to be quite limited (Bongar & Harmatz, 1991; Dexter-Mazza & Freeman, 2003). Similar findings pertain to other professional disciplines (Feldman, 2004; Kubin, 1994; Levin, 1994, as referenced in Bongar, 2002). Survey data suggest that training in suicidology is most often expected to occur outside of graduate training programs (Peruzzi & Bongar, 1999) and through direct clinical experiences with suicidal patients, as cases arise (Berman, 1983). Ironically, data obtained from a sample of clinical training directors have shown that although the study of suicide is considered a relatively important element of clinical graduate training, formal training of *any* kind in suicidology occurred in only 35% of clinical psychology doctoral programs sampled (Bongar & Harmantz, 1989)!

Accordingly, this book represents a considered attempt to replace avoidance and denial with direct focus and thoughtful examination of current knowledge relevant to theory, research, practice, and intervention in the area of adolescent suicide. Our approach to our task has been guided by four working assumptions:

1. There exists a core body of scientific and clinical knowledge in suicidology, particularly strengthened in the last decade by increasingly sophisticated published research on youth suicide, making more reliable its findings and implications for practice. The typical clinician has neither the time nor the interest to keep abreast of developments in this field. Our professional careers (now totaling more than 75 years) have been devoted primarily to this task, to studying suicide and reviewing, summarizing, and integrating what is known to be able to translate empirical findings into usable clinical tools. In presenting the state-of-the-art in suicidology to our readers, we have relied heavily on the most recent empirical work and on well-designed and controlled research from earlier years (see Berman & Cohen-Sandler, 1982a).

2. By its very nature, clinical practice with the suicidal patient is difficult and anxiety-provoking. There are no consensually agreed-on or valid, reliable risk assessment scales or other instruments that have standardized or simplified the task of assessment. There is no agreed-on strategy for intervening in the life-and-death decision of the suicidal mind or for treating the suicidal character. Moreover, with the advent of more effective and safer antidepressants, managed care, and new federal regulations, the context for treating the suicidal adolescent has grown increasingly complex. Our task has been to present strategies for assessment, intervention, prevention, and postvention that the clinician can choose and apply according to individual style, theoretical orientation, and proclivity within this changed environment.

3. There simply is no typical suicidal adolescent. Tom's case is an example illustrating some risk factors captured by the nomothetic net, and, at the same time, it is an idiographic statement.

Every one of the approximately 4,000 15- to 24-year-olds who complete suicide in the United States annually presents a unique contribution to the group as a whole. And yet the group as a whole has some definable properties and attributes of import to us. We have much to learn from both the statistical set (and its scientific base) and the individual case (and the art of working with it). Our task has been to preserve and integrate the science and art of clinical suicidology. To humanize the science of suicidology, where possible, we have made every effort to liberally illustrate principles and findings with case examples, a number of which have been added in this new edition.

4. In the 15 years since we drafted the first edition of this book, a dozen new national nonprofit organizations dealing with suicide prevention have begun collaborative work in the United States (such as the National Council for Suicide Prevention, www.ncsp.org). At the time of this writing, almost every state in the country is either developing or implementing a suicide prevention plan, and 10 nations across our globe have similarly established national suicide prevention plans in recognition that suicide is preventable (see www.sprc.org and www.iasp.info). Embedded within the context of these developing strategies is the unprecedented activism of a community of survivors who daily are turning their losses and grief into mobilized efforts to initiate legislative policy, new programs, and funding for suicide prevention.

In recognition of these developments, we have not only significantly expanded our first edition's treatment of suicide prevention , but we have also written a standalone chapter on postvention. This prevention chapter is singularly important to today's clinician, who often is called out of the office and away from the individual patient to consult in the community on a more programmatic level and to participate in state and community suicide prevention task forces. This work has benefited appreciably from the addition of our third author, Mort Silverman, who brings a wealth of public health experience in suicide prevention to our task. The postvention chapter is particularly important for clinicians who increasingly are seeing survivors as patients and who may face being survivor themselves.

Every chapter in this volume has been thoughtfully reconsidered and dramatically altered. We have made current the epidemiologic data on youth suicide and broadened it, where possible, to include international statistics. These data fuel our understanding of demographic groups at risk and establish meaningful social correlates of suicide risk on the basis of nonclinical samples. The heart of this book, the two chapters on assessment and treatment, remain of most direct clinical import to the practitioner. These two chapters have received considerable attention in light of strategies developed and refined over the past decade. These chapters are nested in reviews of the theoretical and empirical contexts for understanding the suicidal adolescent, the latter benefiting immeasurably from the past decade's research. Last, in recognition of an increasingly litigious culture, we have written a standalone chapter on forensic suicidology, primarily to offer guidance to the clinician appropriately concerned about potential malpractice actions when dealing with at-risk youth.

Suicidology is a field of diversity with a rapidly growing knowledge base. We respect—even thrive on—the differing approaches brought to bear on the assessment and treatment of suicidal adolescents. We have tried to reflect what is current and promising in working with the suicidal adolescent while recognizing the spectrum of options open to the practitioner. At the same time, we have tried not to give short-shrift to any subject of clinical relevance; for example, where we felt a "closer look" at an issue was deserved, we have offered boxed asides for that greater depth. Although we have tried in this volume to remain free from bias, we may not have succeeded absolutely. Also, as we were aware in writing the first edition, what we have committed to paper today must be regarded in the context of a rapidly and continually developing literature in the field. It is just this dynamism that has made our study of suicidology both the motivation and reward for this effort. With this in mind, we have added as an appendix to this volume a list of (and Web sites for) current resources that clinicians might consult to keep current of the ever-evolving state of knowledge and practice.

Our charge 15 years ago from the American Psychological Association was to draft a reasonably short monograph, typical of this series of books. We hoped then that our effort toward brevity did not shortchange our effort toward clarity. With the expanded pages afforded us in the new edition, we similarly hope we have kept focus while deepening understanding and information.

NOTE

Case illustrations are based on actual patients. To maintain confidentiality, all names have been changed.

I

RESEARCH AND CLINICAL PRACTICE

1

THE EPIDEMIOLOGY OF ADOLESCENT SUICIDE

SUICIDE THIRD LEADING CAUSE OF DEATH AMONG TEENS

SUICIDE RATES AMONG 15- TO 19-YEAR-OLDS MORE THAN TRIPLE SINCE MID-CENTURY

WYOMING LEADS NATION IN SUICIDES

Statistics based on epidemiological methods have been used with great success to guide the development of clinical public health interventions and, for example, to help lower death rates from heart disease and cancer. Similar approaches based on sound epidemiological surveillance have increasingly been applied to deaths resulting from suicide, particularly youth suicides. For example, the increasing rate of youth suicide over the last part of the 20th century (c.f., Maris, Berman, & Silverman, 2000) led the U.S. Department of Health and Human Services to establish specific federal health objectives to lower the suicide rate among 15- to 24-year-olds by certain target years. Epidemiologic studies have defined our failure to meet these objectives in 1990 and 2000, leading to reestablished goals for the year 2010 (U.S. Department of Health and Human Services, 2000; see chap. 6). Epidemiological research techniques clearly represent a major force in the study and prevention of suicide, on both macro and micro levels.

A clinician reading this may wonder of what value epidemiologic data can be to the task of assessing suicide risk and treating at-risk adolescents. First and foremost, we believe that clinicians should understand the aforementioned role epidemiologic research plays in defining and highlighting risk factors. A *risk factor* is a statistically based association between some characteristic or attribute of an individual, group, or environment and an increased probability of certain diseases or disease-related phenomena or outcomes (Klerman, 1987). Epidemiologically defined risk factors are of great use as they help identify high-risk patients so that clinicians may better assess and treat these individuals.

Risk factors may be described as either fixed or variable (Kraemer et al., 1997), and as either proximal or distal (Moscicki, 1995):

- A *fixed risk factor* is one that cannot be manipulated or readily changed (e.g., a person's genetic makeup, age, race, or gender).
- A *variable risk factor* is one that changes spontaneously or through some intervention (e.g., depression treated through psychotherapy or medication). If the manipulation of a variable risk factor changes the outcome (e.g., if it reduces the likelihood of suicide), then the variable risk factor may be viewed as a *causal risk factor*.
- *Proximal risk factors* are those situational or life events that are closely related in time to the suicide (hence, they are called *proximal*) and that may precipitate or trigger suicidal behavior.
- For suicide to occur, these proximal risk factors require that a person has a predisposition or vulnerability (or a *distal risk factor*) to being suicidal, such as a mental disorder or character trait such as impulsivity.

We will discuss these risk factors more fully in chapter 3.

Epidemiologic data also can help clinicians develop an understanding of base rates of suicide for given populations so that they may better assess clients' potential suicidal behavior. For example, on the basis of epidemiologic data, a depressed male should be considered in a high-risk category. In time, we expect to develop more sophisticated profiles of high-risk subgroups identified from epidemiologic data. These in turn will guide treatment protocols targeted specifically to these high-risk groups.

Epidemiologic data also helps us to heighten awareness among members of high-risk groups and their families, to encourage closer observation, and to promote help-seeking behavior.

Headlines like those introducing this chapter—prevalent in the popular press—result from the published surveillance data of epidemiologists. *Epidemiology* is the study of disease among populations. Generally speaking, varied kinds of epidemiological investigations with different populations provide data that help determine which groups are more or less prone to (at risk for) particular diseases, disorders, and dysfunctions. Knowledge about risk and protective factors for certain populations is then used to develop public health policies and programming to prevent diseases and to promote health, especially in those populations most at risk or those most likely to develop increased risk at some future time. In the case of suicide, epidemiologists most often use information provided on death certificates to study the variations in suicide rates within and among various populations. Similarly, information on death certificates may be used to investigate a variety of demographic variables relevant to suicide, such as age, gender, and race. Epidemiologists also conduct large-scale surveys, such as the Youth Risk Behavior Survey (YRBS), and merge large data sets, such as in the National Violent Death Reporting System (NVDRS), both of which we will discuss later in this chapter. Thus, descriptive epidemiology attempts to identify and characterize the scope of the problem by determining rates, trends, and groups at higher risk.

To monitor these variables, descriptive epidemiology focuses on the prevalence and incidence of a disorder:

- *Prevalence* refers to the number of (in this case) suicides (or non-fatal suicide attempts, etc.) determined in a defined community at any point of time. For example, in 2000, there were 3,994 suicides in the United States of people under the age of 25. Of these, 1,621 (41%) were 19 years old and younger, and 300 were between the ages of 10 and 14 (National Center for Injury Prevention and Control, 2005). Prevalence allows for relative comparisons, such as where suicide ranks as a cause of death. As the headlines that introduced the chapter proclaim, in 2000, suicide ranked as the third leading cause of death among 15- to 24-year-olds in the United States (see Figure 1.1).
- *Lifetime prevalence* refers to the percentage of individuals who have ever had (or will have) a disorder; for example, about 7% of depressed males will die by suicide at some point in time (Blair-West, Cantor, Mellsop, & Eyeson-Annan, 1999), whereas the number is 4% for both genders combined (Luoma, Martin, & Pearson, 2002).
- The *incidence* or *rate* of suicide refers to the number of new cases of the disorder at a point in time as a proportion of all those in that particular class of individuals, standardized to a base of 100,000. For example, the rate of suicide in the year 2000 among 15- to 19-year-olds was 8.2 per 100,000; among 15- to 24-year-olds it was 10.4 per 100,000 (National Center for Injury Prevention and Control, 2005). Rates allow clinicians to make comparisons among subgroups (e.g., White males vs. Black males), different populations (e.g., Americans vs. Australians), and across time spans (e.g., rates among 15- to 19-year-olds in 1950 vs. in 1990).

Age Groups

Rank	<1	1-4	5-9	10-14	15-24	25-34	35-44	45-54	55-64	65+	All Ages
1	Congenital Anomalies 5,743	Unintentional Injury 1,826	Unintentional Injury 1,391	Unintentional Injury 1,588	Unintentional Injury 14,113	Unintentional Injury 11,769	Malignant Neoplasms 16,520	Malignant Neoplasms 48,034	Malignant Neoplasms 89,005	Heart Disease 593,707	Heart Disease 710,760
2	Short Gestation 4,397	Congenital Anomalies 495	Malignant Neoplasms 489	Malignant Neoplasms 525	Homicide 4,939	Suicide 4,792	Unintentional Injury 15,413	Heart Disease 35,480	Heart Disease 63,399	Malignant Neoplasms 392,366	Malignant Neoplasms 553,091
3	SIDS 2,523	Malignant Neoplasms 420	Congenital Anomalies 198	Suicide 300	Suicide 3,994	Homicide 4,164	Heart Disease 13,688	Unintentional Injury 12,275	Chronic Low Respiratory Disease	Cerebrovascular	Malignant Neoplasms 553,091
4	Maternal Pregnancy Comp. 1,404	Homicide 356	Homicide 140	Homicide 231	Malignant Neoplasms 1,713	Malignant Neoplasms 3,916	Suicide 6,562	Cerebrovascular 6,654	Cerebrovascular 9,956	Chronic Low Respiratory Disease 106,375	Chronic Low Respiratory Disease 122,009
5	Placenta Cord Membranes 1,062	Heart Disease 181	Heart Disease 106	Congenital Anomalies 201	Heart Disease 1,031	Heart Disease 2,958	HIV 5,919	Cerebrovascular 6,011	Diabetes Mellitus 9,186	Influenza & Pneumonia 58,557	Unintentional Injury 97,900
6	Respiratory Distress 999	Influenza & Pneumonia 103	Benign Neoplasms 62	Heart Disease 165	Congenital Anomalies 441	HIV 2,437	Liver Disease 3,371	Suicide 5,437	Unintentional Injury 7,505	Diabetes Mellitus 9,186	Diabetes Mellitus 69,301
7	Unintentional Injury 881	Septicemia 99	Chronic Low Respiratory Disease 48	Chronic Low Respiratory Disease 91	Cerebrovascular 199	Diabetes Mellitus 623	Homicide 3,219	Diabetes Mellitus 4,954	Liver Disease 5,774	Alzheimer's Disease 48,993	Influenza & Pneumonia 65,313
8	Bacterial Sepsis 768	Perinatal Period 79	Influenza & Pneumonia 47	Cerebrovascular 51	Chronic Low Respiratory Disease 190	Cerebrovascular 602	Cerebrovascular 2,599	HIV 4,142	Nephritis 3,100	Nephritis 3,100	Alzheimer's Disease 49,558
9	Circulatory System Disease 663	Benign Neoplasms 53	Septicemia 38	Influenza & Pneumonia 40	Influenza & Pneumonia 189	Congenital Anomalies 477	Diabetes Mellitus 1,926	Chronic Low Respiratory Disease 3,251	Suicide 2,945	Unintentional Injury 31,051	Nephritis 37,251
10	Intrauterine Hypoxia 630	Chronic Low Respiratory Disease 51	Two Field 25	Benign Neoplasms 37	HIV 179	Liver Disease 415	Influenza & Pneumonia 1,068	Viral Hepatitis 1,894	Septicemia 2,699	Septicemia 24,786	Septicemia 31,224

Figure 1.1. Ten leading causes of U.S. death by age group, 2000. From *Web-based Injury Statistics Query and Reporting System* (WISQARS™) *Fatal Injuries: Mortality Reports,* 2005, by the National Center for Injury Prevention and Control. In the public domain.

Comparative rates also allow clinicians to define parameters for case-control research. For example, in a suicide case-control research study on subpopulations with observed high rates of suicide, male suicides in Lithuania (cases) might be identified and then compared to appropriate subpopulations with relatively lower rates (matched controls), such as male suicides in Sweden, to help isolate risk factors or correlates of higher suicide risk in the Lithuanian group.

OFFICIAL STATISTICS: CONSTRAINTS AND LIMITATIONS

Whereas the epidemiological study of suicide has undoubtedly provided some of our most valuable information to date, some of the inherent constraints and limitations of the approach should be noted. Consider, for example, the constraints of the death certificate itself. The death certificate fundamentally provides the raw data for the epidemiological study of causes and manners of death. With regard to nonnatural deaths, *cause of death* refers to the mechanism that produced the death, such as "blunt force trauma," which, in turn, may be a consequence of a fall from a height or a gunshot wound. *Manner of death* is a classification of that death based on the circumstances surrounding a particular cause of death and how that death came into play, that is, by accident (e.g., a fall from a high place), suicide (e.g., a jump from a high place), or homicide (e.g., a push off a high place).

Death certificates are collated by state vital statistics offices based on medical examiner and coroner determinations. These state vital statistics offices then summarize the data they report to establish both state and national mortality trends. As a primarily legal document, the standard death certificate provides only a limited amount of mostly demographic information and simply does not account for some of the most important variables that significantly bear on a suicide, such as psychological variables or premorbid history. Attempts to modify the standard document to include additional information have been met with clear resistance. Issues as mundane as the size of file drawers have been raised to oppose the expansion of the existing form (Working Group on the Classification and Reporting of Suicide, 1984)! To change this state of affairs, pilot-testing of a prototype of the NVDRS by the Centers for Disease Control and Prevention was initiated in 2001. The NVDRS is intended to collect and link detailed information from death certificates, police investigations, coroners' reports, and so on into a useable database to help answer critical questions about suicide and homicide. If implemented on a national level (as of 2004, the NVDRS was funded in 16 states and 8 metropolitan areas), this system would help us obtain such information as the incidence of homicide-suicides and suicide pacts, which types of firearms are used in suicides and how and when they were purchased, and what proportion of youth suicides were intoxicated at the time of death. These types of questions cannot be answered by our current system of death registration, which relies on a single document, the death certificate.

In a much broader sense, the interpretive value of certain types of epidemiological research may be limited in that the validity and reliability of officially reported suicide statistics have been widely questioned and debated in the literature (Jobes, Berman, & Josselson, 1987; Mohler & Earls, 2001; O'Carroll, 1989; Pescosolido & Mendelsohn, 1986). The gist of this debate centers on whether official rates of suicide tend to underestimate the actual rates of suicide, thus calling into question results of epidemiological studies that use official reported rates.

A questionnaire survey of 195 practicing medical examiners supported reason for these doubts (Jobes & Berman, 1984). The majority (58%) of medical examiners surveyed either "agreed" or "strongly agreed" that "the actual suicide rate is probably 2 times the reported rate." Furthermore, when asked to rate the accuracy of mortality figures reported by the National Center of Health Statistics (NCHS) on a scale from 1 (*absolutely accurate*) to 100 (*absolutely inaccurate*), the medical examiners rated the accuracy at a mean of only 46.73. Moreover, a study of experienced physician medical examiners and coroners (Goodin & Hanzlick, 1997; Hanzlick & Goodin, 1997) found substantial disagreement in the manner of death classifications in 23 case scenarios, with differences noted from state to state. These studies noted the need for published guidelines and more uniform training.

It is quite possible that some underreporting does occur (see Maris et al., 2000, p. 72). For example, there are indeed cases in which a family with sufficient political influence has convinced local officials to cover up a suicide of their child for reasons such as the fear of being labeled "bad parents."

Medical examiners and coroners do not have the same level of training, education, and backgrounds and vary in these characteristics from jurisdiction to jurisdiction. In addition, they do not use standardized definitions to certify a suicidal death. Coroners, who are generally not trained in forensic investigation, might unintentionally label a suicide as an accident, for example when there is a single car motor vehicle accident or a drug overdose, by simply not doing a sufficient amount of investigation. Studies that have examined this issue suggest that (a) whereas some underreporting likely does occur, it may be counterbalanced by some overreporting (Kleck, 1988); (b) underreporting occurs more in subgroups where official rates are lower (i.e., Black individuals and women; Phillips & Ruth, 1993); and (c) overall, underreporting is probably in the range of 10% to 18% at most (Kleck, 1988; Speechley & Stavraky, 1991). Thus, we should be reasonably comfortable with the validity of reported statistics.

Yet another consideration is that there is typically a 2- to 3-year delay in the reporting of official death statistics. The lag between the actual occurrence of a death and its official reporting is a reality-based constraint that forces researchers, policymakers, suicide prevention program developers, and suicide prevention advocates to continuously use out-of-date raw data. Note, for example, that in this volume, drafted in 2003 and 2004, we are using official statistics from the year 2000, the most recent available at the time we began this second edition.

Criticisms of epidemiological data and techniques have been widely discussed in the literature and demand interpretive caution when considering the use of and reliance on these data. Nevertheless, the overwhelming strength and value of epidemiological studies of suicide clearly outweigh the various constraints and limitations inherent in this approach.

Last, we should note that the epidemiologic data reported in this chapter will cover three distinct yet overlapping groups: suicide completers, nonfatal suicide attempters, and suicide ideators. More shall be said about these groups and the suicide nomenclature that defines them later in this book.

ADOLESCENT SUICIDE STATISTICS

The suicidal behavior of adolescents over the past 50 years has generated a great deal of concern among public health officials, mental health practitioners, educators, and the public at large. Whereas concern is clearly warranted, hyperbole about an "epidemic" of youth suicide has led to some instances of reporting inaccurate "facts" about youth suicide, resulting in misperceptions and distortions. Let us therefore duly consider the empirical data.

As noted above, in 2000, there were 3,994 officially recorded suicides for young people between the ages of 15 and 24 (National Center for Health Statistics, 2002). For every 100,000 young people in this age group, there were 10.4 suicides in 2000. As noted in Figure 1.2, rates for this age group have waxed and waned throughout the last century, showing increases between 1900 and 1910, 1920 and 1930, and 1940 and 1990, and decreases between 1910 and 1920, 1930 and 1940, and 1990 and 2000. A true appreciation of the epidemiology of youth suicide must therefore take into account the historical trends of the phenomenon. A true understanding of the phenomenon of youth suicide will be guided in part by the social correlates of these observed trends.

In 1957, the adolescent (15- to 24-year-old) suicide rate was 4.0 per 100,000 (Berman & Jobes, 1991). This stands in sharp contrast to the 1977 peak rate for this age group of 13.3 (Rosenberg, Smith, Davidson, & Conn, 1987). Between 1950 and 2000, suicide rates for young people increased, whereas for people 45 years and older, rates declined. It was this striking jump (more than a tripling) in rates that led to the professional and public outcry during the 1980s to prevent adolescent suicide and thereby reverse the trend. Epidemiology begot the call for prevention!

Figure 1.3 displays fluctuations in suicide rates over the past 2 decades for 15- to 19-year-olds and 20- to 24-year-olds. As depicted, rates for the younger age cohort, although consistently lower than those for the older

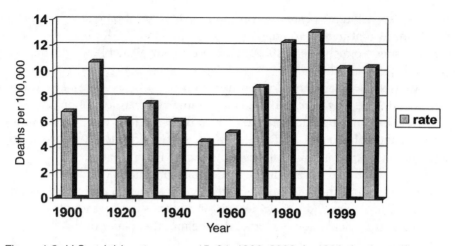

Figure 1.2. U.S. suicide rates, ages 15–24, 1900–2000. In 1900 death certificates were officially collected from only 10 states and Washington, DC. All contiguous states were in the system by 1933. Data from National Center for Health Statistics, various years of *DHHS, Mortality Statistics Branch, Annual Report.*

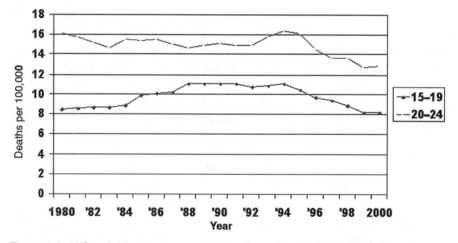

Figure 1.3. U.S. suicide rates, ages 15–19 versus 20–24, 1980–2000. Data from National Center for Health Statistics, various years of *DHHS, Mortality Statistics Branch, Annual Report.*

cohort, followed a somewhat different pattern. Rates for 15- to 19-year-olds rose from 1987 through 1991 to a level approximately 20% above that of 1980, then plateaued before beginning to decline in 1995. The 2000 rate for this age group is essentially what it was in 1980.

Rates for the 20- to 24-year-old age group followed a slightly different course. Starting in 1980 at 16.1 per 100,000, they declined slightly and held essentially steady at lower levels until 1993, when they rose again to their 1980 level, only then to decline once again to a 2000 rate (12.8/100,000) 20% below that of 1980 (National Center for Injury Prevention and Control, 2005).

Looked at another way and from a broader temporal perspective, Figure 1.4 depicts suicide rates for different age groups at 10-year markers from 1950 to 2000. As can be noted from the figure, suicide rates for adolescents in both the 15- to 19-year-old and 20- to 24-year-old cohorts were higher with each passing decade through 1990. It is only in the past decade, particularly in the last five years, that we have witnessed a different and lower pattern. We would like to believe that this is evidence of attention having been paid to adolescent suicide and the subsequent preventive efforts that have been instituted (see chap. 7).

The Study of Historical Trends

Imagine yourself sitting at a symposium on adolescent suicide called in response to media reports of an alarming increase in the incidence of youth suicide. An interdisciplinary panel of distinguished speakers has gathered to present views and explanations for the problem and suggestions for its resolution. The panel focuses on the schools and the intensely competitive pressures of the times as sources of stress. Youth suicide is noted by some panelists to be an international problem. Others question the validity and adequacy of official statistics; still others comment on the problem of journalistic sensationalism. Concerns are raised about suicide clusters, the role of suggestibility and imitation, as well as the availability of guns. Various preventive and intervention strategies are proposed, and the educational system is singled out as uniquely positioned to play a key role in prevention.

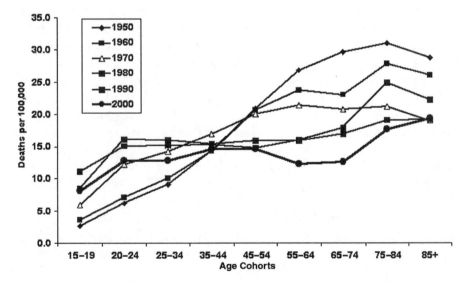

Figure 1.4. U.S. suicide rates by age, 1950–2000. Data from National Center for Health Statistics, various years of DHHS, Mortality Statistics Branch, Annual Report.

Although the themes and insights discussed at this symposium appear contemporary, what is most remarkable about this meeting is that it was held over 95 years ago! The year was 1910 and the location was Vienna, Austria. The chair of this symposium was none other than Sigmund Freud, and the distinguished panel of scholars was made up of members of the Vienna Psychoanalytic Society. This symposium on suicide was one of the last meetings of the original "Wednesday Night Group," which was presided over by Freud and held in his living room (Berman, 1986b; Friedman, 1967).

As discussed by Rosenberg et al. (1987), the early efforts at suicide surveillance among young populations took a variety of forms. For example, Bailey (1903) examined state registry statistics, whereas Miner (1922) attempted to tally over 29,000 newspaper accounts of suicide. Dublin and Bunzel (1933) took yet another approach in their study of insurance records. Data they obtained regarding the last quarter of the 19th century underscores important differences in patterns of adolescent suicide in comparison to more contemporary data.

Holinger and his colleagues (Holinger, 1979; Holinger & Offer, 1981, 1982; Holinger, Offer, & Zola, 1988) pioneered the use of population models as well as predictive models that attempted to project anticipated rates based on historical trends. Accordingly, Holinger et al. (1988) showed that increases and decreases in suicide rates were in parallel to the proportion of adolescents in the U.S. population. The reason for these trends relative to the size of the adolescent cohort is based on the theory of economic strain; that is, as a group's size increases, there is greater competition for available resources (e.g., available jobs, places in size-limited groups such as teams), and these resources do not necessarily expand parallel to the expansion of the cohort. Thus, there follows more failure experiences among the competitively disadvantaged in the cohort—those individuals concurrently being disadvantaged because they are more vulnerable for other reasons (e.g., they possess greater dysfunctionality because of mental disorders). Holinger et al.'s (1988) consequent projection anticipated a decline in observed rates until the mid-1990s, followed by an upturn in rates. However, rates continued to climb until 1994, then, as we have just noted, a 4- to 5-year decline took place. Correspondingly, and contrary to these researchers' predictions, the population of the 15- to 24-year-old cohort actually decreased slightly until 1994; between then and the year 2000, this cohort increased 6% in size. So much for prediction! Figure 1.5 displays a comparison of suicide rates by individuals at each age between 10 and 24 for the periods 1994 to 1995 and 1999 to 2000.

Among the explanatory hypotheses for these temporal changes in adolescent suicide, which we will explore in this and subsequent chapters, are the greater prevalence and earlier age of onset of mental disorders; the greater prevalence of *comorbidity* (i.e., coexisting debilitating physical or mental disorders); changes in rates of substance use and abuse and patterns of acute intoxication; the increased accessibility and availability of firearms;

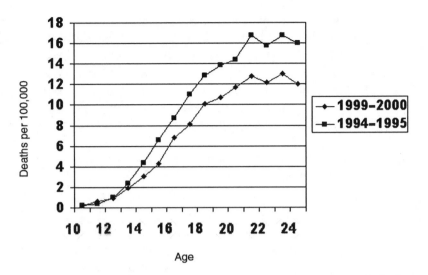

Figure 1.5. U.S. suicide rates, ages 10–24, 1994–1995 versus 1999–2000. Data from National Center for Health Statistics, various years of *DHHS, Mortality Statistics Branch, Annual Report.*

gender differences in help-seeking behavior and stress tolerance; changes in the nuclear family structure and consequent effects on children; and a greater acceptability of suicide as an option (c.f., Hawton, 1998).

Other Causes of Death

Each year the National Center for Health Statistics publishes a variety of reports related to mortality in the United States. Reports of vital health statistics include a range of demographic information as well as data concerning the leading causes of death. As shown in Figure 1.1, suicide is the third leading cause of death among adolescents ages 15 to 24 (following unintentional injury [accident] and homicide). These three forms of violent death, taken together, account for almost three fourths of all deaths in the United States of people up to the age of 25.

Demographic Data

Beyond tracking mortality trends and changes in causes of death over time, epidemiological research can provide a wealth of useful demographic information. Relevant to adolescent suicide, we will briefly consider the demographic variables of race, gender, age, geography, and socioeconomic status.

Race

Youth suicide rates in the United States have always been higher among White than among Black individuals. However, as seen in Table 1.1, the rates for Black males ages 15 to 19 have increased most dramatically, more than tripling (up 234%) in the years between 1960 and 2000. Similarly, the suicide rate for 15- to 19-year-old White males (who remain the modal race and sex group of completers) more than doubled over the same 1960 to 2000 interval. Although rates for females in this age group (see the following section on gender) are now less than one fourth those for males, both White and Black female rates remain more than 60% greater than what they were in 1960.

TABLE 1.1
U.S. Suicide Rates, Ages 15–19, by Gender and Race, 1960–2000

Year/race-gender	WM	WF	BM	BF
1960	5.9	1.6	2.9	1.1
2000	13.9	2.9	9.7	1.5
% increases	+136	+81	+234	+36

Note. Data from National Center for Health Statistics, various years of DHHS, Mortality Statistics Branch, Annual Report.

All forms of violent death in Black adolescent populations have risen sharply over the past 20 years (National Center for Injury Prevention and Control, 2005). Unfortunately, little data is available on completed suicides among other ethnic groups. Hispanic populations, for example, appear to be at significant risk for violent deaths (Centers for Disease Control, 1986), but rates of suicide are lower than for Anglos (Gould & Kramer, 2001). Similarly, Native Americans represent a subgroup at very high risk for alcoholism and violent death, especially suicide. Two thirds of decedents ages 15 to 24 among a 19-year sample of Native American suicides in three New Mexico tribes were found to have a positive blood alcohol level at time of death (May et al., 2002). Suicides among American Indians occur predominantly among the young (Middlebrook, LeMaster, Beals, Novins, & Manson, 2001). The rates for Native American and Alaska Natives between the ages of 15 and 24 have been consistently over 20 per 100,000 for all years but one since 1980 and, on average, more than twice that for all 15- to 24-year-olds during these years. However, there are great variations in rates by geography, tribe, and reservation.

Case Illustration

As reported by Berman (1979), the Duck Valley Indian Reservation, straddling the border of Idaho and Nevada, housed a population of slightly over 1,000 mixed Shoshone and Paiute Indians during the 1970s. Between January 1970 and September 30, 1978, a period of 8.75 years, there were 38 deaths among tribal members. Fifteen of these deaths (40%) were by suicide. Correspondingly, for the United States as a whole, suicides account for about 1.5% of deaths annually. Twenty-eight (74%) of Duck Valley's deaths were nonnatural.

Jurisdictionally, Duck Valley is situated in the state of Nevada. In Nevada, the death rate from alcohol and alcohol-related causes for American Indians in the 1970s was 5 times that of non-Indians. The rate of violent death (nonnatural causes) among American Indians was 2.5 times that of non-Indians. Although Duck Valley's rate of violent death was similar to that of Nevada Indians as a whole, its suicide rate was 3 times greater! Fourteen of the 15 Duck Valley suicides were alcohol-related. The median age of these Duck Valley suicides was only 23 years. All but one were males; 11 of the 15 suicides (73%) were by firearms.

In the year 1977 alone, there were 10 deaths at Duck Valley: four suicides, two accidental deaths (one of which was alcohol-related), one homicide (the only one of the decade), two natural deaths (one of which was alcohol-related), and one undetermined death (an alcoholic, schizophrenic male with a history of three prior suicide attempts).

Among the several explanatory causes given for such high rates of suicide and violent death at Duck Valley were: (a) the relative youth of the male population (on average, 5.5 years younger than other Nevada Indians); (b) high rates of alcoholism and depression; (c) the prevalence of guns (the typical household owned five firearms); (d) high unemployment (more than 80% for most of the year); (e) the isolation of the reservation; (f) the destruction of traditional tribal cultures; and (g) community norms of intolerance of individualism (including an anti-success norm), nonsupport for educational achievement, nonsupport for intra- or extra-governmental leadership, a lack of help-seeking behavior, a lack of systematic help giving (resources, intrasystem communication, and so on), noninterference in others' affairs, and cultural sanctions against the direct externalization of rage against others—although passive–aggressive behavior was normative.

Gender

The ratio of male to female suicide ages 15 to 19 in the United States in 1970 was 3:1; that is, there were three male suicides for every one female suicide (Centers for Disease Control, 1985). In 2000, this ratio increased to 4.7:1 (National Center for Injury Prevention and Control, 2005). Among 20- to 24-year-olds, the ratio of male to female suicide rates increased from 3.4:1 in 1970 to

6.6:1 in 2000. These increases are even more profound when compared to decades earlier, when the ratio was more in the range of 2:1. The increases noted are primarily the result of dramatic increases in young male suicide and only slight decreases in female suicide. Conversely, as we shall see, it appears that adolescent females more frequently attempt suicide, at estimated ratios ranging from 2:1 to 3:1 (Oregon State Health Division[1], 2000; Centers for Disease Control and Prevention, 2002c) in comparison to males.

When race and gender are examined together, gender clearly exerts a greater influence. At both age levels we have been examining, 15 to 19 and 20 to 24, both White and Black males have higher rates than females of both races. As will be noted, there are other considerable gender differences, particularly with regard to the differential use of weapons for completed and attempted suicide, as well as differences in predisposing mental disorders, including substance use, and in overall levels of functioning.

From an international perspective, male youth suicide rates exceed those of females in all countries except in selected rural and urban areas of China (see Table 1.2). Moreover, in some countries, the ratio of male to female suicide rates in this age group is as high as 10:1 (Belarus). Slovakia, Poland, Latvia, the Russian Federation, and Romania all have male to female ratios equal to or greater than that of the United States. (see Table 1.2). (All international rates for various years by gender can be found at www.who.int/mental_health/prevention/suicide.)

Reasons for the high male to female suicide ratio in the United States have been outlined and supported with empirical evidence by Maris et al. (2000). These include males having higher rates of significant suicide risk factors (e.g., alcohol abuse, access to firearms, and shame at failure) and also include males being less likely to engage in a number of protective behaviors (e.g., seeking help, being aware of warning signs, having flexible coping skills, building social support systems, and so on).

Age

Returning to Figures 1.3 and 1.5, the reader will readily note that there are distinct age differences in suicide rates between younger (ages 15–19) and older (ages 20–24) adolescents and at each and every age starting at puberty. Whereas the largest percentage increases over time have been observed in the 15- to 19-year-old age group, the actual rates are considerably higher for the 20- to 24-year-old age group. According to 2000 statistics, the rate of suicide per 100,000 was 8.2 for all 15- to 19-year-olds, whereas the rate for 20- to 24-year-olds was 12.8. In 2000, almost 60% of all suicides under the age of 25 were completed by 20- to 24-year-olds, whereas five of every six suicides completed by all people 19 years old and younger were by 15- to 19-year-olds.

---

[1]The state of Oregon has been a model in the United States for its surveillance of nonfatal suicidal behaviors and will be referenced frequently throughout this chapter.

TABLE 1.2

World Suicide Rates (Latest Year Available), Ages 15–24 (min. $N = 30$), by Gender and Male–Female Ratio

Country	Year	Male	Female	Total	M:F Ratio
Austria	2001	20.8	3.8	12.4	5.5:1
Belarus	2000	38.9	4.8	22.2	8.1:1
Czech Republic	2000	17.4	3.3	10.5	5.3:1
Denmark	1998	10.4	2.8	6.7	3.7:1
Estonia	2000	29.6	6.1	18.1	4.8:1
Finland	2000	31.1	8.1	19.9	3.8:1
France	1999	12.3	3.4	7.9	3.6:1
Germany	1999	12.7	3.0	11.2	3.2:1
Greece	1999	4.4	2.1	3.2	2.1:1
Hungary	2001	17.7	4.3	11.2	4.1:1
Ireland	1999	25.7	5.3	15.7	5.1:1
Kazakstan	1999	45.1	9.1	27.1	5.0:1
Kyrgyzstan	1999	18.5	5.0	11.8	3.7:1
Latvia	2000	30.5	4.8	17.9	6.4:1
Lithuania	2000	49.0	9.6	29.5	5.1:1
Netherlands	1999	8.5	4.4	6.5	1.9:1
Norway	1999	28.3	8.9	18.8	3.2:1
Poland	2000	19.5	3.0	11.4	6.5:1
Republic of Moldova	2000	11.4	2.5	7.0	4.6:1
Romania	2001	10.2	1.8	6.1	5.7:1
Russian Federation	2000	57.7	9.1	33.7	6.3:1
Slovakia	2000	14.1	2.0	8.2	7.1:1
Slovenia	1999	23.5	7.0	15.4	3.4:1
Spain	1999	7.2	2.1	4.7	3.4:1
Sweden	1999	14.8	6.4	10.7	2.3:1
Switzerland	1999	20.1	5.2	12.8	3.9:1
Tajikistan	1999	3.9	2.4	3.1	1.6:1
Ukraine	2000	29.3	5.4	17.5	5.4:1
United Kingdom of Great Britain and Northern Ireland	1999	10.6	2.5	6.7	4.2:1
Canada	1998	21.6	5.1	13.5	4.2:1
USA	1999	17.2	3.1	10.3	5.5:1
Australia	1999	22.1	5.3	13.9	4.2:1
China (selected rural areas)	1999	8.0	12.9	10.4	0.6:1
China (selected urban areas)	1999	3.0	4.1	3.5	0.7:1
China (Hong Kong SAR)	1999	9.0	6.8	7.9	1.3:1
Japan	1999	16.5	7.3	12.0	2.3:1
New Zealand	2000	29.9	5.8	18.1	5.2:1
Republic of Korea	2000	10.2	7.0	8.7	1.5:1
Singapore	2000	6.5	7.7	7.1	0.8:1

Note. From the World Health Organization. In the public domain.

When age and race are examined together, age is a stronger predictor of suicide rates than is race. Between 1983 and 2000, in the United States, rates for older Black males ages 20 to 24 consistently exceeded those for younger White males ages 15 to 19. When age and gender are examined together, gender again appears to have a greater influence on suicide rates than does age (e.g., the rate for 13-year-old males is higher than the rate for 14-year-old females).

Although the increases in youth suicide have been dramatic, it may be surprising to know that other age groups historically have always had much higher rates of suicide. In 2000, those 65 years old and older had the highest rates of suicide in the United States, with an aggregate rate of 15.3 per 100,000. Those 65 years old and older accounted for 18.1% of all suicides in 2000, although they comprised only 12.6% of the population. Concurrently, those 24 years old and younger accounted for 13.6% of all suicides while comprising an equal proportion (13.9%) of the population (McIntosh, 2003).

In epidemiological analyses, relative changes in age-specific suicide rates over time are called *age effects*. Age effects may be caused by changes in physiology, role, or societal age discrimination (Wasserman, 1987). *Period effects* are changes in rates of suicide associated with historical time periods, such as differences in the social environment (economic depression, war, and so on) that exert influence on all age groups. Included as period effects are documented changes in measurement (i.e., changes in the manner in which suicide is certified by coroners and medical examiners). However, it appears that there would be no appreciable change in suicide rates if deaths that remained undetermined in intent were, actually, determined to be suicides. In 2000, for example, were all undetermined deaths among 15- to 24-year-olds in the United States actually determined to be intentional (a highly unlikely outcome), the total number of documented suicides would only increase by 9%.

Geography, Geopolitics, and Culture

Geographic and related sociocultural influences have been widely studied and linked to various trends in international suicide rates. In terms of youth suicide, it appears that observed increases, and even the recent declines, in the U.S. rates are not a uniquely American phenomenon; rather, there are similar increases (and decreases) in many Western European countries and similar historical trends (Diekstra, 1996). Similar patterns have been observed in other parts of the world as well (Lester, 1988).

During the period in which youth suicide rates were increasing in the United States, similar findings were noted internationally. Trends in international rates for youth suicide between 1970 and 1980 for nations with populations of at least one million that also had at least 100 overall suicides were studied by Lester (1988). He reported that suicide rates for 15- to 24-year-old youths had increased in 23 of 29 countries that met the selection criteria. However, these increases varied widely among nations, and some increases were limited to one gender. Hawton (1998) also reported increased rates of suicide among the young in several European countries, Australia, and New Zealand. Similarly, Cantor and Baume (1998) provided data documenting increases in suicides among males ages 15 to 24 between 1960 and 1992 for England and Wales, Ireland and Northern Ireland, Spain, Austria, Belgium, and France, with practically no parallel increase noted in rates of female suicide in these countries. Diekstra (1989) reported increases in 15- to 19-year-old suicides in 9 of 13 countries between 1970 and 1985, with the most dramatic increase (800%!) occurring in Ireland during this period. Noted by Diekstra were correlated social changes in Ireland in rates of illegitimacy, alcohol dependency, unemployment, crime, and divorce, suggesting that youth suicide may be associated with economic instability, a breakdown of family structure, interpersonal violence, and substance abuse. We will return to these themes in chapter 3 when we discuss research-based risk factors.

Differences in surveillance systems, case ascertainment methods, tracking procedures, and the quality of the death certification and registration (record-keeping) systems make international comparisons difficult (e.g., refer to Robins & Kulbok, 1988; Sainsbury & Jenkins, 1982). Table 1.2 compares total suicide rates (latest available years) and both male and female youth (15–24) suicide rates for more than 40 countries around the world, including the United States. Most notable are the observed rates among the various countries formerly affiliated with the USSR (Russian Federation, Lithuania, Kazakstan, and Belarus) all of which have equally high rates for males.

Figure 1.6 depicts state differences in youth suicide rates for 15- to 19-year-olds in the United States from 1994 to 1998. As shown, youth suicide rates are, and have been consistently, highest in the Western states and Alaska and lowest in the Northeastern states (Gould & Kramer, 2001). For example, the 1991–2000 suicide rates for 15- to 19-year-olds and 20- to 24-year-olds in Alaska were 39.6 and 50.7 per 100,000, respectively. These rates were some 8 and 6 times greater than the respective rates over the same time period in New Jersey (4.64/ and 8.81/100,000).

Seiden (1983) first noted that the western region of the United States had the highest rates of youth suicide. He postulated that these states had in common low population densities, suggesting that "undercrowding," a geographical

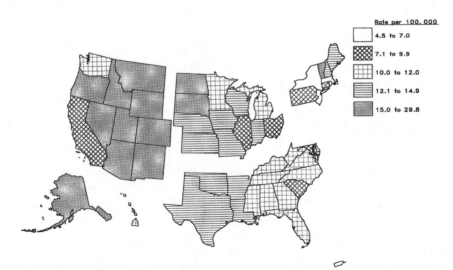

Rate per 100,000

☐	4.5 to 7.0
▨	7.1 to 9.9
▦	10.0 to 12.0
▥	12.1 to 14.9
▦	15.0 to 29.8

Figure 1.6. U.S. suicide rates, ages 15–19, 1994–1998. Data from National Center for Health Statistics, various years of *DHHS, Mortality Statistics Branch, Annual Report.*

isolation leading to social isolation, may be causally related to these high rates. When examined with more recent data, the 10 states with the highest suicide rates among 15- to 24-year-olds during the 1991 to 1998 period have a mean population density of only 12 people per square mile (www.demographia.com, 2004). In addition, these 10 states are located west of the Mississippi; they include the eight intermountain states and both Dakotas. In contrast, the 10 states with the lowest suicide rates during these years (all still east of the Mississippi) had a mean population density of 1,508 people per square mile (see Table 1.3). Left noncontrolled in Seiden's study, however, were potential confounding variables related to both suicide and low population density, such as alcohol consumption and binge drinking, population differences in gender ratio, and the proportion of the population made up of American Indians. Additionally, these data may again represent false differences caused by variability in data collection and medical-legal certification of suicide (see Nelson, Farberow, & MacKinnon, 1978). In line with this, suicide rates typically are consistently higher in rural areas than in urban areas across the country (Fingerhut, 2003). Exhibit 1.1 offers brief profiles of youth suicide in two rural U. S. states.

TABLE 1.3
Suicide Rates and Population Density: Top and Bottom
10 States, Ages 15–24, 1991–1998

State	Rate	Pop. density	State	Rate	Pop. density
AK	32.71	1.0	NJ	6.77	1041.9
WY	26.97	4.7	RI	8.21	960.3
SD	23.39	9.2	MA	8.20	767.6
MT	23.24	5.5	NY	8.31	381.0
NV	23.21	10.9	DC	8.98	9949.2
NM	22.88	12.5	DE	9.31	340.8
AZ	20.2	32.3	IL	10.03	205.6
ND	19.04	9.3	CT	10.08	678.5
ID	18.86	12.2	MD	10.44	489.1
UT	18.81	21.0	OH	10.44	264.9

Note. Data from National Center for Health Statistics, various years of *DHHS, Mortality Statistics Branch, Annual Report*; www.demographia.com, 2004. Pop. = population.

Socioeconomic Status

It has been said that suicide is a truly democratic phenomenon—no race or economic class is immune. As a generalization, this has been largely true. Rates among various socioeconomic classes tend to wax and wane over time and social conditions; for example, economic deprivations and recessions will have a greater effect on those who have something to lose than on those who are already economically disadvantaged. Empirical data concerning the exact

EXHIBIT 1.1
Two State Profiles

Werenko, Olson, Fullerton-Gleason, Zumwalt, and Sklar (2000) have offered an epidemiological snapshot of child and adolescent suicide deaths (ages 9–19) in New Mexico for the years 1990 through 1994, based on a retrospective review of all medical examiner autopsies. During these years, the suicide rate for these ages was more than twice the national average. Eighty-five percent of decedents were male (a 5:1 ratio). Suicide rates increased with age; the rate for 15- to 19-year-olds (22.3) was 6 times that for 10- to 14-year-olds (3.8). Two out of three (67% of) youth suicides were by firearms, with males and non-Hispanic Whites being overrepresented among firearm deaths. Three fourths of these firearms were owned either by a family member or the decedent. More than half (51%) of the decedents had alcohol or drugs present at the time of death; the proportion of American Indian/Alaska Natives who had alcohol or drugs present was 74%. Youth who used a firearm, however, were less likely to be intoxicated or using drugs at the time of their death.

Gessner (1997) used death certificate and U.S. census data to profile suicides among Alaskan youth 14 to 19 years of age during the years 1979 and 1993. Whereas the average rate among these youth was 31.3 per 100,000, about 3 times greater than that of the lower 48 states, Gessner reported significant differences in suicide rates by age, with rates being almost 3 times higher among those age 18 to 19 (46.5) than among those age 14 to 15 (16.0). He also reported significant differences in suicide rates among Alaska Natives (76.9) and, particularly, Alaska Native males, whose rate (120.3) was 4 times that of White males (31.0). Gessner also reported an increase in the use of firearms to complete suicide (84% of suicides in 1989–1993 vs. 64% in 1984–1988), as well as variances in suicide rates across regions of the state, with census areas located in the northern and western regions of the state having the highest rates.

---

influence of socioeconomic status have been somewhat mixed and contradictory. However, the overall picture tends to suggest an inverse association between socioeconomic status and suicide rates, both in the United States and internationally (Stack, 2000). Qin, Agerbo, and Mortenson (2003) addressed socioeconomic differences among more than 20,000 Danish suicides and reported that individuals with incomes in the lowest quartile had more than 5 times the risk of dying by suicide.

Cohort effects are changes in the rates of suicide throughout the lifetime of those affected who share a temporal experience. One example of a cohort effect hypothesized by Easterlin (1978) is that cohorts of greater size will have higher suicide rates (throughout their lifetime) than smaller-sized cohorts. Thus, for example, as the post–World War II "baby boomers" move toward old age, they may be expected to bring with them problems inherent in larger birth cohorts, such as higher rates of suicide. The large proportionate size of the postwar birth cohorts has provided one explanatory cause for the dramatic increases in youth suicide up to the late 1970s. Several studies (see Newman & Dyck, 1988) have found increasing suicide rates with each successive cohort during the 1950 to 1979 period. However, Newman and Dyck (1988) have noted that it is difficult to distinguish period from cohort effects in these studies. Subsequent studies have demonstrated cohort effects in England and Wales (Gunnell, Middleton, Whitely, Dorling, & Frankl, 2003) and Lithuania (Kalediene, 1999), although not in Australia (Morrell, Page, & Taylor, 2003; Snowden & Hunt, 2002).

Easterlin's (1980) work on relative cohort size suggests that changes in the economic well-being of youth—the gap between economic aspirations and reality—led to increased stress and consequent aggression. Specifically, the relative cohort size may serve as one measure of the supply of young labor in the economic marketplace. When an increasing number of adolescents vie for a nonincreasing supply of jobs, the cohort as a whole will experience greater stress and consequent inadequacy, depression, hopelessness, and rage. The latter may explode in the form of increased and self-directed aggression. In one test of this hypothesis, Stack (1997) confirmed this relation, but only in market economies (e.g., the United States and Canada) and mixed economies (e.g., Sweden), but not in command economies (e.g., Hungary). He hypothesized therefore that relative cohort size may have negative consequences only in capitalist nations (as compared to welfare capitalist nations, where full employment and redistributive measures may cushion stress).

Finally, studies of attempted suicide in youth provide little useful data regarding differences in socioeconomic status. These reports invariably are setting-specific (e.g., consecutive admissions at one urban hospital emergency room). In this example, there may be considerable class differences between the relative frequency of emergency room use for medical consequences of an attempt and the use of private physicians, from whom little data on attempters has been collected. Similarly, issues such as the lack of mental health parity in health insurance and other barriers to accessing health care may have differential impacts depending on relative financial means.

THE WHEN, WHERE, AND HOW OF ADOLESCENT SUICIDE

Interpretatively, the when, where, and how of adolescent suicide tell much about the motivation and intention inherent in a young person's suicidal behavior. For example, a teenager who ingests a handful of aspirin in front of her mother following an argument is clearly different from a young man who sneaks out of his house at night, hikes into a heavily wooded park, and shoots himself in the head. Revealed in these examples are distinctly different levels of behavioral motivation, suicidal intent, and lethality of method, which places both individuals "attempting suicide" on opposite ends of the suicide behavior continuum.

The When

There have been a number of studies that have examined temporal variations in the completion of suicide (Blachly & Fairley, 1989; Lester, 1979; Zung & Green, 1974), none of which, however, have been specific to adolescence. Summary U.S. data for the years 1989 through 1996, across all ages, shows suicides occurring most often in the 6 months between March and September (grand mean: 86.85/day vs. 82.13/day for September to February), with no particular month standing out as a peak month (Newslink, 2001). What is notable, however, is that one month, December, stands alone as singularly deviant, with the fewest recorded suicides per day (76.3; Newslink, 2001). Research has also shown that suicide rates tend to dip before and during significant holidays and rise thereafter (Phillips & Feldman, 1973).

In some regions, however, where the regional economy is highly tied to seasonal employment, e.g., in seasonal farming, adult suicides may increase during periods of unemployment. Some seasonal occupations, e.g., commercial fishing, may lead to large paychecks and related celebratory binge drinking, thus suicides as well. How these economic factors might influence the timing of adolescent suicides is unknown.

The Centers for Disease Control and Prevention, in collaboration with the U.S. Departments of Education and Justice, has analyzed monthly school-associated suicide events. They have reported that for the 1992 to 1999 school years, campus-related suicide event rates were higher during the spring semester than during the fall semester (Centers for Disease Control and Prevention, 2001b).

Monday ("Blue Monday"?) appears to be the day of the week on which most suicides occur; suicides generally occur least often on weekends (Brådvik & Berglund, 2003). In terms of the time of day, Hoberman and Garfinkel (1988a) and Shafii and Shafii (1982) found that the majority of completed youth suicides took place in the afternoon or evening. It is important to note that some of the research in temporal trends may need to be interpreted with caution, as death certificates (from which much of the data are gleaned) may not accurately reflect when the act of suicide actually occurred. As Rich, Young, Fowler, and Rosenfeld (1984) have noted, there may be as much as a 6-day difference between the date of the act and the date recorded on the death certificate.

The Where

According to the limited data available on completers of suicide, it appears that most adolescent suicides occur in the home, where the primary means for suicide are available. For example, Hoberman and Garfinkel (1988b) found that 70% of their sample of completers killed themselves at home and 22% killed themselves outdoors. Similarly, 80% of all nonfatal attempts by 12- to 17-year-olds resulting in hospital-based treatment in the state of Oregon in 1999 occurred in the home (Oregon State Health Division, 2000). Given that the majority of adolescent suicides involve firearms stored in the home and the majority of nonfatal attempts by adolescents involve ingesting drugs typically kept in the home, these findings should not surprise us. As we shall discuss more fully below, most firearms involved in self-inflicted injuries come from the adolescent's home (Grossman, Reay, & Baker, 1999). Case-control studies clearly document that the presence of a gun in the home substantially increases the risk of suicide (Brent et al., 1991, 1993) and among suicidal adolescents it increases the risk of suicide as much as 75 times that of those who live in homes without guns (Rosenberg, Mercy, & Houk, 1991).

The How: Methods of Adolescent Suicide

As will be discussed more thoroughly in chapter 4, risk of suicidal behaviors is often defined as a function of psychological intention. Intention is closely linked to the choice of method to be used in an attempt or completion. In general, the more the decedent intends to produce death as a consequence of his or her behavior, the greater the potential lethality of the method selected to carry out that intention. This is especially true in the planned (vs. impulsive) use of particular methods. For example, firearms and hanging are more lethal methods than are overdose ingestion, carbon monoxide poisoning, or wrist cutting.

In addition to issues of intent and lethality, the "choice" of a method of self-destruction is strongly influenced by a number of factors working independently and in combination. As described by Berman, Litman, and Diller (1989), these include the following:

1. *Accessibility and readiness for use*. For example, in jail settings, where other means are limited, hanging is the predictable method of choice.
2. *Knowledge, experience, and familiarity*. Socialization to gun use and ownership, for example, is greatest in the southern United States, where gun use for suicide is also greatest.
3. *Meaning, symbolism, and cultural significance*. Females use drug ingestion as a method of suicide and suicide attempt considerably more often than do males. This has long been theorized to be caused by acculturated concerns for maintaining appearance and avoiding disfigurement. Also, drugs have long been associated with peaceful sleep, a symbolic equivalent to death.
4. *The state of mind of the person at risk for suicide*. For example, the need to communicate one's last moments of thinking appears to be associated with method selection. In a study of young suicides, Peck (1986) found that those using more passive and low-lethality methods (e.g., alcohol and barbiturates or carbon monoxide poisoning) were more likely than those using active and highly lethal methods (e.g., firearms or hanging) to leave suicide notes. Bizarre methods are used almost exclusively by individuals with psychotic disorders.

Suicide methods vary among countries. Worldwide, hanging is the most frequently used method of suicide. In New Zealand, for example, hanging accounted for 54% of youth suicides in 1997, a proportion similar to that of firearms in the United States. In Australia, hanging is the leading method of suicide in young people, accounting for 36% of young male and female suicides (1994 data); however, until 1989, firearm suicide rates exceeded those of hanging among the young (Cantor & Baume, 1998). In some countries, particularly in large agrarian societies, the use of pesticides is most common as a method of suicide (Eddleston & Phillips, 2004). One disturbing trend observed internationally is that of an increasing proportion of young females using more violent methods (World Health Organization, 2000).

Statistics on methods of completed suicide by youth in the United States reflect both consistency and change over time. In 2000, the overwhelming method of choice was that of firearms and explosives, accounting for 57% of all suicides among 15- to 24-year-olds (National Center for Injury Prevention and Control, 2005). Three fourths (75%) of these self-inflicted gunshot wound deaths were accomplished by White males. Firearms are the modal method used by adolescent males to complete suicide, and, contrary to most people's beliefs, firearms are also the modal method used by adolescent females to complete suicide. In 1964, 48% of all U.S. suicides by females between 15 and 19 years of age were by poisoning (ingestion) and 35% were by firearms (Seiden, 1969). In 2000, females showed a 14% increase in the use of a firearm to complete suicide (now 39% of all suicides of females age 15–19) and a 69% *decline* in deaths by poisoning (15% of suicides of females age 15–19; National Center for Injury Prevention and Control, 2005). As data from the NVDRS is reported, much will be learned regarding the drugs of choice used by adolescents who complete suicide by ingestion. Preliminary data from 196 ingestion suicides 24 years old and younger in 2001 (in three U.S. states and two metropolitan areas) for whom toxicology results were known indicated 10% tested positive for antidepressants and 26% tested positive for alcohol (C. Barber, personal communication, November 5, 2004).

Figure 1.7 and Figure 1.8 depict the leading causes (methods) of suicide among males and females, respectively, in the United States. The reader will note the increased use of firearms and the decreased use of suffocation (generally hanging) as people grow older. However, in the last

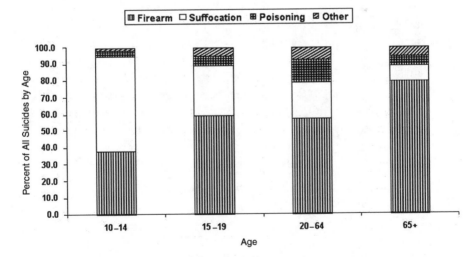

Figure 1.7. Leading causes of suicide among males by age, 2000. Data from National Center for Health Statistics, various years of *DHHS, Mortality Statistics Branch, Annual Report.*

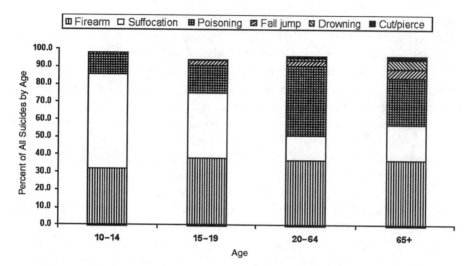

Figure 1.8. Leading causes of suicide among females by age, 2000. Data from National Center for Health Statistics, various years of *DHHS, Mortality Statistics Branch, Annual Report.*

decade, as the proportion of adolescent suicides by firearm has peaked and subsequently declined, there has been an increase in the use of suffocation (again, primarily hanging). Figure 1.9 shows these proportionate trends among 15- to 19-year-old males between 1992 and 2000.

Firearms have been the modal method of suicide, with only slight variation, over the last half-century. Firearm suicide rates in the 15- to 19-year-old age group peaked in 1994 at 9.18 per 100,000, 22% higher than the rate in 1985

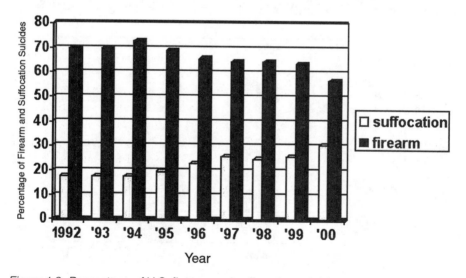

Figure 1.9. Percentage of U.S. firearm and suffocation suicides, males, ages 15–19, 1992–2000. Data from *Web-based Injury Statistics Query and Reporting System* (WISQARS™) *Fatal Injuries: Mortality Reports,* 2005, by the National Center for Injury Prevention and Control.

(7.55/100,000); had declined 32% by 2000 to a level (4.51) below the 1985 rates (6.77/100,000). As noted in Table 1.4, however, these shifts have not been uniform. While rates of firearm suicide have declined for White males, rates of firearm suicide among Black males in this age group have actually increased dramatically (30%), making firearms the most significant correlate of observed increases in overall Black male youth suicide (MMWR, 1998).

TABLE 1.4
U.S. Firearm Suicide Rates, Males, Ages 15–19, 1985 and 2000

	2000	1985
Total males, all races	7.8	6.0
White	8.4	10.5
Black	**7.0**	**5.4**
Hispanic	5.3	6.7

Note. Data from Web-based *Injury Statistics Query and Reporting System* (WISQARS™) *Leading Causes of Death Reports*, 2005, by the National Center for Injury Prevention and Control.

A cross-national study of rates of suicide by firearm between 1990 and 1995 among 15- to 24-year-olds in 34 countries (Johnson, Krug, & Potter, 2000) found that they ranged from 0 per 100,000 in Mauritius, Hong Kong, and Kuwait to 11.4 per 100,000 in Finland. The United States ranked second among these countries in rates of firearm suicide yet had the highest proportion of suicides by firearm relative to all other methods. Suicide by firearm ranks as the third leading cause of death by injury among 15- to 24-year-olds in the United States, trailing only motor vehicle traffic deaths and homicide by firearms. Boyd (1983) argued that the greater availability and accessibility of guns in the United States has had a direct, measurable, and explanatory effect on observed increases in youth suicide over these years. A 1990 study of firearm suicides in King County, Washington (Sloan, Rivara, Reay, Ferris, & Kellerman, 1990), documented that the ready access to handguns among teenagers was, indeed, associated with a somewhat higher rate of suicide. Boyd and Moscicki (1986); the Centers for Disease Control (1986); Kellerman et al. (1993); Brent et al. (1991, 1993); and Kachur, Potter, Powell, and Rosenberg (1995) have clearly shown that increases in the rate of (and the numbers of deaths by) suicide over the latter half of the 20th century were largely due to the use of firearms as a method. A review of the literature on gun availability and suicide concludes that "the preponderance of current evidence indicates that gun availability is a risk factor for youth suicide in the United States" (Miller & Hemenway, 1998, p. 73). Indeed, as noted earlier, the most common location for the occurrence of a firearm suicide by youth is in the home (Brent et al., 1993). Moreover, the risk conferred by guns in the home has been shown to be proportional to their accessibility (e.g., loaded and unsecured) and the number of guns in the home, for youth both with and without identifiable mental health problems or suicidal risk factors (Brent et al., 1993; Kellerman et al., 1993). Firearm ownership levels have a stronger relationship with youth suicide than with suicide among older adults (Brickmayer & Hemenway, 2001).

Recent research (Hemenway, Azrael, & Miller, 2000) showed that in households with children, women frequently did not know that there was a gun in the home, and when they did, they often believed it to be stored safely when it was not. It has been estimated that eliminating access to guns would prevent as much as 32% of completed suicides among minors (Shenassa, Caitlin, & Buka, 2003).

SUICIDE ATTEMPTING BEHAVIORS

As a final consideration related to the extent and nature of the problem, we must briefly address the topic of nonfatal suicidal behaviors. Whereas the prevalence and incidence of completed suicide can be established through records provided by coroners and medical examiners, attempted suicide is difficult to measure epidemiologically. Attempts requiring medical treatment may be observed and counted through emergency room admissions, as they are mandated in the state of Oregon, or cooperating physicians' offices. Those occurring in institutional settings (e.g., jails and psychiatric wards) can be tabulated. However, the great majority of youth suicide attempts (about seven of every eight) are of such low lethality as to not require medical or other attention and are never reported. Thus, data relevant to these behaviors tend to be extrapolations and estimates based mostly on self-report surveys.

Prior to 1990, data on nonfatal suicide attempts was derived almost exclusively from individual research surveys and self-report data. As noted by Velting, Rathnus, and Asnis (1998), adolescent self-reports of previous suicide attempts may not provide sufficiently valid or reliable data, reflecting confused interpretations of the questions asked or careless response styles. In a similar vein, study results may be difficult to compare if operational definitions of terms are not offered and questions are not standardized in wording and format (O'Carroll et al., 1996).

In early surveys of high school students, Smith and Crawford (1986) and Harkavy-Friedman, Asnis, Boeck, and DiFiore (1987) found that approximately 60% reported having some degree of suicidal ideation in their lifetime and that 8.9% had made one or more suicide attempts in any one year. Later studies published in the early 1990s with large samples of high school students suggested slightly lower estimates ranging from 4.5% (Felts, Chenier, & Barnes, 1992) to 7.5% (Garrison, McKeown, Valois, & Vincent, 1993). Studies of American Indian and Alaska-Native youth (c.f., Borowsky, Resnick, Ireland, & Blum, 1999) suggest considerably higher rates of nonfatal suicide attempt.

Since 1990, the Centers for Disease Control and Prevention has monitored nonfatal suicidal behaviors among nationally representative samples of high school students in the United States through its biannual Youth Risk Behavior Surveys (YRBS; Brener, Krug, & Simon, 2000; Grunbaum et al., 2004; Kann et al., 2000). One advantage to this survey is that the research method and the format and wording of questions have been standardized, allowing for meaningful temporal comparisons (c.f., Watson, Goldney, Fisher, & Merritt, 2001). A second advantage is that sample sizes have been large, ranging between 12,000 and 16,000 students across the six surveys conducted between 1991 and 2003. Four questions have been asked consistently across the five surveys. Two questions address suicide ideation: "During the past 12 months, did you ever (a) consider attempting suicide" and (b) "...make a plan about how you would attempt suicide?" Two additional questions, focusing on the same "last 12 months," covered suicide attempts: (a) "How many times did you actually attempt suicide?" and (b) If you attempted suicide... did any attempt actually result in an injury, poisoning, or overdose that had to be treated by a doctor?"

Between 1991 and 2003, significant linear decreases in suicide ideation and ideation with a plan have been documented through the YRBS. The percentage of high school students who say they have considered suicide has declined from 29% to 17% (see Figure 1.10), and those who state they made a plan declined from 18.6% to 16.5% (Grunbaum et al., 2004). This decrease has been most pronounced among female and

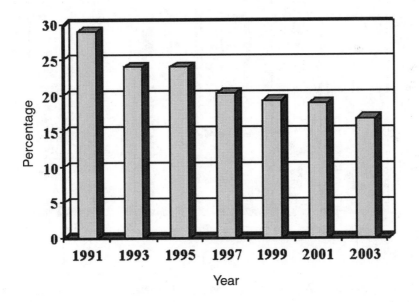

Figure 1.10. Youth Risk Behavior Surveys, 1991–2003, considered suicide. Data from National Center for Chronic Disease Prevention and Health Promotion (2004).

White students. Concurrently, there has been essentially no change in the percentage claiming a suicide attempt in the last year, with the range from 7.3% to 8.7% and the average being 8.1%. Most important, there was a significant increase between 1991 and 1993 in the percentage reporting making a medically injurious attempt, and that increase has remained through 2003 (2.9% in 2003), with about 3 in 10 attempts currently requiring treatment (see Figure 1.11). Disturbingly, this last increase has been shown to be most pronounced among the younger (ninth-grade) students (Grunbaum et al., 2004). Figure 1.12 displays the 2003 YRBS data across the four suicide-related questions addressed to students.

If these self-report data are to be believed, then in a typical high school class of approximately 30 students, in any one year, six will seriously consider suicide, two to three (one boy and two girls) will attempt suicide, and one of these will make an attempt sufficiently harmful to require medical attention (King, 1997).

The data for students in alternative high schools, those serving students at risk for failing or dropping out of regular high school or who have been expelled from regular high school because of illegal activities or emotional or behavioral problems, is even more compelling. When compared to students in regular high schools, these students were 1.5 times more likely to report having seriously considered attempting suicide or having made a plan to do so, almost twice as likely to report having made an attempt, and

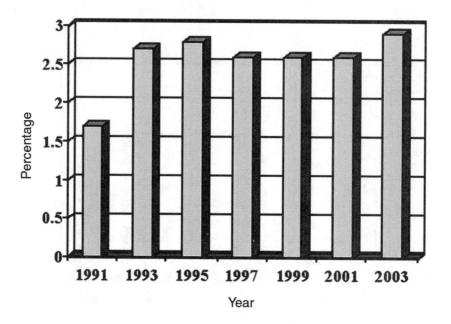

Figure 1.11. Youth Risk Behavior Surveys, 1991–2003, made an injurious suicide attempt. Data from National Center for Chronic Disease Prevention and Health Promotion (2004).

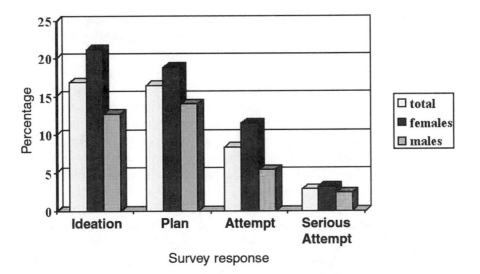

Figure 1.12. Youth Risk Behavior Surveys, 2003. Data from National Center for Chronic Disease Prevention and Health Promotion (2004).

3 times as likely to report having made a suicide attempt serious enough to require medical attention (Grunbaum et al., 1999).

Adolescents have the highest ratio of nonfatal suicide attempts to suicide completions of all age groups (King, 1997). Estimates of the ratio of attempts to completions in adolescence have ranged from about 100:1 (Jacobziner, 1965) to about 350:1, based on a sample of self-referred attempters from more rural locations (Garfinkel, 1989). However, extrapolating data from the YRBS to the population of adolescents in the same age group suggests that the ratio may be more than 800:1 for self-reported attempts and close to 300:1 for those requiring medical attention. On the other hand, data from the state of Oregon for adolescents age 15 to 17 show a much more conservative count of medically serious attempts, giving a ratio to completions ranging from 28:1 between 1988 and 1993 to 43:1 in 1999 (Centers for Disease Control and Prevention, 1995a; Oregon State Health Division, 2000). This discrepancy is considerably greater among female adolescents (1999 Oregon data: 190:1).

Spicer and Miller (2000) analyzed data on both suicides and hospital-admitted attempters from eight U.S. states. Attempters were drawn from two groups: those admitted to the hospital (excluding those who died) and those treated in the emergency department and released to their homes. Among 15- to 19-year-olds in these eight states, there were 55 adolescents hospitalized and 46 adolescents treated and released from the emergency department, a total of 101 medically serious attempters for every one completed suicide. Among 10- to 14-year-olds, the ratio of hospitalized and emergency depart-ment–treated youth to those completing suicide in the same study period was 208:1; among 20- to 24-year-olds, this same comparative ratio was 65:1.

Between the ages of 10 and 24, 87% of those seen at the hospital ingested drugs or poison. Across all ages, these researchers estimated that the case fatality rate from ingestion was only 1.5% as compared to 82.5% by firearm.

Similarly, in Europe, the average annual rate of nonfatal suicide attempts requiring medical attention among females ages 15 to 24 has been estimated at 283 per 100,000 (Kerkhof, 2000). One study monitoring hospital-referred suicide attempts in Gent, Belgium, showed that 1998 rates of attempted suicides among adolescent males were actually higher than those among females (van Heeringen, 2001). In a multicountry study of patients hospitalized for nonfatal suicidal behavior, the female to male ratio was 1.66:1 (Bille-Brahe et al., 1997).

These studies perhaps only highlight how poor our efforts at surveillance of nonfatal suicide behavior have been both in the United States and internationally. Accordingly, the Surgeon General's National Strategy for Suicide Prevention specifically targeted improving surveillance of these behaviors as a year 2005 objective (see chap. 7).

Research on methods of nonfatal suicide attempts in the United States and the United Kingdom has yielded rather consistent results, with intentional overdose occurring most often, typically involving antidepressants and acetaminophen (paracetamol in the United Kingdom; Townsend, Hawton, Harriss, Bale, & Bond, 2001), followed by wrist cutting (Brent, 1987; Hawton, 1986; Lewinsohn, Rohde, & Seeley, 1996; Reynolds & Mazza, 1994; Spirito, Stark, Fristad, Hart, & Owens-Stively, 1987). Females use each of these leading methods more often than do males.

The typical youthful suicide attempter is a young female who ingests drugs at home in front of others (i.e., engages in low-lethality behavior). As will be discussed in chapter 3, however, once an attempt is made at any level of lethality, the risk for future and more serious attempts and completion increases significantly. These estimates may represent only the tip of the iceberg—a sobering thought about the actual scope of the adolescent suicide phenomenon.

CONCLUSION

The epidemiological study of youth suicide spreads the nomothetic net across the problem of youth suicide and captures some of the defining macro variables. Its significance is in highlighting both what is happening and among whom. With the canvas so brushed, we begin to develop a picture of at-risk groups. More important, we can pose some beginning hypotheses, based on the social correlates of epidemiological trends. What we find common to temporal variations and differences between groups that are more versus less at risk allows us to focus our assessment and treatment efforts on those in need. We now must further attempt to understand, for example, what makes some and not other members of the class of White males at risk.

2

THE THEORETICAL CONTEXT

INTUITIVE MODELS

To talk of adolescence and of adolescents nomothetically blurs the uniqueness of every teenager in a developmental period variably described as "caught between" childhood and adulthood. To talk of these individuals idiographically makes all the more difficult our task of arriving at general principles and universal variables. Because clinicians are often inclined to focus on the individual, it is perhaps best to begin our understanding with an idiographic approach. To that end, let us briefly introduce two adolescents.

Case Illustration

Bill is 17, a senior in high school. A good student, hard working, some would say "driven," Bill has achieved well and is hoping to go to either Harvard or Stanford next year. He also is hopeful that his college career will lead him to medical school and a career as a surgeon like his father. Bill is a tall, handsome boy, attractive to girls but surprisingly shy among them. When he socializes, he prefers to hang out in groups rather than date; in these groups, he is likely to be seen deep in introspective discussions with one girl or another. Introspection has no place on the school football team, where this past season Bill led all receivers in pass catches. Nor does he appear at all the quiet type in his new sports car, a gift from his parents on his 17th birthday. The elder of two sons, Bill has always been close to his parents, and a "good son." Perhaps for these reasons, he has been increasingly preoccupied as verbalized threats of separation and divorce become common in his parents' increasingly frequent conflicts. These worries he has kept largely to himself.

Jenny is 15, a sophomore at a large urban high school. Attractive but about 20 pounds overweight, Jenny is mostly a loner—that is, with two exceptions. Since the beginning of this school year, she has had a relationship with a blind classmate for whom she takes notes and has helped around school. And she has just broken up with her first boyfriend, a ninth-grader who took her out on a date after weeks of awkward telephone calls. Jenny is an average student, taking clerical subjects with hopes of getting a job upon graduation from high school as a clerk-typist at one of the insurance companies downtown. She is the fourth of seven children. Her mother is a homemaker and her father a master carpenter.

Bill and Jenny could be two kids from Anytown, U.S.A. One average, the other a star, each is prototypical, perhaps, of adolescents we have known; neither is prototypical of all adolescents. Each can be described in terms of strengths and weaknesses; each triggers impressions, associations, and value judgments within us as observers.

But Bill and Jenny are not typical adolescents. Bill's body was brought to the local medical examiner's office; he put his father's .22-caliber handgun to his head and ended his life in an instant. Jenny was brought by her mother to the local hospital emergency room after she was found bleeding from both forearms, having slashed them with a razor blade.

Why? What could possibly drive these two youths to self-destructive acts? We might hypothesize about Bill's world being about to undergo great change, about the stress of graduating and starting to prove himself anew in a much higher level of competition, about his lack of preparedness to deal with any threat to success or status, about his fears of losing his parents and the protection and security of a predictable family unit. We might pose the idea that his family had not taught him to deal well with loss or change, that he was too enmeshed, too close, too identified. We might wonder about his rigidity and his need to be perfect; no doubt, he even accomplished his suicide with characteristic perfection.

In contrast, it is tempting to construe Jenny's behavior as a "cry for help," a dramatic and powerful statement to her interpersonal surround that she wanted to be attended to and noticed. She was a lost child, in the middle of several siblings, not standing out, keeping her distance from others, invisible even to the one peer she had befriended. Maybe she fantasized about her recent relationship with her first boyfriend in Cinderella-like terms, only to have the dream dashed when the glass slipper fell and broke.

Then, again, we might tell you that none of the above happened, that Bill and Jenny continue on pace toward their chosen futures, each alive and thriving in his or her own way. At once, figure and ground shift. What "explained" the suicide of one now recedes into background noise to an otherwise successful career. What gave ominous meaning to the other's behavior now simply describes ongoing life challenges in an otherwise average teen's struggle toward adulthood.

In great measure, this is how we learn about suicide and suicidal behaviors. Suicide is rarely studied prospectively. Our theories, our hypotheses, our assumptions are generally built on retrospective analyses of behaviors and character studies. The potential for uncorrectable distortion is great. Dead bodies only indirectly answer our question, "Why?" Surviving family members, friends, and others have reason for denial and selective attention in reporting to us their impressions of the decedent. Suicide notes, where available, may be misleading (Leenaars, 1988).

Even those who survive an attempt and are therefore available to give us answers do not do so in ways we believe. Hawton (1987) has reported results of interviews with hospitalized overdose patients and documented the reasons they gave for their attempts. When the same questions were posed to these patients' psychiatrists, quite different motivations were ascribed to their patients' attempts. Indeed, among college counseling center students with suicidal ideation, the perceptions of the student-clients pertaining to suicide are often not matched by the students' counselors (Jobes, Jacoby, Cimbolic, & Hustead, 1997). Routinely, counselors overestimate the psychological risk and pain of the clients while they paradoxically underestimate the clients' emotional upset and urgency.

The reasons for these discordant views are manifold. They involve our implicit assumptions about human behavior, some predetermined thinking about suicide, our attempts to apply the nomothetic theory to the idiographic case, sometimes requiring us to shift figure and ground for our convenience. As with the blind men describing the elephant according to the shape of the trunk versus the ear versus the body, so it is that what we come to believe about suicide, what theories we construct to give meaning to "the ultimate philosophical problem" (Sartre, 1956), and how we assess and treat those who remain alive, begin with the data available to us. An understanding of this context is important to our grasp of the numerous theories of suicidal behavior from which we might choose to guide our clinical work.

OVERVIEW OF THEORIES

Some of the most distinguished practitioners, researchers, theoreticians, and scholars in the fields of psychology, psychiatry, sociology, and biology have contributed a wide range of theories to explain suicidal behavior. Although a number of attempts have been made to develop viable and heuristic theories of suicidal behaviors, conceptually adequate and applicable theories in the field of suicidology have remained elusive. Only limited progress has been made toward the goal of constructing a comprehensive theory of life-threatening behavior (see discussions by Berman, 1986a; Lester, 1994; Shneidman, 1992). Accordingly, most of the major theories in the suicide literature discretely describe different aspects of suicidal behaviors using the characteristic language and construct domains of a particular theoretical orientation or discipline.

The major theories of suicide may be conceptually grouped under the following broad headings: (a) sociological theories, (b) psychological theories, and (c) neurobiological and genetic theories. Although many of the major theories were not specifically constructed to explain youthful suicide per se, they are nevertheless usually applicable to young people. However, some theories have been developed with youth suicide as a particular focus and will be mentioned under the appropriate conceptual headings. In our summary of major theories, we will also consider the increasing emphasis on integrative theoretical approaches and models before shifting our attention to key developmental aspects that come to bear on adolescent suicidality.

Sociological Theories of Suicide

Sociologists were among the first to formally develop theories pertaining to suicide (see Durkheim, 1897/1951). Indeed, sociological theories of suicide have been central to the growth and development of suicidology, right through to the present day.

Case Illustration

The partially decomposed body of Frank, a 19-year-old male, was found hanging by a noose in a condemned apartment building. Residents of the neighborhood reported that Frank, a high school dropout, was often seen loitering in the area, but kept to himself and had not been seen of late. There were no known family or friends to contact for funeral arrangements.

Kemal was a 20-year-old member of an extremist religious group passionately opposed to Western influences in his homeland. In protest, he strapped five sticks of dynamite to his body and walked into a busy market where he detonated the dynamite, killing himself and wounding three bystanders.

Kathy, a 15-year-old high school freshman, took a fatal overdose of barbiturates and was found in her bed after her mother noticed she had not gotten up for school that morning. Kathy had been very depressed about breaking up with her boyfriend of 2 years. The night of her death she had seen him with another girl at a party. A bitter argument ensued in which she threatened to kill herself if he refused to get back together with her.

Bill, a 17-year-old juvenile delinquent, was found hanging in his room at the detention center after being arrested for a drunk-driving incident in which he hit and killed three pedestrians. This arrest followed a series of previous arrests for armed robbery, assault, and possession of drugs. Hours before his death, a peer told Bill that he would probably be tried as an adult and receive a stiff prison sentence.

Each of the preceding four cases of suicide could be theoretically explained and conceptually understood in terms of Emile Durkheim's sociological theory of suicide. As previously noted, Durkheim's classic work *Suicide: A Study in Sociology* (1897/1951) established an important model of sociological study of suicide, which has led to an extensive line of research and subsequent theory construction. Durkheim argued that suicide results from society's strength or weakness of control over the individual. He identified four basic types of suicide that reflect the individual's relationship to society: egoistic, altruistic, anomic, and fatalistic.

Frank's death is an example of an egoistic suicide, which is thought to stem from an individual's lack of integration into society. Largely left to themselves, victims of egoistic suicide are neither connected with, nor dependent on, their community. Kemal's death is an example of an altruistic suicide. In altruistic suicide, the individual is overly integrated into a group so that he or she feels no sacrifice is too great for the larger group. Japanese kamikaze pilots in World War II or religious fundamentalists who kill themselves in the act of attacking their enemy are clear examples of altruistic suicide. Kathy's suicide is an example of anomic suicide. The victim of anomic suicide is not capable of dealing with a crisis in a rational manner and therefore chooses suicide as the solution to a problem. Anomic suicide occurs when the individual's accustomed relationship with society is suddenly and shockingly altered. Finally, Bill's death is an example of fatalistic suicide. Fatalistic suicides are thought to be caused by excessive societal regulation that fundamentally restricts an individual's freedom. Victims of fatalistic suicide feel that they have no viable future.

Many scholars have followed the sociological study of suicide established by Durkheim. Some have used Durkheim's research methodology (Cavan, 1926; Henry & Short, 1954; Sainsbury, 1955; Schmid, 1928), whereas others have developed and extended his theoretical tradition (Douglas, 1967; Gibbs & Martin, 1964). One notable contribution is Maris's (1981) notion of "suicidal careers." Maris's empirically based theory moves away from a static, structural focus and emphasizes a dynamic, developmental model of suicide. By focusing on a multivariate analysis of a large sample of suicide completers in developing this model, Maris was able to simultaneously develop and test his primary thesis that the suicidal individual's "career," or life history, establishes a vulnerability to suicide. Additionally, Maris's work moved traditional sociological research and theory, limited in its exclusive emphasis on societal influences, toward a broad integration with more psychological foci (refer also to Maris, Berman, & Silverman, 2000).

Social–Psychological Approaches

To address some of the limitations of purely sociological approaches, some theories have attempted to synthesize both interpersonal and intrapersonal variables that may bear on suicidal behaviors. For example, Petzel and Riddle (1981), in an extensive review of the literature, conceptualized adolescent suicide as a social and psychological phenomenon. These authors asserted that adolescent suicide is related to interactions of multiple social factors (e.g., family conflict, school adjustment, and social relationships) and cognitively based psychological factors (e.g., conceptions of death, hopelessness, intention, and motivation). On the basis of empirical research with college students, Jobes (1995a; 2000) has theorized that suicidality can often be understood in terms of a continuum between two fundamentally different psychological orientations to suicide. At one end of the continuum are individuals who have an *intrapsychic* orientation to suicide (i.e., people who are highly internalized with a primary suicidal focus on their intrasubjective psychological pain). At the other end of the continuum are individuals who have an *interpsychic* orientation to suicide (i.e., people who are relationally oriented with a suicidal focus that centers on interpersonal issues).

The implications of these theoretical orientations speak to fundamentally different psychologies about suicide, with distinct implications for clinical treatment and prospective behaviors. For example, the intrapsychic type would more typically be a male who is not treatment-seeking and ultimately at more risk for *completing* suicide. On the other hand, the interpsychic type would more typically be a female who is much more inclined to seek treatment and ultimately more at risk for *attempting* suicide. Paradoxically, preliminary data with college students has shown that intrapsychic types are less likely to seek treatment but may well be more likely to respond to clinical care, whereas interpsychic types tend to seek treatment more readily but may be more refractory to medication and psychotherapeutic intervention (refer to Jobes et al., 1997).

Hendin's (1987) theory of youth suicide attempts to explain the phenomenon from both epidemiological and psychodynamic perspectives. Central to Hendin's perspective are trends in the demographic occurrence of youthful suicide, the relation of violence to suicide, and the impact of family influences on young people who become preoccupied with death and suicide. Hendin asserts that integrative social and psychological conceptualizations of youthful suicide provide a framework for understanding the personal meaning of life and death (and related behaviors that exist within a particular culture or subculture).

David Lester (1988a, 1988b) has proposed a social-psychological perspective that attempts to explain youthful suicidal behaviors as a function of quality of life. Lester (1984) has shown that nations with a higher quality of life have higher suicide rates, a finding that he has linked to Henry and Short's (1954) theory of homicide and suicide. These authors have asserted that when people have a clear external source of blame for their misfortune, they are more likely to be angry and assaultive, and thereby less depressed and suicidal. However, although Lester has observed the quality of life effect in other populations, he has not been able to corroborate the effect within youthful samples to a statistically significant degree (Lester, 1988a).

In a different vein, Lester (1987) has also attempted to explain youthful suicides in relation to the concept of social subcultures. Building on a case presentation, Lester describes various defining elements of a "teenage suicidal subculture." In this particular case example, the subculture was made up of five teenagers with heavy substance-abuse problems, poor parental relationships, poor self-image, shyness and dependency on peers, loss of lovers, and a deep involvement in heavy-metal rock music and related fantasies. Lester asserts that this self-contained group generated a great deal of suicidal preoccupation and acting out in their student peers. Lester thus argues that this smaller group "tapped into a suicidal vein among other students," revealing the existence of a "peer culture" that transcends the specific peer group. Accordingly, what we know as the natural experimentation and competition of adolescents within a peer group or culture that becomes a suicidal subculture through social shaping may inevitably lead young people to perform overt suicidal acts.

Dr. Thomas Joiner, a 2003 recipient of the J. S. Guggenheim Memorial Foundation Award, has become one of the field's leading contemporary theorists. His "Interpersonal-Psychological Theory of Attempted and Completed Suicide" is a unique compilation of empirical perspective, clinically based insight, and far-reaching integrative theory building. Joiner (2003a) contends that serious suicidal behavior requires each of three specific interpersonal-psychological precursors. These precursors include (a) an acquired capacity to enact lethal self-injury, (b) a sense that one has become a burden to loved ones, and (c) a sense that one is not interpersonally connected with a group or relationship. The role of *fear* is central to Joiner's thesis. Joiner writes,

> It is right to fear suicide—it leads to death, is often painful and shocking, and is associated with stigma and even taboo. Those who go on to die by suicide have lost their fear of it. Few want to die by suicide, but even among those who want to, few can, because few have acquired the ability to enact lethal self-injury—the ability to beat down the instinct to live. (Joiner, 2003b, p.1)

Joiner (2004) argues that although the acquired ability to commit suicide is necessary, it is not sufficient for a terminal outcome because the person has to *want* to die by suicide. As indicated above, Joiner argues that the essential desire (the want to die aspect of suicide) comes from two important sources: the person's sense of being ineffective and therefore being a burden to others, *and* the person's sense that they are disconnected from others in a relational sense (see Figure 2.1). Critically, within this theory, actual suicide attempts and completions arise from the overlapping and synergistic impact of the acquired ability (desire) for suicide, the perception of being relationally burdensome to others, and a sense of thwarted belongingness—the absence of closeness—to key relationships or groups.

Joiner's (2003a) ambitious theory-building is constructed around what he refers to as "key suicide-related facts." These theory-relevant facts include the prevalence of completed suicide and the associations of completed suicide with age, gender, race, neurobiological indices, previous suicide attempts, mental disorders and substance abuse, impulsivity, and childhood adversity. In addition, his theory is designed to address additional phenomena such as suicide clusters and so called "suicide contagion."

Joiner's theorizing is an excellent and relatively rare example of an effort to build a comprehensive theory of suicide. His work has clear implications for extant conceptualizations of suicidality and is designed to inform and further shape future empirical studies of theory-driven constructs. Moreover, this interpersonal-psychological approach has obvious implications for clinical assessment and treatments as well as for larger suicide prevention efforts.

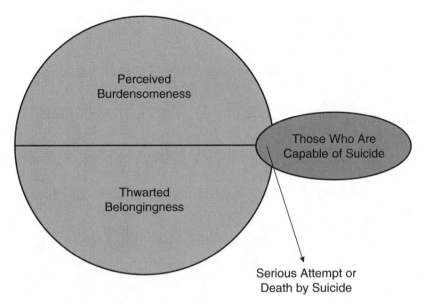

Serious Attempt or
Death by Suicide

Figure 2.1. Those who desire suicide. Reprinted by permission of the publisher from the forthcoming title, *Why People Die by Suicide* by Thomas Joiner, Cambridge, MA, Harvard University Press. Copyright 2005 by the President and Fellows of Harvard College. Used by special arrangement. All rights reserved.

Psychological Theories of Suicide

Following on the heels of sociologists, psychologists, psychiatrists, and other mental health theorists have developed a wide range of psychological theories of suicide. As we shall see, for virtually every school of psychological thought there is a theoretical view on suicide.

Case Illustration

Daniel, an 18-year-old college freshman, was the eldest of three children. Throughout his childhood, Daniel was physically beaten on a regular basis by his alcoholic father. Daniel saw himself as the protector of his younger siblings and was the only child his father abused. The abuse was perhaps related to his father's jealousy of the extremely close relationship Daniel had with his mother, whom Daniel idealized as a saint. At the age of 13, Daniel chose to leave with his divorcing mother while his two siblings stayed in the family home with his father. Daniel and his mother barely scraped by through the subsequent years as his mother worked as a secretary. The family was bitterly divided and his father refused to pay his mother any alimony. Daniel's scholastic abilities earned him an academic scholarship at a local university. In the summer prior to his freshman year, Daniel's mother was diagnosed as having inoperable stomach cancer, from which she died a month prior to the start of school. Daniel was devastated but was determined to attend college to fulfill his mother's dream. His Thanksgiving visit to his father's home was a disaster. Daniel returned to school a day early. On the night of his return, Daniel called his father and during an argument on the phone, shot himself in the head with a revolver he had apparently taken from his father's home. Daniel's last words to his father prior to the fatal gunshot were, "I hate me and I hate you—it's time for the big payback, Dad."

The case of Daniel may be best explained by one of the various psychological theories of suicide. In contrast to the purely societal influences emphasized by sociologically oriented theories, psychological theories of suicide emphasize intrapsychic processes as well as cognitive, emotional, and personality variables. As noted, various psychological theories of suicide reflect perspectives from virtually all the major theoretical orientations in the field (e.g., psychoanalytically oriented, cognitive–behavioral, and family systems theories).

Psychoanalytically Oriented Theory

As with many theoretical considerations in psychology, theorizing on the psychological nature of suicide must fundamentally begin with the thoughts of Sigmund Freud. Although Freud never wrote a paper specifically about suicide, he did see a number of suicidal patients and indirectly provided some important perspectives on the topic. Freud's (1917/1957) classic work *Mourning and Melancholia* outlines the psychological mechanisms involved in turning hostility against the self, which explains the self-reproach and suicidal ideation often seen in melancholic depressions. As summarized by Shneidman (1980), the central Freudian position on suicide was that it represents "murder in the 180th degree." Because people identify with and internalize the objects of their love with ambivalence, they may direct their own aggressive impulses against the internalized love-object whom they both love and hate.

Although this concept of "retroflexed rage" was primary to Freud's considerations of suicide, Tabachnick (1971) notes that his construct of the death instinct is also implicated. As described in *Beyond the Pleasure Principle* (Freud, 1920), the death instinct represents a primary instinctual force in all living matter to return to a state of complete inertia. However, the force of the life instinct as well as societal forces and values generally interfere, albeit temporarily, with the expression of the death instinct. As it relates to suicide, the death instinct (through the superego) was seen to have the capacity to drive the ego into death (Tabachnick, 1971).

In contrast to Freud's indirect and largely contextual discussions of suicide, Karl Menninger considered suicide in more direct and comprehensive fashion. Menninger's psychoanalytic theory of suicide represents an important elaboration and extension of some of Freud's ideas, which he combined with his own seminal thoughts on the topic. Menninger's (1938) classic text *Man Against Himself* represents one of the most important, eloquent, and comprehensive theoretical considerations of suicide to date. Through discussion and case example, Menninger delineates analytic perspectives on hostility and the death instinct. Most notably, Menninger explains the psychodynamics of hostility and suicide in relationship to (a) the wish to kill, (b) the wish to be killed, and (c) the wish to die. Each of these three "wishes" is present in every suicide, Menninger argued, with one predominating in each. As is evident in Daniel's suicide, his wish to punish his father (the wish to kill) ultimately dominated, although both other motivations, the wish to die (to reunite with his mother) and to be killed (self-punishment— "I hate me") are in evidence.

Menninger further elaborated the role of the death instinct through his examination of the construct as it relates to physical illnesses. Menninger also theoretically defined different forms of suicidal expression contributing to a broader conceptualization of suicidal behaviors. One form of expression described by Menninger is "chronic suicide," in which long-term, life-threatening, and indirect self-destructive behavior (e.g., chronic substance abuse) reveals a latent death wish. Similarly, "focal suicide" reveals self-destructive impulses through focused self-destructive acts (e.g., nonlethal cutting behaviors; see chap. 3).

As discussed by Shneidman (1980), Gregory Zilboorg further refined Menninger's hypothesis, asserting that every case of suicide contains strong unconscious hostility combined with an unusual lack of capacity to love others. Zilboorg (1936) also considered narcissistic aspects of suicide, conceptualizing suicide as a primitive act in which one attempts to achieve a fantasized immortality. Asserting that the role of a broken home in suicide proneness reflects both internal and external etiological influences, Zilboorg was one of the first theorists to extend conceptualizations of suicide from purely intrapsychic dynamics to the external world.

A number of the neoanalytic theorists considered both interpsychic and intrapsychic aspects of suicide. Adler (1958) viewed suicide as an interpersonal act: because of insufficient social interest, a suicidal individual hurts others by inflicting injury upon himself or herself. Sullivan similarly emphasized the interactive aspects of suicide, asserting that suicide is usually an interpersonally destructive activity that reflects a hateful and hostile type of integration with others (Green, 1961). Karen Horney argued that most suicides represent a failure in social as well as individual growth, fundamentally reflecting a failure in the development of the self (De Rosis, 1961). In the Jungian tradition, Wahl (1957) hypothesized that suicide represents a desire for rebirth or resurrection to a new and better life. Suicide is conceptualized as a magical and omnipotent act of regression toward a rebirth of a new self (see Jung, 1959). Some suicide notes are explicit in these types of references, such as that of a 13-year-old male who wrote, "Mom and Dad, I'm going to a new life.... I always wanted a second chance."

Other dynamically oriented theorists have offered additional perspectives to explain the nature of suicidal behavior. Some have conceptualized suicide as a means of resolution to problems of separation and individuation (Wade, 1987). As discussed by Jan-Tausch (1963), aggressive acts and suicide attempts can lead to temporary relief of painful affect through the experience of the body as a separate self from an overenmeshed primary object relation. Wade's (1987) study of adolescent girls has indicated that relief from abandonment depression and feelings of separateness is achieved by using suicide as a means for regression to the safety of an earlier symbiotic state. Thus, suicide may represent a resolution of separation–individuation from parental objects, which reestablishes narcissistic equilibrium.

Leonard (1967) has constructed a theory of suicide that similarly emphasizes separation and individuation issues of the first years of life. Inadequate resolution of this phase of development is thought to lead to a lack of separate identity, inadequate impulse control, and rigidity. Leonard theorized that these three factors may increase the individual's vulnerability to suicide later in life under certain precipitating stresses.

Smith (1985) proposed the notion of "ego vulnerabilities" as a means of understanding suicidal behavior. Central to this perspective is the contention that death is the ego's ultimate tool of denial, in that suicide is an act that both preserves (and allows) the realization of the preferred self–other image while negating (attacking) the frustrating and devaluing object. Certain aspects of Smith's approach are reflected in Baumeister's (1990) theory of suicide as an escape from an intolerable experience of self. According to Baumeister, one's negative views of the self can become so unbearable—the self-loathing and self-hatred so extreme—that suicide becomes a compelling means of escape.

Not surprisingly, psychoanalytic constructs have been widely applied to varied and specific aspects of suicidal behavior, from implications in suicide among the elderly (Achte, 1988), to youth (Jobes, 1995b), to clinical risk assessment of suicide (Maltsberger, 1986, 1988), to predictive models of suicidal behavior (Leenaars & Balance, 1984). Clearly, the psychoanalytic tradition, both past and present, has greatly contributed to suicide theory building and our understanding of the phenomenon.

Developmental Theory

Much of the theorizing of psychoanalytically oriented scholars has been used to generate developmental perspectives that are relevant to adolescent suicidal behaviors. These theories tend to emphasize developmental issues that are unique to adolescence, such as simultaneous and competing needs inherent to this stage of life. As Berman (1984) noted, the adolescent is developmentally caught between two worlds: Needs for autonomy and independence paradoxically conflict with dependency needs and a desire to be a part of the family. Often adolescent developmental issues are interactive with the family system, which may foster a shared family regression. Ultimately, a shared family regression may lead to feelings of abandonment, rage, or both, which may in turn lead to self-destructive acting out (Shapiro & Freedman, 1987).

In a broader context, Emery (1983) proposed a developmental perspective that emphasizes identity formation through psychosocial development and epigenetic maturational processes unique to adolescence and the individual. To more fully understand the nature of adolescent depression and suicide, Emery emphasizes the importance of examining a variety of developmental dimensions. Although the unfolding of the adolescent's identity within the social context may be central (c.f., Erikson, 1959), Emery asserts that cognitive, learning, and moral development must be considered as well. As the youth passes through the developmental stage of adolescence, a variety of complex psychological functions are involved in what Emery refers to as the "progression/regression ratio." Building on the work of Erikson (1959) and Bowlby (1973), Emery describes various phases in the development of adolescent identity that may include behaviors that reflect adolescent protest, despair, and detachment. Critically, adolescent attempts to struggle through the various developmental phases inherent in identity formation may lead to depressive symptomatology or suicidal behaviors.

Family Systems Theory

A related line of theorizing arises from the family systems perspective (Minuchin, 1974). Joseph Richman (1984, 1986) is perhaps the most noted author of the family systems approach to suicide and its application to family therapy treatment of suicidal individuals. The essence of this perspective (Richman, 1986) is that disturbances in the family structure—including role conflicts and blurring of role boundaries, dysfunctional alliances across boundaries, secretiveness and failures of communication, and rigidity with inability to accept change or tolerate crisis—promote suicidal acting out within the family system. In their discussion of this approach, Trautman and Shaffer (1984) point out a "chicken or egg" dilemma inherent in family theory in that it is unclear whether the dysfunctional family system produces suicidal behavior or whether individual factors lead to suicidal behavior and a dysfunctional family.

Also implicated in family theories are the potential influence of parental psychopathology and the influence of conscious and unconscious wishes by the parent to "kill off" the child, which may lead to the child's suicidal acting out (Weissman, Paykel, & Klerman, 1972). Relevant to this perspective is Sabbath's (1969) notion of the "expendable child" who is driven to self-destruction by a pathogenic family system. In their review of family dynamics of adolescent suicide, Shapiro and Freedman (1987) assert that adolescent suicidal behavior may be seen as a consequence of ego deficits or faulty internalizations, but emphasize the importance of the youth's response to certain unconscious dynamics within the family system.

More recently Wagner (1997) has theoretically speculated about three potential profiles of suicidal youths and their families based on his extensive review of the empirical literature. These profiles include (a) the "child-driven" profile, (b) the "reciprocal" profile, and (c) the "parent-driven" profile. The child-driven profile pertains to a case in which parental caregiving is relatively competent and supportive but the child needs to escape the pain of severe psychopathology—there is no interpersonal motivation per se. In the reciprocal profile, both the child and the parents have pre-existing vulnerabilities; suicidal behaviors of the child occur from an interaction of child vulnerabilities and a dysfunctional family environment. Finally, in the parent-driven profile, unsupportive parents with poor communication, poor problem-solving skills, and psychopathology lead a child to self-destructive behaviors that communicate an angry message to parents that may elicit guilt or concern in the parent for the child.

In his review Wagner (1997) notes that although family-oriented theories of adolescent suicide have obvious intuitive and clinical appeal, empirical support for these approaches is not definitive. Indeed, empirical data that family dysfunction actually *causes* adolescent suicidal behaviors is only implicitly supported by research. Although there is evidence that poor family or parent-child communications, loss of caregiver to separation or death, and psychopathology in first-degree relatives are correlates of adolescent suicidality, whether these family risk factors actually *preceded* the development of suicidal symptoms in adolescents has not been well established by empirical research (Wagner, 1997).

Behavioral and Cognitive Theory

Over the past 40 years, a number of theorists have addressed the topic of suicide from both a behavioral (learning) and cognitive perspective. For example, from a purely behavioral perspective, Ferster (1973) provided an early provocative discussion of the incidence of depression and associated suicidal behaviors in relation to environmental reinforcement contingencies. Alternatively, Frederick and Resnick (1971) applied the principles of learning theory to describe how suicidal behaviors are actually learned. These authors argued that a variety of stimulus-response relations account for the production of suicidal behaviors, and, therefore, behavior therapy approaches can be effectively used to treat suicidal individuals to extinguish these learned behaviors.

Although behaviorists initially addressed some important ideas related to understanding and treating suicidality, the primary emphasis over the past 40 years has tended to center on *cognitive* aspects of suicide. Neuringer (1964) and Shneidman (1980, 1985) were among the first to address some of the various and unique cognitive aspects of suicide in their discussions of cognitive constriction, ambivalence, rigidity, and dichotomous thinking. Generally speaking, however, cognitive aspects of suicide have been most fully and fundamentally defined by the seminal thinking of Dr. Aaron T. Beck, the founder of cognitive therapy. For many years, Beck and his colleagues (e.g., Beck, Steer, Kovacs, & Garrison, 1985; Rush & Beck, 1978) have emphasized the key role that cognitive errors and distorted thinking play in suicidal behaviors. Beck's concept of the "cognitive triad" (negative thoughts about oneself, the future, and others) is central to the cognitive theory of depression with distinct implications for suicide. Within the cognitive perspective, hopelessness has been found to be perhaps the single most relevant clinical variable implicated in suicidal behavior. Beyond theorizing, empirical investigation has indeed confirmed the importance of hopelessness as an integral feature of suicide (Beck, Brown, & Steer, 1989; Brown, Beck, Steer, & Grisham, 2000). Extensive theoretical and subsequent empirical work by Beck and his colleagues (Henriques, Beck, & Brown, 2003) has recently led to an impressive 10-session cognitive treatment approach for adolescent and young adult suicide attempters, which we will discuss further in chapter 4.

One notable and recent contribution to cognitive–behavioral theorizing has been offered by Rudd, Joiner, and Rajab (2001). As described in their important book *Treating Suicidal Behavior*, Rudd et al. argue that a viable cognitive–behavioral approach to suicidality must use a theoretically based conceptual model with the following 10 requirements (pp. 23–24):

1. The model needs to address those variables (across all domains of functioning including cognitive, affective, behavioral, motivational) in a fashion unique to the patient's presentation and in a manner understandable to the patient. In other words, the model will serve as a parsimonious explanatory *map* of the presenting psychopathology. It needs to account for and communicate to both the therapist and patient the symptomatic presentation, relevant developmental history and trauma,

prominent maladaptive personality traits, identifiable stressors, and behavioral responses in an integrative, rather than isolated, fashion. Consistent with the notion of a *treatment map*, it needs to explain for the therapist and patient how the patient got from point A (nonsuicidal) to point B (suicidal) and how he or she gets to point C (recovery).

2. The model needs to communicate the transient, time-limited nature of suicidal crises, even for those exhibiting recurrent and chronic suicidal behavior. By definition, crises are self-limiting. Even those individuals who present with chronic suicidal behavior are at imminent risk for only limited periods, consistent with Litman's (1990a, 1990b) idea of the *suicide zone*.

3. The model needs to identify individual vulnerabilities that predispose an individual to multiple suicidal crises or recurrent behavior, acknowledging the importance of Axis I and II diagnoses and related comorbidity, along with developmental trauma and personal history.

4. The model needs to provide a means of distinguishing among suicidal, self-destructive, and self-mutilatory behaviors, accounting for distinct differences in the three across each domain of functioning.

5. The model needs to integrate the role of triggering events, accounting for acute and chronic stressors as well as personality disturbance. In particular, the model needs to acknowledge the potentially significant role of *internal* triggers (i.e., thoughts, images, feelings, and physical sensations).

6. The model needs to integrate the importance of emotion regulation, emotional dysphoria, and distress tolerance in the suicidal process.

7. The model needs to address the importance of interpersonal factors and social reinforcement in maintaining the behavior or facilitating recovery.

8. The model needs to provide sufficient explanatory detail so as to translate into a specific treatment plan (i.e., identifiable treatment targets across all domains of functioning).

9. The model needs to facilitate self-monitoring and self-awareness, providing flexibility in explaining day-to-day functioning. This can only be accomplished if the model is straightforward and easy to understand, relying on well-defined theoretical constructs.

10. The model needs to account for the process of change in suicidality over time, not just in terms of presenting symptoms.

It needs to incorporate the idea of skill acquisition, development, and refinement (i.e., personality change). It needs to reflect this change at multiple levels and across multiple domains of functioning.

As an elaboration and application of Beck's (1996) theorizing about modes and psychopathology, Rudd et al.'s (2001) approach emphasizes the interactions of different systems of personality (i.e., cognitive, affective, behavioral, and motivational schemas) that make up the structure or suborganizations that define and shape the suicidal mode. At the individual level, the suicidal mode can be seen as an interactive model that can be used to help identify the specific structural content of a patient's suicidal mode (see Figure 2.2). Critically, the practical assessment of suicide risk that is derived from this model can directly inform specific treatments and targets for treatments that exist within the structure of the suicidal mode.

A final cognitive perspective comes from British psychologist Dr. Mark Williams, who offers a unique and valuable perspective on suicidal thinking processes. In his discussion of suicidal ideation and attempt behaviors, Williams (2001) contends that what has been commonly referred to historically as a "cry for help" is as actually a "cry of pain." As Williams notes,

> ...the cry for help, which many have misinterpreted as a lack of genuineness, is better seen as a cry of pain. Suicidal behavior can have a communication outcome without communication being the main motive. The behavior is elicited by a situation in which the person feels trapped. As with the animal in a trap that cries in pain, the fact that the behavior affects the behavior of other members of the species does not mean that the only motive for the cry was to seek help. Suicidal behavior may be overtly communicative in a minority of cases, but mainly it is "elicited" by the pain of a situation with which the person cannot cope—it is a cry of pain first, and only after that a cry for help. (p. 148)

This notion naturally leads to a central point offered by Williams, which is that most suicidal people are not motivated by a wish to die as much as they are motivated by a wish to escape from an otherwise unbearable situation. According to Williams, feelings of being trapped are further fueled and maintained by biological and psychological changes. Williams argues that a sense of *entrapment* is central to suicidal behavior (i.e., anything that stops an animal or human from getting away when there is a desire to flee). Williams notes that in many suicidal people there is a combination of both defeat and the lack of escape (entrapment). Williams's work with "memory traps" is important because there is evidence that a depressed or suicidal person's autobiographical memory may reduce

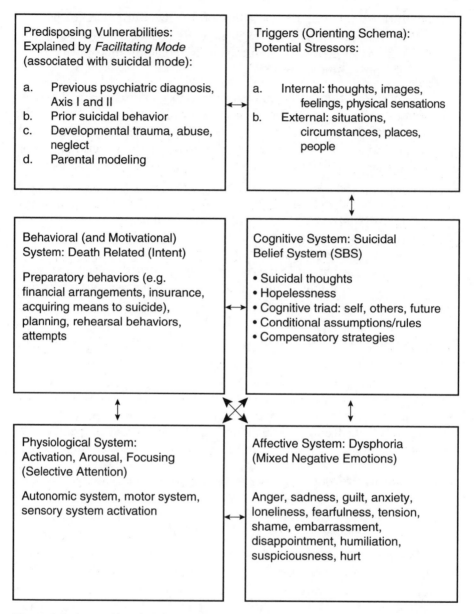

Figure 2.2. A cognitive–behavioral therapy model of suicidality: The suicidal mode. From *Treating Suicidal Behavior* (p. 31), by M. D. Rudd, T. Joiner, and H. Rajab, 2001, New York: Guilford Press. Copyright 2001 by Guilford Press. Reprinted with permission.

their ability to problem-solve and may restrict their capacity to consider the future. Williams concludes the following:

> An inability to be specific in retrieval of personal memories may signal a history of negative events, a history which is unprocessed and still has

power to interrupt the present with intrusive thoughts. Such general memories lead to a situation in which people are vague about the future and fail to produce good, effective problem-solving alternatives. It sets the context against which the final straw, that event which produces a global summary of the emptiness of one's life, may have its devastating consequences. If life circumstances are the factors that put a person in a cage, it is memory that springs the door closed. (2001, p. 173)

Williams's approach has obvious implications for clinical care. In this regard, he argues for the use of structured cognitive therapy with a particular emphasis on *mindfulness* (Segal, Williams, & Teasdale, 2002). A structured psychotherapeutic approach can fundamentally address issues related to memory traps, a sense of personal defeat, psychological entrapment, and a lack of future thinking which may ultimately lead to better problem solving and an improved capacity to cope.

Finally, no discussion of cognitive–behavior theory, suicide, and self-destructive behaviors would be complete without considering the major contributions of Dr. Marsha Linehan (1993; Linehan, Armstrong, Suarez, Allman, & Heard, 1991). At the heart of her dialectical behavior therapy (DBT) is the notion that suicide and self-destructive behaviors represent a basic effort to cope with low distress tolerance and limited coping resources. Linehan persuasively argues that maladaptive coping skills (e.g., cutting or attempting suicide) should be behaviorally extinguished while more adaptive coping skills are taught, substituted, and positively reinforced. A clinical translation of this theory may include informed consent at the start of treatment that there will be no contact with the treatment team for 24 hours following a suicide attempt (i.e., extinguishing the maladaptive behavior) while improvements in communication, help-seeking, and assertiveness are heavily reinforced (i.e., positive reinforcement for development of improved coping skills). Although DBT was principally developed for the treatment of patients with borderline personality disorder, the implications for the broader field of suicidology have been far-reaching indeed (Jobes, 2000). Extensions of Linehan's theorizing and further applications of DBT principles have provided valuable contributions to the clinical suicidology literature (e.g., Chiles & Strosahl, 1995; Miller, 1999).

Integrative Psychological Models

Some psychological theories integrate a range of perspectives and potential influences on suicidal behavior. Farber (1968), for example, conceptualizes suicide as a disease of hope in which social influences (subcultural tolerance for suicide, availability of succorance, demands for interpersonal giving, and demands for exercising competence) are interactive with psychological influence (e.g., future time perspective). Farber contends that the interrelation of perceptual, social, interpersonal, psychological, and cultural variables defines the hopelessness that accounts for suicide.

From a somewhat different perspective, Edwin Shneidman has developed a novel theoretical model based on 10 common psychological variables associated with suicidal death (Shneidman, 1985). Shneidman (1988) posits that the etiology of suicide can be conceptually understood schematically in terms of a suicidal cube. The three surfaces of the cube are respectively labeled *Pain*, *Press*, and *Perturbation* (see Figure 2.3).

Pain is described as the subjective experience of unbearable psychological pain (idiosyncratically defined by the individual) and can range from 1 (*little pain*) to 5 (*intolerable pain*). In more recent years, Shneidman (1996) has further developed the notion of psychological pain in terms of "psychache"—a unique and intense level of psychological suffering that is central to every completed suicide.

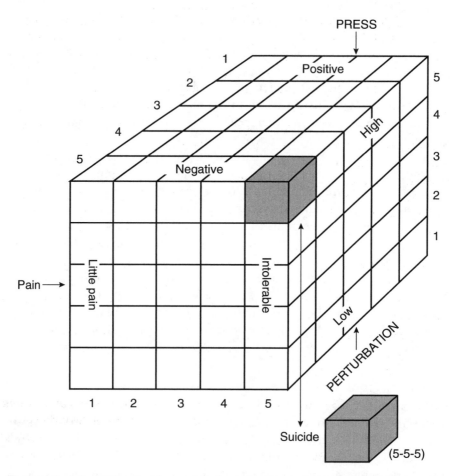

Figure 2.3. A theoretical cubic model of suicide. From *Cataclysms, Crises, and Catastrophes* (p. 175), by G. R. VandenBos and B. K. Bryant (Eds.), 1987, Washington, DC: American Psychological Association. Copyright 1987 by the American Psychological Association.

Press is seen as everything that is done to an individual that affects an individual's response to virtually anything. As discussed by Shneidman's mentor, Henry Murray (1938), presses are those pressures and influences that affect an individual's feelings, thoughts, and behaviors. From an integrative perspective, interpersonal and societal influences on the individual can be conceptualized as presses as well as internal presses (e.g., command hallucinations). In terms of the schematic suicidal cube model, presses range from 1 (*potentially positive*) to 5 (*negative and stressful*).

Shneidman (1985) has described perturbation as the individual's general state of emotional upset and cognitive constriction—a key psychological feature necessary for a lethal suicide attempt to occur. Perturbation is reflected in poor impulse control, agitation, and propensity for precipitous action. With regard to the schematic model, perturbation can range from 1 (*mildly upset*) to 5 (*extremely agitated and emotionally upset*).

Finally, according to Shneidman's model, the corner "suicidal cubelet" (the 5-5-5 blackened portion of the cube) represents the maximum combination of pain, press, and perturbation—the most dangerous and acute suicidal risk. Shneidman asserts that every suicide occurs in relation to a lethal combination of these three interactive components. Shneidman further asserts that the uniquely psychological nature of suicide is motivated by psychological pain (psychache), which in turn is initiated and maintained by blocked psychological needs. This theoretical model thus defines suicide as a death fundamentally caused by a synergy of intense psychological pain, overwhelming pressures, and intense emotional energy and upset.

With a similar phenomenological emphasis on psychological pain, Jobes (2001) has offered another structural model that emphasizes a progression of affective and cognitive activation that leads to actual suicidal behaviors (see Figure 2.4). Beginning with the basic superordinate influences of any one person's biology, sociology, and psychology, this model conceptualizes any suicidal condition as beginning with core mental pain that is then subsequently shaped by internal and relational orientations to suicide as a viable means of coping with psychological pain. In the course of cognitive decision making, various reasons for living and dying are debated and subsequently shape any suicidal behaviors that may follow.

A final integrative model is proposed by Rogers (2001), who offers an existential–constructivist model that explains pathways leading to suicide (see Figure 2.5). This models posits that in our quest for existential meaning and interpersonal connectedness, there are constructions of "worldview" as well as additional constructions of "self," "others," and "relationships." Within this model, given the motivational backdrop of the existential exigencies of death, meaninglessness, and isolation, there are three distinct responses to significant environmental challenges to one's constructions of the world, self, others, and relationships: (a) an alteration of one's constructions, (b) a retention of one's constructions, or (c) suicide.

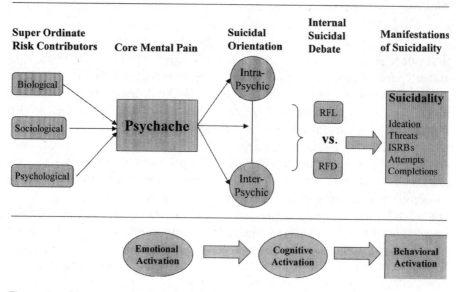

Figure 2.4. Phenomenological model of suicidality.

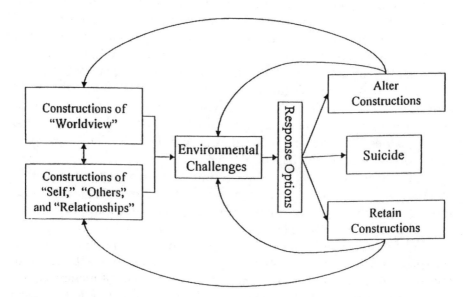

Figure 2.5. Constructivist pathways leading to suicide. From "Theoretical Grounding: The 'Missing Link' in Suicide Research," by J. Rogers, in *Journal of Counseling and Development*, 79, p. 21. Copyright 2001 by the American Counseling Association. Reprinted with permission. No further reproduction authorized without written permission of the American Counseling Association.

Neurobiological and Genetic Theories of Suicide

Since the last edition of this book, perhaps one of the fastest-growing areas of empirical research in suicidology falls under the broad heading of biology. According to Maris et al. (2000), research into the biology and neurobiology of suicide can be organized into four areas of study: (a) genetic studies, (b) studies of populations at risk, (c) biochemistry and anatomy studies, and (d) radiological studies. As basic research, much of the work in this area is necessarily exploratory and descriptive, and therefore it is often not theoretically driven. Nevertheless, there are some important guiding theoretical notions that shape empirical inquiry, which in turn will shape our biological theorizing.

As discussed by Joiner, Johnson, and Soderstrom (2002), there is great promise in the prospect of looking for specific genetic vulnerabilities to suicide. Studies such as Brent, Johnson, and Connolly's (1996) controlled family study of adolescent suicide victims are providing persuasive evidence that propensities toward suicidal behaviors may well be familially transmitted as a trait independent of Axis I and II disorders in terms of suicidal attempts and completions. Buoyed by recent and exciting research of the human genome, biologically oriented suicide researchers have increasingly studied potential links between suicidal behaviors and specific genes. Much of the initial work in this area (e.g., Nielson et al., 1994) has centered on the tryptophan hydroxylase (TPH) gene, which has been found to be associated with suicide. Subsequent research has sought to replicate this finding, and further study is being done on the TPH gene, and allelic variations of the gene, which is involved in the production of the neurotransmitter serotonin. Researchers theorize that further investigations using twins, family histories, and adopted children will lead to a detailed level of understanding about which genes are implicated in suicide, how these genes vary, and therefore who may be uniquely at risk for suicidal behaviors with potential prevention and treatment implications therein.

Beyond genetic research, most of the biological study of suicide has centered on biochemical investigations of certain neurotransmitters in at-risk populations. In this regard, the most promising line of brain biochemistry research has involved neurotransmitter monoamine metabolites, particularly the serotonin metabolite 5-hydroxyindoleacetic acid (5-HIAA), which appears to be correlated with suicidal behavior. Noting that antidepressant treatment enhances serotonin transmission, early lines of experimental inquiry focused on the question of whether serotonin transmission is disordered in depression (Asberg, 1990). Studies of depressed patients indicate a bimodal distribution of 5-HIAA in their lumbar cerebrospinal fluid (CSF), in contrast to a normal distribution in nondepressed patients. Suicidal patients, especially completers who died using violent methods, were noted to aggregate among those with low CSF-5-HIAA. Depressed (unipolar) suicide attempters had 5-HIAA concentrations 25% lower than those of control participants. Similar findings have been reported among suicide-attempting nondepressed patients—those with personality disorders (e.g., criminal offenders) and schizophrenia (Asberg, 1989, 1990). As summarized by Maris et al. (2000), the exact role that serotonin plays in self-destructive behaviors is not completely understood and requires further investigation. These authors suggest that serotonin is somehow involved in the pathway from genetic predisposition and environmental stimulus to the development of psychopathology that is so implicated in suicidality.

Postmortem anatomical and neurochemical studies have some potential for helping us understand the neurobiology of suicide. Studies of suicide victim brain tissue have intensively examined serotonergic, noradrenergic, and dopaminergic neurotransmitter systems (e.g., Stanley, Mann, & Cohen, 1986), but these studies are not yet conclusive. Nevertheless, Mann (1998) has proposed that the ventral prefrontal cortex is an area that may be highly associated with suicidal behaviors. He asserts that abnormalities in this region of the brain may affect the executive functioning, specifically in terms of inhibition and disinhibition. It thus follows that a reduction of serotonergic activity in this part of the brain may impair one's ability to *not* act on powerful aggressive or suicidal feelings. Mann's (1998) work in the neurobiology of suicide has led to the development of a stress–diathesis model of suicidal behavior and the hypothesized roles of serotonergic and noradrenergic activity in suicidal behaviors that are trait and state dependent (Mann & Arango, 1992).

Summary of Suicide Theories

We have only briefly highlighted a sample of broad theoretical considerations of suicide that may be loosely organized under the conceptual headings of sociological, psychological, and neurobiology–genetics. It is important to note that across these domains, there is an increasing emphasis on theoretical integration, particularly among psychological theorizing. Further examples of theoretical integration include those offered by Blumenthal and Kupfer (1990), whose "overlap model" (see Figure 2.6) emphasizes the interactive and overlapping influences of biology, psychiatric disorder, family history and genetics, personality traits, and psychosocial life events/chronic medical illness.

In contrast to this relatively simple and intuitive integrative approach, a more complex and comprehensive model has been developed by Maris, Berman, and Maltsberger (1992; see Figure 2.7). Within this general model of suicidal behaviors, the complexities of interactions among psychiatry, biology, psychology, and sociology are noted and broken down into more specific variables. In addition, this model addresses the life course of a suicidal person from birth to death, and furthermore addresses

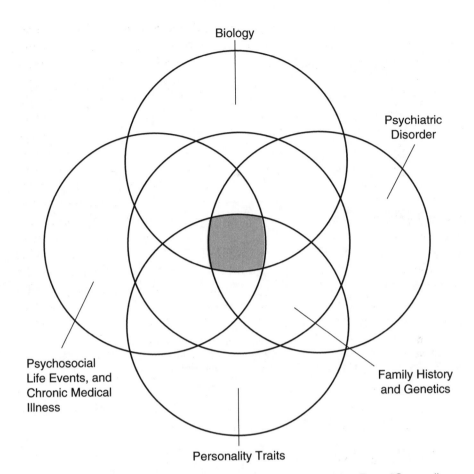

Biology

Psychiatric
Disorder

Psychosocial
Life Events, and
Chronic Medical
Illness

Family History
and Genetics

Personality Traits

Figure 2.6. Overlap model for understanding suicidal behavior. From "Generaliz-able Treatment Strategies for Suicidal Behavior," by S. J. Blumenthal and D. J. Kup-per, 1986, *Annals of the New York Academy of Sciences: Psychobiology of Suicidal Behavior*, 487, p. 329. Copyright 1986 by the New York Academy of Sciences, U.S.A. Reprinted with permission.

different levels of prevention. Completed suicides thus occur in the absence of prevention, when the interactive interplay of psychiatric illness, biology, psychology, and sociology leads a person into a dangerous suicide zone, where certain triggers may cause a critical threshold to be crossed; a suicidal career then ends with death.

Despite increased interest and progress in theory building, further the-orizing and integration of existing and new theories remains an important frontier in the field of suicidology. Having considered the theories relevant and specific to suicide, it is now important to conceptualize these perspec-tives within the larger context of adolescent development itself to better understand who suicidal adolescents are and who they are not.

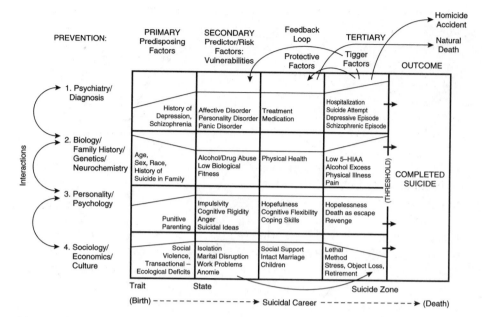

PREVENTION:	PRIMARY Predisposing Factors	SECONDARY Predictor/Risk Factors: Vulnerabilities	Feedback Loop / Protective Factors	TERTIARY / Tigger Factors	OUTCOME
1. Psychiatry/ Diagnosis	History of Depression, Schizophrenia	Affective Disorder Personality Disorder Panic Disorder	Treatment Medication	Hospitalization Suicide Attempt Depressive Episode Schizophrenic Episode	
2. Biology/ Family History/ Genetics/ Neurochemistry	Age, Sex, Race, History of Suicide in Family	Alcohol/Drug Abuse Low Biological Fitness	Physical Health	Low 5–HIAA Alcohol Excess Physical Illness Pain	COMPLETED SUICIDE
3. Personality/ Psychology	Punitive Parenting	Impulsivity Cognitive Rigidity Anger Suicidal Ideas	Hopefulness Cognitive Flexibility Coping Skills	Hopelessness Death as escape Revenge	
4. Sociology/ Economics/ Culture	Social Violence, Transactional – Ecological Deficits	Isolation Marital Disruption Work Problems Anomie	Social Support Intact Marriage Children	Lethal Method Stress, Object Loss, Retirement	

Homicide Accident — Natural Death

Interactions

(THRESHOLD)

Trait State Suicide Zone

(Birth) - - - - - - - - - - - - - ▶ Suicidal Career - - - - - - - - - - - - ▶ (Death)

Figure 2.7. A general model of suicidal behaviors. From *A General Model of Suicidal Behaviors* (p. 668), by R. Maris, A. Berman, and J. Maltsberger, 1992, New York: Guilford Press. Copyright 1992 by The Guilford Press. Reprinted with permission.

THE DEVELOPMENTAL CONTEXT

As Lively (1987) notes,

> Children are not like us. They are beings apart: impenetrable, unapproachable. They inhabit not our world but a world we have lost and can never recover. We do not remember childhood—we imagine it. We search for it, in vain, through layers of obscuring dust, and recover some bedraggled shreds of what we think it was. And all the while the inhabitants of this world are among us, like Aborigines, like Minoans, people from elsewhere safe in their own time-capsule. (pp. 42–43)

In the first edition of this book, we endeavored to challenge readers to reconsider what they thought they knew about adolescence as a developmental period because we felt that emphasizing the developmental context of adolescent suicide was critical to effectively understanding and preventing it. In this section we thus critiqued the commonly held views promulgated by the mass media that teenagers are widely seen as rebellious, angst-ridden, and downright ornery. Moreover, we argued that much of this conventional wisdom did not hold up to empirical examination, limited as it was in the late 1980s. Since that time, however, there has been a great deal more empirical research leading to new and exciting conceptualizations of adolescence as well as evolving models of adolescent psychopathology.

These considerations are particularly clear when we consider changing ideas about the "storm and stress" (or *Sturm und Drang*) approach to describing adolescent development. First presented by G. Stanley Hall (1904) at the turn of the last century, Hall argued that adolescence is inherently a time when teenagers question and contradict their parents, have disruptions in moods, and show a propensity for recklessness and antisocial behavior. Although Hall is widely recognized as the promoter of this model, Arnett (1999) has asserted that Hall was actually more nuanced in his thinking; individual differences exist and culture and biology have a meaningful impact on and shape adolescent storm and stress.

In contrast to Hall's relativistic approach, Anna Freud had a much more emphatic view that storm and stress is universal and immutable; indeed, its absence could actually signify psychopathology. In the years since Hall and Freud, theorists and researchers have debated the universality, incidence, and magnitude of adolescent storm and stress. Arnett (1999) persuasively argues that more recent empirical data is leading to a modified and more balanced understanding of adolescent storm and stress. What has emerged in this area is that adolescence is in fact a difficult period of life (Buchanan et al., 1990). These difficulties are said to focus on three key areas: (a) conflicts with parents, (b) mood disruptions, and (c) risk behaviors. The emerging data thus tend to challenge relatively recent and revisionistic notions that adolescent storm and stress is a myth and does not really find empirical support (a position we argued to some extent in the first edition). In truth, however, the reality is something in between. The empirical data (discussed further in the next chapter) now tend to provide sufficient evidence of meaningful challenges that make adolescence a difficult period of life. Alternatively, however, it would be inaccurate to describe adolescence as only a time of storm and stress—the data suggest that even amidst the challenges of adolescence, many young people nevertheless take pleasure in their lives, are satisfied with relationships, and have hope for the future (Offer, 1987; Offer & Schonert-Reichel, 1992).

Adolescent Psychology

How many generations who have preceded us were convinced that their cohort of teenagers were truly different than any cohort ever previously seen? Certainly the parents of teens during the tumultuous years of the 1960s felt that way about young people who grew their hair, wore strange clothes, and questioned/rejected many mainstream conventional values that were spawned in the post–World War II era. So, in a contemporary sense, we feel some measure of wariness in declaring that contemporary adolescents are any more unique than cohorts of previous generations.

Yet, in the wake of September 11 terrorist attacks on New York and Washington, we are hard-pressed to not consider how today's world is uniquely affecting a fundamentally different adolescent psychology. Indeed, some argue that there are in fact a number of distinct and important differences in today's youth experience that uniquely shape their psychology (Taffel, 2001). Could it be that the routine exposure that contemporary youth have to violence, video games, sex, drugs, and alcohol in conjunction with their largely unsupervised and invisible exploration of cyberspace creates a whole new—never before seen—level of information, awareness, and potential vulnerability among teens? Maybe it is simply a generational perceptual given that the elders of a youth cohort will see contemporary youth as unique and fundamentally different from themselves at the same age. Whatever the case, it still behooves us to understand those themes that are common *and* specific to an adolescent cohort if we are to understand and contextualize the psychological fabric of a young life that may be threatened by a suicidal death.

As noted, the field of adolescent psychology, as well as the evolving field of adolescent psychopathology, has grown rapidly over recent years, and a great deal more theoretical perspectives and empirical data are now available. Although much of the original ground-breaking adolescent theorizing came from the psychoanalytic stance, numerous other perspectives have emerged from a variety of theoretical frameworks and disciplines, including psychology, psychiatry, sociology, education, rehabilitation, and, more recently, from neuroscience. The primary theoretical models of adolescence now include psychoanalytic, developmental, learning, and neurobiological perspectives. Each respective theory contributes a unique and valuable lens through which we can better examine and understand the developmental stage of adolescence.

The classic analytic model of adolescence emphasized instinctual drives and the primacy of the genital stage of psychosexual development (Freud, 1905/1957). Subsequent analytic theories such as Anna Freud's (1958) "storm and stress" model emphasized the interaction of the ego and instinctual drives, which creates anxiety and dread. Later theories have de-emphasized instinctual and biological drives as the focus has shifted toward object-relations (Guntrip, 1974; Winnicott, 1965) and the development of the self (Kohut, 1971, 1977).

Developmental theories of adolescence have evolved along two traditional lines: (a) Erikson's (1968) psychoanalytically based psychosocial stage theory of development, which emphasizes the "identity crisis" of adolescence, and (b) Piaget's theory of cognitive development, which emphasizes the "formal operations" phase of an adolescent's cognitive development. In addition, learning theories of adolescence provide an empirical paradigm from which adolescent behaviors can be examined in terms of operant or classical conditioning. From this perspective, adolescence has been conceptualized as an especially significant period of learning, which may be reflected in the individuality of adolescent response styles and behaviors (Gross & Lewin, 1987).

Perhaps one of the most exciting contemporary areas of theoretical development is in the form of integrated models in developmental psychopathology (e.g., Cichetti & Toth, 1995). Critical to these emerging approaches is a growing appreciation for the evolving nature of neurocognitive development in adolescence and the importance of emotion regulation and the role of emotion socialization (Zahn-Waxler, Klimes-Dougan, & Kendziora, 1998). Of course, longstanding theoretical work has consistently emphasized the importance of pubescent biological change as well as psychological development (e.g., Kestenberg, 1968; Peterson & Taylor, 1980).

Adolescents, Death, and Suicide

In our examination of theoretical aspects of adolescence and suicide, it may be useful to briefly consider how adolescents conceptualize death. Kastenbaum (1986) notes that "[i]t is in adolescence that we glimpse for the first time what we and the world might be" (p. 13). Therein lies a paradox, for in adolescence we may also realize what we might *not* be. With the completion of cognitive development and the interactions between various physical and intrapersonal and interpersonal changes of adolescence, questions of life and death become both real and profound. Indeed, there are those who may spend the balance of their life attempting to conceal or forget a deep sense of existential vulnerability that emerges during adolescence (Kastenbaum, 1986).

The pushes and pulls of life and death are commonly reflected in the music of adolescence (Attig, 1986) and in historically reported fears and preoccupations, such as with nuclear war (Goodman, Mack, Beardslee, & Snow, 1983; Snow, 1984). Typically, latency-aged children and early adolescents begin to develop an increasing awareness of death as a reality. Gordon (1986) refers to this process of an evolving death awareness as the wearing away of the naive child's "cloak of immortality." Through exposure, experience, and subsequent awareness, the older adolescent begins to attempt to impart meaning to death (and, thereby, life) in such a way as to instill a sense of hope in living. Not surprisingly, it is the absence of hope in life that is often observed as a central feature of the suicidal adolescent's inner world.

Adolescent Perceptions of Suicide

In the first edition of this book, we reported on a range of empirical studies investigating adolescent perceptions and attitudes toward suicide. For example, one early study provided data that suggested the possibility that young people (when compared to their parents) have a more accepting attitude toward suicide (Boldt, 1982). To account for this possibility, Baron and Byrne (1984) suggested that unlike previous generations, contemporary young people watch a great deal more television and see movies that contain many depictions of suicide. A desensitization effect was therefore hypothesized: If young people are exposed to numerous portrayals of self-destruction, then the act of suicide may therefore become less mysterious, threatening, and aversive. An alternative explanation cited by numerous authors (see chap. 6) emphasizes the possibility of suicide modeling effects, by which knowledge of suicidal behaviors (particularly in young people) may foster a sense that suicide is a viable escape from unpleasant realities. Accordingly, Allen (1987) argues that death may be less real to an adolescent and suicide may be more acceptable. In effect, an adolescent may fantasize that it is possible to return to life after a suicide, just as one can return from a drug-induced escape from reality.

Empirical research in this area was initially addressed in a line of studies conducted by Domino and colleagues. The Suicide Opinion Questionnaire (SOQ) was extensively used with samples of young people as well as other populations (Domino, 1980, 1981, 1985). For example, Domino and Leenaars (1989) used the SOQ to compare attitudes toward suicide among Canadian and American college students. Their study produced data that addressed suicide-related themes such as motivation, religion, impulsivity, recidivism, and various misconceptions. Results from their study suggested that college students from both countries perceived suicidal acts as manipulative, did not see suicide attempts as impulsive acts, and strongly endorsed the notion that once a person makes a suicide attempt, he or she is more likely to make a second attempt.

More recent research in this domain has examined perceptions and feelings toward suicide as well as different psychological constructs that may bear on suicidality. For example, Orbach, Kedem, Gorchover, Apter, and Tyano (1993) examined the fear of death among suicidal and nonsuicidal adolescents and have found that fear of death is processed and experienced differently by suicidal and nonsuicidal adolescents (i.e., fear of death serves as a facilitator or an inhibitor of suicidal behaviors). Cotton and Range (1996) conducted a study of suicidality, hopelessness, and attitudes toward life and death among clinical and nonclinical teens. In their study, they found that the best predictors of suicidality were related to feelings of hopelessness, repulsion toward life, and feelings of rejection by the family.

Other contemporary research has looked at additional attitudes related to suicide. Marion and Range (2003) studied the attitudes of young African American women, who as a population have very low rates of suicide. These researchers asked their subjects to imagine extenuating circumstances (e.g., a terminal illness) to determine whether their attitudes toward suicide could be swayed by such circumstances. They found that African American women's attitudes toward suicide remained steadfastly negative across circumstances; religiosity was found to be inversely correlated with suicide acceptability. In contrast, King, Hampton, Bernstein, and Schichor's (1996) study of college students demonstrated higher levels of acceptability for suicide given extenuating circumstances.

At a national level, a study conducted by Renberg and Jacobsson (2003) in Sweden attempted to assess broad population-based attitudes toward suicide. At the individual level, subjects who themselves had engaged in suicidal behaviors had more permissive and understanding attitudes toward suicide than did nonsuicidal members of the sample (see also similar findings of Stein, Brom, Elizur, & Witztum, 1998). Empirical research about individual as well as national attitudes and perceptions of suicide continues to be of interest because suicidal behaviors do not occur within a vacuum; clearly, the way a society/culture and an individual views suicide is critical to our ongoing efforts to better understand suicide so that we may better prevent it.

The Interpersonal Context

As a final consideration in this theory-oriented chapter, the interpersonal aspects of adolescent suicide are important to note. Intuitively, we know that a young person's suicidal behaviors will be influenced largely by their attitudes and perceptions of suicide. A young person who views suicide as an enticing and dramatic means of escape is clearly at more risk to act out self-destructively than is a young person who perceives suicide as an unacceptable and abhorrent act. Critically, the formation, maintenance, and change of such attitudes and perceptions occur within, and are interactive with, an interpersonal context.

As an example, the effects of overt and covert labeling within a family, educational, or peer group system can be devastating and may precede subsequent suicidal behaviors. Behavioral and emotional problems may lead parents to label and scapegoat their child as the family's "black sheep." Teachers may come to identify a struggling youth as a "problem child" or a "discipline problem." Members of an adolescent peer group may taunt and reject a disturbed cohort, tagging them with cruel names and derision. Such labeling has the potential to become self-reinforcing, leading to further negative attention-seeking and self-fulfilling prophecies that a young person may become compelled to confirm.

Along these lines, Bostock and Williams (1974) suggested from a behavioral perspective that suicidal behavior can be viewed as an operant that is reinforced and maintained by consequent interpersonal contingencies. This view underscores the interpersonal dilemma of a recipient of a suicidal communication. Responding to depressive or suicidal messages may reinforce the behavior, through the reward of social attention, and thereby increase the frequency of this behavior. Alternatively, to ignore the depressive or suicidal communication in an attempt to extinguish the behavior may serve to prompt feelings of rejection and more severe behavioral outcomes (e.g., an actual suicide attempt).

The role of peers was perhaps never more dramatically displayed than in the horrors of the shootings in Columbine High School. Although not a focus of the media's attention, suicidologists were struck that Dylan Klebolt and Eric Harris were prototypic suicidal teenage boys, replete with conduct, mood, and family problems. In hindsight, their suicidal and subsequent homicidal rage was profoundly fueled by the teasing and taunts of their high school peers.

It is important to note that therapists are certainly not immune to labeling their patients or participating in interactive dynamics that may be pathogenic (Berman & Cohen-Sandler, 1983; Jobes, 2000). By and large, therapists expect patients to be motivated to use offered help, follow therapeutic advice, and actively engage in the therapeutic process on their own behalf. Suicidal patients, however, frequently do not meet such expectations. The negativity, hopelessness, and inability to change that are endemic to suicide are frequently interpreted and subsequently labeled by therapists as *resistance*. Because we may blame a patient for not changing a behavior that we may see as within his or her control, there is a risk that we fail to understand the nature of the patient's experience and thereby engage in a nontherapeutic interactive feedback loop. Inadvertently, a therapist's negative responses to a patient may increase as the patient's suicide intention increases. Therefore, the patient's irritating behavior—perhaps the very reason that the patient needs the therapist's help—exemplifies the process by which these individuals gradually alienate other potential helpers in their world, thereby maintaining their depression and heightening both their isolation and hopelessness. Accordingly, the distancing and help-rejecting behaviors presented by suicidal patients must be relabeled not as resistance but as the reason for treatment (see chap. 5 for further discussion on this topic).

As mentioned earlier, various authors have discussed interactive issues within the family system, where a child's role can become one of acting out the family's psychopathology (Richman, 1986; Sabbath, 1969; Wagner, 1997). Peer-group relationships and interactions appear to play a significant role in that lack of peer involvement and conflictual relationships are commonly associated with adolescent suicide (see Topol & Reznikoff, 1982).

On a more directly interactive level, there is evidence that a peer-group subculture can lead to a series of suicidal behaviors. Robbins and Conroy (1983) cite one case example related to a series of suicidal behaviors among members of a small peer group of adolescents in Chappaqua, New York. In 1978, this small suburban community experienced two adolescent suicide deaths within a 6-month period, followed by five admissions for suicide attempts and an admission for suicidal ideation within 7 weeks of the second suicide. The six suicidal patients were found to be a group of students from the same high school who had visited each other during their hospitalizations for suicidal behavior. The clear implication is that these peers seemed to have influenced or served as models for suicidal behaviors, thus triggering subsequent imitation of suicidal acting out. Although the specifics of possible interactive or interpersonal effects remain unclear, it is apparent that adolescent suicidal behaviors do not occur in an interpersonal vacuum.

CONCLUSION

We opened this chapter with the stories of Bill and Jenny, whose suicidal behaviors had some obvious and not-so-obvious explanations. Depending on the lenses we use to examine their cases, each suicidal behavior takes on a different meaning. For the sake of simplicity, it is tempting to understand suicidal behavior from a theoretical perspective, yet it appears that the most comprehensive understanding requires sensitivity to a broad range of variables, including social, psychological, neurobiological, and genetic influences that are increasingly being considered integratively. Moreover, a comprehensive understanding of adolescent suicide requires a larger context, that of adolescence itself and those aspects that are unique to this stage of development. To that end we have endeavored to describe what is both typical and atypical of adolescence, thus setting the stage to discern what is unique to adolescents who are suicidal. However, to see these youth more clearly, we must go beyond theory and turn our focus to the empirical research on which the potential validity of these and subsequent theories must depend.

3

THE EMPIRICAL CONTEXT

DIFFICULTIES OF SUICIDE RESEARCH

To be sure, the challenges to conducting empirical research in suicide are considerable. As discussed in the first edition of this book, the first generation of research in adolescent suicide was plagued by inadequate methodologies that led to misleading findings (refer to discussions by Berman & Carroll, 1984; Berman & Cohen-Sandler, 1982a; Pfeffer, 1989). Many earlier studies of suicide (including studies of adolescent suicide) lacked acceptable definitions of basic research variables (e.g., the definition of "suicide attempt") or failed to use appropriate control comparison groups. However, over the years since the first edition of this book was published, there has been a gradual improvement in research methodologies and empirical rigor in the study of suicide. For example, O'Carroll et al. (1996) proposed a nomenclature that has sparked significant interest and debate in developing more exacting terms for how we think about and describe the full spectrum of suicidal behaviors (see Silverman, Berman, Tanney, Jobes, & Sandall, 2005; Wagner, Wong, & Jobes, 2002). Routine use of case-control comparisons has become the rule rather than the exception in youth suicide research (e.g., Adams, Overholser, & Spirito, 1994; Brent, Perper, Moritz, Allman, et al., 1993; Brent, Perper, Moritz, Baugher, et al., 1993; Gould, Fisher, Parides, Flory, & Shaffer, 1996; Spirito, Francis, Overholser, & Frank, 1996).

Nevertheless, from an empirical perspective, suicide remains a remarkably difficult phenomenon to study. Suicide research is fundamentally limited by the deaths of its subjects. The people who are most important to understand are, by definition, unavailable to the suicide researcher. Use of standard scientific methodology, such as randomly selected samples or rigorously controlled experiments, is often prohibited by the unique constraints inherent in suicide phenomena. Indeed, as Linehan (1998) has observed, clinical treatment trials of psychiatric populations have routinely and explicitly *excluded* high-risk suicidal patients because of inherent risks and potential for litigation. It is important to note, however, that some changes in this area are underway. For example, the National Institute of Mental Health (NIMH) has provided key leadership in helping move empirical research with high-risk suicidal populations forward, dealing with various ethical and methodological issues that are inherent in doing research with high-risk groups (refer to the NIMH Web site at http://www.nimh.nih.gov/research/highrisksuicide.cfm).

Nevertheless, studying suicidal individuals often requires the use of creative approaches or less than elegant research designs. Given the importance of suicide, some feel that the *relevance* of certain constructs may need to be considered at the potential cost of scientific *rigor* (see discussion by Jobes et al., 2004). In considering the broad range of empirical work performed in this field, it is our sense that a balance must be found between external and internal validity, and we believe that this balance is increasingly being better struck in contemporary suicide research.

Given obvious methodological and ethical constraints, many investigators retrospectively study data obtained by medical examiners and coroners or data gathered through post hoc interviews, suicide notes, or medical records. As an alternative, many suicidologists choose to study living suicide ideators or surviving attempters. However, as depicted in Figure 3.1, data obtained from attempters and ideators is often not readily generalizable to completers, who represent a markedly different population (Linehan, 1986).

Prospective studies (cf., Motto, 1984), desirable from a purely scientific perspective, are difficult, if not impossible, to conduct because of the ethical constraints involved (e.g., interviewing a potential suicidal individual and waiting to see whether that person commits suicide with no effort to intervene). Moreover, there are considerable sample and resource considerations; suicide research is often limited because collecting data on samples large enough to be meaningfully interpretable is usually quite difficult.

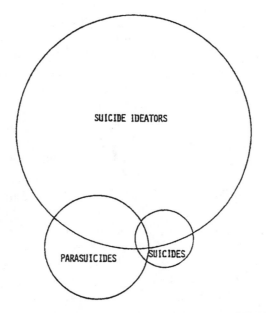

Figure 3.1. Linehan's overlapping populations model. From "Suicidal People: One Population or Two," by M. M. Lineham, 1986, *Annals of the New York Academy of Sciences: Psychobiology of Suicidal Behavior, 487*, p. 21. Copyright 1986 by the New York Academy of Sciences, U.S.A. Reprinted by permission.

The Statistical Approach

From a purely statistical perspective, suicidal behaviors are rare. This fact greatly limits the researcher's ability to empirically identify those demographic, sociocultural, and clinical variables that might provide the means to validly and reliably predict suicidal behaviors (a goal shared by many suicidologists). Even were we able to develop tests with high specificity and sensitivity,[1] the prediction of suicide at a definite or indefinite future time would lead to an intolerable number of false positives and false negatives, and inadequate levels of reliability (Kaplan, Kottler, & Frances, 1982; Murphy, 1983; Pokorny, 1983). The consequences of relying on a predictive (statistical) approach, therefore, places an unacceptable number of patients on suicide watch with associated restrictions in personal liberty (false negatives) or accepting an unacceptable number of otherwise preventable deaths (false positives). As a "low base-rate" event, valid and reliable prediction of suicide at a definite or indefinite future time is virtually impossible.

---

[1]Sensitivity refers to the proportion of correctly identified positive cases, defined as 100 times the ratio of true positives divided by the sum of true positives and false negatives. Specificity refers to the proportion of correctly identified negative cases, that is, 100 times the ratio of true negatives divided by the sum of true positives and true negatives (Galen & Gambino, 1975).

As an illustration, consider the following example (cf. Rosen, 1959). Imagine we had available for our use a 10-item checklist or "suicide assessment scale," which, given a cutoff score, could correctly identify 95% of potential adolescent suicide completers and attempters. For the sake of our discussion, let us assume that in a population of 100,000 adolescents, we could expect 20 completed suicides and 2,000 attempts in any given year. Therefore, the application of our scale should lead to the correct identification of 95% of 2,020 suicidal adolescents per year, or 1,919 adolescents in need of early intervention and treatment. However, the same scale would incorrectly identify 5% of this population as at risk, totaling 4,899 false positives also in need of personal intervention on the basis of statistics. If all these youngsters were deemed in need of hospitalization for observation and treatment, we would need 6,818 inpatient beds each year! To complete this example, we would also miss 1,001 adolescents who were statistically at risk, but who would be offered no treatment in the course of this kind of research.

Also, suicidal urges and behaviors are largely temporally and situationally specific. Suicidal intent is not constant within an individual. The urge to act in a self-harmful or destructive manner is state-dependent. It waxes, wanes, disappears, and returns (Murphy, 1983). The interaction of factors specific to the individual, the environment, and the situational and temporal context determine, in an idiosyncratic and dynamic manner, the "if and when" of both the urge to commit suicide and the action to accomplish it. Therefore, any attempt to apply a statistical model through the use of scales, questionnaires, psychological tests, and so forth to the assessment of possible suicidal behavior must account for these dynamic interactions—refer to a more in-depth discussion of this topic in chapter 4, particularly in reference to Goldston's (2003) excellent review of suicide scales. Given issues around predicting suicidality, there has been an increasing emphasis over more recent years on *screening* populations of children to identify potential psychopathology and suicide risk (e.g., the Columbia Teen Screen—Shaffer, Wilcox, et al., 1996).

The Descriptive Approach

Statistical and clinical models of assessment share a common strategy. The diagnosis of pathology or the prediction of certain behaviors depends on the similarity between that which is observed in a patient and that which is known (through the study of other patients already defined) to be associated with the diagnosis or the behavior. Thus, a patient with an affective disorder may be so diagnosed because said patient has observable symptoms or characteristics that are similar to those of patients reliably and validly diagnosed as having an affective disorder.

In the context of suicide assessment, this strategy calls for an understanding of those characteristics descriptive of known suicidal individuals—that is, those who have completed suicide. Possible future suicidal individuals, then, are defined by the degree to which they share these characteristics. Furthermore, this strategy allows for an evaluative hierarchy. Levels of risk (e.g., low, moderate, high) can be established on the basis of the degree of similarity (e.g., a weighted number of shared factors) observed. Again, this strategy at best provides a static definition of risk (i.e., defining someone as "in the ballpark" and needing further observation and evaluation).

With regard to suicidal adolescents, a wide range of associated characteristics has been noted and described (cf. Berman, 1986a; Berman & Carroll, 1984; Boergers, Spirito, & Donaldson, 1998; Goldston et al., 1998, 1999, 2001; Klimes-Dougan et al., 1999; Wagner, 1997). Most of these factors, however, are derived from the study of low-lethality attempters (e.g., female drug ingesters who are most available for study because of their postattempt hospitalization and compliance with treatment regimens), who, as we shall see, may only slightly resemble adolescents at risk for serious self-harm or death. Thus, we may be faced with the most paradoxical of strategies—attempting to assess an adolescent at mortal risk using strategies and approaches on the basis of characteristics common to those with minimal intent to die who engage in behaviors unlikely to produce a lethal outcome.

From the preceding discussion, it should be quite clear that the methodological and statistical problems inherent in suicide research are considerable but not prohibitive. Increasingly, youth suicide researchers are improving their ability to address the various challenges of this topic through creative approaches and the use of better methodologies and scientific rigor. Moreover, in recognition of the issues involved in studying behaviors such as suicide, ethical notions are evolving pertaining to research conducted with high-risk patients (e.g., the NIMH has increasingly provided direction and support for researchers who receive government support to pursue research with high-risk samples).

RESEARCH METHODOLOGY: REVIEW AND CRITIQUE

As discussed in the preceding section, the methods of suicide research are limited to two fundamental approaches: (a) those studies that pertain to completed suicide and (b) those that pertain to attempters or ideators. As discussed by Robins and Kulbok (1986) and Stack (1987a), within the study of completed suicides, the following two traditions are evident: (a) the "ecological" or macro approach, which uses large samples of aggregate data to address larger epidemiological considerations and social correlates of suicide, and (b) the "case study" or micro approach, which retrospectively examines records or interview data of individual suicides to provide important clinical data pertaining to completed suicides. Within the attempting and ideator studies, a range of methodologies is used with inpatient and outpatient samples to describe characteristics unique to these populations.

Completed Suicide Research

The best data about completed suicides come from studies that have directly examined completed suicides. In this regard, a range of methodologies has been used to obtain valuable data about adolescents who kill themselves.

Ecological Methods of Research

In their review of methodological strategies in suicide, Robins and Kulbok (1986) refer to "ecological analyses" as those studies that compare officially reported suicide mortality statistics between nations, or within a nation, across various demographic variables such as age, gender, and race. A variety of trend analyses are used to examine patterns of suicide in various populations over time.

Emil Durkheim's (1897/1951) pioneering sociological studies of national suicide rates have led to an extensive line of empirical investigation. However, Durkheim's statistical approach has also sparked an extended scientific debate among subsequent investigators about the use of officially reported suicide statistics for studying epidemiological trends and social correlates of suicide (see Jobes, Berman, & Josselson, 1987; Kreitman, 1988; Pescosolido & Mendelsohn, 1986). Great concern has been expressed about the process by which suicide is investigated, determined, and subsequently reported as a mortality statistic (O'Carroll, 1989). The variability observed in medicolegal practice (e.g., Jobes et al., 1987) and recording procedures (e.g., Hlady & Middaugh, 1988) has led to fundamental questions as to whether officially reported suicide statistics are a valid and reliable source of basic epidemiological data (see also discussion by Phillips & Ruth, 1993).

The resulting "social constructionist" argument asserts that the alleged underlying inaccuracies of officially reported suicide statistics invalidate research results that rely on this database (Douglas, 1967). In response to this argument, others (Pescosolido & Mendelsohn, 1986; Sainsbury & Jenkins, 1982) have argued that officially reported rates are indeed appropriate for research purposes. These authors contend that the error variation in the reporting of suicide statistics is randomized in such a way as to not invalidate comparisons made between different suicide rates or conclusions made about social correlates of suicide.

Whereas the actual extent and impact of potential inaccuracies of suicide statistics will probably continue to be debated, the sheer weight and import of this research cannot be denied. The caution of the social constructionists may or may not be warranted, yet there is much to be offered by ecological studies. Indeed, it is fair to say that much of what is thought to be empirically known about completed adolescent suicide comes from this line of empirical investigation (see chap. 1).

Social Correlate Approaches

Related to demographic research of risk factors are studies that seek to determine "social correlates" of suicide. As discussed earlier, although there has been a great deal of debate about the validity and reliability of this research, the social correlate method of study has been widely used by sociologists to explain suicidal behavior in terms of social influences. One example of this approach is seen in the attempts to measure the effects of modeling of suicidal behavior, or the "Werther Effect," which is described later in this chapter. In a broad sense, some of this research has followed the Durkheimian tradition with its emphasis on social integration and the influence of society (Durkheim, 1897/1951; Maris, 1981). Although social correlate methods of study are widely used and published, these methods are also hotly debated and criticized (Cohen, 1986; Rustad, Small, Jobes, Safer, & Peterson, 2003).

For many years, the social correlate approach to understanding suicide has been critiqued in relation to the *ecological fallacy*. The critique centers on the proposition that major social forces originally discussed by Durkheim may play a key role in suicidal behaviors among groups and individuals, particularly in relation to celebrity modeling effects (e.g., Phillips, 1985), suicide contagion (e.g., Gould, Wallenstein, & Davidson, 1989), or media influences on suicidal behaviors (e.g., Stack, Gundlach, & Reeves, 1994). The specific criticism of this approach pertains to the widely understood statistical notion that *correlation does not equal causation*, meaning that increases in suicidal behaviors that appear to be temporally related to media reports of suicide or suicides of others do not mean that these reported suicides directly *caused* any additional suicides. Although this sociological approach has been championed and widely embraced by the field for many years, some data do not necessarily conform to the theory. For example, research conducted by Jobes, Berman, O'Carroll, Eastgard, and Knickmeyer (1996) and Martin and Koo (1996) did *not* demonstrate widely expected increases in either local or national suicide rates following the suicide of rock star Kurt Cobain.

In an effort to better isolate the potential causal effect of media influences, Jobes and colleagues (Jobes, Small, Peterson, Rustad, & Safer, 2000) have conducted a series of laboratory experiments with college students to determine whether rock music with suicidal lyrics has any impact on perceptions or attitudes toward suicide or any discernable effect on mood or acceptance of suicide. These studies have produced some interesting and potentially controversial results (Jobes et al., 2000; Rustad et al., 2003; Small, Jobes, & Peterson, 2003). To summarize, studies of rock music videos and songs by bands such as Pearl Jam, Stabbing Westward, and Alice in Chains have shown that songs with suicidal lyrics (in comparison to songs without suicidal lyrics) *do* have a psychological impact on certain experimental participants. Specifically, suicidal lyrics seem to generate suicide-related cognitions in the minds of certain college student subjects and appear to prompt some degree of dysphoria and negative affect among these subjects. However, the effect is not uniform; personality vulnerability appears to play a part in the impact of these lyrics (i.e., the effect is mediated by the psychological vulnerability of the beholder). Moreover, although there were "negative" effects of this music, for a subsample of participants, there was also a prosocial "positive" impact (i.e., some listeners experienced increased concern for others and gained perspective on their own problems after being exposed to suicidal lyrics). As discussed by Rustad et al. (2003), such data are obviously controversial and open to interpretation and debate. However, so far, the widely held conclusion that suicidal lyrics in rock music are "bad" for all youth listeners is not completely clear from this laboratory-based research, prompting the never-ending call for additional research to help us better understand the correlational versus causal nature of media and social influences on suicidality.

Case Study Method of Research

Whereas macro-oriented ecological research uses aggregate data to define correlates of suicide, micro-oriented case study approaches use individual data to identify more specific risk variables. A range of case-control designs has been used to identify the most salient risk variables associated with suicidal death (e.g., Brent, Perper, Moritz, Allman, Friend, et al., 1993; Brent, Baugher, Bridge, Chen, & Beery, 1999; Shaffer, Gould, et al., 1996). Ideally, these studies use control comparison samples such as matched samples of accidental deaths or living cohorts to help distinguish those variables that are unique and specific to suicidal death. From a purely empirical perspective, retrospective designs are not as preferable as prospective designs. Practical considerations such as economic, resource, and ethical limitations, however, usually require the use of post hoc methodologies.

Medical Examiner and Coroner Data

Perhaps the most straightforward case study method involves the direct examination and analysis of medical examiner and coroner data. Some of the initial studies in this area simply examined data appearing on death certificates (e.g., Brent, Perper, & Allman, 1987), whereas other studies directly examined the investigatory records of medical examiners and coroners (e.g., Hoberman & Garfinkel, 1988a). An additional approach has been used to collect data relevant to suicide and accidental deaths directly from medicolegal officials by having them complete a standardized data-collection form following their investigation of a case (Jobes, Casey, Berman, & Wright, 1991).

Psychological Autopsies

The psychological autopsy was originally developed as a method to assist in the medicolegal investigation of "equivocal" suicide cases (Litman, Curphey, Shneidman, Farberow, & Tabachnick, 1963; Shneidman & Farberow, 1961). Although the medicolegal utility of the technique has been clearly demonstrated (Jobes, Berman, & Josselson, 1986), the psychological autopsy has been increasingly used as an effective and valuable research tool (Brent et al., 1999; Gould et al., 1996; Shaffer, Gould, et al., 1996). Whether used for medicolegal or research purposes, the psychological autopsy technique involves the systematic collection of psychological data through structured interviews of the decedent's family members, friends, coworkers, fellow students, and other associates. Although the specific format may vary, most investigators collect data relevant to the decedent's behavior, personality, style of coping, cognitive processes, psychiatric history, and general emotional life, so that a rich psychological mosaic of the decedent can be assembled.

As with any post hoc analysis, use of the psychological autopsy method is wrought with potential methodological problems (Brent, 1989; Brent, Perper, Kolko, & Zelenak, 1988). For example, concerns about reliability and validity are obvious when data are collected retrospectively from the recollections of grieving family members and friends. Although the inherent methodological issues are considerable, the information produced through well-controlled and rigorously conducted psychological autopsy studies has provided suicidologists with some of the most valuable data collected to date (Brent et al., 1999; Gould et al., 1996; Rich, Young, & Fowler, 1986; Shaffer & Gould, 1987; Shaffer, Gould, et al., 1996; Shafii, Carrigan, Whittinghill, & Derrick, 1985).

Suicide Notes

The systematic analysis of suicide notes is yet another case study method of investigation. This method of study was first systematically used by Shneidman and Farberow (1957). Leenaars (1988, 1989) has applied some novel procedures to the study of suicide notes, but most of the published studies have focused on adult note writers. Leenaars (1989) has identified gender differences among young adult note writers and has further found that young adult note writers are different from older adult note writers in degree—not in the presence or absence—of observed thematic patterns. For example, young adult women are more concerned than are men about their object relations; in contrast, men express more concern about ego functioning than do women. Additional research, however, has under-scored the pervasiveness of content *commonalities* across age ranges rather than unique age-specific differences (Bauer et al., 1997).

Postmortem Studies

A final case study approach is used to study potential biological mark-ers that may contribute to suicidal behavior (however, most of this research thus far has focused on adult samples). Over the last decades, various studies of cerebral spinal fluid (Brown et al., 1982), neuroendocrine functioning (Ostroff et al., 1982; Rich, 1986), and brain lesions (Achte, Lonnqvist, & Hillbomi, 1971) have been conducted postmortem on individuals who have completed suicide. From a more contemporary standpoint, there are now a large number of postmortem studies of the brain tissue of suicide victims that examine neurobiological correlates of completed suicide—refer to Mann (1998) and Kamali, Oquendo, and Mann (2001) for thorough reviews of this more recent work.

Attempter and Ideator Research

Although suicide completers are fundamentally different from attempters, attempter-oriented and ideator-oriented research is nevertheless quite valuable. As many suicide completers have made previous attempts or have previously thought about suicide, the study of attempters or ideators can provide important data about those variables that may uniquely con-tribute to an eventual suicide. On a more pragmatic level, it is much easier to study suicide vis-à-vis attempters because they are still alive and able to provide data. The relative ease of studying living subjects versus deceased subjects is probably most responsible for the heavy emphasis on attempter-oriented research in the empirical literature.

As noted at the start of this chapter, a common problem with a num-ber of previous studies of suicide attempters involves the absence of clear operational definitions (i.e., suicide ideators and attempters were often combined into a single suicidal group). In response to both clinical and research confusion created by our inexact nomenclature, an initiative was first launched by the American Association of Suicidology and subse-quently followed up with leadership from the NIMH. The resulting work (O'Carroll et al., 1996) was published in the journal *Suicide and Life-Threatening Behavior* and is widely known in the field as the "Tower of Babel Nomenclature."

As shown in Figure 3.2, this new nomenclature created terms for describing all suicide-related behaviors as determined by intent, instrumen-tal (i.e., interpersonal) thinking, and outcome (i.e., no injury, nonfatal injury, and death). A recent study conducted by Wagner et al. (2002) specif-ically examined the ambiguity in the term "suicide attempt" and empirically

Terms for suicide-related behaviors				Intent to die from suicide[¶]	Instru-mental thinking	Outcome		
						No injury	Nonfatal injury	Death
SUICIDE-RELATED BEHAVIOR	BEHAVIOR	INSTRUMENTAL BEHAVIOR	Instrumental suicide-related behavior					
			-with injuries	No	Yes		✓	
			-without injuries	No	Yes	✓		
			-with fatal outcome[§]	No	Yes			✓
		SUICIDAL ACTS	Suicide attempt					
			-with injuries	Yes	+/–		✓	
			-without injuries	Yes	+/–	✓		
			Completed suicide	Yes	+/–			✓

Figure 3.2. An illustration of the proposed nomenclature for suicide-related behavior, in terms of outcome and intent to die from suicide. ¶Conscious intent to end one's life through the suicidal behavior. §A fatal outcome of instrumental behavior is properly considered accidental death, because by definition there is no intent to die from suicide. From "Beyond the Tower of Babel: A Nomenclature for Suicidology," by P. W. O'Carroll, A. L. Berman, R. W. Maris, and E. K. Moscicki, 1989, *Suicide and Life-Threatening Behavior, 26*, p. 246. Copyright by Guilford Press. Reprinted with permission.

established the critical role of perceived intent and lethality in defining the construct. These authors have underscored the importance of better defining our understanding of suicide attempts and have proposed the use of a "fuzzy" natural language conceptualization of suicide attempts. At a minimum, the increased effort to use psychometric measures (e.g., Berman, Shepherd, & Silverman, 2003; Smith, Conroy, & Ehler, 1984; Weisman & Worden, 1972) to operationally define the lethality of attempters has been a welcome development in research.

In this vein, the Wagner et al. (2002) study attempted to investigate the sometimes ambiguous nature of suicide attempts among adolescent samples. In their study, Wagner et al. used expert and general clinician samples to investigate so-called "fuzzy" cases of adolescents who engaged in a range of self-destructive behaviors. The following two cases from their study may shed some light on the gray area between the black and white of clearly nonlethal suicidal "gestures" and obvious high-lethality "genuine" attempts.

Case Illustration

The father of a 17-year-old believed his son had intentionally damaged the father's bicycle, but his son insisted it was an accident. The father hit his son in a drunken rage, and his son ran to a secluded storage shed. He placed a noose around his neck, but the shed was terribly cluttered, and he failed to find a solid beam to which he could securely fasten the rope. After a short while he gave up trying. He told no one until later in the evening, when he revealed the incident to his therapist. He could not agree to a "no-suicide" contract.

With few exceptions, the experts found the case to be a difficult one to judge. Those who decided that it was *not* a suicide attempt focused on the lack of medical lethality and the lack of persistence involved, which they took to be signs of ambivalence (e.g.: "No actual harm done"; "Unclear if he was ambivalent about hanging himself or was truly thwarted by [circumstances]"; "Considered lethal behavior but didn't engage [in it]…similar to getting a gun but not firing it"). Yet, more than half of the experts did classify the behavior as a suicide attempt. For example, one expert in the sample with 5 decades of experience stated: "Easy call—intent and method, failed suicide."

Case Illustration

A 17-year-old girl threatened suicide to a boyfriend who repeatedly called her because she was trying to break up with him, saying she would overdose if he did not stop telephoning. When he told her, "Fine, go ahead, I don't care," she took 15 Imipramine but immediately told her mother, who drove her to the hospital. After arriving, she had several seizures and was in an intensive care unit (ICU) for 4 days. She later reported that it had been an impulsive act, she had not wished to die, and she had not thought that the overdose would kill her.

In this case, suicidal intent was low, but the self-harm behavior was of medium lethality. Most of the participants grappled with the discrepancy between suicidal intent and medical lethality. For some judges, the behavior was too serious to dismiss as a nonattempt. For example, one sample expert wrote, "Anyone who spends 4 days in an ICU has engaged in serious self-destruction." Another wrote, "Despite comments to the contrary, her behavior indicates that at least briefly she was willing to risk her life." Another stated, "Lethality of pills makes it serious, but unclear intent makes it difficult." For other judges, the lack of suicidal intent precluded a "Yes" (suicide attempt) judgment. One expert indicated, "Instrumental motive, denies intent to die." Several cited the lack of self-reported suicidal intent and the girl's impulsivity in explaining their decision to not classify the behavior as a suicide attempt. Clearly, cases such as these underscore the complexity of defining self-destructive behaviors with implications for research and clinical practice.

Inpatient Samples

Studies using adolescent inpatient samples of suicide attempters and ideators have been widely reported in the literature (Brand, King, Olson, Ghaziuddin, & Naylor, 1996; Cohen et al., 1996; Cohen-Sandler, Berman, King, 1982a; Goldston et al., 1998). Many of the original clinical reports in the literature were essentially descriptive and case-oriented in nature; in more recent years, more sophisticated empirical approaches have been used.

"Normal" Samples

Efforts have been made to gain some empirical perspective on suicidal thoughts and behaviors among "normal" (nonpsychiatric) samples. Much of this research is conducted through descriptive surveys with more accessible populations. For example, a number of investigators have surveyed high school and college students to determine the prevalence of suicidal ideation (Centers for Disease Control and Prevention, 2002c; Harkavy-Friedman, Asnis, Boeck, & DiFiore, 1987; Rudd, 1989; Smith & Crawford, 1986). As discussed in chapter 1, the surveillance research conducted by the Youth Risk Behavior Survey has provided some of our most valuable data pertaining to suicidality in normal samples.

Historically, studies have measured college student attitudes toward suicide (Domino & Leenaars, 1989) and suicide survivorship (Reynolds & Cimbolic, 1988–1989), whereas other research has been conducted to develop predictive models of suicidal ideation and behavior on the basis of data obtained from college students (Bonner & Rich, 1987). The difficulty of gaining access to "normal" subjects and participation consent from their parents greatly limits the scope of suicide research efforts with nonhospitalized populations. However, some investigators are still able to navigate through some of these difficulties to make useful contributions to the literature (e.g., Wagner, Cole, & Schwartzman, 1996).

Clinical Treatment Research

As discussed in more depth in chapter 5, clinical treatment research for suicidal youth has been slow to develop but has nevertheless produced some promising data. At this point, a handful of studies using random assignment and control groups with adolescent and young adult samples have shown support for short-term cognitive–behavioral problem-solving treatments for reducing suicidal ideation, hopelessness, and depression (Harrington, Kerfoot, et al., 1998; Joiner, Voelz, & Rudd, 2001; Lerner & Clum, 1990; A. Miller, 1999; Miller, Rathus, Linehan, Wetzler, & Leigh, 1997; Rotherham-Borus, Piacentini, Miller, Graee, & Castro-Blanco, 1994; Rudd, Rajab, et al., 1996; Trautman, 1995). Although this research is still limited and inherently difficult to conduct, Rudd, Joiner, Jobes, and King (1999) contend that there is now enough preliminary empirical data to begin shaping treatment recommendations as to what constitutes effective clinical care for suicidal patients.

Critique of Suicide Research

Perhaps one of the encouraging developments in the field of youth suicide prevention since the first edition of our book has been the continuing growth and improvement in the area of empirical research. As long-time consulting editors to the field's top scientific journal—*Suicide and Life-Threatening Behavior*—we can directly attest to the explosion of higher-quality research in the field. Indeed, as one of us (MMS) serves as editor-in-chief, there is direct evidence of a 300% increase in submissions to the journal since the early 1990s; many of these submitted papers pertain to adolescent suicide. Perhaps most critically, beyond the growth of our empirical literature, we are also seeing both better science and increasing relevance; in our view, both the internal and external validity of our research has markedly improved since the first edition of this book. However, what may be most striking about this research literature is that it still remains remarkably underdeveloped given the pervasiveness of youth suicidality and the gravity of the issue.

SUICIDAL BEHAVIORS

Completed Suicide

A completed suicide is certified by a coroner or medical examiner on the basis of evidence indicating intentional, self-inflicted death. The assessment of intentionality often is difficult (Jobes et al., 1986) but rests on evidence that the decedent "had in mind" that the self-inflicted action would produce death. Thus, when we study retrospectively those adolescents who have died by suicide, we derive factors common to youth with high degrees of both lethality and intention to die.

In 2000, there were 300 certified suicides by those age 10 to 14 in the United States, and 3,994 suicides by those age 15 to 24 (National Center for Health Statistics, 2002). For many years, we knew very little about the psychological characteristics of these youthful completers. Fortunately, the psychological autopsy technique first developed by Litman et al. (1963) has become a major research tool in the study of youthful completers (Brent, Perper, Moritz, Allman, et al., 1993; Brent, Perper, Moritz, Baugher, et al., 1993; Brent, Perper, Moritz, Baugher, Schweers, & Roth, 1994; Brent et al., 1999; Rich et al., 1986; Shaffer, Gould, et al., 1996; Shafii et al., 1985). Together these studies have helped us appreciate that upward of 90% of adolescent suicide completers have diagnosable psychopathology at the time of their death (see Table 3.1).

TABLE 3.1
Most Common Teen Suicide Diagnoses—Controlled
Psychological Autopsy Studies

Disorder	Male (%)	Female (%)
	(N = 213)	(N = 46)
Mood disorder	50	69
Antisocial disorder	43	24
Substance abuse	38	17
Anxiety disorder	19	48

Note. From Shaffer, Gould, et al. (1996); Brent et al. (1999).

There is also evidence that seriously suicidal youth often display antisocial behavior or conduct disorders (or both) in greater frequency than affective disorders (which are more associated with less lethal suicidal youth). With some youngsters, as in the following case, it is difficult to distinguish the core etiology, as a diagnosis of attention-deficit disorder may serve to mask an underlying depression.

Case Illustration

David, a 12-year-old sixth grader, was found dead by asphyxiation, hanging from a clothes rod in his bedroom closet. The third of four children, David had a history of hyperactivity, low frustration tolerance, and aggressive behavior. He was in frequent combative relationships with peers and often was taunted by them. As a result, he was often angry and frequently in tears. In school, his inability to maintain attention to task resulted in special placement in a class for the learning disabled. He believed this further marked him as a "loser," giving rise to a continuous cycle of pain, frustration, anger, and acting out. In the last week, he told his grandfather that he would kill himself "some day." His parents, when told of this comment, denied the seriousness of both his intention and his difficulties. With their knowledge, David was not complying with the recommended treatment for his diagnosed attention-deficit disorder. On the day of his death, David had been excluded from eating with some classmates and, at recess, had mud thrown on his new jacket, one he especially had wanted and had appeared proud to display.

The concept of intent central to the definition of suicide posed here makes clear that a variety of self-destructive behaviors, each with increased risk for premature death, are not suicidal. For example, people experiencing anorexia, substance abuse disorders, alcoholism, and even self-mutilators and auto-castrators typically do not seek a cessation of life or of conscious experience through their behavior. Each has a more focal concern (e.g., to alter one's body, to anesthetize pain, to seek pleasure, etc.) having nothing in common with a goal of ending life.

Self-Mutilation

The study of self-mutilators has been given increasing attention (Favazza, 1989; Suyemoto, 1998; Walsh & Rosen, 1988; Zlotnick, Donaldson, Spirito, & Pearlstein, 1997). Self-mutilation most commonly receives clinical attention through self-inflicted wrist cuts and cigarette burns. More extreme forms, such as genital castration and eye enucleation, are indicative of major psychopathology (e.g., schizophrenia and mania). As described by Walsh and Rosen (1988), the function of mutilative cutting, for example, is to decrease tension or other intense affect, diminish a sense of alienation, or terminate dissociation ("I bleed, therefore I am"). Favazza (1989) lists a dozen different goals articulated by patients to explain their mutilative behaviors. In adolescence, the conditions that commonly trigger moderate mutilative behavior are (a) losses that reactivate earlier losses; (b) peer conflict and intimacy problems; (c) body alienation (e.g., distress over sexual identity); and (d) impulse-control problems (often modeled by parents)—themes quite similar to those we find with more directly suicidal youngsters. The most frequent diagnostic frames for these patients are those of borderline personality disorder, often with a comorbid mood disorder, and dissociative disorder.

It is important to note that self-mutilators also make serious suicide attempts. In fact, each of the conditions noted as self-destructive (e.g., eating disorders, substance abuse) are known to be associated with increased risk for suicidal behavior, perhaps as a consequence of the despair experienced when other desired goals fail to be achieved. Thus, as defined, these behaviors are dissimilar from the criterion behaviors we seek to assess as suicidal and are not directly suicidal, yet they are significantly risk-related (see Farberow, 1985 for a classic and excellent compilation of articles on "indirect self-destructive behaviors"). The following cases illustrate the dynamics and comorbid psychopathologies common to adolescent self-mutilators.

Case Illustration

Suzanne, age 19, presented for outpatient treatment complaining of not coping well and of feeling "locked up" and scared. She wished to avoid repeating a hospitalization of 2 years earlier, which had been precipitated by a "hysterical spell" accompanied by visual hallucinations (menacing male figures that would make sexual advances toward her). Suzanne had a long history of multiple somatic complaints, including dizziness, headaches, and irregular menses since puberty. She was considerably overweight and had entered two inpatient programs in an effort to control this problem. It was during one of these programs that her earlier hospitalization had occurred. She had become increasingly agitated by her observations of polymorphous perverse sexual behavior among fellow program patients and felt pressure to equally act out. In response, she experienced fainting spells and had considerable suicide ideation.

The favorite child of her father, who appeared to dote on her, Suzanne felt guilt over his attention; she both wanted his affection but also felt uncomfortable receiving it. At the same time, she described a number of self-imposed strict and rigid rules for her acceptability (to be perfect, to be healthy, and to not show problems or feelings). She described her mother as a perfectionist who harped on Suzanne's lack of attractiveness as a developing female because of her weight and, in particular, her large breasts. To cope, Suzanne steadfastly denied her own needs and attempted to sublimate them by counseling her peers, a role that reinforced her wish to hide her own pain. However, the tension of trying to meet impossible standards became overwhelming. Were she to expose herself to a peer, she would feel overwhelmingly guilty and then would hear voices urging her to hurt herself because she had been "bad." She then would dissociate (during which time she might engage in trance writing or drawing) and, ultimately, end the dissociative episode by cutting herself or burning herself with cigarettes. It was noted that she would attempt to cut or burn herself only in places on her body hidden from public view (reinforcing the norm of hiding) and that this fulfilled her mother's competition with her sexuality (she would cut her breasts and burn herself in the genital area), as she secondarily attempted to maintain a prepubescent and dependent role in her family. Of similar interest, her one known suicide attempt was at the age of 13 with her mother's Xanax pills.

Case Illustration

Millie, age 19, presented as depressed, socially anxious, and isolated. She had no friends and saw herself as "only capable of driving others away." She did not trust others, yet she desperately wished to have and be loved by a boyfriend. Although she spent considerable time alone, she was frightened of being alone. Since childhood, when she would cower at the creakings of an old house, she had repeatedly checked behind the shower curtain and under her bed before going to sleep to assure herself that there were no burglars in her house. Once asleep, she would have frequent nightmares.

Millie described feeling both empty and "rotten" inside. She described her parents as rigid perfectionists who were opinionated and intolerant. Her only success in being acceptable to them was through academics, at which she excelled, maintaining a straight-A average. She filled her aloneness and emptiness by binging on high-calorie foods, sometimes consuming 5,000 calories at a sitting, before subsequently purging the food. Motivated by "irresistible urges," she relieved herself of overwhelming pressure and tension by punching the walls of her apartment and by repetitively slicing her wrists. These cuts had never been severe enough to require medical intervention, nor had she ever been psychiatrically hospitalized; she equated coming for treatment with confirmation of herself as a failure.

Attempted Suicide

What is complicating about the definitional approach is that the great majority of what gets labeled as "attempted suicide" by definition is not. Attempted suicide is an inchoate act—that is, an attempt to die by self-inflicted means. Thus, a true suicide attempter has both intent to die and sufficient lethality in the method to accomplish that intent, but either fails or is foiled (e.g., through rescue or intervention). Neither of these conditions pertains to the great majority of those adolescents who are treated in emergency rooms or referred for psychiatric consultation after self-harm behavior.

The typical adolescent attempter is a female who ingests pills in front of her family after an argument (Wagner, 1997). In fact, the overwhelming majority of attempters are female (by a ratio of about 4:1) and, similarly, pill takers (between 71% and 93%; Bond, Riggs, Spirito, & Fritz, 1988; Goldston et al., 1996; Lewinsohn, Rohde, & Seeley, 1993). These modal descriptors are quite different from those of the typical adolescent completer, almost two thirds of whom are male victims of gunshot-wounds.

Moreover, Linehan (1985) and Cross and Hirschfeld (1985) have described clear differences in the personalities of high- and low-intent attempters, with the latter appearing more deviant. Given the heterogeneity of this group, therefore, it would be helpful were research studies of adolescent attempters to distinguish different subgroups for comparative study. Some typologies have been proposed (e.g., Peck, 1985; Wagner, 1997), but confirmatory research has yet to follow. Perhaps the most useful empirically based perspective on attempt history comes from the work of Rudd, Joiner, and Rajab (1996), who have demonstrated differential and increasing prospective risk for suicidal behavior among patients with no attempt history, versus a single attempt, versus multiple attempts. Although their research applied to adults, these data have been replicated by others (refer to Overholser & Spirito, 2003) and intuitively such findings may well extend to suicidal youth.

As it is apparent that attempters are not homogeneous, with obvious difficulties distinguishing among intentions that adolescents often deny on questioning, the term "parasuicide" (Kreitman, 1977) has been used over the past decades to denote all deliberate self-harming behaviors. Although the term "parasuicide" had enjoyed some measured use (particularly among European suicidologists), many have argued for alternative terms. For example, Canetto and Lester (1995) have suggested the term "nonfatal suicidal behaviors," whereas others have promoted the use of the term "deliberate self-harm behavior" (see discussion by Hawton & van Heeringen, 2000). O'Carroll et al. (1996) coined the term "instrumental suicide-related behavior" (ISRB), which emphasizes potentially self-injurious behaviors for which there is no evidence that the person intended to kill himself or herself, in lieu of wishing to use the appearance of suicidal intent to thereby reach an interpersonal goal.

Case Illustration

Janet was an 18-year-old high school senior who was suddenly dumped by her boyfriend of 6 months. Janet's father was a physician and her mother was a nurse. With plans of studying nursing in college, Janet already had considerable knowledge about medications, particularly psychiatric medications, which she had been taking for over 2 years. Given two past overdoses, Janet's psychiatrist prescribed only selective serotonin reuptake inhibitors (SSRIs) to treat her depression and told her that these were not lethal medications taken in overdose.

In a fight at her ex-boyfriend's house, Janet took a handful of her Prozac in front of her ex-boyfriend and barricaded herself in a bathroom. The parents of the ex-boyfriend called 911 and the police had to break down the door to get to Janet. After a struggle with police and emergency medical technicians, Janet was subdued and strapped to a stretcher. As she was being wheeled out of the home, she told her ex-boyfriend, "Tell my mother I tried to commit suicide, but I don't want to see her!"

The reader should not misconstrue that those who attempt suicide are not to be taken seriously, because there is an overlap between groups of those who complete and those who attempt. With regard to the relationship between attempters and completers, for example, Brent (1987) has documented that those who make medically lethal attempts are similar to those who complete suicide. And, as we shall note, a prior attempt has been found in psychological autopsy studies to be one of the more important risk factors among completers (Shafii et al., 1985). Also, a significant number of attempters ultimately complete suicide (Goldacre & Hawton, 1985; Motto, 1984). Thus, a history of suicidal behavior may be significantly tied to risk for completion, and the lethality of an attempt is related to its intentionality (see chap. 4).

Whereas the intentionality of a completer is presumed to be that of death or ending life, such is not always the case. Some adolescents, lacking intent to die, gamble with the possibility and lose. Others lack sufficient knowledge to calculate accurately, for example, less-than-toxic dosages of ingested medication. Indeed, in a study performed by Harris and Myers (1997), 50% of adolescents in one community sample ($n = 569$) overestimated by twofold the amount of acetaminophen needed to achieve a fatal outcome. Conversely, some who intend to die are rescued, interrupted, or lack access to lethal means and therefore survive.

The intent of most adolescent sublethal self-destructive behavior appears to be interpersonal and instrumental, for example, to mobilize or effect change in another's behavior. For many, their stated intent may not be congruent with that evaluated by a clinical interviewer. For example, Hawton, Cole, O'Grady, and Osborn (1982) reported that of 50 adolescents hospitalized for deliberate self-poisoning, one third stated that they wished to die at the time of the overdose. However, the clinical interviewer believed that only seven (14%) of these patients had intent to die.

Where intent is interpersonal and designed to effect change in another's behavior and where lethality is low, the behavior of the adolescent may involve initiating movements toward an attempt. These low-lethality behaviors are often called suicide "gestures" or "rehearsal" behaviors. Whatever the case, such actions are equivalent to behavioral threats. Thus, the adolescent may make hesitation cuts to the wrist or swallow a decidedly nontoxic dosage of medication to scare others into a different response. As is evident in the following case, such low-toxicity ingestions often represent attempts to exert power in a context of perceived powerlessness.

Case Illustration

Linda, age 15, argued with her grandmother, with whom she had lived for the 7 years since her mother died, when she was told she could not go on a family outing because she had not completed her chores. Upset, she ran to the bathroom, thinking she would end her life. Grabbing a bottle of Extra Strength Tylenol, Linda took and swallowed six pills. Later she asked her grandmother in a calm and controlled voice, "What would happen if I killed myself?" In discussing her ingestion at the hospital, she related that when she actually took the pills, she was hoping that she would get sick and, in consequence, that her family would change their attitude toward her.

Reliable estimates of the incidence of low-lethality self-destructive behavior among adolescents are difficult to establish and, for the most part, are formed on the basis of hospital admissions. As noted in chapter 1, surveys of U.S. high school students indicate that approximately 8% to 9% of students sampled admitted to one or more "attempts," yet only about 1 in 3 of these attempters reported receiving medical attention following their attempt. Thus, simply relying on hospital records to index attempts leaves unaccounted many self-destructive behaviors of relatively low intent and lethality.

Repeat Attempters

In relation to clinical assessment, one subgroup of youth who participate in sublethal suicide attempt behaviors is of special interest (Overholser & Spirito, 2003). This group is composed of those who engage in chronic, habitual self-destructive behavior. Estimates of the percentage of attempters across all ages repeating an episode within 1 year of the first attempt range from 14 to 26% (Reynolds & Eaton, 1986). The majority of adult repeaters have been found to be younger (under 30), and the frequency of repetitive attempts appears greater at younger ages (under 19; Eyman & Smith, 1986). These patients may use such behaviors as a regular means of coping with stress and are significantly demanding of the treatment system. In clinical settings, repeatedly hospitalized patients of this type may be pejoratively referred to as "frequent flyers." Such patients also appear to have more chronic symptoms, poorer coping histories, and more family histories positive for suicidal behavior and substance abuse (Reynolds & Eaton, 1986; Wagner, 1997).

The chaotic and chronic dysfunctional family patterns common to lives of repeat suicide attempters is clearly evident in the following case. Although repeat suicide attempters' first attempts are generally milder, once a more seriously lethal attempt is made, subsequent attempts remain seriously lethal (Eyman & Smith, 1986). Thus, this group remains at high risk for completing suicide. In fact, one report from Finland indicates that after an approximately 5-year period of follow-up, 5% of adolescent repeaters had completed suicide as compared to only 1% of "first-timers" (Kotila & Lonnqvist, 1987). As previously noted, research by Rudd and Joiner (Joiner & Rudd, 2000; Rudd, Joiner, & Rajab, 1996) is particularly germane here; a history of multiple attempts is among the most pernicious of risk factors for future suicidal behaviors.

Case Illustration

Cassie, age 15, was brought to the emergency room by her mother after she ingested multiple medications. Her overdose was precipitated by a fight with her mother, during which Cassie was confronted with being truant from school five times in the previous week. Concurrently, Cassie's mother reported dramatic changes in Cassie's behavior and personality over the previous few months, including an escalating series of altercations with friends and a significant drop in school interest and performance. Although Cassie denied using drugs herself, her boyfriend had recently been sentenced to 30 months in jail for drug possession.

This was Cassie's fifth emergency room visit for self-harm behavior since age 10, when she deliberately splashed hot grease on her arms, ending a furious fight with her older sister. This sister recently had been indicted for assault and battery. Cassie's mother has a history of hospitalizations for schizophrenia, including visual hallucinations. Her father deserted the family when Cassie was 7 years old.

Threateners

Two categories of suicidal actors and actions remain to be described in our array of defined suicidal behaviors. These involve verbal behavior—one public and the other subvocal. Those who make suicidal threats, or "threateners," are those who alert their interpersonal context, most often during crises, to the possibility of suicide. As we will learn, the great majority of attempts and completions, perhaps as much as 80%, are preceded by such threats or warnings. Conversely, the great majority of threats are not followed by actions, are often not intended to be so followed, or are deterred from being acted on by their contingent reinforcers (e.g., desired attention from others). However, we would be remiss if the following point did not strike the reader as a *déjà entendu* before the end of this book: All threats and communications about suicide should be taken seriously, responded to, and evaluated as indicators of potential clinical significance and potential risk. To not do so and to be proved wrong by eventual suicidal behavior is a cost we believe to be most preventable and unacceptable.

Suicide Ideators

As noted earlier, transient thoughts about the meaning of life and even suicide may be normative in adolescence, with up to 63% of high school students reporting any degree of ideation (Smith & Crawford, 1986). More recent data from the previously mentioned Youth Risk Behavior Survey indicates that 16.9% of high school youth ($n = 15,240$) seriously considered attempting suicide (Centers for Disease Control and Prevention, 2003). Suicidal ideation becomes clinically significant when it is more than transient, possibly a preoccupation, or when it is accompanied by the possibility of being translated into behavioral actions (see chap. 4). Current ideation, when there is a history of past attempt, is significantly related to reattempt (Brent, Perper, Moritz, Allman, et al., 1993; Goldston et al., 1999; Lewinsohn, Rohde, & Seeley, 1996).

It may be presumed, a priori, that thoughts of suicide precede suicidal behavior, although this may not be conscious for some. Although most adolescent attempters report contemplating their attempts only a relatively short time before engaging in the behavior (Hawton et al., 1982), most who make an attempt report much longer histories of wishing to die, often extending back to early childhood (Berman & Schwartz, 1990). Adolescents reporting "troubling" levels of suicidal ideation have been found more likely to also report an attempt and, compared to nonideators, more negative and total life stress, less support, and poorer adjustment (Dubow, Blum, & Reed, 1988). Suicide ideation also has an obvious and significant relation to both major depressive and borderline personality disorders, of which it is one of the defining criteria for diagnosis (American Psychiatric Association, 1990). However, as Jobes (2000) has pointed out, the relation between major psychiatric illnesses and suicidality is not always clear. Indeed, there are certainly cases of severe mood spectrum disorders in which suicide is never entertained; alternatively, there are cases of relatively neurotic "worried well" individuals who may be plagued by suicidal thoughts and fantasies. Moreover, Rosenberg (1999) presented data of a subset of suicide attempts and completions that appear to happen quite suddenly with a remarkably short time span from initial ideation to behavior (less than 5 minutes) and in the presence of relatively nominal preexisting psychopathology.

The mysteries of suicidal ideation, behaviors, and the exact role of psychopathology are considerable. Nevertheless, there are various lines of contemporary research that are studying in greater depth those aspects of suicidal suffering that are unique or different from the suffering that one may experience in a unipolar depression with no suicidal ideation. For example, Orbach and colleagues (Orbach, Mikulincer, Gilboa-Schechtman, & Sirota, 2003; Orbach, Mikulincer, Sirota, & Gilboa-Schechtman, 2003) have developed a line of empirical research studying the nuances of psychological pain. In addition, Rudd (2003) has conducted research examining the differential nature of suicidal cognitions. Studies of psychological pain, perfectionism, hopelessness, and future thinking represent an exciting frontier in contemporary suicidology (Jobes et al., 2004; O'Connor et al., 2004; Williams, 2001).

Recent qualitative research by Jobes and Mann (1999, 2000) has provided some useful perspectives on the nature and specific content of suicidal thoughts among young people. Their research with outpatient suicidal college students (n = 201; mean age = 21) involved a method in which students were asked to describe their various reasons for wanting to live versus their reasons for wanting to die (Jobes & Mann, 1999; Mann, 2002). As part of a clinical assessment protocol, these patients were encouraged to think about and then write in their own words up to five reasons for living and five reasons for dying. Hundreds of such written responses were then organized into reliable response coding categories (Kappa's > .80). As shown below in Table 3.2, these responses provide a unique window into the content of thoughts that suicidal college students have in their considerations of the life versus death suicidal dialectic (Mann, 2002).

TABLE 3.2
SSF Reasons for Living Versus Reasons for Dying

Reasons for living	Reasons for dying
■ Family	■ Others (retribution)
■ Friends	■ Unburdening others
■ Responsibility to others	■ Loneliness
■ Burdening others with suicide	■ Hopelessness
■ Unrealized plans and goals	■ Issues about self
■ Hope for the future	■ General escape
■ Enjoyable things	■ Escape the past
■ Beliefs (religion)	■ Escape the pain
■ Preservation of self	■ Escape responsibility

Note. Reliable coding categories (Kappa's > .80). From *Reasons for Living vs. Reasons for Dying: The Development of Suicidal Typologies for Predicting Treatment Outcomes*, Table 2, by R. Mann. Unpublished doctoral dissertation. Reprinted by permission of the author.

As noted earlier, suicidal ideation often precedes threats and attempts, and a single attempt is significantly related to both a repeat attempt and completed suicide. Both retrospective and prospective studies of adolescent suicidal behavior note significant overlap among these behaviors.

In early studies of completed suicides across all age groups, including youth, prior suicide attempts consistently stand out. For example, Maris (1981) found the number of prior attempts to be the predictor with the strongest beta value when comparing both attempters and completers with normal control subjects. With a particular focus on adolescence, Farberow's (1989) summary found prior behavior (attempts, threats, ideation, or a combination of these) to be "one of the strongest indicators of high risk in adolescents," with reported frequencies varying from 22% to 71% of those making subsequent attempts. Similarly, Shafii et al. (1985) concluded that a prior attempt was the single most important risk factor for ultimate completion.

Thus, the adage that the best predictor of future behavior is past behavior appears applicable to suicidal behavior among both adolescents and adults. As Marks and Haller (1977) could not distinguish adolescent threateners from attempters, and as the preceding brief review makes clear that there is significant overlap among attempts and completions, the at-risk adolescent, first and foremost, is so identified by any of the various prior suicidal behaviors. However, as noted by Clark and Gibbons (1987), the association between past and future suicidal behaviors is mostly explained by the individual's predispositional attributes (from genetic to characterologic). What remains for us to identify, therefore, are those factors denoting risk that can be identified before any self-harm action occurs.

RISK FACTORS

Risk factors are those attributes or characteristics of the index group (i.e., suicidal adolescents) that describe membership in that group. As such, the identification of such attributes in an as-yet nonsuicidal adolescent should alert us to the possibility that this adolescent may become a member of the group already identified as suicidal. These attributes will not describe all suicidal adolescents, but they should identify a significant proportion. Also, identified attributes are most significant when they are derived from control group studies—that is, they differentiate suicidal adolescents from nonsuicidal adolescents.

As noted by Berman and Cohen-Sandler (1982a), a finding of frequency—for example, an occurrence common to 60% of a sample of suicidal adolescents—may be useful for generating testable hypotheses but has little meaning as a specific risk factor if that frequency is not significantly greater than that of a relevant control group. For these reasons, in the following discussion of risk factors we will attempt to highlight only those research-based findings that have been found to discriminate suicidal adolescents from others, and to note high-frequency attributes as worthy of more controlled study.

Psychopathology and Personality Characteristics

As we discussed in the first edition of this book, research on the presence of Axis I and Axis II disorders in cases of completed suicide has been an important area of study. Indeed, one might argue that the most important research in adolescent suicide in the past 20 years has been groundbreaking psychological autopsy studies that have established that upwards of 90% of adolescent suicide completers have a diagnosable Axis I or Axis II disorder (e.g., Brent et al., 1999; Shaffer, Gould, et al., 1996). It is interesting to note that whereas importance of diagnosis has been clearly established in adolescent suicidality, recent work has suggested that a singular focus on psychiatric diagnosis sometimes precludes examining other crucial constructs more broadly (Jobes, 2000). Indeed, Spirito (2003) has argued that beyond diagnosis, there is value in studying broader psychological characteristics such as cognitive, behavioral, emotional, and environmental factors associated with adolescent suicide. While acknowledging the importance of diagnosis, these authors advocate focusing on psychological characteristics because,

...the implications for an individual adolescent can be more prescriptive without negating the treatment course necessary for the underlying psychiatric disorder. The focus on psychological characteristics may help the clinician more clearly identify those factors—such as impulsivity, anxiety, aggression—which result in the suicide attempt, even among persons with the same diagnosis, such as depression. Alternatively, certain characteristics, such as impulsivity, may be risk factors for some psychiatric diagnoses, such as alcohol abuse, but not others, such as depression. (pp. 10–11)

Similarly, our sense is that *both* approaches are important to fully understanding the complexity of adolescent suicide, so we will thoroughly consider both diagnostically related risk factors as well as broader psychological characteristics.

Psychiatric Diagnoses

Although a variety of pathologies have been noted, three types of disorders tend to predominate in reports of completed and attempted suicide among adolescents: mood disorders, substance abuse disorders, and conduct disorders.

A diagnosis of depression, both unipolar and bipolar, has been frequently reported among both completers (Brent, Perper, Goldstein, et al., 1988; Lonnqvist et al., 1995) and nonfatal attempts (Kerfoot, Dyer, Harrington, Woodham, & Harrington, 1996; Lewinsohn, Rohde, & Seeley, 1994), with rates being higher among psychiatric inpatients than among medically hospitalized samples (Spirito, Brown, Overholser, & Fritz, 1989). Shaffer, Gould, et al. (1996) found that the odds of suicide among those with a mood disorder were more than 10 times greater than those of adolescents without mood disorders.

The relation between depression and suicidality, however, is complex. Depression appears most directly related to suicide ideation (Sanchez & Le, 2001; Velez & Cohen, 1988; Wetzler et al., 1996), but the great majority of depressed youth are not suicidal. Shaffer and Bacon (1989) have estimated that among males, the ratio of nondepressed to depressed suicidal adolescents is approximately 660:1. Depressives with suicidal ideation have been differentiated from those without ideation primarily in terms of the former having more disturbed intrafamilial relationships (Kosky, Silburn, & Zubrick, 1986). In addition, the relation between depression and suicidal ideation may be mediated both by deficits in cognitive coping strategies and hopelessness (see below).

Substance abuse is clinically associated with depression in adolescence. Alcohol and other drug use and abuse, again, have been found with great frequency among completers (Brent, Perper, Moritz, Baugher, et al., 1993; Brent, Perper, Moritz, Baugher, Schweers, & Roth, 1994) and among lethal and sublethal attempters (Overholser, Freheit, & DiFilippo, 1997).

Substance abuse histories have been noted in 15% to 33% of adolescent completers (Hoberman & Garfinkel, 1988b; Poteet, 1987). In studies of adolescent substance users, suicide attempts have been found to occur at rates 3 times those of control subjects, with the "wish to die" increasing dramatically after the onset of substance use (Berman & Schwartz, 1990). Most important, substance use at the time of suicidal behavior has been found to be related to the lethality of the method used (Brent et al., 1987).

Rosenstock (1985) has reported on a 9-year longitudinal analysis of consecutive adolescent psychiatric inpatient admissions, finding concurrent increases in admission diagnoses of depression (350%), substance abuse (200%), and suicidal ideation (300%). Embedded as intervening variables among and common to these symptom presentations are cognitive distortions, impulsiveness, frequent and serious interpersonal loss, and family pathology. More will be said about these and related themes descriptive of the common threads between pathological states and suicidal behaviors later in the book.

Related to both depression and substance abuse disorders is the third commonly found pathology, conduct disorder. Shafii et al. (1985) found that 70% of their psychological autopsy subjects had exhibited antisocial behavior (vs. 24% of control subjects). These youth had come into conflict with legal authorities and had been involved in a variety of antisocial behaviors, from shoplifting to drug selling to prostitution. Shaffer and Gould (1987) similarly note a preponderance of antisocial behaviors among completers and that conduct disorders increased the odds of completed suicide by threefold in comparison to those without this diagnosis (Shaffer, Gould, et al., 1996). The role of conduct disorder in adolescent suicidal behavior may be even greater than that of depression. Apter, Bleich, Plutchik, Mendelsohn, and Tyano (1988) found higher-scale scores for suicidality on the Kiddie Schedule for Affective Disorders and Schizophrenia (K–SADS) for conduct-disordered adolescents than for those with major depressive disorder, even though those with conduct disorders were less depressed (see also Andrews & Lewinsohn, 1992; Beautrais, Joyce, & Mulder, 1998).

Relatedly, aggressive symptoms are common to hospitalized attempters (Garfinkel, Froese, & Hood, 1982) and characterize one of two types of child attempters described by Pfeffer, Plutchik, and Mizruchi (1983). The importance of aggression to suicidality has been highlighted by Plutchik, van Praag, and Conte (1989), who proposed that suicide risk is heightened when aggressive impulses are triggered, then amplified by forces such as substance abuse and not attenuated by opposing forces such as appeasement from others. In a 3-month follow-up study, Spirito et al. (1992) found that 23% of adolescent suicide attempters were involved in physical fights, with 14% running away.

Conduct disorders, depression, and substance abuse disorders frequently present comorbidly, with the frequency and lethality of attempts increasing with the degree of comorbidity (Frances & Blumenthal, 1989). Indeed, Wagner, Cole, and Schwartzman (1996) have found a synergy between depression, conduct problems, and substance abuse that can be linked to a history of attempts, whereas any one of these problems does not retrospectively identify history of suicide attempts. Depression and anxiety symptoms have been noted to be corelated among samples of suicidal adolescents (cf. Bernstein & Garfinkel, 1984; Mattison, 1988), as have depression and conduct disorders (Alessi, McManus, Brickman, & Grapentine, 1984).

Related as well is borderline personality disorder, a diagnosis more common among those who engage in sublethal self-harm behaviors (Crumley, 1979). Friedman, Clarkin, and Corn (1982) found the most suicidal of their sample of adolescents to be those with both borderline pathology and depression. It is important to note that this relation was sustained even once the suicide criterion was removed from those criteria used to make the *Diagnostic and Statistical Manual of Mental Disorders, Third Edition* (*DSM–III*; American Psychiatric Association, 1980) diagnosis of borderline personality disorder.

In terms of other personality characteristics, Beautrais, Joyce, and Mulder (1999) conducted a case-control study of personality traits and cognitive styles among youth suicide attempters and found elevated levels of hopelessness, neuroticism, and external locus of control as significant risk factors for serious suicide attempts. Common across these various personality-related diagnoses and constructs are a range of distinct behaviors related to affect dysregulation, intense rage, impulsiveness, and aggressiveness, which are often seen among suicidal adolescents (Esposito, Spirito, & Overholser, 2003).

In terms of cognitions, a particularly crucial variable across the suicide research literature pertains to the concept of hopelessness. On the basis of Beck's findings with adult samples (Beck, Steer, Kovacs, & Garrison, 1985), hopelessness has been found at significantly higher levels in samples of adolescent ideators and attempters in comparison to control samples (Negron, Piacentini, Graae, Davies, & Shaffer, 1997; Swedo et al., 1991). Although the relation between hopelessness and suicidality in adolescence has not been upheld universally (Asaranow, Carlson, & Guthrie, 1987; Beautrais et al., 1999; Carlson & Cantwell, 1982; Kerfoot et al., 1996; Rotheram-Borus & Trautman, 1988), recent research of adolescent inpatients at 18 months follow-up has shown that a combination of persistent depression and hopelessness does appear to predict prospective attempt behaviors (Brinkman-Sull, Overholser, & Silverman, 2000).

As we shall note in the next chapter, there is no typical suicidal adolescent. Indeed, in addition to these primary diagnostic types, a variety of other diagnoses can be found among those adolescents at risk. Shaffer, Garland, Gould, Fisher, and Trautman (1988) note finding a subgroup of completers showing evidence of anxiety, perfectionism, and distress at times of change and dislocation. This description might best fit the high-achieving "star" whose suicide invariably shocks the community of survivors as beyond reason and worthy of front-page news coverage. Shaffer, Garland, Gould, et al. (1988) also report learning disabilities and schizophrenia as characterizing completers. The most common descriptors applied to Hoberman and Garfinkel's (1988a) sample of adolescent completers were "withdrawn," "lonely," and "supersensitive," labels remarkably similar to those Shafii et al. (1985) found in two thirds of their subjects. However, in the latter study, this withdrawn, inhibited personality was not found significantly more often among the suicides when compared to control subjects.

Adolescent Suicide and Sexual Orientation

Over the years, there has been some measure of controversy over the potential role of homosexuality in relation to adolescent suicidality. From an empirical perspective, recent research has shed some light on the true role of sexual orientation among suicidal youth. Some recent data does provide links between homosexuality and increased suicide ideation and behaviors (e.g., Remafedi, 1998; Russell & Joyner, 2001; van Heeringen & Vincke, 2000), but to date no empirical data has clearly linked *completed* suicide to homosexual orientation.

Behavioral Characteristics

The withdrawal noted among suicidal adolescents may be a sign of depression or a coping strategy (Grolholt, Ekeberg, Wichstrom, & Haldorsen, 2000). As such, much research is yet needed to discriminate between suicidal and nonsuicidal depressed adolescents. Social isolation and social alienation, however, consistently identify the suicidal adolescent in a number of studies (cf. Farberow, 1989; Hawton, Fagg, & Simkin, 1996; Spirito et al., 1996).

Alienation from, and a lessened involvement in, the school milieu have also been found (Mazza & Eggert, 2001) but, again, may be predictive more generally of emotional disturbance (Cohen-Sandler et al., 1982a) and of depression in particular. Consistent with findings of both depression and acting-out behavior, school disciplinary problems, poorer school performance, underachievement, and dropping out of school have all been noted among suicidal adolescents (cf. Berman & Carroll, 1984; Mazza & Eggert, 2001).

Although there is understandable popular interest in the potential relationship between bullying and suicidality, the empirical literature in this area is relatively limited. One notable exception is a large survey conducted in secondary schools in two regions of Finland (Kaltiala-Heino, Rimpela,

Marttunenen, Rimpela, & Rantanen, 1999). Using a large sample (n = 16,410) of 14- to 16-year-olds, Kaltiala-Heino et al. (1999) found an increased level of depression and severe suicidal ideation among *both* those who were bullied and those who were bullies. Indeed, when these authors controlled for symptoms of depression, suicidal ideation was actually most pronounced among adolescents who were the bullies! Obviously, more research is needed before we can fully understand the dynamics of bullying as it may pertain to adolescent suicidality.

Runaway street youth have been compared to nonrunaway peers with findings of greater depression, prior and current suicidality, and other psychopathology, including substance abuse (Rotherham-Borus, 1993; Smart & Ogborne, 1994; Unger, Kipke, Simon, Montgomery, & Johnson, 1997; Yoder, 1999). Stiffman (1989) found that 30% of the St. Louis-area runaways she studied reported a past suicide attempt. Multiple regression analyses revealed that runaways who had attempted suicide differed from those who had not in terms of greater substance abuse, more behavior problems, family instability (including drug abuse, suicidality, depression, and antisocial behavior), and female gender. Running away from home is inherently a sign of family conflict, a variable of significance we shall discuss. However, it is important to note that in studies of children and latency-age youth (e.g., Pfeffer, Conte, Plutchik, & Jerrett, 1980), running away is a sign of emotional disturbance and is not pathognomonic of suicidality. Furthermore, characteristic of these younger adolescents is a family enmeshment that makes it difficult for them to pull away from familial and parental problems. It has been postulated that in these families, a suicide attempt may be the youngster's way of wrenching away from a fused system (Cohen-Sandler, Berman, & King, 1982b).

Family and Parental Characteristics

Among the most studied of variables relating to adolescent suicide is the influence of the family, and the parental system in particular (e.g., Wagner, 1997; Wagner, Silverman, & Martin, 2003). As role models, as sources of praise and reinforcement, and as nurturers and caretakers, parents have obvious roles in the development of healthy and ultimately autonomous children. When parents, individually or together, have serious conflicts or problems, the adolescent's press for autonomy and growth may be seriously affected.

Compared to normal adolescents, suicidal adolescents report poorer familial relationships and more interpersonal conflict with parents with less affection (Brent, Perper, Moritz, Baugher, et al., 1993; Slap, Vorters, Chaudhuri, & Centor, 1989; Wagner, Cole, & Schwartzman, 1995; Wagner et al., 2003). They describe time spent with their families as less enjoyable and hold more negative views of their parents (McKenry, Tishler, & Kelly, 1983).

In their review of this literature, Wagner et al. (2003) found the following six major lines of empirical research that capture contemporary considerations of adolescent suicide and family factors:

1. *Family communications and problem solving.* There is a fair amount of evidence that problems between parents and children are implicated in adolescent suicide completions (Brent, Perper, Morritz, Baugher, et al., 1993; Gould et al., 1996; Gould, Shaffer, Fisher, & Garfinkel, 1998). In terms of attempted suicide and suicidal ideation, dysfunction in the whole family system has been observed in several prospective studies (e.g., King et al., 1995; McKeown et al., 1998).

2. *Scapegoating or the expendable child.* The view that suicidal adolescents are perceived as "expendable" or are differentially treated negatively within a family system dates back to work conducted by Sabbath (1969). Empirical literature linking negative treatment to completed suicide is limited, but there is more evidence that suicidal teen attempters and ideators may be singled out within a family, particularly in relation to physical and sexual abuse (e.g., Brown, Cohen, Johnson, & Smailes, 1999; Fergusson, Woodward, & Horwood, 2000).

3. *Attachment to caregiver.* Many studies have focused on attachment-related issues such as separation, loss, or quality of parent–child attachments. Data linking attachment issues to completed suicide is limited. Suicide attempts and ideation do seem to occur more in single-family homes (e.g., Wagner et al., 1995), but the data are mixed and sometimes contradictory. In terms of quality of attachment, some data suggest an association between suicidality and lower parental care and availability (West, Spreng, Rose, & Adam, 1999), whereas other research has not shown that attachment status prospectively predicts suicidality (Klimes-Dougan et al., 1999).

4. *Family psychopathology.* Evidence of family psychopathology in first-degree relatives is also somewhat mixed. Some data suggest higher rates of psychopathology among family members of adolescent suicide completers (Brent, Bridge, Johnson, & Connolly, 1996), attempters, and ideators (Fergusson et al., 2000; Klimes-Dougan et al., 1999), whereas other prospective studies have failed to link suicidal attempts and ideation with family psychopathology (Brent, Kolko, et al., 1993).

5. *Other evidence of family transmission.* Family studies of adult probands and behavioral genetics have yielded interesting results. For example, research among the Amish has supported the notion of familial transmission of suicidal behaviors (Egeland

& Sussex, 1985). Moreover, genetic studies of twins versus studies of adopted siblings provide consistent evidence of genetic influences on suicidal behaviors (Papadimitriou, Linkowski, Delabre, & Medeleuicz, 1991; Roy & Seigel, 2001).

6. *Molecular genetics research.* Behavioral genetic research has inspired a contemporary line of study examining specific mechanisms for transmission of suicidal behaviors. These studies tend to focus on serotonin influences (e.g., Arango & Underwood, 1997) and on the serotonin transporter gene (Mann et al., 1997). This largely retrospective line of research needs replication to further clarify conflicting results.

Stressful Life Events

Among suicidal adolescents, significantly increased levels of life stress have been found (Adams et al., 1994; Huff, 1999). Overholser (2003) has organized empirical research on the types of life stressors as follows: (a) interpersonal; (b) death, separation, divorce; and (c) physical illness. Overall, the past and current empirical data provide support for a link between life stressors and suicidality (e.g., Beautrais, Joyce, & Mulder, 1997; Cohen-Sandler, Berman, & King, 1982a). Interpersonal conflict and social isolation are clearly associated with adolescent suicidality (Brent, Perper, Moritz, Baugher, et al., 1993; Gould et al., 1996; Lewinsohn et al., 1994). Thus far, data linking increased suicide risk with parental death, separation, or divorce have not been found (Overholser, 2003). However, Hawton et al. (1996) have linked chronic physical illness to increased suicidal behaviors. Critical to our consideration of life stressors is that the mere presence of life stressors does not necessarily cause adolescent suicidality; rather, life stressors may serve as triggers to a vulnerable youth who may already be at risk (e.g., a multiple attempter).

Cognitive Strategies

The very occurrence of suicidal behavior in a context of life stress strongly implicates the absence or ineffectiveness of behavioral controls (coping strategies) and alternative cognitive problem solving. Adult suicide has often been described as problem-solving behavior (Beck, Rush, Shaw, & Emery, 1979) related to distorted patterns of thinking. In addition to patterns already discussed (impulsivity and hopelessness), the focus has been on dichotomous (polarized) thinking, rigidity, inflexibility, and constriction (Levenson & Neuringer, 1971; Neuringer, 1976).

Deficits in problem-solving skills among suicidal children (Asaranow et al., 1987; Cohen-Sandler, Berman, & King, 1982b; Orbach, Rosenheim, &

Hary, 1987), adolescents (Klimes-Dougan et al., 1999), and college students (Yang & Clum, 1994) have long been documented, particularly in terms of generating fewer alternative solutions to situations of interpersonal conflict. Early on, Corder, Schorr, and Corder (1974) found that suicidal adolescents feel less control over their environment. Consequently, these adolescents responded with greater rigidity and more attempts to structure. At the more extreme end, Tishler, McKenry, and Morgan (1981) found that their sample of suicidal adolescents displayed poorer reality testing and more psychotic thinking.

The reader interested in the extensive literature on cognitions and suicidal behavior might consult Esposito, Johnson, Wolfsdorf, and Spirito (2003) for a contemporary review of this work. For our purposes, it is important to note that the adolescent deficit in these problem-solving skills is more likely to distort his or her perception of problem situations, narrow the range of alternatives to deal with the situation, express greater hopelessness, and behave with more impulsivity. Again we are stuck with a chicken-or-egg–type problem etiologically, as these observations may reflect either the cause or the effect of psychopathology.

Imitation and Suggestibility

Generally speaking, exposure to the suicidal behavior of another person in the social networks or families of completers (Shafii et al., 1985) or attempters (Garfinkel et al., 1982) appears more common in these groups than in control groups. Attempters (as illustrated in the following case) and ideators identified through high school surveys of nonpatient adolescents report more frequently knowing a peer, friend, or family member who had attempted suicide (Harkavy-Friedman et al., 1987; Smith & Crawford, 1986).

Case Illustration

Darlene, age 15, ingested 30 Sudafed tablets after hearing that her "best friend" had attempted suicide by overdose earlier in the day. Darlene had shown signs of a depressive disorder, including insomnia, weight loss, and suicide ideation, for 3 weeks since problems began developing with her boyfriend. One of her presenting problems was that she had no friends.

As we have noted, a family history of suicide should be considered significant as an alerting sign to suicide risk in adolescence (e.g., Gould et al., 1996). Murphy and Wetzel (1982), after reviewing the literature, estimated that 6% to 8% of those who attempted suicide had a family history of suicide. The most significant findings regarding family history of suicidal behavior are with adult samples. As one example, Roy (1983) found that of 243 psychiatric inpatients with a definite history of suicide in a first- or second-degree relative, almost half had attempted suicide, more than half had a depressive disorder, and more than a third had a recurrent affective disorder. In a 7-1/2-year follow-up, 3% of these patients had completed suicide. Both identification and genetic explanations have been posed to explain these findings.

Exposure to another's suicide may be considered an accelerating risk factor among those already predisposed to be at risk. That is, exposure by itself is not sufficient to cause a suicide that otherwise would not have occurred. Two sources of research provide a basis for this perspective: studies of media influence and cluster suicides.

Suicide Clusters and Media Influence

When suicidal events occur close together in space and time or when suicidal events share characteristics (e.g., a similarity of method), beyond what would be normally expected in a given community, such connections suggest an influence among events or triggering by one or more of the preceding events. In epidemiology, such a closely grouped series of phenomena is termed a "cluster," and with regard to suicide has been further defined by the Centers for Disease Control as requiring three or more events in the series, although some have criticized this definition as not precise enough epidemiologically (Clark, 1989).

The primary mechanism by which exposure affects a follow-up suicide is through imitation or modeling. The degree to which the second person identifies with or feels similar to the model has been suggested as a possible modifier of the degree of influence exerted (Davidson & Gould, 1989; Davidson, Rosenberg, Mercy, Franklin, & Simmons, 1989; Gould, Jamieson, & Romer, 2003). Adolescents, in general, are highly susceptible to suggestion and imitative behavior, as these are primary modes of social learning and identity formation. To a disturbed youngster, particularly one with pre-existing suicidal impulses and diffuse ego boundaries, the perceived attention given to a suicidal event might easily lead to any of several irrational cognitions. Most powerful among these is the belief that the attention and notoriety given to the preceding suicide will be achieved by their own and that, even in death, they somehow will be able to appreciate that attention. Where the model suicide is that of a star, one believed to have everything going for him or her, the model's suicide may precipitate or exacerbate a sense of hopelessness ("If he or she couldn't hack it, what chance do I have?") or be permission-giving ("If you feel like I did, here's the way to solve the problem").

Where exposure to another's suicide has been used to explain such phenomena, such exposure may be direct, where the subsequent suicidal youngster actually knew the victim of a preceding suicide, or indirect, where knowledge was garnered through word of mouth, news, or fictional accounts.

The majority of research studies have been in the area of indirect exposure, with the focus on nonfictional and fictional media accounts of suicide as stimuli. As summarized by Gould, Jamieson, and Romer (2003), the effect of publicized suicides on imitative behavior has been most consistently documented in studies of the nonfictional, print, and television news media. Primarily on the basis of the work of sociologist David Phillips (1985), the significant increases in suicides noted after publication of front-page suicide stories has been termed the "Werther Effect," referring to an alleged rash of imitative youth suicides following publication of Goethe's *The Sorrows of Young Werther* in 1774. Other researchers have extended Phillips's work and reported that stories of celebrity suicides, particularly those of entertainment celebrities, had the most significant effect; this effect was specific to those in a similar social role (Berman, 1988). Thus, for example, Phillips (1985) reported that in the month following Marilyn Monroe's suicide, there was an extraordinary increase (12%) of suicides nationwide, particularly among young women. Similarly, Berman (1987) was able to demonstrate a statistically significant increase in gunshot-wound suicides in Los Angeles County in the 7 days following comedian Freddie Prinze's suicide by gunshot wound in 1977. However, additional work in this area (Kessler, Downey, Milavsky, & Stipp, 1988), using more refined methods of analysis, has raised some critical questions about whether any observed effect on adolescent suicides is indeed imitative.

Although the bulk of the research in this area supports evidence for the Werther Effect, it is important to note that there is still no conclusive evidence that media effects actually *cause* subsequent suicides among the young. Indeed, a number of studies since the 1980s have *not* found evidence for imitative effects (Berman, 1988; Jobes et al., 1996; Kessler et al., 1988; Martin & Koo, 1996; Phillips & Paight, 1987). Indeed, of particular note is one carefully performed case-control study by Mercy et al. (2001) that indicates that exposure to suicide may actually be *protective*, suggesting an anti-imitation effect. Clearly, this is a controversial area of research in need of additional study.

Controversies in this area of research have continued with the unexpected findings of Jobes et al. (1996) and Martin and Koo (1996) related to the celebrity suicide death of rock star Kurt Cobain. Jobes et al. (1996) used an interrupted time-series analysis methodology to study King County (Seattle, Washington) medical examiner data. To their surprise, these researchers found that there was no statistically significant increase in completed suicides following Cobain's suicide in 1994 (refer to Figure 3.3) when data were compared to the control years of 1993 and 1995.

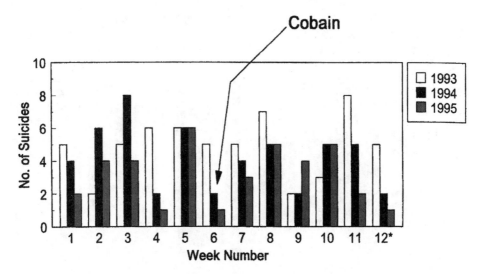

Figure 3.3. Suicides in King County, Washington, by week, late February to mid-May, several years. *Partial week. Data from Medical Examiner's Office, King County, Washington. From "The Kurt Cobain Suicide Crisis: Perspectives From Research, Public Health, and the News Media," by D. A. Jobes, A. L. Berman, P. W. O'Carroll, S. Eastgard, and S. Knickmeyer, 1996, *Suicide and Life-Threatening Behavior, 26*, p. 263. Copyright 1996 by Guilford Press. Adapted with permission.

Interestingly, in this same study, there was a statistically significant increase in suicidal crisis calls to the Seattle Crisis Center in comparison to control years (see Figure 3.4).

These authors speculated that there were perhaps some unique aspects to the Cobain case related to responsible media coverage, a potentially important (and possibly suicide-preventive) memorial service held in Seattle, and the grisly circumstances of Cobain's method (a shotgun blast to the head). Beyond this local study in Seattle, Washington, Martin and Koo (1996), using national mortality data in Australia, found no significant increase in completed suicides in that country following Cobain's suicide.

Given the inherent controversies of this area, the development of media guidelines in 2001, through a collaboration of the American Foundation for Suicide Prevention, the American Association of Suicidology, the Suicide Prevention Advocacy Network, and the Annenberg Public Policy Center (among others), is notable as a means of providing guidance to reporters on responsible reporting of suicide in the media (American Foundation for Suicide Prevention, 2004).

Means of Death

As noted in chapter 1, the majority of both male and female adolescent suicide completers died by firearms and explosives, with handguns

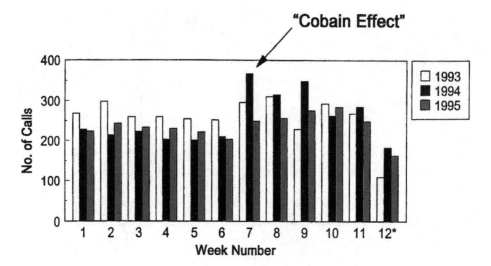

Figure 3.4. Suicide crisis calls to the Seattle Crisis Clinic by week, late February to mid-May, several years. *Partial week. Data from Seattle Crisis Clinic. From "The Kurt Cobain Suicide Crisis: Perspectives From Research, Public Health, and the News Media," by D. A. Jobes, A. L. Berman, P. W. O'Carroll, S. Eastgard, and S. Knickmeyer, 1996, *Suicide and Life-Threatening Behavior, 26*, p. 263. Copyright 1996 by Guilford Press. Adapted with permission.

predominating. Hanging has been more frequent among males, with ingestions predominating among females. The overwhelming majority of sublethal self-harming behaviors involve the ingestion of pills as the modal method of attempt (Wagner, 1997). As Wagner notes, there are a number of factors that have been posited to explain the choice of method used. These are

1. availability and accessibility (i.e., ease to obtain);
2. sociocultural acceptance (i.e., normative use);
3. knowledgeability (i.e., familiarity with use);
4. social or behavioral suggestion (e.g., modeling);
5. saliency (e.g., suggested by publicity);
6. personal or symbolic meaning of act or setting (e.g., a landmark jumping site such as the Golden Gate Bridge); and
7. intentionality and rescuability (if intent is high, methods of choice will be those most lethal, most efficient, and least likely to be interfered with).

Given a context for suicidal action—that is, an otherwise predisposed youth in a situation of precipitating stress—the ready availability or accessibility of a method of suicide may be a sufficient triggering mechanism to promote impulsive suicidal behavior. To this end, Brent and colleagues (Brent, Perper, Moritz, Baugher, Schweers, & Roth, 1993) have clearly shown that the risk of suicide significantly increases in a home where there is a firearm; the risk is similarly increased whether the gun is loaded or unloaded. Given the research in this area, it is imperative that a focus on methods of possible use by adolescents be considered along with the exploration of other sociopsychological risk factors.

Protective Factors: Contraindications to Risk

It seems inherently obvious and tautological that the absence of risk factors noted above should serve to protect the adolescent from self-harm potential. However, in recent years, a great deal of interest has centered on the notion of "protective factors" that may significantly decrease suicide risk in the face of other extant risk factors. As discussed by Beautrais (2003),

> ...even among those with high levels of exposure to risk factors, a substantial proportion fail to develop suicidal behaviors...[S]uch findings suggest the presence of various protective or resiliency factors that act to mitigate the effects of exposure to risk factors...[T]hese factors [may] include adaptable temperament; internal locus of control; good self-esteem, self-image, self-confidence, and self-efficacy; good problem-solving skills; good social support and social networks; a good emotional relationship with at least one person in the family; positive school experiences; and spiritual faith. (p. 1147)

Although work in this area has been increasing (e.g., Borowsky, Resnick, Ireland, & Blum, 1999; Davis, 1999; Quinn, 1999; Resnick, 2000; Resnick et al., 1997), relatively little is known about the exact factors that might mitigate risk factors for suicidal behaviors. This important and promising area of empirical inquiry is no doubt an important frontier in our efforts to understand the dialectic between those who are inexorably drawn to suicide versus those who appear to fend off suicidality even in the face of considerable factors that tend to correlate highly with suicidality.

COMMON THEMES: RISK FACTORS

Embedded in the foregoing summary of research-based risk factors are some common themes. Attention to these "between the lines" issues makes the intuitive process of assessment, the art of risk assessment (see chap. 4), rest appropriately on its scientific foundation. Concurrently, it allows the clinician to move away from an overly concrete focus on a checklist of risk factors, only a few of which will describe any one suicidal adolescent.

It is difficult to describe these common themes succinctly or in any ordered fashion, as many of them operate synergistically. It is also difficult to describe these themes in terms of necessary and sufficient conditions, as, for the most part, none of them are either necessary or sufficient. It is also difficult to propose a schematic model, for example that of interlocking Venn diagrams proposed by Blumenthal and Kupfer (1989), as such schemata tend to concretize dynamic processes. In the context of this premise, it is therefore easiest simply to list and summarize these themes from Blumenthal and Kupfer (1989) as follows:

1. A *negative personal history.* This includes early life events and stressors such as narcissistic injuries, significant skill deficits (particularly interpersonal and social), negative models for coping, and a genetic–biochemical vulnerability. Obviously, family history of suicidality and parental psychopathology are central to this theme. Also, prior self-harm behavior in response to real or anticipated losses is noteworthy.

2. *Psychopathology and significant negative personality attributes.* This includes evidence of sufficient symptomatology or personality characteristics to define either an Axis I or Axis II diagnosis or attributes that diminish healthy attachments to systems, structures, or object relations. Particularly important are comorbid psychopathologies including or exacerbated by significant substance abuse. Examples of personality attributes of concern include aggression, low frustration tolerance, loneliness, and impulsivity.

3. *Stress.* This includes environmental, psychosocial affect-arousing stimuli that threaten the adolescent's ability to maintain self-esteem and to cope effectively. Often these stressors are anticipated rather than real, but they pose unacceptable rejection, humiliation, or feared punishment.

4. *Breakdown of defenses; affect and behavior dysregulation.* This includes evidence of cognitive rigidity, irrationality, thought disturbance, loss of reality testing, irrationality, and acute behavioral change, including initiated or heightened substance abuse, panic, heightened anxiety, disorientation, and rage.

5. *Social and interpersonal isolation and alienation.* This includes behavioral withdrawal, isolation, and alienation from typical attachments; help-rejecting and noncompliant behavior; antagonism toward alliances with systems, authority, or mainstream associations; and alternative identifications with fringe and marginal groups identified by their alienation from mainstream society.

6. *Self-deprecatory ideation, dysphoria, and hopelessness.* This includes statements of unhappiness, pessimism, and irritability; feelings of worthlessness, uselessness, and stupidity; negative

views of self; the inability to derive pleasure or to be pleased by others; and death-related and suicidal fantasies.

7. *Method availability, accessibility, and knowledgeability.* This includes sufficient impulse toward self-destructive action or with intent to die or to use self-harm for some instrumental or interpersonal gain. An adolescent particularly may find the availability and accessibility of a weapon—one that he or she knows how to use—an irresistible call to action.

CONCLUSION

In philosophy, empiricism is a doctrine stating that all knowledge derives from experience. In the behavioral sciences, experience (observations) must be provable by experiment. Within the context of both limited observation of suicidal adolescents and significant methodological difficulties in adequately studying these youth, it is perhaps remarkable that we have come so far in so short a time in identifying empirically based risk factors. Our experience thus far ought to encourage us that significantly more refined observations, and their practical application, are within our grasp. Indeed, the growth of empirical research since the publication of the first edition of this text is quite notable and promising; the field has notably blossomed in the past 10 years, with much more and better-quality research. As we continue to focus our lens of understanding, both the contours and nuances of our subject matter sharpen under our watchful gaze. Our focus now shifts to the dynamic interface of these data with the assessment of the potentially self-destructive possibilities we endeavor to prevent.

4

ASSESSMENT

Case Illustration

Soon after Michael, age 17, was caught shoplifting, his parents referred him to a psychologist for "anger management." Michael had been chronically angry, particularly with his mother, blaming her for a wide range of alleged wrongdoings and for practically all his problems. His parents believed that the shoplifting incident, Michael's first, was his way of asking for help.

The psychologist observed that Michael's relationship with his parents was not close and aligned himself with Michael to gain increased independence. He further noted that Michael's parents were verbally abusive and that the shoplifting incident was symptomatic of the pressure Michael felt from them to complete his college applications. Observing Michael's unhappiness, he referred him to a psychiatric colleague for consideration of antidepressant medication.

On the psychiatrist's intake questionnaire, Michael checked a large number of symptoms and behaviors of concern. Among these were alcohol use, anger, anxiety, body image, decreased attention, distractibility, hopelessness, loneliness, low energy, outbursts, physically violent, poor impulse control, and thoughts of suicide. In the intake interview, Michael elaborated that he smoked cigarettes; had been drinking since the age of 13, more than once "past the point of vomiting"; currently used downers, uppers, and pot (2–3 times/week); and had a history of self-cutting. He stated that both his parents had histories of depression and that his dad had a drinking problem. The psychiatrist diagnosed Michael as having a major depressive disorder and prescribed a selective serotonin reuptake inhibitor (SSRI).

Neither caregiver evaluated further Michael's past self-harm behavior, the nature of his current suicide ideation, or his risk for future suicidal behavior. Two months later, Michael was found dead, a result of a self-inflicted hanging.

The significance of a suicide risk assessment is never more tragically apparent than after the suicidal death of a young person in treatment, and, most strikingly, when the treating clinician did not thoroughly evaluate the possibility of suicidal behavior (Bongar et al., 1998). In Michael's case, two clinicians were negligent in considering his danger to self. These failures to evaluate his risk were compounded by the fact that red flags to his risk abounded (suicide ideation, hopelessness, depression, substance abuse, prior self-harm behavior, loneliness, legal problems, poorly controlled rage, etc.).

An adolescent's risk for suicide should be assessed (and documented)

- at intake (i.e., for all new patients);
- at mention, observance, or report of suicide ideation or past suicidal behavior;
- when there are signs of change in mental status;
- during increased environmental stressor-worsening symptoms;
- when there exists predisposition to be suicidal;
- immediately after self-harm behavior; and
- at times of management transition (e.g., rotation of psychiatric residents, therapist vacations, discharge planning, etc.) when there is history or signs of emotional reactivity and behavioral instability.

The importance of assessing suicide risk goes beyond the obvious need to protect the adolescent from self-harm, when risk appears present. Assessment of risk informs treatment planning and management. First, risk assessment helps define the locus of treatment (inpatient or outpatient) and the intensity of safeguarding—that is, the need for closer observation and monitoring; consideration (costs and benefits) of the need for hospitalization, or, alternatively, for increased frequency of outpatient therapeutic intervention; and the clear demand to restrict access to accessible means for suicide, particularly firearms.

Second, it is best to treat suicidal adolescents by first targeting for treatment the adolescent's suicidality (Jobes, Berman, & Martin, 2000; Rudd, Joiner, & Rajab, 2001). Risk factors that are variable or malleable, in contrast to fixed or unchangeable, need to be specifically identified for defined interventions (see chap. 5).

THE REFERRAL SOURCE

As we will note in chapter 5, adolescents rarely initiate direct help-seeking behaviors. The majority of suicidal youth receive help only after the referrals of others. Virtually anyone that comes into contact with a potentially suicidal adolescent may encounter a suicidal threat that could lead to a referral. However, those who most commonly make a referral are those who have the most contact with a young person, such as friends, family members, or teachers. Others with less frequent contact may nevertheless be uniquely situated to detect and refer a suicidal youth. Some common "gatekeepers" include school administrators, guidance counselors, juvenile justice officials (e.g., judges, lawyers, probation officers), religious leaders (e.g., priests, ministers, rabbis), coaches, community youth workers, or health professionals. Primary care physicians (pediatricians), in particular, are often in a position to detect depressive symptomatology and associated suicidal feelings.

Intervention in, and the prevention of, an adolescent suicide often fundamentally depends on the degree of awareness and sensitivity of key people in the young person's life who seriously respond to obvious or veiled suicidal cues and make referrals to those who can help. The vast majority of young people who kill themselves provide a variety of verbal and nonverbal clues about their imminent suicidal behavior to those in a position to notice. Indeed, Brent, Perper, Goldstein, et al. (1988) found in their sample of adolescent completers that 83.3% had made suicidal threats to others in the week prior to their death. Perhaps one of the most tragic aspects of adolescent suicide is that suicidal clues and threats are often not taken seriously, are denied, or are simply missed by potential respondents.

Once observed, the adolescent at possible risk must be referred for professional assessment and treatment. Those who might first notice suicidal cues (e.g., friends and family) are usually not mental health professionals and may not be aware of the process of making an appropriate referral to a professional. One ironic note is that those individuals who are probably most often exposed to suicidal threats may be the least prepared to respond responsibly. According to the Brent, Perper, Goldstein, et al. (1988) study, up to half of the adolescent completers who made a threat made their suicidal intentions known only to a peer or sibling. Unfortunately, suicidal threats expressed only to a peer or sibling may not lead to appropriate referrals to a professional. This may be true particularly when a youthful subculture emphasizes the importance of maintaining confidences (i.e., keeping secrets from adult authority figures). Accordingly, our preventive outreach efforts with young people have aimed to drive home the idea that it is better to lose a friendship because of sharing such a secret with a responsible adult than to lose a friend to suicide because of keeping such a secret from an adult.

Therefore, the journey an adolescent must make between feeling, contemplating, and expressing suicidal impulses and being subsequently referred for professional assessment and treatment may be dangerously circuitous or, more tragically, never made. Prior to our discussion of the clinical assessment of suicide risk, it is important that we briefly consider the context of a referral that leads to that assessment.

THE REFERRAL CONTEXT

The context or circumstances of the referral vary widely as there is no one pathway whereby a suicidal adolescent comes to be seen by a mental health practitioner. Perhaps most commonly, school officials or parents refer an adolescent to a professional when they detect noticeable depressive symptoms, suicidal threats, or acting-out behaviors. In a school setting, for example, an internal referral to a school psychologist or guidance counselor may occur when a teacher notices that a top student has failed three consecutive quizzes and appears lethargic and sad. The school psychologist or counselor may then assess and treat the student or refer him or her to another professional. Alternatively, a parent may seek out treatment for his or her child at a community mental health center in response to the child's vague suicidal threats or recent substance abuse.

Although perhaps less common, other individuals may also facilitate a potentially life-saving referral. An astute pediatrician finding evidence of an eating disorder and superficial cut marks on the wrists of an adolescent in a physical examination may recommend to the parent referral to a private practitioner. A compassionate judge may detect emotional difficulties underlying a juvenile's petty crime and recommend a psychological evaluation and treatment. A child-protection worker sent into the home of a reported child abuser may suspect a risk of suicidal acting out in an adolescent victim and accordingly recommend an assessment.

Clearly there are an infinite number of ways that a troubled adolescent may come to be seen by a clinician. The early detection and subsequent referral to a clinical professional provides some important preassessment data that bear on the adolescent's psychological, social, cognitive, and emotional resources; potential for compliance (see chap. 5); and ability to seek and receive help. It therefore behooves the mental health professional to consider briefly both the source and the context of the referral before conducting the actual assessment of suicide risk.

Case Illustration

Susie, an 18-year-old first-semester college freshman, is referred by her art professor to the University Counseling Center. On intake, she reports feeling depressed and believes she is unable to take her upcoming final exams. She states that she has been sleeping poorly and is unable to concentrate on her studies. She eats infrequently and lightly and has lost several pounds in the last month without intention to do so. She describes herself as listless. Furthermore, she notes that she has withdrawn from friends and avoided practically all contact. A friend who accompanied her to the center corroborates that Susie has not returned phone calls and has refused offers to talk. Her communications, when offered, have reflected a preoccupation with death and dying; her jokes have been morbid. Susie states that she has indeed been obsessed with thoughts of death, preferring a "peaceful ending" to a life of pain. She does not believe she will be alive by Christmas. Her major semester project for art, which led to her referral, was a painting of a young female sprawled at the foot of a tall building. It was entitled *Susie-cide*.

The experienced clinician may have little difficulty noting the presence of both a diagnosable affective disorder and suicidal ideation, as in the case of Susie. But perhaps the most difficult and anxiety-provoking aspect of a clinical evaluation is that of assessing whether, at some future time, there is risk for suicidal behavior. Research has documented a significant relation between depression and suicide ideation; however, the association between these factors and future suicidal behavior is limited (Carlson & Cantwell, 1982). For example, Shaffer and Bacon (1989) reported the ratio of depressed adolescents to depressed suicides was approximately 660:1. As well, Motto (1984) reported a long-term (5- to 15-year) follow-up of teen-agers admitted to San Francisco Bay–area hospitals after a suicide attempt or with serious depression. Certain risk factors were found to be *proportionately* more common among those who later took their own lives; however, at the same time, the same factors were *numerically* many times more common in those who would not. Thus, the presence of an affective disorder, even one with concurrent suicide ideation, is not sufficiently discriminative to allow a dynamic assessment of risk for future, potentially lethal behavior.

At the same time, such a case presentation illustrates the concept of early detection. Clinicians alert to risk factors associated with suicidal behavior in adolescence (see chap. 3) must use this awareness to "red flag" (Blumenthal & Kupfer, 1989) youth at risk for future suicidal behavior. Such attention allows for further assessment and identification of a youth at risk. In turn, such an identification is, obviously, the first step toward offering that youth treatment that, if accepted and implemented successfully, may well lead to the prevention of suicidal death (Eddy, Wolpert, & Rosenberg, 1989b).

SUICIDE RISK ASSESSMENT

Suicide risk assessment involves active inquiry in four major areas of patient functioning and history:

1. Predisposing vulnerabilities
2. Triggers or precipitating events
3. Mental status: affective, cognitive, and behavioral states
4. Contraindications: coping skills and resources versus failed protections

In addition, on the basis of the foregoing and further questioning, suicide risk assessment requires an evaluation of the adolescent's

1. suicidal intent, reasons or motivations for suicide, and lethality.
2. compliance.

These observations and judgments made by a skilled clinician using active and empathic inquiry allow for an overall assessment of acute versus chronic risk for suicidal behavior. The final judgment of acute risk (and more discrete judgments regarding the potential for imminent suicidal behavior) is formed on the basis of a combination of observations regarding the patient's vulnerability to be suicidal, readiness to act, acceptability of suicide, factors known to increase risk, and failed protections, especially including loss of supports.

Case Illustration

Kathy's early years were marked first by her father's abandonment before she was born and the subsequent rage her mother could not hide—rage at her husband for leaving and at Kathy for being "too old" to abort.

Forced to work, Kathy's mother delivered Kathy and her sister to her own mother, who lovingly raised the girls throughout their early years. When Kathy was 10, her father returned and kidnapped the girls from their grandmother's house. During the next 2 years, Kathy was frequently and severely abused physically by her father; and twice she was nearly strangled to unconsciousness by her sister, who years later would be diagnosed and institutionalized as a paranoid schizophrenic. When Kathy was found and returned to her mother's custody, she learned of her grandmother's precipitous death 3 months earlier. Believing that her mother neither loved nor wanted her, still suffering the effects of her abuse, and now, deeply mourning the loss of the only person by whom she felt valued, Kathy openly expressed her wish to join her grandmother. On her 13th birthday, Kathy ingested a "cocktail" of some 85 pills culled from her mother's medicine chest.

As evidenced by Kathy's case, suicidal adolescents have suffered, among other things, serious blows to their self-esteem, their sense of self, and their ability to cope, often because of years of conflictual, stressful, or traumatic experience. Family history is an essential aspect of an adequate assessment of suicidal risk. Familial (and genetic), biophysical, sociocultural, psychopathological, and related factors determine the context for how an adolescent will respond to later demands for adjustment. In Kathy's case, her early experiences predisposed her to be especially vulnerable later in adolescence to precipitating loss, abuse, and rejection.

Case continued

Kathy was rescued and briefly hospitalized after her ingestion attempt. For the next several years, she ambivalently chose life as she struggled to find a stable and healthier sense of self.

She was bright and found some self-worth through academic successes. However, she was understandably unable to trust and, consequently, formed few significant friendships—until her senior year in high school, when she met Carl, with whom she had her first significant love relationship. However, Carl soon showed his instability. As arguments and coercion replaced the blush of first love, Kathy attempted to break off the relationship with Carl. Carl responded by severely beating and raping Kathy. At 2 a.m. the following morning, Kathy entered her mother's car in the closed garage of her home and ran the engine, hoping that the carbon-monoxide fumes would bring her the peace of death. In a single behavior, she was protesting a life in which she felt helplessly entrapped and a future that promised only more of the same. She felt compelled by an urgent and intense need to end her psychological pain.

Stories of abuse, neglect, and instability such as Kathy's tragically are all too common among those reporting for emergency medical treatment consequent to a suicide attempt. The following case of Rowena, perhaps, is typical of how chaotic, pathological, and despairing these lives often are. As noted in chapter 3 and as illustrated by Rowena's case, it is often difficult to distinguish the suicidal adolescent from the matrix of family turmoil, violence, and pathology that predispose him or her to be suicidal.

Case Illustration

Rowena, age 16, made her third visit to the emergency room in 2 years after ingesting 48 Extra Strength Tylenol (500 mg) behind a locked bathroom door (lethality rating = 7.0; see discussion of lethality ratings in this chap.). Each of her prior visits was for a suicide attempt, one by overdose and the other by ingestion of rubbing alcohol. The current attempt was in response to an argument with her sister, the latest in a series of disputes beginning with her being punched in the face by her father and stabbed with a pair of scissors by her mother 9 days prior to this admission. On intake, Rowena stated unequivocally that she hoped to die (high intent).

Rowena was the younger of two girls born to her father, an unemployed heroin abuser, and her mother, who abandoned her after several years of early physical abuse. At the age of 14, when her father threatened to kill her, Rowena was removed by court order to a group home. At the time of the current incident, she lived with her grandmother and sister. Her father, forbidden by the court to see Rowena, lived downstairs with his second wife. At the time of admission, Rowena had been suspended from school because of repetitive assaultive behavior toward her peers.

Psychopathology

As noted in the discussion on risk factors in chapter 3, a large number of studies have documented that mental disorders have been retrospectively diagnosed in an overwhelming majority of adolescent suicides. Controlled psychological autopsy studies in the United States (c.f. Brent, 1987; Brent et al., 1999; Rich, Young, & Fowler, 1986; Shaffer, Gould, et al., 1996; Shaffer & Gould, 1987; Shafii, Carrigan, Whittinghill, & Derrick, 1985) have reported that an average of 90% of teen suicides have an acute psychiatric (Axis I *DSM–IV*) disorder. This prevalence appears to be about 4 times greater than that found in control groups. In European samples, the prevalence of psychiatric disorders has been found to be somewhat lower (70%; Houston, Hawton, & Shepperd, 2001), although still quite significant.

Shaffer and Gould (1987) found psychiatric symptoms among all but a small proportion of completers and also found that approximately one half of all suicides in their psychological autopsy study had had previous contact with a mental health professional. Luoma, Martin, and Pearson (2002) found that 15% of people under the age of 35 had been in treatment with a mental health professional within 1 month of their suicide. In a similarly older sample of young people (ages 15–29; Runeson, 1989), only one of 58 cases of Swedish completers did not have either an Axis I or Axis II diagnosis, and 72% had a history of prior care from a mental health professional. More than one third of Houston et al.'s (2001) sample from the United Kingdom were in treatment at the time of their death.

The most common diagnostic disorders among suicidal adolescents are mood disorders. In males, a diagnosis of depression is most often comorbid with disruptive or conduct disorders or substance abuse. The rate of depression in completed suicide among males is lower and the comorbidity of substance abuse is higher than corresponding rates for females (Shaffer, Gould, et al., 1996). Depressed girls are more likely to withdraw and become silent and inactive; depressed boys tend toward more disruptive and aggressive behavior (World Health Organization, 2000).

Although prevalent among those who become suicidal, depression is neither a necessary nor a sufficient condition for suicidal behavior. A proportion of adolescents complete suicide with no discernible depressive symptoms, and a large proportion of depressed teens never engage in suicidal behavior.

The typological approach focuses more on diagnostic similarities drawn from clusters of research-based findings. As outlined in chapter 3, the following diagnostic groups appear to be commonly found among suicidal adolescents and thus are to be considered more at risk for suicidal behavior than others:

1. The *depressed* adolescent, readily diagnosed using research-based criteria
2. The *substance-abusing* adolescent, who may turn to drugs or alcohol to anesthetize depression
3. The *borderline* or *schizotypal* adolescent, who has a history of rage, impulsivity, and interpersonal instability
4. The *antisocial, acting-out,* or *conduct-disordered* adolescent, whose behavior signals a lack of alliance with or allegiance to healthy objects and systems
5. The *marginal, isolated loner,* who exists on the fringes of a peer system, separate from a peer system, or in groups of marginal others (e.g., with other runaways)
6. The *rigid, unifocal perfectionist,* the "star" who operates with depressogenic logic when threatened with not achieving at self- or other-demanded levels of performance
7. The *psychotic* adolescent, whose behavior is governed by either command hallucinations or an intense panic in anticipation of a self-perceived decompensation
8. The *in-crisis* adolescent, whose stress-provoked behavior is driven by impulsivity and irrationality

As suggested by both empirically derived risk factors and the typology of suicidal adolescents discussed above, a number of mental disorders are found among suicidal adolescents. Often, not one disorder is apparent; frequently, disorders are comorbid, such as borderline personality and mood disorders, as illustrated by Kathy's case. At times, one set of symptoms or behaviors may shadow an underlying disorder, such as a teenager's increasing alcohol or drug abuse used to drown out an underlying depression. Certain diagnoses have been clearly associated with increased rates of suicide (e.g., mood disorders, schizophrenia, and alcohol abuse among adults; conduct disorders, mood disorders, and substance abuse among adolescents). More important, certain diagnoses indicate the need for pharmacotherapeutic intervention, thereby regulating, for example, a thought disorder or bolstering behavioral control.

The most prevalent *DSM–IV* Axis I diagnoses, among a wide range reported across many studies of both attempters and completers, appear to be conduct disorder, mood disorder, and substance use disorders. However, concomitant disorders are common, such as mood and substance abuse disorders (Brent, Perper, Goldstein, et al., 1988; Shafii, Steltz-Lenarsky, Derrick, Beckner, & Whittinghill, 1988). Different studies report markedly different prevalences of the same disorder. For example, only 2% of Hoberman & Garfinkel's (1988a) sample of completers were classified as having bipolar affective disorder as compared to the 22% observed by Brent et al. (1988). Lastly, some commonly observed symptom presentations, such as intense anxiety during an acute crisis or rigid perfectionism in the high-achieving student, may not be sufficient to meet defined criteria for the diagnosis of a mental disorder such as anxiety disorder (Mattison, 1988; Shaffer, Garland, Gould, Fisher, & Trautman, 1988).

Substance abuse disorders appear more commonly in American samples of adolescent suicide than in European samples (Brent, Perper, Moritz, Allman, et al., 1993; Houston et al., 2001; Martunnen, Aro, Henrikksson, & Lonnqvist, 1991; Shaffer, Gould, et al., 1996). Risk for suicide appears to increase when heavy substance use is (a) comorbid, especially with depression; (b) active and frequent; (c) accompanied by recent or anticipated loss of a close relationship; (d) evidenced by deteriorated social status or decreased work or school performance; co-occurring with (e) chronic social isolation.

Case Illustration

Carla, age 12, was admitted to the intensive care unit unconscious and unstable after ingesting eight of her mother's 50-mg Elavil tablets, an unknown quantity of amytryptiline, and approximately 20 tablets of Tylenol #3 (with codeine). This attempt, her first, came after arguing with her father over chores and restrictions imposed because her grades were so bad. She reported going to the medicine chest and ingesting everything she could find because "it became too much" and she "did not want to live."

For the previous month, she had displayed a noticeable change of mood, behaving with more instability and depression, feeling worthless and hopeless. In this period she had lost her appetite and had dropped two dress sizes. She increasingly had isolated herself, staying alone in her room. Her school performance, for which her father had grounded her, had declined from Bs the previous term to Ds. Both her mother and maternal grandmother had histories of affective disorder.

Case Illustration

Mila, age 15, was admitted to the emergency room in a delirious, disoriented, agitated, and combative state after ingesting multiple medications, including an estimated 16 160-mg Flexoril tablets. This was her third known parasuicidal behavior, all by ingestion, in 18 months. Mila had a long record of delinquent activity that included occasional fights and the stabbings just two weeks earlier of two boys who were beating up her older brother. Because of this latter offense, she had been removed to a group home, in which she allegedly was propositioned sexually; this incident led to her anxious and tearful return home just hours prior to this attempt.

Case Illustration

Stan, age 20, tested his outpatient therapist by phoning him at 4:00 a.m. on Sunday morning, stating, "I just took all of them, you quack, quack, quack" and hanging up. A 3-day hospitalization ensued in response to his overdose. In explaining his attempt, Stan related that he had been criticized by his boss and had stayed up all night drinking, hating himself and everyone else. He felt alone, empty, "a failure at everything"; his rage knew no boundaries.

Stan had a long history of intense rage, directed primarily at his mother, who he claimed sexually provoked him throughout his adolescence, but also at his father for not protecting him from "the witch." He felt chronically empty, anxious, and hopeless. He harbored considerable confusion over his sexual identity, frequently testing homosexual urges under the influence of alcohol, but disowning them when sober. His therapist reported that Stan often behaved provocatively, idealizing him one moment and denigrating him the next. His chronic tension and self-deprecatory rumination made concentration difficult, resulting in much inefficient work performance. Additionally, his uneasiness with others allowed only transient relationships to develop, proof to Stan of his unworthiness.

Case Illustration

Larry, age 18, became depressed, hopeless, and increasingly suicidal after breaking up with his girlfriend while home from college over Christmas break. He blamed himself for the breakup, as he had been dating other girls at school during his first term away. With his return to school, he found himself increasingly unable to attend to and concentrate on his studies. Additionally, he felt anhedonic and anergic, had poor appetite and insomnia with early morning awakening, feelings of help-lessness, hopelessness, and low self-esteem. He began to drink heavily, binging three to four nights a week until he blacked out. His academic performance deteriorated considerably. Associated with these changes, he felt paranoid and had visual hallucina-tions and ideas of reference.

As his depression worsened and he increasingly felt suicidal (he purchased razor blades in anticipation of cutting himself), Larry sought the help of a pastoral counselor, who recommended hospi-talization. After 2 days, however, his parents signed him out against medical advice and returned him to their care at home. Within a week, he overdosed with an unknown quantity of his prescribed medications. Several days after his second hospital admission, he was still unable to give a coherent history of what happened.

Personality Traits

Axis II diagnoses are commonly observed and occur concomitant with both substance abuse and mood disorders; almost 30% of Houston et al.'s (2001) sample of completed suicides had a diagnosed personality disorder. However, per-sonality disorders (e.g., borderline personality disorders) are more difficult to diagnose in adolescence than in adulthood. Diagnoses unto themselves lack suf-ficient specificity to significantly improve our assessment of an adolescent's risk for suicidal behavior. Nevertheless, maladaptive personality traits (e.g., para-noid) may be reasonably common among those at risk (Houston et al., 2001). Beautrais, Joyce, and Mulder (1999), for example, found that neuroticism and external locus of control were significant risk factors for serious suicide attempts.

Apter (2000), on the basis of studies, both postmortem and clinical, of suicidal adolescents in Israel, has posed a typology of the following three maladaptive personality constellations in suicidal behavior:

1. *Narcissistic–perfectionistic type*. This adolescent has an inabil-ity to tolerate failure and imperfection. Combined with an

underlying isolative, private, or even schizoid personality structure, he or she does not ask for help or support and tries to maintain a positive impression on others while harboring shame.

2. *Impulsive–aggressive type.* An oversensitivity to minor hassles and life stressors leads this adolescent to react with anger and anxiety, then to develop a secondary depression and suicidal behavior. Frequently abused as younger children, these adolescents typically will be diagnosed as having a borderline personality disorder and will have a concomitant substance abuse history or problem.

3. *Mental disorder–hopelessness type.* This adolescent is driven to suicide by a combination of significant Axis I psychopathology and hopelessness.

Family History and Family Pathology

A family history of suicide and current or past parental psychopathology, especially a mood or other significant Axis I diagnosis, are particularly related to increased risk for suicide in adolescents (Gould & Kramer, 2001). Houston et al. (2001) found a family history of psychiatric disorder in more than half of the completed suicides they psychologically autopsied. Similarly, risk increases with histories of family violence and abuse and poor communication between the adolescent and his or her parents. Conflict with parents, also, is a common precipitant of adolescent suicidal behavior (see "Triggers" section later in this chapter).

Past History of Suicide Attempt

If there is one truism in evaluating risk for future behavior, it is that the most significant predictor of future behavior is past behavior. The importance of prior suicide attempts, single or recurrent, as a predisposing risk factor is supported by numerous research studies (e.g., Rudd, Joiner, & Rajab, 1996). Stoelb and Chiriboga (1998) reported that a high school student who has made one suicide attempt is 18 times more likely to make another within 12 months. About one third of completed suicides have made a known prior attempt (Brent et al., 1999; Shaffer, Gould, et al., 1996), with the prevalence of past attempts being more common among females. For example, Shaffer and Gould (1987) reported that 21% of males and 33% of females in their study of New York–area completers had made a prior attempt. In spite of the significance of prior suicidal behavior, the clinician should not lose sight of the fact that the majority of suicide completers are first-time attempters.

Prior suicidal behavior is more clinically significant to a current assessment when it was relatively recent, relatively lethal, or more death-intentioned; did not lead to a positive therapeutic experience or consequence; or was one of multiple, repetitive nonfatal attempts.

Developmental Trauma

As illustrated in Kathy's case, a history of physical or sexual abuse, punitive parenting, or neglect are related to increased risk for suicide attempt or completion among adolescents (Brent et al., 1999; Brent, Perper, et al., 1994; Fergusson et al., 1995; Gould et al., 1996; Kaplan et al., 1997; Kerfoot, Dyer, Harrington, Woodham, & Harrington, 1996; Kosky et al., 1990; Reinherz et al., 1995).

Those variables that describe the adolescent's early childhood (e.g., developmental trauma) and genetic history (e.g., family history of violence, suicide, or mental disorder) are also characterized as "perpetuating risk factors" in that they cannot be changed (Felner & Silverman, 1989).

Triggers (Precipitants)

In the context of predisposing vulnerability, stressful life events are significant as "final straws" in precipitating suicidal behavior (Brent et al., 1999; de Wilde, Kienhorst, Diekstra, & Wolters, 1992; Gould et al., 1996). Common among the significant precipitants found in studies of adolescent suicidal behavior are interpersonal discord and conflicts (e.g., a disciplinary crisis) and losses (Brent, Perper, Goldstein, et al., 1988). For younger adolescents, these more frequently involve a parent; for older adolescents, a romantic attachment (Brent et al., 1999).

Seventy percent of attempts and completions reported by Brent, Perper, Goldstein, et al. (1988) were precipitated by interpersonal conflict. Hoberman and Garfinkel (1988a) found that precipitating arguments with parents were most often about drug use, parenting issues, academic performance, and dating. School problems, disappointments, and problems with the police were also commonly found. In Houston et al.'s (2001) sample of British adolescent suicides, significant life events occurred within the week of death in 16 of 27 cases, with more than one third of these experiencing two or more significant life events in that week.

Triggering events may best be characterized by those that threaten

- losses of valued or desired attachments (triggering feelings of abandonment or rejection);
- acute disappointments;
- legal action or incarceration, especially for youth with conduct disorder and substance abuse problems; and
- embarrassment, humiliation, or a threat to status.

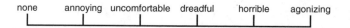

| none | annoying | uncomfortable | dreadful | horrible | agonizing |

Figure 4.1. Likert pain scale. From *Pain Clinic Manual* (2nd ed., p. 63), by M. McCaffery and C. Pasero, 1999, Philadelphia: Elsevier. Copyright 1999 by Elsevier. Adapted with permission.

MENTAL STATUS EVALUATION

Among the most observable clues to suicide risk are those made discernible by a thorough mental status evaluation. Particularly when suicide ideation is not directly expressed, the risk that thoughts of death and suicide are being harbored, and might be acted on, increases when affective and cognitive signs are present. The presence of these signs should alert the clinician to return to the question of suicide ideation, to probe once again as to its presence under conditions of great psychic pain or hopelessness.

Affective System

How might the adolescent's affective state hint at increased potential for suicide? Perhaps most obviously, risk increases when signs of sadness or dysphoria are present. Dysphoria involves a mixture of painful feelings in addition to sadness: feelings of anxiety, tension, fearfulness, anger, guilt, loneliness, shame, humiliation, and so on. These negative or painful affects may predispose the adolescent to seek escape from pain.

As defined by Shneidman (1999), psychological pain is mental suffering or inner torment, a hurt or misery, an ache in the mind ("psychache"). It can range from feeling blue to unbearable distress. McCaffery and Passero (1999, pp. 68–73) offer a helpful seven-point Likert pain scale descriptive of an ordinal continuum of psychological pain ranging from *none* to *agonizing* as shown in Figure 4.1.

Shame and humiliation may be particularly insidious feelings. Often harbored by adolescents who perceive failure to meet expectations of their parents or who are especially sensitive to signs that they are not accepted by or fitting in with their peers, these feelings further feed a sense of oneself as a sham—presenting a persona to others that is discordant with one's self view. Loneliness is a state of pained aloneness. As a phenomenological state, it can be experienced deeply by adolescents who appear overtly to very much be part of and active in a peer group. Highly sensitive to negative cues and harboring an inner sense of being unloved, however, they never truly incorporate a sense of belongingness and attachment.

In this regard, consider the writings of Luke (age 17) whose inner turmoil, psychic pain, and disappointments fed thoughts of suicide that dominated the pages of his private diaries and poems:

These are the last words I write

Because I will take my life tonight.

A good son I was not

A good son you have always sought

I could have been a better friend

Instead I was all pretend

I was a horrible lover

Such that I could never recover

I could have been someone better

I wish I could have been someone better

Now I've taken the pills

And I'm starting to get the chills

The knife gleams

And my blood streams

I'm getting tired

Hatred is all I've inspired

After my eyes close

My blood no longer flows

Because my heart needs a jump start

I wish I could wait and see

What I must be

When these negative affects are particularly intense or poorly controlled, the risk for impulsive or explosive and violent behavior increases. Perhaps the most tragic examples of this truism is documented in our studies of school shooters, most notably Dylan Klebold and Eric Harris, who took the lives of 11 others before taking their own lives at Columbine High School in suburban Denver in 1999.

Case Illustration

Eric Harris and Dylan Klebold were isolated, socially alienated, and full of rage. They banded together with others as part of the "Trench Coat Mafia," achieving a measure of power in their retributive fantasies and shared differences. Harris, the dominant of the two, had a diagnosed depression for which he had been prescribed an antidepressant. He recently had been arrested for breaking and entering (perhaps suggesting a possible conduct disorder, as well). He displayed violent fantasies in school writings and a video produced for a school project. He also had an obsessive fascination with violent video games, identified and worshiped Adolph Hitler and all things Nazi, and had ready access to an arsenal of available firearms. Together, Harris and Klebold built pipe bombs in Harris's garage. In his diary, Harris wrote of his and Klebold's expectation (after the school shootings) to commandeer an airplane and crash it into Manhattan. If this failed, Harris wrote, they would end their lives in a hail of police gunfire.

Cognitive System

As a mood disorder deepens, cognitive processing tends to become more primitive. Distortions in thinking emerge; grays become dichotomized into blacks or whites, perceptions generalize, thinking styles rigidify. Core beliefs define feelings of helplessness ("I can't do anything to make things better"), worthlessness ("I don't deserve..."), and an inability to tolerate distress ("I can't stand feeling this way anymore"; Rudd et al., 2001). In turn, these beliefs define the thoughts and associated feelings we ascribe to hopelessness ("Things will never change").

Hopelessness is correlated with depressed mood, but, more important and significant, with suicide intent. Hopelessness predicts repeat attempts and suicide completions even with psychopathological disorders being controlled (Beck, Steer, et al., 1985; Kerfoot et al., 1996). In contrast, hope (see below) is one of several protective factors mitigating against suicide.

Suicide ideation usually comes to the clinician's attention through reported threats. Communicated suicidal ideation (see below), although a cardinal indicator heightening risk for potential overt behavior, is neither a necessary nor a sufficient condition for the assessment of risk for that behavior. At the same time, it is important to remind ourselves that considerable trust must be gained before adolescents harboring such thoughts will be willing to share them. Gaining entry into the inner world of the at-risk adolescent is an art (Shea, 1999) requiring formidable technical skill.

Suicidal thoughts range from passive wishes to die (or to be made dead) to active and planful thoughts. They also vary along a continuum from fleeting and transient to pervasive and ruminative. Over time, the more active and pervasive the suicidal ideation, the more likely a suicide attempt will occur (Lewinsohn, Rohde, & Seeley, 1996). Similarly, when suicide ideations are intense, vivid, or uncontrollable, risk for self-harm behavior increases.

When suicide ideation is noted, an evaluation of the adolescent's wish to die (or his or her suicide intent) is immediately called for. *Suicide intent* refers to the desired and expected consequences of a contemplated behavior. In part, intent may be discerned by the degree to which the adolescent has planned suicidal behavior. In general, the more concrete and thorough the planning, the more acute the risk. The clinician must ask specific questions relating to the adolescent's plan (when, where, how) and the availability and accessibility of means necessary to accomplish that plan. The clinician also needs to understand the adolescent's seriousness by addressing aspects of a planned action that suggest a low likelihood of rescue or reversibility were the plan put into effect. Adolescents who rehearse or make preparations by obtaining planned means (securing a a gun, hoarding pills, etc.) or testing out a planned means (visiting a bridge, making a noose and placing it around one's neck, etc.) figuratively have engaged in a dress rehearsal for the real thing. It is important that the clinician understand how far the rehearsal went and what made the adolescent stop the behavior from being carried out. Questions should be raised regarding efforts to conceal low-lethality attempts or rehearsal behaviors.

In adolescence, most often the stated intent of a suicidal motive is both interpersonal and instrumental. That is, the wish is to alter life circumstances, to communicate an otherwise unaccepted message, to mobilize or to change others, to coerce others' behavior through threat or guilt, or to seek revenge. That these intentions are not death-seeking does not necessarily diminish the possibility that the adolescent will bet his or her survival or sacrifice his or her life to accomplish any of these ends. The functional analysis of such motives, however, is most important to therapeutic planning should the adolescent be available for such intervention.

The clinician, furthermore, needs to attend to the meaning of suicidal behavior or intent as expressed by the adolescent. Hawton (1987) has documented that reasons given by overdose patients to explain their attempts are quite different from those ascribed to these behaviors by the patients' psychiatrists. These discrepancies do not define one or the other view as more valid; rather, they indicate that for the sake of empathic communication, pairing, and rapport, clinicians should listen carefully to their patients. When one so attends, themes of escape and relief, control and power frequently appear. The latter two motives often are described when the adolescent is asked whether he or she has any fantasies of how others would react were he or she to die. In general, the intended goals of suicidal behavior involve attempts to replace the experience of pain, helplessness, hopelessness, or powerlessness—affects and cognitions common to the suicidal state.

The clinician should note that suicide ideation in the absence of a plan does not necessarily suggest less risk. This is particularly true in cases where behavioral activation (e.g., impulsivity) is potentially high.

Suicide ideation also includes thoughts about how one's death may affect others and, in particular, wishes for others to be affected in specific ways (e.g., to feel guilty for perceived maltreatment; see "Reasons for Suicide" below). Moreover, when ideation is currently denied but recently expressed or reported, it is imperative that the clinician understand what motivated the recent ideation, the presence or absence of similar motivating conditions, and the adolescent's perspective on what has changed between the time ideation was expressed and the present.

Suicide intent may also be discerned by asking what the adolescent would wish to accomplish were he or she to act on their ideation. The intended aim, purpose, or goal of suicidal behavior, moreover, may establish specific targets for treatment, as these ends may be reasonable and descriptive of the adolescent's unmet needs, which might be met without having to engage in suicidal behavior.

Reasons for suicide are also important to assess. These reasons, or motivations, refer to the functional meaning of suicidal actions to the adolescent contemplating them. The range of possible reasons is broad and includes the following:

1. Escape from pain (no feeling is better than bad feeling),
2. Revenge (to aggress against an aggressor—"They'll be sorry…"),
3. Rebirth (magical thinking that with death comes a new life, a second chance),
4. Control and power (an act of mastery to replace feeling helpless),
5. Reunion (with a deceased loved one; to replace a disrupted attachment),
6. Self-punishment (for feelings of guilt or sinfulness).

Hjelmeland et al. (2002) interviewed more than 1,600 European patients who had made a suicide attempt and categorized their self-reported intentions. They found four main themes:

1. *Care-seeking*: "I wanted to show someone how much I loved him or her"; "I wanted others to know how desperate I felt"; "I wanted to get help from someone"; "I wanted to know if someone really cared about me."
2. *Influencing others (revenge, punishment, manipulation)*: "I wanted others to pay for the way they treated me"; "I wanted to make someone feel guilty"; "I wanted to persuade someone to change his or her mind."

3. *Temporary escape*: "I wanted to get away for a while from an unacceptable situation"; "I wanted to sleep for a while."
4. *Final exit*: "The situation was so unbearable that I could not think of any alternative"; "My thoughts were so unbearable that I could not endure them any longer"; "I wanted to die"; "I wanted to make things easier for others."

A residual, more impulsive, less self-aware characterization was expressed by some patients: "It seemed that I lost control of myself, and I do not know why I did it." The reader will note that the first two themes reported above are decidedly interpersonal and instrumental, whereas the latter two themes speak more to the theme of escape from pain.

Behavioral Activation and Arousal

A fair proportion of adolescent suicidal behaviors occur on impulse, with little or no evident planning. In one study of a slightly older population (ages 13–34), Simon et al. (2001) found that 24% of nearly lethal suicide attempters report a lag of only 5 minutes or less between the impulse to die by suicide and the behavior. Problems of affect regulation, hostility, and impulsive aggression are highly associated with suicidal behavior (Brent, Johnson, et al., 1993, 1994). Signs of poor impulse control and rage indicate suicidal risk, and a number of diagnostic types noted in the previous section have in common a lack of control over expression of impulse. However, because expressions of rage may be other-directed, self-directed, or free-floating, near-term predictions of suicide risk become difficult. A history of assaultive, violent behavior strongly implicates the potential for such behavior without directionality.

Often, suicidal adolescents have been observed to be as full of rage toward others as toward themselves, providing evidence of the free-floating nature of their aggression. For example, Cairns, Peterson, and Neckerman (1988) compared a sample of emotionally disturbed, assaultive children (ages 4–18) with histories of serious suicide attempts to a matched sample of nonattempters and found no difference between the groups on the frequency of severity of other-directed violence. As in the following case, free-floating rage also exerts a most powerful interpersonal control.

Case Illustration

Leon, age 11, was brought to the emergency room after threatening to ingest his mother's Xanax. Since his parents'

> divorce 3 1/2 years ago, Leon began developing symptoms of
> anxiety and depression, including frightening nightmares.
> Recently, he attempted to hit his mother with a table lamp, yell-
> ing, "I want to kill you!" For the past month he had been carry-
> ing a kitchen knife, threatening others to "stay away from [me]!"

When impulsivity and rage are documented, or when there exists a loosening of controls because of pathology or substance abuse, and when there exists a context to believe that suicidal intent is present (see the next section), risk for near-term suicidal behavior is high. In concert with a readily available or accessible method, the possibility of imminent suicidal behavior is great, as is the need for hospitalization to protect the adolescent from himself or herself.

Communications

As noted earlier in this chapter, the possibility of imminent suicidal behavior may be, and often is, signaled by verbal or behavioral messages. Adolescents in particular, although less frequently writers of suicide notes than adults, communicate in words, school essays, poems, diaries, journals, and artwork (like Susie's in the Case Illustration on p. 123) a preoccupation with themes of death, dying, the afterlife, or suicide. Questions about death or suicide, asked out of context or with more than ordinary interest, or communicated dreams about death should alert the observer to follow up with appropriate concern. When such signals are present, the interviewer should explore for further evidence of suicide ideation, especially the existence of a plan and the possibility of rehearsal behavior or preparations (e.g., the hoarding of pills or knowledge of how to secure a lethal weapon).

It is essential to establish this approach to all suicidal communications—that is, that they deserve, no less require, further inquiry and through such inquiry the possibility of intervention. Clinicians, given to analytic and interpretive readings of patient communications, should be careful not to prematurely interpret an adolescent's communication as signaling suicidal risk or not. All communications need to be placed in a contextual frame best supplied by the adolescent himself or herself and by that adolescent's history.

The following cases describe the range and variety of forms of communication, from poems to journal entries to drawings. The reader should note that each was a signal meant for observation and discovery.

Case Illustration

Cheryl, age 17, wrote the following poem for her high school English class three days prior to her overdose attempt:

A Plea

My world is a lonely world

A world devoid of love, laughter, and life

A world full of despair and darkness…

A world in need of a knife

My life is a lonely life

No more friends or happiness do I have

The only thing left in my life

Is cold, dark loneliness and sadness

No need for worry

No need for despair

Don't worry for her life

For Cheryl is already dead inside

The job has been done by her knife.

Case Illustration

Patty, a 15-year-old repetitive wrist-cutter, kept a journal in which she frequently wrote introspectively and self-disclosingly of her pain. After being gang-raped on her birthday, about which she told no one, she wrote the following passage expressing her despair and emptiness, then cut herself:

The house. The house was once happy, when the man had his wife and children. Now it is empty… except for the old man. Once he was young and happy. He was at peace. Now he is alone. When his wife died, and then, when his son died, he felt rage. Then he felt sad. Now he can no longer

> feel the pain. Now he is empty. Nothing lasts, everything can be taken away. Soon the old man will die and the house will be sad. Maybe he will find peace in the skies. No one cares about the house.

The following letter was sent to the central office of the American Association of Suicidology after the association's name and address appeared as a trailer to a public service television announcement about teen suicide:

Case Illustration

I am 12 years old and I don't know if I have the power to live much longer. My parents pay attention to my 15-year-old sister. She blames everything on me and I don't know anything about it and I get into trouble. My teachers know I'm thinking about it cause I starve myself and I cut in my skin. My teachers had a conference with my parents about it. I've told two of my friends about it, one doesn't believe me, the other tells me "Don't do it." If things don't change, I will commit suicide. I have the date marked on my calendar. I get the feeling that my parents don't want me. They say they love me but I know they don't. So that is why I'm going to commit suicide. I'm going to give them a present on my birthday.

Case Illustration

Barb, a 19-year-old college sophomore who acknowledged being depressed, brought her diary to her new therapist, suggesting that his reading of it might give him added insight into her problems. After only two meetings, during which Barb presented herself in a most guarded manner, speaking in a monotone and only in response to directives and questions, he was eager to have such an opportunity to read her written thoughts. When he turned to her most recent entries, dated the evening before this session, instead of introspective writing he found drawings on facing pages, as shown in Figures 4.2 and 4.3.

Figure 4.2. First of two pages in Barb's journal reflecting her suicide ideation.

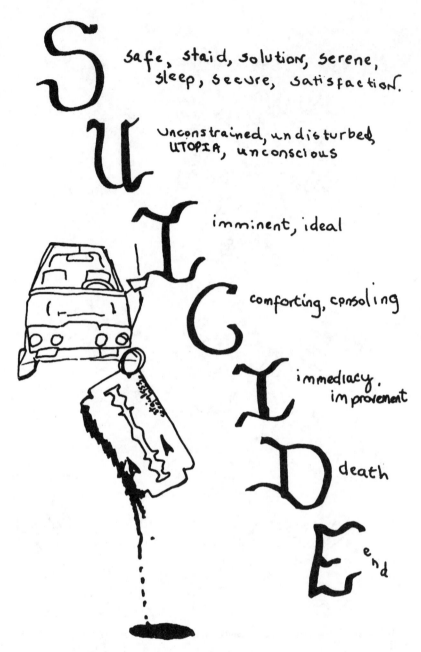

Safe, staid, solution, serene, sleep, secure, satisfaction.

Unconstrained, undisturbed UTOPIA, unconscious

imminent, ideal

comforting, consoling

immediacy, improvement

death

end

Figure 4.3. Corresponding page in Barb's journal. Original drawing has bright red ink dripping off of razor blade.

Case Illustration

The parents of Stan, an 18-year-old college freshman, found a spiral notebook their son left after being home from school over Christmas break. In it they discovered the following poem, which caused them to be concerned:

My search continues for a blade.

    A razor's edge to skin the fox

to determine the entrail's configuration,

    to ascertain the color of his blood.

My hand jerks down and immortality

    rises within my soul. With fright

the dial sweeps from left to right

    propelling me toward ecstasy again.

My eyes scrutinize the frictionless surface.

    A meticulous search for the final obstacle

that will jettison my corporeal body

    from reality to hell, via mutilation.

But I will not have existed without fear,

    a surname for insanity, delight.

In my final, wild ride I change dimensions

    entering through a violent, scarlet porthole.

In consultation, Stan's parents related that their son had always lived recklessly (e.g., he had been stopped over five times for speeding), had run away from home several times during his adolescence, and had been in more than a few physical altercations with his father. Although they had found a bong in his bedroom, they had accepted his denial of drug use and his explanation that he was merely "holding it for a friend."

Our admonition to the reader to avoid premature interpretation is most evident here, as the brief background given on Stan leaves open several competing meanings of his poem. These range from that of a suicidal message to that depicting the thrill of the behavioral gambler (excessive risk-taker) to that of masturbatory fantasy. Furthermore, we do not know for sure that this communication even reflects his own thinking, as there yet exists the possibility, albeit remote, that it is related to academic course work, or was transcribed from some other source. As always, we are left with the need for more information.

Behavioral Communications

The possibility of suicidal behavior appears greatest, and is most difficult to predict temporally, when there are signs of poor impulse control and rage. A number of the diagnostic types noted in the previous section (e.g., borderline personality disorder, substance abuse) have in common a lack of control over expression of impulse. In particular, they have in common a history of assaultive, violent behavior.

The most significant of behavioral markers or communications is prior suicidal behavior, with perhaps 9% of those once attempting going on to complete suicide within 10 years (Motto, 1984). As reviewed earlier, Shaffer and Gould's (1987) preliminary report of New York-area completers found that 21% of males and 33% of females have a history of attempt. Of the 27 suicides investigated by Houston et al. (2001) in the United Kingdom, 25 of whom were males, 63% had a history of previous self-harm, and the majority had histories of repetitive self-harm. As noted earlier, prior suicidal behavior is more clinically significant to a current assessment when it is relatively recent, relatively lethal, death-intentioned, not responded to with clinical intervention, or the last in a sequence of repeated parasuicidal behaviors.

Other behavioral messages are often direct substitutes for verbal communications. For example, termination behaviors such as writing a will, giving away favored possessions, and making preparations for death are infrequently observed in adolescents, but they are clear markers of suicidal intentions when they do occur.

One indirect behavioral sign of note is that of acute behavioral change. Even in adolescence, there are relatively stable behavioral patterns. Significant changes in behavior, particularly those out of character and persistent that are otherwise unexplained, demand a context of understanding. Absent that understanding, the possibility exists that the behavior is masking and concurrently signaling a significant mood shift (depression or anxiety), any of a number of concurrent pathologies (e.g., substance abuse), or some cognitive disturbance in need of further evaluation. Examples for such changes in behavior that warrant further observation and evaluation are changes in sleep cycles, eating patterns, intensity of anger, irritability, withdrawal, dress, hygiene, grooming, body piercing, and so on.

Symptomatic cues to the presence of increased reactivity and behavioral activation might be (a) insomnia, (b) panic, agitation, (c) impaired attention and concentration, and (d) acute intoxication.

LETHALITY

As previously noted, the level of sophistication in both definition and research in suicidology makes it impossible for us to adequately establish risk factors particular to levels of lethality. In spite of this, an assessment of lethality, the expected medicobiological consequence of a performed or contemplated act, is important so that we may evaluate dangerousness to self and determine the proper response to that evaluation. "High lethality" refers to the significant possibility of a life-threatening effect secondary to self-harm behavior. As a corresponding reference point, "low lethality" refers to minimal medical danger consequent to self-inflicted action.

An excellent resource for understanding the concept of lethality was first presented by Smith, Conroy, and Ehler (1984) and recently revised by Berman, Shepherd, and Silverman (2003). On the basis of the likely impact of specific actions, and modified by the circumstances surrounding the intended action (e.g., probable rescuability), these researchers have provided the clinician with a defined procedure for scaling lethality of attempts or planned actions that does not rely on the patient's stated intent. Ratings of lethality are made on an 11-point equal interval scale having nine anchor points ranging from 0.0 (*death is an impossible result*) to 10.0 (*survival only by fortuitous circumstance and rigorous intervention*). Ease of use and reliability of ratings are enhanced by illustrative examples and by method (e.g., ingestion, cutting) for each anchor point. For example, an attempt contemplated by a patient having small doses of potentially lethal medication (e.g., 10–15 50-mg Thorazine [chlorpromazine] tablets) is rated 2.0; one ingesting 15 to 20 lithium carbonate tablets is rated 3.5. Ratings of suicidal behavior above scale point 3.5 are considered "serious." The following case illustrates a highly lethal attempt (10.0 on this scale) because of the adolescent's use of a shotgun, in spite of the high probability of rescue and the stated nonlethal intent:

Case Illustration

Sam was 17 when he approached the front stoop of his girlfriend's house with a borrowed shotgun in hand. Angered by her threat to end their yearlong relationship, he intended to prove to her how much he loved her. As he claimed later, he had "carefully researched" just where to aim the shotgun in order not to hit any vital organs. After ringing her doorbell and hearing her approaching footsteps, he shot himself in the abdomen. As planned and gambled, he survived his wounds, spending close to 3 weeks in the hospital recovering.

The following two cases would be rated 7.0 and 1.0, respectively, on the Smith et al. (1984) Lethality of Suicide Attempt Rating Scale:

Case Illustration

Bob, age 15, was severely reprimanded by his grandmother when he returned from being with his girlfriend because he had told no one where he was. (His grandmother, who had raised him almost from birth after his mother had abandoned him, had grown increasingly anxious about Bob ever since his first suicide attempt, which had occurred over 1 year earlier, soon after his father, a drug addict, announced he was leaving.) Feeling totally unsupported, Bob went to his bedroom to listen to his stereo. He soon complained of a headache and asked for some aspirin. At the hospital, he reflected back on the next several minutes as "blank"; but, at best count, he took 72 aspirin, telling no one until he later developed shortness of breath and called out to his grandmother, who called for emergency medical treatment.

Case Illustration

Patrice, age 16, attempted to kill herself by ingesting six antibiotic pills to avoid being sent by her father to live with his sister in another state. Patrice had a long history of behavioral problems, including substance abuse, runaway behavior, truancy, sexual promiscuity, and two prior overdoses. Additionally, she had been repeatedly assaulted by her substance-abusing boyfriend.

The case of Patrice is illustrative of the distinction between lethality and intent, where the former is low but the intent and its predisposing conditions are serious. Intent refers to the purpose or goal of the self-harm behavior. The clinical relationship between intent and lethality has been described as ranging from "robust" (Brent, 1987) to mixed (Goldston, 2000). When the goal is to escape a painful condition or context by seeking a condition of nonpain (i.e., by wanting death), intent is high. Similarly, when the motive of suicidal behavior is passage to a new existence, such as reuniting with a deceased love object, going to a desired afterlife, or being reborn, the likelihood of death (as the end of bodily life) being sought through high-lethality behavior is great. Such was the obvious consequence of Timmy's magical thinking in the following case.

CONTRAINDICATIONS

Suicidal adolescents never present in such a way as to lead clinicians to unequivocally assess risk. Juxtaposed to both situational and characterological conditions suggesting levels of risk are a number of factors that must be considered as potentially abating risk. These include available coping skills and resources as well as a positive history of compliance. Where there is a future time perspective including a desired object or goal; where the adolescent demonstrates some ability to tolerate frustration, to assess his or her emotional state as on a continuum that varies according to situation and time; where there is a good history of compliance and a nonhostile, nonrejecting cooperation with the intake interviewer, there exists an increased likelihood that imminent risk is not present. Similarly, where there is a supportive home environment and open channels of communication from family members to the mental health caregiver, risk may be maximally monitored and lessened.

Coping Skills and Resources

Suicidal behavior may be construed as an end result of despair and hopelessness, self-contempt, rage, and the unavailability of sustaining resources (Maltsberger, 1986). Alternatively stated, the risk of suicidal behavior is lessened when the youngster has available both internal (e.g., cognitive) and external (e.g., interpersonal) resources for coping successfully with stress and conflict.

The availability and accessibility of interpersonal resources and supports are essential, first, in the short-term monitoring of an in-crisis adolescent, and second, in the long-term alliances that inherently reduce the adolescent's intolerable feelings of aloneness while increasing the likelihood of rational problem solving to deal with the suicidogenic context.

The cognitive strategies used by the adolescent determine the degree to which alternative routes to desired goals can be considered and possibly accomplished. What problem-solving strategies have been used in the past or applied to the current problem? How rational or irrational is the adolescent in attempting to cope with the current problem? How able is the adolescent, in the interview condition, to use cognitive rehearsal, to think hierarchically, to assess self, and to tolerate ambivalence?

Noting that ambivalence is a common affect of the nonfatal completer or ideator, it is helpful for the clinician to focus with the adolescent on what has kept him or her alive to this point. Linehan, Goodstein, Nielsen, and Chiles (1983) developed the Reasons for Living (RFL) Inventory (see chap. 3), which has been revised and validated with an adolescent population (Osman et al., 1996) and is of use in this assessment. Adolescent psychiatric patients with recent suicide attempts have been found to have fewer reasons for living than do nonsuicidal adolescents (Gutierrez et al., 2000). Jobes and Mann (1999) have advocated for a more integrated approach to understanding suicidality by addressing what sustains (reasons for living) and what moves suicidal individuals to escape (reasons for dying), offering the most frequent reasons for both on the basis of a sample of university counseling center patients.

An alternative way to conceptualize coping-skill deficits is to conceptualize these as "failed protections." Just as there are correlates of suicide that we speak of as risk factors, there are protective factors that strengthen our resolve to sustain ourselves through difficulty and pain. Garmezy and Masten (1986) noted that despite exposure to stressful events, some individuals maintain competencies. Being able to turn to interpersonal supports to ask for and accept help, for example, may be what best explains why females have significantly lower rates of suicide than males, whose gender socialization is antagonistic to these behaviors. Behaving impulsively signals deficits both in cognitive problem solving and impulse control.

Thus, concurrent with an inventory of risk factors, it is important to assess those protective factors available to and displayed by the adolescent. When these are strong and exercised, predisposing risk should be well contained. For example, Rubenstein, Heeren, Housman, Rubin, and Stechler (1989) reported that, in particular, family cohesion and adaptability offset the effects of increased stress in the lives of at-risk youngsters. In addition to those coping skills noted above, we might address the adolescent's

- self-esteem (areas of conflict-free, positively valenced attitudes toward self);
- personal control (confidence in coping skills);
- sense of self-efficacy;
- sense of humor;
- internal sustaining attachments (e.g., religiosity) that may also exert a constraining influence in promoting the unacceptability of suicide;
- external attachments (e.g., to interest groups, healthy peer networks, etc.);

- views of the environment as predictable and life as basically positive;
- ability to elicit positive responses from the environment;
- close personal bonds (i.e., is one present with at least one family member?); and
- school environment (i.e., is it a positive one?).

It is imperative that risk assessment screens reflect an awareness of both risk and protective factors in arriving at judgments of risk for suicidal behavior.

COMPLIANCE

Crucial to the decision not to hospitalize a youth in crisis is the assessment of that youth's compliance with recommended outpatient treatment regimens. Perhaps as crucial to that compliance is the support of family members in effecting compliance. Past behavior may again be the best predictor of future behavior. The correlates of noncompliance with past treatment recommendations (e.g., hopelessness, more severe psychopathology, higher suicidal intent) are associated with higher risk for attempted and completed suicide (Brent, 2001). The issue of compliance will be more fully discussed in chapter 5.

Information essential to the assessment of compliance is available in the assessment interview itself. One of the better measures of possible future compliance is the adolescent's cooperation with the assessment interview. In contrast, an angry, resistive, difficult-to-interview youngster evidences in his or her behavior an inability to form an alliance with a gatekeeper to the helping system. Motto's report (1984) that future adolescent male completers—significantly more often than control subjects— were rated as having a negative or ambivalent attitude toward the psychiatric interviewer at the time of intake underscores the importance of the adolescent's interpersonal alliances to the overall assessment of risk.

Similarly, the adolescent's willingness to form a short-term, renewable "no-suicide agreement" in order for therapeutic interventions to be instituted signals whether help offered can be help received. Such agreements or "contracts" are verbal or written statements of expectancy and contingency for both patient and therapist and serve as a first step in a treatment plan (see chap. 5). It should be noted, however, that agreements formed with some patients cannot be reasonably accepted. Adolescents with a history of lying and distrustful relationships with authority, evidence of a thought disorder, or patterns of emotional and behavioral reactivity (e.g., panic or impulsivity) are often unable to comply readily with such an agreement (Boggiano, 1988).

Case continued

When Sam entered outpatient treatment, he denied his suicidal intent in describing his shotgun attempt. Reports by others of his frequent suicidal threats and a yearlong history of alcohol abuse similarly were denied. A combative and manipulative relationship with a rigid, authoritarian father was the prototype for the transference relationship he formed in therapy. In this context, his response to an offer of a no-suicide agreement—"I am here, aren't I?"—understandably was the best he could give.

THE PSYCHOMETRIC ASSESSMENT OF SUICIDE RISK

No doubt thousands of pages of scientific journals have been dedicated to the presentation of different instruments, tools, measures, and tests that have been developed to assess suicide risk and constructs related to suicidality (e.g., hopelessness or risk-taking behaviors). Although various researchers have dedicated themselves to test construction work, these measures or the use of psychological tests for assessing suicide (e.g., the Rorschach Inkblot Test or the Minnesota Multiphasic Personality Inventory [MMPI]) may not be widely used or found to be particularly useful (refer to survey by Jobes, Eyman, & Yufit, 1995). Many clinicians appear to prefer the use of clinical interviews, asking key questions and making certain observations over using assessment tools. From our bias, multiple sources of data can often work synergistically to create a more comprehensive assessment. Moreover, assessment tools added to the medical record make for a more complete level of documentation that may prove protective in malpractice litigation (see chap. 7). Although an exhaustive review of all the extant instruments is not possible, we will nevertheless highlight some aspects of these tools. First we will consider those risk assessment measures that are constructed through quantitative and multivariate methodologies before turning our attention to more qualitative approaches to suicide risk assessment.

Quantitative Risk Assessment Tools

Goldston (2003), under commission from the National Institute of Mental Health, has published an extensive review of psychometric assessment instruments used to evaluate suicidal behaviors in children and adolescents up to age 18. Similarly, Range and Knott (1997) published evaluations and recommendations on 20 relatively new assessment instruments, some of which focused on children and adolescents. These works follow an earlier review by Lewinsohn, Garrison, Langhinrichsen, and Marsteller (1989).

Goldston included in his review more than 60 instruments that assessed (a) the presence of suicidal behaviors, (b) the risk or propensity for suicidal behaviors, (c) the intentionality and medical lethality of suicidal behaviors, and (d) miscellaneous others. This review is particularly valuable because psychometric properties (reliability, internal consistency, concurrent validity, factor analyses, and predictive validity) are reported and referenced for each instrument. Whereas in the earlier review (Lewinsohn et al., 1989) the majority of the 29 scales reported on had insufficient attention to issues such as validity, it is quite evident that considerable psychometric test construction work has occurred over the last decade in the development of these instruments.

All scales have some strengths and some weaknesses. Most important, as Goldston notes (2003, p. 199), "very few of these instruments...have been demonstrated to be predictive of attempted suicide, much less completed suicide." He continues by saying that those "that are marketed as being able to identify individuals at future risk of suicide are falsely advertised—claims about identifying risk are speculation, or perhaps, wishful thinking, but not conclusions based in empirical data." Exhibit 4.1 briefly describes two scales that are highly recommended.

EXHIBIT 4.1
Two Recommended Scales

Both Goldston (2003) and Range and Knott (1997) recommend Beck's Scale for Suicide Ideation (Beck & Steer, 1991) and Linehan's Reasons for Living (RFL) Inventory (Linehan et al., 1983). Beck's Scale for Suicide Ideation is a 21-item self-report questionnaire addressing the adolescent's wish to die, wish to live, reasons to live versus reasons to die, and both active and passive suicidal ideation. When ideation is present, follow-up questions probe duration and frequency of thoughts, ambivalence, deterrents, and so on. The RFL has been adapted for use with adolescents as a 52-item measure of adaptive or life-maintaining beliefs and includes a number of newer questions. A brief version (BRFL–A; Osman et al., 1996) has a more tolerable 14 items and a factor structure consistent with the original RFL.

Global, objective personality measures have also been used to identify predisposing suicide risk. Indeed, there is some evidence that patients are more likely to disclose suicide ideation on a self-report measure than in a clinical interview (Kaplan et al., 1994). Johnson, Lall, Bongar, and Nordlung (1999) reviewed nine objective personality inventories and concluded that there was very little evidence for predictive utility for any of the reviewed scales, including the MMPI. Additionally, only a few studies have been reported regarding the use of these inventories with adolescents (Jobes et al., 1995).

Given the continuing problems these measures have with regard to unacceptable rates of false positives and false negatives and inadequate ability to differentiate groups, it appears best to conclude that their use remains informative within a battery of instruments used as part of a comprehensive evaluation of suicide risk that includes both testing and in-depth psychiatric interview.

Qualitative Assessment of Suicide Risk

Although suicide risk assessment instruments constructed using quantitative multivariate approaches have been predominant in the field, there has more recently been increased work using a more qualitative approach to suicide risk assessment. For example, Jobes et al. (2004) have argued that given the incidence and seriousness of suicidality in clinical practice, there is an ongoing need for new and better ways to assess suicide risk. Jobes (2000) has suggested that some clinicians may not routinely use quantitatively developed suicide risk tools because they may fail to capture something essential about the suicidal patient's *experience*. To this end, Jobes and colleagues have pursued a line of *qualitative* assessments of suicide risk to gain a different perspective on the suicidal patient's experience using written responses to different stimulus prompts (e.g., Jobes & Mann, 1999).

In one recent study, Jobes et al. (2004) conducted an exploratory investigation examining a range of open-ended qualitative written responses—a modified sentence completion task—made by suicidal outpatients to five assessment prompts from the Suicide Status Form (SSF). The quantitative aspects of the SSF are discussed elsewhere (see Jobes, Jacoby, Cimbolic, & Hustead, 1997 and the discussion of the Collaborative Assessment and Management of Suicidality [CAMS] in chap. 5). Of particular concern here are the qualitative assessments built into this clinical tool. As shown in Figure 4.4, the first five SSF constructs include psychological pain, press, perturbation, hopelessness, and self-hate; for each construct, the patient is asked to rate the construct on a Likert scale and then to further respond to the stimulus prompts (e.g., the prompt for the Psychological Pain construct is, "What I find most painful is_____"). The 18-year-old suicidal college freshman who completed the assessment shown in Figure 4.4, writes in his own words: "never having a girlfriend."

Given their experience studying these types of open-ended responses, Jobes et al. (2004) set out to develop reliable coding categories that could capture and describe the unique assessment data garnered through this approach. Thus, they acquired data from two different clinical samples of suicidal outpatients seeking treatment, suicidal college students ($n = 119$) and active duty U.S. Air Force personnel ($n = 33$), who provided a wide range of patient-written responses to the five SSF prompts. A qualitative

Suicide Status Form-SSF II (Initial Session)

Client: _____ Clinician: _____ Date: 8/4/03 Time: 10 AM

Section A (Client):

I have thoughts of ending my life: 0 1 (2) 3 4
(0=Never; 1=Rarely; 2=Sometimes; 3=Frequently; 4=Always)

Rate and fill out each item according to how you feel right now.
Then rank in order of importance 1 to 5 (1=most important to 5=least important).

Rank

8 — 1) RATE PSYCHOLOGICAL PAIN (hurt, anguish, or misery in your mind, not stress, not physical pain):
Low pain: 1 2 3 (4) 5 :High pain
What I find most painful is: Never having a girlfriend

1 — 2) RATE STRESS (your general feeling of being pressured or overwhelmed):
Low stress: 1 2 3 4 (5) :High stress
What I find most stressful is: school — I just can't get motivated

4 — 3) RATE AGITATION (emotional urgency; feeling that you need to take action; not irritation; not annoyance):
Low agitation: 1 2 3 (4) 5 :High agitation
I most need to take action when: I lie awake at night, thinking of problems

3 — 4) RATE HOPELESSNESS (your expectation that things will not get better no matter what you do):
Low hopelessness: 1 2 3 (4) 5 :High hopelessness
I am most hopeless about: My life ever really being happy

5 — 5) RATE SELF-HATE (your general feeling of disliking yourself; having no self-esteem; having no self-respect):
Low self-hate: 1 2 (3) 4 5 :High self-hate
What I hate most about myself is: I can't get myself to do what I want

N/A — 6) RATE OVERALL RISK OF SUICIDE: Extremely low risk: 1 2 (3) 4 5 :Extremely high risk
(will not kill self) (will kill self)

1) How much is being suicidal related to thoughts and feelings about yourself? Not at all: 1 2 3 (4) 5 : completely
2) How much is being suicidal related to thoughts and feelings about others? Not at all: 1 2 3 (4) 5 : completely

Please list your reasons for wanting to live and your reasons for wanting to die. Then rank in order of importance 1 to 5.

Rank	REASONS FOR LIVING	Rank	REASONS FOR DYING
1	My mom	3	My life is a mess
2	My Gramma	4	no girlfriend
4	I'm smart	5	I'm flunking school
5	Maybe things could be okay	2	I need relief
3	I have potential	1	ESCAPE!

I wish to live to the following extent: Not at all: 1 2 3 4 (5) 6 7 : Very much
I wish to die to the following extent: Not at all: 1 2 (3) 4 5 6 7 : Very much
The one thing that would help me no longer feel suicidal would be: a girlfriend who could love me for who I really am.

Figure 4.4. Suicide Status Form (SSF II, initial session).

coding manual was then developed through a step-by-step methodology, and two naive coders were trained to use the coding system. Ultimately, this coding system was used to sort and categorize each of the 636 patient-written responses to the SSF prompts from the two samples with high interrater reliability (Kappa's > .80). The coding categories that make up this system appear in Table 4.1.

TABLE 4.1

Definitions of SSF Coding Categories and Example Responses

Category	Definition	Examples
1. Relational[a]	Any references to specific relationship problems or issues with family, friends, significant others, or any other social interaction. Any responses that speak to being hurt by others, hurting others, or being alone and isolated go here as well.	"Loss of my father." "Loneliness."
2. Self[b]	Responses that are specific to one's self, or when a reference to one's self is clearly inferred. These can be statements about feelings or qualities about the self. These tend to be descriptors of core attributes or harsh self-critiques of external descriptors.	"I hate myself." "I'm a bad person."
3. Helpless[c]	Any implied or specific references to feeling out of control, lost, trapped, or directionless. Includes statements about hopelessness about one's ability to cope, function, or achieve in the future.	"Being out of control." "There's no way out."
4. Global/General[a]	Any nonspecific, broad statements that are completely inclusive and therefore vague. These responses indicate a general overarching sense of being overwhelmed or unable to cope.	"Everything." "Overwhelmingness."
5. Unpleasant Internal States[b]	Statements referring to specific, discrete descriptions of hurting, distress, suffering, pain, or other negative emotions.	"Anxiety." "Hurting and misery."
6. Unsure/Unable to Articulate[a]	Statements in which the person indicates he or she is uncertain or unable to respond. This may include responses that seem purposely evasive, avoidant, or apathetic.	"Unsure." "I don't know."
7. Role Responsibilities[a]	Common adult role expectations including the roles of worker, homemaker, or student. Responses related to academic concerns, financial burdens, or job concerns are included here. Specific future-oriented statements regarding career are also included.	"I'm a bad parent." "I'm failing a class."
8. Situation Specific[d]	Any reference made about a specific situation or circumstance, or any references made to a certain place, time, or events.	"When I awake." "When I come home alone."
9. Compelled to Act[e]	Statements in which the person expresses an explicit desire to urgently change his or her life, a quick solution, a need to take action, or a feeling of being stuck.	"This needs to end." "I can't take it anymore."

TABLE 4.1 (Continued)

Category	Definition	Examples
10. Future[f] Experiences	Statements relating to specific dreams, skills, events, or with a clear reference to the future (except career or school, see Role/Responsibilities).	"My future." "Achieving my dreams."
11. Internal Descriptors[g]	Statements relating to a lack of positive qualities or the presence of negative qualities in himself or herself; feelings about the self; and inner descriptors of the self.	"I'm a coward." "I'm an idiot"
12. External Descriptors[g]	Statements relating to external aspects of the self, such as personal appearance, body, or behaviors in which he or she is engaging.	"I'm fat." "My drug use."

Note. From "Describing Suicidality: An Investigation of Qualitative SSF Responses," by D. A. Jobes, K. N. Nelson, E. M. Peterson, D. Pentiuc, V. Downing, K. Francini, and A. Kiernan, 2004, *Suicide and Life-Threatening Behavior, 34*, p. 105. Copyright 2004 by Guilford Press. Adapted with permission. [a] Applies to pain, press, perturbation, hopelessness, and self-hate. [b] Applies to pain, press, perturbation, and hopelessness. [c] Applies to pain, press, perturbation, and self-hate. [d] Applies to press and perturbation. [e] Applies to perturbation only. [f] Applies to hopelessness only. [g] Applies to self-hate only.

Using this approach, these researchers found that some types of written qualitative responses by these suicidal patients were more frequent than others, both within and across the five SSF constructs. Among a range of specific exploratory findings, one general finding was that two thirds of the 636 obtained written responses could be reliably categorized under four major content headings: *Relational* (22%), *Role Responsibilities* (20%), *Self* (15%), and *Unpleasant Internal States* (10%). Jobes, Wong, Conrad, Drozd, and Neal-Walden (in press) argue that one major virtue of this line of research is that assessment data is gathered directly from patients—using a "bottom-up" approach—where the patients write in their own words about their suicidal experience. Further research may show that this approach provides a useful, alternative way to understand and assess suicide risk that is different from the "top-down"—purely multivariate–quantitative—assessment approach. Ultimately, this research underscores the potential value of gaining both quantitative *and* qualitative assessment data as meaningfully different reference points that bear on a thorough assessment of suicidal risk.

BIOLOGICAL MARKERS

With increasing focus being placed on biological correlates of suicide (see chap. 6), especially among adult suicides, markers identifying those at risk remain elusive. Some preliminary and small sample studies, particularly of low concentrations of 5-HIAA (hydroxyindoleacetic acid) in the cerebrospinal fluid (CSF), have been conducted with adolescent suicide attempters, leading some researchers (American Academy of Child and Adolescent Psychiatry, 2001) to be optimistic that routine CSF monitoring after an attempt may be useful in the prevention of subsequent suicidal behavior where patients with abnormally low levels are given special care and treatment.

DEMOGRAPHIC RISK VARIABLES

We should note that certain static risk variables, such as gender, need to be considered in the overall risk assessment, but that their applicability to the individual case only exists as they interact with more dynamic variables. That is to say, for example, that we know that, as a group, Black females, compared to all other race–sex subgroups, have the lowest rates of suicide. However, in the instance of a single Black female being assessed by a clinician, the presence of multiple dynamic risk factors for suicide significantly discounts her group membership. This being said, generally speaking, older adolescents have higher rates of suicide than do younger adolescents, male adolescents have higher rates of suicide than do female adolescents, and White adolescents have higher rates of suicide than do Black adolescents (see epidemiology, chap. 2).

ASSESSMENT BY PARAPROFESSIONALS AND REFERRAL GUIDELINES: TRAINING TIPS

Earlier in this chapter we noted that nonclinicians, paraprofessionals, and adolescent peers are often "first finders" of suicidal messages, and that knowledge of some simple rules for making appropriate assessment referrals to the mental health system may be beneficial to fostering early detection and treatment. Clinicians in a position to consult with and train these groups (e.g., crisis center and school personnel) need to consider helping the community make effective referrals. To aid in this process, it behooves such groups to have designated ahead of time those who are familiar and comfortable with treating suicidal adolescents. Professionals who can be trusted to work well with this population ought to be so designated first by the referral source, whose experience has been positive, or second on the recommendation of trusted others. Also, it is imperative that nonprofessionals know the limits of their competence.

As should be apparent from the preceding two chapters, the problems of suicidal adolescents should not be telescoped into mere temporal exaggerations of everyday problems of living. It takes a well-trained and experienced mental health professional to work with these issues and with the interpersonal struggles the suicidal adolescent typically brings to treatment. Those with insufficient training should be involved only to the point of gathering sufficient information to make an effective assessment on which a referral can be based.

Paraprofessionals need to be trained in communication and interview skills to the point of understanding some simple do's and don'ts and knowing what kind of information is most pertinent to effect a referral. Learning to be calm in an anxiety-provoking interaction, not to negate or apply verbal pablum to the affect or reasons espoused by suicidal youngsters for their suicidal thoughts or impulses, and not to engage in a philosophical or moral debate takes considerable practice and supervised training. Learning to collect assessment data, particularly on the persistence, duration, and intensity of the adolescent's suicidal urges, predisposing and precipitating conditions for these urges, and sufficient background data regarding available interpersonal supports demands an awareness of what to ask as well as to how to ask. These practices should be construed as *skills* by those responsible for training of mental health professionals, monitored consistently through supervision, and bolstered by repeat training opportunities over time.

THE SCREENING OF SUICIDE RISK

With attention to the foregoing observations, the clinician now has sufficient data to make reasoned judgments of the adolescent's potential for acting in a self-harmful manner and for developing a treatment plan. As the cliche goes, "A good surgeon does not need to make a large incision": The better the assessment, the easier it is to develop intervention strategies.

Risk Assessment Categorization

Rudd et al. (2001) outline two approaches to rating risk severity. The first categorizes risk as chronic, acute, or chronic with acute exacerbation. The last categorization is similar to the notion of a double depression, wherein a patient with a dysthymic disorder may have an acute manifestation in the form of a major depressive episode. The assessment of *acute risk* for suicidal behavior is essentially made on the basis of the presence of a current crisis or prominent symptoms, significant stressors, and current suicide ideation. Adolescents with a past history of suicidal behavior maintain a lifetime *chronic risk* for subsequent suicidal behavior. Even in the absence of a crisis, prominent symptoms, significant stressors, and current suicide ideation, however, they remain at chronic risk. Those who have made a prior attempt (chronic risk) and who have a current crisis or prominent symptoms, significant stressors, and suicide ideation would be categorized as *chronic risk with acute exacerbation*.

Adolescents with chronic risk need to be carefully watched for symptom exacerbations, for notable changes in behavior and emotional regulation, for how they currently cope under conditions of increased stress, and so on. They live in a "suicide zone" (Litman, 1990) wherein they maintain a greater vulnerability to retrogress to past and suicidal modes of coping than do healthier adolescents. Triggers may reactivate conflicts and a breakdown of sustaining resources and coping skills, producing an acute suicidality. Acute exacerbations of risk are typically time-limited, but, by definition, potentially life-threatening. Adolescents in an acute phase, also by definition, are at high and possibly imminent risk for suicidal behaviors.

Severity of Risk

There is no agreed-on rating system for establishing the severity of suicide risk, but clinicians tend to conceptualize risk on an ordinal continuum ranging from *no risk* to something akin to *high and imminent risk*. J. Somers-Flanagan and R. Somers-Flanagan (1995), and as modified by Rudd et al. (2001), propose a 5-point scale from *nonexistent* to *extreme*. Each and every risk variable outlined above, observed as present (versus absent), needs to be addressed along some sort of continuum (e.g., low, medium, high; or mild, moderate, extreme). For example, suicide ideation may range from vague, passive, or transient to intense, preoccupying, uncontrollable, or insistent. Ideation with a definitive and accessible plan is clearly at the more clinically significant end of the continuum than is ideation without a plan; however, ideation without a plan—where there is agitation, poor control, and consequent impulsiveness—may be equally of concern.

In the previous edition of this book, we offered a three-level screening (Level I: potential for self-harm behavior, Level II: possibility for self-harm behavior, and Level III: imminent probability of self-harm behavior), attempting to discriminate the potential for suicidal behavior (nonfatal attempt or completion) were the adolescent to act in the context of risk. We present it here because, in our view, it still has utility, clinical relevance, and heuristic value:

Level I Risk

The first screen represents the "red flag" level of assessment, wherein the patient presents with one or more perpetuating (historical) or predisposing (current life) risk factors. For example, these might include a family history of suicidal behavior, a history of prior attempt, family psychopathology, or the exposure to suicidal behavior of a peer. Additionally, current diagnosed psychopathology or symptomatic behavior (e.g., depression, acting-out behavior, substance abuse), behavioral patterns that signal underlying problems (e.g., a rigid cognitive style, heightened anxiety), or high levels of observable stress or familial conflict should alert the clinician to pay close attention to the possibility of suicidal behavior.

Level II Risk

The possibility of suicidal behavior increases dramatically when there is evidence that death, dying, or, explicitly, suicide is on the patient's mind. Expressions of ideation and communications of these ideas through writings, drawings, questions about death out of context, preoccupations with images of death (including obsessive fascination with death-related rock music), or behavior signaling an identification with deceased others should alert the clinician to probe more deeply and observe more closely.

Ideas in and of themselves are not dangerous. However, in the context of poor impulse control, ideas can readily turn into behaviors. By analogy, sexual fantasies and attractions are considered healthy expressions of libido. However, lacking appropriate controls, such fantasies can be acted on inappropriately, intrusively, impulsively, and, possibly, even violently.

Several of the diagnoses commonly seen among suicidal adolescents signal a common theme regarding poor impulse control. Substance abusers, those with borderline personality disorders and antisocial personality disorders, and psychotics, for example, will display difficulties controlling their behavior. Any evidence of impulsiveness, rageful, assaultive behavior toward others, or high degrees of anxiety suggest a potentially dangerous lack of control.

Two other variables are particularly significant in screening the possibility of suicidal behavior at this level. The first, cognitive constriction, reflects a rigid, inflexible ideational life. The adolescent whose thinking is constricted will tend to dichotomize observations, use a binary system with which to construe problems and solutions, and develop what suicidologists refer to as "psychological myopia" or "tunnel vision." If life is bad, then this rationale dictates that death is the option. Gray areas, alternative solutions, and compromise positions are not tolerated. One extreme form of this constriction is hopelessness. Hopelessness, when expressed as the patient's dominant way of construing self, others, and the future, is a signal of severe cognitive rigidity and constriction. Without the flexibility to perceive portholes in a wall, otherwise seen as increasingly entrapping the adolescent, both panic and despair are likely to increase. It should be noted, however, that in perhaps the only nonconfirmatory study (Rotheram-Borus & Trautman, 1988), no empirical support was found for hopelessness as a predictor of intent in a sample of adolescent *minority* female attempters.

Similarly, evidence of social isolation or alienation suggests that the adolescent is lacking needed buffers, objects with whom catharsis may occur or from whom support can be received. When the family context is one of unavailability, nonsupport, or pathology (particularly involving abuse or violence), the adolescent must turn elsewhere. When peers are themselves troubled or identified by their discongruency with family (e.g., other runaways or substance abusers) or marginality (e.g., heavy-metal rock and rollers), the support available to the adolescent at risk is colored by the effects of these problems (e.g., low self-esteem, substance abuse).

Level III Risk

Whether a self-harmful intent will be acted on, given the foregoing levels of risk, at this level depends on a number of situational and characterological factors. Suicide risk may be situationally specific; that is, it may wax under conditions of threat and stress and wane when the adolescent is removed from those conditions. It is for this reason that brief hospitalization may serve to temporarily reduce risk, and discharge back to unresolved conditions of stress may bring the patient back to the emergency room as a result of a repetitive suicidal behavior.

The availability and accessibility of a method of self-harm, under conditions of a developed suicidal intent or reason for suicidal behavior, may be sufficient stimulus for suicidal behavior to occur. On impulse, an individual lacking ego controls will view the gun in the nightstand or vials of pills as sirens irresistibly beckoning an end to pain. Alternatively, those who develop a plan for their suicide must include a method sufficient to accomplish their ends. That method undoubtedly will be that most accessible or readily obtainable and about which the potential suicide has some knowledge or experience. As noted in chapter 1, the most common method used by adolescents who die by suicide is firearms. The most common location for the occurrence of a firearm suicide of a youth is in the home (Brent, Perper, Moritz, Baugher, Schweers, et al., 1993), and the accessibility and availability of a firearm in the home and the number of firearms in the home have been found to be positively associated with suicidal risk among adolescents (Brent et al., 1993; Kellerman et al., 1992)

Absent intense panic or a psychotic break, potential suicides tend to choose methods of suicide that are syntonic with their character. For example, those characterologically in need of presenting well to others, and conversely intolerant of not looking good, will rarely choose a method that promises disfigurement. Similarly, planful types do not choose methods common to impulsive characters like young children (e.g., running into oncoming traffic).

Characterologically, suicidal actions occur either on impulse, in a moment of provocation by an individual predisposed to act self-harmfully;

or planfully, as a result of a developed and organized set of actions designed to accomplish suicidal goals. Thus, individuals giving evidence of suicidal predisposition and the inability to avoid acting in a suicidal manner, or evidence of a concrete and specific plan including a lethal weapon of self-destruction, must be taken most seriously. Included in the former group must be those adolescents displaying command hallucinations. Also, those who are intoxicated and threatened with humiliation or punishment, such as the typical jail suicide, must be closely watched. With regard to the latter group, the clinician should be alert to the availability or obtainability of the method, the planned conditions of its use (rescuability), and the likely consequences of its use (lethality).

When a suicide note already has been drafted, risk is imminent. As stated earlier, notes are written in the past tense or from the perspective of death having been accomplished. The discovery of such a document prior to suicidal action is an undeniable signal of imminent risk.

Imminent Risk

Richman (1986) presented four characteristics common to the assessment of suicide risk: (a) the exhaustion of personal resources such as hope and energy and the breakdown of usual defenses, (b) the exhaustion of familial resources, (c) a state of intolerable stress, and (d) the perception of suicide as a viable solution. These reflect a focus similar to our common theme—the breakdown of typical defenses and consequent lack of control, interpersonal alienation or isolation, and cognitive constriction under conditions of situational stress or predisposing pathology. Given these conditions, the individual has options to attempt to change intolerable conditions but lacks resources to make mature choices. Thus, limited, more primitive coping patterns emerge, primarily those of flight (suicidal death) or fight (suicidal behavior to affect others, perhaps changing their behavior). Where these ends are readily accomplished through self-harm behavior, we have imminent risk.

Imminent suicide risk involves a constellation of

- *predisposing vulnerability* to being suicidal (prior suicidality, current psychopathology);
- *readiness* to act (triggers, arousal, ideation with plan or high impulsivity, acute symptoms);
- *acceptability* of suicide (reasons for dying, attraction to death as an escape from pained life, models for suicide, hopelessness);
- *loss of supports* (social isolation, loss of attachments to self-worth, low help-seeking behavior); and
- *failed protections* (poor behavioral controls, intoxication, aggression, conflictual attachments, availability of means).

Case Illustration

Walter, age 13, was seen for assessment under court order after he had been picked up by the police for running away from home with a loaded shotgun. He lived with his divorced mother; their relationship was described as "tumultuous." He had not seen his father since his parents divorced when he was 8.

At intake, he presented with sleep problems; hopelessness; low self-esteem; recent but currently denied suicide ideation; low energy; low motivation; decreased appetite; weight loss; daily mood swings (to mild grandiosity, elation, expansiveness, some racing thoughts, and tangentiality); panic attacks; and hallucinogenic flashbacks (visual when on drugs). His affect was flat, his concentration was mildly impaired, and his judgment and insight were poor. Axis V Global Assessment of Functioning (GAF) was rated at 29.

Walter had a history of diagnosed depressive episodes with mood swings, attention-deficit disorder, poly-substance use (pot since age 10, daily; ecstasy, heroin, LSD, amphetamines, etc.), runaway behavior, and panic attacks. In addition, he had made four prior suicide attempts in the last 3 years. The first was at age 11 by hanging; this was followed by two overdose attempts and one wrist-cutting. Each past nonfatal attempt was believed to be of low risk and high rescuability. There was a strong family and, in particular, parental history of depression. His maternal great-grandfather completed suicide.

Current diagnostic impressions were those of Axis I, Depressive Disorder Not Otherwise Specified, Poly-substance Abuse, Oppositional Disorder, and Attention-Deficit/Hyperactivity Disorder; and Axis II, Borderline and Narcissistic Personality Disorders.

In making a summary risk assessment, we find that Walter had chronic high risk with acute exacerbation. He had a history of low-lethality suicide attempts, a large number of predisposing risk factors, and acute symptomatology in a context of little to no protective factors. Although current suicide ideation was denied, with his history, current depression, mood swings, anxiety, and racing thoughts, the possibility of imminent suicidal behavior would remain high until such time as he stabilized. Thus, immediate hospitalization should be considered to accomplish this goal.

HOSPITALIZATION

Assessment represents the first step in the process of treatment and, if done well, eases the transition into successful treatment. By understanding the psychological state of the potential suicide, the interviewer is in a position both to effect the necessary external controls to reduce the likelihood of a self-inflicted, lethal solution to current problems, and to provide the adolescent with the initial hope that these problems may be resolvable through a number of nonlethal interventions. In this sense, the assessment interview should be interactional. It serves both as an opportunity to observe and gather necessary information, and as a structuring vehicle to stabilize the adolescent through feedback, shared conceptual understanding, and empathy.

Should intent and the risk of imminent suicide remain high despite initial interventions, hospitalization should be considered to provide sufficient sanctuary and time to achieve stabilization. This consideration should be made on the basis of other observations as well, such as (a) high levels of unresolvable stress; (b) the presence of a thought disorder (e.g., delusions or command hallucinations) or impending ego decompensation; (c) other symptoms of loss of control (e.g., disorientation, dissociation, high impulsivity); (d) high levels of rage, panic, or uncontrollable violent behavior; (e) the absence of a supportive family or surrogate interpersonal system able to monitor and maintain sufficient watch over the adolescent through the period of crisis (or the presence of an abusive, substance-abusing, or seriously mentally disordered parent); or (f) the unobtainability of an alliance in the context of assessed risk for suicidal behavior (cf. Comstock, 1977).

Landau-Stanton and Stanton (1985) pose three additional criteria: (a) an attempt made by a male, (b) a family history of completion, or (c) an attempt made in secret that is clearly not a cry for help from significant others. These authors further argue that an overnight hospitalization may be warranted even in low-lethality attempts to lessen intensity and pressure in the adolescent's life. Clearly, hospitalization has both benefits and costs (see chap. 5 for comparisons of inpatient vs. outpatient treatment) that need to be weighed carefully on a case-by-case basis. The decision to hospitalize, as in the following case, is demanded when help-seeking for either medical or psychological need is necessary but not voluntarily acted on.

Case Illustration

John, age 19, a college sophomore transfer student, slashed his wrists and forearms with a razor blade after being rebuffed by his roommate. He later reported that he had been feeling down and had wanted to talk, but his roommate angrily demanded that he be left alone. Feeling more depressed, rageful, and worthless as a result, John proceeded to slash his arms eight or nine times in front of his roommate. When his roommate, remarkably, did not respond, John wrote "I HATE ME!" in blood on the walls of their apartment, then locked himself in his bedroom. It was not until the following afternoon, when his roommate returned from classes and noticed that John's door was still shut and locked and that John was not responsive to his calls, that the police were called to forcibly open the door. Conscious but groggy, John was taken by the police for emergency evaluation.

On intake, John's wounds were considered superficial and bleeding had stopped. John then denied feeling depressed but did state that he felt alone and lonely and that he had no one to share his feelings with (in transferring colleges, he also left his ongoing outpatient therapy). He stated that he had no friends, that he could not talk with his parents, and that his suicide attempts—he claimed the current one to be his fifth but the first that resulted in a hospitalization—were attempts to get away from his loneliness. Mental status evaluation found John to have slightly depressed affect but no vegetative signs of depression. He was fully oriented and showed no signs of a thought disorder. Insight was rated as limited and judgment impaired. He was admitted for protective observation and milieu therapy with provisional diagnoses of dysthymic disorder (Axis I) and avoidant personality disorder (Axis II).

Initially, John was under close observation with nursing checks every 15 minutes. He participated in nursing counseling, ward activities, and group therapy. After 3 days of hospitalization, he was considered stabilized and improved and showed no signs of continued risk. He was discharged contingent on meeting with or accepting a referral from his outpatient therapist. (We will continue our discussion of John's case, describing his treatment, in chap. 5).

CONCLUSION

The assessment of the adolescent at risk for suicidal behavior has been likened to finding a needle in a haystack. By being alert as to what to observe and by observing alertly, the size and brilliance of that needle increase, thereby correspondingly increasing the likelihood of its discovery. Translating the metaphor into practical application requires that the clinician first be attuned to risk factors as red flags. With a focus on multiple assessments and a screening system with which to sift observations, the clinician becomes both capable of making reasoned judgments regarding the need for intervention and integral to the process of that intervention.

The assessment of suicide risk in adolescence is central to treatment planning—first, because treatment requires a live body, and second, because much of the foregoing assessment analysis provides the clinician with invaluable data with which to establish meaningful goals for treatment. As noted at the outset of this chapter, the suicidal urge is not static; neither, therefore, can the assessment of that urge be static. In addition to its importance to early intervention, the assessment of suicidal risk should be made and documented with frequency during ongoing treatment, especially at times of impending transition, heightened stress, or changes in environmental supports. With such attention, it is presumed a priori that treatment will continue to have the time and opportunity to make a noticeable difference in the lives of these youngsters.

5

THE TREATMENT OF THE
SUICIDAL ADOLESCENT

There is perhaps no topic since the first edition of this book that has undergone more fundamental change than the domain of treatment. The advent of managed (mental health) care, significantly shorter periods of inpatient hospitalization, the extensive contemporary use of psychotropic medications, and exponential increases in malpractice litigation following a patient's suicide have all created tremendous change, upheaval, and uncertainty in an already challenging area of clinical intervention. Since the period of European enlightenment, it has been axiomatic that self-destructive individuals should be protected from themselves, which has customarily been accomplished by placing them in some form of a "protective asylum" (i.e., an inpatient hospital setting). It was not so long ago that suicidal patients were hospitalized for weeks, months, or even years. Indeed, it was not so long ago that even relatively low suicidal risk routinely prompted an immediate inpatient admission.

The impact of contemporary changes in clinical care are clearly evident in the following case.

Case Illustration

A clinician receives a call from the desperate mother of Jim, a 16-year-old substance-abusing, conduct-disordered teen whose behavior is clearly out of control. Jim has made a series of suicide attempts, including two overdoses, a failed hanging, and one recent incident involving his father's handgun. He has been hospitalized four times over the past 2 years. Each hospitalization was extremely brief—lengths of stay ranged from 1 to 4 days—and his parents' insurance carrier now refuses to precertify any additional hospitalizations until the new year (it is now September). Jim has seen four different psychiatrists in these 2 years and has received a range of medications, including various antidepressants, mood stabilizers, antipsychotics, and benzodiazapines. He is currently prescribed Prozac and Zyprexa, but he struggles with his parents over taking his medications at all, let alone reliably. Jim's attendance at school has been irregular and he recently announced that he was going to drop out and find a job. In one recent behavioral outburst, he chased his mother around the house with a saw from his father's workshop when she confronted him about his messy room. Incredibly, Jim's mother reports that Jim has neither been in any form of individual psychotherapy nor has the family ever pursued family psychotherapy. She is thus desperately seeking some kind of "behavioral management" psychotherapy for her child (on the recommendation of a friend). However, after contacting five different outpatient clinicians, she is still not able to locate anyone who either has an opening or is willing to see her troubled son. Jim's mother reports that she herself has become increasingly depressed and that her marriage is falling apart over struggles with their son.

In a recent series of studies, Olfson et al. (Olfson, Marcus, Druss, Elinson, et al., 2002; Olfson, Marcus, Druss, & Pincus, 2002) have analyzed data from the household sections of the 1987 National Medical Expenditure Survey ($n = 34,459$) and the 1997 Medical Expenditure Panel Survey ($n = 32,636$). Trends in the rate of psychotherapy use from these nationally representative samples were analyzed by age, gender, race and ethnicity, marital status, education, employment status, clinical diagnosis, and income. Although there was no statistically significant change in the overall rate of psychotherapy use between 1987 and 1997, some significant findings were noted. Psychotherapy was increasingly administered by physicians and provided in conjunction with psychotropic medications.

The rate of outpatient treatment for depression increased from 0.73 per 100 people in 1987 to 2.33 per 100 persons in 1997 ($p < .001$). The proportion of treated individuals who used antidepressant medications increased from 37.3% to 74.5% ($p < .001$), whereas the proportion who received psychotherapy declined (71.1% vs. 60.2%, $p = .006$). The mean number of depression treatment visits per user declined from 12.6 to 8.7 per year ($p = .05$). An increasingly large proportion of patients were treated by physicians for their condition (68.9% vs. 87.3%, $p < .001$), and treatment costs were more often covered by third-party payers (39.3% vs. 55.2%, $p < .001$). Between 1987 and 1997, there was a marked increase in the proportion of the population who received outpatient treatment for depression. Treatment became characterized by greater involvement of physicians, greater use of psychotropic medications, and expanding availability of third-party payment, but fewer outpatient visits and less use of psychotherapy. These changes coincided with the advent of better-tolerated antidepressant medications, the increased use of managed care, and the development of rapid and efficient procedures for diagnosing depression in clinical practice.

Olfson, Marcus, et al. (2003) subsequently examined relationships between parental depression and children's mental health problems and health care use in the 1997 Medical Expenditure Panel Survey data. This data was derived from a nationally representative sample of children 3 to 18 years of age ($n = 8,360$) with one or more parents living in the household. Children of parents with depression were approximately twice as likely as children of parents without depression to have a variety of mental health problems and were 2.8 times more likely to use mental health services in adjusted analyses. Children of parents with depression are at increased risk for a range of health problems, and parental depression is related to increased child health and mental health service use and expenditure.

Suffice to say, over the last 10 to 15 years, we have witnessed dramatic changes in mental health practice. Rising health care costs and managed mental health care have essentially overturned well over a hundred years of what was unchallenged clinical wisdom and routine practice. In a contemporary managed care environment, it has become increasingly difficult when working with insurance carriers to precertify a patient for inpatient care or, furthermore, to keep a patient in the hospital. In truth, imminent and acute high-risk suicidality is about the only presentation that can still be used to justify inpatient care; active, acute, and unrelenting suicidal risk is about the only thing that may extend a hospital stay for perhaps a day or two. With average length of hospital stays being drastically reduced, there is little time for stabilization or meaningful clinical care.

In the typical contemporary inpatient scenario, utilization review personnel appear on the unit shortly after admission to push for discharge planning long before the patient is fully evaluated and often before clinical staff feel the patient is ready to leave. What usually ensues is a peculiar dance whereby the inpatient nursing staff and attending doctor exact from the patient a "safety contract" lasting until their next outpatient appointment. This routine intervention has become increasingly odd. All too often, contemporary safety contracts are neither contractual, in any legal sense, nor do they typically address important issues of actual outpatient safety (i.e., these contracts tend to emphasize what a patient will *not* do vs. what he or she *will* do should he or she feel impulsive or self-destructive; M. C. Miller, 1999). Moreover, research has shown that the "next outpatient appointment" provision in the safety contract, which links the patient to future clinical care, is all too often an appointment that patients do not make (Trautman, Stewart, & Morishima, 1993).

Fortunately, the field of clinical suicidology has not stood still in the face of dramatic changes in clinical practice. For example, as discussed by Jobes (2000), various theorists and clinical researchers have increasingly examined the cognitive, behavioral, and affective underpinnings of suicidal states, asking important research questions with clear implications for clinical practice. Over the past decade, we have seen an increasing emphasis on the phenomenology of suicide—what does suicide *mean* to the individual and how does suicidality differ among individuals? What do suicidal people (adolescents) feel and think, and how do they ultimately behave when they get psychologically stuck in a state of acute crisis? How does suicidal thinking cognitively break down? How do suffering people get trapped in psychological spaces where their need for escape becomes overwhelming?

In our view, at the heart of virtually every suicidal struggle is an intense need for escape and relief from psychological pain and suffering (Shneidman, 1993). Clearly, suicidal individuals—both youth and adults—desperately need asylum or sanctuary, which presents a considerable clinical challenge in contemporary practice. As noted, a number of emerging studies are helping to elucidate the psychology of suicide, particularly in terms of a potential suicidal adolescent's hopelessness, absence of future thinking, lack of problem-solving skills, tendency toward impulsivity, and presence of psychological pain. These larger conceptual constructs are not necessarily diagnosis-specific (Jobes, 2003a; Henriques, Beck, & Brown, 2003; Salkovskis, 2001) and are suggesting new directions in clinical practice (Jobes, 2000, 2003b).

As the data suggest, there has been a growing de-emphasis on the importance of the clinical (psychotherapy) relationship, perhaps because of various managed care influences and the exponential increase in the prescribing of psychotropic medicines. However, we remain convinced that most suicidal adolescents (in particular) have distinct relational, familial, and peer-based conflicts. At the center of many suicidal states is a fundamental struggle related to the presence or absence of certain key relationships, and how those relationships are perceived by the suicidal individual. We believe that, increasingly, suicidal teens often need "contemporary asylum," and that may actually be better found in a well-formed and carefully monitored *outpatient* therapeutic alliance (Goldsmith, Pellmar, Kleinman, & Bunney, 2002; Jobes, 2003a).

Clearly, there are different types of suicidal teens; a "one-size treatment" does not fit all. In our experience, suicidal teenagers often need a full range of interventions—psychotherapy, medication, family therapy, engagement of peers, even spiritual and existential consideration. However, more tailored and individualized interventions cannot be applied until we become more sophisticated about assessing, understanding, and conceptualizing different types of suicidal states, and in appreciating the idiosyncratic nuances of the suicidal mind as manifested in a young person.

Evidence-based research in the provision of mental health care has consistently shown that a combination of psychotherapy and medication is more efficacious than either approach by itself (TADS Team, 2004). Beyond the demonstrated benefits of appropriately administered psychopharmacology, most suicidal patients can directly benefit from good psychotherapy that specifically helps them solve problems, cope, and develop a thicker and more resilient "psychological skin." Clinicians can listen, understand, and help improve coping skills so that suicidal patients can develop a better "psychological toolkit" so that they may find alternative ways of handling suffering and distress, short of ending their life forever. Beyond this, through the power of corrective therapeutic relationships, we may also help suicidal adolescents find a way to make their life more livable—a crucial bottom line. We believe that suicidal youth must be helped in such a manner that they actually become active and integral players in their own therapeutic process—collaborative partners in preventing (their own) suicide (Jobes, 2003a).

According to Rudd, Joiner, Jobes, and King (1999), two interdependent forces have emerged in the last decade that have significantly altered the nature of care for suicidal patients: the aforementioned advent of managed care and the development of clinical practice guidelines. They argue that psychotherapy as provided in today's mental health arena will almost necessarily be time-limited in some form or fashion. Treatment time limitations are most frequently imposed externally—that is, by the managed care company or insurance provider involved, restricting the frequency, duration, or actual type of care provided. The dilemma many clinicians confront today is how to provide effective psychotherapeutic services for high-risk individuals within such rigid constraints—particularly for those patients who are suicidal—all the while balancing escalating liabilities.

Rudd et al. (1999) have pointed out that practice guidelines have simultaneously emerged that drive the very nature of care provided and that directly affect the clinician's day-to-day work. Despite considerable disagreement as to their appropriateness, scientific foundation, and clinical utility, guidelines continue to emerge and will probably persist (American Psychiatric Association, 2003; Ashworth, 2001; Shaffer & Pfeffer, 2001). Various authors (e.g., Garfield, 1996; Havik & VandenBos, 1996; Nathan, 1998) have advocated for focused clinical effectiveness studies addressing the duration of therapy for different disorders and related cost–benefit analyses. This is particularly true for suicidal patients, the majority of whom present with a broad range of diagnoses and considerable comorbidity across *Diagnostic and Statistical Manual of Mental Disorders, Fourth Edition* (*DSM–IV;* American Psychiatric Association, 1994) Axes I, II, and III (e.g., Linehan, 1993a, 1993b; Rudd, Dahm, & Rajab, 1993; Rudd, Joiner, & Rajab, 1996). Rudd et al. (1999) observe that

> Changes in the nature of the psychotherapy delivery system have been particularly challenging for those clinicians treating suicidal patients. Others have documented the negative impact of managed care on the overall sense of well-being and satisfaction experienced by practitioners in today's mental health marketplace (Hersch, 1995; Sherman & Thelen, 1998). This problem is compounded by the complexity of clinical and practical demands presented by suicidal patients. With considerable restrictions in access to inpatient care or long-term psychotherapy, those clinicians and treatment centers that provide outpatient services to suicidal patients are left with no proven treatment alternatives (e.g., Maltsberger, 1993, 1994; Rudd & Joiner, 1998). (p. 438)

CULTURE, RACE, ETHNICITY, AND RELIGION

As noted in chapter 1, suicide rates vary across racial, ethnic, and religious groups, as they do throughout the life span (Goldsmith et al., 2002). Racial and ethnic differences as well as religious orientation and belief systems may influence views of death, dying, and suicidal behaviors (Group for the Advancement of Psychiatry, 1989). In some groups, suicide can be considered a traditionally accepted way of dealing with shame, distress, or physical illness (Tseng, 2001). In some cultures, suicidal ideation may be considered a disgraceful or private matter that should be denied. In addition, acculturative stressors may contribute to suicidal behaviors (Hovey, 2000).

Knowledge of and sensitivity to different racial and ethnic perspectives related to suicidality as well as cultural differences in belief systems about death and suicide become important in the assessment, treatment, and management of suicidal risk (American Psychiatric Association, 2003).

As noted by Shiang (2000), every individual in a particular cultural milieu learns to use culturally specific coping strategies to promote health and development. Patients also must be understood within their specific cultural context. Hence, a suicidal act may well depend on the specific cultural scripts of the group, the degree of social influence of the act, the social position held by the suicidal individuals and their family members, and how the act can be interpreted in light of the predominant gender script. Collaborations of mental health professionals with culturally relevant providers, including the clergy and spiritual ministers, may be effective in maximizing treatment effectiveness and to reach otherwise underserved groups (Marsella & Yamada, 2000).

Thus, in the face of many contemporary treatment changes and developments, we are faced with some significant reconsiderations as we approach the topic of treating adolescent suicide and suicidal behaviors in the current edition. To bring meaning and sense to this dynamic area of change, this chapter first considers the empirical treatment literature and then reviews the established major approaches to treatment. In chapter 6, we will present our "integrative–eclectic" treatment approach to clinical work with suicidal adolescents.

EMPIRICAL TREATMENT LITERATURE

There are several different types of psychotherapies, including behavioral therapy, psychodynamic therapy, and supportive therapy. Behavioral therapies, including cognitive–behavioral therapy, focus on restructuring current thoughts, perceptions, and beliefs to facilitate behavioral and emotional change. Psychodynamic, or insight-oriented, therapies focus on increasing self-understanding and linking current situations and reactions to past events. Supportive therapies focus on providing advice, attention, and sympathy in a nonjudgmental environment (Goldsmith et al., 2002). All of these techniques and their modifications have strengths and weaknesses as they relate to directly altering suicidal ideation, intent, plans, and actions.

As discussed in the first edition of this book, the relatively limited empirical treatment literature of the 1980s suggested that various forms of structured, primarily cognitive–behavioral (problem-solving) treatments held the greatest promise for certain types of suicidal (adolescent) patients (refer to Rudd et al., 1999, for a thorough review of this earlier work). In the ensuing years, we have observed continued empirical support for the cognitive–behavioral therapy approaches (Lerner & Clum, 1990; Linehan, Armstrong, Suarez, Allmon, & Heard, 1991; Rudd, Rajab, et al., 1996; Salkovskis, 1996). However, as observed by Jobes, Jacoby, Cimbolic, and Hustead (1997), these studies primarily tested theory-driven structured treatments for particular subtypes of suicidal clients; virtually no studies have examined general clinical assessment and treatment of a range of suicidal clients seen in typical outpatient settings.

Much of the extant treatment literature is not specific to adolescent suicidality; indeed, outpatient treatment studies that target depressed adolescents generally exclude adolescents with suicidal behaviors (e.g., Kroll, Harrington, Jayson, Fraser, & Gowers, 1996; Lewinsohn, Clarke, Hops, & Andrews, 1990; Mufson et al., 1994; Wood, Harrington, & Moore, 1996). One clear exception to the tendency to exclude suicidal adolescents is Brent et al.'s (1997) comparison of individual cognitive–behavioral therapy (CBT), systemic behavior family therapy (SBFT), and individual nondirective supportive therapy (NST) on adolescents' depressive symptoms, suicidality, and functional impairment. Results from their study indicated that CBT was more efficacious than SBFT or NST at reducing depression during the acute phase of treatment, although all three conditions showed significant reductions in suicidality and functional impairment. However, only 31% of the study participants had suicidal features, thus limiting the generalizability of these findings (Rathus & Miller, 2002).

Other treatment-related issues have been increasingly investigated by adolescent suicide researchers. For example, as many as 50% of adolescent suicide attempters fail to receive follow-up mental health treatment (Spirito, Brown, Overholser, & Fritz, 1989) and, of those who do receive treatment, up to 77% do not attend therapy appointments or fail to complete treatment (Trautman et al., 1993). Although some preliminary data exist concerning those suicidal clients who drop out of outpatient treatment (Jobes et al., 1997; Rudd, Joiner, & Rajab, 1996), there are virtually no empirical process-and-outcome research studies using actual clinical samples that pertain to suicidal clients who remain in treatment. Thus, clinicians who are treating suicidal patients in ongoing psychotherapy are often forced to rely on the suicide-focused treatment literature that is principally case-based and largely anecdotal (Jobes, 1995a).

However, in response to some of the previously discussed changes in clinical practice, there has recently been more focus on the identification of empirically based outpatient treatment protocols. For example, Olfson, Marcus, Druss, and Pincus (2002) have pursued research related to the increasing use of psychotropic medications over the past decade. Treatment by medication is less expensive and usually requires much less frequent direct clinical contact, an obvious plus in a managed-care world. However, the medication compliance literature should give us pause in that some data suggest that many patients fail to fill prescriptions, often fail to take medicine as prescribed, and may not achieve or maintain therapeutic levels (Dwyer, Levy, & Meander, 1986; Haynes, McKibbon, & Kanani, 1996; Horowitz & Horowitz, 1993).

In reviewing the empirical literature addressing the psychotherapeutic treatment of suicidality, Rudd (2000) has identified a number of important questions that need to be addressed by suicide treatment researchers. These include the following:

- What treatments have demonstrated effectiveness for treating suicidality?
- Within identified treatments, are there *core interventions* associated with positive outcome?
- Are there identified treatments that clearly should *not* be used as a result of consistently poor outcome data?
- Can high-risk suicidal patients be treated safely *and* effectively on an outpatient basis?
- Are there prohibitive features of particular treatments, such as exorbitant costs, duration, frequency, intensity, risks, or side effects?
- Are there differential dropout rates for specific treatment approaches that need to be considered?
- Does treatment setting influence outcome?
- Does treatment *delay* (i.e., the period of time from suicidal crisis to the onset of treatment) predict treatment outcome?
- Is treatment duration associated with outcome (i.e., are short-term treatments more or less effective than longer ones)?
- Do particular subgroups (e.g., multiple attempters or those with comorbid problems across both Axis I and Axis II) require specific treatment approaches?
- Does treatment effect endure (i.e., what are the observed relapse rates)?
- Are there identified approaches specifically targeting those who relapse?
- Does diagnostic comorbidity affect treatment selection, prognosis, or outcome (i.e., treatment matching)?
- How should treatment response or outcome be conceptualized?
- How can treatment compliance be maximized?
- How can treatment fidelity be maintained across clinicians for specific treatment approaches? (p. 48)

Since the first edition of this book, there has been a great deal more specific interest and focus on the *lack* of research in the treatment of suicidality (e.g., Hawton et al., 1998; Linehan, 1997; Rudd et al., 1999). Comprehensive reviews of the treatment literature by these authors has led to an increased level of awareness about various challenges, limits, and needs for pursuing treatment-oriented research. For example, Linehan (1997) scrutinized all investigations that have included randomized clinical trials (RCTs) of psychosocial and behavioral interventions for treatment of suicidal behaviors (adults and adolescents). At that time, only 20 studies were found in the extant literature that randomly assigned individuals to treatment conditions (i.e., experimental treatment groups, treatment-as-usual groups, and control groups). Four of the 20 studies showed a significant effect for psychosocial interventions and another for pharmacotherapy. More recently, Linehan (2004) has reviewed an additional 10 randomized clinical trial studies, with overall findings remaining largely the same. Prominent among the findings of these reviews was that the psychosocial interventions were most effective with those at high risk for suicidal behaviors. Linehan (2004) concluded, however, that despite the above results, relatively little is still known about how we might lower suicide *completions*. In contrast, much more is known with regard to *nonfatal* suicidal behaviors, where focused behavioral interventions appear to hold the greatest promise for reducing suicide attempts and other nonfatal suicidal behaviors. With the following noteworthy exceptions, the extant treatment literature typically does not focus specifically on *adolescent* suicidality, with the majority of studies focusing on adult samples (see Leenaars, Maltsberger, & Neimeyer, 1994; Spirito & Overholser, 2003; Zimmerman & Asnis, 1995).

As reviewed by Rathus and Miller (2002), however, two randomized controlled studies have specifically targeted suicidality in adolescents. Cotgrove, Zirinsky, Black, and Weston (1995) compared standard outpatient care to an experimental condition comprised of standard care plus a "greencard" given to adolescents that permitted immediate readmission to an inpatient unit at a local hospital if they felt actively suicidal. Results indicated no differences between groups on measures of repeated self-injurious behavior. Harrington, Kerfoot, and colleagues (1998) compared a three- to four-session, home-based family problem-solving therapy to treatment as usual with adolescent suicide attempters. Results of this study indicated that the experimental intervention was more effective than routine care in reducing suicidal ideation only among attempters who did not meet criteria for major depression.

Rotheram-Borus and colleagues (Rotheram-Borus, Piacentini, Van Rossem, Graee, et al. 1996, Rotheram-Borus, Piacentini, Cantwell, Belin, & Juwon, 2000; Rotheram-Borus, Piacentini, Miller, Graee, & Castro-Blanco, 1994), using a quasi-experimental design, have reported that the effects of a specialized emergency room program improved subsequent treatment adherence among female adolescent suicide attempters to a six-session, family-based cognitive–behavioral outpatient program called Successful Negotiation/Acting Positively (SNAP). Among a larger sample, 18-month follow-up data showed improvement on mental health indices among subjects in both conditions; however, rates of suicide ideation and reattempts did not differ across treatment conditions.

Rathus and Miller (2002) have concluded that none of the aforementioned studies have demonstrated the superiority of a treatment focusing exclusively on suicidal adolescents relative to a comparison group in terms of reducing suicidal behavior and psychiatric inpatient admissions along with treatment dropout rates. Such variables are clearly essential in our evaluation of treatments for suicidal youth.

Until recently, little had been known about the relative or combined effectiveness of CBT and selective serotonin reuptake inhibitors (SSRIs). The Treatment for Adolescents with Depression Study (TADS) was a randomized controlled trial of a volunteer sample of 439 patients between the ages of 12 to 17 with a primary *DSM–IV* diagnosis of major depressive disorder. The trial was conducted at 13 U.S. academic and community clinics between spring 2000 and summer 2003 (TADS Team, 2004).

The interventions consisted of 12 weeks of (a) fluoxetine alone (10–40 mg/d), (b) CBT alone, (c) CBT with fluoxetine (10–40 mg/d), or (d) placebo (equivalent to 10–40 mg/d). Placebo and fluoxetine alone were administered double-blind; CBT alone and CBT with fluoxetine were administered unblinded.

They found that, compared with placebo, the combination of fluoxetine with CBT was statistically significant on the Children's Depression Rating Scale–Revised. Compared with fluoxetine alone and CBT alone, treatment of fluoxetine with CBT was superior, whereas fluoxetine alone is a superior treatment to CBT alone. Rates of response for fluoxetine with CBT were 71.0%; fluoxetine alone, 60.6%; CBT alone, 43.2%; and placebo, 34.8% Clinically significant suicidal thinking, which was present in 29% of the sample at baseline, improved significantly in all four treatment groups. Fluoxetine with CBT showed the greatest reduction. Seven (1.6%) of 439 patients attempted suicide; there were no completed suicides.

The authors commented that

> With respect to risk, suicidality decreased substantially with treatment. Improvement in suicidality was greatest for patients receiving fluoxetine with CBT and least for fluoxetine alone. While fluoxetine did not appear to increase suicidal ideation, harm-related adverse events may occur more frequently in fluoxetine-treated patients and CBT may protect against these events. Taking risks and benefits into account, the combination of fluoxetine with CBT appears superior as a short-term treatment for MDD [major depressive disorder] in adolescents. (p. 816)

As of this writing, no scientific studies have found a specific causal association between treatment of major depressive disorder with an SSRI and increased risk of suicidal ideation or attempt. Controversy about the possible increase in suicidality with the use of SSRIs in children and adolescents led the regulatory agency of the British Medicines and Healthcare to contraindicate all drugs in this class (except fluoxetine) for use in pediatric patients with major depressive disorder because of an unfavorable risk-to-benefit ratio (Committee on Safety of Medicines Web site, 2004, http://medicines.mhra.gov.uk/aboutagency/regframework/csm/csmhomemain.htm).

On October 15, 2004, the U.S. Food and Drug Administration directed pharmaceutical companies to place "black box warnings" on the package inserts for all antidepressant drugs. The "warnings" alert health care providers to an increased risk of suicidality (suicidal thinking and behavior) in children and adolescents and state that patients should be provided with a patient medication guide advising them of risks and precautions (U.S. Food and Drug Administration, 2004). As of this writing, among the SSRIs, only fluoxetine is approved for use in treating major depressive disorder in pediatric patients.

The TADS study found that the impact of treatment with fluoxetine on reduction of suicidal ideation was identical to that of placebo, suggesting that fluoxetine on average did not increase suicidal ideation. They note that suicidal crises and nonsuicidal self-harming behaviors were not uncommon in this population of depressed adolescents. The TADS findings are consistent with other research that found that CBT has a specific beneficial effect on suicidal ideation and that CBT combined with fluoxetine may confer a protective effect not only against suicidal ideation, but also on harm-related behaviors (Barbe, Bridge, Birmaher, Kolko, & Brent, 2004).

Thus, although progress has been made in the empirical study of treating suicidality, there is still a tremendous need for growth in the science of clinical suicidology. As discussed by Rudd (2000), with fewer than two dozen studies in the world's literature that approach sound research criteria for randomness or control, we are still in our infancy in terms of pursuit of empirical research in this area. Both Linehan (1997) and Rudd (2000) have highlighted a central common problem in the scientific study of suicidality to date—namely, patient-subjects evidencing some form of suicidality (ideation, intent, prior or current attempt) are ordinarily and routinely *excluded* from clinical trial research (both addressing medication and psychotherapy) because of their "high-risk" status. As discussed in chapter 4, the National Institute of Mental Health has recently developed guidelines that outline criteria for the inclusion of high-risk suicidal individuals in clinical trial research. The inclusion of suicidal adolescents in clinical control trials is critical in those studies that evaluate the effectiveness and efficacy of psychotropic medications administered to adolescents for the treatment of depression, anxiety, panic disorders, and eating disorders.

MAJOR TREATMENT APPROACHES

A variety of major treatment approaches for working with suicidal adolescents have been put forward in the literature. Our goal is to first present and describe the primary clinical approaches as a prelude to our discussion of our own integrative–eclectic approach to adolescent suicidality (see chap. 6). We have divided the current discussion of major clinical approaches into the following treatment modalities: (a) individual psychotherapy, (b) family psychotherapy, (c) group psychotherapy, and (d) psychopharmacological treatments.

Individual Psychotherapy

Reflecting perhaps our own clinical biases, we begin our discussion of the major treatment approaches with individual psychotherapy. Adolescent suicidal risk is, of course, influenced by many forces—family, peers, culture, genetics, and physical, cognitive, and emotional development, to name but a few. However, within the professional literature, the principle approach to the clinical treatment of suicidal individuals has centered on individual therapy, often in combination with other modalities and interventions. In this regard, some significant headway has been made over the past 20 years in the development of specific clinical approaches as well as different types of interventions that may help treat the suicidal youth.

Psychodynamic Psychotherapy

Historically, psychodynamic approaches dating back to Freud have more longevity than other approaches we will discuss. Not surprisingly, various psychodynamic approaches—even specific to adolescent suicide—have been discussed throughout the clinical literature (refer to discussions by Jobes, 1995a; Jobes & Karmel, 1996). Moreover, many practicing clinicians are still psychodynamically trained and routinely use dynamic treatment approaches with their patients, including (we presume) their suicidal adolescent patients. Beyond theoretical and clinical discussions, there is unfortunately no direct empirical support for the specific efficacy of psychodynamic treatment for suicidal teens. Given the empirical bias that is displayed throughout this book, we will therefore discuss psychodynamic approaches to treating adolescent suicidality with a measure of prudence. Although we do not dispute that clinically and conceptually psychodynamic theories have much to offer the practitioner and the patient, we are mindful that until data more clearly support the value of this type of therapy (in cases of suicidal adults in general or more specific to suicidal teens), some necessary caution about its potential usefulness and efficacy is in order.

With this caution in mind, psychodynamic treatments for suicidal adolescents do have many compelling features that are quite germane to the topic at hand. For example, treatments in the psychodynamic theoretical tradition tend to routinely emphasize the importance of development (e.g., Erikson, 1968); the impact of family relationships on personality development and one's ability to relate to others (e.g., Fairbairn, 1952; Guntrip, 1968); the development of the self (e.g., Kohut & Wolf, 1978); and, of course, the central healing role of the clinical relationship (e.g., Freud, 1917/1957; Goldsmith et al., 2002; Kohut, 1977).

Across the many lines of psychodynamic approaches, there are different ways that therapeutic healing is thought to occur (King, 2003). For example, from an object–relations perspective, the recovery process of psychotherapy can be understood as a three-stage process (Guntrip, 1968). First, during rapport development, the patient needs a parent figure as a protector against intrapsychic pain and anxiety (i.e., a dependable rescuer from hopeless losing battles with problems the patient does not understand). The second stage, involving the development and analysis of transference, addresses how and why basic needs were (and are) not met in past (and present) relationships with the patient's actual parents and social network. Finally, in the third stage of regrowth and maturing, the patient begins to feel the impact of nonerotic stable parental love, which enables the child within to grow and possess its own individuality. In this final stage, there is a maturing sense of selfhood that helps the patient to be separate without feeling cut off from key object relations.

Other psychodynamic schools of thought speak to the importance of gaining conscious insight into anxiety-provoking unconscious conflict that is often associated with certain key developmental periods (i.e., a more orthodox-driven theory of psychoanalysis). Yet other schools speak to the need to redress childhood emotional deficits (e.g., the absence of empathic affirmation from reliable and responsive parents, or even overt abuse and neglect). Within self-psychology, an empathically oriented form of psychotherapy is thought to lead to corrective self-object transferences that then lead to a kind of therapeutic reparenting that is thought to help a fractured sense of self become more cohesive, whole, and viable.

Given the aforementioned lack of empirical support, we will limit further discussion about specific psychodynamic approaches, opting to pepper our discussions throughout this chapter and book with psychodynamic constructs and ideas when they are appropriate and relevant to the discussion at hand. Although empirical data supporting psychodynamic approaches to adolescent suicide is wanting, we nevertheless are inclined to conclude that

> …a psychodynamic approach to the assessment, management, and treatment of suicidal adolescents can be quite effective…there is much in psychoanalytic tradition to help guide one's clinical interventions. Perhaps most important, beyond crisis-management, a psychodynamic approach to this clinical work holds the promise of actually treating (and resolving) the underlying causes of suicidality within the young person. (Jobes, 1995a, p. 152)

Having briefly discussed this principle yet obvious nonempirically supported therapeutic approach, let us now shift our focus to considerations of more empirically derived and validated approaches to the clinical treatment of suicidal youth.

Problem-Solving Approaches

As suggested earlier, a variety of studies have emphasized the potential therapeutic worth of problem-oriented psychotherapy. Some approaches discussed further on (e.g., Beck's approach to cognitive therapy) have at the heart of their treatment a problem-solving emphasis. In this regard, literature in this vein has tended to emphasize cognitive and behavioral aspects of clinical treatment. We will thus talk generically about various types of problem-solving interventions before turning our focus to major treatment approaches that use problem solving in an integral way.

In relation to cognition, Salkovskis (2001) has identified prominent cognitive mechanisms in patients who have made suicide attempts. The first of these mechanisms involves deficits in problem-solving skills, particularly with regard to interpersonal problem solving. Second, there is evidence of a bias toward retrieval of overgeneral (as opposed to specific) memories. In addition, there is evidence of a third factor, which is the association between feelings of hopelessness and actual suicide. It follows that clinical treatments that modify such factors should be effective in helping people who are troubled by suicidal ideation and in reducing both the rate of repeat attempts and the rate of actual suicide. These three psychological maintaining factors are not fully independent. The identification of links between the maintaining factors may hold the key to the development of a focused and integrated psychological treatment. Fortunately, effective treatment need not await resolution of all these issues because problem-solving training with a cognitive–behavioral emphasis is likely to deal not only with problem-solving deficits per se, but also with impairments in the ability to generate specific (as opposed to overgeneral) memories.

Although an explicit problem-solving strategy is usually modified to fit with the particular person being helped, it generally follows a format that includes (Salkovskis, 2001)

1. making a problem list;
2. prioritizing problems to be dealt with, not only on the basis of importance and impact but also on the basis of likely short-term effectiveness;
3. deciding on a range of possible solutions, usually involving an element of unconstrained "brainstorming," in which the person is encouraged to consider freely any possible solution;
4. selecting a particular solution, often by systematically reviewing the pros and cons of the most likely solutions available;

5. breaking down the implementation of the chosen solution into smaller, more manageable steps;
6. anticipating and identifying obstacles to each step (including not only practical difficulties but also cognitive and emotional difficulties); and
7. systematically reviewing progress between steps before deciding whether to move on to the next step.

Throughout this process, the importance of specificity in thinking about solutions and their implementation is emphasized. In this way, both problem-solving deficits and deficits in specificity of recall may be corrected by treatment. It also seems likely that problem solving has the effect of reducing hopelessness in people who have previously been unable to see any way out of what had seemed to be insoluble situations (Salkovskis, 1996).

In his consideration of cognitive and behavioral problem-solving approaches, Rudd (2000) has observed

> There appears to be an emerging trend for the efficacy of CBT, both over the short- and the long-term. It appears that CBT, integrating problem-solving as a core intervention, is effective at reducing suicidal ideation and related symptoms over the short-term. Reducing attempts appears to require longer-term and more intensive treatment, with a specific focus on skill deficits and related personality dysfunction. (p. 57)

Cognitive–Behavioral Therapy

Particularly useful with younger patients, cognitive therapy (Beck, Rush, Shaw, & Emery, 1979) has deservedly gained a reputation as a primary treatment modality of choice with depressed and suicidal patients. This is especially true when depressive symptoms make introspection difficult. Similar to depressed suicidal adults, suicidal adolescents often experience negative cognitions about themselves, their environment, and their future. To this end, cognitive–behavioral therapy (CBT) has been shown to be an effective intervention for depressive symptoms (Clarke, Rohde, Lewinsohn, Hops, & Seeley, 1999). Although work in CBT and related research with teenagers is more limited, Beck and colleagues are beginning to make important inroads with youthful populations (e.g., Henriques et al., 2003). It has become increasingly self-evident, however, that young patients must first learn to recognize and alter their cognitions before they can use and benefit from more insight-oriented treatments.

Beck's model of treatment is highly structured and collaborative. Although not touted as such, it makes maximum use of the relationship between patient and therapist, wherein the latter plays roles ranging from teacher to cheerleader. Most important, the cognitive therapist works to develop "collaborative empiricism" (Beck, Hollon, Young, Bedrosian, & Budenz, 1985). The notion of collaborative empiricism embraces a cooperative scientific–investigative relationship between clinician and patient to identify those maladaptive cognitions and underlying assumptions maintaining the patient's negative mood, to test and analyze the validity of those assumptions, and to target, jointly, goals for changing those found invalid.

As noted, depressed and suicidal adolescents exhibit a number of cognitive deficits. The cognitive model of treatment strictly focuses on these and the distorted and negative cognitions that are used by the patient. Cognitive therapy postulates three primary areas of maladaptive thinking for attention: (a) the "cognitive triad," the idiosyncratic and negative view of self, experience, and future; (b) "schemas," stable patterns of molding data or events into cognitions; and (c) "systematic errors" in thinking that establish and maintain a depressed mood and the hopelessness that Beck believes is "at the core of the suicidal wishes" (Beck et al., 1979, p. 151).

From an empirical perspective, short-term CBT appeared to be more effective than family or supportive therapy with depressed teenagers (Brent et al., 1997). However, after 2 years, the apparent differences between these therapies were no longer apparent (Birmaher et al., 2000). The efficacy of CBT with suicidal adolescents has not yet been examined, but in the cited studies, all therapies reduced suicidal ideation.

Brent and colleagues have created and revised a CBT treatment manual (Brent & Poling, 1997), modifying the approach of Beck, Rush, Shaw, and Emery (1979) for depressed adolescents. The treatment is comprised of 12 to 16 weekly sessions followed by a 6-month booster phase of monthly or bimonthly sessions. Parents and adolescents receive a psychoeducational manual about mood disorders and their treatments. The active intervention is described as a collaborative "guided discovery" to monitor and modify automatic thoughts, assumptions, and beliefs (Brent, 1997). Because suicidal individuals are thought to often have difficulty in communicating and negotiating their needs and wishes (McLeavey, Daly, Ludgate, & Murray, 1994) and to frequently resort to passive-avoidant coping strategies (Adams & Adams, 1991), Brent's treatment model encourages more assertive and direct methods of communicating, as well as increasing the teenager's ability to conceptualize alternative solutions to problems (Shaffer & Pfeffer, 2001).

Brent's study provides no evidence of the efficacy of CBT for teenagers who have made a suicide attempt. This group of adolescents was not included in this study. However, the intervention was reported to be as effective as systemic family therapy and nondirective supportive therapy in reducing suicidal ideation in depressed adolescents during the 12- to 16-week treatment period (Brent et al., 1997).

In the cognitive–behavioral model of treatment, the adolescent is taught to monitor his or her own behavior and thoughts through a diary of daily activities and pleasurable thoughts (Harrington & Saleem, 2003). From these observations might be constructed activity schedules, or systematic plans for decreasing negative and increasing positive thoughts and activities.

Through graded homework tasks, the patient is taught mastery (the opposite of helplessness) through small-step goal-attainment experiences and pleasure (the opposite of dysphoria) by engaging in reinforcing experiences. Dysfunctional cognitions are restructured, attributions are appropriately refocused, and self-evaluations are modified as appropriate to more rational beliefs and interpretations of more scientifically observed data.

Teaching the adolescent to observe the immediate social environment, collect data through accomplishable homework assignments, and bring those observations into the therapy session for collaborative interpretation is akin to teaching college students the scientific method: (a) establish a research hypothesis, (b) pose a way to test and measure that hypothesis, (c) collect data in an unbiased manner, and (d) analyze and interpret results to prove the hypothesis (or if the null hypothesis is accepted, establish a new research hypothesis). By teaching the scientific method to suicidal adolescents, the therapist is proposing both a model of rational thinking and participant observation in one's personal–social world and that control in that world is possible. For example, a suicidal adolescent who reports that her parents singularly ignore her during family dinner might be instructed to closely observe in 1-minute units who initiates conversation, who responds to whom, and so on over several mealtime gatherings, and to bring this "data" to the next session. With these "baseline observations" in hand and interpreted with the therapist's guidance, any of several "experiments" might be conducted to see what stimuli produce what responses from whom. With these additional new data in hand, specific behaviors might be targeted by this adolescent as more or less effective in accomplishing desired goals in her relationship with her parents.

Some researchers report that the effectiveness of the cognitive model has been demonstrated with adults to be at least equal to that of tricyclic antidepressants in modifying depressed mood (Beck, Hollon, et al., 1985). However, these same authors caution that it is not for use with patients diagnosed as having a schizoaffective disorder or a borderline personality disorder. Reynolds and Coats (1986) reported on a 5-week, 10-session CBT program with 30 high-school-age depressives. Their self-control skills-training model produced significant improvements as rated on a number of measures of depression as compared to a no-treatment control group. A similar approach has been tested by Rehm (1987), whose treatment model focuses on self-evaluation and self-reinforcement as essential aspects of self-control training.

Beck and his associates (Henriques et al., 2003) have recently developed a specific 10-session cognitive therapy intervention for adolescent and young adult suicide attempters. A novel element of the therapy is that the treatment can be applied to individuals exhibiting suicidal behavior, regardless of psychiatric diagnosis. Another central philosophical element is the notion that the suicidal behavior is both understandable given the patient's frame of reference but ultimately disadvantageous to the patient.

The intervention owes much to the cognitive model of emotional disorders in general and depression in particular, as well as the large empirical literature linking hopelessness with suicidal behavior (e.g., Beck, Steer, Kovacs, & Garrison, 1985). In accordance with cognitive theory, the central feature of the intervention is the identification of proximal thoughts and associated core beliefs that were activated just prior to the patient's suicide attempt. With the particular cognitive components identified, cognitive and behavioral strategies are applied to help individuals develop more adaptive ways of thinking about their situation and more functional ways of responding during periods of acute emotional distress. The focus of the therapy is on reducing suicidal behavior, and key elements of the intervention include (a) developing specific ways to address hopelessness and target suicidal behavior, (b) developing effective ways for engaging patients quickly in the treatment to reduce dropout, (c) increasing adaptive use of other health services, and (d) increasing the adaptive use of social support.

The intervention is a 10-session protocol with specific strategies developed for the early, middle, and late phases of the treatment. The therapist plays an active and directive role in working with the patient in a collaborative manner to explore the individual's perceptions, interpretations, and explanations related to suicidal behavior. The structure of the therapy sessions consists of agenda setting; checking symptoms such as mood, suicidal ideation, and behavior; monitoring use of substances; monitoring compliance with other treatments; building bridges between past sessions with a particular focus on beliefs related to the suicide attempt; making capsule summaries; eliciting feedback throughout the session; and assigning homework.

As with other proscribed modalities, they underscore the importance of using a flexible approach in implementing the procedures described here. Under optimal circumstances, patients are motivated for treatment, attend each session on time, and complete all their homework assignments. However, these optimal circumstances are uncommon, especially among teenagers. In making clinical decisions, the therapist is encouraged to individualize therapy to the styles, capacities, and needs of patients, as opposed to just "getting through" the material.

The main goals in the early phase of treatment (Sessions 1–3) are to (a) engage the patient in treatment, (b) have the patient "tell his or her story" about the suicide attempt, (c) assess the patient for risk for suicidal behavior, (d) develop a safety plan for suicidal emergencies, (e) orient the patient to the cognitive model, (f) begin to develop a cognitive conceptualization of the suicide attempt, (g) begin to develop a problem list and goals for the therapy, and (h) convey a sense of hope to the patient.

The middle phase of treatment (Sessions 4–7) focuses on developing new skills for reacting to distressing situations with a focus on cognitive restructuring and behavioral change. Components include (a) changing maladaptive beliefs and automatic thoughts, (b) construction of a "Hope

Kit," (c) building affective coping skills, (d) addressing impulsivity, (e) increasing social support, and (f) increasing compliance with adjunctive health and social services.

The final phase consists of a formal assessment of increased cognitive-behavioral skills. A guided imagery relapse prevention task (RPT) can serve as an endpoint assessment. The objective is to prime (i.e., expose) in the session as many of the thoughts, images, and feelings (i.e., triggers) associated with prior suicide attempts as possible and to determine whether the patient is able to respond to problems in an adaptive way. The RPT consists of five stages:

1. The first stage is describing the task, which consists of imagining both past and possible future sequences of events that result in the patient becoming suicidal. The imagery exercise serves as a chance to practice coping in imagination, which might help coping in real-life situations.

2. In the second stage, the therapist has the patient imagine the sequence of events and concomitant thoughts and feelings that led up to the suicide attempt. The therapist sets up the scene, reviewing the situational and personal triggers associated with previous attempts.

3. The third stage involves using the same format as before but this time responding to maladaptive thoughts and images with the tools learned in therapy. This step aims to test whether the patient can, in imagery, produce alternative ways of responding.

4. In the fourth stage, the therapist uses the patient's conceptualization to develop a scenario that the patient might face in the future that would likely lead to suicidal thinking. The therapist uses guided imagery to direct the patient through a possible sequence of events and concomitant thoughts and feelings. As the patient generates possible solutions and activates learned coping strategies, the therapist praises (i.e., reinforces) the patient for adaptive responding but also proposes additional challenges.

5. The final stage involves debriefing patients. After the relapse prevention task is given, patients are then asked to return to the therapy session and describe how they feel. Any suicidal ideation activated by the task is explored, and the patient remains in the session until all such thoughts have subsided.

A final consideration under the heading of CBT is an approach developed by Rudd, Joiner, and Rajab (2001), who have extended Beck's original theorizing about the "suicidal mode." Rudd et al. have written an important and valuable treatment guide entitled *Treating Suicidal Behavior: An Effective*

Time-Limited Approach. This text is one of the first that may truly be considered a treatment manual specific to suicide. In their book, these authors comprehensively and specifically present an initial theoretical (CBT) model of suicidality, and build a system of clinical assessment on the basis of this model. The assessment then logically leads to a clinical approach for dealing with crisis intervention and symptom management that seamlessly evolves into a clinical treatment designed to eliminate suicidal behaviors through skill building and the development of enduring adaptive modes. Although not specifically developed for work with suicidal youth, this manualized CBT approach nevertheless is one of the first "A to Z efforts" to comprehensively and conceptually target and treat suicidality within a cohesive and coherent theoretical model that directly shapes clinical assessment and treatment.

Dialectical Behavior Therapy (DBT)

Dialectical behavior therapy (DBT; Linehan, 1993a, 1993b) is an evidence-based outpatient psychotherapy for chronically parasuicidal adults diagnosed with borderline personality disorder. Parasuicide is defined as acute, deliberate, nonfatal self-injury or harm that includes suicide attempts and nonsuicidal self-injurious behaviors (Linehan, 1993a). Suicidal behaviors are considered to be maladaptive solutions to painful negative emotions but that also have affect-regulating qualities and elicit help from others.

This approach shares many features and procedures of cognitive–behavioral problem solving, but it is much more broadly based. Linehan identifies emotional dysregulation as a key factor that arises from biologically vulnerable patients being exposed at an early age to invalidating environments. The resulting affective instability then interacts with instability in behavioral, interpersonal, and cognitive domains to produce the pattern of reactions that are characteristic of such patients, including parasuicidal behavior.

DBT treatment focuses on validation and empowerment, consistent with the philosophy of cognitive–behavioral approaches to *DSM–IV* Axis I major psychiatric disorders. In DBT, the therapist aims to help the patient to modulate his or her emotional reactions, to reduce the associated extreme behaviors, and to accept his or her own reactions. Problem solving is a core skills-training strategy, supplemented by a range of ancillary treatments, supportive group sessions, and telephone consultations. There is considerably greater emphasis on working on and with the therapeutic relationship (more in the style of cognitive therapy than psychodynamic psychotherapy). Other core skills taught in DBT include mindfulness training, interpersonal effectiveness skills, and techniques designed to deal with psychological distress (including well-validated cognitive and behavioral techniques designed to deal with depression, anxiety, and posttraumatic stress).

These techniques are applied in an integrated and formulation-driven way, adapted for use with this particular group of patients in ways that take their particular sensitivities into account.

In a randomized clinical trial comparing DBT with treatment as usual, DBT was more effective in reducing suicide attempts, other parasuicidal acts, number of inpatient psychiatric hospitalization days, and anger, while improving social adjustment, treatment compliance, and treatment dropout rate (Linehan et al., 1991). Recent replication efforts of DBT have shown promising preliminary results (Koons et al., 1998; Linehan et al., 1998).

Dialectical Behavior Therapy for Adolescents. Recently, a modified and manual-based form of DBT has been used with suicidal adolescents with a diagnosis of borderline personality disorder (Miller, Rathus, Linehan, Wetzler, & Leigh, 1997). DBT for adolescents (DBT-A) requires the participation of an adolescent's relative in the skills-training group who is charged with improving the home environment and teaching other relatives to model and reinforce adaptive behaviors for the adolescent. DBT-A has been reduced from 1 year to two 12-week stages, covers fewer skills, and uses simpler language for skills training. In a nonrandomized comparative-treatment study with adolescents who were suicidal and diagnosed as borderline, there was a suggestion that DBT-A is acceptable to teenagers and reduces rates of psychiatric hospitalization (Miller et al., 1997).

In a recent study, Rathus and Miller (2002) compared an adolescent adaptation of DBT (Miller et al., 1997) to treatment as usual for suicidal adolescents using a quasi-experimental design. They hypothesized that DBT appeared appropriate for suicidal adolescents with borderline personality features because of its targets of reducing life-threatening behaviors, decreasing therapy-interfering behaviors, and decreasing quality-of-life–interfering behaviors. Furthermore, behavioral skills targeted in treatment (emotional regulation, interpersonal effectiveness, distress tolerance, and mindfulness and attentional control) closely correspond to core issues of adolescent development (e.g., mood lability, unstable relationships, impulsive behaviors, identity confusion), which are only intensified for adolescents presenting for treatment. They found that DBT was more effective than treatment as usual in reducing psychiatric hospitalizations and increasing treatment completion rates. They found that patients receiving DBT showed reductions in suicidal ideation, general psychiatric symptoms, and borderline personality symptomatology.

Interpersonal Psychotherapy

The focus of interpersonal therapy (IPT) is on the link between the onset of depressive symptoms and current interpersonal problems. The emphasis of change strategies is on the person's immediate personal context, his or her reaction to life events and current social dysfunction, and how these factors relate to symptom formation. No attempt is made to deal with more enduring aspects of personality. Having established links between interpersonal functioning and depressive symptoms, specific intervention strategies are used according to a detailed manual developed by Klerman and Weissman (1989). This 12- to 16-week therapy focuses on the style and effectiveness of interpersonal interactions.

Similar to previously discussed approaches, skills training is a major part of the later stages of interpersonal psychotherapy, making it attractive as a potential treatment for adolescents who make suicide attempts. Some of the interpersonal issues that are addressed by IPT for Adolescents (IPT–A) include separation from parents, conflicts with parental authority, development of close relationships with members of the opposite sex, initial experience with death of a relative or friend, and peer pressures (Mufson, Moreau, Weissman, & Klerman, 1993; Mufson, Weissman, Moreau, & Garfinkel, 1999).

IPT may be a useful treatment for addressing the adolescent's use of suicidal behavior as a means of communicating anger or distress or of resolving conflict. The adolescent's ability to establish a therapeutic alliance and commit to informing the therapist about suicidal preoccupations and intent, and going to an emergency service, if necessary, is central to IPT. However, as yet there have been no published results of its specific effectiveness among suicidal youth, although IPT has been found to be effective in the treatment of depression.

Comparisons of Problem-Solving, CBT, DBT, and IPT Approaches

Salkovskis (2001) has thoughtfully compared the four approaches we have just considered. According to Salkovskis, an active psychological treatment needs to meet the following criteria if it is to have any chance of being successful in reducing the repetition rate of attempted suicide and diminishing the number of completed suicides:

1. It must help the patient to feel understood (including, but not confined to, the use of "nonspecific" therapy factors such as empathy, genuineness, and nonpossessive warmth, and also including aspects of patient empowerment).
2. The main focus of therapeutic efforts should be on factors understood (through empirically grounded theory) to be generally involved in the experience and maintenance of intense and persistent distress in particular patient groups (including, but not confined to, those who meet criteria for particular diagnoses).
3. Therapy should be adapted to target the particular specific and idiosyncratic manifestations of the generally identified maintaining factors (i.e., the way in which the general maintaining

factors affect the particular patient who the therapist is seeking to help).

4. Therapy should have been demonstrated to be more effective than a waiting list or treatment as usual.

Currently, only CBT with a problem-solving emphasis and DBT meet all of these criteria. Both standard cognitive therapy for depression and interpersonal therapy currently meet the first three criteria. Salkovskis (2001) observes that examination of the details of all four approaches suggests common elements in terms of the following:

1. A focus on the "here and now",
2. Attention to negative emotions as a guide to the appropriate focus of therapy,
3. A major element of both problem-solving training and skills training being included in the treatment package,
4. The emphasis being on engaging the person in an empathic, active, and collaborative therapeutic relationship to empower him or her to make changes to the current situation.

Collaborative Assessment and Management of Suicidality

The Collaborative Assessment and Management of Suicidality (CAMS) approach is specifically designed to quickly identify and effectively engage suicidal outpatients in their own clinical assessment and care (Jobes, 2000, 2003a; Jobes & Drozd, 2004; Jobes, Wong, Drozd, Conrad, & Neal-Walden, in press). CAMS is intended to modify and change *clinician* behaviors in how they initially identify, engage, assess, conceptualize, plan a treatment, and manage suicidal outpatients (Jobes, 2003b; Jobes, Luoma, Jacoby, & Mann, 1998).

The CAMS approach emphasizes a thorough and *collaborative* assessment of the patient's suicidality that ultimately leads to a problem-solving approach to suicide-specific treatment planning; in effect, the clinician and suicidal patient *coauthor* an outpatient treatment plan. CAMS is specifically designed to form and launch a strong therapeutic alliance creating an effective and superior treatment trajectory (Jobes & Drozd, 2004; Jobes et al., in press). Thus, the heart of the CAMS approach is a strong therapeutic alliance where both parties work together to develop a shared phenomenological understanding of the patient's suicidality.

Use of the Suicide Status Form (SSF) is central to CAMS. The psychometric validity and reliability of SSF quantitative (Jobes et al., 1997) and qualitative assessments are discussed in depth elsewhere (Jobes & Mann, 1999, 2000; Jobes et al., 2004; Nunno, Jobes, Peterson, Pentiuc, & Kiernan, 2002). Within the CAMS approach, the clinician asks permission to literally take a seat next to the patient to work together in the completion of the SSF assessment. The interactive assessment process is used to build the clinical partnership; what is learned through this assessment is then used to directly shape the outpatient treatment plan.

In adult outpatient samples, preliminary research has shown that CAMS may be used to quickly and economically decrease outpatient suicidal ideation and may actually decrease the use of non–mental health medical utilization (Drozd, Jobes, & Luoma, 2000; Jobes, Drozd, Neal-Walden, Wong, & Kiernan, 2003; Jobes et al., in press; Wong, 2003).

It is important to note that the CAMS approach conceptualizes the assessment and treatment of suicidal patients in a fundamentally different way than current conventional approaches (Jobes, 2000). As shown in Figure 5.1, suicidality has been traditionally viewed as a *symptom* of some central psychiatric illness (e.g., depression). This Kraepelinian approach thus emphasizes primary treatment of the diagnosed psychiatric illness with the assumption that treating the major illness will reduce the symptom of suicidality. In contemporary care, this typically means that the suicidal patient is prescribed medication for the diagnosed illness with the expectation that successful pharmacological treatment of the major illness will also include reduction of the suicidal symptom.

As depicted in Figure 5.2, CAMS embodies a different emphasis where the treatment focus and target is *suicidality*, independent of diagnosis. Through collaborative assessment and deconstruction of the patient's suicidality, important problems and goals naturally emerge; the key is for the clinician to see the world—and the seduction of suicide—through the eyes of the patient. Collaborative assessment leads to collaborative treatment planning that emphasizes a problem-oriented approach designed to reconstruct more viable ways of coping and living. In this regard, certain aspects

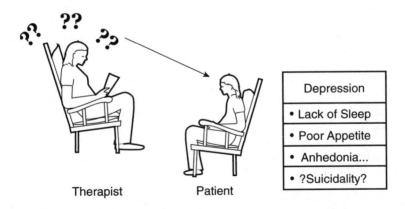

Figure 5.1. The Kraepelinian model: suicidality as a symptom of psychiatric illness. From "Collaborating to Prevent Suicide: A Clinical-Research Perspective," by D. A. Jobes, 2000, *Suicide and Life-Threatening Behavior, 30*, p. 14. Copyright 2000 by Guilford Press. Adapted with permission.

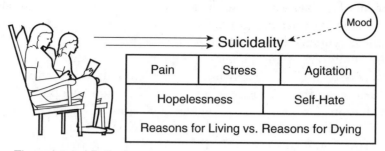

Pain	Stress	Agitation
Hopelessness		Self-Hate
Reasons for Living vs. Reasons for Dying		

Therapist and Patient

Figure 5.2. The Collaborative Assessment and Management of Suicidality (CAMS) approach. From "Collaborating to Prevent Suicide: A Clinical-Research Perspective," by D. A. Jobes, 2000, *Suicide and Life-Threatening Behavior, 30,* p. 14. Copyright 2000 by Guilford Press. Adapted with permission.

of CAMS are philosophically and strategically akin to aspects of Linehan's (1993a, 1993b) DBT and Beck's recent cognitive therapy approach to relapse prevention in suicide attempters (Henriques et al., 2003). It is important to note, however, that CAMS is flexible and facilitates therapeutic work, independent of theoretical orientation or clinical techniques. The protocol does *not* usurp clinical judgment or autonomy but does provide helpful front-end guidance on how to handle suicidality quickly and directly without getting into an adversarial struggle.

Thus, the CAMS approach uses a range of behavioral, cognitive, psychodynamic, humanistic, existential, and interpersonal approaches to assess, understand, manage, and intervene with suicidality. Critically, the approach embraces some overarching assumptions about suicidality. For example, within the CAMS approach there is a fundamental understanding that virtually all suicidality seen in patients represents some effort to cope or solve problems, although it is a very dramatic and extreme form of coping or problem solving. From this perspective, clinicians must approach suicidality in an empathic, matter-of-fact, and nonjudgmental fashion. Ironically, the clinician's ability to understand the viability and attraction of suicide as a coping option seems to provide the essential glue for forming a strong therapeutic alliance where more adaptive methods of coping can be evaluated, explored, and tested. The use of CAMS therefore prompts early identification of suicidality, a thorough assessment of the risk, development of a suicide-specific treatment plan, clinical tracking, and documentation through treatment until suicidality is resolved. The specific steps within CAMS are as follows:

1. Early identification of risk,
2. Collaborative assessment using the SSF,
3. Collaborative treatment planning,

4. Clinical tracking of "suicide status" at each session using the SSF suicide tracking form,
5. Clinical resolution of suicide status.

In summary, CAMS engages the suicidal patient differently than conventional individual psychotherapeutic approaches, thereby creating a different treatment trajectory. This trajectory is fundamentally shaped by an enhanced therapeutic alliance forged in the shared pursuit of trying to assess and understand what it *means* for the patient to be suicidal, and with that shared knowledge determining how that risk will be clinically managed. Given the challenges of clinical work with suicidality, increased concerns about malpractice liability, and the decreased use of inpatient hospitalization, CAMS may provide a promising new approach to effective clinical work with suicidal individuals on an outpatient basis (Jobes & Drozd, 2004).

CAMS—*Problem-Solving Treatment.* Jobes (2004a) has recently proposed a new development in the CAMS approach to suicidality. The Collaborative Assessment and Management of Suicidality—Problem-Solving Treatment (CAMS–PST) is a new 12-session, freestanding treatment module for suicidal outpatients. As noted above, CAMS was originally conceived as a clinical aid that could be used with a variety of treatment approaches. This eclectic and flexible use of CAMS has virtue in terms of not dictating the treatment that *must* be used. In this regard, the eclectic use of CAMS enables it to be applied to almost any theoretical orientation or treatment. However, in this sense, CAMS is not really a clinical treatment that can be readily studied in a prospective randomized clinical trial design where manualized care is necessary and treatment fidelity must be assured.

Therefore, ongoing efforts to further study CAMS required the development of a specific treatment. Accordingly, CAMS–PST emphasizes many elements of the original CAMS approach but further builds on previous research with a distinct emphasis on problem-solving aspects of care that are specific to suicide risk. In the course of 12 sessions, the CAMS–PST clinician and patient address the following five clinical domains:

1. Collaborative SSF assessment,
2. Collaborative SSF treatment planning,
3. Collaborative deconstruction of suicidogenic problems,
4. Collaborative problem-solving interventions,
5. Collaborative development of reasons for living.

Prospective research is being pursued to study the impact of CAMS–PST in comparison to treatment as usual in youthful samples targeting suicidal ideation and related behaviors. Thus, the evolution of CAMS initially led to an assessment-oriented eclectic use of CAMS (Jobes, 2004b) and has subsequently led to the development of CAMS–PST as a new short-term treatment module for suicidal outpatients (Jobes, 2004a).

Family Psychotherapy

Although individual psychotherapy is the mainstay of treating the suicidal adolescent, there are cases where family therapy may be considered the treatment of choice. This may be particularly true in cases where family conflict or pathology is central to the adolescent's continued suicidality or where family enmeshment of the adolescent is central to the adolescent's struggle toward autonomy. Thus, even with the older adolescent, family therapy should be considered and implemented, if possible, to help liberate the adolescent from a dysfunctional family system.

Family discord, poor communication, disagreements, lack of cohesive values and goals, and irregular routines and activities (Miller, King, Shain, & Naylor, 1992) are common in suicidal children and adolescents, who often feel isolated within the family. Some have suggested that suicidal teens may view themselves as expendable to the family, which becomes a central motivating force for self-annihilation (Miller et al., 1992; Pfeffer, 1986; Sabbath, 1969). Family intervention may decrease such problems, enhance effective family problem solving and conflict resolution, and reduce blame directed toward the suicidal child or adolescent (Shaffer & Pfeffer, 2001).

Brown (1985) has asserted that an adolescent's suicidal behavior frequently is reflective of a "profound deficit in the family system," causing the ultimately suicidal child "to be devoid of a deeply felt sense of being a lovable and valued person" (p. 71). As noted in chapter 3, this observation is supported by the plethora of research findings related to disturbed familial and parental systems within which the suicidal adolescent lives, from which he or she struggles for independence, and the high frequency with which a conflict or argument between the adolescent and parent precipitates suicidal behavior. The importance of the family to the etiology of the suicidal condition bespeaks its importance in the therapeutic process. Fishman (1988) goes so far as to label as "absurd" the idea of treating the troubled adolescent apart from his or her ongoing social context. Thus, it is imperative that therapists who treat adolescents at risk for suicidal behavior have knowledge of family processes and the characteristics of suicidal families in particular, and the skill to work with the family in (or, alternatively, to refer the family for) family therapy. In fact, failure to involve parents, parent surrogates, or other family members in the treatment of an adolescent can be construed as clinical therapeutic practice that is below the acceptable standard of care (see chap. 7).

The principal goals of family therapy with suicidal adolescents are modifying communication patterns and pathological interactions among family members, increasing support for the adolescent's attempts at self-care and tolerance for separation, and improving the family's problem-solving behavior. Subsidiary to these goals are those of increasing flexibility and decreasing patterns of rigidity, reinforcing family strengths and teaching reinforcement strategies for use among family members, and reframing the family's understanding of the communication and interactive patterns of the adolescent (as well as those of the parents and siblings of the adolescent). Perhaps most important, a central goal is to develop an understanding within the family of the meaning of the adolescent's suicidal behavior and the possible death wishes held by family members toward the suicidal adolescent. In this vein, Richman's (1986) psychoanalytically oriented approach to family therapy seeks to help suicidal families differentiate and accept what he terms "the terror of change," as well as opening an otherwise closed dysfunctional system.

Family-based cognitive therapy aims to reframe the family's understanding of their problems, to alter the family's maladaptive problem-solving techniques, and to encourage significant support at home and determine whether there is someone who can take action if the adolescent's behavior or mood deteriorates. Clearly, where parental pathology is intrinsic to the adolescent's suicidality, an appropriately therapeutic focus on these suicidogenic conditions is necessary. The therapist should keep in mind that a lack of observed motivation or a noncompliance of families to be involved in recommended psychotherapeutic interventions (referred to earlier) is contraindicative of family therapy. Individual psychotherapy is indicated instead of family therapy when the adolescent is older and when therapeutic issues relate primarily to the adolescent's peer system.

Harrington, Kerfoot, et al. (1998) used a brief, home-based intervention targeting family-based problem solving. The positive effects of these interventions held even among high-risk, multiple-attempt patients and patients with comorbid mood and anxiety disorders (Joiner, Voelz, & Rudd, 2001; Rudd, Rajab, et al., 1996). In addition, treatment adherence in such interventions appears to be greater for high-risk, multiple-attempt patients. However, these interventions do not appear to have a significant impact on the long-term rate of suicide attempts. Harrington and colleagues (1998) also found that their short-term family-based therapy specifically reduced suicidal ideation for those youth without major depression, pointing to a need for more research on the differential effects of interventions on suicidal subtypes (Goldsmith et al., 2002).

In some instances, parents who are noncompliant with a recommendation for family therapy will force their child (the "identified patient") into individual therapy. In such a case, it is incumbent on the psychotherapist not to collude with the parents. The potential for life-threatening, iatrogenic effects is too great. In the case that follows, the therapist's position and understanding of his patient was not one of empathy.

Case Illustration

Sally, age 15, was sent to analytic psychotherapy by her divorced mother. Sally had a history of depression and rageful acting-out behavior that included the destruction of her bedroom and one suicide attempt by overdose. Her parents, neither of whom would agree to enter either individual or family therapy themselves, were appropriately described by Sally (and others) as "intrusive, invading, overcontrolling, manipulative, narcissistic, erratic, and megalomanic." After several months of frustrating thrice-weekly sessions, Sally vehemently refused to come to treatment, stating both that she had no after-school time for herself and that it was her parents who needed treatment, not her. Her analyst maintained an analytic posture, interpreting her treatment resistance as "transferential rage"; he did not see her behavior as appropriate to either her view or her entrapment.

As noted, teaching reinforcement strategies to parents is an important aspect of family therapy. Parents can be taught to provide contingent reinforcement to the adolescent's behavior, particularly to reinforce appropriate behaviors and not to reward, primarily through attention, noncompliant and provocative behaviors. As observed by Wagner (1997), the synergy of individual therapy *and* family therapy often makes this combination of approaches the treatment of choice for many suicidal teens.

Group Psychotherapy

Group psychotherapy, with its emphasis on verbal versus physical expression and ventilation of affect, communication- and listening-skills development, peer support, and role modeling, is also a significant modality of choice, where available and led by a competent and trained group therapist.

In contrast to a variety of group-based skill-enhancement programs (to be described later), homogeneous group psychotherapy with at-risk adolescents is a relatively underreported treatment modality, given the numbers of patients necessary, and one most easily accomplished in inpatient hospital or partial hospitalization settings. Ross and Motto (1984) have described their experiences with an open-ended, mixed-gender outpatient group with eight high-risk adolescents, six of whom had made prior suicide attempts. The primary themes that emerged in the group were those relating to family and peer relationships and the control of potentially overwhelming affects and impulses. Through group support and befriending, group members learned alternative strategies for stress and affect management and improved both self-control and self-esteem. Although no operational measures of outcome were presented, the authors were encouraged by their experience with this model and suggested its use as a supplemental modality and of particular benefit where family therapy is not feasible. Similarly, Glaser (1978) has argued that group therapy is a useful alternative when the adolescent attempter is in florid rebellion against his or her parents. On the other hand, Hengeveld, Jonker, and Rooijmans (1996) have reported on difficulties in organizing short-term, high-frequency group treatments for recurrent suicide attempters with personality disorders.

Psychopharmacology: General Considerations

The use of medications can play a role in the therapy of suicidal adolescents. Although there is no agent that serves as an "antisuicide pill," medication may be helpful in cases where the diagnostic condition and related symptoms can be therapeutically targeted with the use of certain medicines (refer to Maris, Berman, & Silverman, 2000, for a more detailed review of the biology of suicide). This may be particularly true in a case where a needed level of symptom reduction allows for greater accessibility and success to verbal modes of clinical intervention. For example, antidepressants, or, more specifically, SSRIs (e.g., paroxetine, fluoxetine, sertraline) may be indicated should a major depressive disorder be diagnosed. Alternatively, major tranquilizers can be used if there is evidence of bipolar disorder or schizophrenia. Should antipsychotic neuroleptics be indicated, intramuscular injections of prolixin decanoate or halperidol may be considered to be preferable to pills, particularly to ensure compliance, although newer novel antipsychotic medications are now available in injectable form.

It should be noted, however, that only a few well-controlled drug studies with adolescent patients have appeared to date in the literature (TADS Team 2004; Trautman, 1989). Nonmedically oriented therapists need to be cautious in taking an antimedication stance a priori, because the standard of care in the treatment of the suicidal condition demands consideration of possible beneficial effects of pharmacological intervention (see chap. 8) (Goldsmith et al., 2002).

When medications are prescribed, careful monitoring of their administration to the suicidal adolescent is essential. Dosage levels must be considered carefully and hoarding of pills by the patient prevented. In a similar sense, access to medications by a suicidal adolescent must be severely limited. Pills should be administered by a trusted and available significant other, with specific instructions given to carefully guard against the easy availability of these medications to the adolescent at risk. Although medications may be essential in stabilizing and treating the suicidal child and adolescent, all administration must be carefully monitored by a third party who can report any unexpected change of mood, increase in agitation or emergency state, or unwanted side effects, and who can regulate dosage (Shaffer & Pfeffer, 2001).

When no trustworthy significant other is available—for example, in the case where parental pathology is evident—physicians should be warned to maintain control over available supplies of medications through scheduled weekly office visits and weekly control over the quantity of medications made available to the adolescent. When the therapist is not a physician but rather works with a physician who prescribes medication for referred patients, it is essential that interactive lines of communication remain open. The therapist should be familiar with the common dosages, properties, and effects, particularly adverse and side effects, of prescribed medications. Moreover, the clinician must be on top of the case and cognizant of all treatments provided to his or her patient; those who provide concurrent treatments should be informed of significant changes in the patient's behavior, significant events threatening behavioral response, and any observed responses to medication (lack of compliance, side effects, etc.) that are perhaps not reported directly to the psychopharmacologist by the youthful patient or his or her parents.

As discussed in chapter 2, one of the most exciting advances in understanding the genetic and biological bases for suicidal behavior is J. John Mann's proposed stress–diathesis model of suicide, which is formed on the basis of research findings in neurobiology (Mann, 2003; Mann, Waternaux, Haas, & Malone, 1999). Basic neurobiological research about the role of neurotransmitters (e.g., serotonin, dopamine, norepinephrine) in modulating brain function has led to the theoretical proposition that a vulnerability to suicidality may exist independently of those stressors (or risk factors) that have been correlated with suicidal behavior (especially psychiatric disorders such as mood disorders, schizophrenia, anxiety disorder, substance abuse disorders, and certain personality disorders). Mann et al. (1999) propose that there is a diathesis, or predisposition to suicidal behavior, that has distinct biological underpinnings. They contend that there are biological correlates of this diathesis for suicidal behavior as well as biological correlates of the stressors for suicidal behavior, such as major psychiatric disorders (Mann, 1998). These two domains have different biological correlates leading to different therapeutic approaches.

Empirical evidence is mounting that the most common diagnostic condition related to suicide, major depressive disorder, is clearly associated with impaired serotonergic function involving different brain regions (predominantly the ventral prefrontal cortex) but is *independent* of the serotonergic abnormality associated with the vulnerability or diathesis for suicidal behavior (Mann & Arango, 2001). The familial transmission of the stressors (i.e., psychiatric illnesses) is independent of the familial transmission of the diathesis for suicidal behavior. Hence, these authors postulate that there are familial, and almost certainly genetic, factors related to the diathesis for suicidal behavior. The consequence of such genetic factors most likely is a biological abnormality or phenotype.

Decreased brain serotonin function (as measured by CSF 5-HIAA) has been found in suicidal patients, independent of their psychiatric disorders. Hopelessness, low self-esteem, social isolation, and inadequate control of aggressive impulses may be core symptoms of such individuals (Ahrens & Linden, 1996). Of note is that people who exhibit aggressive or impulsive behavior toward others are also more prone to self directed, impulsive, aggressive, and suicidal behaviors (Verkes & Cowen, 2000). A long line of empirical research has established decreased brain serotonin function in those with mood disorders (especially major depressive disorder), which may explain why the majority of depressed individuals do not engage in suicidal behaviors and why only approximately 60% of individuals who complete suicide have a diagnosis of major depressive disorder at the time of their death (see chap. 3).

Olfson et al. (1998) conducted separate analyses of physician-reported data from the 1985 and 1993–1994 National Ambulatory Medical Care Survey, a nationally representative survey of office-based medical practices (all physicians), focusing on visits to office-based psychiatrists. The proportion of outpatient psychiatric visits in which an antidepressant was prescribed increased from 23.1% (95% confidence interval [CI], 19.7%–26.5%) in 1985 to 48.6% (95% CI, 47.5%–49.7%) in 1993–1994. After controlling for several patient variables, psychiatric patients were approximately 2.3 (95% CI, 1.8–2.9) times more likely to receive an antidepressant in 1993–1994 than in 1985. In 1993–1994, SSRIs accounted for approximately half of the psychiatric visits with an antidepressant prescription. Increases in the rate of antidepressant prescription were particularly evident for children and young adults, White persons, new patients, and patients with adjustment disorders, personality disorders, depression not otherwise specified or dysthymia, and some anxiety disorders.

Olfson, Marcus, Weissman, and Jensen (2002) analyzed medication-use data from two nationally representative surveys (1987 and 1996) of the general population, focusing on children 18 years of age and younger who used one or more prescribed psychotropic medications during the survey years. The overall annual rate of psychotropic medication use by children increased from 1.4 per 100 people in 1987 to 3.9 per 100 people in 1996 ($p < .0001$). Significant increases were found for the rate of stimulant use (0.6/100 people to 2.4/100 people), antidepressant use (0.3/100 people to 1.0/100 people), other psychotropic medications (0.6/100 people to 1.2/100 people), and prescription of different classes of psychotropic medications (0.03/100 people to 0.23/100 people), especially antidepressants and stimulants. Rates of antipsychotic and benzodiazepine use remained stable. In 1996, stimulant use was especially common in children age 6 to 14 (4.1/100 people), and antidepressant use was common in children age 15 to 18 (2/100 people). Between 1987 and 1996, there was a marked expansion in use of psychotropic medications by children, especially stimulants and antidepressants.

One brief note relates to both the patient–physician relationship and the therapist–physician relationship as being critical to the successful implementation, maintenance, and success of psychopharmacological treatments. As discussed elsewhere in this chapter, issues of transference and countertransference influence the degree to which patients are compliant with medications. Furthermore, transference and countertransference issues may also become significant in the relationship between therapist (nonphysician) and the physician (primary care physician or psychiatrist) charged with medicating the patient. Our best advice is to always be aware of these dynamics and to discuss them on a regular basis. Open and frequent communication between and among therapist, physician (psychopharmacologist), patient, and the patient's support network are key to the success of the treatment.

In fact, the majority of time, nonphysician clinicians or therapists work with a general practitioner or pediatrician in the office-based treatment of youths that involves utilizing psychotropic medications. Goodwin, Gould, Blanco, and Olfson (2001) collected data from the National Ambulatory Medical Care Survey (1992–1996) to determine prescribing patterns and clinical management approaches with visits during which psychotropic medications were prescribed to patients age 19 or under. Psychotropic medications were prescribed during 2.2% of all visits. A majority of the prescriptions for psychotropic medications (84.8%) were provided by general practitioners or pediatricians. For the visits during which a psychotropic medication was prescribed, stimulants were the most commonly prescribed (53.9% of such visits), but prescription of other classes of medications was not uncommon: antidepressants (30%), anxiolytics (7.2%), antipsychotics (7.2%), and mood stabilizers (12.7%).

Clinical Use of Psychopharmaceuticals

The use of the three major classes of psychopharmaceuticals (antidepressants, anxiolytics, and antipsychotics) for the treatment of suicidal individuals will be briefly reviewed here as they relate to the treatment of major psychiatric disorders.

Mood Spectrum Disorders

We will initially consider pharmacological treatments for unipolar (depressive) disorders before turning our attention to the psychotropic treatment of bipolar (manic–depressive) disorders.

Medications for Depressive Disorders. Antidepressants have been shown to be clearly effective in the treatment of major depressive disorders. Some studies suggest that the use of antidepressants has lowered suicide rates in clinical populations (Gunnell & Ashby, 2004; Isacsson, Bergman, & Rich, 1996; Olfson, Shaffer, et al., 2003), although these studies need to be prospectively replicated and carefully controlled.

There are well over 20 antidepressants currently available for use, only a few of which are SSRIs. Hence, global statements about causal mechanisms cannot be made because truly rigorous studies have not been undertaken. Furthermore, there is a controversy as to whether certain classes of antidepressants can be associated with the worsening, or even the emergence, of suicidal ideation or behavior in the early weeks of treatment (Jick, Kaye, & Jick 2004; Khan, Khan, Kolts, & Brown, 2003; Mann & Kapur, 1991; Montgomery, Dunner, & Dunbar, 1995). In July 2003, the Medicines and Healthcare Products Regulatory Authority (MHRA) published warnings about the use of paroxetine for those patients in the under-18 age group because of a possible increased risk of suicidal impulses. New data from various clinical trials showed episodes of self-harm and potentially suicidal behavior were between 1.5 and 3.2 times higher in patients younger than 18 taking the medication versus those receiving a placebo. As with many other drugs in this class, paroxetine does not have a license for use in the under-18 age group, but physicians have widely prescribed it (and other psychopharmaceuticals) for this age group. SSRIs are the preferred psychopharmacological treatment for adolescent depression, with the caution that suicidal youth on SSRIs must be watched for any increase in agitation or suicidality, especially in the early phase of treatment (Montgomery, 1997).

As noted earlier in the chapter, in October 2004, the U.S. Food and Drug Administration (FDA) directed manufacturers of all antidepressant drugs to revise the labeling for their products to include a boxed warning and expanded warning statements that alert health care providers to an increased risk of suicidality (suicidal thinking and behavior) in children and adolescents being treated with these agents, and to include additional information about the results of pediatric studies. The FDA also informed these manufacturers that a patient medication guide (or "MedGuide"), which will be given to patients receiving the drugs to advise them of the risk and precautions that can be taken, must be given when these drugs are prescribed. These labeling changes are consistent with the recommendations made to the FDA at a joint meeting of the Psychopharmacologic Drugs Advisory Committee and the Pediatric Drugs Advisory Committee on September 13 to 14, 2004.

The risk of suicidality for these drugs was identified in a combined analysis of short-term (up to 4-month) placebo-controlled trials of nine antidepressant drugs, including SSRIs and others, in children and adolescents with major depressive disorder, obsessive–compulsive disorder, or other psychiatric disorders. A total of 24 trials involving over 4,400 patients were included. The analysis showed a greater risk of suicidality during the first few months of treatment in those receiving antidepressants. The average risk of such events for patients on such drugs was 4%, twice the placebo risk of 2%. No suicides occurred in these trials. On the basis of these data, the FDA has determined that the following points are appropriate for inclusion in the boxed warning:

1. Antidepressants increase the risk of suicidal thinking and behavior (suicidality) in children and adolescents with major depressive disorder and other psychiatric disorders.
2. Anyone considering the use of an antidepressant in a child or adolescent for any clinical use must balance the risk of increased suicidality with the clinical need.
3. Patients who are started on drug therapy should be observed closely for clinical worsening, suicidality, or unusual changes in behavior.
4. Families and caregivers should be advised to closely observe the patient and to communicate with the prescriber.

In addition, the warning must include information as to whether the particular drug is approved for any pediatric indication(s) and, if so, which one(s).

Among the antidepressants, only fluoxetine is approved for use in treating major depressive disorder in pediatric patients. Fluoxetine, sertraline, fluvoxamine, and clomipramine are approved for obsessive–compulsive disorder in pediatric patients. None of the drugs is approved for other psychiatric indications in children.

As noted, the FDA recommended that pediatric patients being treated with antidepressants for any indication should be closely observed for clinical worsening as well as agitation, irritability, suicidality, and unusual changes in behavior, especially during the initial few months of a course of drug therapy or at times of dose changes (either increases or decreases). This monitoring should include daily observation by families and caregivers and frequent contact with the physician. It is also recommended that prescriptions for antidepressants be written for the smallest quantity of tablets consistent with good patient management to reduce the risk of overdose.

In addition to the boxed warning and other information in professional labeling on antidepressants, MedGuides are being prepared for all of the antidepressants to provide information to patients and their families and caregivers about the risk of suicidality in children and adolescents. MedGuides are intended to be distributed by the pharmacist with each prescription or refill of a medication.

As noted before, research on the efficacy of specific pharmacologic agents for preventing suicides is scant because many prior studies excluded patients who are at high risk for suicide. In addition, most clinical drug trials exclude children and adolescents. However, there are very good reasons to believe that SSRIs might reduce suicidality in children and adolescents, including their potential to reduce irritability, affective response to stress, hypersensitivity, depression, and anxiety. It remains unclear whether SSRIs might specifically increase the propensity toward suicidal ideation and action in some children and adolescents. If they do, even in a very small percentage of patients, it would speak to the use of concomitant medications to address this side effect (at least during the initial phases of antidepressant medication treatment), close monitoring over the initial few months, and a review with the adolescent and his or her family of potential adverse reactions and side effects prior to the initiation of treatment.

Medications for Bipolar Disorders. Not only has lithium been shown to be effective in the treatment of bipolar disorder, but it also has been shown to significantly reduce suicide attempt rates (Dunner, 2004; Tondo, Jamison, & Baldessarini, 1997). Other studies suggest that lithium may exert antisuicidal effects independent of its mood-stabilizing properties (Müller-Oerlinghausen, Müser-Causemann, & Volk, 1992; Schou, 1999). It is unknown what the exact mechanism is, although there is some speculation that the antisuicidal effect goes beyond the pharmacokinetics alone and relates to the increased contact and monitoring that occur when patients are prescribed lithium.

Psychotic Disorders

Suicide in patients with schizophrenia is strongly associated with depressive symptoms (Harkavy-Friedman, Nelson, Venarde, & Mann, 2004). Meltzer and Okayli (1995) found that among patients with schizophrenia who were resistant to treatment with conventional medications, treatment with clozapine improved depression and significantly lowered suicide attempts. Clozapine recently became the first drug ever approved by the FDA for reducing the risk of suicidal behavior, specifically in mood-disordered patients with schizophrenia. The recent International Suicide Prevention Trial found that clozapine significantly reduced the number of suicide attempts in a group of 980 patients with schizophrenia ($n = 609$) or schizoaffective disorder ($n = 371$), compared to olanzapine ($p < 0.005$). Patients were assessed weekly for 6 months and then biweekly for 18 months in this randomized multicenter trial. Hospitalizations or rescue interventions to prevent suicide were also reduced in the clozapine-treated group. However, the study was conducted in adults and it is not clear how these results will affect treatment of children and adolescents.

Anxiety Disorders

Patients with primary anxiety disorders (generalized anxiety disorder, panic disorder, phobias, obsessive–compulsive disorder, and posttraumatic stress disorder) have increased risk for suicide, independent of a comorbid depressive disorder. Fawcett (1988) has shown that the suicide risk is higher in patients with both anxiety symptoms and affective disorders, compared to patients who only suffer from affective disorders without anxiety. Fawcett et al. (1997) have concluded that prompt and adequate treatment of severe anxiety with anxiolytics or sedating antidepressants will lower agitation, impulsivity, and the acute risk of suicide. Nevertheless, clinicians should be cautious about prescribing medications that may reduce self-control, such as benzodiazepines. Montgomery (1997) noted that benzodiazepines may disinhibit some individuals who then exhibit aggression and suicide attempts.

Fawcett (2001) has postulated that SSRIs stimulate serotonin-2 receptors, resulting in a worsening of a patient's perception of anxiety during the first few weeks of treatment. The combination of increased anxiety and simultaneous relaxation of psychomotor inhibition elevates the risk of self-destructive acts such as suicide attempts and suicide. Fawcett argues for a need for extra vigilance on the part of physicians, therapists, and family members during the first weeks of treatment for depression with marked anxiety.

Medications and Personality Disorders

As noted, patients with borderline personality disorders are prone to a range of suicidal behaviors, including threats, gestures, self-injury, and attempts. Some of the SSRIs seem to be effective in decreasing anger, irritability, aggression, and impulsivity (Coccaro & Kavousi, 1997; Salzman et al., 1995), as well as suicide attempts (Verkes et al., 1998). To date, however, there is scant literature that directly investigates the potential use of medications for particular personality disorders.

CONCLUSION

Since the first edition of this text, there has been considerable progress in the development of various treatments relevant to suicidality. As noted early on, there is perhaps no area in the field that has undergone more changes than treatments for suicidal patients. We have reviewed the range of psychosocial modalities that are relevant to working with suicidal patients and the potential merits—and controversies—of using psychotropic medications. Although much work has been done, a great deal more is yet needed. In our next chapter, we will present our own integrative approach to treatment that we believe builds on the evolving empirical research and our collective clinical wisdom on how to best treat the suicidal adolescent.

6

AN INTEGRATIVE–ECLECTIC
APPROACH TO TREATMENT

Given the preceding review in chapter 5, we feel strongly that an integrative and eclectic approach to working with suicidal adolescents is crucial. Clearly, "one-size treatment" does not fit all, and there is tremendous value in judiciously combining theoretical perspectives, treatments, and interventions from across the spectrum of options. In this regard, our approach is fundamentally shaped by the extant empirical literature, our own considerable clinical experience, and an overriding sense that using more treatment options in a synthesized manner is superior to rigidly adhering to only one or two approaches (King & Apter, 2003). Thus, this chapter will highlight the following areas: (a) a pragmatic problem-solving treatment orientation, (b) the therapeutic encounter, (c) the role of the family, (d) the clinical alliance, (e) crisis intervention and general clinical considerations, (f) general considerations of outpatient treatment, (g) specific outpatient strategies and interventions, (h) ongoing clinical treatment, (i) termination, (j) potential pitfalls, and (k) final practice recommendations. Our in-depth consideration of all these areas should provide a valuable and pragmatic approach, as well as a useful perspective, on the full range of practice options for treating suicidal youth.

A PRAGMATIC PROBLEM-SOLVING TREATMENT ORIENTATION

It is our strong clinical bias that adolescent suicidality is best addressed with a clear bottom-line emphasis on problem solving. Indeed, as will be discussed later in the chapter, the very crux of crisis-intervention work is that of pragmatic problem solving. This stage of clinical work invariably involves a relatively brief and intensive course of sessions that are strategically pursued with a specific focus on reducing suicidality through creative problem solving. This goal is largely accomplished through a pragmatic collaborative effort—a "two heads are better than one" approach—following a relatively standardized and strategic process of exploring the problem, defining the problem, generating alternative solutions, testing hypotheses, and pursuing a resolution.

Exploring the Problem

The exploration phase of problem solving involves understanding the pertinent aspects of the precipitating event(s) and the adolescent's response(s) (emotional, cognitive, and behavioral). Through structured and semistructured questions, the therapist must carefully explore the pervasiveness, duration, and frequency of events that set off the current crisis response and threaten a loss of control. Most important, the antecedent and reinforcing conditions for suicidal ideation or behavior must be developed as framed from the patient's perspective. It is essential during this phase that reflective comments ("mirroring") be made to the adolescent to convey that a common frame of reference is being established and that his or her emotional responses are understandable and therefore valid.

For the suicidal adolescent patient, this is an opportunity for ventilation and catharsis—narcissistic gratification for both what he or she has to say and how he or she feels. For the therapist, this is an opportunity to forge an alliance and to selectively listen. Most patients "spill" their problems, prompting some of our colleagues to refer to this stage of intervention as "mess solving." Nevertheless, it is the therapist's task to skillfully identify the essential and manageable elements of the crisis situation to identify and define what is within the patient's and the therapist's capacity to modify quickly.

Defining the Problem

Defining the problem should be a natural outgrowth of the foregoing exploration. The goal of exploration is to identify and clarify the problem and to describe the problem in terms that the adolescent can accept. Such a description needs to focus on the role the adolescent's suicidality has played as one of many possible solutions. Note that the adolescent's suicidality is not presented to the patient as the problem but as a potential solution—it is the goal of problem solving to arrive at a more effective solution to the problem being defined.

The therapist's role in the problem-solving intervention is to actively lend an ego to the patient. The adolescent is confused, overwhelmed, frightened, and dysfunctional. Inappropriate solutions are grasped at as futile attempts to change a situation that is causing intense pain. The therapist offers a "third eye" and a "second brain" to better perceive and abstract the essential elements of the situation causing pain. Once defined within manageable terms, the task then shifts to a thoughtful (vs. an impulsive) consideration of various alternative solutions to the problem. It is helpful therefore to present the problem in terms of separate but integrated parts and solutions in terms of achievable steps toward an agreed-on goal.

Generating Alternative Solutions

By understanding the goal or instrumental purpose of the suicidal behavior (or the "functional analysis of motive"), the therapist can steer the patient toward available, alternative behaviors. Typically, the goal of suicidal behavior is reasonable. It is designed to satisfy some unmet need, to change some intolerable situation, to effect change in others, or to reduce painful affect. Indeed, Shneidman (1993) observes that suicidal patients often view self-destructive behavior as a viable solution to apparently intolerable and seemingly unchangeable states of psychological pain. To be therapeutic we need to help the adolescent appreciate that his or her suicidal behavior typically does not change problems for the better; in fact, it typically perpetuates and deepens problems. The therapeutic task is to arrive at more effective alternative solutions that do not require the end of one's biological existence or self-injury; however, this task first requires not acting on the suicidal urge.

One model for problem definition we have found readily understandable to adolescents is a simplified and debased psychological explanation: Stress (antecedent and precipitating events) leads to pain (feelings of hurt and fear) leads to defense (attempts to escape pain). It is often useful to schematize this on paper with the adolescent to illustrate clearly that, for example, suicidal behavior has merely been the adolescent's attempted solution (defense) to change another's unwanted behavior (stress) that has made the adolescent feel unloved, humiliated, or rejected (pain).

With this explanation and a reasonable assessment of the function of suicidal behavior, consensual goal setting can often be achieved. For example, when an adolescent has attempted suicide to decrease affective distress, the short-term goal might be to seek ways to remove the adolescent from the stress-provoking situation and to decrease the intrusiveness of anxiety symptoms. The longer-term goals might involve teaching stress-inoculation techniques, anger-management skills, or tension-reduction skills. It is in this context that short-term use of anxiolytic medications has been shown to be effective in lowering agitation and impulsivity (Fawcett, Scheftner, & Fogg, 1990).

Generating alternative strategies of problem resolution should be presented as a joint enterprise between patient and therapist, although in truth, this stage of intervention involves considerable and careful direction by the therapist. The therapist has clearer perceptions and more rational perspectives. He or she has tools to lend to the adolescent. Advice should be given. Directives and suggestions are warranted. This phase of problem-solving treatment is not the time for more passive or inactive therapeutic postures. The adolescent needs to arrive at a relatively immediate structure both with which to understand what has happened and to make some change occur.

Alternatives generated under the guidance of the therapist should involve consideration of the availability of significant others who are not part of the matrix of factors making the patient suicidal; available community resources; and the adolescent's history of and currently available coping skills. The adolescent should be exhorted to generate possible alternative solutions first, without regard to evaluating their effectiveness. The cognitive rigidity common to the suicidal mind needs to be pushed toward flexibility. The therapist should sell the model that it is better to discard choices in hand than to limit oneself to only one alternative. The therapist needs to be prepared to counter the adolescent's attempts to reject the therapist as "not understanding" when the adolescent presents merely one maladaptive choice by iterating the problem defined earlier. The therapist should maintain a focus on generating, together with the patient, as many alternatives as possible. In contrast, it should go without saying that any appropriate and creative responses should be reinforced with praise and encouragement.

Cognitive rehearsal and role playing of alternatives often helps clarify the pros and cons of, and foreseeable roadblocks to, the various ideas generated. What is sought is a hierarchy of choices available to the adolescent for hypothesis testing. Suicide should be affirmed as one of these choices, although it is hoped that this choice is seen as one of relative ineffectiveness, and a last resort—if all else fails.

Testing Hypotheses

Hypothesis testing is simply a directed and structured scientific technique of trying alternative approaches to accomplish a short-term goal. Small and accomplishable homework assignments can be structured to try this or observe that. Revisions and modifications to initial hypotheses often occur as information is collected and observations analyzed. New information should lead to modified approaches. Critically, when clinician and adolescent are engaged in a problem-solving intervention, the adolescent has actually joined with the therapist in working on the defined problems and is, by definition, no longer acutely and impulsively trying to end the problems through suicidal behavior.

Pursuing a Resolution

At this point in the collaborative process the clinician and the client have set the stage for pursuing the very issue that brought the client to the clinician in the first place—a resolution to the suicidal behaviors or suicidal crisis. The initial problems of heightened lethality and perturbation are essentially resolved, provided continued treatment can occur and the dialogue remains ongoing. It is at this point that the broader perspectives and goals of individual therapy can be approached.

THE THERAPEUTIC ENCOUNTER

It is axiomatic that the adolescent identified to be at risk for suicide needs help. However, adolescents are notoriously reluctant to seek help, particularly from mental health professionals, who are frequently viewed as helpers of "last resort" (Aaronson, Underwood, Gaffney, & Rotheram-Borus, 1989). Much of this resistance is borne out of any of a number of irrational but well-defended beliefs. Some adolescents believe that others will find out they are seeing a "shrink," either through some breach in confidentiality (the possibility of which is suggested by any number of illustrative examples all too readily offered by the adolescent) or by the adolescent's projected introspection, which gives rise to the notion that "others are paying as much attention to me as I do to myself," a process akin to the "imaginary audience" described by Elkind (1980). Elkind describes a corollary to this belief, the "personal fable," which further reinforces the adolescent's rejection of the mental health caregiver. The personal fable refers to the adolescent's belief that his or her emotional experiences are unique, a belief affirmed by the "fact" that others (the imaginary audience) are so concerned with them. This fable of uniqueness may then lead the adolescent to believe that others, including and *especially* the therapist, could not truly understand his or her problems.

Suicidal adolescents report feeling intense, painful, and distressing depression and worthlessness; anger; anxiety; and a hopeless inability to change or find a solution to frustrating circumstances (Kienhorst, Wilde, Diekstra, & Wolters, 1995; Ohring et al., 1996). Often they respond impulsively to their sense of desperation by attempting a potentially self-destructive act. Hence, psychotherapeutic techniques aim to decrease such intolerable feelings and thoughts and to reorient the cognitive and emotional perspectives of the suicidal child or adolescent (Kernberg, 1994; Spirito, 1997; Spirito & Overholser, 2003). Although this is all well and good from the clinician's bias, issues pertaining to adolescent autonomy can fly in the face of what might be a desirable treatment intervention.

Indeed, issues of autonomy underlie yet another and perhaps more distressing observation regarding the adolescent's reluctance to seek help, particularly in situations where clinical intervention has been prompted by a suicidal act. Of those adolescents seen in emergency rooms for medical and psychological intervention after self-harm behavior, only a minority have been observed to comply with recommended follow-up appointments (Rotheram-Borus, Piacentini, Cantwell, Belin, & Juwon, 2000; Rotheram-Borus, Piacentini, Miller, Graee, & Castro-Blanco, 1994, Rotheram-Borus, Piacentini, Van Rossem, et al., 1996). The remarkably high rate of noncompliance with follow-up treatment referrals may validate the notion that many suicide-related behaviors are interpersonal (instrumental), coercive, and attention getting in their intent. Therefore, once an event has received an initial clinical response, the behavior has served its intended purpose to alter the existing contingencies in the adolescent's interpersonal world. The adolescent may not have bargained for the possibility that they may now be labeled as a "psychiatric patient" or that they may be diagnosed with a mental disorder. Often, in the adolescent's mind, nothing more is to be gained by further involvement with the mental health treatment system (see the Case Illustration of Angela).

Alternatively, adolescents are quick to feign a restored equilibrium after an acute emotional upset out of fear of having more permanently changed a family system's dynamics. The same dynamics that serve to keep a battered spouse in an abusive relationship may similarly apply to the adolescent attempter, who may quickly move to restore the unacceptable but familiar homeostasis that existed before the attempt. This systemic enmeshment and felt responsibility for the family as a whole is the very opposite of the drive toward autonomy that may promote some suicide-related behavior.

Case Illustration

Angela, age 15, was treated in the emergency room after ingesting a "handful" of ampicillin in front of her mother and younger sister. This she did in retribution for being reprimanded and hit by her mother for staying out late. In the intake interview, she denied current suicidal ideation and stated that she was "glad" that her mother was worried. Once medically cleared, she was given an appointment with the outpatient psychiatry clinic for 9 days later, an appointment that was never kept. The nurse who attempted to contact the family by phone to follow up learned that the phone number given at intake had been disconnected for over 2 months.

THE ROLE OF THE FAMILY

Adolescents, like children, are almost never self-referred for psychotherapy. Most are brought to therapy by adults—their parents or guardians. This is true particularly in cases of suicide-related behaviors, which acutely signals the family system to act in the adolescent's behalf. Therefore, most referrals for follow-up care are made with the awareness of the parent or parent surrogate who originally brought the adolescent into the emergency room and was present during the emergency phase of intervention. The high rate of noncompliance to follow-up recommendations, then, more probably reflects the more serious denial or collusion of the larger family system. With the literal wound repaired, families of suicidal youth often act as if the emotional wound had healed and the system's reparation were remarkably complete without any further observation or need for further treatment.

Sometimes, as in the following case of Brenda, the family's denial persists in spite of overwhelming evidence of the need for treatment.

Case Illustration

Brenda, age 15, was accompanied to the emergency room by her aunt after ingesting approximately 20 aspirin and 15 Claritin. Her ingestion came at the end of a rageful loss of control in response to her mother's refusal to allow her to sleep in the basement. Brenda became enraged, assaulted her younger sister, broke several pieces of furniture, and tore the sheets off all the beds. She then locked herself in the bathroom, threatening to kill herself while ingesting what she could find in the medicine chest. Her mother eventually called the fire department to intercede and break down the door to the bathroom. Brenda was not brought for treatment until 6 hours later, when she complained to her aunt of abdominal discomfort. Although her attempt was seen as impulsive, she was evaluated as remaining at high risk at intake. She was unable to assure the staff that she would not overdose again, she spoke of feeling hopeless, her affect remained depressed and shallow, and she was confused and alluded to hearing voices while in the bathroom urging her to "Do it! Do it!" Additionally, she described a long history of explosive rage and assaultive behavior toward her sister. In spite of Brenda's precarious mental status, her mother refused to allow a voluntary admission into an inpatient psychiatry unit.

As in the following case of Marcie, the consequence of parental denial and noncompliance is the maintenance of the adolescent as the "bad seed" and as the identified patient (Sabbath, 1969; Shapiro & Freedman, 1987).

Case Illustration

Marcie, age 13, was brought to the emergency room by her cousin after overdosing on an unknown quantity of unknown pills. The precipitating event for the ingestion was a dispute with her mother in which Marcie was hit in the face and threatened with being put into foster care. When Marcie's mother was contacted by phone, she denied the alleged beating, stating instead that Marcie was an unmanageable child who stayed out all night with unknown boys with whom she was sexually promiscuous. She refused to come to the hospital to meet with the treatment team.

One significant consequence of parental noncompliance is a maintained probability of further suicidal behavior on the part of the adolescent, perhaps in an increasingly lethal cycle of cause-and-effect behavior among family members. In Litt, Cuskey, and Rudd's (1983) study, 60% of noncompliant adolescents had made a prior suicide attempt; none of the compliant adolescent patients had made a prior attempt. This cycle, then, appears to underlie repetitive suicide attempts and defines a major task of therapy if and when a therapeutic alliance can be secured. This task is to help the family of the adolescent interpret their child's behavior as a family event and (particularly for the older adolescent or where family pathology is significant) help the adolescent truly gain autonomy from the family (Wagner, 1997; Wagner, Silverman, & Martin, 2003).

Perhaps it is tautological to suggest that one way to accomplish this end is to offer the adolescent individual psychotherapy in addition to or, if necessary, instead of family therapy. More to the point and irrespective of modality, the success of any treatment effort depends on securing the initial compliance of the adolescent and his or her family and then establishing an effective working relationship with the adolescent that strives to develop mutually agreed-on, nonsuicidal, non-self-destructive alternatives for coping.

THE CLINICAL ALLIANCE

Throughout the psychotherapy research literature, the quality of the therapeutic alliance is consistently cited as the most critical factor in successful psychotherapy process and outcome (Goldfried, 1980). In our pursuit of developing quality alliances with adolescent patients, it is important to remember some basic facts and some critical interpersonal dynamics. Adolescents, particularly those in suicidal crisis, are much more like children than adults. At one and the same time, they paradoxically ask permission to act like adults and seek excuses from responsibility when they have acted like children. Yet, like adults, they wish to have their independent thoughts respected, their feelings validated, and their personhood affirmed—all reasonable and appropriate needs.

Beyond these developmental issues, there are important generational challenges as well when a clinician endeavors to form an alliance with an adolescent. It is essential to remember that (a) the clinician is automatically and generically perceived by the teen as being a member of the same generation from which the adolescent is seeking autonomy; that (b) the adolescent's associations to seeing a "doctor" may have a long history that, more than likely, is antagonistic to the type of relationship both necessary to and sought by the clinician; that and (c) the doctor's office is a foreign, often formal place connoting role distinction and pomposity—not exactly the most inviting environment for your average troubled teen. Perhaps most critically, at the start of treatment the clinician is almost always viewed by the adolescent suspiciously as the parent's (or guardian's) "henchman"—a parental proxy or agent who is hired and paid exorbitant fees to fix the adolescent (i.e., taking the parent's side in all matters and finding a way to make the child behave as the parents wish). Given the various issues of adolescent development, distrustful perceptions, and often distorted assumptions, it takes a great deal of care and skill to win the trust of a teen, let alone build a viable therapeutic alliance.

Enhancing the Clinical Alliance

Fortunately, there are a variety of methods for fostering, deepening, and enhancing clinical alliances with adolescent patients. Fundamentally, therapists must be capable of being a "good-enough parent." Clinical management of the delicate balance between maintaining authority and being humanly accessible may be augmented by use of warmth within limits, appropriate self-disclosure, appropriate use of humor, and general flexibility (e.g., shorter or longer sessions depending on the patient's tolerance). A collaborative and more interactive approach often is useful. A clear understanding about confidentiality should be established—what will and what will not be disclosed to parents can be a crucial and contentious issue (which we will discuss later in this chapter). Ideally, the adolescent patient should be actively involved in treatment planning. The therapist's accessibility and availability to the patient and criteria for contacting the clinician between sessions should be clearly negotiated and understood as well. It is perhaps self-evident that empathic listening paired with active verbal validation and recognition of the teen's feelings and perspective are critical to alliance formation.

Although we need to work to actively foster an alliance with adolescent patients, we must nevertheless balance these efforts by maintaining a necessary sense of professional authority and role. For some clinicians it is tempting to "buddy-up" to the adolescent patient, potentially aligning themselves against the parents to strategically win the trust of the adolescent. It is a tightrope walk between working to form intimacy and trust with the suicidal adolescent while also maintaining a sense of balance by preserving one's authority and professionalism. Walking the proverbial tightrope between these roles is often difficult and perhaps can best be accomplished with idiosyncratic style. Although we have little reason to suggest how individual therapists should decorate their offices or present themselves to their patients, there are some generic considerations we would like to propose:

1. The physician's white lab coat belongs only in hospital settings, and only then when appropriate to role and function.
2. Doctors should be introduced as "Doctor..." and not by first name. Role expertise should be fostered while interpersonal distance reduced. For example, a face-to-face or angular seating arrangement is greatly preferable to that which places an office desk between patient and doctor.
3. Flexibility in session length is often useful; sessions may be limited to 30 to 45 minutes or potentially go longer when the adolescent gives evidence of tolerating more time with the clinician.
4. Adolescent patients may be encouraged to come to treatment, if they wish, with a friend who will wait for them and

with whom they can leave at the end of the session. There may be virtue in considering having the friend join the session, if seen as appropriate by both patient and therapist (Bernstein, 1989).

5. Warmth and comfort in the office setting are important. This implies flexibility on the clinician's part regarding rules for such things as snacking and drinking soft-drinks during sessions.

6. Warmth within the limits of the clinical role likewise is important. It can be helpful for the therapist to thoughtfully self-disclose where relevant, to use humor where appropriate, and to appreciate and reinforce the adolescent's humor, even as more often cynically expressed.

7. Within reason and good judgment it can sometimes be helpful to change the routine or be more flexible in how therapy is done. For example, leaving the confines of the clinical office setting by going for a walk with the teenage patient can be very affective and positive. Of course, "indulging" the adolescent patient by changing one's routine or modifying one's rules must be done with care and forethought.

Generally speaking, working with suicidal adolescents is best done by a clinician who is available to the suicidal patient and family. Such clinicians need to have skills and training in managing suicidal crises. A clear goal is to relate to the adolescent patient in an honest and consistent manner, providing an objective understanding of the patient's attitudes and life problems, and conveying a sense of optimism and activity (Katz, 1995; Pfeffer, 1990).

The Initial Clinical Contact

Forming a viable clinical alliance with a suicidal adolescent often depends on how one orchestrates the initial clinical contact with the adolescent and the responsible adults in the adolescent's life. At a minimum, an overview of clinical treatment should be provided in the initial clinical contact; information about the frequency of meetings, the expected course of treatment (with a particular focus on early goals), cancellations, and some statement about termination of treatment should be readily provided. As noted earlier and as we will discuss in more depth later in the chapter, issues of confidentiality and communication with parents about what is discussed in treatment should be made particularly clear to all parties. The adolescent and parents need to be presented with an absolutely clear statement regarding the therapist's rules for confidentiality and under what conditions and circumstances significant adults (particularly parents) will be involved or receive communications.

We have often found it helpful to anticipate the adolescent's distrust of these statements and to acknowledge that time together will have to prove the measure of the therapist's trustworthiness with regard to these issues. Similarly, the therapist's criteria for considering hospitalization may be presented while strategically aligning with the adolescent's (typical) wish not to be hospitalized. That is, hospital intervention can be presented as one of "last resort" to maximize the adolescent's alliance and compliance with outpatient work.

The therapist's availability and accessibility to the child and parents also should be explicitly discussed, as should the expected use of the telephone as an adjunct to the time spent in the practice office. Finally, it is very important to specifically provide the opportunity for the adolescent and responsible adults to ask any questions they may have about the treatment process.

Transference

Adolescent suicidal patients are often demanding and dependent, and may well replicate earlier disturbed relationships through transference. Therapists should accept and work through various projections and transferences, and strive to provide a potentially novel and stable good object relationship experience for the adolescent. For example, clinicians should give a clear and consistent message that they want to hear about, and can tolerate, the patient's painful affect. As Guntrip (1968) noted, basic "ego relatedness" is possible when the therapist shares in the patient's painful inner world as a consistent, real, and good object.

Ideally, the clinician's major transferential role will be that of the good parent who does not expect behavior beyond the child's level of emotional maturity. Because adolescents typically struggle with issues of separation, helplessness, and dependency, these issues should be expected, accepted, and tolerated by the therapist. Critically, good parents (clinicians) nurture and gratify needs, but always within limits. Therefore, limit setting is equally crucial to the patient, the therapist, and the overall efficacy of the psychotherapy.

Countertransference

Suicidal adolescents may regress and become increasingly demanding as dependency on the therapist evolves. Moreover, they may express anger and aggression as well as passivity—various behaviors that will test a therapist's patience and resolve and, perhaps, confirm the patient's own sense that he or she is undeserving of care or love. It is important to note that most therapists typically expect their patients to be motivated to use therapeutic help and actively engage in the process on their own behalf. Unfortunately, suicidal patients (particularly adolescents) often do not readily fit into the good patient role. Therapists confronted with such patients may respond with a variety of negative attitudes and feelings, such as mild irritation, exasperation, wishes to be rid of the patient, and even countertransferential hate (Maltsberger & Buie, 1974). If these attitudes and feelings are left unchecked, there may be iatrogenic effects via therapist withdrawal, malice, and avoidance (Jobes & Maltsberger, 1995).

To address countertransference, therapists should attempt to limit the number of seriously suicidal patients within their caseload to no more than a few at a time. It is also crucial that professional consultation be ready and available at all times. It is further helpful for therapists to keep abreast of institutional policies and procedures as well as relevant laws and statutes related to suicide and commitment procedures. Finally, self-monitoring and good record keeping are essential to bring to awareness unconscious negative thoughts and impulses that may interfere with effective psychotherapy.

Modestin (1987) has argued that "the best protection…is constant self-monitoring…along with the ability to allow negative impulses to become conscious and to keep them in consciousness without excessive shame or guilt" (p. 384). Not all countertransference responses are negative. Some reactions, when both tolerated and understood, can be effective tools in understanding both the patient and others' reactions to the patient (Maltsberger, 1986). Paralleling the therapist's tolerance of his or her own negative affect (e.g., anxiety, anger, despair), the therapist must endeavor to give a clear and consistent message that he or she can tolerate the patient's painful affect; a stance which may markedly contrast parents who may not be able to tolerate the patient's painful affect (Hynes, 1989). When the clinician demonstrates a capacity to tolerate and metabolize painful affective material, the net result may prove to be an enhanced therapeutic alliance.

One important way to accomplish this kind of tolerance is to keep in mind what we know about both adolescence and suicidality (i.e., that neither is constant). It is critical that we do not succumb to false expectations and suffer ultimate disappointment when expectations are potentially dashed. For example, a therapist cannot afford to be lulled into comfort and self-congratulation by the first report of improvement from a suicidal adolescent. Because the suicidal urge is state-dependent and therefore tends to wax and wane contingent on the adolescent's environmental context, mental status, and so on, the patient is quite likely to express suicidal feelings again. Accordingly, a continuous focus by the therapist on risk assessment should help to reduce the potential for surprising developments or disappointment.

As already noted, the therapist's expectations must continue to include a clear and consistent awareness that the suicidal adolescent enters treatment with a transferential set of perceptions already in hand. The patient, irrespective of age, may often behave like a helpless child, lacking in skills or resources to effectively cope with the exigencies of everyday life. These deficits may exist either because the adolescent has yet to learn more adaptive problem-solving skills or potentially because the adolescent is temporarily out of control (because of overwhelming stress or psychopathology). Such patients may become demanding and dependent on the therapist or, as noted before, will replicate earlier disturbed relationships, harboring and acting out fantasies the therapist cannot, in reality, fulfill (refer to Jobes & Karmel, 1996, for an in-depth case example).

On one level, it is imperative that the therapist not share the patient's delusions (e.g., of the therapist's omnipotence). On another level, it is important that the therapist accept the transferential relationship and play the part of the good parent. Good parents do not expect behavior beyond the level of the patient's emotional maturity. Adolescents, in general, develop asynchronously; physical, emotional, and cognitive development do not keep equally apace. Suicidal adolescents have the added problems of dependency and helplessness, which need to be accepted as givens and tolerated by the therapist. Good parents nurture and gratify needs but maintain a sense of judgment, decency, and appropriate limits. Thus, appropriate limit setting is both in the interest of the adolescent patient and clinician to ensure the healthy management of negative countertransferential reactions. In a similar vein, it is essential that the therapist examine his or her attributions regarding the cause of the patient's difficulties. There is an important distinction, for example, between (a) viewing suicidal patients as ill and therefore entitled to treatment by an expert and (b) seeing suicidal behavior as an attempt to solve the problem of pain stemming from skill deficits or psychopathology that are treatable. From the latter perspective, the patient can receive help without a label of weakness or culpability and can participate in using that help in a manner that enhances autonomy and self-esteem (Berman, 2003; Berman & Cohen-Sandler, 1982b).

As a corollary, the tendency of some therapists to use pejorative labels to describe therapeutic impasses and undesirable patient behavior serves only to distance the therapist and create transferential and countertransferential problems. When the patient displays distancing, help-rejecting behaviors, he or she is expressing dynamics learned and inherent in relationships in existence long before the establishment of the therapeutic relationship. So-called resistance usually identifies a primary reason for the patient to *be in treatment* rather than an obstacle to treatment. To blame the patient for displaying behavior that illustrates why he or she is in the situation precipitating therapy clearly displays the therapist's problem more than the patient's. Resistance is simply a learned defense, and such defenses serve a protective function (S. Lerner & H. E. Lerner, 1983). It is a reflection of the patient's problematic, yet potentially understandable, adaptation to his or her often chaotic interpersonal environment, and, as such, it should be expected by the therapist and not pejoratively labeled.

Indeed, to label the suicidal patient's behavior as "manipulative" similarly can often lead to a withdrawal of therapeutic contact when it may provide reason for intensifying therapeutic involvement. In the same vein, we have often noted how often exasperating clinicians may label—often inappropriately—nearly any and all difficult and manipulative patients as "borderlines." Some observers have astutely remarked that "it is noteworthy...that only patients are called manipulative" (Hamilton, Decker, & Rumbaut, 1986). Manipulation is operationally defined as efforts to influence, manage, operate, or control "shrewdly or deviously" (Morris, 1973). Obviously, it is the deviousness of the adolescent's attempt to control another's (including the therapist's) behavior that gives rise to the negative responses related to this behavior. Yet, were adolescents capable of accomplishing their goals "shrewdly," they would, again, have little reason to need therapy. The suicidal adolescent should therefore be *expected* to manipulate others; in turn, clinicians should overtly establish as an objective of treatment helping the adolescent accomplish a more effective and more direct control over his or her interpersonal world. Moreover, troubled teens also need to learn to accept and appreciate those situations in which such control is unlikely to ever be exercised successfully. This critical reframing demands greater, rather than less, involvement in the treatment of the suicidal adolescent. With particular reference to the patient using suicidal behavior as a method of influence and control (i.e., instrumental behavior), clear and consistent limit setting by the therapist, including a matter-of-fact, nonreinforcing response to any suicidal behavior by the patient, needs to be emphasized.

CRISIS INTERVENTION AND GENERAL CLINICAL CONSIDERATIONS

There is only one goal of crisis intervention: namely, to keep the patient physically safe and alive until the crisis situation has resolved. Therefore, extraordinary means of maintaining safety and stability are sometimes necessary, including voluntary or even involuntary inpatient hospitalization. Various authors have discussed at length the range of responses that make up what we generally associate with crisis intervention with suicidal youth. For example, these responses typically include protection from self-harm using the following types of crisis interventions: (a) restricting access to means of death; (b) decreasing the patient's interpersonal isolation; (c) removing or decreasing agitation, anxiety, and sleep loss; (d) structuring the treatment (e.g., increasing number of sessions); (e) working on problem-solving skills; (f) providing accessibility and availability to the patient; (g) creating future linkages; (h) negotiating the maintenance of safety and the development of a contingency plan; and (i) using inpatient hospitalization in cases of clear and imminent suicide risk (Cimbolic & Jobes, 1990; Jobes & Berman, 1993). As in the first edition of this book, we will highlight again many of these interventions in the current section, but there are also some new additions and modifications to crisis intervention that have emerged over the past 15 years.

To begin our discussion of crisis intervention, we must first underscore that the acute suicidal crisis is produced by a unique synergy of intrapersonal, environmental, social, and situational variables. As a response to life crises, suicide and self-destructive behaviors occur among people of every age, gender, race, religion, and economic and social class. Because patients may respond to life crises with suicidal behaviors, clinicians must be prepared to face the immediate tasks of assessing possible and imminent self-harm behavior while concurrently protecting against that possibility. Often these tasks must be accomplished under conditions of incongruent expectations and goals. As previously noted, suicidal people tend to defy the health professional's expectation that fostering and maintaining life is a shared goal of patient and doctor (Hoff, 1994). Suicidal individuals, especially adolescents, are invariably brought to treatment by others under conditions of acute distress and a volitional threat to life. As discussed, these are not at all the characteristics of the "good patient"; instead, these qualities bring tension and instability to (and potentially impede) the necessary working alliance with the caregiver (Vlasek, 1975). Thus, working with depressed and suicidal people can be a frightening and difficult undertaking. Indeed, the assessment, treatment, and general management of an acute suicidal crisis are perhaps among the most difficult challenges faced by any mental health professional, despite attempted suicide being one of the most frequently encountered of all mental health emergencies (Roberts, 1991; Schein, 1976).

Consistent with the commonly accepted definition of *crisis* (e.g., Slaikeu, 1990) is the notion that acute emotional upset, dysphoria, and the associated sense of urgency to act in a self-destructive and potentially life-ending way will usually subside with adequate time and protective constraints (e.g., hospitalization in cases of imminent danger). Underlying skill deficits in emotion regulation, distress tolerance, interpersonal dysfunction, impulsivity, problem solving, and related cognitive distortion and rigidity typically do not "spontaneously remit"; these issues and deficits usually require appropriate clinical intervention and targeted care (e.g., Rudd, 1998).

It is well established that suicidal impulses and behaviors are largely temporal, transient, and situation-specific. As stated above, suicide intent is state-dependent and tends to wax and wane. Empirical research indicates that most people who kill themselves give some form of prior warning (see Shafii, Carrigan, Whittinghill, & Derrick, 1985) and often desire an outcome other than the termination of their biological existence (Shneidman, 1995). The crisis clinician is thus in a pivotal, potentially life-saving, position. Accurate clinical risk assessment and appropriate interventions can literally make a life-or-death difference.

As described by Roberts (1991), clinicians may effectively respond to an individual in crisis by working through seven stages of intervention: (a) assessing lethality and safety needs, (b) establishing rapport and communication, (c) identifying major problems, (d) dealing with feelings and providing support, (e) exploring possible alternatives, (f) formulating an action plan, and (g) providing follow-up. Roberts's seven-stage model was developed to apply broadly to a range of crises, but it is clearly applicable to specific interventions with suicidal youth.

Following a suicidal event, Shaffer and Pfeffer (2001) offer a useful checklist of steps a clinician should follow in determining whether a suicidal adolescent can be discharged from an emergency setting. For example, they suggest that children and adolescents should never be discharged from the emergency service without the child's or adolescent's caretaker having verified the child's or adolescent's account. The clinician should also see the caretaker to discuss making firearms and lethal medications inaccessible to the child (Kruesi et al., 1999). There is empirical evidence that unless this discussion is held, parents will not, on their own initiative, take the necessary precautions (McManus et al., 1997). Parents who own firearms are usually more willing to secure firearms than to remove them.

Limiting the adolescent's access to alcohol or other potentially disinhibiting substances should also be discussed with the adolescent and family. Before discharge, the clinician must have a good understanding of the amount of support that will be available for the child or adolescent if he or she is discharged to home. The clinician should recognize that treatment recommendations are more likely to be followed if they match the expectations of the family, if they are economically feasible, and if the parent is well and available enough to support attendance. The family's experience in the emergency room may also color the referral process (Rotheram-Borus, Piacentini, Miller, et al., 1996; Rotheram-Borus, Piacentini, Van Rossem, et al., 1996).

It is important to note that training in suicidal crisis intervention and specific systems of crisis intervention has become increasingly popular since the first edition of this text. For example, a group of suicidologists located in Calgary, Canada, has developed a very popular community gatekeeper training called ASIST (Applied Suicide Intervention Skills Training; www.livingworks.net). This particular crisis-intervention approach is taught in intensive training workshops emphasizing role-playing among ordinary community gatekeepers who may be uniquely positioned to intervene with a suicidal person (e.g., ministers, priests, rabbis, police officers, and school personnel). Similarly, Paul Quinnett has developed the Question, Persuade, and Refer (QPR) approach, which is designed to train community gatekeepers on how to help someone in a suicidal crisis using the Question, Persuade, and Refer action steps. The QPR gatekeeper training program is now available through an interactive, Web-enabled CD-ROM (see www.qprinstitute.com).

Clear and Imminent Danger and the Role of Hospitalization

The bottom-line "tail that wags the dog" of crisis intervention involves the prospect of "clear and imminent" danger. As discussed elsewhere (Jobes & Maltsberger, 1995), what exactly constitutes "clear and imminent" is both cloudy and time-indeterminable, yet the requisite actions linked to this notion are considerable, with implications for the patient's civil liberties and personal freedom. Our sense is that the "clear and imminent" call requires, and always will require, subjective judgment about the potential for physical danger within the next few hours. How imminent is "imminent" may perhaps extend over 24 hours; the term simply has defied reasonable definition. Whatever the case, clinicians are charged with the responsibility of making this determination and, if so judged, of pursuing the safety afforded by an inpatient setting, preferably through voluntary admission or alternatively through involuntary commitment if necessary.

Hospitalization

Given the various issues—including stigma, managed-care constraints, and the significantly reduced numbers of available adolescent inpatient beds—the need for hospitalization, management while hospitalized, and post-discharge planning are tinged with medicolegal implications and liability issues for clinician, hospital staff, and hospital administration. Suffice it to say that the decision to hospitalize an adolescent is never an easy one.

Recently, the American Academy of Child and Adolescent Psychiatry released a "Practice Parameter for the Assessment and Treatment of Children and Adolescents with Suicidal Behavior" (Shaffer & Pfeffer, 2001). Regarding the criteria for hospitalization, they state

> Mental status features predictive of short-term difficulty include the inability to form an alliance with the clinician, a lack of truthfulness or inability to discuss or regulate emotion and behavior, psychotic thinking, current intoxication from drugs or alcohol, or multiple previous serious suicide attempts. (p. 585)

The clinician should ask himself or herself whether the patient can form an alliance to report suicidal intent or suicidal plans. Can the clinician identify and decrease potential sources of noncompliance, provide adequate family psychoeducation to limit family conflicts and aberrant communication, reduce social-skill and problem-solving deficits, and focus on co-occurring psychopathology (Berman & Jobes, 1991; Brent, 1997; Brent & Perper, 1995; Piacentini et al., 1995)?

The need for emergency medical care, the presence of significant or volatile psychopathology, the use of a highly lethal or unusual method, or the assessed imminent and unabated risk of suicide are additional indicators for hospital admission and the inpatient treatment of the suicidal adolescent. Inpatient psychiatric care allows for complete medical management of any injuries sustained from an attempt. In addition, inpatient care provides for (a) the removal of the adolescent from sources of environmental stress and the immediate change in patient–systems (family, peer, etc.) dynamics, (b) maximum control over the possibility of unresisted self-harm behavior, (c) multiple sources of observation and assessment; (d) 24-hour support, (e) decreased interpersonal isolation and increased behavioral activity through multimodal treatments and required participant interactions (e.g., milieu therapy; formal and informal peer group meetings; ward government; point-system contingent reward programs; art, music, and recreational therapies; intensive psychotherapy [individual and family]; and pharmacotherapies), and (f) a stepwise attainment of goals leading to a planned discharge to follow-up outpatient care.

Once stabilized and out of crisis, the adolescent can ideally be transitioned into outpatient care (notwithstanding the previously noted challenges in follow-up outpatient compliance). Our bias is that shorter hospital stays are preferable given the possibility of reinforcing regression through an institutional dependency, the intrusive depersonalization and stigmata attendant to the need to be hospitalized, and being removed from one's everyday social milieu.

As discussed earlier in this chapter, the opportunity to maintain an adolescent on an inpatient psychiatric unit long enough to benefit from multimodal interventions has become severely limited in more recent years. Moreover, postdischarge planning is often fraught with multiple layers of concern. Attention to issues of safety nets and returning patients to safe environments is critical, especially because the rate of mortality from suicide is elevated beginning as early as 1 week to about 1 year after discharge. Initiating and maintaining social-support networks and professional contact postdischarge is often critical to the success of a hospitalization and challenging to achieve.

The American Association of Suicidology (AAS; 2003) has recently developed specific recommendations for consideration prior to therapeutic passes, trial leaves, or discharge. These recommendations are appropriate for inpatient psychiatric units in general hospitals, psychiatric hospitals, and residential treatment centers. It is important to note that the AAS recommendations are not comprehensive treatment guidelines regarding suicidal people and are not a substitute for the clinical decisions that arise from the treatment relationship. Moreover, empirical support for these recommendations is less than conclusive. However, on the basis of the literature that does exist, and in the collective clinical experience of the AAS authors, these recommendations represent current best practices. Obviously these recommendations are subject to change as additional research is published and new knowledge is gained.

Generally speaking, trial leaves, passes, and discharges are transitions that necessarily result in a reduction in the level of monitoring of patients known to be at elevated risk for suicidal behaviors. Frequently, some or many clinical or environmental risk factors remain to at least some degree. Vulnerability to suicide may persist and may be exacerbated while the individual is on pass or leave, or after discharge from an inpatient or residential setting. Although the use of trial leaves and passes has declined significantly because of changes in the system of financing for inpatient care, they still warrant selective use but with an understanding that they require a careful balancing of risks and benefits.

For patients at significant risk of suicide, risk may also be exacerbated during the period following discharge from an inpatient setting. That risk is most elevated in the month following discharge, with about half of all post-discharge suicides occurring in the week following discharge (Appleby et al., 1999; Ho, 2003). It is also clear that patients do not always accurately self-report suicidal ideation to mental health professionals, increasing the importance of communication and coordination between families and the treatment team (Busch, Fawcett, & Jacobs, 2003). To minimize suicide risk during these periods of transition, the American Association of Suicidology issued the recommendations shown in Exhibit 6.1.

EXHIBIT 6.1

AAS Recommendations for Inpatient and Residential Patients Known to Be at Elevated Risk for Suicide

1. Treatment providers should reevaluate suicide risk prior to approving a pass or discharge.

2. The decision to grant a pass or discharge should include a risk–benefit analysis to support the clinical decision. This decision should be based, at minimum, on a consideration of the following: (a) response to treatment, (b) external support(s), (c) current mental status, (d) presence of current suicidal ideation, (e) availability of means to suicide (including firearms), (f) patient's adherence to treatment, (g) history of impulsivity, and (h) past suicide attempts. The assessment should also include a review of the crisis that precipitated the admission, whether the precipitating crisis has abated or been resolved, and whether any new potential precipitants have arisen during hospitalization. The crisis precipitating admission may have been resolved but profound distress may be arising for additional reasons.

3. The simple denial of suicidal ideation is insufficient evidence to determine an absence of suicide risk. One recent study of 76 suicides that occurred during inpatient hospitalization or immediately after discharge reported that 78% of the patients had denied suicidal ideation when last assessed (Busch et al., 2003)

4. Reliance on a so-called no-suicide contract should not be considered, by itself, to be a sufficient intervention on which to make a pass or discharge recommendation.

EXHIBIT 6.1 (Continued)

5. The availability of the family and other sources of support should be assessed, as well as their willingness and ability to provide such support.

6. A family session should routinely be recommended.

7. Both the patient and the family or significant others should be given instructions regarding suicide and its associated risks, including, but not limited to, the following: (a) warning signs of suicide, (b) the increased risk for suicide during pass or following discharge, (c) the need for medication and other treatment adherence, (d) explanation of how psychiatric symptoms may impair judgment, (e) explanation of the need for the patient to avoid use of intoxicants and how intoxicants increase risk, (f) the need for the removal of the means for suicide, and (g) the particular risk associated with firearms.

8. The patient and family or significant others should be given explicit instructions on how to access the treating physician or therapist regarding questions, observations, or concerns, and should be given information regarding how to access treating clinicians after office hours as well as any limitations on their availability. Emergency phone numbers that are available 24 hours a day, 7 days a week, such as psychiatric emergency services and crisis lines, should also be given.

9. If family members or significant others are asked to assist in the outpatient monitoring of risk, specific instructions should be given, including action steps to be taken in the event of felt concern or the development of a crisis. Consideration should be given to providing these in writing, as oral instructions may be difficult to recall accurately in the midst of a crisis.

10. Where permitted by law, and with the patient's written permission, the patient's family members or significant others should be alerted to the patient's history of suicidal thinking, feeling, behavior, and nonfatal suicide attempts.

11. Every effort should be made to assure that the clinicians with responsibility for treating the patient following discharge receive a copy of the patient's discharge summary.

12. The patient should have an outpatient follow-up appointment scheduled before discharge.

13. Prescription of psychiatric medications at pass and discharge transitions should be undertaken with consideration of the potential for overdose.

14. All clinical and residential staff should have training in the assessment and management of suicidal risk, and the identification and promotion of protective factors.

Note. © American Association of Suicidology, 2003. Reprinted with permission.

Partial Hospitalization

In more recent years, partial hospitalization (sometimes referred to as "day treatment") offers a viable alternative to inpatient hospitalization by offering a form of intensive multidisciplinary treatments and skilled observation and support that does not include overnight stays associated with traditional inpatient treatment. Partial hospitalization can be an excellent alternative to acute psychiatric inpatient hospitalization if the child or adolescent is considered to be disturbed but stable, or containable enough in a supportive home or other residential setting. Because of the decreased costs involved, partial hospitalization may provide longer treatment than acute hospitalization to stabilize the emotional condition and address environmental stresses and problems of the patient. It may also be used as a "step down" from acute psychiatric hospitalization to transition the patient back into full involvement in school and family activities (Shaffer & Pfeffer, 2001).

GENERAL CONSIDERATIONS OF OUTPATIENT TREATMENT WITH SUICIDAL ADOLESCENTS

Without definitive research-based guidelines for effective treatment models, clinicians must decide for themselves on a logical treatment plan based on a theory of intervention and a thorough understanding of the suicidal adolescent, both generic and specific to the presenting case. Most therapists provide a particular type of therapy to their patients that may be independent of patient diagnosis. In other words, patients are most likely to get the type and format of psychotherapy in which the therapist is most experienced, trained, or devoted (Beutler, 1989). This is not necessarily problematic in that psychotherapy research has shown that much of the treatment outcome variance may be attributable more to the therapist–patient compatibility than to specific therapeutic approaches or techniques (Beutler & Mitchell, 1981).

Nevertheless, when treating suicidal adolescents, the therapist needs a specific therapeutic plan that identifies problems, goals, and interventions that will provide both short- and long-term antidotes to the problems of the suicidal adolescent. At a minimum, the therapeutic plan needs to address the site of treatment (e.g., outpatient psychotherapy practice), the involved therapeutic agents (e.g., primary and adjunct therapists and therapies), and the multimodality of approach to treatment (e.g., primarily individual, group or family therapy, as well as pharmacotherapy). The treatment plan must also overtly identify the therapeutic strategies that will be used to target and attain specific treatment goals (see the Case of Rhonda below). Critically, the specific features just described need to appear explicitly in written form as a central component of the patient's medical record.

Case Illustration

Rhonda, age 17, ingested the contents of her family medicine chest (primarily antihistamines and analgesics) at 3 a.m. She was brought to the emergency room by her father, who found her confused and difficult to awaken for school in the morning. On intake, Rhonda stated that she had wanted "to drown out the pain" and that she had been preoccupied for several days with ending bad feelings she had about herself, ever since her "boyfriend" tried to drown himself. This relationship not only served to precipitate her suicide attempt but was also prototypical of the predisposing condition to her suicidality. Rhonda was enmeshed with this friend, Tommy, who was either an asexual or bisexual classmate and who was described as both confused and mesmerizing, like a cult leader. Each of them, in turn, had triangulated this relationship with a 15-year-old male who appeared to be of sexual interest more to Tommy than to Rhonda. Rhonda's bad feelings about herself were in part stimulated by Tommy's competitive strivings and attempts to control Rhonda's involvement with this younger male.

Underlying this enmeshment was Rhonda's fusion with her father, to whom she told all, including sexual secrets and behaviors. In turn, her father related his extramarital affairs to Rhonda. Without discomfort, Rhonda shared that both she and her father were "perpetually horny." Although there was no intimation of overt incestuous behavior, Rhonda had clearly displaced her mother (who was described as meek, naive, and socially unskilled).

Treatment goals were established through individual and family outpatient therapy and included concurrent individual therapy for her father, as well as marital therapy. Family therapy focused on the establishment of appropriate boundaries and role responsibilities. Marital therapy attempted to increase the parental union and develop an appropriate sexual relationship.

Rhonda's individual work focused on increasingly differentiating from her father and from Tommy, while increasing her involvement with healthy peer supports and youth groups. Definitions of self-worth were established to be dependent not on pleasing a dominant male (either her father or Tommy), but on aspects of self-control and self-determination.

One of the clear benefits of outpatient psychotherapy is that it allows for in-vivo maintenance and observation of the adolescent's routine functioning and interactions. In contrast to inpatient care, outpatient treatment additionally provides (a) support for the adolescent's autonomy and self-esteem to endure under difficult conditions and to function successfully,

(b) the long-term involvement of both a consistent therapist and available community services, and (c) the potential coordination with the adolescent's school (e.g., teachers and counselors) and other professionals in the resource network available to the adolescent. Given all of the above considerations, we are strongly biased on the side of pursuing *outpatient* care over inpatient hospitalization.

Indeed, we would even say that inpatient intervention should be avoided if it is at all possible to substitute intensive and appropriate outpatient care (Jobes, 2003a). In this vein we want to argue both sides of the fence. On the one hand we believe that inpatient treatment can be appropriate, necessary, and life-saving in certain extreme cases. On the other hand, we believe that the vast majority of cases can and should be handled on an outpatient basis if treatment can be appropriately structured and sufficient outpatient safety is achieved. To this end, the remainder of this section will focus on appropriate interventions that can be routinely applied in outpatient treatment.

It is of course our bias that certain outpatient approaches and clinical attitudes will optimize therapeutic success with suicidal youth. For example, in the short term, we concur with Trautman (1989), who suggests that effective work with suicidal youth should be active, assertive, explanatory, and responsive. These qualities are attributes common to briefer, problem-solving oriented (primarily cognitive–behavioral) therapies. Moreover, it is our experience that adolescent suicidal patients tend to respond best to structured forms of psychotherapy, particularly those that teach new coping skills and techniques. As will be apparent, however, there remains considerable room for a more interpretive psychodynamically oriented approach to treatment, particularly in longer-term treatment scenarios.

SPECIFIC OUTPATIENT STRATEGIES AND INTERVENTIONS

What follows are considerations that we believe are the key elements of what constitutes viable outpatient care with suicidal youth. Given the potential seriousness of suicidal ideation and suicidal behaviors, each of the following elements should at least be considered as part of a comprehensive plan of outpatient care.

Structuring the Treatment

The adolescent in crisis needs handles onto which he or she may grab for security and stabilization. Linkage with the therapist begins to accomplish that goal. Linkage with treatment represents a sustaining alliance with both the therapist and the future, of which the adolescent's perspective may be severely limited by past experience, overwhelming affect, and cognitive constriction.

Treatment structuring, or therapy pretraining, can occur in a number of significant ways. The initial contact is just that—the first of an indefinite number in a sequence of further contacts. The goal of the initial contact must clearly be stated between therapist and patient: to formulate and define the problem so as to intervene with a successful solution. The long-term goal may also be stated: to achieve significant change where deemed necessary to improve the adolescent's sense of self and relationship to others. To accomplish these ends, the therapist structures for the adolescent their mutual responsibilities (the patient to stay alive and come to therapy; the therapist to provide therapy). The therapist further structures future sessions (e.g., the when, where, frequency, time limits) and describes the process of therapy (e.g., in the beginning, mutual problem solving to reduce the patient's suicidality; issues of confidentiality). Together, the dyad must establish the therapeutic goals, with the therapist carefully attending to make sure that these goals are within the patient's capability to achieve.

When necessary, the therapist should provide factual information to the adolescent, replacing confusing experiences with clarity and labels. Symptoms need to be named and syndromes described as clusters of symptoms and experiences with which the adolescent can identify. It is helpful to place such diagnostic structures in the frame of hope; that is, the therapist must emphasize that the disorder can be treated (analogies to physical illness may be helpful in this regard), and that some symptoms or diagnostic conditions are caused by biochemistry, which can be regulated, others by negative learnings and nonnurturant environments, which are changeable, and still others by the effects of skill deficits, which are remediable. None of these frames convey the typical suicidal adolescent belief that what is at the core of his or her experience is an awful, very bad, no-good person!

The therapist needs to play soothsayer as well, providing some statements about what the adolescent can expect. These include a longer-term statement about the termination of therapy and, more immediately, an understanding that the suicidal urge waxes, wanes, and returns. This understanding prepares the adolescent not to be disappointed following inappropriate expectations early in treatment.

Case Illustration

Ellen, age 15, was a sophomore in high school when she was referred for outpatient treatment 5 weeks after cutting her wrists at home. A tall, physically well-developed girl, she was cooperative in the initial interview, fully oriented, but clearly depressed. She reported that she cut herself because she was "mad at herself" because she was "doing nothing right." Few specific referents were given to explain what standards were not being met to her satisfaction.

Ellen described a long history of self-harm behavior, beginning in the fifth grade, when she first scratched hesitation marks into her wrist with the point of a school compass after being reprimanded by her parents. Her second episode occurred 2 years later, when she ingested a number of different medications from her parents' medicine chest. This was the only one of her several gestures and attempts that required medical attention and led to her first course of outpatient psychotherapy. She reported that this attempt was in response to her "wanting attention" at a time when her parents were involved with her older brother (age 19), who had been arrested for stealing a car. Two other low-lethality attempts occurred over the subsequent 2 years and prior to the latest, one by cutting and one by overdose. Both these attempts were in response to conflicts within her family, feelings of intense guilt, and an apparent need to punish herself. With regard to self-punishment, she stated that she often "craved pain" and that she accomplished this by digging her long nails deep into her skin or repeatedly scratching herself.

Ellen was the youngest of three children and the only girl. Her oldest brother was expelled from high school soon after his arrest for car theft. He currently lived in a halfway house for recovering drug abusers. He also had a history of self-harm behavior. Her 18-year-old brother quit high school and was currently in the Army.

Ellen's father had battled a 20-year history of depression, for which he had been treated with medication during most of that time. In her early childhood, he frequently physically abused her, although no incidents were reported in the last 7 years. His father was reported to be depressed as well. Ellen's mother, who had become pregnant at 17, was the daughter of an alcoholic mother. Her father had died of cancer when she was 8. She was the oldest of three; her brother was a drug-addicted bisexual and her sister had been sexually abused by her stepfather.

Ellen, once a straight-A student, was currently performing at a C average. She was sexually active and, with her mother's permission, had begun taking the pill at age 12. In spite of this precaution, she had had two pregnancies and two miscarriages in the last 3 years. She was currently involved with and having daily sexual relations with a sometime employed, 21-year-old Danny. Ellen had experimented with LSD, PCP, cocaine, and marijuana. She drank regularly on the weekends with her boyfriend and smoked a pack of cigarettes each day.

Ellen exemplified well Maltsberger's (1986) "unendurable affect states." As a child of abuse, her introjections were hostile. She was the bad child, worthless, guilty, and fearful. She had great difficulty trusting others and was convinced she was beyond lovability. She was contemptuous of herself and unable to express her rage externally. Only slight refuge came from her retreat into drugs or alcohol. The following journal entry illustrated well Ellen's sense of painful entrapment in a world of confusion and guilt:

Case Illustration

Why does it have to be me with the problems, emotions so hard to handle? Why should he have to handle them, problems that I imagine? Because supposedly there are no problems. Why can't I see that and just be happy? No, I am not allowed...something will not allow me to be happy.

They each have their own place to be put, but I can't figure out where they belong. It is like a puzzle and I have the wrong pieces. Or do I just not fit? I want to die. Why should they have to put up with my problems? Why do they have to, or do they? Do they know what's going on? Do I know?

The treatment plan outlined for Ellen consisted of individual and group outpatient psychotherapy, with goals of decreasing suicidal tendencies and depression, decreasing substance abuse, and enhancing self-worth and self-esteem. A cognitive approach was taken to decrease depressogenic thinking, inappropriate guilt, and self-blame. Group psychotherapy focused on establishing a peer support system, on defining ways Ellen could establish her sense of lovability other than through a sexual relationship with a "must-have" boyfriend, and on establishing greater self-respect in her relationships in general. Anticipatory problem-solving training allowed her to increasingly approach a number of difficult interactions with forethought rather than impulsivity. Inherent in her treatment was a greater appreciation of her father's and grandfather's depressions and her parents' unintended reinforcement of her early and active sexuality. This was accomplished through monthly family sessions that also allowed discussion of the effects of her brother's acting out on both her and her parents.

In the course of an 18-month treatment, prior to a 6-month termination and follow-up phase (see "Termination" section), Ellen was able to establish much of her self-worth on evidence of self-control—no further self-harm episodes occurred—and on her academic performance, which improved to consistent honor roll status. She got and maintained a part-time job, the earnings from which went primarily toward the purchase and support of a used car. She eventually felt strong enough to risk leaving her long-standing relationship with Danny, after first becoming pregnant and making a difficult decision to have an abortion; thereafter she chose a series of increasingly respectful boyfriends. In these relationships, sex was not the reason for contact. After several early episodes of drug experimentation, including one frightening experience of freebasing cocaine, she essentially had been drug-free during the last several months of therapy, except for occasional beer-drinking at parties. Treatment ended at the end of her senior year, soon after her acceptance to college.

The following case of John similarly outlines a treatment process.

Case Illustration

The initial goals of John's (see Case Illustration, chap. 4, p. 165) outpatient treatment consisted of decreasing his suicidality, his depression, and his sensitivity or reactivity to perceived rejections. Concurrently, a primary focus was established on increasing interpersonal skills. Treatment was multimodal in focus, including both cognitive and behavioral approaches and much insight-oriented discussion of early wounds and disappointments by his parents. Because John's parents were several hundred miles away from his college and because of his age, no family therapy was offered. However, directives for dealing with and reframing his parents' involvement were given when home visits were to occur.

Six weeks after initiating outpatient therapy, John became increasingly agitated and took a low-lethality overdose of sleeping pills. He rejected the need for hospitalization. Instead, he implied through multiple references to a secret he was not ready to share, but which defined his self-hate and aloneness, that this attempt was meant to relieve the tension created by this withholding. Within a week, he shared that he was gay "at least in spirit." Over the next several months, he began experimenting sexually, acting with disregard for directives about safe sex and proclaiming relief that "the chains were off." He refused to use recommended resources to learn about the gay world and to enter a group composed of gay men his age who were "coming out." Instead, he increasingly behaved inappropriately, choosing as a liaison anyone who would approach him at a gay bar. He soon developed a preoccupation with a fellow student whom he began to idealize in spite of receiving clearly rejecting responses, including an off-putting suggestion, "Why don't you just kill yourself and leave me alone." After this, John ingested more than 50 Extra Strength Tylenol and immediately called for an emergency therapy appointment in which he divulged his ingestion and accepted immediate hospitalization.

In spite of this, his sixth suicide attempt and second hospitalization, John's therapist viewed this as a pivotal period in his therapy. For the first time, John had opened the door to a long-held secret and reason for self-hate, and he no longer rejected hospital care. His ingestion was followed by an immediate seeking of help and intervention.

John's 10-day inpatient treatment involved intensive individual therapy; milieu therapy, including structured ward meetings; and the usual range of group therapies, including recreational, art, and occupational groups. His outpatient therapist, although not the primary treating therapist, continued to meet with John while he was hospitalized and consulted with the inpatient staff on treatment decisions. On discharge, John returned to outpatient care, now meeting twice weekly. After another 3 weeks of tenuous stabilization, John gradually accepted his therapist's recommendations to accept the several referrals to support groups in the gay community. With this involvement came increasing contact with gay friends who were not sexual partners, and within 4 months, a coming-out with his parents, who were surprisingly accepting, informing John that they had suspected he was gay for the past few years. Through this period of adjustment, John was able to accept the metaphor of "the ugly duckling" to explain his earlier social anxiety and self-hate. Two years after beginning therapy, John was involved in a healthy gay relationship of some 4 months' duration and began terminating ongoing treatment.

Temporal Linkages

Insight-oriented therapies are constructed on a foundation of the past—in fact, the distant past, rooted in the influences of early childhood. Irrespective of the type of therapy, it is important that suicidal adolescents, whose perspectives are severely constricted by the pain of the immediate precipitant and the demands of suicidal urges, have the proverbial blinders removed so that they may appreciate that the current intense moment is but a moment in time. Time stretches from early childhood through the present and into the future.

There are a number of orientation techniques that reinforce the idea of temporality to the adolescent. Whenever impulses can be thwarted by delay, time—perhaps the most powerful of therapeutics—can work to provide a lessened sense of urgency. The therapeutic pitch to be sold to the adolescent is simply, "What can be done in May can be done in December." Future time perspective is reinforced by discussions about the course or process of treatment and by rehearsal strategies to deal with the recurrence of suicidal urges, as well as any of a multitude of situations one might foresee and for which responses might be predeveloped.

As noted, continuity with the past is the hallmark of classical therapies and is also appropriate to the newer, more behavioral treatments, which still must allow for the role of prior learning and patterns developed over time. These should be shared with the adolescent patient, particularly as they help explain the problems presented and help attribute causes to something other than the adolescent's inadequacy. The fact that the adolescent has weathered past crises and depressions also needs to be affirmed, although one has to be careful not to stimulate the adolescent's tendency to interpret such feedback as evidence of how long he or she has struggled to no avail and therefore as evidence of ultimate failure.

Of note in this context is the importance of interpretation. Interpretations, particularly those relating to the transference relationship, provide essential links between current observation and early childhood referents. Borderline patients especially will both attack and idealize the therapist, often rapidly shifting these projections. Interpreted connections to early parental introjections and their resulting masochistic and destructive transference reactions help the patient come to give up unrealistic expectations of both himself or herself and others. As a result, we might expect less idealization and need to attack, as self and therapist are viewed more realistically.

The relationship between the "now" and future time can be reinforced between sessions by the assignment of concrete, accomplishable homework assignments that link session (x) to session $(x + 1)$ and by between-session telephone contacts. Anxiety about the short-term future can be diffused by such "connectors" or bridging maneuvers. Another example is a long-held technique designed to stimulate curiosity and to bridge sessions, in which patient-initiated content, introduced toward the end of a session, is held for discussion at the start of the next session, as suggested by the therapist's statement, "That's really worth spending some time talking about. But we have so little time left today, let's make sure we start Tuesday's session on that note. I've got some thoughts about that I'd really like to share with you then."

Protection From Self-Harm

One obvious initial target goal in any therapeutic plan must be that of protecting the adolescent from possible self-harm behaviors. As discussed in the following section, clinical efforts to decrease lethality and perturbation (Shneidman, 1985) must be central to the treatment plan. Intrapsychic, interpersonal, biological, and environmental factors that predispose the patient to be at risk must be individually identified and targeted in treatment. In extreme cases, this may require removal from a stressful to a nonstressful environment (e.g., hospitalization), but more often than not, this involves an active engagement of mutual problem solving. In addition to problem solving, interpersonal support, caring, and warmth, otherwise felt to be absent in the adolescent's network of significant others, must be offered.

Decreasing Perturbation

As we have discussed, external stressors often overwhelm the adolescent's potential resources and coping skills; predisposing conditions may make a patient highly vulnerable to otherwise minor events, not unlike the acute pain experienced when iodine is used to cleanse an open skin wound. The level of upset and reactivity can severely constrict the adolescent's ability to process information and use cognitive resources to solve problems. Particularly where symptoms of acute anxiety and insomnia are concerned, immediate attention must be given to settling down the patient's level of upset. Consideration of well-monitored medication, and the active removal of external sources of stress and perturbation, should be sought. Often, immediate cognitive–behavioral attention to anxiety-provoking cognitions, such as those that lead to anticipatory fears of impending decompensation, can be dramatically helpful to the suicidal youth.

Accessibility and Availability

It follows that protection from self-harm implicates the clinician's accessibility and availability to the patient. As noted before, individual sessions may need to be scheduled as often as deemed necessary, particularly in the early stages of treatment. Appropriate contact with the therapist should be encouraged and reinforced to occur between sessions and particularly during periods of heightened affect and reactivity. By definition, accessibility means the possibility of contact at any time of the day or night. Obviously, this means that the telephone or Internet can serve as adjunctive means of contact between therapist and patient. This does not mean that the therapist should feel constrained to be available 24 hours a day, nor that demands for contact, no matter how unreasonable, will be met. The following are some guidelines for maximizing the appropriate use of this means of contact:

1. Give your phone number and those of at least two others of use should you be unreachable. One of these should be that of a 24-hour telephone service (suicide prevention center, hotline, crisis center) that you have screened to be well administered. Make sure your patient retains these numbers, for example, on a wallet card.
2. Teach your patient how, when, and where to reach you. For example, providing on paper a picture of your typical weekly schedule helps the adolescent understand that you may be teaching on one day, typically at home writing on another, and so on. Inform them when you usually check your e-mail.
3. Educate your patient as to what to expect when and if he or she calls. For example, an answering machine (or service) at the office or at home may answer when you are unavailable, or if you are reached at 2 a.m., you may be groggy, speak unintelligibly for the first few moments, and so forth. These directives should include contingency instructions—that is, "If this happens, then do the following…," that you do not always check your e-mail at a certain time, and that this method of communication may not be the most confidential, reliable, or timely manner of connecting with you.
4. Educate your patient as to what to expect should they call a crisis service. It may be helpful to explore his or her attitudes toward and history of using a hotline. It may be helpful to role-play or, better yet, to have an in-vivo phone call to a hotline to desensitize any discomfort with this resource and to dispel concerns about flashing red lights suddenly appearing and sirens sounding at the front door.
5. Remind the adolescent that he or she is to call *before* acting on any suicidal wish and that he or she does not have to feel suicidal to call.
6. Encourage noncrisis phone contacts, such as immediate follow-ups to homework assignments, or brief between-session check-ins. These contacts should be kept brief, less than 5 minutes, and can be scheduled if necessary to occur at defined times of mutual convenience. Over time, these calls can be channeled into prearranged contacts, thereby reinforcing the

adolescent's tolerance for distress until the appointed hour of contact.

7. Do not assume a priori that this telephone accessibility will be abused. Interpret for your patient, at the appropriate time, that too-frequent late-night or early-morning telephone calls indicate to you that the therapy has yet to sufficiently help the patient get needed rest and sleep; that what has prompted calls overnight could have been handled perhaps even better in the morning (again, "tolerating" some distress); and that such frequent need to connect may indicate that office sessions are currently scheduled too infrequently and that, therefore, either more sessions must be scheduled or, if at the limit of what is feasible to arrange, hospitalization needs to be considered.

8. Use the telephone proactively. With perhaps no more of an agenda than "I was thinking about how what we talked about in our last session went…," find reason to reinforce a message of your constancy and care for your patient as a nonsuicidal person. These calls also should be kept quite brief and used as a link between in-office contacts.

9. Last, as insurance, be sure that you have available and accessible names and addresses of significant others (family and friends) should, in the midst of a suicidal crisis, you need to contact the adolescent's supports to help effect a rescue. Nothing can feel more agonizing, short of news of a completed suicide, than to attempt to deal with such an event without any way to help emergency medical personnel locate an uncooperative patient.

The Coping Card Approach

Various authors have discussed variations of what Judith Beck (1995) has called a "coping card" (refer to approaches discussed by Chiles & Strosahl, 1995; Jobes, 2003b; Rudd, Joiner, & Rajab, 2001). The spirit of this approach is to create an opportunity for the patient to develop and learn about coping and self-soothing. More specifically, the clinician may use the back of their business card to have the patient identify five (therapeutic) things they can do to cope with distress (e.g., go for a walk, listen to music, talk to a friend). With support and guidance from the clinician, a thorough list is discussed and created. The clinician then adds the phone numbers as the sixth item for coping. The clinician then encourages and seeks a good-faith commitment on the patient's part to go through and use each of the five initial coping strategies *before* they seek to call the clinician.

The message here is wonderfully mixed; the patient can literally learn to cope on their own by progressively using successive strategies that were conceived in therapy, and the clinician is still available to them should those strategies not succeed in resolving the crisis. Figuratively speaking, the clinician is still there for the patient, but he or she is simply the sixth means of coping rather than the first. With successive effort and modification, patients can learn to rely on their own ability to cope without necessarily engaging the therapist immediately, yet the clinician remains available and supportive (albeit at the bottom of the coping list).

The Strategic Use of E-Mail

The use of e-mail presents yet another interesting and contemporary point of discussion. Much has been written about the assumptions inherent in the use of e-mail as a prime mode of communication—especially as it relates to regular contact and psychiatric emergencies (Hsiung, 2002). As the use of e-mail as a communication tool in the general population has increased dramatically over the past decade, so, too, although to a lesser degree, has its use as a tool for communication between clinicians and patients. Recently, the American Medical Informatics Association (AMIA) developed guidelines for the use of e-mail in clinical settings, and this set of guidelines was made accessible to physicians by the American Medical Association.

Silk and Yager (2003) reviewed these guidelines and, from clinical and administrative viewpoints, attempted to apply them to the mental health field. The authors felt that, prior to any e-mail communications between physicians and patients, informed consent forms should be used and the limits and appropriateness of e-mail communications be delineated to patients (e.g., some describe e-mail as electronic postcards that do not afford confidentiality that patients routinely expect). They related that patients need to know what the expected turnaround time was for replies from the physician and whether e-mails were read by the physician during weekends. They also spoke about the issue of privacy, including sharing e-mails with third parties, the issue of encryption of e-mails, and alerting physicians to log off their computers when away from them. Clinicians and patients also need to establish the kind of e-mails that would be appropriate. It was suggested that topics related to medication management, including dosages, side effects, and renewal of prescriptions, would be appropriate. Psychodynamic psychotherapy was deemed not appropriate to be conducted via e-mail.

However, the authors noted some special exceptions in this area. The authors also discussed the appropriate contents of the subject line and identification parts of the e-mail as well as advising that physicians develop an automatic reply system to acknowledge receipt of e-mail messages. Clinicians were also advised to reply to e-mail messages when they were read and acted on and that all patient e-mail, including the clinician response, should be kept as part of the patients' medical records. The authors then addressed the issue of tone of e-mail and the boundary difficulties inherent in this regard. The issue of whether e-mail communications should be subject to being billed for was also discussed. The authors concluded that for e-mail communication with patients, therapists should pay particular attention to issues of confidentiality, boundary issues, and communicative tone. They felt that e-mail could potentially provide a useful tool for enhancing communication between clinicians and their patients.

Interactive Journaling

For patients who enjoy writing and find this activity potentially therapeutic, we suggest that the clinical dyad consider the use of interactive journaling. This approach simply involves a session-by-session exchange of journal notebooks that provide an opportunity for a between-session written dialog to occur. Often patients write more than the clinician about their therapy, questions, concerns, and worries. Clinicians in turn may make shorter entries that tend to comment on the patient's entries. For patients who enjoy writing, interactive journaling can be a powerful and effective adjunct to ongoing psychotherapy.

The Use of Therapeutic Contracts

As noted at the beginning of this chapter, a recent and contentious issue in contemporary suicidology is the problematic and potentially countertherapeutic use of what are commonly called "no-suicide contracts" or, alternatively, "safety contracts." As discussed by Jobes (2003a),

> ...among mental health providers there are tremendous needs for more evolved clinical knowledge...(for example) struggles around hospitalization also interact with the problematic use of "safety contracts," where patients and doctors dance around "commitments to safety." In truth, these safety contracts are neither contractual nor do they ensure genuine safety, because they tend to emphasize what patients *won't* do versus what they *will* do (should they feel desperate, impulsive, or self-destructive). Clinicians need to develop better outpatient treatment plans that are specific to suicide—what patients (and clinicians) will do if the patient feels impulsive, out of control, and self-destructive. (p. 3)

Basically the critique is not so much of the desired goal of insuring outpatient safety and stability, but rather our perception of what we consider to be a particularly problematic use of such contracts. Specifically, the problem arises when a clinician uses these contracts to *extract* promises of safety from a patient when the patient knows that the only alternative to not agreeing to the contract conditions will be a hospitalization (or civil commitment). As the party in the position of control, clinicians can exert tremendous pressure and coercion to achieve a safety contract from their patients (Simon, 1999). However, this inappropriate use of safety contracting all too often leap-frogs over the most important focus of what may ensure outpatient safety—namely, a carefully negotiated, appropriate, and viable outpatient treatment plan (M. C. Miller, 1999). We fear that, all too often, clinicians are lulled into a false sense of security and relief, perceiving that they are actually protecting themselves from malpractice liability because they have successfully extracted promises of safety from their patients. We have routinely seen in forensic cases where clinicians cling to their use of a safety contract to defend the complete absence of a written and viable outpatient treatment plan in the medical record—something that is typically not lost on the plaintiff's expert and lawyer.

As a more viable alternative consideration, Rudd et al. (2001) advocate the use of a "crisis response plan" and argue that clinicians should exert their considerable influence to encourage patients to commit to their treatment or to commit to the specific interventions that make up the crisis response plan. Our point in this discussion is to raise concerns about the distorted use or potentially countertherapeutic overreliance on safety contracts. We feel strongly that clinicians should be emphasizing therapeutic interventions, actively engaging the patients in therapeutic negotiations that specifically and precisely focus on how the patient will cope, remain stable, and maintain genuine safety. Having shared our experience and biases, let us now continue with a balanced consideration of what may be positive and potentially negative about the use of traditional safety contracts.

Generally speaking, in outpatient settings, no-suicide or safety contracts are routinely used as a major element of treatment, particularly in the early stages of clinical care. A written or verbal "no-suicide" contract is commonly negotiated at the start of treatment in the hope that it will improve treatment compliance and reduce the likelihood of further suicidal behavior (Brent, 1997; Rotheram, 1987). Traditionally, no-suicide contracts have been used as a "probe" to understand the patient's and family's ability to institute change and to "test" the degree to which the patient has made a commitment to the therapy and to the goal of no further self-destructive behaviors. The appropriate use of contracts or (better yet) therapeutic "agreements" with adolescents can both structure the link between clinician and patient while simultaneously providing valuable assessment data. Where the patient's response is equivocal (the "I'll try" or "Maybe" variety), the therapist has significant information regarding the patient's relative ambivalence about truly engaging in treatment, potentially opening the door for consideration of more restrictive treatment alternatives (e.g., hospitalization). To date, however, no empirical studies have evaluated the actual efficacy of traditional safety contracting (Reid, 1998).

As previously noted, the traditional use of safety contracts involves having the child or adolescent promise not to engage in suicidal behavior (self-harm behaviors of any type). Linked to this promise is often an additional commitment that the child or adolescent will inform his or her parents, the therapist, or some other responsible adult if he or she has thoughts of suicide, develops plans to commit suicide, or feels unable to maintain his or her safety (Simon, 1991). Again, we need to emphasize that a safety contract should never serve as a substitute for a carefully designed outpatient treatment plan that includes a variety of different types of safety-oriented interventions (M. C. Miller, 1999). Indeed, in cases where there is a disturbance of mental status, the clinician should never be solely reliant on the no-suicide contract (Egan, Rivera, Robillard, & Hanson, 1997; Fergusson & Lynskey, 1995).

Although traditional use of no-suicide or safety contracts can be quite reassuring to family members and clinicians, there is increasing concern about various limitations that must be considered when using one (Miller, Jacobs, & Gutheil, 1998). Clearly, safety contracts should be used only if a comprehensive assessment of the suicidal patient's mental state and a consideration of the developmental state indicate that the patient understands what commitment actually means. Such contracts should never be seen as anything more than an adjunct to the management of patients with low intent. To be sure, even if the patient agrees to such a contract, the suicide risk may still persist. Moreover, it is important to note that a traditional no-suicide contract may actually lessen a patient's communication of stress and dysphoria, decrease the potential for developing a therapeutic alliance, and impair risk management (Shaffer & Pfeffer, 2001).

As noted previously, coercive communications, such as "Unless you promise not to attempt suicide, I will keep you in the hospital or tell your parents about your behavior," should never be used; such threats may actually inspire deceit and defiance. In spite of the best efforts of patients and their families, there are occasions when the patient or members of the family support system are not always able to adhere to the contract for various reasons (e.g., when patients are feeling overwhelmed or are experiencing cognitive distortions or coexistent pathologies). Furthermore, traditional safety contracts assume that the clinician is always available to respond to the call from the patient, his or her family members, or the emergency room when a patient activates the aspects of the contract. Needless to say, the contract potentially puts too much of a burden on support systems, the family, and the therapist. Given all these potential problems and pitfalls, we ultimately concur with Rudd et al. (2001) in their emphasis on encouraging the adolescent patient to commit to the therapy or specific in-crisis intervention rather than merely promising "safety."

In our professional training experience, we have found that many clinicians find themselves uncomfortable with recent critiques of safety contracting, insisting that this approach is a tried-and-true way of engaging the patient on the side of staying safe. For those who still value the approach,

Ashworth (2001) has offered the following common-sense recommendations to optimize the use of safety contracts:

1. Contract parameters must be clear, in writing, and checked and updated regularly.
2. Family members and supportive others should be included in negotiating the safety plan and contract. This planning is best undertaken in an open forum with all support people present.
3. Access to lethal means to self-harm (i.e., guns and medications in the home) must be prevented in agreement with family members.
4. Twenty-four-hour availability of the mental health clinician or backup in case of a crisis situation is needed. This coverage signals to the client and his or her family that the clinician is concerned about the seriousness of the situation (M. C. Miller, 1999).

Thus, to come full circle, we do not advocate the traditional use of no-suicide or safety contracts (agreements) to improve treatment compliance, and we are wary that such contracts are all too often used to provide the *clinician* with a false sense of assurance that a patient will not engage in self-destructive behaviors while under a clinician's care. We feel much more inclined to support Rudd et al.'s (2001) notion of carefully developing an outpatient crisis response plan and having both the patient and clinician commit to that plan for safety and to the treatment endeavor in which they are both engaged (see also discussion by Jobes & Drozd, 2004).

Restricting Access to Lethal Means

As noted in chapter 1, suicidal behavior requires access to, the availability of, and often knowledge of a potentially lethal method. Additionally, readily available methods of self-destruction are those overwhelmingly chosen to be used by suicidal people either on impulse or by design. Such a patient is immediately confronted with a new problem at a time of cognitive constriction and inflexibility, thereby limiting the application of good problem-solving skills. The potential for significant self-harm is severely reduced when these means are either unavailable or inaccessible to the suicidal patient (cf., Lester, 1989). Therefore, the clinician, personally or through available significant others, should ask about and subsequently take the necessary steps to remove available means (e.g., firearms, pills) from the adolescent's access or, at a minimum, arrange for significant delay in their ready access to the patient.

Where significant others are involved in control over means availability, they need to be educated in the significance of this responsibility and guided by the therapist's directives only. Firearms kept in the home can be safely stored under locked conditions or can be removed from the home and handed over to significant others for safekeeping, literally placed in a safe-deposit box or car trunk (with the key under another's control), or brought to the therapist for control. Ammunition can be stored separately and under lock-and-key. Triggers can be removed to inactivate the firearm. Medicine chests need to be purged of old and unnecessary prescriptions and over-the-counter remedies, and all pills placed in the care of a significant other (Berman, Shepherd, & Silverman, 2003).

When the adolescent (or his or her parent) is asked to take responsible steps toward control, it often is helpful to place this directive in a self-disclosing frame, such as "It makes me uncomfortable...," with statements to the patient that such anxiety on the therapist's part would undesirably interfere with the therapist's helpfulness. In some cases, such as the following of Ray, there is almost a literal scream for protection from self-destructive urges, only to have that communication remain apparently unheard by others in a position to act on behalf of the adolescent.

Case Illustration

Ray, age 14, had made three suicide attempts prior to completing his suicide. Each time there had been someone there to stop him. He communicated often about his intent, remarking that "Life's a bitch" and asking others about which way they thought it would be better to kill oneself. The day before his death, he asked his mother whether it would be better to stick a gun "in your mouth or in your temple?" He chose the latter, using a .357 Magnum that had been kept, fully loaded, in his mother's nightstand.

Decreasing Social Isolation

During the suicidal crisis, it is imperative that the adolescent not be left alone. The patient should effectively be under "suicide watch" by a significant other. Significant others must be explicitly told not to leave the patient alone during the crisis phase. Pills can be popped quickly, acquiring and discharging a firearm can occur in minutes, and brain damage (anoxia) by hanging can occur within 5 minutes. In cases where family or friends are unavailable, hospitalization may necessarily have to be considered. Various other interventions can and should be used to help decrease social isolation.

Support Linkages

The therapist often becomes the primary support in the suicidal patient's life. Too often, we learn just how significant this bond is through the unfortunate consequence of a completed suicide. It is one of the therapist's primary responsibilities to recognize the power of his or her role and function for patients, and to use that power to broaden the patient's attachments beyond the therapeutic office. For example, it is hoped that with the therapist as an ally, the adolescent can realign with his or her family, if appropriate, or separate to the world of peer alliances. Increasingly, therapy should be directed toward the identification of available and healthy significant others and promotion of those linkages. As the support network develops and is trusted, the adolescent's interpersonal isolation is diffused, and adjunct "therapists" become available among whom the demands of the suicidal adolescent can be spread.

Where relevant in the adolescent's natural environment, cultural interests, hobbies, or religious group involvement may be available. Where they were once of value but decathected as the adolescent increasingly alienated himself or herself, they may be reattached as emotional energy becomes freed up and available. In some settings, such as high schools or colleges, supports may be created by adjunctive lay therapists. For example, trained volunteers may serve as "companions" (McCarthy, Wasserman, & Ferree, 1975) or befrienders, or surrogate siblings who provide both basic support functions and social-skills training to the adolescent patient. Furthermore, various therapy modalities are built on a premise of broadened support. For example, group therapy and inpatient ward meetings serve similar support functions, as do telephone hotlines.

Social-Skills Training

The lack of available social supports and resources and the difficulties in allying with available resources have been noted frequently as areas of deficit among suicidal adolescents. These deficits often underlie those adolescent suicide-related behaviors that are intended to control others or gain control over the responses of others. However, these behaviors, designed to accomplish a worthwhile goal, are often counterproductive (e.g., they only alienate others more) and unnecessarily destructive. It is therefore appropriate to consider and incorporate into treatment structured models to ameliorate these deficits in interpersonal and social skills.

Social-skills training procedures have been developed by a number of researcher-clinicians. Through modeling, role playing, role reversal, reinforcements (both tangible and social), and practice, skills can be developed and enhanced to give the adolescent the tools to manage and accomplish relationships with others more effectively and rewardingly. Typically, specific behaviors are targeted: assertiveness, conversational skills, and problem-solving skills.

Situation-specific social skills—for example those relevant to entry to a new social system such as a high school or a college campus—can be taught by trained peer companions, as noted before.

Hansen, Watson-Perczel, and Christopher (1989) have provided an overview of social-skills training with adolescents, finding general support for the effectiveness of these interventions. In addition, they discuss a number of clinical issues (e.g., dealing with compliance with and resistance to these procedures) of importance to implementing these procedures as components in a more comprehensive treatment model.

The Treatment of Loneliness

Joiner, Lewinsohn, and Seeley (2002) have noted that loneliness may be defined by both a lack of pleasurable engagement to, and painful disconnection from, others. The core of loneliness, they found, was a lack of pleasurable engagement, and this, in turn, predicted social impairment and the course of depression in adolescents. Interventions to alleviate loneliness serve to facilitate more rewarding social interactions and to teach skills of being alone when necessary but without negative affect such as anxiety, panic, or sadness. Young (1982) has developed a treatment model, based in cognitive theory, that focuses on those cognitions (e.g., automatic thoughts such as "There's something wrong with me" and maladaptive assumptions such as "If someone leaves me, there must be something wrong with me"); behaviors (e.g., avoidance, lack of assertiveness); and emotions (e.g., boredom, sadness, hopelessness) that predispose the adolescent to feel lonely and maintain loneliness.

Managing Anger, Aggression, and Impulsivity

Most of the behavioral treatments of suicidal adolescents derive from their focus on depression and its underlying cognitions and behaviors as a target symptom or diagnosis. Consistent with its central role in the psychodynamics of depression and self-destructive behavior, aggression (the behavioral expression of rage, anger, or hostility) often needs to be considered a primary target for intervention. This is true irrespective of whether aggression is seen as a primary or contributing factor to the adolescent's suicidality.

Novaco (1979) and colleagues (Robins & Novaco, 1999) were among the first to develop a behavioral intervention to deal with anger and cope with provocation. Techniques of anger management, meaning the regulation rather than the suppression of anger, taught to the adolescent include cognitive controls (understanding one's own and others' feelings, self-statements in preparation for and confronting arousal), emotional controls (relaxation, humor), and behavioral controls (effective communication, assertion training, task-oriented problem solving).

Aggression may also be controlled through medication, anxiety-management procedures, and other approaches to improving impulse-control problems common to the suicidal condition. Central to the control of aggression and to the observed risk for suicide is the involvement of drugs or alcohol. Thus it is essential, where substance is involved, that these be targeted as foci for self-management. Cognitive self-control procedures simply cannot succeed when the adolescent patient uses self-medication to alleviate distress, deaden emotional pain, or gain entry to a peer group. As such, changing the adolescent's social system might be required, including an intervening period of increased loneliness before new relationships are formed. Group psychotherapy and available forms of Alcoholics Anonymous and Narcotics Anonymous groups should be considered as networks of support while the focus of treatment addresses decreasing substance-use-related cues and substituting aversive consequences for positive reinforcers to substance use.

Finally, the regulation of intense affect must include attention to the overinvolvement of everyday stimulants (e.g., caffeine, nicotine), effects of nutritional deficiencies, and intrusions in sleep regulation, the results of which invariably will be increased confusion, irrationality, and poor behavioral control. The increased use of exercise, even low-level physical activity, can do much to modulate arousal and increase adaptive energy. The judicious and modeled use of humor—where natural, appropriate to the situation, and not self-deprecatory—serves as a tension releaser, a healthy stimulant (particularly of affect incompatible with depression or anger), and a mechanism promoting the therapeutic alliance.

ONGOING CLINICAL TREATMENT WITH SUICIDAL ADOLESCENTS

Beyond crisis intervention and the establishment of initial outpatient stabilization, ongoing clinical work with suicidal adolescents poses its own unique challenges and rewards. If one has the opportunity to continue ongoing treatment with an adolescent patient on the other side of a suicidal crisis, then clinical work can increasingly focus on broadening the adolescent's linkages beyond the here and now crises (temporal linkages) to a wider network of intrapersonal as well as interpersonal resources (support linkages). Moreover, ongoing treatment often affords the opportunity to address those predisposing conditions that made the adolescent vulnerable to suicidality in the first place. Thus, ongoing work may focus on a continued effort to reduce the effects of psychopathology perhaps through a combination of psychotherapy and appropriate psychopharmacology. In terms of psychotherapy, maladaptive cognitions and problematic behaviors can be addressed and further modified. Beyond changes in behaviors and cognitions, ongoing psychotherapy can often address deeper affective issues and may begin to address deeper concerns pertaining to self-esteem, self-worth, and relational well-being.

Psychodynamically trained psychotherapists often refer to "working through" as that stage of treatment where the fruits of clinical hard work, time, trust, intimacy, and support may be seen. Psychodynamic treatment of suicidality within the adolescent can sometimes require a significant working-through period of intensive psychotherapy. Indeed, this working-through phase may last from a few months to years depending on the degree of psychopathology. Of course other therapeutic modalities may continue to be used to supplement individual work. As previously discussed, ongoing or even strategic and intermittent use of family therapy, in particular, may prove to be a powerful adjunct to individual work (Brown, 1985; Richman, 1986). Whatever the case, the potential for the clinical alliance to be the proverbial "corrective emotional experience" perhaps holds the greatest long-term promise for good clinical outcomes and long-term psychological health.

TERMINATION

Because attachment issues, and therefore separation and individuation issues, are primary in the genesis of suicidality, termination is a crucial phase of the treatment process. Therapists experienced in working with suicidal patients know well to be aware of the patient's increasing separation anxiety, and the patient's denial of same, as termination becomes a reality. Also, this is one of the causal explanations offered for suicides that occur soon after hospital discharge. For this reason, termination perhaps ought to be labeled "weaning." Termination with a once-suicidal adolescent begins as the adolescent stabilizes—that is, as the risk of suicidal behavior abates—and continues through the end of formal, weekly in-office contacts over a potentially long period of follow-up. It is the adolescent who ultimately leaves therapy, much as it is the adolescent who ultimately leaves home.

Sessions initially scheduled with greater frequency should be scheduled with greater infrequency, but with continued regularity, over time. Thus, as therapy goals are attained, twice-weekly contacts may be reduced to weekly contacts, then to twice monthly, and so forth. Decisions to wean are made on the basis of an ongoing assessment of goals: (a) there has been no further imminent risk for self-harm over an extended period of observation and contact; (b) the probability of self-harm, assessed continuously throughout treatment, has reduced to a level of minimal or no risk, particularly as evidenced by no self-harm behavior over the term of treatment and during stressful times and situations; (c) skill enhancement has occurred as appropriate to treatment goals; and (d) the quality of life (e.g., mood, self-image, supports) has improved such that the adolescent is behaving unambivalently on the side of life versus death (e.g., hope has replaced hopelessness).

Particular attention must be paid to helping the adolescent cope with feelings of loss inherent in the developing separation from therapy. Issues of loss need to be framed within the context of gains in both therapeutic goals and specifically in strengthened bonds with others outside the therapy session. It has been our experience that weaning may extend well into the future. As appropriate, sessions can be scheduled on a monthly basis, then on a quarterly basis, and so on. In addition, and particularly should the adolescent leave home to attend school, for example, contact can be maintained by infrequent postcards between the adolescent and the therapist. These contacts serve to provide a follow-up monitoring of treatment benefits, a continued link (therapist constancy) should the adolescent ever need to reconnect, or a basis for referral-making in the adolescent's new environment should the need arise. Also, follow-up sessions are useful as "booster shots" to smooth rough edges or to retrain specific skills if needed or in anticipation of anniversary dates of importance in the history of the adolescent's suicidality.

POTENTIAL PITFALLS

There are, of course, many potential pitfalls that make clinical work with suicidal adolescents challenging and sometimes perilous. For example, for psychodynamically trained psychotherapists, there are major risks for clinicians who may follow a more orthodox traditional drive-theory approach to therapy. In our experience, what is clearly *not* needed is an overly intellectual blank-screen, impersonal, or classically neutral psychotherapist. It is perhaps self-evident, but suicidal thoughts should never be interpreted as mere fantasy or wish fulfillment. Such thoughts must always be taken very seriously and discussed as a potential reality. On another front, both adolescents and suicidality demand that the therapist take a more engaging, often directive, and active role in treatment than might be expected in some forms of dynamic therapy.

For the purely cognitively oriented therapists, some adolescents may feel a need to go beyond their thinking processes with needs to talk about deep feelings and painful affects. As previously discussed, it behooves the clinician to be flexible, creative, and open to the adolescent's emerging treatment agenda. Throughout this chapter we cannot emphasize enough the importance of clinical collaboration, where temporary departure from a more structured cognitive–behavioral protocol is valuable in the service of deepening a shared sense of collaborative care. It is important to appreciate that for certain disorders with certain maladaptive behaviors (e.g., substance abuse, eating disorders, or a suicidal depression), it is often difficult for patients to give up certain behaviors because of the value the behavior has to the patient. Even though abusing alcohol, binging and purging, and attempting suicide are objectively unhealthy from the clinician's perspective, these behaviors nevertheless provide the patient intoxication, short-term relief, and a sense of perceived control. There is increasing evidence that purely directive clinical approaches may not work as well with certain problems in contrast to more collaborative approaches that overtly engage the patient as a key player in his or her own care (Geller, Brown, Zaitsoff, Goodrich, & Hastings, 2003; Jobes, Drozd, Neal-Walden, Wong, & Kiernan, 2003; Jobes, Wong, Conrad, Drozd, & Neal-Waldon, in press).

Another potential pitfall is that adolescents will often express ambivalence about potential change for the better and, more often, expectations of further disappointment. Common to their dynamics, these patients are likely to behave regressively and with a demanding dependency on the therapist. Furthermore, they are prone to express anger and aggression, as well as passivity, behaviors destined to test the tolerance of the best of therapists if not merely validate their own sense of unlovability. For some, like Sam in the following case, their identity is rooted fragilely in their reactive autonomy, an oxymoronic dynamic reflecting a sense of personal control simulated by a fear of being controlled by a transferential object.

Case Illustration

By age 19, Sam (see Case Illustration, chap. 4, p. 147) had a history of chronic depression, including multiple suicide attempts of low intentionality but high lethality. These attempts were typically coercive in response to a girlfriend's termination of a short but intense relationship in which Sam's lovability was demanded rather than earned. He entered outpatient therapy on the appeal of his latest girlfriend, who stated that Sam had been threatening to kill himself with a gun in his possession if she would not "give him a chance."

Sam had left home at the age of 16, living in a succession of group homes while living off the streets and involving himself in peer groups defined by drug use and experimentation. The stimulus for his leaving home was his antagonistic relationship with his father, whom he described as punitive, rejecting, controlling, and contentious. Sam both rebelled against and identified with his father, describing himself as both stubborn and controlling. When the therapist, an older male, tested Sam's willingness to agree to an initial contract, Sam responded that he would make no commitments, that he would reject any attempt to control him, including any contract about his gun, his drinking or pot use, and so forth.

He refused to consider a voluntary hospitalization. Furthermore, he stated that the therapist would have to take time to get to know him, that "you'll just have to accept me on my terms," and that "we'll take this thing just one session at a time."

The persistently suicidal patient—as we have noted a high risk for ultimate completion—is another example of the "bad patient" who stimulates an iatrogenic response. These patients, such as Sue Ellen in the following case, often are pejoratively referred to as "pseudocides" or "scare-a-cides," reflecting the staff's conditioning not to take seriously the significance of these behaviors. Unfortunately, the most serious consequence of such iatrogenesis is that of a completed suicide.

Case Illustration

Sue Ellen, age 16, is well known by the emergency room staff, who invariably are called on to treat her for an overdose or wrist-cutting attempt on a Saturday night busy with the usual trauma patients common to a city hospital. When she arrives for the sixth time, for a low-lethality attempt, the staff, impatient with and frustrated by her for manipulating their attention away from patients "really" in need, treat her with disdain. One over-taxed member of the treatment team says within Sue Ellen's earshot, "If she really wants to do it, she should get it over with already!" Two months later, after learning of her suicidal death, this same staff member responded with surprise.

FINAL PRACTICE RECOMMENDATIONS

Rudd et al.'s (1999) review of the treatment literature was only able to tentatively answer a few of the most fundamental questions regarding the treatment of suicidality. Nevertheless, these authors provide a useful set of 28 practice recommendations that make intuitive and clinical sense. These recommendations represent a first-generation effort to develop empirically relevant considerations and provide a useful focus and organization about clinical treatment aspects pertaining to suicidal patients (including youth), which are worth noting as we bring this chapter to a close.

Intervention

1. Intensive follow-up, case management, telephone contacts, or home visits may improve treatment compliance over the short term for lower-risk cases.
2. Improved ease of access (i.e., a clearly stated crisis plan) to emergency services can potentially reduce subsequent attempts and service demand by first-time suicide attempters.

Treatment

1. Intensive follow-up treatment following an attempt is most appropriate and effective for those identified as *high risk*. High risk is indicated by multiple attempts, psychiatric history, and diagnostic comorbidity.
2. Short-term cognitive–behavioral therapy that integrates problem solving as a core intervention is effective at reducing suicidal ideation, depression, and hopelessness over periods of up to 1 year. Such brief approaches do not appear effective in reducing attempts over enduring time frames.
3. Reducing suicide attempts requires longer-term treatment and treatment modalities that target specific skill deficits such as emotion regulation, poor distress tolerance (i.e., impulsivity), anger management, interpersonal assertiveness, as well as other enduring problems, such as interpersonal relationships and self-image disturbance.
4. High-risk suicidal patients can be safely and effectively treated on an outpatient basis if acute hospitalization is available and accessible.

Clinical Practice

1. When imminent risk does not dictate hospitalization, the intensity of outpatient treatment (i.e., more frequent appointments, telephone contacts, concurrent individual and group treatment) should vary in accordance with risk indicators for those identified as high risk.
2. If the target goal is a reduction in suicide attempts and related behaviors, treatment should be conceptualized as long-term and target identified skills deficits (e.g., emotion regulation, distress tolerance, impulsivity, problem solving, interpersonal assertiveness, anger management) in addition to other salient treatment issues.

3. If therapy is brief and the target variables are suicidal ideation or related symptomatology such as depression, hopelessness, or loneliness, a problem-solving component should be used in some form or fashion as a core intervention.
4. Regardless of therapeutic orientation, an explanatory model should be detailed, identifying treatment targets, both direct (i.e., suicidal ideation, attempts, related self-destructive and self-mutilatory behaviors) and indirect (depression, hopelessness, anxiety, and anger; interpersonal relationship dysfunction; low self-esteem and poor self-image; and day-to-day functioning at work and home).
5. In an effort to enhance compliance and reduce risk for subsequent attempts, use of a standardized follow-up and referral procedure (e.g., letters or phone calls) is recommended for those dropping out of treatment prematurely.
6. The lack of definitive data regarding the efficacy of one approach over another should be reviewed with the patient as a component of informed consent.

Informed Consent

1. Provide informed consent pertaining to limits of confidentiality in relation to clear and imminent suicide risk and offer a detailed review of available treatment options, fees for service (both short- and long-term), risks and benefits, and the likely duration of treatment (especially for multiple attempters and those evidencing chronic psychiatric problems).
2. Provide an extended evaluation prior to specific treatment recommendations when patients present with more complex diagnostic issues or chronic suicidality.

Diagnosis

1. Evaluate for *DSM–IV* Axis I and Axis II diagnoses and document supporting symptomatology.
2. Provide diagnostic and symptom-specific treatment recommendations.

Monitoring Suicidality

1. Routinely monitor, assess, and document a patient's initial and ongoing suicide risk and document interventions for maintaining outpatient safety until suicidality has clinically resolved.

2. For cases of chronic suicidality, monitor, assess, and document ongoing risk of suicidality and document interventions that address the chronic nature of the suicidal preoccupations. It is important to note the chronicity of some symptoms (e.g., specific suicidal thoughts with a definitive plan), indicating factors that escalate risk (i.e., emergence of intent) versus those that diminish risk (e.g., lack of intent).

Treatment Duration

1. For acute crisis cases of suicidality (particularly in the presence of an Axis I disorder), provide a relatively short-term psychotherapy that is directive and crisis-focused, emphasizing problem solving and skill building as core interventions.
2. For chronic cases of suicidality (particularly in the presence of an Axis II disorder), provide a relatively long-term psychotherapy in which relationship issues, interpersonal communication, and self-image issues are the predominant focus of treatment when crises have resolved.

Therapeutic Relationship

1. Develop a strong therapeutic alliance with the suicidal patient and make the clinical relationship central to the outpatient treatment plan (e.g., negotiating access, using the relationship as a source of safety and support during crises, attending to the patient's sense of profound loneliness).
2. Monitor and respond to countertransference reactions to the suicidal patient (particularly those that are chronically suicidal) and routinely seek professional consultation, supervision, and support for difficult cases.

Treatment Outcome Monitoring

1. Use a clearly articulated scheme for identifying, classifying, and discussing suicidal behaviors in treatment (e.g., that provided by O'Carroll et al., 1996).
2. Use a consistent approach to assessing treatment outcome, incorporating both direct (i.e., suicidal ideation, suicide attempts, instrumental behaviors) and indirect markers of suicidality (i.e., markers of symptomatology, personality traits, or general level of day-to-day functioning).

3. Assess treatment outcome at predictable intervals, using psychometrically sound instruments to complement and balance patient self-report.

Specific Considerations for Treatment of Adolescents

1. Involve parents or guardians in the clinical assessment, treatment planning, and ongoing suicide risk assessment process. Acknowledge their helpful contributions and empower them to have positive influences in their roles as parents and caregivers.
2. Evaluate the parent or caregiver's ability to fulfill essential parental functions such as the provision of food and shelter and the maintenance of a safe, nonabusive home environment for the suicidal adolescent. If there exists a concern about the adolescent's basic care and safety, address it with parents or caregivers directly and notify protective services if appropriate.
3. Evaluate the parent's or caregiver's ability to fulfill other parental functions such as consistent limit setting with follow-through, healthy communication with the adolescent, and positive role modeling. Recommend treatment for severe, identifiable parental psychopathology and recommend interventions as needed to (a) assist and empower parents in fulfilling their supportive and limit-setting functions, and (b) assist family members in improving their communication skills and relationships with each other.

CONCLUSION

As Rudd (2000) has concluded, there is adequate support in the existing scientific literature for the following:

1. Intensive follow-up treatment following an attempt is most appropriate and effective for those identified as high risk, as indicated by multiple attempts, psychiatric history, and diagnostic comorbidity.
2. Short-term cognitive–behavioral therapy, integrating problem solving as a *core intervention*, is effective at reducing suicidal ideation, depression, and hopelessness over periods of up to 1 year. Such brief approaches do not appear effective at reducing attempts over much longer time frames.
3. Reducing suicide attempts requires longer-term treatment and treatment modalities targeting specific skills deficits, such as

emotion regulation, poor distress tolerance (i.e., impulsivity), anger management, and interpersonal assertiveness, as well as other enduring problems such as interpersonal relationships and self-image disturbance (i.e., personality disorders).

4. High-risk suicidal patients can be safely and effectively treated on an outpatient basis if acute hospitalization is available and accessible. (pp. 56–57)

As Salkovskis (2001) has pointed out, only two focused psychotherapeutic approaches (cognitive–behavioral therapy and dialectical behavior therapy) so far have been found to be helpful with people at risk of attempting suicide, although risk-factor research suggests that techniques of interpersonal psychotherapy may also prove helpful. One recent meta-analysis (Hawton et al., 1998) of randomized controlled clinical trials in which repetition of deliberate self-harm—including attempted suicide—was the outcome measure found a significant reduction in repetition of self-harm behaviors among patients participating in dialectical behavior therapy. Although these data are encouraging, there is a clear need for a great deal more research in this important area of study.

In our discussion of treating suicidal adolescents, two overriding major themes have emerged. One is that relatedness and attachment are central to both the etiology of suicidal problems and, in turn, relationships may prove to be pivotal to successful clinical outcomes. Our integrative–eclectic approach emphasizes various aspects of the help-seeking, -giving, and -receiving clinical process. For example, we have noted that suicidal adolescents are often unfamiliar with effective working alliances with significant adults; therapists much therefore gently but firmly forge cooperative clinical partnerships with their adolescent patients that may ultimately generalize to multiple attachments in the community at large. Thus, from beginning to end, treatment demands attention to issues of linkage, attachment, and relatedness, and the potential success of treatment is largely dependent on these themes.

A second major theme is the therapist's need for a pragmatic, problem-solving, and strategic approach to treatment that takes into account idiographic aspects of each presenting case. A thorough understanding of the full range of helpful clinical strategies and techniques form the armamentarium from which the therapist may selectively or liberally cull and apply any and all strategies deemed appropriate for optimal clinical care. On the basis of a pragmatic functional analysis of the suicidal adolescent's motives and a complete assessment of the suicidal adolescent, these various applied clinical interventions and strategies can translate into effective treatment that leads to successful suicide prevention at the individual clinical level. This theme of suicide prevention is now one that we will more broadly consider in chapter 8.

7

STANDARDS OF CARE AND MALPRACTICE IN SUICIDE TREATMENT

Evaluating and treating patients at risk for suicidal behavior is complex and difficult work. Clinicians, intent on providing high-quality care to their patients, have responsibilities to ensure that they are current in the available scientific and professional knowledge pertaining to at-risk patients; that they act to safeguard the welfare of their patients and, of course, do no harm; that they behave within the ethical standards of their professions; and that they strive to use their best judgment and make cost–benefit-based decisions with regard to their patients.

Clinicians owe a duty of care to their patients. A *duty of care* is a legal concept, derived from the existence of a doctor–patient relationship. This relationship is established in outpatient and inpatient settings, in emergency interventions and settings, and the like. With regard to at-risk patients, the duty of care carries with it responsibilities to act affirmatively to protect a patient from his or her own violent acts. The scope of that duty may vary from setting to setting and the nature of the therapeutic relationship. The court holds clear expectations of the therapist. Foremost among these expectations is the duty to attempt reasonably to prevent the suicide of the patient. If the court finds that this duty was breached through negligence, either through an act of omission or commission relative to the standard of care, and this breach was proximately related to the patient's suicide or suicidal behavior, a finding of negligence or malpractice may result. Rachlin (1984, p. 303) has summarized the four elements of proof necessary to prove negligence with a **4D** mnemonic: The plaintiff must establish that there was a **D**ereliction (breach) of a **D**uty (to care) that **D**irectly (proximately caused) **D**amages (a compensable injury).

The **standard of care** is also a legal concept, defined by statutes that vary from state to state. Typically, the standard of care specifies the clinician's duty to exercise that degree of skill and care customarily used in similar circumstances by similar clinicians (Simon, 2004). The standard of care is established by judgment and opinion as to whether the care provided was *reasonable*—that is, not significantly and indefensibly deviant from that of reasonable professionals of similar training and experience. Opinions regarding the possible deviation from standard care are provided by expert witnesses, professionals purporting to have some expertise in treating and understanding suicidal patients, hired by opposing attorneys. Therein lies the rub. Even in nuisance suits, where the defendant psychotherapist is convinced that his or her behavior was reasonable, both the plaintiff and the defendant will have their experts, each testifying honestly to their opinion that the therapist did or did not practice negligently. In this regard, experts become advocates for their own opinions and, as noted by Jensen (1993, p. 192), most attorneys "would go into a lawsuit with an objective uncommitted independent expert about as willingly as [they] would occupy a foxhole with a couple of noncombatant soldiers." For this reason, it behooves the clinician to understand well what the court, through case law, asks in addressing the question of reasonable care.

Essentially, there are two factors that determine liability in a suicidal death: *foreseeability* and *reasonable care*. Foreseeability has nothing to do with crystal-ball gazing or predicting suicide. It has everything to do with the assessment of risk. Failing to assess risk is an egregious professional failing on the part of the therapist. Because suicidal behavior is not predictable, the assessment of risk should be made and documented for all patients. The assessment of risk involves, at a minimum, attention to the possibility of suicidal behavior through the asking of questions about suicidal thoughts, plans, intent, and actions, in addition to known risk factors; and the making and documentation of judgments made on the basis of these observations. One cannot be held liable for incorrect judgment (unless it is formed on the basis of an egregious minimization of presented evidence). One might argue that the very fact that a suicide has occurred (when not correctly foreseen) is, by definition, highly suggestive that clinical judgments were incorrect. Judgments should be reasonable, formed on the basis of the data observed, and the data observed should be reasonably sought.

Inherent in this focus is a very important subtheme of documentation: the recording of observations and judgments. The failure to keep proper and contemporaneous records is a violation of customary procedure and ethical standards. However, more important, the lack of careful documentation severely undermines the caregiver's defense, as there is no corroborating evidence of asserted reasonable practices. A lack of proper documentation by itself cannot be a proximate cause of a patient's suicide; however, it makes defending oneself in a malpractice action difficult to say the least. Even worse, notes written after the fact of a patient's suicide will appear, and be read, as purely self-serving. Consider, in the following case, the believability of Dr. Smith's assertions regarding his treatment sessions reconstructed from memory after the suicide of his patient.

Case Illustration

Following the suicide of a 17-year-old patient, a malpractice suit was filed by the patient's family against Dr. Smith. When his records were subpoenaed and examined, it was noted that Dr. Smith had billed his patient's parents for a total of 13 sessions. However, he had maintained contemporaneous clinical notes for only six of these sessions. In deposition, he claimed that he had a very busy practice and often did not have time to write notes when he saw his patients. Instead, he claimed that he could reconstruct what transpired in these sessions and offered testimony regarding these sessions, now 3 years later, from memory.

(Note: With the 2003 enactment of Health Information and Portability and Accountability Act [HIPAA] legislation, clinicians now must be particularly sensitive to and cautious about regulated distinctions between clinical [medical] records or progress notes and psychotherapy process notes.)

The second factor determining liability, reasonable care, connotes that a treatment plan should be developed consistent with the patient's diagnoses and assessed suicide risk, and that the treatment plan should include appropriate precautions as dictated by evaluated risk. Where suicide risk is elevated because of a clinical depression, for example, the treatment plan should include consideration of therapeutic and pharmacologic interventions. Should an adolescent be judged to be at high and acute risk, precautions against the adolescent acting in some self-harm manner must be considered and attempted. A high-risk adolescent cannot be sent home unmonitored or given medications in sufficient quantity to kill himself or herself. Where recommendations for follow-up behavior are made but not acted upon by the adolescent and the parents, this noncompliance needs to be documented in the patient's record and alternative interventions should then be formulated and instituted. Calculated risks taken for presumed therapeutic gain are within the standard of care and also benefit the therapist if rationales for these risks are documented.

Last, a breach of duty to protect the patient ("abandonment") may be found if the therapist did not act to have ordered precautions carried out with *dependability*. Dependable follow-through is a component of reasonable care. Thus, for example, the therapist who orders a suicide watch of a patient on the inpatient ward will be held responsible if that watch is not carried out by the nursing staff responsible for its accomplishment.

As noted, the standard of care is primarily determined by the testimony of experts, but it is informed by available practice guidelines, codes of ethics, relevant professional literature and authoritative sources, institutional policies and procedures, and legal precedent. Guidelines, unto themselves, do not define standards of care; rather, they establish reasonable and prudent behaviors. With regard to at-risk patients, practice guidelines (cf., American Academy of Child and Adolescent Psychiatry, 2001) establish parameters for the clinician to attend reasonably to the adolescent patient in the following areas:

INTAKE ASSESSMENT

The standard of care requires mental health clinicians to adequately assess suicide risk. Thus, the reasonable and prudent clinician would systematically evaluate the patient's presenting symptoms and complaints, note both distal and proximal suicide risk factors, delineate the presence and strength of current protective factors, conduct a mental status exam via interview procedures, and consider the need for psychological testing to complement interview data. Inherent in this assessment are (a) consideration of the patient's past medical and psychological history, inclusive of prior suicidal behaviors, treatment, and treatment compliance, and (b) family history of mental disorders and psychiatric hospitalization, suicidality, substance abuse, and so on. Where relevant and possible, collateral family interviews should be conducted (see below) to augment information supplied by the adolescent patient.

With this data, differential diagnoses should be established in accordance with *Diagnostic and Statistical Manual of Mental Disorders, Fourth Edition* (*DSM–IV*; American Psychiatric Association, 1994) criteria, and suicide risk should be evaluated and documented. As identified earlier in the book, suicide risk assessment goes well beyond asking adolescents whether they are thinking of suicide and documenting "patient denies suicidal thoughts." In studies of adult suicides, the majority of patients denied suicide ideation in response to questions asked during their final interview (Busch, Fawcett, & Jacobs, 2003; Isometsa et al., 1995). Suicidal risk assessment assesses the degree of acute risk and identifies modifiable and treatable risk factors as well as protective factors that may be strengthened, making the suicide risk assessment integral to treatment planning.

TREATMENT PLANNING

Where suicide risk has been judged present, a treatment and management plan commensurate with that evaluation of suicidality (and underlying predisposing risk factors and assessed protective factors) needs to be established and documented. Inherent in this planning are (a) considerations of the need for psychopharmacological management of any underlying disorder, and (b) the setting (e.g., the need for hospitalization inclusive of the need for close observation and monitoring) and the frequency and type of psychotherapeutic intervention best suited to diminishing factors influencing risk and enhancing factors that are protective. Where relevant and possible, records of prior treatment should be sought, as these may be informative with regard to undisclosed history and observations of patient compliance with prior recommended interventions.

PROVIDING TREATMENT

The principle of reasonable and prudent care requires the clinician to implement treatment in accordance with the treatment plan. To accomplish this, the clinician should attempt to facilitate the adolescent patient's adherence to and cooperation with recommended treatments. This, of course, is further facilitated by building a therapeutic alliance with the patient and the patient's family. The following recommendations may help accomplish these goals:

- Communicate information to the patient and family (or appointed guardians) regarding diagnosis and associated treatment recommendations.
- Provide information on alternative treatments, where applicable.
- Refer the patient for a physical examination, including appropriate lab tests, to rule out organic causes for presenting symptoms.
- Educate family members about the treatment strategy and about the importance of having realistic expectations.
- Assuming outpatient care, educate parents about safeguarding the home, particularly with regard to removing firearms from ready availability and accessibility.

- Assuming outpatient care, educate parents regarding the need to monitor their child, and communicate observations of change or concern. To accomplish this, it is important that the clinician evaluate the parental or other caregiver system's ability to fulfill essential observational, limit-setting, and supportive functions, and to make recommendations and referrals where indicated to empower parents to fulfill these functions.

When indicated by diagnosis, psychopharmacologic interventions may need to be considered, leading to referral for appropriate medical or psychiatric consultations. When these referrals lead to collateral treatments, the standard of care would require documentation of collaboration and communication, for example, between the psychologist and psychiatrist. Significant treatment observations should be shared and treatment decisions coordinated between collateral caregivers. It is singularly important and good risk-management strategy to document these communications. Where medications are prescribed, the nonmedical clinician maintains a responsibility to report patient-communicated side effects and adverse reactions to the physician in addition to observed changes in mental status after initiation of drug treatment. Conversely, changes in dosage or medications prescribed during the course of treatment should be communicated to and recorded in the nonmedical caregiver's records. In this regard, it behooves the nonmedical caregiver to be knowledgeable about prescribed medications and, in particular, about medications with published evidence of efficacy in reducing observed suicidal behaviors (cf., Meltzer, 1999; Tondo, Jamison, & Baldessarini, 1997b). Given, however, recent federal warnings about the potential for selective serotonin reuptake inhibitors (SSRIs) to exacerbate suicidality in youth, caution must be exercised in monitoring these drugs with these patients. In the case of a malpractice action against a prescribing physician that alleges negligent prescribing, the collaborating psychologist is at risk of being deemed equally negligent where such negligent actions should have been known by the psychologist.

Caregivers treating at-risk adolescents have a responsibility to maintain reasonable accessibility to the patient and his or her family. Reasonableness in this regard is open to interpretation and expert opinion (one expert in trial opined that the therapist must carry a beeper at all times—we disagree), but, at a minimum, should include instructions of what the patient and family or guardian should do if one is not immediately accessible in an emergency. There is little question that reasonableness would command that coverage be arranged when the caregiver is unavailable or unreachable, as on holiday.

Inherent in providing reasonable and prudent care to at-risk adolescent patients is the need for caregivers to manage (monitor and respond to) countertransferential reactions (cf., Maltsberger & Buie, 1974), behave within professional ethical standards (see below), and modify treatment plans or seek consultation if no improvement is evident. It is also important to stress that ongoing assessment of suicide risk is part of treatment. Assessing risk of increased suicidality is particularly important at times of discharge or termination from treatment, at management transitions (e.g., therapist vacations and staff rotations in hospitals), and at times of significant shifts in environmental stressors.

We need to iterate that keeping contemporaneous records of observations, judgments, rationales, collaborative caregiver communications, treatment plans, and interventions is essential to clinically based risk management. As noted by Simon (2004), "some courts have held that [what] was not recorded was not done: document, document, document" (p. 21).

Table 7.1 expands on the above points relative to the responsibilities of inpatient clinicians to adolescents at risk. For a more in-depth consideration of these guidelines, we recommend the reader consult Bongar (2002), from which this table has been reprinted, and Bongar et al. (1998), in which these common failures and recommendations were earlier delineated.

TABLE 7.1
Commonly Alleged Failures in Meeting Standards of Care for Suicidal Inpatients: Duties and Responsibilities of the Clinician

Alleged failures	Remedies
	Foreseeability
Appropriately diagnose patient.	Obtain history of current and past problems.
	Perform physical examination.
	Perform mental status exam.
	Conduct assessment of suicidality to determine suicidal risk.
	Reach tentative diagnosis.
	Provide risk-benefit analysis of treatment options to support critical clinical and administrative management decisions.
	Consider least restrictive environment options.
	Develop initial treatment plan.
	Discuss treatment plan with patient.
	Obtain informed consent.
	Discuss limits of confidentiality with patient.
	Communicate treatment plan to all relevant staff by writing orders.
	Obtain and review past medical and psychiatric/ psychological records when reasonably possible.
	Obtain collateral information from patient's support network with patient's consent.
	Order appropriate tests and evaluations to establish suicidal intent.

TABLE 7.1 (Continued)

Alleged failures	Remedies
	Foreseeability
Appropriately foresee future behavioral problems.	Reassess regularly the diagnosis, level of suicidality, and appropriateness of all aspects of the treatment plan. Communicate regularly with staff in writing and orally. Reassess regularly the patient's competencies and capacities for complying with the treatment plan. Be aware of the hospital's policy and procedure manual regarding the management of suicidal patients. Monitor adherence to the treatment plan by staff. Read the medical chart entries regularly. Obtain consultation when indicated.
	Causation
Provide protection against harm.	Implement treatment plan. Monitor treatment plan results. Provide informed consent about changes in treatment plan. Discuss confidentiality with patient.
Control, supervise, observe, and restrain patient.	Offer alternative therapeutic approaches and discuss advantages/disadvantages with patient.
Provide safe, secure, and protective environment.	Consider appropriate installation of privileges, restrictions, and precautions. Determine frequency of surveillance. Remove all known means of self-harm from unit.
Treat conditions associated with suicidal behaviors (including use of medication and all other appropriate therapeutic modalities).	Consider consultation when indicated. Provide plan-specific interventions.
Carry out treatment orders as written.	Monitor adherence to treatment plan.
Document clinical decisions.	Determine frequency of clinical availability. Review regularly pass and privilege policies and procedures.
Communicate among staff.	Adhere to hospital manual on policies and procedures.
Retain patient in hospital until no longer actively suicidal.	Arrange for alternative secure environment if prolonged hospitalization is not financially feasible.
Provide postdischarge plans.	Engage in discharge planning. Encourage adherence to aftercare plans.

TABLE 7.1 (Continued)

Alleged failures	Remedies
	Causation
Provide postdischarge care.	Educate patient's support network about risk management. Maximize support network's attention to ensuring patient's compliance with aftercare recommendations.

The following case illustrates a number of alleged "failures" or breaches in the standard of care.

Case Illustration

On a Saturday afternoon, Juan, a 19-year-old single male, was brought by the police to the emergency department of a large city hospital on a "certificate of evaluation." A cousin of Juan's had called Juan's outpatient psychiatrist a few hours earlier and reported a terrifying conversation she had had with Juan. Juan, she said, had told her that his meds weren't helping and had never helped, that he was going to be evicted from his apartment if he didn't have rent money by Sunday, and that this was his last weekend and that he would not be around on Sunday. Juan further told her that he heard voices telling him to cut himself or cause a gas explosion, and that he planned to kill himself by a gas explosion, predicting "It's going to be a messy scene." When his cousin asked how he felt should others get harmed in the explosion (he lived in a small apartment building), he said, "I'll be dead; I don't care."

When he failed to appear for his scheduled outpatient psychiatric appointment later that morning, the psychiatrist called the police, expressed concern over her patient's increasing hopelessness and suicide risk, and asked them to go to his apartment and escort him immediately to the hospital for an evaluation.

Juan had two prior admissions to this hospital. He was first admitted, at age 12, with a history of school vandalism and stealing, enuresis (1–2 times/week), and morbid obesity. At this admission he also admitted to having increasing suicide ideation. He was diagnosed as having a major depression and was hospitalized for an extended period of time. In addition to his depression, secondary targets for treatment were his body image, anxiety, anger, and social withdrawal.

His second hospitalization occurred at age 17. Brought to the hospital by his mother for episodes of angry outbursts, paranoia (he feared he was being watched through holes in their apartment wall), self-cutting ("Xs" on his arms "in honor of those who had turned against me"), and visual hallucinations, he was involuntarily admitted. After 4 days he was discharged with an Axis I diagnosis, Adjustment Disorder with Mixed Disturbances of Emotions and Conduct, and an Axis II diagnosis, Borderline Personality Disorder.

In the emergency department this day, Juan related to the psychiatric resident that he had been unemployed for 6 months and had given up looking for work. He reportedly ran out of marijuana 3 days earlier and said he was "going crazy." He said that during his high school years he had dealt drugs and was dependent on amphetamines. He currently was taking Depakote (250 mg bid) and Zoloft (100 mg, PO qd).

Juan now minimized his statements to his cousin, stating, "I worried a lot of people today," that he did not want to harm himself, and that he was "just frustrated about [his] situation." He said that he had threatened to cause a gas explosion to get attention—"to rile [his] family up," and that he needed and wanted to look for work.

He was calm and cooperative, oriented to time, place, and person, and organized and goal-directed in his thinking. His mood was appropriate; he denied both audio and visual hallucinations and delusional thinking. He did admit to some paranoid thoughts regarding "people standing behind me."

The psychiatric resident offered Juan the option of hospitalization, but he declined, observing that he would not be able to seek work if he were hospitalized, saying "I want to spend Sunday searching the paper's classifieds." He furthermore stated that his rent had been extended by Goodwill Industries.

After consulting with the attending psychiatrist and reporting on Juan's current mental status, the psychiatric resident was directed to discharge Juan to the care of his outpatient psychiatrist—with instruction to Juan to arrange a follow-up outpatient appointment the following Monday.

On Sunday, Juan died by a self-inflicted gas explosion in his apartment. The four-unit building, although demolished, was otherwise uninhabited at the time.

Within months, Juan's mother brought suit against the psychiatric resident, the attending psychiatrist, and the hospital. Charging negligence and malpractice, the complaint alleged that there were multiple failures on the part of these (now) defendants:

- Failure to assess risk for suicide,
- Failure to detain for further evaluation,
- Failure to consult with referral source (his psychiatrist),
- Failure to secure medical records and to inform self of prior psychiatric history,
- Failure to implement a treatment plan commensurate with suicide risk,
- Failure to consider need for pharmacologic intervention and to implement same,
- Failure to protect patient from known danger to self,
- Failure to possess adequate degree of skill and training to adequately assess and treat suicidal patients.

In defense of these alleged failures, an expert might forcefully argue that Juan's current mental status would not have allowed for involuntary hospitalization. He showed no signs of acute suicidality at the time of interview, denied suicidal thinking, and appeared calm and not psychotic. Whatever had precipitated his agitating behavior earlier in the day clearly had passed. As he refused voluntary hospitalization and with his agreement to follow up with his outpatient psychiatrist, there simply was no other choice but to discharge him.

On the other hand, one might counterargue that, at a minimum, his outpatient psychiatrist should have been consulted for her input such that discordant observations could be discussed and evaluated, the reported resolution of stressors might have been corroborated through outreach phone calls, a drug screen could have been ordered, treatment records could have been retrieved and examined, and a more intensive evaluation of Juan's recent noncompliance with treatment and medications could have been conducted. Moreover, a thorough reconsideration of his medication regimen could have been considered. All of these strategies of good evaluation and management would have taken some time, within what state statutes would have allowed, and would have allowed for a more thorough evaluation of his suicide risk, the true intent of his threats, the quality of his therapeutic and familial alliances, and so on.

A BRIEF NOTE ON ETHICAL ISSUES

Motto (1983) observed that philosophical views of suicide and those of the clinical practitioner, the potential healer of self-destructive individuals, are vastly different. One deals with suicide within the frame of rationality and the ideal, the other through the eyes of his or her patient—eyes clouded by confusion, mental disturbance, and a chaotic reality. The philosopher can establish criteria to determine whether a given suicide would be an ethical act, a morally defensible decision to maintain autonomy, have a rational choice, or free oneself from overwhelming pain. The clinician, on the other hand, establishes criteria to restrict autonomy (i.e., hospitalize, even involuntarily) on the basis of the patient's lack of rationality or inability to tolerate pain without intervention.

We substantially agree with Clements, Sider, and Perlmutter (1983) that the crucial question for clinicians is not whether suicide is justifiable, but rather whether suicide intervention is justifiable. These authors argue, correctly, that clinicians *must*—in fact, as discussed above, are legally *expected* to—have an affirmative stance toward intervention. A patient in therapy has entered a therapeutic value system that defines, in part, what is in the best interests of that individual.

Suicide is rarely in the best interest of the individual, especially the young patient. Because the data presented in this book support the view that youth suicide is the consequence of a complex system of interacting forces, ranging from psychopathology to irrational cognitions to disturbed family systems, and even biological dysfunction, it is difficult to defend the suicidal act as one of autonomous choice. An empathic understanding of the suicidal adolescent demands that those conditions making the adolescent suicidal be treated; with that treatment it is reasonable to expect a decrease in that patient's suicidality.

Thus, the important clinical and ethical questions are those related to what kind of treatments or interventions will best accomplish that outcome. In this vein, the best intervention is not always coercive prevention or even hospitalization (Jobes, 2000; Linehan, 1993a). The clinical goal is to reduce risk for suicide at an acceptable cost. We believe that the myopia of the suicidal adolescent demands whatever cost is necessary to establish time and treatment to help create a truly autonomous individual.

THE MALPRACTICE SCRIPT

As will be described in chapter 9, the act of suicide visits upon bereaved survivors some unique traumata and reactions to the caregiver. Among these is anger and an implicit, if not explicit, blameworthiness for (a) not being good enough to have made the decedent value life sufficiently to remain alive (an act of omission) or (b) having done something to have made the decedent wish to take his or her life (an act of commission). In this context, it is understandable that surviving family members might readily direct their anger and blame toward caregivers who allegedly had the opportunity to intervene in, and prevent, a suicide that had been threatened. Indeed, one recent survey found that the majority of family survivors of a loved one in treatment at the time of his or her suicide considered contacting an attorney; 25% actually did (Peterson, Luoma, & Dunne, 2002). In Juan's case (p. 267), his cousin's concern and anxiety, stimulated by his threats, prompted an appropriate intervention by his psychiatrist. That he was discharged so soon after his admission to the emergency department without involvement of either his psychiatrist or cousin in both understanding the judgments and rationale of the psychiatric team, and in being given aftercare instructions, was an invitation to a malpractice action.

It should be noted that the defendants in Juan's case will most likely mount a defense to a malpractice complaint, primarily built around the constraints posed by managed care. In today's health care environment, managed care decision makers demand significant evidence of imminent danger or inability to care for self as conditions for approving hospital admission or granting extended inpatient days. On the basis of Juan's mental status at the time he was evaluated in the emergency department, these criteria would have been very difficult to meet. Nevertheless, the clinician's responsibility is first and foremost to care for the patient and to use his or her independent judgment, not to cede that autonomy to managed-care policies or procedures.

For psychotherapists, a patient's suicide is a catastrophic event. It brings much the same sequelae as that experienced by family members— that is, feelings of loss, helplessness, anger, guilt, and self-incrimination, and for an estimated one third of these therapists, severe distress (Hendin, Haas, Maltsberger, Szanto, & Rabinowicz, 2004). Additionally, given their professional role, psychotherapists often fear being humiliated in some public way among their colleagues or among referral sources. In some cases, negative reactions from the therapist's institution feed their distress (Hendin et al., 2004). The most feared sequela of a patient's suicide, however, is the threat of a lawsuit alleging malpractice.

Modern legal considerations have shifted from viewing suicide as a punishable wrong (because the state was deprived of something or someone of value) to viewing suicide as a product of mental disorder requiring treatment, and to the recognition of pain and suffering among those bereaved by the loss (Litman, 1987). Those charged with the care and treatment of patients are, de facto, charged with the task of preventing the suicide of that patient. This responsibility makes psychotherapists ripe targets for the externalization of survivors' rage.

Litman (1982) has estimated that 1 in 3 suicides by patients in inpatient care results in a lawsuit. Although he further estimates that only about

1 in 10 of these ever makes it to the courtroom, even "nuisance" suits pose threats of considerable media exposure, in addition to the costs in time and expense to the therapist to mount an effective defense. As noted in the introduction to this text, psychologist practitioners have more than a 1 in 5 chance (and psychiatrists a 1 in 2 chance) of having one or more patients complete suicide during the course of their professional career. Kleespies, Penk, and Forsyth (1993), moreover, found that 1 of every 9 psychology interns or trainees had to cope with the completed suicide of a patient, the majority during their internship year. Therefore, there appears to be considerable reason for therapists at all levels to be alert to, and protective against, the possibility of such litigation. Whereas in years past the great majority of malpractice claims were lodged against inpatient practitioners and institutions, we have noted a shift over the past 20 years toward a dramatic increase in suits against outpatient practitioners (Jobes & Berman, 1993; Bongar et al., 1998).

As is apparent from the research-based findings describing characteristics of the suicidal adolescent, these patients generally do not fit the model of the ideal patient. By the time they are seen in therapy, typically not of their own volition, they have developed a character pathology or self-destructive behavior patterns (drug use, sexual promiscuity, eating disorders, vandalism, etc.) or dual diagnosis presentations (e.g., conduct disorder issues and substance dependence) that make positive working relationships difficult at best. At the same time, the parent of the suicidal adolescent often will indeed make and hold the therapist responsible for what they have not thus far been able to accomplish on their own. When that adolescent dies by suicide, parental blame and responsibility will understandably be denied and externalized to the therapist.

In the earlier edition of this book we noted that such claims were number one on the hierarchy of suits brought against psychiatrists in the United States (Gutheil, 1989) and, as of July 1988, the sixth most frequent type of claim (and the second most costly) filed against psychologists (Pope, 1989). More important, these actions were increasing in frequency and, correspondingly, in legal costs (Berman, 1990a). As described by Bongar (2002, p. 50), more recent claims data are not available, as insurance carriers no longer disclose the number of malpractice claims for suicide or wrongful death; however, Gutheil (1999) has asserted that "suicide remains the most common cause of litigation against all mental health professionals" (p. 561). Placed within an international context, we should note that the United States has had a longer and much more litigious history regarding malpractice claims than other countries have had; however, significant increases in litigation following a suicide have been noted across the globe (Leenaars et al., 2003).

When a surviving family member consults a personal injury attorney alleging malpractice by a caregiver with regard to the assessment and treatment of a deceased loved one, that attorney will seek the patient's clinical chart. That record will then be sent to an expert, who will be asked to render an oral opinion as to whether there was a breach in the standard of care of the patient-decedent. Should that opinion support the survivor's allegations, a formal complaint will be lodged with the court and a malpractice action has begun.

The survivors now are known as plaintiffs and the caregiver now is a defendant. The wise caregiver will have contacted his or her liability insurance carrier after receiving the plaintiff attorney's subpoena; this defense attorney will, similarly, seek out an expert who will be willing to provide opinions in defense of the caregiver and in refutation of those opinions presented by the plaintiff's expert. Typically, there are multiple defendants (as in Juan's case), each with his or her own experts and attorneys in the developing script.

What typically plays out at this point is a series of legal maneuverings, briefs, and what can be an extended period of "discovery" during which other records are sought, interrogatories (formal questions) are rendered and responded to, and depositions of all knowledgeable and involved parties are taken. In some cases, this process can stretch into years.

For a plaintiff to prove malpractice on the part of a caregiver, four essential elements must be demonstrated. First, evidence must be presented that there existed a duty to care. This is readily established by the fact that the care-giver provided usual and customary services to the patient, held himself or herself out as a professional licensable by the state, and so on. Second, the plaintiff must demonstrate that there was a dereliction in the performance of that duty. This, as we have described above, is established by expert opinion relative to the concept of standard of care. Third, it must be shown that damages occurred. This is readily established by the fact of a suicide or a nonfatal attempt; it is also established by secondary losses (financial, consortium, etc.). Last, it must be established that these damages were caused by the alleged dereliction of duty. This is known as "proximate" or "direct causation." The following case integrates these concepts of alleged failures in the standard of care.

Case Illustration

Cameron was a 15-year-old male who was referred to a psychologist, Dr. Dodge, for reasons of exacerbating and negative interactions with his father and stepmother. These conflicts had worsened, particularly in the form of rageful interactions with his stepmother, in the several months since the death from cancer of his natural mother, with whom he had been especially close.

During her terminal illness, Cameron participated in caring for her (including changing her colostomy bag), and after her death, he participated in bathing her. He spoke to at least two family members regarding fantasies of reuniting with his mother, which he mentioned to Dr. Dodge at intake.

Cameron had a several-year history of oppositional behavior, lying, school truancy (including poor attendance and tardiness), shoplifting, runaway behavior, and drug use (pot, alcohol, LSD). For several years prior to this referral, Cameron had seen a number of caregivers for one or another of these behavioral problems. Moreover, he described recent problems with sleeping, declining grades, and passive suicide ideation (wishes to be killed).

Dr. Dodge saw Cameron five times individually, nine times overall, as sessions often involved his father or his step-mother, or both, or his younger brother. Yet other sessions were held just with his father and stepmother. In deposition, Dr. Dodge claimed that she was providing family therapy, that treatment "varied as each new member [of the family] came in," and that therapy was ruled by "the crisis of the day," wherein she mediated family conflicts.

Toward the end of the third month of treatment, so as to relieve family tension and on Cameron's request, Dr. Dodge rec-ommended that he be allowed to live at his aunt's house for a few weeks. Unbeknownst to Dr. Dodge, his aunt's family had a particularly violent history, open drug use by the parents, and an arsenal of unsecured firearms. It was while living there that Cameron stole his uncle's shotgun, ran away, and killed himself. Dr. Dodge met three times with various family members after Cameron's death to discuss her observations and express her condolences. Cameron's family subsequently filed a malpractice suit against Dr. Dodge.

After reviewing the clinical records, the plaintiff's expert expressed the following opinions about Dr. Dodge's care and treatment of Cameron:

- *Failure to adequately evaluate, diagnose, and treat:* There was no documented assessment of Cameron's presenting problems; no evidence of a mental status exam having been conducted; no evidence of a complete and thorough developmental, social, and psychiatric history, including his history of substance abuse, sleep problems, and so on. There was no effort to secure prior treatment records. There was no documented diagnostic assessment; there was no attempt to explore and consider alternative diagnostic formulations, particularly possible comorbidity among diagnoses of major depression, substance abuse, or conduct disorder; and there was no multiaxial diagnostic assessment.

Furthermore, the plaintiff's expert concluded that no treatment plan was developed, and no treatment goals were established. The treatment that Cameron received was not tied to a diagnostic formulation. Cameron was in need of individual psychotherapy but did not receive this. There was no evident treatment strategy that focused on Cameron's problems or individual needs. Allegedly, family therapy was provided, but never was the entire family seen together at one time. Dr. Dodge was never in control of the treatment; it was dictated by whomever the patient was that day. Cameron, a severely disturbed adolescent, was seen only five times alone and only a total of nine times over a 3-month period.

In spite of the presence of multiple risk factors for suicide (and possibly others never asked about), the plaintiff's expert found that there was no effort to conduct a thorough risk assessment and to base treatment interventions accordingly. There was also no effort to consider suicide risk within the context of his diagnoses, particularly with the possibility of comorbidity.

In addition, Dr. Dodge recommended that Cameron move to his aunt's household without adequately assessing this family; with (available) knowledge of significant family violence and alcohol and drug use in this family; and without exploring (and having removed) the availability of a firearm in the context of Cameron's suicide ideation.

- *Failure to protect confidentiality*: The plaintiff's expert found that Dr. Dodge failed to follow ethical standards and to maintain appropriate clinician–patient boundaries. Specifically, information gained from one or another family member in sessions not attended by others was shared with those others.

- *Fraudulent fees and insurance statements*: The plaintiff's expert found that Dr. Dodge fraudulently billed the family's insurance company: double-billing for a single session, claiming more than one individual therapy session when two members of the family were seen together, and billing in Cameron's name after his death. All sessions were billed to the insurance company as individual psychotherapy in spite of Cameron being seen alone only five times.

Dr. Dodge's liability insurance company settled this suit for several hundred thousand dollars.

The following case similarly describes alleged multiple breaches in the standard of care in the treatment of an adolescent on an inpatient unit.

Case Illustration

Marshall, a 13-year-old male, was admitted to a private psychiatric hospital on a 90-day order granted at a judicial hearing following an acute stay at another local hospital for running away with a friend and with a loaded shotgun.

On admission, he was given multiple *DSM* Axis I diagnoses, depressive disorder not otherwise specified, poly-substance abuse, oppositional disorder, and attention-deficit/hyperactivity disorder (ADHD), and two Axis II diagnoses, borderline and narcissistic personality disorders.

Marshall's history of depressive episodes is similar to that described in chapter 4's Case Illustration on page 164. A drug screen at admission was negative. Chart notes reflected that he was admitted to "contain suicidal impulses."

Marshall was placed on 30-minute observational precautions. Marshall contracted for safety with nursing staff. The comprehensive treatment plan, written 2 days after admission, established four problem-area foci: (a) impaired social relationships, social withdrawal, and excessive talk about bizarre topics; (b) anger management; (c) substance abuse; and (d) family conflict. Orders were written for Prozac (20 mg.), family therapy (2–3 times/week), group therapy, recreational therapy, activity therapy, substance abuse group therapy, anger-management therapy, and so on.

Ten days after admission, nursing staff noted superficial scratches on both of Marshall's wrists and lower forearms. Marshall reported feeling depressed and "wanting to die" the night before. It was unknown what object was used. Marshall was assigned an individual goal by the hospital administrator, a psychologist new to, and not yet licensed by, the state, to "list 101 ways I could kill myself," as a paradoxical intervention "to take the mystique out of it."

Four weeks after admission, after Marshall had been particularly disruptive in a group meeting, his room was searched and evidence was found that he had been hoarding and crushing his medication and snorting it. He was removed to a secluded time-out room located at the back of the patient care unit, isolated from his peers at the end of a hallway where he was to remain until he completed three individual goal's and showed decreased disruptive behavior. The room had a mattress and sheet; all personal belongings remained in his bedroom.

Three nights later, a family therapy session was held with Marshall and his mother, in which Marshall's "self-sabotaging behaviors" were discussed. Both Marshall and his mother cried during the session. After the session, his mother told the social worker, "I think he'll try to kill himself just to prove us all wrong." In response, the social worker placed Marshall again on 30-minute suicide precautions. Even before the order was written, however, Marshall had hanged himself with his bed sheet from a door hinge in the seclusion room.

Upon filing a malpractice claim against the hospital, the psychologist-administrator, and the social worker, the following were listed among the breaches in the standard of care alleged by plaintiff's experts:

- Failure to provide proper treatment,
- Negligent provision of punitive behavioral treatment; treatment intervention provided by nonclinical staff,
- Failure to provide a coherent treatment plan for Marshall's depression,
- Failure to manage medication; failure to consider a faster-acting medication or a potentiating drug such as lithium,
- Failure to safeguard (time-out room neither visible to staff nor suicide-proofed),

> - Failure to follow hospital policies and procedures limiting time-out to a maximum of 1 hour (vs. 3 days),
> - Failure to institute suicide precautions in a timely manner,
> - Callous disregard for and failure to assess suicide risk.

As an appendix to this chapter, we present to you the case of Bill, in which experts' opinions for both the plaintiff and the defense are offered for you to consider in formulating your own opinion.

CONFIDENTIALITY

In an era dictated by Health Information and Portability and Accountability Act (HIPAA) regulations, it is important that we speak to related questions of confidentiality. Each of the major mental health disciplines has specific guidelines of ethical principles that bear on a patient's right to confidentiality. For psychologists, the American Psychological Association's (American Psychological Association, 2002) Ethics Code describes the various circumstances and conditions in which a patient's right to confidentiality may be broken (no matter what their age). In essence, the patient's confidentiality is protected at all times except for circumstances in which there is clear and imminent danger to self or others (in some circumstances, substantial inability to care for oneself and cases of ongoing sexual abuse of a minor will warrant a break in confidentiality). Similarly, the American Psychiatric Association's (2001) Ethical Code, Section 4.8, specifies that confidential information may be revealed "in order to protect the patient or the community from imminent danger"; and the National Association of Social Workers Code of Ethics (National Association of Social Workers, 1999), Standard 1.07 on privacy and confidentiality, "does not apply when disclosure is necessary to prevent serious, foreseeable, and imminent harm to a client."

With the advent of HIPAA, all health professionals are required to be mindful of issues pertaining to privacy and security of personal health information. With full HIPAA compliance having commenced on April 14, 2003, a considerable emphasis is now being made to inform patient consumers about privacy issues and explanations of how their personal health information is being handled and communicated. For practitioners, HIPAA has increased awareness about those elements that constitute an adequate and complete medical record and the importance of how one handles confidential material (from how records are literally stored to how personal information is to be communicated to other providers or insurance companies). At the time of this writing, HIPAA and its various and considerable provisions are being sorted out. What ultimately HIPAA means to patient and practitioner may not be known for many years until litigation and case law further clarifies what is essential about this significant development in the health care industry.

Generally speaking, evidence of clear and imminent danger to self (in the absence of a clear commitment to safety) requires the clinician to take whatever steps are necessary to ensure the physical safety of the patient. Necessary steps may include hospitalization, initiation of commitment procedures, or notification of law-enforcement officials. As will be discussed in the following section, parents of a minor at clear and imminent risk must be informed as well.

Confidentiality and Minors

As outlined in previous chapters, the determination of clear and imminent danger is a clinical judgment. There simply is no actuarial approach to this assessment. Thus, the clinician must use best judgment as a guide as to when parents of a minor must be informed of their child's assessed risk. Our belief is that it is best to align parents with the treatment of their child, and an open discussion of their child's assessed risk is important to that alignment. Further, it is best to align the adolescent with this strategy at the beginning of treatment. This is both good practice and a good risk-management practice.

Whereas the need to break confidence is evident in situations where assessed risk of harm is high, clear, or imminent, there may be somewhat less clarity about issues of confidentiality in ongoing clinical work with minors. Under current statutes, with few exceptions, the law deems adolescents (under 18 years of age) not sufficiently mature to make treatment decisions. Conversely, parents of a minor child retain the legal authority to permit or refuse treatment of their child. As parents are legally responsible for the welfare of their children, they are in the position to grant informed consent and make key decisions about their child's treatment. In the eyes of the law, parents technically have a right to any and all information obtained in an evaluation or treatment of their child. Therefore, while the child is the recipient of treatment, the parents in effect become the clients of the provider (Brewer & Faitak, 1989).

Counterbalancing the laws pertaining to minors and their lack of rights to informed consent and confidentiality are the various professional association's codes of ethics, which protect the privacy and confidentiality of information gathered in treatment. Clinicians must take special care to protect the overall welfare and best interests of the adolescent patient. To this end, clinicians who work with minors must find a balance between respecting the legal rights of the parents while ensuring the best possible care for their child. Parents should therefore be fully informed of their legal rights as well as the clinical issues that bear on the best interests (i.e., the treatment) of their child.

Although parents may technically have a right to any information shared in treatment, successful therapy may be undermined if adolescents believe that anything they say may be readily and inappropriately disclosed to their parents. For treatment to be effective, adolescents must be able to trust the therapist with their most private thoughts and feelings and, wherever possible, have their autonomy respected. Conversely, parents must trust the therapist's judgment to disclose relevant information in an amount and manner that best serves their child's treatment.

To address the inherent issues, thoughtful, thorough, and proactive treatment planning, ideally with both the parents and the adolescent, is essential to laying the foundation for successful treatment of a minor. All the major professional associations' codes of ethics specify the relevant limits of confidentiality. Similarly, these ethics codes speak to principles of informed consent, meaning that issues of confidentiality and conditions under which it would not apply should be thoroughly discussed with both minors and their parents prior to the onset of treatment. At a minimum, it is considered reasonable to inform parents of their child's diagnosis, associated symptoms or problem description, the nature and purpose of the proposed treatment, the risks and consequences of the proposed treatment, the viable alternatives to the proposed treatment, and the prognosis should the proposed treatment be accepted or not (Bongar, 2002). We believe it is important to have these discussions regarding confidentiality, ground rules, the initial treatment plan and rationale, and so on conjointly with the parents and their child, if possible at the end of the first session, or, if not, at the second session (i.e., before the treatment plan actually is initiated).

The nature, timing, and extent of disclosure of clinical information to the parents should be specifically discussed and understood by all parties. Periodic meetings to update and modify the treatment should be planned as well. When working with a suicidal youth, it is sometimes valuable to discuss problem-solving strategies that might enlist the support of the parents should the adolescent become actively suicidal. The goal is to think through and plan around potential hurdles in advance and thereby begin to build a team approach to working through the inherent issues. In a similar vein, Taylor and Adelman (1989) describe reframing approaches that motivate the patient to share information when it is considered to be in his or her best interest. It is with the adolescent's best interest in mind that these ethical and legal issues frame good clinical practice.

More than this, there are good clinical rationales for involving the family. First and foremost is the recognition of the social matrix of suicide, with the family being most influential in the developmental pathway of the adolescent.

Second is the ongoing role the family must play in the therapeutic work of the adolescent patient (Wagner, 1997).

Regarding the former, the clinician has a duty to seek corroborative information from the parents at the time of an emergency triage evaluation. It behooves the clinician as well to conduct an evaluation of the youth in the context of his or her family; such an evaluation provides a wealth of information regarding parental psychopathology, impaired family communications, hostility, inflexible problem solving, symbiotic relationships, scapegoating, and so on. Observations of family functioning inform treatment planning that might require collateral family therapy or parallel therapies of one or both parents. In some cases, observations of family pathology might necessitate treatment decisions to protect the patient from the parents (Jacobson, 1999).

Regardless of whether the family might constitute part of the adolescent's risk for suicide, the family is an important contributor to the protection of the child. Parents must be sought as allies of the caregiver and the treatment goals; as observer-reporters of the adolescent's mental status and behavior outside of the therapeutic hour; as collateral caregivers in monitoring medication compliance, where called for; as motivators and supporters of their child's attachment to and compliance with the treatment plan; and as guardians of their child's safety with regard, for example, to making available firearms inaccessible, and so on. Furthermore, parents must be informed at the termination of outpatient treatment or at the dispositional transition from inpatient to outpatient care of (a) the potential return of pretreatment suicidal risk, (b) specific issues or stresses that could precipitate further suicidal behavior, (c) the importance of maintaining realistic expectations, (d) what to be observant of, and (e) what to do if and when such observations are noted.

Practice parameters specific to emergency or crisis service interventions, and triage decisions before discharging an adolescent who has made a nonfatal suicide attempt, have been published by the American Academy of Child and Adolescent Psychiatry (2001). At a minimum, we believe these reflect the standard of care at this juncture of working with a suicidal adolescent. Table 7.2 reflects these recommendations.

A strong, positive alliance with the adolescent's family may be the caregiver's best defense against the initiation of malpractice litigation. Where parents have been reasonably informed of the seriousness and complexity of the problems presented by their child, in particular of their child's self-destructive potential and the caregiver's efforts to reduce risk during treatment, the likelihood of these parents alleging negligence after the death of their child would appear to diminish greatly. Anticipating and acknowledging the risk inherent in working with a disturbed adolescent while affirming the patient's strengths to the adolescent patient's parents works to align the parents with

TABLE 7.2
Emergency Discharge Planning Checklist for Adolescent Attempters
and Families

- Have caretaker verify adolescent's account of attempt
- Discuss with caretaker how to effectively secure or remove firearms and lethal medications
- Caution caretaker to limit access to potentially disinhibiting substances (alcohol or drugs)
- Educate caretakers on the need for their support, observation, and monitoring
- Identify potential precipitants and how to prevent reoccurrences
- Obtain commitment from both adolescent and caretakers to attend scheduled follow-up appointment(s)

Note. Data adapted from *Practice Parameters and Guidelines: Suicide* (p. 40S), by the American Academy of Child and Adolescent Psychiatry, 2001, Washington, DC: Author. Copyright 2001 by the American Academy of Child and Adolescent Psychiatry. Adapted with permission.

the therapist and shared goals. Last, where the caregiver attends the funeral and expresses shared grief, rather than defensiveness, risk of a malpractice action is reasonably managed. In this regard it is interesting to note that the Peterson et al. (2002) survey found that survivors reputedly were less litigious when clinicians made contact after the suicide of their loved one; however, as a rule, defense attorneys tend to strongly discourage clinicians from having contact with the family of the deceased after a suicide. As a related issue, clinicians must understand that the psychotherapist–patient privilege survives the death of a patient; thus, confidentiality restrictions on patient records continue after the death of a patient unless expressly waived by the decedent's duly appointed legal representative (Stromberg et al., 1993).

CONCLUSION

It is impossible to sufficiently describe the range of potential acts of omission or commission that can occur in the treatment of a potentially suicidal patient. Such patients' problems and dynamics are notably complex and often difficult to treat. For these reasons, the essential task of the caregiver is to adequately assess and maximally design and implement a treatment plan consistent with that assessment. The therapist needs a protocol, a plan of treatment that takes into account the idiographic aspects of each presenting case, an understanding of potentially helpful strategies and techniques, and the therapeutic armamentarium from which to selectively cull and apply strategies deemed appropriate. On the basis of a functional analysis of the suicidal adolescent's motives and a complete assessment of the suicidal adolescent, these applied interventions translate treatment into prevention, a theme to be more broadly considered in our next chapter.

It is, perhaps, unfortunate that the work of a clinical practitioner must occur under the watchful eye of the legal community; however, this is an inescapable reality of modern American life. Parents have a right to expect that their children will be fairly treated and to ask practitioners to use reasonable judgment in making treatment decisions. In this regard, the otherwise intrusive thought of potential litigation has an upside. It forces practitioners to be more observant and cautious, more attentive to what they are doing, and more focused on actively working to reduce observed risk and enabling available protections for their adolescent patients. We view these consequences not as promoting "defensive medicine" but as improving standards of care. The best risk management regarding the potential for a malpractice suit after the suicide of a patient is simply that of good practice. The consequence of good practice is proper attention to our patients' well-being and a considerably diminished likelihood of needing to attend to the potential for litigation.

Case Illustration

Bill was 12 years old when he was found hanging in the family garage the first week of August. The third of four children in a middle-class family, Bill had a 2-year history of conduct-based problems, depression, and substance abuse. He had been performing poorly in school for years and was going to be held back from seventh grade in the coming fall. The family had a fair amount of marital and family discord. Bill's two older siblings (a brother and sister) had been seen with some success by Dr. Nelson, a clinical psychologist with expertise in adolescence and family psychotherapy. Bill began seeing Dr. Nelson in May after a particularly poor year in school and a recent foiled "suicide attempt." Bill's dad had walked into his room while Bill was trying to affix a hanger to a nail on his wall to hang himself. Bill's dad did not take this attempt seriously—the small nail would never have supported Bill's weight.

Dr. Nelson met with Bill's parents shortly after this event; he subsequently saw Bill for a total of five sessions, rather irregularly over the course of the summer. After the initial session, Dr. Nelson diagnosed Bill with unipolar depression and poly-substance abuse. His assessment of Bill's suicidality was relatively thorough and fairly well documented (his initial note ran three full pages). Dr. Nelson promptly referred Bill to Dr. Kelly, a psychiatrist colleague of his for over 20 years, who saw Bill for two sessions and prescribed Paxil for depression. Dr. Nelson and Dr. Kelly never actually conferred about the case over the course of care.

Dr. Nelson's treatment plan was modest: close parental supervision of contraband drugs and acting-out behaviors, referral for substance-abuse evaluation, increased behavioral activity including sports (with his father in particular), and possible tutoring for academic difficulties. Dr. Nelson explained to Bill his policy on emergencies, gave him his card with all available numbers, and reported having made a solemn contract with Bill that he would call if he felt suicidal. Clinician and patient shook hands on the deal and Dr. Nelson felt confident about Bill's outpatient safety.

By all accounts, Bill's mood and behavior improved over the course of care. He attended his first sessions and seemed committed to improving his behaviors and stopping all alcohol and marijuana use. He was spending more time with his dad and elected to take a firearm safety course with him. Bill and his dad enjoyed some hunting trips together and Bill enjoyed a 2-week sports camp that he attended with his younger brother. In the beginning of July, Bill went to spend 3 weeks with his grandparents out of state. These weeks went by unremarkably; letters home to his parents were upbeat; he really enjoyed swimming, boating, and fishing with his grandfather. Although the sports camp and trip interrupted Bill's outpatient therapy, Dr. Nelson did not object given Bill's steady improvement and positive reports.

Following his return in late July, Bill met (for the last time) with Dr. Nelson. He seemed a little glum about coming home but reported looking forward to a fresh start in school. Dr. Nelson asked about and Bill denied having any suicidal thoughts. One week later, Bill failed his gun-safety exam, which was terribly disappointing to him. The following day Bill's mother called home from work during lunch to check on Bill and got no answer. Worried, she contacted her husband, asking him to swing by the house to check on Bill. Bill's father found him hanging in the garage by a cord nailed to a crossbeam. Dr. Nelson learned of Bill's suicide later that day and immediately contacted the family; he then sent a condolence card and attended the funeral. He indicated to the parents that he was stunned by the tragedy as they all agreed that Bill was doing so much better. Given these circumstances, Dr. Nelson was even more stunned when, 6 months later, he was informed that a malpractice suit had been filed alleging that his care of Bill had breached the standard of care. The complaints included

- failure to adequately assess and diagnose the risk of suicide;
- failure to develop an adequate treatment plan specific to suicide;
- failure to coordinate care with medicating psychiatrist;
- failure to address academic concerns sufficiently; and
- failure to hospitalize patient following the initial suicide attempt.

Experts were engaged to review the case by both the plaintiff's and defense attorneys. The plaintiff's expert contended that Dr. Nelson failed to meet the standard of care on a number of fronts. First, he did not sufficiently assess the risk of suicide (neither assessment tools nor psychological tests were administered), and there was sufficient risk to warrant an initial hospitalization and thorough evaluation in an inpatient setting. Second, he asserted that Dr. Nelson's treatment plan was too modest; there were not enough suicide-specific aspects addressed and interventions applied to assure outpatient safety. Third, the failure to communicate and coordinate care with the psychiatrist was presented as a major professional and ethical failing.

In turn, the defense expert disputed the alleged failing in coordinating care with the psychiatrist, arguing that both clinicians relied on their 20-year working relationship to alert each other if and when the case warranted concern. In the case of Bill, both clinicians thought the case was going well and substantiated that with their records. Citing literature on the poor quality of care in general practice, the defense expert argued that Dr. Nelson's assessment of suicidality was typical, if not superior, and that his documentation was unusually detailed. Although the treatment plan was indeed limited, a viable plan was documented and appeared to be working up to the time Bill died. The defense expert further contended that care could have perhaps been better in hindsight; however, on virtually all aspects (but for failing to consult with his colleague), Dr. Nelson either met or exceeded the standard of care. Given that neither practitioner saw reason for concern, and both could document improvements, however, this failing to consult with each other was not in any way causative of Bill's suicide. Yet, tragically, Bill died.

Was Bill's care acceptable or below the standard of care? Given the wisdom of hindsight, you might well agree with the plaintiff's expert that Bill should have received any and all possible assessments and treatments and that, had these been instituted, Bill's suicide might have been averted. On the other hand, given his notable improvement and that the standard of care does not require *optimal* clinical behavior, on what reasonable grounds would you argue, as did the plaintiff's expert, that Dr. Nelson clearly performed inadequately and that the alleged breaches in the standard of care proximally caused Bill's suicide? Should Dr. Nelson be found negligent in the case of Bill?

II

PREVENTION AND POSTVENTION

8

PREVENTION

In the last 15 years there have been major developments in our conceptualization and implementation of suicide prevention programs. The typical mental health clinical practitioner usually thinks of prevention and health promotion one person at a time—as individual patients who file through our various practice settings. The typical prevention-oriented professional usually thinks of prevention and health promotion many people at a time, targeting the population, groups, and subgroups at risk in the larger community. On closer examination, however, we shall see that broad-based suicide prevention uses many of the same principles and approaches used on a more individualized scale in clinical practice. As clinicians, we typically await problems, symptoms, and syndromes to be brought to us by patients; these are the targets of our interventions. But as clinicians who have gained extensive prevention-oriented experience, we seek to broaden our perspective to meld the mental health with the public health approaches in ways that can prove to be interactive and complimentary.

As this text is primarily written for clinical practitioners, the reader may wonder why we have added a whole new chapter on prevention in this edition of our book. We believe the dramatic contemporary evolution in adolescent suicide prevention programs and thinking can have a critical impact on the way clinicians conceptualize problems and interventions, particularly forging greater collaboration and out-of-the-box thinking in matters of timing and focus of our work. Moreover, we hope that an understanding of the larger youth suicide prevention efforts will compel clinician readers to extend their work beyond the confines of the clinical office and get involved with this important and essential effort. There can be tremendous professional satisfaction in working synergistically at both an individual (clinical) level as well as at a population or group (prevention) level. Considering the scope of the problem, we clearly have a need for both.

DEVELOPMENTS IN THE YOUTH SUICIDE PREVENTION MOVEMENT

Beginning with the publication of the four-volume U.S. Department of Health and Human Services *Secretary's Task Force on Youth Suicide* in 1989 (Alcohol, Drug Abuse, and Mental Health Administration, 1989) (including an entire volume entitled "Strategies for the Prevention of Youth Suicide"), the decade of the 1990s was marked by a concentrated focus on exploring the potential for the prevention of suicide and suicidal behaviors across the life span, with a particular emphasis on youth and adolescents. The approaches ranged from national strategies to school-based programs to interventions for high-risk youth (runaways, dropouts, the incarcerated).

On the international level, the International Association for Suicide Prevention (IASP), the United Nations (UN), and the World Health Organization (WHO) have shown leadership with support for community interventions, and recently, the World Psychiatric Association (WPA) established a section on Suicidology. Suicide is now widely accepted as an international public health problem, and suicidal behaviors are seen to be preventable (World Health Organization, 2002). To document this, in September 2003, the WHO teamed with IASP to sponsor the first World Suicide Prevention Day and moved toward making this an annual event to occur in all countries across the globe.

Back in the United States, some of the major public and private organizations that have spearheaded these efforts include the American Association of Suicidology (AAS), the American Foundation for Suicide Prevention (AFSP), and the Suicide Prevention Action Network (SPAN USA). In addition, leaders among a dozen national nonprofit organizations doing work in suicide prevention and several federal departments (especially the departments of Health and Human Services, Education, and Defense) have been actively involved in suicide prevention efforts. In the last few years, major reports regarding suicide prevention have emanated from the National Academy of Sciences/Institute of Medicine (NAS/IOM; Goldsmith, Pellmar, Kleinman, & Bunney, 2002), the President's New Freedom Commission on Mental Health (2003), and the Office of the Surgeon General (U.S. Public Health Service, 1999, 2001). In connection with these efforts, a Federal Steering Group (FSG) within the U.S. Public Health Service has been formed (DeMartino et al., 2003).

The emerging field of suicide prevention has been chronicled by a number of major books and monographs (Berman, 1990a; Hawton & van Heeringen, 2000; Hendin & Mann, 2001; Jacobs, 1999; Kosky, Eshkevari, Goldney, & Hassan, 1998; Lester, 2001; Maris, Berman, & Silverman, 2000; Silverman & Maris, 1995a; Upanne, 2001; Vijayakumar, 2003). A number of national programs (e.g., in Australia, Finland, New Zealand) and state programs (e.g., in Oregon, Washington, Maine) have focused on youth suicide prevention. Public health concepts of disease prevention and health promotion have been applied to the challenge of suicide prevention, most notably concepts and techniques of injury prevention (Potter, Powell, & Kachur, 1995; Sanddal, Sanddal, Berman, & Silverman, 2003; Silverman & Maris, 1995a). In 1998, the Centers for Disease Control and Prevention funded the first Suicide Prevention Research Center, and in 2002, the Substance Abuse, Mental Health Services Administration (SAMHSA) funded the first National Suicide Prevention Technical Resource Center.

Beginning with the following Case Illustration, this chapter will provide an overview of the theory of prevention from a public health perspective (disease prevention and health promotion) and will review existing, promising, and evaluated suicide prevention programs specifically targeted at youth and adolescents.

Case Illustration

In March 1987, Bergenfield, New Jersey, gained instant celebrity, no doubt one it neither desired nor appreciated. Four teenagers—two boys and two sisters ranging in age from 16 to 19—died in a group suicide pact by carbon-monoxide poisoning in a car in a closed garage. While waiting to die, each took turns writing notes on a brown paper bag.

In published reports of their deaths, these four teens were variously described as "deeply troubled," "losers," and "pain-in-the-ass type kids" (Martz, 1987). Indeed, all had significant histories of alcohol and drug abuse, all were estranged from their conflict-ridden families, three had dropped out of school and the fourth had recently been suspended, and all four advocated punk styles and were into heavy-metal rock music. Perhaps of most profound importance, all had been friendly with another school dropout, an 18-year-old boy who, in an alcohol-related incident, either fell or jumped to his death off the New Jersey Palisades along the Hudson River the year before. One of the girls had dated this boy, and one of the male suicide victims had witnessed that death. The other boy had seen his father kill himself 4 years earlier.

During the prior year, three other Bergenfield youths had died equivocal deaths, each certified by the coroner as an accident. Two of these youngsters, best friends, were hit by freight trains in alcohol-related incidents within 3 weeks of each other (Cantor, 1989). In the days immediately succeeding the "Bergenfield Four" deaths, a 20-year-old man died by carbon-monoxide poisoning in his family car at home, 20 miles southwest of Bergenfield; within hours of this death, a psychiatrically disturbed 20-year-old woman, with three prior attempts, and her 17-year-old boyfriend were interrupted and rescued in the midst of their carbon-monoxide suicide attempt in the same garage as the Bergenfield Four!

In Chicago on the day after the first Bergenfield suicide incident, two girls, age 17 and 19, described as "inseparable," carried out their planned suicide pact. This occurred also by carbon-monoxide poisoning, under the influence of alcohol, and, apparently, was inspired by the publicity from the Bergenfield suicides (Martz, 1987). As many as a dozen other "copycat suicides" were alleged to have occurred over the following several months (Diegmuller, 1987). In many ways, these events renewed national interest in the phenomena of suicide clusters and the prevention of suicide in youth.

The phenomenological experience of a suicide cluster in a community or school typically mobilizes responsible people in the community to initiate preventive programming. Such crisis-initiated problem-solving behavior probably has reinforced the unfortunate use of the word "contagion" to describe the process of clustering, as if anyone and everyone in the community were now susceptible to catching the suicide bug!

Although the youths in the previous case may have had in common what we know now to be risk factors for completed suicide, the commonality in their method and in the apparent suggestibility of their suicidal actions is most striking. What mechanisms might underlie such a rash of suicidal actions? Shared delusions, a magical belief that in death one can appreciate the attention of the media to such events, or simply a legitimizing—a permission-giving to an action otherwise still latent—stirred by the model of another?

As clinicians, we know that some adolescents are symbiotically bonded with another; the death of the one may therefore compel the death of the other; this is done to avoid an unwanted separation (Gould, Greenberg, Belting, & Shaffer, 2003). Others are compelled to suicide as penance because they feel overwhelming guilt and responsibility for not preventing the death of the first. Each mechanism is apparent in the Bergenfield suicide pact and the influencing deaths that preceded the pact.

There is little dispute that clusters do occur and that suicidal youths within a cluster have known risk factors that can identify them with some precision. By identifying adolescents at risk for an imitative suicide and those closely bonded with suicidal others, steps can be taken to interrupt pathways of influence (Hawton et al., 1999; Schmidtke & Schaller, 2000). As was discussed in chapter 3 and as will be discussed later in this chapter, the 1994 suicide of Kurt Cobain, lead singer of the band Nirvana, led many experts to fear a rash of copycat adolescent suicides would occur (Jobes, Berman, O'Carroll, Eastgard, & Knickmeyer, 1996). In this case, however, media guidelines on how to handle suicide stories may have made a difference in the aftermath of the rock icon's death. In this regard, community-wide models for the prevention and containment of suicide clusters have been proposed by the Centers for Disease Control (1988), and related recommendations for the media responses to suicidal events have been recently revised (Centers for Disease Control and Prevention, 2002a). There is a growing sense in the suicide prevention community that broad-based prevention efforts *can* make a difference, proving that causal relationships between interventions and decreased suicide is nevertheless an elusive goal.

OVERVIEW TO PREVENTION THEORY

There is extensive theorizing in the field of prevention that shapes and guides prevention efforts. Generally speaking, the defining features of prevention programs include their timing, the level of analysis they target, and the conditions that are the first- and second-order (most direct) targets of change (Silverman & Felner, 1995).

The field of public health has traditionally held twin goals: disease prevention and health promotion. Public health is grounded in the science of epidemiology. Hence, as shown in Exhibit 8.1, we begin with the standard tripartite epidemiological definitions of prevention: primary, secondary, and tertiary (Caplan, 1964).

EXHIBIT 8.1
Epidemiological Definitions of Prevention

Prevalence = Incidence x Duration
Incidence = $\dfrac{\text{Prevalence}}{\text{Duration}}$
Primary Prevention: Reduce Prevalence by Reducing *Incidence*
Secondary Prevention: Reduce Prevalence by Reducing *Duration*
Tertiary Prevention: Reduce Prevalence by Reducing *Reoccurrence*

Note. From *Encyclopedia of Primary Prevention and Health Promotion* (p. 28), by T. Gulotta and M. Bloom, 2003, New York: Kluwer Academic/Plenum Publishers. Copyright 2003 by Kluwer Academic/Plenum Publishers. Adapted with permission.

Primary prevention reduces the prevalence of a disorder or dysfunction by reducing the number of new cases (*incidence*) that appear in a defined population. Secondary prevention reduces the prevalence of a disorder by reducing the *duration* of a disorder or dysfunction in individuals who have expressed signs and symptoms of that disorder. Tertiary prevention reduces the prevalence of a disorder by reducing the *reoccurrence* of episodes.

Berman and Jobes (1995; see Exhibit 8.2) have applied these concepts to adolescents at risk for suicide. Primary prevention traditionally has focused predominantly on the modalities of information and education. Early recognition, identification, and intervention define secondary prevention efforts. Tertiary prevention is designed to prevent recurrent episodes. Generally speaking, by definition, clinicians are most typically involved with secondary or tertiary levels of intervention. For example, primary prevention in the school system would include a health class that everyone takes that focuses on health promotion, disease prevention, stress reduction, and utilization of a range of coping skills. Secondary prevention includes the early identification of students at increased risk for suicidal behaviors, as well as arranging for an assessment and intervention. Such increased risk factors include the onset of depressive symptoms, the use of alcohol or other drugs, truancy, or openly talking about death and dying. Tertiary prevention is the treatment of adolescents who have already attempted suicide. The concept implies a restoration to a level of prior healthy functioning.

THE ANATOMY OF PREVENTION MODELS

When looking at a model for the prevention of suicide or suicidal behaviors, it must account for the following variables: (a) it must be applicable to *specific settings* in which one would find groups of individuals at risk

A Conceptual Model of Prevention Strategies

	Individual Predisposition	Social Milieu	Proximal Agents
Primary Prevention	Depression management Anger management Loneliness prevention Problem-solving training Competency enhancement Critical viewing skills Help-seeking training	Dropout prevention Early detection and referral of parental pathology Surrogate role models Media guidance	Gun-safety training for parents and pediatricians Suicide awareness among health care providers Federal firearms prevention education
Secondary Prevention	Triage programs Volunteerism Outpatient treatment	Gatekeeper training Peer counseling Parental pathology Case finding Caregiver training	Medication emetics Environmental safety Decrease access to guns
Tertiary Prevention	Psychiatric treatment Substance abuse treatment	Community mental health treatment Juvenile justice programs Case management follow-up	Selective serotonin reuptake inhibitor (SSRI) treatment Psychotherapy for depression Neuroleptics for psychosis

Note. From *Suicide Prevention: Toward the Year 2000* (p. 149), by M. M. Silverman and R. W. Maris (Eds.), 1995, New York: Guilford Press. Copyright 1995 by Guilford Press. Adapted with permission.

for the behaviors; (b) it must be adaptable to various *developmental stages and phases* of groups of individuals, or be specifically focused on a target population known to be at high risk for the behaviors; (c) it must be *adaptable to various settings* where groups of people congregate; (d) it must *specifically address the etiology, pathogenesis, and known risk factors* associated with the targeted behavior; (e) it must clearly *identify the goal of its activity* (i.e., primary prevention, early intervention, secondary prevention or pretreatment); (f) it must allow for the use of multiple types of interventions over time; and (g) it must be testable, in that its components can be measured and easily defined (Silverman & Koretz, 1989).

Felner, Felner, and Silverman (2000) identified a critical set of tasks that must be addressed in the design of preventive efforts. These tasks are (a) to assess the ways in which normal developmental processes have been disrupted in the target population, (b) to identify those conditions that lead to these disruptions and distortions, and (c) to create interventions whose goals are to modify or "correct" these distortions until they closely approximate those that lead to "healthy" development and healthy outcomes.

To effectively mount a successful preventive intervention program, it is incumbent to first measure the extent of the problem (epidemiology), identify who is at risk (risk assessment), decide how and where to target interventions (needs assessment), identify local resources and support networks (ecological assessment), and be prepared to provide immediate interventions for those identified at most risk (treatment; Silverman & Koretz, 1989).

When evaluating prevention models, researchers must be clear about what *precisely* is being prevented, and what *precisely* is being measured, to determine to what extent the intervention has been successful at achieving that specific goal. Any successful intervention aimed at reducing the prevalence of suicidal ideation in the adolescent population, for example, must start with baseline data (e.g., the Youth Risk Behavior Survey [see chap. 1] regarding self-reported suicidal ideation) and the assurance that the measures being used to gauge the targeted outcome (suicidal ideation) preintervention are robust, reliable, and valid. Once the intervention is established, those same tools, techniques, and measurement instruments must be used to measure change over time.

One must start by defining features of prevention that must be present in any model: (a) interventions are timed to be "before the fact" (i.e., before the expression of the targeted disorder or symptom) and hence are directed at essentially "well" populations; (b) the level of analysis is at the population, group, or community level; (c) the focus of the change efforts is on preconditions, antecedent conditions, precipitating conditions, perpetuating conditions, and so on; (d) efforts are directed at promoting strengths, well-being, and positive developmental outcomes or reducing psychological maladjustment; and (e) a sensitivity to the physical, emotional, and psychological developmental stages of the targeted behavior must be present (Cowen, 1983; Felner et al., 2000).

THE INTERFACE BETWEEN SUICIDAL BEHAVIORS AND PREVENTION MODELS

Inasmuch as most suicidal behaviors are multicausal and multifactorial in etiology, so must the preventive interventions themselves be multifocal in terms of the behaviors and etiological agents they are designed to target. Any serious discussion of preventive efforts directed at adolescent suicide must first define those behaviors that (a) define the targeted behaviors to be prevented, (b) define the pathological continuum associated with suicide, and (c) represent the frequently observed signs and symptoms found to be highly associated with suicide and suicidal behaviors. Effective prevention outcomes are predicated on intervening before the targeted disorder or illness becomes a reality. However, predicting future behavior, even in a high-risk population, is not easy to do—if not impossible.

For example, a summary of the research literature suggests that approximately 10% to 15% of suicide attempters have a lifetime risk of eventually dying by suicide, whereas only 30% to 40% of those who die by suicide have had a prior history of suicide attempts (Maris et al., 2000). Although these numbers suggest that there is a small, but significant, group of suicide attempters who warrant our attention and intervention, there is also a larger group of individuals for whom we need other markers to identify their risk for eventual suicide.

Thus, a number of basic assumptions fundamentally define prevention, and these assumptions altogether parallel certain assumptions made in clinical practice. Exhibit 8.3 lists various basic assumptions that are used to develop preventive interventions and prevention models.

EXHIBIT 8.3
Basic Assumptions About Prevention

We know

- how to define the risk condition and behavior.
- who is at risk.
- how to identify who is at most risk.
- why an individual is at risk.
- when an individual is at most risk.
- which situations, settings, and behaviors place an individual at most risk.
- which interventions lower an individual's risk status.
- when interventions are to be applied to lower an individual's risk.
- which outcomes are to be measured.

Note. From *Encyclopedia of Primary Prevention and Health Promotion* (p. 32), by T. Gulotta and M. Bloom, 2003, New York: Kluwer Academic/Plenum Publishers. Copyright 2003 by Kluwer Academic/Plenum Publishers. Adapted with permission.

In the broadest sense, virtually all prevention approaches assume the existence of (a) interrelationships among theories of disease expression; (b) epidemiologically established risk factors (both causative and correlational); (c) effective, efficacious, and efficient interventions specifically targeted at those risk factors; (d) culturally sensitive and population-focused interventions that will be readily received and adopted; and (e) the existence of outcome measures that are sensitive and specific to measuring the outcomes that are linked to the specific interventions. As shown in Exhibit 8.4, these conditions allow us to reach decision points about which preventive interventions to select (Silverman, 1996).

EXHIBIT 8.4
Decision Points in Selecting Preventive Interventions

- Which points in the causal chain are particularly vulnerable to interruption?
- Which interventions are likely to contribute to the prevention of a large proportion of a disorder?
- Which interventions are likely to be effective across different (but related) types of disorders?
- What sorts of interventions will result in *immediate* reductions in such disorders?
- What sorts of interventions will result in *long-term* reductions in such disorders?
- Which of the potential interventions are *feasible* and most readily adopted?
- What are the costs of the various promising interventions, relative to their likely *effectiveness*?

Note. Adapted from Third National Injury Control Conference (Department of Health and Human Services, 1992). In the public domain.

THE PUBLIC HEALTH APPROACH AS APPLIED TO SUICIDE PREVENTION

Once again we see distinct parallels between a clinical approach to intervention and a more comprehensive public health approach to prevention. As such, clinical approaches and techniques often generalize well into a prevention-oriented approach to a problem such as youth suicide.

Clearly Defining the Problem

The first step in the public health approach is collecting information about incidence of suicide and suicidal behavior. This step is referred to as *surveillance* and refers to gathering information on the characteristics of individuals who express suicidal behaviors (the circumstances surrounding these incidents, the events that may have precipitated the act, the adequacy of social support and health services received, and the severity and cost of injuries to individuals and society). In addition, this first step provides information on the prevalence of the disorder in the community (the total number of incidents or cases that occur during a fixed time frame or within a well-defined population). This step provides answers to whether a problem is an epidemic or a pandemic, whether it is a burden to the community, and whether it is increasing or decreasing in numbers or rates within defined geographical regions, age groups, or populations. This step covers the who, what, when, where, how, and how many of the identified problem.

Identifying Causes and Protective Factors

The second step focuses on determining why the problem exists in the community and why it may have become a problem of increased concern. During this step, risk factors that may contribute to the expression of suicide and suicidal behaviors are identified. Such risk factors include the degree of depression and alcohol and other drug abuse within the community, barriers to accessing mental health treatment, easy access to lethal means or methods, and impulsive or aggressive tendencies. This step also may be used to define groups of people at increased risk for suicide and suicidal behaviors. At the same time, protective factors are identified, which can include an individual's genetic or neurobiological makeup, attitudinal or behavioral characteristics, and environmental attributes. Protective factors enhance resiliency and serve to counterbalance risk factors. Protective factors include family and community support; effective and appropriate clinical care for mental, physical, and substance abuse disorders; easy access to effective clinical interventions and support; and the acquisition of learned skills for problem solving, conflict resolution, and nonviolent management of disputes. Understanding the interactive relationship between risk factors and protective factors in suicide and suicidal behaviors and how this interaction can be modified are challenges identified within the public health approach.

Developing and Testing Interventions

Over the years, different approaches have been developed to intervene with populations at risk for the expression of suicide and suicidal behaviors. The traditional triad of primary, secondary, and tertiary approaches has been found to be most effective for physical disorders. Newer conceptualizations have been introduced, such as the triad of universal, indicated, and selected interventions (R. S. Gordon, 1983). This approach focuses on the characteristics of the intervention itself: those interventions that are good for everyone (universal), those targeted to individuals at increased risk for the expression of the problem (indicated), and those highly developed and refined interventions directed at those individuals who are already expressing the disorder or dysfunction (selected). The challenge is to develop and test interventions that are matched to the targeted populations and then to measure the effectiveness of each approach to ensure that the strategies are safe, ethical, and feasible. Pilot testing of some of these interventions may reveal important differences among particular age, gender, ethnic, and cultural groups, helping to determine for whom and when a suicide prevention strategy is best fitted.

Implementing Interventions

The next step is to implement interventions that have demonstrated effectiveness in preventing suicide and suicidal behaviors in larger settings and across broader population groups. Implementation requires data collection (surveillance) as a means to continue evaluating effectiveness of an intervention. Determining effectiveness across settings is important prior to endorsing large-scale implementation of public health campaigns.

Evaluating Interventions

Ongoing evaluation builds the evidence base for refining and extending effective suicide prevention programs. Determining an intervention's cost-effectiveness is an important component of this step, as is measuring its impact on a community. The information gleaned from the evaluation of clinical trials and preventive interventions leads to the refinement of interventions and a better understanding of all the components that contribute to the development, maintenance, and expression of suicide and suicidal behaviors in different age groups, cultural and ethnic populations, gender groups, and geographical locations.

As interventions for preventing suicide are developed and implemented, communities must consider several key factors. Interventions have a much greater likelihood of success if they involve a range of services and providers within the community. This requires community leaders to build effective coalitions across traditionally separate sectors, such as the health care delivery system, the mental health delivery system, faith communities, social services, civic groups, educational institutions, and the public health system. Interventions must be adapted and adopted to support and reflect the experience of survivors of suicide and specific community values, cultures, and standards. They must also be designed to be responsive to multiethnic and culturally diverse participation from all segments of the community, including survivors of suicide. A public health approach to suicide prevention involves the cooperation, collaboration, and coordination of individuals, communities, organizations, and leaders at all levels of society—be they family, community, local, regional, tribal, or national.

YOUTH SUICIDE PREVENTION: FEDERAL AND PUBLIC HEALTH INITIATIVES

In 1983, the Centers for Disease Control and Prevention established a violence prevention unit that brought to public attention a disturbing increase in youth suicide rates. In response, the Secretary of Health and Human Services established the multiyear public and private Secretary's

Task Force on Youth Suicide to review what was known about risk factors for youth suicide as well as promising interventions. As noted earlier in the chapter, the final set of recommendations and supporting papers were published as a four-volume report in January 1989 and, where relevant, have been referenced frequently throughout this book (Alcohol, Drug Abuse, and Mental Health Administration, 1989).

The Secretary's Task Force on Youth Suicide made 33 recommendations in six broad categories: data development, research into risk factors, intervention effectiveness evaluation, increased support for suicide prevention services, public information and education, and broadening the involvement of both public and private sectors in the prevention of youth suicide. Each recommendation was supported by an "action plan," suggesting steps for implementation. To its credit, the task force acknowledged the complexity of the problem of prevention and the necessity for a long-term and cooperative strategy, elements almost impossible to accomplish at the federal level when dealing with shifting administrations, priorities, and personalities. As indicated above, although support for prevention is a lofty activity for all public health–minded politicians, it is a very difficult outcome to measure, especially for a target such as suicide, which has a low base rate. Hence, in terms of showing the general public that federal funds are well spent on a regular basis, other public health prevention targets are often easier to support and document quick results.

Shortly thereafter, an international effort culminated in the United Nations/World Health Organization's 1996 summary, *Prevention of Suicide: Guidelines for the Formulation and Implementation of National Strategies* (United Nations, 1996). In the United States, SPAN USA, a grassroots advocacy organization including suicide survivors (people close to someone who completed suicide), suicide attempt survivors, and community activists, championed these guidelines as a way to encourage development of a national suicide prevention strategy for the United States. Their work to marshal social will for suicide prevention generated Congressional Resolutions recognizing suicide as a national problem and suicide prevention as a national priority. These resolutions provided further impetus to develop a national suicide prevention strategy (U.S. Public Health Service, 2001).

SPAN USA propelled the creation of an innovative public and private partnership to jointly sponsor the National Suicide Prevention Conference, which convened in Reno, Nevada, in October 1998 (Silverman, Davidson, & Potter, 2001). Participating agencies with the U.S. Department of Health and Human Services were the Centers for Disease Control and Prevention, the National Institutes of Health, the Office of the Surgeon General, the Substance Abuse and Mental Health Services Administration, the Health Resources and Services Administration, the Indian Health Service, and the Public Health Service Regional Health

Administrators. Conference participants, including health, mental health, and substance abuse clinicians, researchers, policymakers, suicide survivors, consumers of mental health services, and community activists and leaders, discussed eight background papers that were commissioned to summarize the evidence base for suicide prevention (Silverman, Davidson, & Potter, 2001). Working in regional, multidisciplinary groups, participants at the Reno Conference offered many recommendations for action that were shaped into a list of 81 recommendations by an expert panel.

Moving forward with the work of the Reno Conference, U.S. Surgeon General Dr. David Satcher issued his *Call to Action to Prevent Suicide* in July 1999, emphasizing suicide as a serious public health problem (U.S. Public Health Service, 1999). The Surgeon General's *Call* introduced a blueprint for addressing suicide prevention through awareness, intervention, and methodology (AIM). The blueprint describes 15 broad recommendations, containing goal statements, broad objectives, and recommendations for implementation, consistent with a public health approach to suicide prevention, and represents a consolidation of the highest-ranked of the 81 Reno Conference recommendations according to their scientific evidence, feasibility, and community support.

Continuing attention to suicide prevention issues and the significant role of mental health and substance abuse services in suicide prevention is reflected in the landmark *Mental Health: A Report of the Surgeon General* (U.S. Department of Health and Human Services, 1999) and in the nation's public health agenda, *Healthy People 2010* (see Objectives 18-1 and 18-2; U.S. Department of Health and Human Services, 2000). In early 2000, the Secretary of Health and Human Services officially established the *National Strategy* Federal Steering Group (FSG) to "ensure resources identified...for the purpose of completing the *National* [Suicide Prevention] *Strategy* are coordinated to speed its progress." The FSG carefully reviewed the recommendations of both the Reno meeting and the *Call to Action* with a view to developing a comprehensive plan outlining national goals and objectives that would stimulate the subsequent development of defined activities for local, state, and federal partners. The *National Strategy* leadership consultants met to identify the scope and priorities for these goals and objectives for action as well as the aims of the strategy (Exhibit 8.5). The leadership consultants continued to refine the goals and objectives as part of a broadly inclusive process that invited critical examination by scientific, clinical, and government leaders, other professionals, and the general public.

Revised draft goals and objectives were also posted on the Web, inviting comment. During 2000, public hearings on *Goals and Objectives for Action* were held in Atlanta, Boston, Kansas City, and Portland to provide a face-to-face forum for additional input and clarification. The goals of the National

EXHIBIT 8.5
Aims of the National Strategy

- Prevent premature deaths from suicide across the life span
- Reduce the rates of other suicidal behaviors
- Reduce the harmful aftereffects associated with suicidal behaviors and the traumatic impact of suicide on family and friends
- Promote opportunities and settings to enhance resiliency, resourcefulness, respect, and interconnectedness for individuals, families, and communities

Strategy for Suicide Prevention are listed in Exhibit 8.6. This national effort culminated in the publication of the *National Strategy for Suicide Prevention: Goals and Objectives for Action* in 2001 (U.S. Public Health Service, 2001).

EXHIBIT 8.6
Goals of the National Strategy for Suicide Prevention

- Promote awareness that suicide is a public health problem that is preventable
- Develop broad-based support for suicide prevention
- Develop and implement strategies to reduce the stigma associated with being a consumer of mental health services, substance abuse services, and suicide prevention services
- Develop and implement suicide prevention programs
- Promote efforts to reduce access to lethal means and methods of self-harm
- Implement training for recognition of at-risk behavior and delivery of effective treatment
- Develop and promote effective clinical and professional practices
- Improve access to, and community linkages with, mental health and substance abuse treatment services
- Improve reporting and portrayals of suicidal behavior, mental illness, and substance abuse in the entertainment and news media
- Promote and support research on suicide and suicide prevention
- Improve and expand surveillance systems

In the United States, 1 in 10 children and adolescents suffer from mental illness severe enough to cause some level of impairment (Burns et al., 1995). Yet, in any given year, it is estimated that only about 1 in 5 of such children receive specialty mental health services. In March 2000, the White House held a follow-up meeting to its historic White House Conference on Mental Health, held in June 1999 (U.S. Department of Health and Human Services, 1999). This follow-up meeting specifically addressed the need to improve the diagnoses and treatment of children with emotional and behavioral conditions (U.S. Public Health Service, 2000).

In September 2000, the U.S. Surgeon General (Dr. David Satcher) convened a conference called Children's Mental Health: Developing a National Action Agenda. Dr. Satcher noted that children and families are suffering because of missed opportunities for prevention and early intervention, fragmented services, and low priorities for resources. Overriding these problems is the issue of stigma, which continues to surround mental illness (and suicide; U.S. Public Health Service, 2000). Dr. Satcher emphasized the need to improve early recognition and appropriate identification of mental disorders in children within all systems serving children, and to improve access to services by removing barriers faced by families with mental health needs, with a specific aim to reduce disparities in access to care.

Thus, the *National Strategy for Suicide Prevention* is formed on the basis of existing knowledge about suicidal behavior and suicide prevention. It uses the public health approach, which has helped the nation effectively address problems as diverse as tuberculosis, heart disease, and unintentional injury. The *National Strategy* is designed to be a catalyst for social change with the power to transform attitudes, policies, and services. Representing the combined work of advocates, clinicians, researchers, and survivors, the *National Strategy* lays out a framework for action and guides development of an array of services and programs to be set in motion. It strives to promote and provide direction to efforts to modify the social infrastructure in ways that will affect the most basic attitudes about suicide and its prevention and that will also change judicial, educational, and health care systems. As conceived, the *National Strategy* requires a variety of organizations and individuals to become involved in suicide prevention and emphasizes coordination of resources and culturally appropriate services at all levels of government—federal, state, tribal, and community. The *National Strategy* represents the first attempt in the United States to prevent suicide through a coordinated approach by both the public and private sectors.

Recently, the President's New Freedom Commission on Mental Health (2003) released a report that contained six goals and 19 recommendations that address improving access to mental health assessment, treatment, and management. Many of the recommendations have direct relevance to the prevention of suicide and suicidal behaviors, and the identification, assessment, and treatment of suicidal individuals. Specifically, Recommendation 1.1 calls for the advancement and implementation of the *National Strategy for Suicide Prevention* (see Exhibit 8.7).

EXHIBIT 8.7
Goals and Recommendations in a Transformed Mental Health System

---

**GOAL 1   Americans Understand That Mental Health Is Essential to
Overall Health.**

Recommendations   1.1   Advance and implement a national campaign to
reduce the stigma of seeking care and a national
strategy for suicide prevention.

1.2   Address mental health with the same urgency as
physical health.

GOAL 2   Mental Health Care Is Consumer and Family Driven.

Recommendations   2.1   Develop an individualized plan of care for every adult
with a serious mental illness and child with a serious
emotional disturbance.

2.2   Involve consumers and families fully in orienting the
mental health system toward recovery.

2.3   Align relevant federal programs to improve access
and accountability for mental health services.

2.4   Create a Comprehensive State Mental Health Plan.

2.5   Protect and enhance the rights of people with mental
illnesses.

GOAL 3   Disparities in Mental Health Services Are Eliminated.

Recommendations   3.1   Improve access to quality care that is culturally
competent.

3.2   Improve access to quality care in rural and geograph-
ically remote areas.

**GOAL 4   Early Mental Health Screening, Assessment, and Referral to
Services Are Common Practice.**

Recommendations   4.1   Promote the mental health of young children.

4.2   Improve and expand school mental health programs.

4.3   Screen for co-occurring mental and substance use disorders and link with integrated treatment strategies.

4.4   Screen for mental disorders in primary health care,
across the life span, and connect to treatment and
supports.

**GOAL 5   Excellent Mental Health Care Is Delivered and Research
Is Accelerated.**

Recommendations   5.1   Accelerate research to promote recovery and
resilience, and ultimately to cure and prevent mental
illnesses.

5.2   Advance evidence-based practices using dissemina-
tion and demonstration projects and create a public-
private partnership to guide their implementation.

5.3   Improve and expand the workforce providing
evidence-based mental health services and supports.

5.4   Develop the knowledge base in four understudied
areas: mental health disparities, long-term effects of
medications, trauma, and acute care.

EXHIBIT 8.7 (Continued)

GOAL 6	**Technology Is Used to Access Mental Health Care and Information.**
Recommendations	6.1 Use health technology and telehealth to improve access and coordination of mental health care, especially for Americans in remote areas or in underserved populations.
	6.2 Develop and implement integrated electronic health information systems.

WHAT ARE THE BEST AVAILABLE PREVENTION APPROACHES?

As we have established throughout this text, suicidal behaviors are complex behavioral expressions emanating from multiple etiologies (psychological, biological, genetic, sociological, economic, etc.; Silverman & Felner, 1995). As noted in chapter 3, commonly agreed-on definitions for the range of suicidal behaviors still elude us (O'Carroll et al., 1996). This is particularly true when trying to understand suicidal behaviors when they occur in children. Because suicide is a relatively low base-rate disorder, and because it rarely occurs in children below the age of 11, it has been very difficult to enumerate the common risk factors most often associated with suicidal behavior in this age group (U.S. Public Health Service, 1999).

Gould and Kramer (2001) argue that suicide prevention strategies for youth should be evidence-based and have two general goals: case finding with accompanying referral and treatment, and risk-factor reduction. They list the following as important to the act of case-finding: school-based suicide awareness curricula, screening, gatekeeper training, and crisis centers and hotlines. Regarding risk-factor reduction, they list the importance of restrictions of lethal means, media education, postvention and crisis interventions, and skills training (e.g., symptom management and competency enhancement for youth).

Yet another approach is to focus solely on protective factors, inasmuch as it is often difficult to significantly change risk factors. As we have described, protective factors can include an individual's genetic or neurobiological makeup, attitudinal and behavioral characteristics, and environmental attributes. In addition, protective factors include effective and appropriate clinical care for mental, physical, and substance abuse disorders; easy access to a variety of clinical interventions and support for help seeking; restricted access to highly lethal methods of suicide; family and community support; support from ongoing medical and mental health care relationships; learned skills in problem solving, conflict resolution, and nonviolent handling of disputes; and cultural and religious beliefs that discourage suicide and support self-preservation instincts (U.S. Public Health Service, 1999).

Restricting Access to Lethal Means

Means restriction refers to limiting the availability of firearms and medications. Although there is evidence that these strategies can reduce suicide rates—a number of studies have shown that guns in the home, particularly loaded guns, are associated with increased risk for suicide—it is a politically charged topic. For the clinician, this public health and prevention approach is particularly germane; indeed, one of the most powerful clinical interventions that can be made is the facilitation of removing lethal means from the home environment.

Restricting access to firearms (particularly handguns) was estimated by Holinger (1984) to reduce youth suicide by about 20%. Given the frequency with which firearms are used among youth who complete suicide (at the time of this writing, 57% of completions), their lethality, and their correlated use by high-risk, substance-abusing youth (Brent, Perper, & Allman, 1987), controlling access and availability of guns, particularly to high-risk youth, has compelling logic as a preventive measure (Berman, 1998).

Logic also suggests that restricting access to highly lethal means would allow the impulse to commit suicide to wane or would force the potential youth suicide completer to consider and locate an alternative means, one most likely to be less immediately lethal, therefore allowing opportunity for intervention (Marzuk, Tardiff, & Hirsch, 1992). Support for this approach has come principally from two areas. In 1970, Great Britain changed the source of its domestic heating gas to one containing one sixth the carbon-monoxide content of the earlier supplies. Suicide by carbon-monoxide asphyxiation, which had accounted for over 40% of all British suicides before this transitional detoxification, now accounted for fewer than 10%, with no appreciable increase in the use of alternative methods (Shaffer, Garland, Gould, Fisher, & Trautman, 1988). Second, the mandated introduction of automobile emission-control systems in the United States allowed for a similar naturalistic experiment. In examining before and after rates of suicide by carbon-monoxide asphyxiation, Clarke and Lester (1987) reported a notable decline after installation of these systems.

Cantor (1989) has outlined a number of specific interventions regarding firearms. These range from the politically sensitive and possibly unattainable goal of outright gun control to more limited and feasible measures such as mandatory safety training and mandatory waiting periods for and background checks on those who purchase guns. In the mid-1990s the American Association of Suicidology held a conference with youth suicide researchers, firearms safety groups, and firearms advocacy groups in attendance. The outcome of that meeting was a consensus on the research findings regarding youth suicide by firearms and recommended prevention strategies (Consensus Statement on Youth Suicide by Firearms, 1998) as follows:

- Firearms are the most common method of suicide by youth. This is true for both males and females, younger and older adolescents, and for all races.

- The increase in the rate of youth suicide (and the number of deaths by suicide) over the past four decades is largely related to the use of firearms as a method.

- The most common location for the occurrence of firearm suicides by youth is in the home.

- There is a positive association between the accessibility and availability of firearms in the home and the risk for youth suicide.

- The risk conferred by guns in the home is proportional to the accessibility (e.g., loaded and unsecured firearms) and the number of guns in the home.

- Guns in the home, particularly loaded guns, are associated with increased risk for suicide by youth, both with and without identifiable mental health problems or suicidal risk factors.

- If a gun is used to attempt suicide, a fatal outcome will result 78% to 90% of the time.

- Public policy initiatives that restrict access to guns (especially handguns) are associated with a reduction of firearm suicide and suicide overall, especially among youth. (pp. 89–90)

Similar proposals have been made regarding other commonly available means. Jumping from heights, although accounting for only a small proportion of youth suicides, has been observed to be a most preventable method. One such case example is discussed in Berman (1990a), with experts proposing a number of strategies to restrict access to high places (Figures 8.1 and 8.2). Restricting access to drugs, the most common method of suicide attempt among adolescents, has been proposed by Eddy et al. (1989) and Cantor (1989). One means to reduce the ease of overdose, for example, might be to limit prescription dosages of potentially lethal medications such as antidepressants to a 7-day supply. Another suggestion (Holinger, 1984) is to sell prescription antidepressants along with an emetic or antidote, available for immediate administration should the overdosing adolescent change his or her mind or be found in the midst of an attempt. Hawton (2002) recently reported on a national legislative mandate to decrease the number of acetaminophen tablets (analgesics) that can be purchased in blister packets at any one time. Their analyses indicate a reduction in acetaminophen suicides and overdoses following the introduction of the change.

Figure 8.1. Bridge barriers as means restriction: a closer look. Despite the obvious prevention merits of means restriction, actually implementing prevention barriers in the real world is often complicated and challenging. For example, in Washington, DC, there are two major bridges that traverse the valley of Rock Creek Park—a beautiful public park that runs from north to south right through the heart of the District of Columbia. One of these bridges, the Duke Ellington Bridge, which leads into the Adams Morgan community of DC, has an iron fence with bars that curve inward at the top. This iron fence (a suicide prevention barrier) was added to the Ellington Bridge over many aesthetic objections from members of the community so that would-be jumpers would find it nearly impossible to scale this fence and use this particular bridge as a launching point for diving to their death. Photograph by Alan L. Berman. Reprinted with permission.

Crisis Intervention and Telephone Hotline Services

Crisis center hotlines that provide telephone counseling, drop-in centers, and other services are approaches with anecdotal evidence of effectiveness. However, there are concerns that teens and males, in particular, are less likely to use them. In 1985, Franklin, Comstock, Simmons, and Mason (1989) surveyed almost 400 suicide prevention and intervention programs in the United States, about one third of those identified. The majority of these programs were crisis telephone services and mental health centers having a crisis component. Although reported proportions were considered conservative, suicide-related crisis telephone contacts were estimated at only 6% per year, 8% of these being adolescents. Of walk-in clinics, only an estimated 11% of annual clients were considered suicidal, 8% of which were adolescents.

Figure 8.2. Bridge barriers as means restriction: a closer look. Ironically, however, the nearly adjacent Taft Bridge, which delivers Connecticut Avenue foot and vehicle traffic into the heart of downtown Washington, has no such barrier. Would-be suicide jumpers discouraged by the physical barriers of the nearby Ellington Bridge need only walk less than 2 minutes to easily leap to their deaths from the aesthetically pleasing yet unprotected Taft Bridge. Similar struggles have been noted throughout the United States and the world. Indeed, Japan's Mt. Mihara is a famous suicide site, as is the Eiffel Tower in Paris. However, by far the most infamous site for suicide, perhaps in the world, is San Francisco's Golden Gate Bridge. Since its completion in 1937, the Golden Gate has been linked to well over 1,000 known suicides. Yet the Bay Area community has fought back numerous attempts to erect some form of barrier or safety net to save lives, primarily citing the aesthetic cost to adding this kind of protection to the famous bridge (Friend, 2003). Needless to say, great public health prevention strategies do not necessarily translate into public health realities. Photograph by Alan L. Berman. Reprinted with permission.

Crisis centers and telephone hotlines offer immediate help, with 24-hour availability to resolve crises of a suicidal or potentially suicidogenic nature through active intervention efforts. For teenagers, the anonymity and comfort and familiarity of the telephone and the typically nonprofessional staffing of these services theoretically make this form of entry to the help-giving system more acceptable than direct, face-to-face contact with an office-based professional. With this entry, either crises may be resolved without the need for professional treatment, or referrals for more intensive care can be accomplished when needed. Again, there are clear implications for clinical practice, as use of a crisis hotline as an adjunct to care can be quite helpful. Moreover, there are emergencies where the patient may not be able to reach the clinician; in such cases the planned use of a crisis hotline can prove invaluable.

How effective are these services in preventing suicide? Most studies have been methodologically unsound and lacking in direct evidence of usage, comparing communities before and after the establishment of a program or communities with versus without a program, thus risking the "ecological fallacy" (Shaffer, Garland, Gould, et al., 1988).

As was noted in more depth in chapter 3, the suicide of rock star Kurt Cobain provided a unique naturalistic opportunity to try to prevent prospective suicides through the prompt issuing of media guidelines and making crisis center hotline services well known to the community (Jobes et al., 1996). Within days of the suicide, media guidelines from the Centers for Disease Control were faxed to the Seattle Mayor's office, and the Seattle Crisis Center was intimately involved in a critical public memorial service held in a large Seattle park. Moreover, the researchers were able to try to prospectively address the ecological fallacy issue by working with the King County Medical Examiners office to specifically look at death scene connections to copycat suicides as well as study naturalistically the use of crisis center services in the weeks following Cobain's suicide. The marked increase in calls to the Seattle Crisis Center, referred to as the "Cobain Effect," does not enable us to make causal links between these services and the apparent absence of a subsequent outbreak of copycat suicides. However, these correlational data were nevertheless encouraging for those who believe in the efficacy of hotline crisis prevention services.

Quantitative methods of meta-analysis were applied by Dew, Bromet, Brent, and Greenhouse (1987) to a series of published evaluation studies to determine whether suicide prevention services work. They found that crisis center clients were at higher risk for suicide than those members of the general population and that completed suicides were more likely than members of the general population to have contacted a program. However, taking the series of studies as a set, the establishment of a center had no demonstrable effect on a community's suicide rate.

The relatively low rates of use by suicidal teenagers noted here beg the question of how to encourage increased contact between those in need and those who provide needed services. The answer appears to be in public relations. As the majority of adolescent suicides are males, targeted advertising of these programs to males would be imperative (Shaffer, Garland, Gould, et al., 1988). Currently, SAMHSA has funded two major studies to evaluate both process and outcome measures of crisis hotline effectiveness.

Gatekeeper Training and Screening Programs

As it is well known that teens typically share problems first with other teens, raising the consciousness of teenagers in general to the existence of these programs, particularly their anonymity and confidentiality and their specific services, should have some effect on increasing referrals to them. Until such gatekeeper services attain the level of support necessary to accomplish a sustained marketing of services to the community of adolescents in general as well as those specifically at risk, little significant impact on the overall suicide rate can be expected.

Gatekeeper training targets people who have contact with youth to help them identify and refer students at risk for suicide. It also teaches them how to respond to suicide or other crises. There is strikingly little evidence that such training is effective in reducing suicide, but there is evidence that people trained as gatekeepers are better prepared to intervene.

Postvention programs focus on friends and relatives of people who have committed suicide. Again, there is no sound evidence of their efficacy, but supporting those who have experienced a trauma is a sound idea (refer to chap. 9).

Screening programs use a screening instrument to identify high-risk youth for further assessment and treatment. Shaffer and Croft (1999) have reported on using systematic screening with a self-administered unit for predictors of suicide in a high school population in New York City. Popular programs like Signs of Suicide (SOS) and Teen Screen do offer research findings indicating that they are effective at identifying teens at risk (Aseltine & DeMartino, 2003).

Screening for mood changes, depression, suicide ideation, and substance abuse may be an important tool to identify adolescents at risk for suicide. A self-administered screening test addressing questions of mood (feeling unhappy or sad), anger, temper, suicidal thoughts, and substance abuse can be used. Students who have a positive score on this test are referred for a formal diagnostic interview by a trained mental health professional (e.g., clinical psychologist or psychiatrist) who then makes the diagnostic and risk determination as well as the decision to refer the student for treatment. In this situation, the screening test is the self-administered tool to the high school population, whereas the diagnostic test ("gold standard") is the formal interview by the mental health professional. It is important to remember, this model is only good if there are adequate evaluation and therapy services for referrals and follow-up (Gould & Kramer, 2001).

Educational approaches in which students learn about suicide, its warning signs, and how to seek help seem intuitively correct, but there is only sparse evidence of their effectiveness (Kalafat, 2003). Criticisms of educational programs include concerns over their lack of selectivity, focus on environmental stresses versus mental health, "one-time" (vs. sustained) approach, and the potential for negative reactions from students who have previously attempted or considered suicide (Shaffer, Garland, Vieland, Underwood, & Busner, 1991).

School-Based Prevention Programs

In recent years, the schools have increasingly become sites for a variety of educational prevention models designed to combat a range of public health concerns facing today's youth. Programs in drug abuse prevention, AIDS prevention, child abuse prevention, and sex education have proliferated and compete for time with basic education demands. The school is a logical and natural site for such preventive efforts, given this is where student attention is held relatively captive, where teaching and learning are normative tasks, and where peer interactions can be mobilized around a common theme. With increasing public and community awareness of the reality of adolescent suicide, it is not surprising that suicide prevention education programs have joined the growing list of pressing public health education foci. It is often helpful for clinicians to know about the school environment and how mental health issues are handled when working with an adolescent patient.

Case Illustration

Jimmy and Kevin, age 16 and 17, respectively, were rural youth who were reputed to be into the "gothic scene"—various kids in the school indicated that the boys were into satanic worship, witchcraft, and wizardry. There had been rumors that the boys had been staging satanic ceremonies in the woods behind the school where live animals were being sacrificed. The school community was later shocked to discovery that the two boys had died over the weekend in an apparent suicide pact. Their bodies had been found in a clearing in the woods behind the school where they had built a fire pit and had a campsite.

Word of the double suicide spread like wildfire in the small rural community. The high school principal held a schoolwide assembly about the deaths. He provided little information but said that he and the faculty had decided to have a memorial service later in the week and those students who wanted to attend the funerals would be given excused absences from school. Before the week was over, there were three additional students who had made attempts, one of whom remained in intensive care. A community "expert" was brought in to another schoolwide assembly to talk about satanic cults and suicide. Over the next month, cases of reported suicidal ideation and reputed attempts terrified the small rural community.

As shown in the preceding case, the school setting can serve as center stage where the drama of adolescence may well be played out. In our experience, there can be well-meaning efforts toward prevention, intervention, and postvention, but being "well-meaning" does not guarantee effectiveness. It therefore behooves us to think about how schools can potentially play a key role in suicide prevention.

The typical school-based suicide prevention program is a three- to six-class, classroom-centered, curriculum-based, lecture-discussion program using, to a lesser extent, experiential exercises or films (Goldsmith et al., 2002). Goals typically include heightening awareness about the problem of adolescent suicide and informing (facts and "myths") adolescents about suicide; increasing recognition of signs and symptoms (risk factors) to facilitate case identification; changing attitudes about suicide and about receiving help; and identifying appropriate resources (Zenere & Lazarus, 1997). Additionally, programs often attempt pragmatic skill building in the areas of affect recognition, listening, communication, crisis and stress management, problem solving, and referral making. One common focus is on encouraging "secret sharing" with a responsible and trusted adult, as when a suicidal teen confides to a peer his or her suicidal ideation or plan but only with the caveat that the confidant will "tell no one" (Eggert, Karovsky, & Pike, 1999).

To a greater extent, school-based programs are now focusing principally on gatekeeper education, increasing awareness among teachers, administrators, and other school personnel of warning signs as well as teaching referral skills. Others have encouraged the development of peer counseling programs, emphasizing the natural communication patterns and help-giving system common to the student culture.

To make more normative the notions of "problem solving" as a treatment and of peers as caregivers, these programs attempt to destigmatize suicide by deemphasizing the relation between suicide and psychopathology (e.g., suicide is a "problem in living"). Hoberman and Garfinkel (1988a) have expressed some concern that such attempts to normalize the experiences of suicidal youth invalidate what we know about youth suicide and psychopathology, thereby directly countering the goal of increasing recognition (case finding) of those in need of treatment (psychotherapy). Shaffer, Garland, Gould, et al. (1988) argue furthermore that by so misrepresenting the facts, these programs may heighten the risk of imitation. In their view, the likelihood of suicide being imitated would be lessened if suicide were depicted "as a deviant act by someone with a mental disturbance" (p. 681).

Other criticisms of school-based models have questioned the implicit assumption in these programs that education is synonymous with prevention. Citing unflattering evaluations of attempts in the United States to stem the prevalence of unwanted pregnancy, AIDS, smoking, and drug abuse through school-based prevention models, Berman (1990b) has questioned whether there is any reason to believe that knowledge alone is sufficient to change behavior. In addition, Berman notes that those teens most at risk for these health-endangering behaviors are those who are least likely to attend preventative education programs.

Shaffer, Garland, and Whittle (1988), in their systematic evaluation of three high school programs in New Jersey, confirm that identified high-risk students may be "turned off" by these programs and that behavioral preferences (e.g., what the student would do and to whom the student would talk if depressed) and attitudes about the management of a suicidal problem did not change. On the more positive side, they found no evidence that these programs caused harm, and, in contrast, many students reported that the prevention training served as a source of comfort (confidence boosting) regarding their attempts to help other students.

The Centers for Disease Control and Prevention published a report and recommendations from a panel of specialists in unintentional injury, violence, suicide prevention, school health, and mental health services, entitled "School Health Guidelines to Prevent Unintentional Injuries and Violence" (Centers for Disease Control and Prevention, 2001b). Although youth suicide was considered to be an intentional injury (self-inflicted), this consensus statement was formed on the basis of a review of approximately 200 strategies that schools could implement to prevent unintentional injuries, violence, and suicide. The prevention recommendations address school environment, instruction, services, and personnel (see Exhibit 8.8). Strategies are then listed for implementing the recommendations. The strategies are grouped by guiding principles that describe essential qualities of coordinated school health programs to prevent unintentional injury, violence, and suicide.

The recommendations, guiding principles, and strategies are not prioritized. Instead, they represent the state-of-the-science in school-based unintentional injury, violence, and suicide prevention. However, every recommendation is not appropriate or feasible for every school to implement, nor is it feasible to expect any school to implement all of the recommendations. The Centers for Disease Control and others are developing tools to help schools implement the recommendations and strategies included in this report.

Whether the focus of changing attitudes and knowledge and the attempt to impart skill building in relatively short periods of training can have an impact on the ultimate goal of these models, that of decreasing the incidence of suicidal behavior, has yet to be established. Moreover, given the relative infrequency of suicidal behavior, evidence of decreased rates of attempt or completion requires long-term evaluative outcome research.

The great majority of these programs are targeted school- or grade-wide and have multiple goals ranging from attitude change to knowledge and skill acquisition. On a broader level, these school-based programs pose unanswered questions as to the best use of limited resources in developing future models. What strategy of intervention makes the most sense? Should targets of interventions be limited, for instance, to those most at risk or to parents most in position to observe their children? Should efforts be geared toward primary prevention (e.g., skill development beginning in primary grades and continued through booster training thereafter), or case finding,

EXHIBIT 8.8
Centers for Disease Control and Prevention School Health Recommendations to Prevent Unintentional Injuries, Violence, and Suicide

- **Recommendation 1:** Social environment: Establish a social environment that promotes safety and prevents unintentional injuries, violence, and suicide.

- **Recommendation 2:** Physical environment: Provide a physical environment inside and outside school buildings that promotes safety and prevents unintentional injuries and violence.

- **Recommendation 3:** Health education: Implement health and safety education curricula and instruction that help students develop the knowledge, attitudes, behavioral skills, and confidence needed to adopt and maintain safe lifestyles and to advocate for health and safety.

- **Recommendation 4:** Physical education and physical activity programs: Provide safe physical education and extracurricular physical activity programs.

- **Recommendation 5:** Health services: Provide health, counseling, psychological, and social services to meet the physical, mental, emotional, and social health needs of students.

- **Recommendation 6:** Crisis response: Establish mechanisms for short- and long-term responses to crises, disasters, and injuries that affect the school community.

- **Recommendation 7:** Family and community: Integrate school, family, and community efforts to prevent unintentional injuries, violence, and suicide.

- **Recommendation 8:** Staff members: For all school personnel, provide staff development services that impart the knowledge, skills, and confidence to effectively promote safety and prevent unintentional injuries, violence, and suicide, and support students in their efforts to do the same.

or improving response capabilities of caregivers? Should efforts be directed not at education but perhaps toward changing suicidogenic conditions in the environment or effecting legislation, for example, to deal with issues of gun control or drug abuse? We need a theory of change and an effective public health model with which to define what targets should be approached best by whom and when—and all this at an affordable cost.

It is our belief that the schools are appropriate sites for preventive programming. Furthermore, we believe that clinicians trained in suicidology and understanding of youth suicide should initiate training models with the enlisted cooperation of school personnel. In particular, we believe that the emphasis should be given to the school- and community-based models of intervention that follow. Each suggestion focuses on behavioral change achievable through educational efforts. Each has a somewhat limited scope and target and, therefore, a measurable goal. Together these models promote the idea of the school as a community resource, placing education in a broad frame including the teaching of skills to children, their parents, and the community as a whole.

However, it must be noted that changes in knowledge and attitudes do not necessarily translate into behavior. Research needs to be done that provides evidence for the relationship between these proximal outcomes and such intermediate behavioral outcomes as increased identification and referral of at-risk youth by school-based adults and students. A systemic approach to suicide prevention also requires the effective treatment and follow-up of identified youth (Kalafat, 2001), and there is a dearth of research in this area (Linehan, 1987). Kalafat (2003) points out that to assess distal program effects (reduction of suicide rates), programs must (a) be carefully implemented with fidelity; (b) address multiple levels of school and community contexts (i.e., administrative policies and procedures, education for all school staff, classroom curricula, parent education, connections between school and community gatekeepers); (c) be disseminated to enough sites to obtain large population samples for epidemiological impact assessment; and (d) be institutionalized or sustained over sufficient length of time to detect epidemiological trends.

In a recent review, Kalafat (2003) has observed that because the school is the community institution that has the primary responsibility for the education and socialization of youth, the school context has the potential to moderate the occurrence of risk behaviors and to identify and secure help for at-risk individuals. School education codes and statutes include the mandate to not only educate but also to protect students (Davis & Sandoval, 1991). Thus, schools offer a logical setting for preventive interventions.

Kalafat (2003) finds that there is longitudinal evidence that programs that promote generic protective factors such as social competence, decision making, family connections, and school bonding moderate the appearance of a variety of risk behaviors, including substance abuse, delinquency, violence behavior, and problem sexual behavior and pregnancies (Elias, Gara, Schuyler, Branden-Muller, & Sayette, 1991; Hawkins, Catalano, Kosterman, Abbott, & Hill, 1999; Lonczak, Abbott, Hawkins, Kosterman, & Catalano, 2002; Perry et al., 2000). Although these comprehensive programs have not included suicide in their outcome assessments, there is some evidence for an association between protective factors such as connection with school and prosocial norms and reduced suicidal thoughts and plans (Evans, Smith, Hill, Albers, & Nuefeld, 1996; McBride et al., 1995).

Although these school-based programs do not address suicidal behaviors directly, comorbidity and shared risk factors exist between suicidal behaviors and other problem behaviors that are the targets of many of these existing school-based programs (Gould & Kramer, 2001). However, these comprehensive programs alone will not be sufficient to address the mediators of suicidal behavior. Weissberg and Elias (1993) pointed out that modifying school environments and implementing multigrade social skills and problem-solving programs take a considerable amount of time, and these efforts also must be complemented with instruction specific to particular risk behaviors.

Recently, Davidson and Marshall (2003) developed a school-based suicide prevention guide for schools and the students, families, and communities they serve. They note that state departments of education, school systems, and local schools have complementary and coordinated roles in preventing suicide, although prevention planning is worth initiating at any level. Across the country, wide differences exist in the resources that have been devoted to school suicide prevention, the range of preventive activities that have been tried, the degree to which efforts have been evaluated, and how coordinated and comprehensive that prevention programming has been.

The foundation of specific school-based suicide prevention activities and programs is the elimination or reduction of conditions that place students at risk for suicide and the strengthening of protective factors against suicide. School prevention efforts that address risk and protective factors before problems that students face become overwhelming are more helpful than an exclusively narrow focus on recognition and assistance for students who have already become suicidal. Typical components of a comprehensive school-based suicide prevention program can be found in Exhibit 8.9.

EXHIBIT 8.9
Components of a Comprehensive School-Based Suicide Prevention Plan

- A safe social and physical school environment

- Clear policies and procedures for school personnel to follow

- Designation of trained school personnel for screening, intervention, and referral of students at risk for suicide

- Responsive school support services for at-risk students and school-system linkages with community services providers

- Curriculum and instruction that incorporates positive skills and capabilities associated with the prevention of suicide, other violence, and unintentional injuries, such as problem solving, stress and anger management, refusal and resistance skills, empathy and social perspective taking, decision making, and communication

- Crisis response protocols that include roles for all school personnel and give practical direction for common situations in the aftermath of a suicide, such as appropriate media coverage, notification sequences, and methods of avoiding suicide contagion

- Education for students and families on mental health problems commonly associated with student suicide (such as depressive disorders, substance abuse, and severe behavioral disorders) directed toward (a) early help-seeking and positive attitudes toward help-seeking, (b) guidance in assisting another person to seek help, (c) awareness of school and community access points for help, and (d) recognition of immediate suicide risk with appropriate actions to take.

Note. From Davidson and Marshall (2003).

The following are examples and elaborations of some of the school-based components that comprise a comprehensive suicide prevention program:

1. *Early detection and referral-making skills.* It is appropriate that both faculty and students be taught to be observers of self and others. Specific behaviors associated with suicide risk, particularly signs of psychopathology common to depression and substance abuse as co-related risk conditions, might be widely posted as easily as have been "the warning signs of cancer." Students and faculty should not be expected to intervene directly, but rather to refer a student believed to be at risk to a professional competent to evaluate and treat that student. Referral-making skills are teachable.

2. *Resource identification.* An effective referral rests on having competent professionals in the community to whom referrals can be made. Community resources, agencies, and private practitioners can be evaluated to ensure the competencies of those to whom students at risk may be sent. Students themselves could be trained to serve on consumer investigative teams, sent with appropriate evaluative criteria, to establish a dynamic system, updated annually, of those professionals so identified. In this way also, chances are greater that students would understand and demystify the professional community, thereby increasing probable access and utilization.

3. *Help-seeking behavior.* One of the side benefits to resource identification by students is making more normative the idea of seeking and receiving help. When the community as a whole is perceived as engaged in showing concern for the quality of its services and resources, public awareness of these resources increases, as does destigmatization; that is, there is a greater acceptance of resource utilization. It is possible that compliance with referred treatments might also increase, thereby reducing the frequency of repeat suicide attempts.

4. *Professional education.* Also related to resource identification is the evaluation of the specific training of professionals dealing with youth suicide. When a community's schools view their mission to be the education of the community as a whole, particularly when that education serves to have a positive impact on the educability of students by enhancing their health and minimizing their distress, the upgrading of professional skills becomes part of the school's function.

5. *Parent education.* Again, if the broad view of the school's role is that of educating all segments of the community, parents should be alerted to be observant of risk factors and available

resources to whom they might bring their questions and seek counsel. Outreach programs can be developed to teach responsible gun ownership, particularly to parents of high-risk children. Drug-abuse awareness programs are available to teach parents signs of potential drug use by their children. Parent training classes might be encouraged, even required, of new parents.

6. *Primary prevention.* Taking the long view, the most effective and probably the most cost-effective strategy is that of primary prevention, incorporating any number of programs designed to teach health-enhancing behavior through teaching behavioral skills. These programs must begin in the primary grades, be reinforced through follow-up training, and focus on adaptive skills and competencies. A number of models relevant to mental health goals are in the literature related to self-esteem training, problem-solving training, social-skills training, anxiety-management training, and assertiveness training. Additionally, time-limited, structured educational models for training youth to manage negative affect states such as anger and depression are available (see chap. 6).

Given that a sizable proportion of suicide-prone youngsters display their impending risk through decreased attention to their academics, thereby increasing their likelihood of dropping out of school, and that many suicidal adolescents have already dropped out or have been expelled from school, school-based programs that identify such youth well before they leave school and attempt to attach them more positively to the school environment should be encouraged. Programs designed to enhance the school environment for all students, irrespective of academic skills, increase the likelihood of positive role-model identifications and alternative skill attainment.

7. *School-based postvention.* Preventive functions are served through appropriate interventions after the fact of suicidal behavior. For example, a student hospitalized for a suicide attempt and treated may now need help successfully reintegrating into the academic and social environment of the school without risk of repeat attempt or ultimate completion (see further discussion in the next chapter).

Considerations for an ongoing therapeutic plan and coordination between therapist and school counselor or other liaison are essential. A number of questions need to be adequately addressed. Among these are the following:

- What initial and longer-term academic load should the student carry to minimize stress and maximize a successful reentry?

- How should parents be involved in planning reintegration?
- What attention needs to be given the peer community into which the student will reenter?

Suicide attempters may be viewed with contempt or avoided by others. Attention must be given to sensitizing the peer environment, dealing with fears and anxieties, and smoothing the path of reentry for the returning student.

PRACTICE CONSIDERATIONS IN PREVENTION

Although it may be ideal to attempt to prevent suicidal ideations in youth, this population is in a state of developmental flux (physical, social, emotional, cognitive, psychological), and may require multilayered interventions and approaches to reduce such thoughts from ever occurring. Others have found utility in focusing on the more "immediate" behaviors associated with these ideations (i.e., self-destructive behaviors; Brent, 2003). One approach is to understand the degree to which adolescents have accurate knowledge of the lethality of various suicide methods. This line of study is formed on the basis of the observation that many attempts and deaths may be "accidental" and "unintentional" because youth miscalculate the lethality of suicidal methods or are uninformed of the relative lethality of different methods (Berman, Shepherd, & Silverman 2003).

Whereas most adolescents might accurately perceive the lethality of firearms, their knowledge of lethality of poisons is questionable. Research reflects that adolescents misperceive the dangerousness of poisons such as acetaminophen (Harris & Myers, 1997). Ingestion of poisons is the most common method used in completed adolescent suicides. For example, in a recently published large-scale epidemiological study (Shenassa et al., 2003), 84.7% of adolescents under the age of 18 who completed suicide were found to have ingested poisons. Finally, research suggests that use of less violent means in suicide attempts does not necessarily reflect lower lethality of suicidal intent (Denning, Conwell, King, & Cox, 2000). Hence, a preventive intervention approach might address lowering both the lethality of the ideation and intent as well as the lethality of the methods used (or their avoidance altogether).

PREVENTION STRATEGIES THAT WORK

To date, there are various approaches with sufficient empirical support or practical success to deem them viable youth suicide prevention strategies. As noted earlier, within each approach, there are countless opportunities for mental health clinician involvement—as consultants, trainers, program evaluators, educators, and so on.

State Youth Suicide Prevention Plans

A number of states (Washington, Maine, Georgia, et al.) have taken the lead in developing statewide youth suicide prevention programs. The State of Oregon developed a Youth Suicide Prevention Program beginning in 1997 (Bloodworth, 2000). They will soon report on their evaluation of the program. The 15 strategies that comprise the program are presented in Exhibit 8.10. The plan emphasizes three key prevention approaches: (a) community education, (b) integration of systems serving high-risk youth, and (c) access to a full range of health care, including mental health and alcohol and drug treatment services.

EXHIBIT 8.10
State of Oregon Youth Suicide Prevention Program

- Develop and implement public education campaigns to increase knowledge about symptoms of depression and suicide, response skills, and resources; increase help-seeking behavior; and decrease stigma associated with treatment for behavioral health problems

- Promote efforts to reduce access to lethal means of self-harm

- Educate youth and young adults about suicide prevention

- Reduce harassment in schools and communities

- Provide media education to reduce suicide contagion

- Provide education for professionals in health care, education, and human services

- Provide gatekeeper training to create a network of people trained to recognize and respond to youth in crisis

- Implement screening and referral services

- Increase effectiveness of crisis hot lines

- Enhance crisis services

- Establish and maintain crisis response teams

- Improve access to affordable behavioral health care

- Provide skill-building support groups to increase protective factors and involve families

- Support suicide survivors by fostering the development of bereavement support groups

- Improve follow-up services for suicide attempters

Many of the suicide preventive interventions directed at the adolescent and young adult groups are applicable and appropriate for children and preadolescents. These include (a) means-restriction strategies (limited access to lethal means; firearm disposal or containment; restricted access to alcohol or other drugs), (b) gatekeeper training (health and mental health professionals), (c) health communication campaigns (increase risk-assessment techniques for health professionals; community health awareness campaigns), (d) school gatekeeper training (school nurses, counselors, teachers, coaches), (e) postvention response (interventions directed at survivors of loved ones who die by suicide), and (f) psychotherapeutic interventions (family, psychopharmacology, psychoeducation, group therapy; Grossman & Kruesi, 2000).

The State of Utah has been engaged in a systematic analysis of their youth suicides to develop effective suicide preventive interventions tailored to their at-risk population. The State of Washington's well-recognized, research-based youth suicide prevention program was established in 1995 and includes a youth-focused campaign on suicide prevention. A toolkit (Eastgard, 2000) for Washington schools implementing the campaign includes a checklist (see Exhibit 8.11) for "getting started." Schools using this toolkit typically use campaign materials conceived, designed, and tested in Washington State through the youth suicide prevention program.

EXHIBIT 8.11
Final Design Steps of a Youth Suicide Prevention Campaign

Before implementing a school-based prevention campaign, be sure to

- secure permission to conduct a campaign;
- talk with school administrator or principal;
- address any concerns;
- review concept and design;
- itemize benefits for the students and for the school;
- enlist support of the school's counselors;
- confirm existence of the school's crisis response plan and how to contact and activate crisis response team;
- line up local support resources;
- identify staff (including professional trainers, faculty, students);
- involve parents (through PTA, PTSA, or another parent organization);
- schedule training; and
- confirm that any (outside) presenters are knowledgeable and prepared.

Note. From *Youth Suicide Prevention Program of Washington State*, by Youth Suicide Prevention Program, 2000, Seattle, WA: Author. Copyright 2000 by Youth Suicide Prevention Program. Adapted with permission.

Not surprisingly, review of the state plans for adolescent suicide prevention reveals that funding is a primary challenge. Many states have no funding for suicide prevention efforts, whereas others successfully acquire state appropriations or allocations from state departments of health or mental health. Others find ways to use federal funding sources for suicide prevention. Most common is the use of the Maternal and Child Health Block Grant, but the Emergency Medical Services for Children grant is also used in several states. Some states also use funds from the Substance Abuse Prevention and Treatment Block Grant and the Safe and Drug-Free Schools and Communities Act.

School-Based Programs

As previously noted, Kalafat's (2003) review of school-based approaches to suicide prevention finds that there are a number of published reports on universal programs, none on selective programs, and a single report on an indicated program (see earlier discussion of Gordon's operational model). He points out that current comprehensive universal school-based suicide prevention programs are designed to increase the likelihood that school gatekeepers (administrators, faculty, and staff) and peers who come into contact with at-risk youth can more readily identify them, provide an appropriate initial response to them, will know how to obtain help for them, and are consistently inclined to take such action. The role of schools in this endeavor is critical but limited to the identification and referral to specialized school or community-based mental health services (see Exhibit 8.12).

Examples of universal programs are Adolescent Suicide Awareness Program (ASAP; Ryerson, 1990) and Lifelines (Kalafat & Underwood, 1989), each of which has been evaluated and widely disseminated. An updated combined version, Lifelines ASAP, also has been developed (Kalafat, Ryerson, & Underwood, 2001). Similar comprehensive programs also have been developed in Florida (Zenere & Lazarus, 1997) and Washington (Eastgard, 2000). The Washington program features substantial involvement of students in the development of local peer support and involvement messages and the provision of classroom lessons, which may represent a mediational process superior to the predominant teacher-to-student process.

Eggert and her colleagues developed an indicated prevention program called "Reconnecting Youth" (Eggert, Thompson, Hertine, & Nicholas, 1995). Reconnecting Youth is a school-based prevention program for 14- to 18-year-old youth in grades 9 through 12 who are at risk for school dropout. These youth also may exhibit multiple behavior problems, such as substance abuse, aggression, depression, or suicide risk behaviors. Reconnecting Youth uses a partnership model involving peers, school personnel, and parents to deliver interventions that are organized into four components, including school bonding activities, parent involvement, school crisis-response planning, and a

EXHIBIT 8.12
Universal Programs

The overall goal of universal programs is to create competent school communities in which all members accept responsibility for the safety of each other and can provide an appropriate initial response to those at risk. The specific conceptual and empirical bases for such programs are as follows:

- Most suicidal youths confide their concerns more often to peers than to adults.

- Disturbed youth (e.g., depressed, substance abusers) prefer peer supports as opposed to adults more than their nondisturbed peers.

- Some adolescents, particularly some boys, do not respond to troubled peers in empathic or helpful ways.

- As few as 25% of peer confidants tell an adult about their troubled or suicidal peer.

- Therefore, the inaccessibility of, and reluctance of, adolescents to seek out helpful adults is considered to be a risk factor that contributes to destructive outcomes associated with a variety of adolescent risk behaviors, including suicide.

- Conversely, research has shown that contact with helpful adults may be considered a protective factor for a variety of troubled youth.

- There is also evidence that provision of help by youth may be beneficial to them. Participation in helping interactions can shape prosocial behaviors and reduce problematic behavior and is related to indices of social competencies that can carry over to other challenging situations

Note. Adapted from *School Approaches to Youth Suicide Prevention* (pp. 1211–1223), 2003, Thousand Oaks, CA: Sage. Copyright 2003 by Sage. Adapted with permission.

Reconnecting Youth (RY) class offered for 50 minutes daily during regular school hours for one semester (80 sessions).

Subsequently, Eggert and her colleagues implemented and evaluated briefer versions of the RY class with potential dropout students who were identified as at risk for suicide through a subsequent screening (Randell, Eggert, & Pike, 2001). They found that a brief indicated intervention consisting of a risk assessment, crisis intervention, and enhanced connection with caring adults was sufficient for affecting short-term attitudes and ideation.

In the School-Based Suicide Prevention Guide developed by Davidson and Marshall (2003) is an appendix listing 40 exemplary programs believed to be useful to other school programs in the United States. These 40 school-based suicide prevention programs were found to focus on different aspects of schools. A breakdown by categories indicates that the majority of programs contain elements that are curricular in nature and view the school as the appropriate venue for assessment and referral services:

1. School as environment and organization (11),
2. School curriculum and educational activities (22),
3. School as access point (2),
4. School as service provider (20),
5. Special needs schools (5).

At the time of this writing, one program, the Signs of Suicide (SOS) High School Suicide Prevention Program, has been independently selected by SAMHSA for its National Registry of Effective Programs (NREP).

Guo and Harstall (2002) recently reviewed 10 evaluated school suicide prevention programs and found variation in program content, frequency, duration, delivery, and quality of evaluation, which made it difficult to draw conclusions across studies. Nevertheless, Kalafat (2003) concludes that school personnel may be encouraged by the availability of some conceptually grounded, clearly packaged, field-tested programs. Although there is some initial empirical support for these programs, more systematic evaluation needs to be done that assesses implementation fidelity and the relationships among hypothesized mediating variables (e.g., sense of connection to the school community), moderating variables (e.g., degree of coordination between schools and communities), proximal outcomes (e.g., knowledge and attitudes), and distal outcomes (suicide rates).

International Strategies

The Australian Institute of Family Studies conducted an evaluation of their National Youth Suicide Prevention Strategy in 2000 (Mitchell, 2000). They evaluated the strategy according to "six maps of program logic": (a) primary prevention and cultural change; (b) early intervention; (c) crisis intervention and primary care; (d) treatment, support, and postvention; (e) access to means and injury prevention; and (f) system-level activities. They identified "four maps of achievements": (a) primary prevention and cultural change; (b) early intervention; (c) crisis intervention and primary care; and (d) treatment, support, and postvention. For these four "maps," they evaluated the public health elements of each effort and concluded that they have the highest promise of success.

The U.S. Air Force Suicide Prevention Program

From 1990 to 1995, suicide rates were rising at a statistically significant pace among Air Force personnel overall, and among both Black and White enlisted male subgroups. By the end of the period, the overall rate was reaching all-time record-high levels for the Air Force. Using a data-driven prevention model to guide its search of extant community data, it identified nine factors that were frequently associated with victims of suicide and three factors it concluded were protective. Stigma, cultural norms, and beliefs that combined to discourage help-seeking behavior were identified as major hurdles to successful suicide prevention.

With the support of the Air Force Chief of Staff, the work of implementing 11 recommendations aimed at mitigating risk factors and strengthening the protective factors for suicide was begun. The risk factors identified included problems with the law, finances, intimate relationships, mental health, job performance, and alcohol and other substance abuse. These were often further complicated by social isolation and poor coping skills. The team identified three key protective factors: a sense of social support, effective coping skills, and policies and norms that encourage effective help-seeking behaviors. The 11 Air Force Suicide Prevention Initiatives are as follows:

1. Leadership involvement. Using strong leadership from the Air Force Chief of Staff, this initiative encourages commanders at levels of the organization to actively support suicide prevention.

2. Suicide prevention in professional military education. This initiative requires that suicide prevention information be integrated into Professional Military Education (PME) curricula.

3. Commanders as gatekeepers. This initiative was designed to lead to improved marketing and community awareness regarding use of mental health services, and held commanders as gatekeepers, responsible for the unit climate that makes seeking and using helping services an acceptable thing to do.

4. Community prevention services. This initiative is designed to insure the provision of more preventive services by mental health professionals *outside* clinical settings.

5. Annual suicide prevention training. This initiative requires annual suicide prevention training for *all* active duty, reserve, guard, and civilians in the Air Force organization.

6. Investigative interview handoff policy. This initiative led to a clarification of investigative interview policy requiring that appropriate supervisors make sure that an assessment for suicide potential is conducted following various investigatory procedures of personnel.

7. Critical incident stress management. This initiative requires the establishment of a multidisciplinary critical incident stress management team to respond to completed suicides.

8. Creation of the Integrated Delivery System and the energizing of the Community Action Information Board. This initiative led to the establishment of a seamless system of services across multidisciplinary human service prevention activities. This initiative led to the creation of the Integrated Delivery System and brought new vitality to the existing Community Action Information Board.

9. Established limited patient–psychotherapist privilege. This initiative led to the establishment of a partial psychotherapist–patient privilege for personnel under investigation who may be at risk for suicide.

10. Behavioral Health Survey. This initiative created a tool for assessing behavioral health aspects of a unit, which was available to any commander.
11. Epidemiological database and surveillance system. This initiative led to the development of a central surveillance system for fatal and nonfatal self-injuries (i.e., the Suicide Event Surveillance System).

Whether encountering the breakup of an intimate relationship, financial difficulties, legal problems, or, frequently, some combination of these, Air Force personnel were encouraged to offer assistance where possible and to promote use of community resources when necessary. In effect, this program sought to change an entire culture related to being in trouble and seeking help. The message became: you help a troubled buddy more by getting them to appropriate health services than you do by taking them out and getting them drunk.

In 2000, the best of the "homegrown" programs developed at Air Force installations were carefully reviewed with the help of nationally recognized experts to produce a best practice toolkit for community education. A Web-based epidemiological database was established as well as a unit-based tool to assess aggregate risk among subordinates. Anonymously administered, the Behavioral Health Survey assesses risk along several validated scales and tells the commander how his or her unit compares with the Air Force as a whole. Critical incident stress-management teams were established to serve personnel at every installation, with deployable teams available to provide additional resources to installations hard hit by potentially traumatizing events.

The Chief of Staff required the principle agencies at each geographical location to work together to assess the needs of the population they serve, develop a consolidated plan targeting their collective resources to a prioritized list of those needs, collaboratively market the resources to the community, and evaluate the effectiveness of their plan.

When the project began in 1995, suicide was the second leading cause of death among the 350,000 Air Force members, occurring at an annual rate of 15.8 per 100,000. Since then, the suicide rate has declined significantly over 3 consecutive years, and for the first 6 months in 1999, the annualized rate fell below 3.5 per 100,000. This is more than 50% less than the lowest rate on record prior to 1995, and an 80% drop from the peak rates in the mid-1990s. The suicide rates increased in 2000 and in early 2001, but have declined again since April 2001 and have remained much lower than rates prior to 1995. Statistically significant declines in violent crime, family violence, and deaths from unintentional injuries have also been measured concurrently with the intervention.

The Air Force community shares many characteristics with other American communities, and yet in some ways is quite distinct. For instance, the Air Force, like other communities, has identifiable leaders that can influence community norms and priorities. Human services, including health care, are delivered through a labyrinth of community agencies and organizations that are not well connected. The community has elements of a common identity but at the same time is a collection of widely diverse individuals. There is an established network of gatekeepers—people who open gates to helping resources for individuals in need.

The overarching principles, such as leveraging community leaders to change cultural norms, engaging and training established networks of gate-keepers, improving coordination of broadly diverse human services, and providing educational programs to community members should be trans-portable to any civilian community with some minimal level of organization and cohesion.

College Student Suicide Prevention

The topic of college student suicides has received renewed attention, beginning in 2000 with a spate of well-publicized suicides at nationally known universities. One estimate is that there are close to 1,100 suicides per year on college campuses (NMHA/Jed Foundation, 2002). Many of these tragic deaths have led to lawsuits being filed by grieving parents, contending that the university in question should have done more to prevent the suicide from occurring. Among a number of failures often cited is the expectation that the university should have contacted the parents when the university became aware of the potentially suicidal behavior of the student. Other fail-ures include protecting the student from self-harm. The outcome of these lawsuits will most likely shape the manner in which universities will evaluate and manage students with any form of self-destructive behaviors.

The largest, longest, and most statistically rigorous study of college stu-dent suicides was undertaken from 1980 to 1990 at 11 Midwestern universi-ties, in addition to the Pennsylvania State University (Silverman, Meyer, Sloan, Raffel, & Pratt, 1997). The Big 10 Universities Student Suicide Study analyzed 261 suicides that occurred on these 12 campuses over a 10-year period. Most striking was the finding that the suicide rate on these campuses was exactly 50% lower (7.5/100,000 vs. 15.0/100,000) than that of a control group matched for age, race, and gender. These findings are similar to other less rigorously controlled studies of similar populations. Hence, contrary to what appears in the popular press, suicides are relatively rare events on college campuses. The Jed Foundation, in collaboration with the National Mental Health Association, held an expert panel meeting in 2002 to address vulnera-bility, depressive symptoms, and suicidal behavior on college campuses. They identified essential services for addressing suicidal behaviors on campus (see Exhibit 8.13) and an institutional checklist (see Exhibit 8.14).

- Screening program(s)

- Targeted educational programs for faculty, coaches, clergy, and student and resident advisors

- Broad-based, campus-wide public education

- Educational programs and materials for parents and families

- An onsite counseling center with appropriately trained providers

- Onsite medical services

- Stress-reduction programs

- A nonclinical student support network

- Off-campus referrals, if available

- Emergency services

- Postvention programs

- Medical Leave policies

Note. From *Safeguarding Your Students Against Suicide* (p. 5), by The Jed Foundation, 2002, New York: Author. Copyright 2002 by The Jed Foundation. Adapted with permission.

Much speculation has occurred regarding why the rates for this late adolescent and young adult population are significantly lower than in the matched general population. There is much consensus among university student services personnel that the explanation include the following:

1. Easy and unrestricted access to health care;
2. Fewer restrictions on number of mental health treatment sessions per year;
3. Prohibitions against possession of firearms on university property;
4. Restrictions about and monitoring of alcohol and other drug use and abuse;
5. Geographical availability of community support services, including campus ministers;
6. Enlightened faculty, coaches, trainers, residence hall staff, student service personnel who are comfortable being available to, and supportive of, this population;
7. Professional availability of campus police;
8. Regular monitoring of daily activities (eating, sleeping, personal hygiene, attending classes) especially for those who live in dormitories and residence halls;
9. Regular opportunities for receiving and giving peer social support;
10. Sense of a future regarding the meaning and purpose for being engaged in pursuing academic studies;
11. Appreciation and respect by peers and authority figures for contributions made to the work of the larger community.

EXHIBIT 8.14
Safeguarding Against Suicide—A Checklist for Your Institution

Administrative Policies

___Yes ___No ▪ Do we have a mental health management plan in writing?

___Yes ___No ▪ Have we allocated enough financial resources to accommodate the plan and all of its components?

___Yes ___No ▪ Do we have a Medical Leave policy in place that includes mental health problems?

Risk-Identification Programs

___Yes ___No ▪ Do we have a screening program in place?

___Yes ___No ▪ Do we have a transitional support program in place for parents and families of incoming students who have already been diagnosed with mental health disorders?

___Yes ___No ▪ Have we trained our faculty, coaches, clergy, student advisors, and resident advisors to identify students who may be at risk for suicide or suicidal behaviors?

___Yes ___No ▪ Have we educated our students so that they are able to identify at-risk behaviors within themselves and among their peers?

On-Campus Support Services

___Yes ___No ▪ Do we have an on-site mental health services center?

___Yes ___No ▪ Have we hired providers who are appropriately trained to handle suicidal clients? If not, are we willing to train them?

___Yes ___No ▪ Do we have a 24-hour emergency service that is accessible to students?

___Yes ___No ▪ Do we have a crisis-management plan in place in the event of a suicide or other trauma on campus?

___Yes ___No ▪ Do we provide students with support programs (social, academic, etc.)?

___Yes ___No ▪ Have we made our students and faculty aware of exactly what services are offered on campus and in the community?

___Yes ___No ▪ Have we publicized the names and numbers of on-campus and off-site support providers?

Community-Based Support Services

___Yes ___No ▪ Do we have working relationships with community mental health providers to ensure appropriate off-site referrals? Do we know their appointment hours and fees? Have we arranged for a sliding scale? Do they accept insurance?

___Yes ___No ▪ Have we identified which hospital or center in the community is on call to handle any campus emergencies?

___Yes ___No ▪ Does our university Web site offer links to mental health information and services?

Note. From *Safeguarding Your Students Against Suicide* (p. 8), by The Jed Foundation, 2002, New York: Author. Copyright 2002 by The Jed Foundation. Adapted with permission.

In the fall of 1984, the University of Illinois instituted a suicide prevention program to reduce the rate of suicide among its enrolled students. At the core of this program was a policy that required any student reported to have threatened or attempted suicide to attend four sessions of clinical assessment; one consequence of noncompliance was withdrawal from the university. Over 18 years of implementation and study, the suicide rate among enrolled students decreased 55.4% (Joffe, 2003).

Spurred by the efforts of parent survivors of their college student son's suicide, the Jed Foundation (www.jedfoundation.org) has developed and is disseminating widely on college campuses a Web-based screening instrument (www.ulifeline.org) that allows students to self-assess their own suicidality and be connected directly with campus professionals for help.

PREVENTION STRATEGIES THAT MAY WORK

Evidence is mounting that a focus on family systems and community support building may prove to be effective preventive interventions. Approaches include parent education, healthy family functioning, conflict resolution training, communication skills building, improved access to health care, and access to crisis hotlines. However, definitive empirical support for these methods is still pending.

PREVENTION STRATEGIES THAT DO NOT WORK

There is little emprical evidence that suggests which suicide prevention strategies are most effective with children. However, there is evidence from adolescent suicide prevention studies that certain strategies are *not* effective. They include (a) scare tactic approaches and (b) health-awareness programs that focus solely on suicide prevention (Shaffer et al., 1991). The promulgation of the myth that school-based suicide prevention programs are harmful because talking about suicide with students will promote suicidal behavior is just that, a myth. According to Kalafat (2003), more than 30 years of crisis hotline experience and more than 20 years of school-based suicide prevention programming in which there have been no documented cases of stimulating suicidal behavior through discussion of the topic should lay this myth to rest. The Centers for Disease Control and Prevention have clearly stated this: "There is no evidence of increased suicidal ideation or behavior among program participants" (Centers for Disease Control and Prevention, 1995b, p. 66). Potter, Powell, and Kachur (1995) note that "[f]urthermore, numerous research and intervention efforts have been completed without any reports of harm" (p. 87). Second, talking with youth about suicide will not "plant the idea in their head" because they are well aware of suicide from their experience with suicidal peers and the media. Classroom lessons will not be students' first exposure to this topic (Kalafat & Elias, 1992; Norton, Durlak, & Richards, 1989).

CONCLUSION

We know that many clinicians do little in terms of larger prevention work in the community, perhaps preferring the more direct and intimate work that comes with clinical intervention and prevention efforts that occur at the individual level. However, other clinicians do have involvement beyond their consultation room, working in the larger arena of community-level prevention. Our goal in this chapter has been to fully review and consider the significant range of contemporary efforts that are underway in the field of youth suicide prevention to perhaps inspire more efforts to prevent the suicide of both the one as well as the many.

The greatest need seems to be a greater awareness, recognition, and response to youth in need and in times of crisis. This increased sensitivity befalls parents, educators, school personnel, health care professionals, mental health professionals, clergy, first responders (firefighters, police, emergency technicians), and even youth themselves to the potential for self-injurious behaviors. Suicide is preventable. Resources for providing effective interventions must be available that are affordable, accessible, and age-appropriate. The locus of intervention for youth must be targeted first to the family, community (church and school), and pediatrician's office.

The American Academy of Child and Adolescent Psychiatry (Shaffer & Pfeffer, 2001) identified the following public health approaches to suicide prevention in children and adolescents: (a) crisis hotlines; (b) method restriction; (c) indirect case-finding by educating potential gatekeepers, teachers, parents, clergy, and peers to identify the "warning signs" of an impending suicide; (d) direct case-finding among high school or college students or among the patients of primary practitioners by screening for conditions that place teenagers at risk for suicide; (e) media counseling to minimize imitative suicide; and (f) training professionals to improve recognition and treatment of mood disorders.

Inasmuch as child and adolescent suicide is a multidimensional disorder with a multicausal and multifactorial etiology, the prevention of suicide must encompass a comprehensive, coordinated, and collaborative approach. A biopsychosocial framework seems appropriate to such a challenging enterprise. What with suicide rates being low (albeit underreported), prevention efforts must be sustained and maintained over long periods of time before a reduction in the rate can be measured and attributed to ongoing preventive initiatives. A comprehensive strategy may well encompass two approaches: direct prevention approaches and system-level approaches. Direct prevention approaches include primary prevention and cultural change; early intervention; crisis intervention and primary care; treatment, support, and postvention; and restricting access to means. System-level approaches include policy and planning activities; ongoing research and evaluation; improved and expanded communications and media training; education and training of community gatekeepers and health care professionals; networking and collaboration between and among community organizations and institutions; and community development.

However, it is fairly certain that we will not see a substantial change in the suicide rate if we do not address the common risk factors that have been shown to contribute to a multitude of adolescent disorders and dysfunctions. Such well-known and common risk factors for such disorders include substance misuse and abuse, precocious sexual activity, exposure to violence and crime, involvement in the juvenile justice system, being in foster care, dysfunctional family functioning, marital discord and divorce, undiagnosed and untreated psychiatric disorders, homelessness, chronic physical illness, poverty or lack of access to health care, underachievement in school, lack of mentorship, lack of religious or community affiliation, and an absence of hope and a sense of a future (Dryfoos, 1990; U.S. Public Health Service, 2001). To this list, we would add access to lethal means of self-injury as a risk factor being specific to adolescent suicide.

As Gould, Greenberg, et al. (2003) conclude in their 10-year review of youth suicide preventive intervention studies,

> Given the complexity of the mechanism of youth suicide, it seems likely that no one prevention/intervention strategy, by itself, is enough to combat this critical problem. Rather, a comprehensive, integrated effort, involving multiple domains—the individual, family, school, community, media, and health care system—is needed. (p. 400)

As a society, we may well not be able to eliminate all the risk factors that increase the potential for suicidal behavior. However, as clinicians and public health workers, we all can surely agree that the enhancement of resilience or protective factors are at least as essential as risk reduction in preventing suicide. Such a dual-pronged strategy—at both the clinical *and* public health level—sustained over time, will most likely achieve the outcome we all seek: to effectively reduce the incidence of suicide among our youth.

SURVIVORS OF SUICIDE
AND POSTVENTION

Suicide is a personal and interpersonal disaster. The moment of the disaster's happening is its most dramatic. But it is not its only moment. A tragedy has its warnings and precursors—and it has its sequelae. There is much to be done after an earthquake, explosion, avalanche, tornado, fire, flood—or suicide. Postvention—the events that come after the dramatic event that gives the entire sequence its label—aims to mollify the inimical psychological sequelae in survivor-victims. (p. 154)

—Edwin Shneidman (2001)

Case Illustration

As a high school freshman, Steve was a popular and active 15-year-old, the pride and joy of his loving parents. Outstanding academically, a starter on the varsity baseball team, Steve had a girlfriend and a network of good friends. Hoping to gain entrance to an Ivy League college, Steve transferred to a private school his sophomore year. That was the year everything turned bad.

Inexplicably, Steve had trouble adjusting to the new school environment; his grades began to slip as he began to withdraw into himself. He made few new friends and eventually lost touch with his old friends. His girlfriend broke up with him over Christmas, and Steve appeared to become more and more depressed, withdrawn, and hostile to his parents' attempts to help. When spring approached, he refused to try out for baseball. His parents thought it was just a phase and had planned to transfer him back to his old school in the fall. But Steve would not live that long. One Friday night, his parents came home from a movie to find Steve lying dead after shooting himself in the head with his father's favorite hunting rifle.

His parents were shocked and utterly devastated. Their loss inexplicable, they felt they had no one to whom they could turn. Their mourning was filled with confusing feelings of guilt, hurt, anger, loss, and embarrassment. Steve's two younger sisters were devastated as well. Ashamed about Steve's suicide, his parents hurriedly arranged a brief memorial service and cremated his body within a few days.

Steve's parents found it difficult to talk about the death with their friends and withdrew from active involvement in the community. In the year following Steve's death, his father began to drink heavily, stayed out late, and engaged in frequent arguments with his wife. As the first year's anniversary of Steve's death approached, the situation had further deteriorated; Steve's sisters were acting out in school, his mother remained distraught and depressed, his father's drinking had resulted in two arrests for driving while intoxicated, and the marriage was on the verge of collapsing. Upon a recommendation from their priest, the family went to see a family therapist to begin to sort out and adjust to what had happened to them as individuals and as a family.

OVERVIEW

Suicidology as a field of study is perhaps most fundamentally rooted in, and oriented to, the prevention and intervention of suicidal behaviors. Preventing adolescent suicidality is particularly compelling. Yet despite our best efforts as clinicians, parents, teachers, or friends, we can never ultimately protect a determined individual from self-destructive urges. One of the most devastating outcomes that results in virtually any suicide therefore is the pain experienced by the "survivors"—those who are left behind in the aftermath of a suicide. As adolescent suicide takes the precious lives of teenagers we love, so too are the lives of their survivors taken over by a profound sense of grief related to such a loss. Over the past three decades, suicide survivorship and healing work conducted with survivors has emerged as a major area of attention within the field of suicidology.

The History of Suicide Survivorship

In his poignant discussion of the history of the suicide survivor, Colt (1987) graphically describes the desecration of the corpse of a young man "convicted" of suicide in Paris during the 18th century. The victim's body was dragged by his heels through the city streets and subsequently hung upside-down in the public square as an example to all who would consider such a crime; a crude form of suicide prevention indeed. His body would be denied a proper burial and would be tossed in the sewer or the town's dump. Property, title, and goods of the deceased would all be forfeited to the King, and law would decree that there be no memory of him. Wife and children would leave the town humiliated, hoping to start a new life while always hiding the secret shame of being suicide survivors.

There is a long and ignominious history of stigma connected to suicide and the litany of acts and rituals practiced throughout the world to mark the shameful event (Colt, 1987). To prevent the suicide's ghost from wandering, corpses were decapitated, buried outside city limits or tribal territories, burned, beaten with chains, thrown to wild beasts, or buried at a crossroads with a stake through the heart. In years past, survivors of suicide were often directly punished as accessories to the crime of suicide (because the guilty party was not available). As depicted above, survivors in medieval Britain and France were frequently forced to forfeit both the goods and property of the victim as well as their own. On occasion, family survivors of the victim were required to pay a fine to the suicide's in-laws in redemption for the shame brought to their name.

In England during the 18th century, automatic forfeiture of property to the crown and desecration of the corpse began to be replaced by crude investigations into the cause of death. Trials were held posthumously in a Coroner's Court to determine whether the victim had been insane and therefore innocent (*non compos mentis*) or a criminal against himself or herself (*felo de se*), guilty of crime, and subject to subsequent forfeiture of property and desecration of the body (Colt, 1987). The determination of insanity was thus central to civil disposition of a suspected suicide, and survivors were thereby afforded a modicum of relief from some of the direct blame and punishment. However, rewritten civil law did not release the survivor of the societal stigma of suicide or the superstitions and prejudices associated with madness and insanity.

During the 19th century, however, there was a distinct shift away from the view of suicide as a crime or sin toward a more medical perspective. A major line of research emerged in the area of genetic influences on suicide. Various theories of heredity were proposed that placed survivors at risk of succumbing to genetically influenced suicide (Winslow, 1840). By the mid-20th century, these theories were largely disregarded (Kallman & Anastasia, 1947). However, as discussed by DePaulo (2003), advances over the past 10 years in genetics and neurobiology has led to a great deal of recent interest in the exact influences of genetics on behavior and the development of serious psychopathology, as we have described elsewhere in this volume, that is so often seen in completed suicides. Many of the recent studies in this area tend to focus on serotonergic pathways in the brain that may be linked to impulse-control problems and aggressive traits (DePaulo, 2002).

As researchers developed a more empirical perspective on the topic, a new kind of social stigma for the suicide survivor was ushered in by the Victorian era of respectability (Colt, 1987). Although no longer directly punished in a civil sense, the act of suicide nevertheless marked a family's name, lowered property values, and generally tainted the reputations of the survivors. In response, survivors attempted to conceal the suicide, hastily arranged funerals, and kept the truth from children. Suicide became the family secret, the neighbors' gossip, and a source of blame and public shunning. Survivors were thus doomed to their own private shame, trapped with their feelings of hurt, loss, and anger.

It is striking to note that even with the increased interest in the study of suicide in the last 40 years, suicide survivorship long remained a largely unexamined topic. Professional interest in suicide survivorship began to emerge during the 1960s, when the founders of the Los Angeles Suicide Prevention Center were contracted by the Los Angeles Medical Examiner's Office to conduct psychological autopsies. As an unexpected outgrowth of this procedure, an awareness of the unique psychological needs of survivors emerged. In response to this awareness, Shneidman (1967) coined the term *postvention*, referring to efforts to assist grieving suicide survivors.

Since that time, the body of clinical and empirical literature on survivorship has grown considerably, with a notable increase in publications and empirical research in this area, particularly over the past 10 years. Concurrent with this increased scholarly and professional interest in suicide survivorship and postvention has been the increasingly prominent advocacy role played by suicide survivors who have potently argued for and catalyzed political and social change related to mental illness and suicide prevention. Indeed, the *National Strategy for Suicide Prevention* developed under the tenure of former U.S. Surgeon General Dr. David Satcher (U.S. Public Health Service, 2001) was largely propelled and led by the efforts of the Suicide Prevention Action (nee Advocacy) Network (SPAN), a grassroots organization led by parent survivors Jerry and Elsie Weyrauch. As shown in Exhibit 9.1, the evolution of survivors from being tainted, shamed accessories of a loved one's suicide to becoming a viable and potent political and social force for suicide prevention is one of the more remarkable developments in suicidology over the past 30 years.

EXHIBIT 9.1
A Brief Chronology of the Survivor Movement

The evolution of the survivor movement is one of the most remarkable developments within contemporary suicidology. Beginning in the late 1970s, an inexorable process began that continues to the present day which has helped move survivors of suicide from the shadows of shame and blame into the forefront of suicidology and suicide prevention. The following is a chronology of key events:

- **1977–1980:** There is the formation of the first suicide-specific survivor support groups. These early efforts include "Ray of Hope," founded by Elizabeth ("Betsy") Ross in Iowa City; "Survivors of Suicide," founded by Iris Bolton in Atlanta; "Heartbeat/Survivors After Suicide," founded by LaRita Archibald; and a co-led (survivor and professional) survivor support group at the Los Angeles Suicide Prevention Center.

- **Spring 1980:** Iris Bolton makes first survivor-oriented presentation at the Annual Conference of the American Association of Suicidology (AAS) held in Alburqueque. At same conference, Adina Wrobleski chairs several sessions on surviving suicide.

- **Spring 1983:** At AAS Annual Conference in Dallas, survivors convened and began plans for developing a "Survivors Committee" within AAS. The purpose of this committee was to identify and assert needs of survivors within the Association and to the Board of AAS.

- **1984:** Persistent advocacy and work of survivors Bolton, Wrobleski, Archibald, Stephanie Weber-Harding, Edward Dunne, and Karen Dunne-Maxim led to AAS Board formally recognizing the Survivor Committee as the official postvention arm of AAS.

- **1989:** First AAS-sponsored "Healing After Suicide" conference held in Denver (chaired by LaRita Archibald). Iris Bolton was elected to AAS Board of Directors. Celebrity survivors (e.g., Marriet Hartley, Joan Rivers, and Judy Collins) began to speak out publicly about surviving suicide and became involved in the field. The American Suicide Foundation, later renamed the American Foundation of Suicide Prevention (AFSP), began to mobilize survivor support for generating funding for suicide-related research.

- **1993:** AAS publishes first issue of *Surviving*, as a survivor-specific newsletter.

- **1994:** Survivor Committee becomes Survivor Division within AAS.

- **1996:** SPAN (the Suicide Prevention Advocacy Network) is founded by the Weyrauch family as a survivor-based grassroots advocacy group promoting suicide prevention.

- **1998–2000:** SPAN (with support of CDC and SAMSHA) convened first National Suicide Prevention Conference in Reno, Nevada, to develop a national suicide prevention strategy, which was accepted as a guiding plan by Surgeon General Dr. David Satcher. SPAN's letter-writing campaign and grassroots lobbying efforts on Capitol Hill led to resolutions in both Houses of Congress in support of suicide prevention. Survivors Karen Dunne-Maxim and brother Ed Dunne were elected as successive Presidents of AAS.

EXHIBIT 9.1 (Continued)

- **2001–2002:** Publication of the National Strategy for Suicide Prevention. Federal funding for a Suicide Prevention Resource Center (SPRC) occurs in 2002 (prompted by the National Strategy) following the work of survivors and other suicide prevention advocacy groups.

- **2004:** Enactment of the Garrett Lee Smith Memorial Act provides 82 million dollars of Federal funding for youth suicide prevention (named after the son of suicide survivor and U.S. Senator Gordon Smith from Oregon).

Note. Interviews and recollections of Edwin S. Shneidman, Iris Bolton, LaRita Archibald, Edward Dunne, Karen Dunne-Maxim, Sam Heilig, Jerry and Elsie Weyrauch, Norman Farberow, and Jerry Reed. From *Comprehensive Textbook of Suicidology* (p. 542), by R. Maris, A. Berman, and M. Silverman (Eds.), 2000, New York: Guilford Press. Copyright 2000 by Guilford Press. Adapted with permission.

BEREAVEMENT

Much of the empirical work dedicated to this topic since the first edition of this book has centered on research that endeavors to discern whether suicide bereavement is idiosyncratic or different from bereavement caused by other manners of death, notably sudden deaths like homicides or accidents. Intuitively, it would seem that suicide bereavement would be worse because of the presumed intent of those who die by suicide (i.e., they *chose* their own demise unlike those who die by accidental or homicidal manners of death). However, empirical data bearing out such intuitive differences has offered decidedly mixed results (McIntosh, 1993). To further understand this important and lively area of contemporary research, let us first consider broader notions of bereavement before our specific considerations of suicide bereavement.

Evolving Perspectives on Bereavement

Hauser (1983) defines bereavement as the physiological, psychological, behavioral, and social response patterns displayed by an individual following the loss (usually through a death) of a significant person or thing. Grief and mourning are two distinct components to bereavement. Grief refers to the specific feelings and emotional responses related to bereavement, whereas mourning refers to the social customs and rituals that help the bereaved to grieve—expressing thoughts, feelings, and memories related to the loss of the loved one (Hauser, 1987). Although mourning rituals tend to vary widely, mourning as a means to express grief is common to most cultures (Averill, 1968; Rosenblatt, Jackson, & Walsh, 1972). Culturally based rituals of mourning that facilitate the expression of grief and provide support for the bereaved appear to lead adaptive patterns of bereavement and healing (Hauser, 1987).

For many years, conventional wisdom held that a fairly consistent bereavement process and emotional progression were virtually universal in nature. Well-known bereavement models developed by Elizabeth Kubler-Ross and John Bowlby described various phases of "normal" bereavement in terms of a progression through initial shock, followed by yearning and protest, which leads to disorganization, which is ultimately followed by a working-through and reorganization phase (Bowlby, 1980; Kubler-Ross, 1969).

In more recent years, however, conventional wisdom pertaining to the idea of a universal "normal" linear process of bereavement has not been supported by contemporary empirical research. For example, recent studies by Bonanno and colleagues (Bonanno, Keltner, Holen, & Horowitz, 1995; Bonanno et al., 2002) have clearly shown that it is actually quite difficult to predict the process, nature, or length of time in which any one individual may grieve. Indeed, Bonanno, Papa, and O'Neill (2001) argue that for many years we have overpathologized grief and failed to recognize the pervasiveness of human resiliency in the face of grief. Thus, traditional notions of "normal" grief or a typical progression of bereavement through particular stages has been challenged and largely discounted in lieu of contemporary research. The notion that an individual deviating from a predictable bereavement progression is manifesting a form of "pathological" grief has been virtually abandoned by bereavement researchers (Bonanno et al., 2001; Bonanno et al., 2002). The empirical research literature now clearly shows that although there are many common bereavement experiences and emotions, the specific order, nature, and duration of these experiences varies widely across individuals (Bonanno et al., 2002).

Suicide Bereavement

As suggested earlier, a major emphasis in suicide-specific bereavement research in recent years has focused on the question as to whether suicide bereavement is fundamentally different than bereavement from other manners of sudden death. In our first edition we indicated that the extant literature had not definitively determined specific differences between suicide and other sudden-death bereavements (e.g., van der Wal, 1989–1990). In his review of 16 studies comparing groups of suicide survivors to other control groups of survivors of other sudden deaths, McIntosh (1993) found more similarities than differences. Although McIntosh noted some evidence of a small number of suicide-specific grief reactions (e.g., the course of bereavement), he also found differences between groups largely disappeared by the second year after the death.

These types of counterintuitive and contradictory data have spawned a series of more recent studies into suicide-specific bereavement. In their discussion and critique of this research, Ellenbogen and Gratton (2001) point out a number of fundamental methodological problems that have plagued this line of research, including the following:

1. Concepts are not always operationally defined.
2. Grief is rarely studied longitudinally.
3. Few studies have an adequate control group.
4. Group sizes are usually quite small.
5. Measures used are often not intended for the study of grief, nor are they psychometrically sound.
6. Theories are not explicitly stated.
7. Women and White people of upper socioeconomic class are overrepresented.
8. Refusal rates are high.
9. Sampling methods are suspect.
10. There is rarely control of possible confounding variables.
11. Jordan (2001) reassessed this research literature and suggested that suicide bereavement *is* in fact different in three main areas: (a) thematic aspects of suicide bereavement, (b) social processes surrounding suicide survivors, and (c) the impact of suicide on family systems.

Thematic Aspects

Jordan (2001) argues persuasively that considerable evidence exists for qualitative and thematic differences in suicide bereavement (e.g., Clark & Goldney, 1995; Range, 1998). For example, suicide survivors are more likely to question the meaning of the death (i.e., why did they do it?) than other survivors (Grad & Zavasnik, 1996; Silverman, Range, & Overholser, 1994–1995). Suicide survivors have higher levels of guilt, blame, and responsibility (Cleiren & Diekstra, 1995; Silverman et al., 1994–1995) and also experience more feelings of rejection or abandonment along with anger toward the deceased (Bailley, Kral, & Dunham, 1999; Reed, 1998; Silverman et al., 1994–1995).

Social Processes Surrounding Suicide Survivors

Jordan (2001) further argues that research shows that suicide survivors feel more isolated and stigmatized than other mourners and may be viewed more negatively by others (e.g., Allen, Calhoun, Cann, & Tadeschi, 1993). Other research has shown a tendency for suicide survivors to "self-stigmatize" (e.g., Van Dongen, 1993), leading to more withdrawal from social supports (Seguin, Lesage, & Kiely, 1995). Thus, these data suggest that suicide survivors are in fact viewed more negatively by others, as well as by themselves, thereby uniquely affecting social interactions and their potential for social support.

The Impact of Suicide on Family System

Finally, Jordan (2001) asserts that although data on the impact of death of family systems is more limited, there is at least some evidence that suicides uniquely affect a family system in comparison to other deaths. Citing data from psychological autopsy studies (e.g., Brent, Moritz, Bridge, Perper, & Canobbio, 1996), qualitative research (e.g., Dunn & Morrish-Vidners, 1987–1988), and research pertaining to heightened risk for suicide survivors (e.g., Fekete & Schmidtke, 1996; Ness & Pfeffer, 1990), Jordan argues that there is at least implicit support for the notion that suicide uniquely affects a family system compared to other forms of death. More direct and definitive research is needed in this area to more fully understand the potential differential impact of suicide on a family system.

Taken together, the weight and trends in the empirical research appear to be providing increasing support for the intuitive notion that suicide bereavement is unique in certain ways compared to other forms of bereavement. Increasingly more complex multivariate research (e.g., Bailley et al., 1999) is beginning to more definitively flush out the exact nature of some of these differences, with distinct implications for postvention and clinical care that can be better tailored to survivors of suicidal death.

SURVIVING SUICIDE: CONSIDERATIONS FOR HELP AND HEALING

Having reviewed and explored the history of suicide survivorship, various aspects of general bereavement, and unique aspects of suicide bereavement, we are now prepared to examine helpful responses to suicide survivors that may facilitate a healing process. In our experience, surviving the death of a young person is among one of the most difficult of all burdens to bear, particularly for parent survivors who invariably feel so guilty and blamed. When we consider the literature pertaining to help and healing for survivors, there is never any mention that suffering over the loss is ever really cured. However, in our experience, survivors of suicide are able to experience a process of ongoing healing, typically finding ways to make some measure of meaning from their loss through rituals or activities that preserve and honor the memory of their loved one. But before we can properly consider this healing process, it is first important to consider whom we mean when we refer to "suicide survivors."

Identifying Survivors

As discussed by Jobes, Luoma, Hustead, and Mann (2000), it is important to thoughtfully consider the full range of those who may be considered a suicide survivor. To be clear, virtually no one chooses to become a suicide survivor; by its very nature, suicide survivorship is abruptly thrust on potentially any person who knew and cared about the deceased. One effort to conservatively estimate the numbers of potential suicide survivors in the United States between 1972 and 1995 identified 4.06 million potential survivors of suicide (McIntosh, 1996), which increases by an additional 180,000 (or an estimated average of 6 survivors/suicide) each calendar year (Jobes, Luoma, et al., 2000).

Whether any one individual member of this legion chooses to embrace the identity of "suicide survivor" is of course always up to that individual. In truth, many may never consider acknowledging this identity, yet others may directly reject the notion. Others, genetically linked as survivors to the suicide, may never have known the decedent, as when a parental suicide occurs when a child survivor is an infant; thus, these survivors may not have experienced a moment's bereavement over the death of their parent. However, for many who have faced this type of sudden and traumatic loss, connecting to the identity of being a *survivor* of suicide can often be a critical first step in an important healing journey.

In terms of identifying potential survivors, the most obvious candidates are the decedent's immediate nuclear family; parents and siblings of an adolescent who dies by suicide are the most directly affected. Additional survivors of a suicide, however, may include others who are not so obviously identified. Extended family members such as grandparents, aunts, uncles, and cousins are often deeply affected by a suicide, but their grief may not be as readily recognized as that of the immediate kin. Friends of the deceased represent yet another group of survivors who may be profoundly devastated, especially when the victim is an adolescent peer. As we will discuss later in the chapter, mental health professionals, who may have worked heroically to prevent a suicide, are frequently neglected as legitimate survivors. Formal groups or organizations—a sports team, a church, a class, or a whole grade in school—can be seen as survivors of suicide. Indeed, Zinner's (1985) notion of "group survivorship" conceptualizes groups as extended families (with their own mores, symptoms, goals, hierarchies, and communication networks) that must mourn the loss of a member. Bottom line, virtually anyone touched, moved, or affected by a suicide may potentially be considered a survivor of that suicide.

On this journey, survivors can often find strength, growth, and new sources of comfort and support (Bolton, 1998). We have often heard suicide survivors acknowledge that over time, a kind of personal growth and strength can arise from the ashes of their grievous loss. However, if given a choice, survivors invariably would opt for the return of their lost loved one over this kind of forced growth. This is the essential nature of the suicide survivor's struggle—an unanticipated and unwelcome set of challenges where one is forced to chart a new course though a nightmarish storm of sadness, anger, and loss, or perhaps flounder, even drown, in a sea of guilt, self-blame, and immeasurable grief.

A Suicide Survivor's Journey

As discussed throughout this chapter, many suicide survivors have contributed to the development of the contemporary survivor movement. Among these leaders, Iris Bolton has uniquely provided important guidance and wisdom on the subject of surviving suicide. In the aftermath of her 20-year-old son's suicide, Bolton endeavored to deal with the loss (Bolton, 1983). As a result of working through her own healing process, Bolton has provided comfort and facilitated healing to countless other survivors, both personally and through her public presentations. She is among the first to describe surviving suicide as a *journey* of healing; she routinely recounts what she calls the four tasks of grief that she initially learned at a grief workshop (Bolton, 1998). These tasks include (a) the importance of telling the story, (b) the importance of expressing emotion, (c) the importance of making meaning from the loss, and (d) the importance of making a transition from the physical presence of the person to a new relationship with that person. Through the tireless efforts of Bolton and other survivor leaders, a path through the journey of losing someone to suicide is perhaps a bit clearer, and with the support of fellow survivors this journey does not have to be undertaken alone.

Helping Survivors Survive

Survivors of suicide potentially have special treatment and support needs that may be met through various modalities, different settings, and activities. For our purposes, we will briefly examine four main areas of survivor intervention: (a) group and systems postvention, (b) various forms of clinical response (e.g., psychotherapy), (c) survivor support groups, and (d) training of first responders. In addition, we will conclude this section with a discussion of the emergence of suicide survivor grassroots activism. Suicide survivors taking leadership in the field of suicide prevention is an important contemporary development in the suicide survivor experience (e.g., cases of suicide survivors advocating for suicide prevention legislation, program development, efforts to destigmatize mental illness, etc.).

Group and Systems Postvention

As noted above, entire groups or social systems can be considered survivors of suicide. For example, in one case discussion, Berman, Jacobs, and Jobes (1993) explored postvention approaches in a relatively small professional work setting. Effective postvention in smaller group systems typically involves identifying and recognizing various individuals in the group and providing opportunities for individual responses as well as opportunities for the larger group or perhaps subgroups to meet, process the loss, and develop ways of providing support to each other.

Various protocols and recommendations—specific to adolescent suicide—have been developed for school settings. As we discussed in the first edition of this book, the Centers for Disease Control (1988) published a first-generation model for school-based suicide prevention that incorporated various recommendations for postvention in the event of completed suicide by a student. Key to this model was an a priori emphasis *before* a suicide to anticipate the potential impact of a suicide on a school community, thus leading to the development of a postsuicide crisis response plan. Included in this plan were common-sense recommendations—for example, information should be thoughtfully shared directly in class and not over a public address system. Generally speaking, these recommendations emphasized the importance of a balanced approach to the situation; over-responding can lead to sensationalizing, and underresponding generates suspicion, rumor, and a message that the situation cannot be dealt with directly. Postvention in schools is an important area where well-meaning efforts to help may inadvertently contribute to the romanticization and glorification of suicidal deaths (refer to Callahan, 1996).

Contemporary considerations of school-based postvention can be seen in the recent work of the Task Force for Child Survival and Development (Davidson & Marshall, 2003). In their guide for school-based suicide prevention, Davidson and Marshall emphasize three major areas that pertain to exemplary suicide postvention practices. These key postvention areas include (a) various specific postvention action steps, (b) dealing with the media following a suicide, and (c) post-traumatic loss debriefing.

In terms of specific action steps, should a suicide or suicide-related event occur within a school-based milieu, Davidson and Marshall highlight the outstanding work of the American Association of Suicidology (AAS) Suicide Prevention Programs Committee (Smith, 1998). The summary guidelines from the AAS tend to emphasize the importance of precrisis steps to identify and select a crisis team, the availability of individual and group counseling, and communications with students, faculty, staff, and media. The major summary points of the AAS guidelines are as follows:

1. Plan in advance of any crisis.
2. Select and train a crisis team.
3. Verify any report of suicide from the medical examiner or police.
4. Schedule a meeting with the school principal.
5. Assess the situation and adjust the size of the crisis team accordingly.
6. Disseminate information to faculty, students, and parents. Be sensitive to parents' wishes and always be truthful.
7. Follow victim's classes throughout the day with discussion and counseling.

8. Arrange for counseling rooms in the school building.
9. Invite friends to join the support group or be counseled individually.
10. Check records and provide individual counseling for all identified students at risk.
11. Provide counseling or discussion opportunities for faculty.
12. Arrange for students and faculty to be excused to attend the funeral.
13. Coordinate or consult on memorial plans by the school.
14. Make a home visit to the family of the deceased.
15. Respond to media inquiries.
16. Link with the community as appropriate.
17. Follow up with continued counseling or refer for outside treatment as necessary.

In terms of dealing with the media following a suicide, Davidson and Marshall highlight the original work of O'Carroll and Potter (1994) in the development of first-generation "media guidelines" for handling suicides within a system and working constructively with the news media. The major points of the original media guidelines include the following:

1. Suicide is often newsworthy and it will probably be reported.
2. "No comment" is not a productive response to media representatives who are covering a suicide story.
3. All parties should understand that a scientific basis exists for concern that news coverage of suicide may contribute to the causation of suicide.
4. Some characteristics of news coverage may contribute to contagion, whereas other characteristics may help prevent suicide.
5. School spokespersons and the media must carefully consider what is to be said and reported regarding suicide.
6. Concise, factual reporting of suicide may benefit at-risk persons.

As was discussed in chapter 3, a recent collaboration between several federal agencies and nonprofit groups has produced recommendations to the media regarding coverage of suicides and has made these available on their Web sites.

Finally, Davidson and Marshall recommend post-traumatic loss debriefing as developed by Thompson (1990). This approach emphasizes a stage model for working with trauma following an upsetting event like a completed suicide within a school system. Thompson outlines the following stages in this approach:

1. *Introductory stage.* During this stage, survivors are introduced to the debriefing process.
2. *Fact stage.* During this stage, information is gathered to "recreate the event" from what is known about it.

3. *Life review stage.* A life review of the deceased can be the next focus, if appropriate.
4. *Feeling stage.* During this stage, feelings are identified and integrated into the process.
5. *Reaction stage.* Exploring the physical and cognitive stress reactions to the traumatic event takes place during this stage.
6. *Learning stage.* This stage consists of assisting survivors in learning new coping skills to deal with their grief reactions.
7. *Closure stage.* This stage includes wrapping up loose ends, answering outstanding questions, providing final assurances, and creating a plan of action that is life-centered.

As with any stage model of grief or trauma, these stages provide a framework for expectations, activities, and postvention efforts to help members of a larger system deal with the grief, loss, and trauma of losing one of their own. At the same time, we should note that there is some debate as to the effectiveness of some models of trauma counseling. For example, in reviewing the literature regarding Critical Incident Stress Debriefing (CISD), Beutler (2003) has noted that as many as 20% of those treated by CISD may recover *more slowly* from the effects of trauma than those recovering with no debriefing treatment at all.

Psychotherapy

It has been estimated that up to 50% of completed suicides were in treatment at the time of their death (Robins, 1981). As Dunne (1987) has noted, survivors of suicide often do not seek assistance from mental health professionals, possibly because they feel anger toward the profession for not preventing a loved one's suicide or because they fear the stigma of mental illness. Unfortunately, those who do seek treatment may encounter therapists who are unfamiliar with those aspects of suicide survivor grief that uniquely differentiate it from other forms of grief. In reviews of working with survivors in therapy, Dunne (1987) and more recently Barlow and Morrison (2002) examined both general considerations and specific clinical themes that are relevant to treatment.

Effective work with survivors requires that the therapist be aware of his or her own attitudes about suicide and guard against countertransference responses—especially blaming the client or family. Moreover, therapists should be knowledgeable about normal grief processes and respectful of the time that grief work can require. It may be necessary to work in different modalities, depending on the needs of the survivor. In many cases, family therapy may be particularly useful to work through systemic issues such as blaming, scapegoating, and isolation of family members. Individual or couples therapy may be the treatment of choice for survivors working with alternative sets of issues. Dunne (1987) suggests that often the client is the best barometer of which specific treatment strategy may be most useful.

In terms of clinical themes relevant to working with survivors, Dunne (1987) cites six major themes commonly seen:

1. Surviving suicide often establishes a perpetual need to search for both physical and psychological clues to the reason for the suicide.
2. Whether irrational or appropriate, suicide survivorship often leaves a legacy of profound guilt.
3. Survivorship often profoundly alters one's social relationships as a consequence of real or imagined stigma.
4. Grief following a suicide is often complex and likely to be incomplete.
5. The idea of suicide as a solution to a problem becomes implanted in the survivor's mind.
6. Suicide erodes the survivor's capacity to trust others.

We suggest, in addition, that there may be value in conducting an informal "psychological autopsy" with surviving family members as a means of addressing in some way the compelling and haunting "why?" question (i.e., the need to understand and make sense of the suicide) In this regard, it is also important to address and defuse lingering feelings of guilt and responsibility that family members invariably feel. As with an institutional "root cause analysis," which we will discuss later in the chapter, the goal of thoughtfully reviewing and reconstructing the deceased's suicide is meant to provide understanding, insight, and clarity about what happened. Ultimately, in cases of suicide, developing some sense of what one did and did not do is critical to finding one's way through the survivor's struggle of feeling responsible for the death.

Although these general considerations and themes are by no means exhaustive, they do suggest that there are special considerations relevant to working with suicide survivors. Central to this work is the need for clinicians to be aware of their own attitudes about suicide and the special issues that suicide survivors bring to the therapeutic setting.

Surviving the Suicide of the Therapist

Although the literature is limited on the topic, the tragic event of losing a therapist to suicide poses some unique challenges to bereavement and further professional care. As discussed by Farberow (1993), surviving patients may have unrealistic or distorted perceptions of responsibility for the clinician's death by unduly burdening the therapist with their problems and issues. There are also concomitant feelings of anger and betrayal that this professional who was their guide to hope and health was either a hypocrite, an imposter, or both. The clinician's suicide is obvious evidence of the professional not being able to take his or her own medicine, not applying therapeutic coping to save his or her own life. Moreover, because of the transferential nature of psychotherapy, there may be some concern of an increased suicide risk in the patient through identification with the deceased clinician. Obviously, feelings of abandonment and rejection are natural, and the prospect for believing in the benefits of future psychotherapy is tainted. If one encounters a patient in such circumstances, great effort should be made to reassure the patient that this is a remarkably rare event; most clinicians are able to manage their own problems through psychotherapy and professional consultation. Finally, efforts to resolve any feelings of guilt for having caused the clinician to commit suicide should be thoroughly addressed (Farberow, 1993).

Survivor Support Groups

There has been a virtual explosion in suicide survivor support groups over the past 3 decades (as of August 2003, the AAS listed on their Web site more than 350 groups in North America and the International Association for Suicide Prevention listed approximately 200 groups in Europe), probably because of a general decrease in social taboos related to suicide (Heilig, 1985), the growing public awareness of adolescent suicide (McIntosh, 1987), as well as national attention at the highest levels of government (U.S. Public Health Service, 2001). About 10 years after the birth of the survivor movement, Appel and Wrobleski (1987) observed that suicide survivors were increasingly less secretive and more prepared to seek help. To be sure, the self-help survivor support group by its very nature appears to draw many to seek help who might otherwise avoid traditional mental health modalities (Maxim & Brooks, 1985). As with other self-help movements, the involvement in self-help support groups of mental health professionals who are not themselves survivors has sparked its share of controversy (see Appel & Wrobleski, 1987; Heilig, 1985). Although undoubtedly each side of the argument has legitimate perspectives and concerns, we would support Silverman (1978) and, more recently, Hall and Epp (2001), who have advocated a nonadversarial stance between professionals and self-help leaders to create a partnership in providing compassionate help to survivors of suicide.

In her study of multiple family support groups for survivors, Billow (1987) notes three major implications of the function of these groups. First, survivors clearly have a need to be with other survivors, a key aspect of engaging survivors in treatment. Second, open-ended groups appeared to be particularly effective with regard to survivors who may move away from the group and subsequently return (possibly around significant holidays and anniversaries). A third implication was the way in which members used the group to resolve their feelings of hopelessness through political action and consumer advocacy.

Special Considerations for Child Survivors of Suicide

As discussed by Farberow (2001), there are special considerations when the bereaved is a child. Obviously, the death of a parent is profoundly difficult for school-age children, no matter the manner of death. At what age a child has the developmental capacity to mourn has been a matter of some debate. Indeed, some have argued that there is evidence of mourning in young infants, whereas others assert that true mourning is intimately linked with an understanding about the finality of death, which may not occur until adolescence. The exact role and impact of suicide on children is not deeply understood; losing a parent to suicide can be akin to a post-traumatic stress disorder event in a child's life. Child survivors have a broad range of behavioral outcomes following the suicidal death of a parent—ranging from overfunctioning and being the perfect child to deteriorating behaviors of withdrawal, substance abuse, and conduct-related problems. It is generally held that even young children should be told that the death was a suicide to avoid later confusion and anger. Moreover, the egocentric developmental world of the child can often result in the child feeling like the death was *their* fault (obviously in cases of suicide but also in cases of natural death). Surviving parents and family, perhaps with professional assistance, need to help even young children clarify issues of responsibility, confusion, anger, shame, and guilt. As is true of youth mental health in general, childhood bereavement is most manifest in terms of *behaviors*; surviving family, friends, and members of the child's support system should observe unusual behaviors or conduct problems as a window into the child's bereavement process.

Training of First Responders

A significant development since the first edition of this book has been the increased interest and focus on what have come to be called "first responders" to suicides. First responders typically include police officers, emergency medical technicians, coroner's office investigators, and emergency room personnel (nurses, physicians, and aids). The increased focus on first responders has been driven, in part, by suicide survivors who have had negative experiences with professionals who literally are thrust into the middle of and may exacerbate the initial trauma of the suicide of a loved one. For example, it is not uncommon in the earliest stages of a suicide for a family member to be questioned by the police as a suspect in a possible homicide staged to look like a suicide.

Obviously, the issues in these circumstances are complex; police officers must necessarily secure a death scene so that potential forensic evidence—that is so critical in cases where foul play must first be ruled out—is not disturbed until a thorough investigation of the scene has been performed. Survivors often and understandably reflect back on these initial experiences of losing their loved one as being profoundly traumatizing and humiliating, adding further insult to injury. Given the complexity of these situations, it is encouraging to note that work to increase the sensitivity of first responders to the suicide survivor's experience is being pursued (Earle, 2003; Horgas, 2003). Earle (2003) argues that there is a need to fundamentally shift the mindset of first responders to avoid additional or secondary trauma to suicide survivors. Whereas most first responders (e.g., police) are trained to manage death scenes in a detached way, to solve a crime, a shift in mindset can create a very different experience for the survivor of suicide. Earle (2003) advocates training that emphasizes sensitivity and knowledge about mental illness and suicide, creating a fundamental awareness that

1. suicide is not a crime, nor a crime scene;
2. survivors at the scene need to be treated with professionalism and dignity;
3. survivors are not perpetrators of the death, but victims;
4. survivors are already experiencing trauma and shock; and
5. survivors need assistance, not additional trauma.

In a similar vein, Molock (2003) argues for additional training for clergy. Although members of the clergy may not be immediate first responders, they are nevertheless often uniquely positioned to provide an early and critical healing response to suicide survivors. Molock (2003) asserts that a well-trained member of the clergy who understands issues of mental health and suicide bereavement can make an important pastoral response to a suicide survivor with important implications for future spiritual and emotional adjustment and well-being.

Suicide Survivor Activism

As discussed at the beginning of this chapter, one of the most striking developments in the field of suicidology over the past 30 years has been the birth, growth, and maturation of the survivor movement (Jobes, Luoma, et al., 2000). This movement has advanced and evolved in at least two major ways: (a) the fundamental recognition and general acknowledgment of unique problems, issues, and needs related to losing someone to suicide, and (b) the emergence of suicide survivors as a potent source of grassroots activism and mental health advocacy. In the last decade, there has been a virtual explosion of suicide survivor activism in the formation of various suicide prevention organizations and movements (e.g., the Suicide Prevention Action Network—SPAN USA, Suicide Awareness Voices of Education—SAVE, The Link's National Resource Center, Organization for Attempters and Survivors of Suicide in Interfaith Services—OASSIS, the Yellow Ribbon Campaign, Kristin

Brooks Hope Center, the Jed Foundation, and the JASON Foundation). Moreover, the original "Survivor Committee" of the American Association of Suicidology (AAS) founded in the early 1980s has since evolved into the "Survivor Division"—one of five major membership divisions within AAS. Finally, suicide survivors play a key leadership role in the American Foundation for Suicide Prevention (AFSP), raising money for empirical research in suicide prevention and education (see Appendix A).

There can be no doubt that the activism of suicide survivors has fundamentally changed the entire field of suicidology. In the United States, the tireless work of suicide survivors has directly and indirectly led to the development of a national suicide prevention plan, establishment of a national suicide prevention technical resource center, a plethora of state suicide prevention plans, national suicide prevention hotlines, legislative resolutions in both houses of the U.S. Congress, a major review of suicide research by the Institute of Medicine of the National Academy of Sciences, media guidelines for reporting and covering suicide, and increased private and public funding for suicide research and prevention programming. To date we know of no specific studies that have investigated the impact of this type of activism on the survivor's healing experience. Nevertheless, one can intuitively assume that survivors may directly and indirectly benefit from the knowledge and experience of transforming the pain of their loss into work that may possibly help prevent even one future suicide, and thereby the related suffering that axiomatically accompanies that death (Esposito-Smythers, Jobes, Lester, & Spirito, 2004).

AN INTERNATIONAL PERSPECTIVE

While there have been significant developments in the United States over the past decades in the survivor movement and work in postvention, there have also been significant developments at an international level as well. As discussed by Grad (2003), different countries with different issues and approaches have much to offer to our understanding. Grad highlights in her review the experiences of four countries to illustrate both similarities and differences in approaching surviving suicide and postvention in other parts of the world.

The Australian Perspective

Research conducted with survivors and professionals has identified a number of major themes. Three major themes included

- the need for improved attitudes of professionals and providers to bereaved individuals, including less patronizing services, more compassion, less adversarial coroner examinations, training in not being judgmental, the need to listen better to survivors, and more education;

- the need to address unique bereavement needs of special groups (e.g., children, immigrants, rural communities, etc.); and
- the need to increase the flexibility and availability of services, including more active follow-up after suicide (both short- and long-term), on-demand systems of emotional support (rather than monthly meetings, for example) that can be available after hours and on weekends, and more workplace systems of support.

The Norwegian Perspective

Grad (2003) highlights survivor research from Norway and describes the phenomenon of "social helplessness," which is the social network's failure to respond to and support survivors of suicide. More specifically, survivors in this research recount the experience of anticipated support not coming through; trusted people stayed away and avoided contact. Moreover, survivors described low tolerance in others for addressing grief and pain, thoughtless remarks, and unhelpful advice. Grad proceeds to describe an evolving sense of openness in Norway that has been helpful to survivors (i.e., there is more frank and forthright discussion of suicide and the needs of survivors). Moreover, key political leaders in Norway have opened doors to a new and broader national acceptance of discussing and addressing issues such as suicide, bereavement, and the stigma of mental illness.

The Belgian Perspective

In her review, Grad (2003) summarizes findings from a national study in Belgium on the needs of suicide survivors (Delhaise, Andriessen, & Forceville, 2001). This research revealed that survivors in Belgium seek respect and dignity, need to be taken seriously, and stress the importance of being given sufficient time and support to mourn the death of their loved one. Furthermore, there were strong views about the need for knowledgeable providers who are sensitive to the unique issues and needs of suicide survivors. The notion of "survivor rights" was another clear theme in this research, as were concerns about social reactions and lack of support from others. Concern was also expressed about providers and professionals who do not reach out to surviving family members after a patient dies by suicide. Interestingly, this research also uncovered strong views about clinician survivors, a subject that will be addressed in depth at the end of this chapter.

The Slovenian Perspective

Grad's (2003) discussion of a suicide survivor program in Slovenia underscores the individual differences that exist across different survivors of suicide. These individual differences also give rise to many important questions about working with survivors. For example, how much discussion of complex and contradictory feelings of grief and loss is healthy? Can discussion of these feelings in support groups ever become counterproductive? What role should professionals have in helping the survivor process? Should professionals play a passive and supportive role or a more active and directive role? What emerges from this work is that survivors have *needs* and that these needs are idiosyncratic; some need support and direction, others need to be left alone; some need information and education, still others need to hear about successful survivors who have ultimately found their way through this seemingly impossible experience.

At the end of her review Grad (2003) describes a unique workshop on the topic of surviving suicide and postvention that included 80 participants from around the world. She summarizes,

> The collected wisdom can be condensed into a single line: postvention practices for suicide survivors should not be prescriptive but instead should empower survivors to find their own path. Or as one of the participants concluded the workshop: 'We should not give the survivors rules, but let them find new goals.' (p. 134)

CLINICIAN SURVIVORS

Case Illustration

Stephanie is a 35-year-old clinical psychologist who works at a large university counseling center. As a staff psychologist, she sees a wide range of undergraduate and graduate patients. Stephanie received her PhD about 5 years ago and is licensed in her state of practice. She enjoys her work at the counseling center, has a small private practice on the side, and dabbles in some ongoing clinical research projects. She has worked with many depressed and suicidal patients and believes she has a fairly good working knowledge of suicide.

One afternoon, Stephanie conducted an intake with a 19-year-old sophomore political science major. Her patient, Mike, was a pleasant but emotionally immature young man who appeared to be very depressed. During the course of their first interview, Mike tearfully revealed to Stephanie that he had been in a homosexual relationship with a distant cousin who was 20 years his elder.

The relationship had begun rather innocently when they met for the first time at a large family reunion the summer after

Mike's freshman year at college. Mike, a self-described social introvert, came to idolize his cousin, a schoolteacher who happened to live in the university town where Mike went to college. During the fall of his sophomore year, Mike became quite close to his cousin as they spent hours together talking and going to movies and sporting events. By the end of the fall semester, Mike's cousin became the entire focus of Mike's social life.

Following his return from Christmas break, Mike eagerly went to visit his cousin. His cousin received him warmly and through the course of the evening became quite intoxicated. When Mike got up to leave, his cousin made a sexual advance. Simultaneously terrified and exhilarated by his idol's sexual interest, Mike capitulated.

Thereafter, an ongoing sexual relationship evolved over the following weeks. Although Mike felt confused, he was also flattered and excited by this new development, until one fateful night. Shortly after midterm exams, Mike's cousin took him to a gay bar, an experience that was very upsetting to Mike. After their return home, his cousin initiated sex and Mike refused. After his refusal, Mike's cousin brutally raped him.

This event occurred about 2 weeks prior to Mike seeking treatment at the counseling center. Since that night, Mike had become quite depressed and unable to go to classes. The incident left Mike with a sick feeling, and he felt profoundly guilty and "dirty" about the entire relationship. His cousin repeatedly attempted to call and visit him, but Mike refused to have any contact with him. Each phone call or attempted contact brought a cycle of depression and acute agitation.

Stephanie quickly recognized the depth of injury, the degree of betrayal, and the fragility of Mike's emotional world. She empathically listened to his story and began to focus her assessment around the cycles of depression and upset that followed his cousin's attempts to contact Mike. She astutely asked whether Mike ever felt suicidal in this cycle of depression. Mike quietly confirmed that indeed he thought about suicide a great deal and how he would like to end the pain. When Stephanie appropriately inquired about a plan, Mike said he thought of shooting himself, but he did not have a gun.

Stephanie, concerned about Mike's imminent safety, conducted a thorough assessment of suicide risk and received clear commitments from Mike that he would remain safe and would call her if he felt unsafe. Mike seemed greatly relieved to finally tell his story, and Stephanie sensed a good connection with Mike. She scheduled their next session for later that week and felt fairly confident about his safety. She carefully documented her assessment and consulted with the director of the agency about the case.

Stephanie met with Mike for another 2 weeks and felt that they were making good headway. She continued to assess his suicidality and felt that the alliance was forming quite well. Mike had been able to maintain the boundary with his cousin, who had begun to leave him alone. Stephanie was cautiously encouraged about Mike's progress.

About a month after she had begun to work with Mike, Stephanie received a call from the director of the agency in the early hours of a Monday morning. It seemed that the resident director of Mike's dormitory had called—Mike had been found by his roommate hanging by a belt in his closet. Two notes had been left, one for his parents and one for Stephanie. Her note read,

Dear Stephanie,

I'm so sorry, I know I've let you down. I broke my promise to you, but I had no choice. I can't live with him and I can't live without him—I tried but it hurt too much. You did the best you could, please don't be mad at me. I appreciate all that you tried to do, but it's my life and my choice. Now my pain will end, but his will just begin.

Mike

Despite all her best efforts, her skill and knowledge, her thorough assessment and treatment, Stephanie was unable to save Mike from his own pain and anger. The story of Mike's death serves to remind us of our most fundamental limitations as therapists and as human beings—we can never ultimately predict and prevent every patient's suicide. Such a realization strikes at the very heart of our own narcissism and grandiosity as psychotherapists.

Having applied a number of different lenses through which we have broadly examined the epidemiology, theory, research, assessment, treatment, malpractice liability, and prevention of suicide, we apply yet one more lens. This final lens brings the topic of suicide into a narrow and sharp focus, a focus that is most personal and perhaps most threatening. Therein, our final consideration centers on the therapist's survivorship of an adolescent patient's suicide.

A Personal and Professional Crisis

Jones (1987) asserts that the suicide of a patient in therapy is the most difficult bereavement crisis that therapists may encounter and endure. Litman (1965) has noted that the crisis is compounded because the patient's suicide often presents a personal as well as a professional crisis. The differentiation of personal versus professional issues as it relates to a patient's suicide often becomes quite fuzzy.

Skilled therapists tend to develop very intense and intimate relationships with their patients. Although for the competent and ethical therapist, these relationships remain fundamentally professional and appropriate, they do invariably touch the therapist personally as well. Therapists often come to care sincerely for their patients and, moreover, may become quite invested in their progress. Unarguably, therapists become quite invested in their patients remaining alive. We have found that the personal investment may become especially intense in the case of youthful suicidal patients—"They have so much living yet to do." In our perceived omnipotence and grandiosity, we may be professionally, and personally, drawn to take it upon ourselves to be the savior of a particular young patient. Such a natural and seductive pull may set up a traumatic personal loss for the therapist should the patient choose death over life.

The various and confusing boundaries between professional and personal issues related to working with suicidal patients are further complicated by the specific demands and responsibilities of the professional role. For better or worse, therapists are society's watchdogs, legally bound to protect patients from themselves and others. Thus, the professional role may require breaking the patient's fundamental right to confidentiality or may require hospitalizing a patient against his or her will, limiting personal liberty. Moreover, recent survey data suggest that malpractice litigation is almost automatically considered by the majority of grieving survivors when a loved one in treatment dies by suicide (Peterson, Luoma, & Dunne, 2002), which further adds to stressors endured by clinicians who lose a patient to suicide.

The personal and professional issues inherent in a patient's suicide therefore provide a complex matrix of various manifestations and consequences (see Exhibit 9.2). Fundamentally, surviving a patient's suicide generates a number of essential questions that speak to issues of both personal and professional competence and responsibility: "What could I have done that I did not do? Was it my fault? What did I do that I should not have done?" Readers may find the personal account of Jones (1987) helpful in gaining some perspective on the therapist's personal and professional survival of a patient's suicide.

Resources for Clinician Survivors

At the time the first edition of this book was published, there were remarkably few resources to which clinicians could turn to help sort through

EXHIBIT 9.2
Therapist Reactions to Suicide

Manifestations	Consequences
I. *Personal*	
A. *Affective*	
Anger (deceased, family, supervisor)	Blame
	? suicide rate
Sadness/depression/hopelessness	Fuels guilt, denial, anger
Relief	
B. *Cognitive*	
Denial/Repression/Guilt	Myth-making
Guilt	Obsessive reviewing, fuels professional fears
	Search for meaning
Shame	Fuels professional fears
One-way communications:	
"I won't let you help me"	Anger toward deceased
"You can't help me"	Feelings of inadequacy
C. *Behavioral*	
Loss of patterns of conduct	Impaired professional and personal performance
Partial identification	? suicide rate
II. *Professional*	
Fears—Blame by the family/Lawsuit	Avoid contact with family, avoid attending funeral
—Censure by colleagues	Secrecy and isolation, personally and professionally
—Damage to reputation/publicity	
Doubts regarding adequacy/competence	Conservatism to avoid repeat
	Decline in suicidal patients
	Professional shift or leaving profession altogether
Reorganization: What can I learn?	Formal case review
	Enhanced skills, competence
	Owning responsibilitiy for "mistakes"

Note. Reprinted from "Therapists as Survivors of Client Suicide," by Frank A. Jones, Jr., from *Suicide and its Aftermath: Understanding and Counseling the Survivors* (p. 131), edited by Edward J. Dunne, John L. McIntosh, and Karen Dunne-Maxim, Copyright 1987 by Edward J. Dunne, John L. McIntosh, and Karen Dunne-Maxim. Used by permission of the publisher, W. W. Norton & Company, Inc.

the experience of losing a patient to suicide. In more recent years, however, a group of suicidologists with the AAS formed a task force to address this important area of concern. The AAS Clinician Survivor Task Force has since created many needed resources for clinician survivors. These include a Web site (a link to which can be found on the AAS Web site at www. suicidology.org). The Clinician Survivor Task Force link provides an extensive listing of relevant literature on surviving a patient's suicide, including over 50 citations, vignettes of clinician survivors describing their experience of losing a patient to suicide, and possible contacts to informally consult with members of the task force. In addition, members of the task force are pursuing survey research at the national level to gather basic information about the clinician survivor experience so that additional resources and support services can be developed (McIntosh, Albright, & Jones, 2002).

Although more recent work in this area has been extraordinarily important, much of what was true 10 years ago about getting through the process of losing a patient to suicide remains the same. For example, Marshall (1980) offered some excellent recommendations for facilitating survivorship at the professional group level (e.g., the professional staff of an interdisciplinary team working in an inpatient psychiatric setting). These include three basic conditions for helping a professional staff to survive a patient's loss: (a) a supportive and nonblaming staff atmosphere that ensures that a range of feelings can be expressed and understood, (b) the availability of a neutral consultant or consultation group, and (c) training to supplement prior training and experience with suicidal people. This training should include discussions of personal philosophies concerning suicide, clarification of personal responsibilities, an awareness of limits of responsibility, and knowledge of agency policies relevant to actions taken before and after suicides. For individual clinician survivors, Marshall (1980) similarly recommends outside consultation to provide objectivity and support.

In a somewhat different vein, self-help support groups of therapists who have survived patient suicides have been cited in the literature as being particularly helpful (Binder, 1978; Goldstein & Buongiorno, 1984). As described by Jones (1987), such support groups provide (a) a place to acknowledge and work through personal loss, (b) an opportunity for clinicians to practice what they preach in terms of dealing with and talking about their emotions, and (c) the opportunity to talk to other professionals who have been through a similar experience.

Finally, the work of Maltsberger, Hendin, Hass, and Lipschitz (2003) is worthy of note. Through the auspices of the American Foundation for Suicide Prevention (AFSP), these authors have developed an ongoing databank of suicide case studies, information for which has been obtained directly from clinicians who have lost patients to suicide. By tapping into clinicians as a resource of this information, these investigators have begun to gain a better understanding of the psychology and behaviors pertaining to completed suicide (e.g., precipitating events) of people in treatment at the time of their suicide. As we have already noted, clinicians are certainly not immune to the tragedy of suicide. Relatively recent efforts to help clinicians cope and contribute new knowledge as to what may ultimately prevent future suicides are welcome developments in the field of suicidology.

Institutional Survivorship

The death by suicide of someone in treatment affects both therapists and the institutions that employ them. As it is axiomatic that those most severely at risk for suicide should be hospitalized where protection from their own impulses and maximum observation can be offered, it is to be expected that suicides can and do occur during these inpatient hospitalizations. It has been estimated that 5% to 6% of all suicides occur in hospitals (Busch, Fawcett, & Jacobs, 2003). When such adverse events occur, hospitals and treatment teams are often targets of survivor-initiated litigation (see chap. 7). Whereas malpractice claims target individuals alleged to be responsible for acts of negligence that are causative of suicide, they also target the institution. Common allegations, for example, focus on failures to provide a safe environment, failures to adequately train staff, and so on.

Just as the psychological autopsy is a helpful tool for surviving family members to arrive at some explanatory understanding of their loved one's suicide, hospitals have a similar tool to better understand what went wrong when an inpatient suicide occurs. This tool is called a "root cause analysis," or RCA. The RCA has additional benefits in that it identifies contributory factors that can be tied to quality improvements and a lessened likelihood of future inpatient suicides, thus, as well, additional liability exposure. Similar to the psychological autopsy, the RCA is a structured, retrospective approach to identify systems and organizational issues as they interface with possible human error. Rather than assuming that adverse events are always the result of human error (i.e., character flaws), the philosophy behind the RCA is that errors are system flaws. Individual clinician survivors are generally supported by this human systems approach.

The Joint Commission on the Accreditation of Healthcare Organizations (JCAHO) has collected data on more than 2,000 sentinel (adverse) events that occurred in accredited hospitals between January 1995 and July 2003. Patient suicide was the most frequently reported sentinel event, accounting for 16% of all events. RCAs conducted on these events identified a variety of root causes. Most common among these were problems in the physical environment, followed in order by failures in patient assessment, staff orientation and training, interstaff and system communication breakdowns, problems in the continuum of care, security-system failures, failures in making available essential information (e.g., to family members), inadequate staffing levels, and issues involving the competency or credentialing of staff (for more information, see www.jcaho.org/accredited+organizations/ambulatory+care/sentinel+events/rc+inpatients+suicides.htm). In 1997, the JCAHO mandated the use of RCAs to investigate and take remedial steps to reduce sentinel events in accredited hospitals. The following case provides an example of an RCA.

Case Illustration

Phillip, a 17-year-old high school senior, took a massive overdose of acetaminophen and prescribed medication, intent on ending his life. A cousin intervened and brought him to a local general medical hospital where he was admitted and treated medically for a potentially lethal ingestion. Six days later he was transferred to an acute care psychiatric hospital where he was placed on voluntary admission after admitting to having thoughts of shooting or hanging himself, feeling lonely and isolated, and having both visual and auditory hallucinations and ideas of reference directing him to take his life. He was restricted to the ward, placed in an unlocked single treatment room and on suicide precautions (to be visually checked every 15 minutes, later reduced to 30 minutes). Additionally, he contracted for safety. Suicide precautions were discontinued 4 days later as he stated he "would not hurt himself while in the hospital." The nursing note charted that he continued to feel sad and depressed, minimally interacted with peers, and that he "easily contracted for safety." There was no documented presence or absence of suicide ideation. Later that afternoon, a meeting was held with a social worker, Phillip, and his parents to discuss discharge planning. Early that evening, he approached a nursing assistant and asked for paper and pen, stating he wanted to put his thoughts on paper because he was feeling suicidal and wanted to talk with someone. He wrote a list of images that were preoccupying him and mentioned suicide in the note. He took the note to the nurse's station but found only a secretary at the desk and no nursing staff in sight. Thinking they were too busy to talk to him, he left the note at the desk and returned to his room. He then proceeded to hang himself with a sheet wedged in a closed door leading from his bathroom to his room.

Contributing factors to Phillip's suicide identified by the hospital's RCA team were as follows (each was accompanied by an action plan to remediate the identified problem):

- The availability of cloth sheets and a solid door increased the likelihood that a patient could hang himself or herself (physical environment problem).

- Suicide risk assessment policies and procedures needed to be revised, risk assessment protocols needed to be more empirically based, and staff needed annual training in suicide risk assessment and prevention (human factor—communication and training; polices and procedures).
- Staffing patterns were created on the basis of an outdated (15-year-old) acuity system that increased the likelihood that a patient could commit a dangerous act; the number of staff per shift was inadequate; and there was a heavy reliance on overtime, leading to greater fatigue and burnout (human factor—fatigue and scheduling).
- The ward design was found to be a contributing factor to Phillip's death. Two long intersecting hallways with a centrally located nursing station increased the likelihood that a dangerous act could go undetected (environment and equipment).

CONCLUSION

In conclusion, we concur with Professor Edwin Shneidman's (2001) observation that,

> ...the person who commits suicide puts his psychological skeleton in the survivor's emotional closet; he sentences the survivor to deal with many negative feelings and more, to become obsessed with thoughts regarding the survivor's own actual or possible role in having precipitated the suicidal act or having failed to stop it. It can be a heavy load. (p. 154)

Indeed, for as long as humans have roamed the earth, there have undoubtedly been suicides, and, in turn, with every suicide there are various grieving survivors who are left in its wake. As we have seen, the experience of losing a loved one to suicide is plagued with stigma and notoriety. The European enlightenment ushered in the beginnings of a more compassionate and less pejorative stance toward those who have lost a loved one to suicide. However, more respectful recognition and a more compassionate response to suicide survivors is only a part of relatively recent history. It is poignant to note that with the increased recognition and acknowledgement of the survivor experience, we have seen various survivors emerging into key leadership roles in our efforts to better understand and prevent suicides (particularly among youth).

It is inescapably compelling to find new and better ways to prevent future youth suicides. But because we will probably never be able to completely stem the tide, we must continue to endeavor to find new and better ways to reach, care for, and heal those grieving family members, friends, cohorts, groups, systems, *and* clinicians who are left behind. We owe it to those we lose who could not find their way. We owe it to ourselves to somehow find our way without them. In virtually every suicide, there is a series of tragic actions not taken, words not spoken, realizations that come too late—the maddening clarity of hindsight. But in every tragic suicide there is also always some latent hope that we may still learn, understand, recognize, intervene, and ultimately save some future life that is yet too young and unrealized to be lost so soon to the tragedy of adolescent suicide.

APPENDIX A:
ADOLESCENT SUICIDE RESOURCES

Suicide Prevention Organizations

- American Association of Suicidology (AAS) (www.suicidology.org)
- American Foundation for Suicide Prevention (AFSP) (www.afsp.org)
- Iris Alliance Fund (www.irisfund.org)
- Jason Foundation (www.jasonfoundation.com)
- Jed Foundation (www.jedfoundation.org)
- Kristin Brooks Hope Center (www.hopeline.com)
- Link Counseling Center's National Resource Center for Suicide Prevention (www.thelink.org)
- National Council for Suicide Prevention (NCSP)
- National Organization for People of Color Against Suicide (www.geocites.com/nopcas)
- Organization of Attempters and Survivors of Suicide in Interfaith Services (www.oassis.org)
- Samaritans, Inc.
- Suicide Awareness Voices of Education (www.save.org)
- Suicide Prevention Action Network USA (www.spanusa.org)
- Suicide Prevention Resource Center (www.sprc.org)
- Yellow Ribbon Suicide Prevention Program (www.yellowribbon.org)

Suicide Research Databases and Program Evaluation

- Australian Institute for Suicide Research and Prevention (www.gu.edu.au/gwis/aisrap.htm)
- Center for Therapy and Studies of Suicidal Behavior—Germany (www.uke.uni-hamburg.de/extern/tzs_e.html)
- Centre for Suicide Research (University of Oxford)—United Kingdom (cebmh.warne.ox.ac.uk/csd/)
- European Network on Suicide Research and Prevention—Germany (www.euro.who.int/mentalhealth/depressionandstressrelatedmorbidity/)
- International Academy for Suicide Research (www.uni-wuerzburg.de/IASR/)

- National Plan for Suicide Prevention—Norway
  (www.med.uio.no/psy/ssff/engelsk/menuprevention/
  Mehlum.htm)
- National Suicide Prevention Strategy—United States
  (http://www.mentalhealth.org/suicideprevention/)
- National Suicide Prevention Strategy for England
  (www.dh.gov.uk/publicationsandstatistics/annualreports/
  DHAnnualReports)
- Centre for Suicide Prevention—Canada
  (www.suicideinfo.ca)
- Suicide Prevention Research Center—United States
  (www.sprc.org)
- Suicide Research and Prevention Unit (U. Oslo)—Norway
  (www.med.uio.no/psy/ssff/engelsk/menuprevention/
  Mehlum.htm)
- Training Institute for Suicide Assessment and Clinical
  Interviewing—USA (www.suicideassessment.com)
- University of Oxford Centre for Suicide Research—UK
  (www.cebmh.warne.ox.ac.ik)
- Youth Suicide Prevention Strategy—New Zealand
  (www.myd.govt.nz/sec)
- Suicide Prevention Strategy—Australia
  (www7.health.gov.au/hsdd/mentalhe/sp)

Health Professional Organizations

- American Academy of Family Physicians (www.aafp.org)
- American Academy of Pediatrics (www.aap.org)
  - Injury and Poison Prevention Section
    (www.aap.org/sections/ipp)
- American Association of Poison Control Centers
  (www.aapcc.org)
- American College Health Association (www.acha.org)
- American College of Emergency Physicians (www.acep.org)
- American College of Preventive Medicine (www.acpm.org)
- American Correctional Health Services Association
  (www.corrections.com/achsm/)
- American Medical Association (www.ama-assn.org)
- American Nurses Association (www.nursingworld.org)
- American School Health Association (www.ashaweb.org)
- American Teachers of Preventive Medicine (www.acpm.org)
- Association of Maternal and Child Health Programs
  (www.amchp.org)
- Emergency Medical Services for Children (www.ems-c.org)

- Emergency Nurses Association (www.ena.org)
- National Adolescent Health Information Center (NAHIC) (http://nahic.ucsf.edu)
- National Association of Alcoholism and Drug Abuse Counselors (www.naadac.org)
- National Assembly on School-Based Health Care (www.nasbhc.org)
- National Indian Health Board (www.nihb.org)
- Society for Adolescent Medicine (www.adolescenthealth.org)

Mental Health Organizations

- American Academy of Child and Adolescent Psychiatry (www.aacap.org)
- American Association of Children's Residential Centers (www.aarc-dc.org)
- American Association of Marriage and Family Therapy (www.aamft.org)
- American Association of Private Practice Psychiatrists
- American Counseling Association (www.counseling.org)
- American Pastoral Counselors Association (www.aapc.org)
- American Psychiatric Association (www.psych.org)
- American Psychiatric Nurses Association (www.apna.org)
- American Psychological Association (See Division 12, Section VII: Behavioral Emergencies; www.apa.org)
- American School Counselors Association (www.schoolcounselor.org)
- American Society for Adolescent Psychiatry (www.adolpsych.org)
- Anxiety Disorders Association of America (www.adaa.org)
- Child and Adolescent Bipolar Foundation (www.bpkids.org)
- Children and Adults With Attention Deficit Disorders (www.chadd.org)
- Depression and Bipolar Support Alliance (www.dbsalliance.org)
- Families for Depression Awareness (www.familyaware.org)
- National Alliance for the Mentally Ill (www.nami.org)
- National Association for Rural Mental Health (www.narmh.org)
- National Association of Psychiatric Health Systems (www.naphs.org)
- National Association of Psychiatric Treatment Centers for Children (www.air.org)
- National Association of Social Workers (www.naswdc.org)

- National Depressive and Manic-Depressive Association (www.ndmda.org)
- National Foundation for Depressive Illness (www.depression.org)
- National Mental Health Association (www.nmha.org)

Education Related Organizations

- American Federation of Teachers (www.aft.org)
- Center for the Prevention of School Violence (www.cpsv.org)
- Coalition for America's Children (www.kidscampaign.org)
- National Association of School Nurses (www.nasn.org)
- National Association of School Psychologists (www.nasponline.org)
- National Association of Secondary School Principals (www.nassp.org)
- National Congress of Parents and Teachers (www.pta.org)
- National Education Association (www.nea.org)
- National Parent Teacher Association (www.pta.org)
- Students Against Destructive Decisions (www.sadd.org)

Special Population Organizations

- Alliance for Children and Families (www.alliance1.org)
- American Correctional Association (www.aca.org)
- Child Welfare League of America (www.cwla.org)
- Children's Defense Fund (www.childrensdefense.org)
- Gay and Lesbian Medical Association (www.glma.org)
- National Black Child Development Institute (www.nbcdi.org)
- National Center on Institutions and Alternatives (www.ncianet.org)
- United National Indian Tribal Youth (www.unityinc.org)

International Organizations

- Befrienders International (www.befrienders.org)
- Canadian Association for Suicide Prevention (www.thesupportnetwork.com/CASP/)
- International Association for Suicide Prevention (www.med.uio.no/IASP/)
- Irish Association for Suicidology (www.ias.ie/)
- World Health Organization (www.who.int)

Public Health and Injury Prevention Organizations

- American Association of Public Health Physicians (www.aaphp.org)
- American Public Health Association (Injury Control and Emergency Health Section; www.apha.org)
- Child Trends DataBank (www.childtrendsdatabank.org)
- Children's Safety Network: National Injury and Violence Prevention Resource Center (www.childrenssafetynetwork.org)
- National Organization for Youth Safety (www.noys.org)
- National SAFE KIDS Campaign (www.safekids.org)
- National Youth Violence Prevention Resource Center (NYPRC; www.safeyouth.org)
- Partnership for Prevention (www.prevent.org)
- SafetyLit (www.safetylit.org)
- Society for Public Health Education (www.sophe.org)
- Youth Suicide Prevention Program (www.yspp.org)

Federal Organizations

U.S. Federal Government Organizations

- Administration on Children, Youth, and Families (www.acf.hhs.gov/programs/acyf/)
- Centers for Disease Control and Prevention (www.cdc.gov)
- Health Resources Services Administration (www.hrsa.gov)
- Indian Health Service (www.ihs.gov/medicalprograms/injuryprevention)
- National Center for Health Statistics (www.cdc.gov/nchs)
- National Center for Injury Prevention and Control (www.cdc.gov/ncipc)
- National Institute of Mental Health (www.nimh.nih.gov)
- National Strategy for Suicide Prevention (www.mentalhealth.org/suicideprevention)
- National Technical Assistance Center for Children's Mental Health (www.georgetown.edu/research/gusshd/cassp.htm)
- NIAAA (National Institute on Alcohol Abuse and Alcoholism; www.niaaa.nih.gov)
- NICHD (National Institute on Child Health and Human Development; www.nichd.nih.gov)
- Substance Abuse Mental Health Services Administration (www.samhsa.gov)
- U.S. Department of Education (www.ed.gov)
- Youth Risk Behavior Surveillance Survey (www.cdc.gov/healthyyouth/yrns/index.htm)

Death Certification and Mortality Resources

- National Association of Medical Examiners (www.thename.org)
- National Center on Child Fatality Review (htttp://ican-ncfr.org)

Gun Safety Advocacy Organizations

- Common Sense About Kids and Guns (www.kidsandguns.org)
- Gun Free Kids (www.gunfreekids.policy.net)
- HELP Network (www.helpnetwork.org)
- Stop Handgun Violence (www.stophandgunviolence.com)

Journals

Aggression and Violent Behavior
Annals of Emergency Medicine
Archives of Pediatrics and Adolescent Medicine
Archives of Suicide Research
Crisis
Death Studies
Journal of the American Academy of Child and Adolescent Psychiatry
Suicide and Life-Threatening Behavior

APPENDIX B:
RECOMMENDED READINGS

Bolton, I. (2001). *My son, my son: A guide to healing after death, loss, or suicide.* Atlanta, GA: Bolton Press.

Although self-published, this work is considered by survivors of suicide as the mother of all books on surviving the loss of a child to suicide. Bolton effectively transforms pain into reasons to live for survivors.

Bongar, B. (2002). *The suicidal patient: Clinical and legal standards of care* (2nd ed.). Washington, DC: American Psychological Association.

An excellent and comprehensive manual for practicing clinicians, with particular reference to assessment and treatment practices and tools to manage potential malpractice actions.

Bongar, B., Berman, A. L., Maris, R. W., Silverman, M. M., Harris, E. A., & Packman, W. L. (Eds.). (1998). *Risk management with suicidal patients.* New York: Guilford Press.

Designed to help clinicians minimize risk of successful malpractice litigation, this book brings to the reader a wealth of recommendations regarding standards of care from authors with a wealth of experience as expert witnesses in forensic cases.

Colt, G. H. (1991). *The enigma of suicide.* New York: Summit Books.

A former staff writer for *Life* magazine, Colt has written a most readable and comprehensive overview of contemporary (early 1990s) suicidology and suicide prevention, laced with case studies.

Ellis, T. E., & Newman, C. F. (1996). *Choosing to live: How to defeat suicide through cognitive therapy.* Oakland, CA: New Harbinger.

A practical cognitive–behavioral approach written for suicidal patients (and their therapists) and excellent for bibliotherapy purposes.

Goldsmith, S. K., Pellmar, T. C., Kleinman, A. M., & Bunney, W. (Eds.). (2002). *Reducing suicide: A national imperative.* Washington, DC: National Academy Press.

The consequence of intensive study at the turn of the century, this volume offers a wealth of scientific evidence.

Goldston, D. B. (2003). *Measuring suicidal behavior and risk in children and adolescents.* Washington, DC: American Psychological Association.

A thorough and detailed compendium of psychometric tools for assessing suicide risk among youth.

Hawton, K., & van Heeringen, K. (Eds.). (2000). *The international handbook of suicide and attempted suicide.* Chichester, England: Wiley.

An authoritative edited handbook covering its topic from A to Z and written by a wide range of international contributors.

Jacobs, D. G. (Ed.). (1999). *The Harvard Medical School guide to suicide assessment and intervention.* San Francisco: Jossey-Bass. This edited volume has a number of fine chapters covering a wide range of topics of importance to those working with at-risk patients.

Kleespies, P. M. (Ed.). (1998). *Emergencies in mental health practice: Evaluation and management.* New York: Guilford Press.

An edited compilation of 19 chapters covering all aspects of mental health emergency care.

Linehan, M. (1993). *Cognitive behavioral treatment of borderline personality disorder.* New York: Guilford Press.

Considered by most suicidologist clinicians as an essential read to understand borderline suicidal patients, this volume includes Linehan's innovative and empirically tested dialectical behavior therapy approach to working with them.

Maris, R. W., Berman, A. L., & Silverman, M. M. (2000). *Comprehensive textbook of suicidology.* New York: Guilford Press.

This book offers a broad overview of the current scientific understanding of suicide and its prevention. Described by reviewers as "encyclopedic," it was voted as "Book of the Year 2000" by the Suicide and Parasuicide Web site.

Romer, D. (Ed.). (2003). *Reducing adolescent risk: Toward an integrated approach.* Thousand Oaks, CA: Sage.

An edited volume of selected presentations from a conference on risk-taking behaviors among adolescents that seeks commonalities in risk and prevention strategies.

Rudd, M. D., Joiner, T., & Rajab, M. H. (2001). *Treating suicidal behavior.* New York: Guilford Press.

A cognitive-behavioral manual offering a detailed and empirically supported approach to assessment and treatment. This is a detailed and structured model for conceptualizing and intervening with the suicidal patient.

Shea, S. (1999). *The practical art of suicide assessment: A guide for mental health professionals and substance abuse counselors.* New York: Wiley.

Compelling and elegant, this is a well-written critical guidebook to the art of interviewing the suicidal patient, with particularly good suggestions for getting below the surface presentations to elicit denied but present ideation, dealing with contradictory data, and so on.

Shneidman, E. S. (1998). *The suicidal mind.* New York: Oxford University Press.

Offering theory and Shneidman's unique perspective on psychological pain ("psychache"), this book is structured around three case studies and written in a compelling style.

Spirito, A., & Overholser, J. *Evaluating and treating adolescent suicide attempters: From research to practice.* San Diego, CA: Academic Press.

An excellent, thorough, and empirically informed discussion of adolescent suicide attempters from top researchers in the field.

U.S. Public Health Service. (2001). *National strategy for suicide prevention: Goals and objectives for action.* Washington, DC: Department of Health and Human Services. Available at www.mentalhealth.org/suicideprevention.

Williams, M. (2001). *Suicide and attempted suicide.* London: Penguin Books.

A lucid and thoughtfully written book examining cognitive aspects of suicidal suffering with an emphasis on cognitive treatments and the use of mindfulness.

REFERENCES

Aaronson, S. L., Underwood, M., Gaffney, D., & Rotheram-Borus, M. J. (1989, April). *Reluctance to help-seeking by adolescents.* Paper presented at the annual meeting of the American Association of Suicidology, San Diego, CA.

Achte, K. (1988). Suicidal tendencies in the elderly. *Suicide and Life-Threatening Behavior, 18,* 55–65.

Achte, K. A., Lonnqvist, J., & Hillbomi, E. (1971). Suicides following war brain-injuries. *Acta Psychiatrica Scandinavica, 225,* 3–92.

Adams, D., Overholser, J. C., & Spirito, A. (1994). Stressful life events associated with adolescent suicide attempts. *Canadian Journal of Psychiatry, 39,* 43–48.

Adams, M., & Adams, J. (1991). Life events, depression, and perceived problem solving alternatives in adolescents. *Journal of Child Psychology and Psychiatry, 32,* 811–820.

Adler, A. (1958). Suicide. *Journal of Individual Psychology, 14,* 57–61.

Ahrens, B., & Linden, M. (1996). Is there a suicidality syndrome independent of specific major psychiatric disorder? Results of a split-half multiple regression analysis. *Acta Psychiatrica Scandinavica, 94,* 79–86.

Alcohol, Drug Abuse, and Mental Health Administration. (1989). *Report of the Secretary's Task Force on Youth Suicide: Volumes 1–4.* (DHHS Publication No. ADM 89-1621). Washington, DC: U.S. Government Printing Office.

Alessi, N. E., McManus, M., Brickman, A., & Grapentine, L. (1984). Suicidal behavior among serious juvenile offenders. *American Journal of Psychiatry, 141,* 286–287.

Allen, B. G., Calhoun, L. G., Cann, A., & Tadeschi, R. G. (1993). The effects of cause of death on responses of the bereaved: Suicide compared to accidental and natural causes. *Omega, 28,* 39–48.

Allen, B. P. (1987). Youth suicide. *Adolescence, 22,* 271–290.

American Academy of Child and Adolescent Psychiatry. (2001). Practice parameter for the assessment and treatment of children and adolescents with suicidal behavior. *Journal of the American Academy of Child and Adolescent Psychiatry, 40*(Suppl.), 24S–51S.

American Association of Suicidology. (2003). *AAS recommendations for inpatient and residential patients known to be at elevated risk for suicide.* Unpublished manuscript.

American Foundation for Suicide Prevention. (2004). *Reporting on suicide: Recommendations for the media.* Retrieved June 20, 2005, from http://www.afsp.org/education/recommendations/5/1.htm

American Psychiatric Association. (1994). *Diagnostic and statistical manual of mental disorders* (4th ed.). Washington, DC: Author.

American Psychiatric Association. (2001). *Principles of medical ethics with annotations especially applicable to psychiatry.* Washington, DC: Author.

American Psychiatric Association. (2003). Practice guidelines for the assessment and treatment of patients with suicidal behaviors. *American Journal of Psychiatry, 160*(Suppl. 11), 1–60.

American Psychological Association. (2002) Ethical principles of psychologists. *American Psychologist, 45,* 390–395.

Andrews, J. A., & Lewinsohn, P. M. (1992). Suicidal attempts among older adolescents: Prevalence and co-occurrence with psychiatric disorders. *Journal of the American Academy of Child and Adolescent Psychiatry, 31,* 655–662.

Appel, Y. H., & Wrobleski, A. (1987). Self-help and support groups: Mutual aid for survivors. In E. J. Dunne, J. L. McIntosh, & K. Dunne-Maxim (Eds.), *Suicide and its aftermath* (pp. 215–233). New York: Norton.

Appleby, L., Shaw, J., Amos, T., McDonnell, R., Harris, C., McCann, K., et al. (1999). Suicide within 12 months of contact with mental health services: national clinical survey. *British Medical Journal, 318,* 1235–1239.

Apter, A. (2000). *Personality constellations in suicidal behaviour.* Proceedings of the 5th annual Conference, Irish Association of Suicidology (pp. 14–25). Castlebar, County Mayo, Ireland: Irish Association of Suicidology.

Apter, A., Bleich, A., Plutchik, R., Mendelsohn, S., & Tyano, S. (1988). Suicidal behavior, depression, and conduct disorder in hospitalized adolescents. *Journal of the American Academy of Child and Adolescent Psychiatry, 27,* 696–699.

Arango, V., & Underwood, M. D. (1997). Serotonin chemistry in the brain of suicide victims. In R. Maris, M. Silverman, & S. S. Canetto (Eds.), *Review of suicidology 2000* (1st ed., pp. 237–250). New York: Guilford Press.

Arnett, J. J. (1999). Adolescent storm and stress, reconsidered. *American Psychologist, 54,* 317–326.

Asaranow, J. R., Carlson, G., & Guthrie, D. (1987). Coping strategies, self-perceptions, hopelessness and perceived family environments in depressed and suicidal children. *Journal of Consulting and Clinical Psychology, 55,* 361–366.

Asberg, M. (1989). Neurotransmitter monoamine metabolites in the cerebrospinal fluid as risk factors for suicidal behavior. In *Alcohol, Drug Abuse, and Mental Health Administration, Report of the Secretary's Task Force on Youth Suicide: Vol. 2. Risk factors for youth suicide* (DHHS Publication No. ADM 89-1622, pp. 193–212). Washington, DC: U.S. Government Printing Office.

Asberg, M. (1990, April). *The biology of suicide.* Paper presented at the 23rd annual conference of the American Association of Suicidology, New Orleans, LA.

Aseltine, R., & DeMarino, R. (2004). An outcome evaluation of the SOS suicide prevention program. *American Journal of Public Health, 94,* 446–451.

Ashworth, J. (2001). *Practice guidelines: A guide for mental health clinicians working with suicidal children and youth.* British Columbia, Canada: British Columbia Ministry of Children and Family Development.

Attig, T. (1986). Death themes in adolescent music: The classic years. In C. A. Corr & J. N. McNeil (Eds.), *Adolescence and death* (pp. 32–56). New York: Springer Publishing Company.

Averill, J. R. (1968). Grief: Its nature and significance. *Psychological Bulletin, 70,* 721–748.

Bailey, W. B. (1903). Suicide in the United States, 1897–1901. *Yale Review, 12,* 70–89.

Bailley, S. E., Kral, M. J., & Dunham, K. (1999). Survivors of suicide do grieve differently: Empirical support for a common sense proposition. *Suicide and Life-Threatening Behavior, 29,* 256–271.

Barbe, R. P., Bridge, J., Birmaher, B., Kolko, D., & Brent, D. A. (2004). Suicidality and its relationship to treatment outcome in depressed adolescents. *Suicide and Life-Threatening Behavior, 34,* 44–55.

Barlow, C. A., & Morrison, H. (2002). Survivors of suicide: Emerging counseling strategies. *Journal of Psychosocial Nursing and Mental Health Services, 40,* 28–39.

Baron, R., & Byrne, D. (1984). *Social psychology: Understanding human interaction* (4th ed.). Newton, MA: Allyn & Bacon.

Bauer, M. N., Leenaars, A. A., Berman, A. L., Jobes, D. A., Dixon, J. F., & Bibb, J. L. (1997). Late adulthood suicide: A life-span analysis of suicide notes. *Archives of Suicidology, 3,* 91–108.

Baumeister, R. F. (1990). Suicide as escape from self. *Psychological Review, 97,* 90–113.

Beautrais, A. L. (2003). Suicide and serious suicide attempts in youth: A multiple-group comparison study. *American Journal of Psychiatry, 160,* 1093–1099.

Beautrais, A. L., Joyce, P. R., & Mulder, R. T. (1997). Precipitating factors and life events in serious suicide attempts among youths aged 13–24 years. *Journal of American Academy of Child and Adolescent Psychiatry, 29,* 1543–1551.

Beautrais, A. L., Joyce, P. R., & Mulder, R. T. (1998). Psychiatric illness in a New Zealand sample of young people making serious suicide attempts. *New Zealand Medical Journal, 111,* 44–48.

Beautrais, A. L., Joyce, P. R., & Mulder, R. T. (1999). Personality traits and cognitive styles as risk factors for serious suicide attempts among young people. *Suicide and Life-Threatening Behavior, 29,* 37–47.

Beck, A. T. (1996). Beyond belief: A theory of modes, personality, and psychopathology. In P. Salkovskis (Ed.), *Frontiers of cognitive therapy* (pp. 1–25). New York: Guilford Press.

Beck, A. T., Brown, G., & Steer, R. A. (1989). Prediction of eventual suicide in psychiatric inpatients by clinical rating of hopelessness. *Journal of Consulting and Clinical Psychology, 57,* 309–310.

Beck, A. T., Hollon, S. D., Young, J. E., Bedrosian, R. C., & Budenz, D. (1985). Treatment of depression with cognitive therapy and amitriptyline. *Archives of General Psychiatry, 42,* 142–148.

Beck, A. T., Rush, A., Shaw, B., & Emery, G. (1979). *Cognitive therapy of depression.* New York: Guilford Press.

Beck, A., & Steer, R. (1991). *Manual for the Beck Scale for Suicide Ideation.* San Antonio, TX: Psychological Corporation.

Beck, A. T., Steer, R. A., Kovacs, M., & Garrison, B. (1985). Hopelessness and eventual suicide: A 10-year prospective study of patients hospitalized with suicidal ideation. *American Journal of Psychiatry, 142,* 559–563.

Beck, J. S. (1995). *Cognitive therapy: Basics and beyond.* New York: Guilford Press.

Berman, A. L. (1979). *An analysis of suicidal and non-natural deaths among the Duck Valley Reservation Indians.* Unpublished report to the McCormick Foundation, Chicago, IL.

Berman, A. L. (1983). *Training committee report.* Unpublished manuscript. (Available from the American Association of Suicidology, 5221 Wisconsin Avenue, NW, Washington, DC 20015)

Berman, A. L. (1984, October 3). *The problem of teenage suicide.* Testimony presented before the U.S. Senate, Committee on the Judiciary, Subcommittee on Juvenile Justice.

Berman, A. L. (1986a). Adolescent suicide: Issues and challenges. *Seminars in Adolescent Medicine, 2,* 269–277.

Berman, A. L. (1986b). A critical look at our adolescence: Notes on turning 18 (and 75). *Suicide and Life-Threatening Behavior, 16,* 1–12.

Berman, A. L. (1986c). Helping suicidal adolescents: Needs and responses. In C. Corr & J. McNeil (Eds.), *Adolescence and death* (pp. 151–166). New York: Springer.

Berman, A. L. (1987, May). *Suicide and the mass media.* Paper presented at the annual meeting of the American Association of Suicidology, San Francisco, CA.

Berman, A. L. (1988). Fictional depiction of suicide in television films and imitation effects. *American Journal of Psychiatry, 145,* 982–986.

Berman, A. L. (1989). Mass media and youth suicide prevention. *In Alcohol, Drug Abuse, and Mental Health Administration, Report of the Secretary's Task Force on Youth Suicide: Vol. 3. Prevention and interventions in youth suicide* (DHHS Publication No. ADM 89-1623, pp. 276–284). Washington, DC: U.S. Government Printing Office.

Berman, A. L. (1990a). Standard of care in assessment of suicidal potential. *Psychotherapy in Private Practice, 8,* 35–41.

Berman, A. L. (1990b). Suicide interventions in schools: Critical reflections. In A. A. Leenaars & S. Wenckstern (Eds.), *Suicide prevention in schools* (pp. 243–255), Washington, DC: Hemisphere Publication Services.

Berman, A. L. (1998). Consensus statement on youth suicide by firearms. *Archives of Suicide Research, 4,* 89–94.

Berman, A. L. (2003). An idiographic approach to understanding suicide in the young. In R. A. King & A. Apter (Eds.), *Suicide in children and adolescents* (pp. 198–210). Cambridge, England: Cambridge University Press.

Berman, A. L., & Carroll, T. (1984). Adolescent suicide: A critical review. *Death Education, 8*(Suppl.), 53–64.

Berman, A. L., & Cohen-Sandler, R. (1982a). Childhood and adolescent suicide research: A critique. *Crisis, 3,* 3–15.

Berman, A. L., & Cohen-Sandler, R. (1982b). Suicide and the standard of care: Optimal vs. acceptable. *Suicide and Life-Threatening Behavior, 12,* 114–122.

Berman, A. L., & Cohen-Sandler, R. (1983a). Suicide and malpractice: Expert testimony and the standard of care. *Professional Psychology: Research and Practice, 14,* 6–19.

Berman, A. L., & Cohen-Sandler, R. (1983b, May). *The therapeutic alliance with suicidal patients: Thoughts on attributions of responsibility.* Paper presented at the annual meeting of the American Association of Suicidology, Dallas, TX.

Berman, A. L., Jacobs, D. G., & Jobes, D. A. (1993). Case consultation: Tillie. *Suicide and Life-Threatening Behavior, 23,* 268–272.

Berman, A. L., & Jobes, D. A. (1991). *Adolescent suicide: Assessment and intervention.* Washington, DC: American Psychological Association.

Berman, A. L., & Jobes, D. A. (1995). Suicide prevention in adolescents (age 12–18). In M. M. Silverman & R. W. Maris (Eds.), *Suicide prevention: Toward the year 2000* (pp. 143–154). New York: Guilford Press.

Berman, A. L., Litman, R. E., & Diller, J. (1989). *Equivocal death casebook.* Unpublished manuscript, American University, Washington, DC.

Berman, A. L., & Schwartz, R. (1990). Suicide attempts among adolescent drug users. *American Journal of Diseases of Children, 144,* 310–314.

Berman, A. L., Shepherd, G., & Silverman, M. M. (2003). The LSARS-II: Lethality of Suicide Attempt Rating Scale-Updated. *Suicide and Life-Threatening Behavior, 33,* 261–276.

Bernstein, G. A., & Garfinkel, B. D. (1984). School phobia: The overlap of affective disorders and anxiety disorders. *Journal of the American Academy of Child Psychiatry, 23,* 235–241.

Bernstein, N. I. (1989). Managing the difficult adolescent patient. *The Independent Practitioner, 9,* 30–33.

Beutler, L. E. (1989). Differential treatment selection: The role of diagnosis in psychotherapy. *Psychotherapy, 26,* 271–281.

Beutler, L. (2003, August). *Symposium on the National Center on Disaster Psychology and Terrorism.* Presented at the Annual Convention of the American Psychological Association, Toronto, Ontario, Canada.

Beutler, L. E., & Mitchell, R. (1981). Psychotherapy outcome in depressed and impulsive patients as a function of analytic and experiential treatment procedures. *Psychiatry, 44,* 297–306.

Bille-Brahe, U., Kerkhof, A., DeLeo, D., Schmidtke, A., Cpet, P., Lonnqvist, J., et al. (1997). A repetition-prediction study of European parasuicide populations: A summary of the first report from Part II of the WHO-EURO multicentre study on parasuicide in cooperation with the EC concerted action on attempted suicide. *Acta Psychiatrica Scandinavica, 95,* 81–86.

Billow, C. J. (1987). A multiple family support group for survivors of suicide. In E. J. Dunne, J. L. McIntosh, & K. Dunne-Maxim (Eds.), *Suicide and its aftermath* (pp. 208–214). New York: Norton.

Binder, R. (1978). Dealing with patients' suicides: Letter to the editor. *American Journal of Psychiatry, 135,* 1113.

Birmaher, B., Brent, D. A., Kolko, D., Baugher, M., Bridge, J., Holder, D., et al. (2000). Clinical outcome after short-term psychotherapy for adolescents with major depressive disorder. *Archives of General Psychiatry, 57,* 29–36.

Blachly, P. H., & Fairley, N. (1989). Market analysis for suicide prevention: Relationship of age to suicide on holidays, day of the week and month. *Northwest Medicine, 68,* 232–238.

Blair-West, G. W., Cantor, C. H., Mellsop, G. W., & Eyeson-Annan, M. L. (1999). Lifetime suicide risk in major depression: Sex and age determinants. *Journal of Affective Disorders 55,* 171–178.

Bloodworth, R. (2000). *The Oregon plan for youth suicide prevention: A call to action.* Oregon Department of Human Services: Injury Prevention and Epidemiology Program.

Blumenthal, S. J., & Kupfer, D. J. (1989). Overview of early detection and treatment strategies for suicidal behavior in young people. In *Alcohol, Drug Abuse, and Mental Health Administration, Report of the Secretary's Task Force on Youth Suicide: Vol. 3. Prevention and interventions in youth suicide* (DHHS Publication No. ADM 89-1623, pp. 239–252). Washington, DC: U.S. Government Printing Office.

Blumenthal, S. J., & Kupfer, D. J. (1990). *Suicide over the life cycle: Risk factors, assessment, and treatment of suicidal patients.* Washington, DC: American Psychiatric Publishing.

Boergers, J., Spirito, A., & Donaldson, D. (1998). Reasons for adolescent suicide attempts: Associations with psychological functioning. *Journal of the American Academy of Child and Adolescent Psychiatry, 37,* 1287–1293.

Boggiano, W. E. (1988, April). *When should we accept a "no suicide" pact?* Paper presented at the annual meeting of the American Association of Suicidology, Washington, DC.

Boldt, M. (1982). Normative evaluations of suicide and death: A cross-generational study. *Omega, 13,* 145–157.

Bolton, I. (1983). *My son, my son: A guide to healing after death, loss, or suicide.* Atlanta, GA: Bolton Press.

Bolton, I. (1998). In honor of my father and my son. *Suicide and Life-Threatening Behavior, 28,* 355–357.

Bonanno, G. A., Keltner, D., Holen, A., & Horowitz, M. J. (1995). When avoiding unpleasant emotions might not be such a bad thing: Verbal-autonomic response dissociation and midlife conjugal bereavement. *Journal of Personality and Social Psychology, 69,* 975–989.

Bonanno, G. A., Papa, A., & O'Neill, K. (2001). Loss and human resilience. *Applied and Preventative Psychology, 10,* 193–206.

Bonanno, G. A., Wortman, C. B., Lehman, D. R., Tweed, R. G., Haring, M., Sonnega, J., Carr, D., & Neese, R. M. (2002). Resilience to loss and chronic grief: A prospective study from pre-loss to 18 months post-loss. *Journal of Personality and Social Psychology, 83,* 1150–1164.

Bond, A., Riggs, S., Spirito, A., & Fritz, G. (1988, March). *Adolescent attempts in a pediatric emergency room.* Paper presented at the annual meeting of the Society of Adolescent Medicine, Seattle, WA.

Bongar, B. (2002). *The suicidal patient: Clinical and legal standards of care* (2nd ed.). Washington, DC: American Psychological Association.

Bongar, B., Berman, A. L., Maris, R. W., Silverman, M. M., Harris, E. A., & Packman, W. L. (Eds.). (1998). *Risk management with suicidal patients.* New York: Guilford Press.

Bongar, B., & Harmatz, M. (1989). Graduate training in clinical psychology and the study of suicide. *Professional Psychology: Research and Practice, 20,* 209–213.

Bongar, B., & Harmatz, M. (1991). Clinical psychology graduate education in the study of suicide: Availability, resources, and importance. *Suicide and Life-Threatening Behavior, 21,* 231–244.

Bonner, R. L., & Rich, A. R. (1987). Toward a predictive model of suicidal ideation and behavior: Some preliminary data in college students. *Suicide and Life-Threatening Behavior, 17,* 50–63.

Borowsky, I. W., Resnick, M. D., Ireland, M., & Blum, R. W. (1999). Suicide attempts among American Indian and Alaska Native youth: Risk and protective factors. *Archives of Pediatric and Adolescence Medicine, 153,* 573–580.

Bostock, T., & Williams, C. L. (1974). Attempted suicide as an operant behavior. *Archives of General Psychiatry, 31,* 482–486.

Bowlby, J. (1973). *Attachment and loss: Vol. 11. Separation.* New York: Basic Books.

Bowlby, J. (1980). *Loss: Sadness and depression: Vol. 3. Attachment and loss.* New York: Basic Books.

Boyd, J. H. (1983). The increasing rate of suicide by firearms. *New England Journal of Medicine, 308,* 872–874.

Brådvik, L., & Berglund, M. (2003). A suicide peak after weekends and holidays in patients with alcohol dependence. *Suicide and Life-Threatening Behavior, 33,* 186–191.

Brand, E. F., King, C. A., Olson, E., Ghaziuddin, N., & Naylor, O. (1996). Depressed adolescents with a history of sexual abuse: In diagnostic comorbidity and suicidality. *Journal of American Academy of Child and Adolescent Psychiatry, 35,* 34–41.

Brener, N. D., Krug, E., & Simon, T. (2000). Trends in suicide ideation and suicidal behavior among high school students in the United States, 1991–1997. *Suicide and Life-Threatening Behavior, 30,* 304–312.

Brent, D. A. (1987). Correlates of medical lethality of suicide attempts in children and adolescents. *Journal of the American Academy of Child and Adolescent Psychiatry, 26,* 87–91.

Brent, D. A. (1989). The psychological autopsy: Methodological considerations for the study of adolescent suicide. *Suicide and Life-Threatening Behavior, 19,* 43–57.

Brent, D. A. (1997). The aftercare of adolescents with deliberate self-harm. *Journal of Child Psychology and Psychiatry, 38,* 277–286.

Brent, D. (2001). Assessment and treatment of the youthful suicidal patient. In H. Hendin & J. Mann (Eds.), *The clinical science of suicide prevention* (pp. 106–131). New York: New York Academy of Sciences.

Brent, D. A. (2003). Some strategies to prevent youth suicide. In D. Romer (Ed.), *Reducing adolescent risk: Toward an integrated approach* (pp. 321–324). Newbury Park, CA: Sage.

Brent, D. A., Baugher, M., Bridge, J., Chen, J., & Beery, L. (1999). Age and sex-related risk factors for adolescent suicide. *Journal of the American Academy of Child and Adolescent Psychiatry, 38,* 1497–1505.

Brent, D. A., Bridge, J., Johnson, B. A., & Connolly, J. (1996). Suicidal behavior runs in families. *Archives of General Psychiatry, 53,* 1145–1152.

Brent, D. A., Holder, D., Kolko, D., Birmaher, B., Baugher, M., Roth, C., et al. (1997). A clinical psychotherapy trial for adolescent depression comparing cognitive, family, and supportive therapy. *Archives of General Psychiatry, 54,* 877–885.

Brent, D. A., Johnson, S., Bartle, S., Bridge, J., Rather, C., Matta, J., et al. (1993). Personality disorder, tendency to impulsive violence, and suicidal behavior in adolescents. *Journal of the American Academy of Child and Adolescent Psychiatry, 32,* 69–75.

Brent, D. A., Johnson, B. A., Perper, J., Connolly, J., Bridge, J., Bartle, S., et al. (1994). Personality disorder, personality traits, impulsive violence, and completed suicide in adolescents. *Journal of the American Academy of Child and Adolescent Psychiatry, 33,* 1080–1086.

Brent, D. A., Kolko, D., Wartella, M., Boylan, M., Moritz, G., Baugher, M., et al. (1993). Adolescent psychiatric inpatients' risk of suicide attempt at 6-month follow-up. *Journal of the American Academy of Child and Adolescent Psychiatry, 32,* 95–105.

Brent, D. A., Moritz, G., Bridge, J., Perper, J., & Canobbio, R. (1996). The impact of adolescent suicide on siblings and parents: A longitudinal follow-up. *Suicide and Life-Threatening Behavior, 26,* 253–259.

Brent, D. A., & Perper, J. A. (1995). Research in adolescent suicide: Implications for training, service delivery, and public policy. *Suicide and Life-Threatening Behavior, 25,* 222–230.

Brent, D. A., Perper, J. A., & Allman, C. J. (1987). Alcohol, firearms and suicide among youth: Temporal trends in Allegheny County, Pennsylvania, 1960–1983. *Journal of the American Medical Association, 257,* 3369–3372.

Brent, D. A., Perper, J., Goldstein, C., Kolko, D., Allan, M., Allman, C., et al. (1988). Risk factors for adolescent suicide: A comparison of adolescent suicide victims with suicidal inpatients. *Archives of General Psychiatry, 45,* 581–588.

Brent, D. A., Perper, J. A., Kolko, D. J., & Zelenak, J. P. (1988). The psychological autopsy: Methodological considerations for the study of adolescent suicide. *Journal of the American Academy of Child and Adolescent Psychiatry, 27,* 363–366.

Brent, D. A., Perper, J., Moritz, G., Allman, C., Friend, A., Roth, C., et al. (1993). Psychiatric risk factors for adolescent suicide: A case control study. *Journal of the American Academy of Child and Adolescent Psychiatry, 32,* 521–529.

Brent, D. A., Perper, J. A., Moritz, G., Baugher, M., Roth, C., Barach, L., et al. (1993). Stressful life events, psychopathology, and adolescent suicide: A case control study. *Suicide and Life-Threatening Behavior, 23,* 179–187.

Brent, D. A., Perper, J. A., Moritz, G., Baugher, M., Schweers, J., & Roth, C. (1993). Firearms and adolescent suicide: A community case-control study. *American Journal of Diseases of Children, 147,* 1066–1071.

Brent, D. A., Perper, J. A., Moritz, G., Baugher, M. Schweers, J., & Roth, C. (1994). Suicide in affectively ill adolescents: A case control study. *Journal of Affective Disorders, 31,* 193–202.

Brent, D. A., Perper, J. A., Moritz, G., Liotus, L., Schwears, J., Balach, L., et al. (1994). Familial risk factors for adolescent suicide: A case control study. *Acta Psychiatrica Scandinavica, 89,* 52–58.

Brent, D. A., & Poling, D. (1997). *Cognitive therapy manual for depressed and suicidal youth.* Pittsburgh, PA: Western Psychiatric Institute and Clinic, University of Pittsburgh Medical Center.

Brewer, T., & Faitak, M. T. (1989). Ethical guidelines for inpatient psychiatric care of children. *Professional Psychology: Research and Practice, 20,* 142–147.

Brickmayer, J., & Hemenway, D. (2001). Suicide and firearm prevalence: Are youth disproportionately affected? *Suicide and Life-Threatening Behavior, 31,* 303–310.

Brinkman-Sull, D. C., Overholser, J. C., & Silverman, E. (2000). Risk of future suicide attempts in adolescent psychiatric inpatients at 18-month follow-up. *Suicide and Life-Threatening Behavior, 30,* 327–340.

Brown, G. K., Beck, A. T., Steer, R. A., & Grisham, J. R. (2000). Risk factors for suicide in psychiatric outpatients: A 20-year prospective study. *Journal of Consulting and Clinical Psychology, 68,* 371–377.

Brown, G. L., Ebert, M. E., Goyer, P. F., Jimerson, D. C., Klein, W. J., Bunney, W. E., et al. (1982). Aggression, suicide, and serotonin: Relationships to CSF amine metabolites. *American Journal of Psychiatry, 139,* 741–746.

Brown, H. N. (1987). The impact of suicides in therapists in training. *Comprehensive Psychiatry, 28,* 101–112.

Brown, J., Cohen, P., Johnson, J. G., & Smailes, E. M. (1999). Childhood abuse and neglect: Specificity of effects on adolescent and young adult depression and suicidality. *Journal of the American Academy of Child and Adolescent Psychiatry, 38,* 1490–1496.

Brown, S. (1985). Adolescents and family systems. In M. L. Peck, N. L. Farberow, & R. E. Litman (Eds.), *Youth suicide* (pp. 71–79). New York: Springer Publishing Company.

Buchannan, C. M., Eccles, J. S., Flanagan, C., Midgley, C., Feldlaufer, H., & Harold, R. D. (1990). Parents' and teachers' beliefs about adolescents: Effects of sex and experience. *Journal of Youth and Adolescence, 19,* 363–394.

Burns, B. H., Costello, E. J., Angold, A., Tweed, D., Stangl, D., Farmer, E. M. Z., et al. (1995). Children's mental health service use across service sectors. *Health Affairs, 14,* 147–159.

Busch, K. A., Fawcett, J., & Jacobs, D. G. (2003). Clinical correlates of inpatient suicide. *Journal of Clinical Psychiatry, 64,* 14–19.

Cairns, R. B., Peterson, G., & Neckerman, H. J. (1988). Suicidal behavior in aggressive adolescents. *Journal of Clinical Child Psychology, 17,* 298–309.

Callahan, J. (1996). Negative effects of a school suicide prevention program—a case example. *Crisis, 17,* 108–115.

Canetto, S. S., & Lester, D. (Eds.). (1995). *Women and suicidal behavior.* New York: Springer Publishing Company.

Cantor, C. H., & Baume, P. J. M. (1998). Changing methods of suicide by young Australians, 1974–1994. *Archives of Suicide Research, 4,* 41–50.

Cantor, P. C. (1989). Intervention strategies: Environmental risk reduction for youth suicide. In *Alcohol, Drug Abuse, and Mental Health Administration, Report of the Secretary's Task Force on Youth Suicide: Vol 3. Prevention and interventions in youth suicide.* (DHHS Publication No. ADM 89-1623, pp. 285–293). Washington, DC: U.S. Government Printing Office.

Caplan, G. (1964). *Principles of preventive psychiatry.* New York: Basic Books.

Carlson, G. A., & Cantwell, D. P. (1982). Suicidal behavior and depression in children and adolescents. *Journal of the American Academy of Child Psychiatry, 21,* 361–368.

Cavan, R. S. (1926). *Suicide.* Chicago: University of Chicago Press.

Centers for Disease Control. (1985). *Suicide surveillance report, United States, 1970–1980.* Atlanta, GA: Author.

Centers for Disease Control. (1986). *Youth suicide in the United States, 1970–1980.* Atlanta, GA: Author.

Centers for Disease Control. (1988). Centers for Disease Control recommendations for a community plan for the prevention and containment of suicide clusters. *Morbidity and Mortality Weekly Report, 37*(Suppl. S-6), 1–12.

Centers for Disease Control and Prevention. (1995a, April 28). Fatal and nonfatal suicide attempts among adolescents, 1988–1993. *Mortality and Morbidity Weekly Report, 44*(16), 312–315, 321–323.

Centers for Disease Control and Prevention. (1995b). Suicide among children, adolescents, and young adults. *Morbidity and Mortality Weekly Report, 44,* 289–291.

Centers for Disease Control and Prevention. (1998). Suicide among black youths, United States, 1980–1995. *Morbidity and Mortality Weekly Report, 47*(10), 193–196.

Centers for Disease Control and Prevention. (2001a). Deaths: Preliminary data for 1999. *National Vital Statistics Reports, 49*(3).

Centers for Disease Control and Prevention. (2001b). School health guidelines to prevent unintentional injuries and violence. *Morbidity and Mortality Weekly Report, 50,* 1–74.

Centers for Disease Control and Prevention. (2001c). Temporal variations in school-associated homicide and suicide events, United States, 1992–1999. *Morbidity and Mortality Weekly Report, 50*(31), 657–660.

Centers for Disease Control and Prevention. (2002a). *Reporting on suicide: Recommendations for the media.* Retrieved April 17, 2003, from http://www.nimh.nih.gov/research/suicidemedia

Centers for Disease Control and Prevention. (2002b). Surveillance summaries. *Morbidity and Mortality Weekly Report, 51*(4).

Centers for Disease Control and Prevention. (2002c). Youth risk behavior surveillance, United States, 2001. *Mortality and Morbidity Review, 51,* 1–64.

Centers for Disease Control and Prevention. (2003). Youth risk behavior surveillance—United States, 2003. *Morbidity and Mortality Weekly Report, 53,* SS-2.

Chemtob, C. M., Hamada, R. S., Bauer, G. B., Kinney, B., & Torigoe, R. Y. (1988). Patient suicide: Frequency and impact on psychologists. *Professional Psychology: Research and Practice, 19,* 421–425.

Chiles, J. A., & Strosahl, K. D. (1995). *The suicidal patient: Principles of assessment, treatment, and case management.* Washington, DC: American Psychiatric Association.

Cimbolic, P., & Jobes, D. A. (1990). *Youth suicide: Assessment, intervention, and issues.* Springfield, IL: Charles C Thomas.

Clark, D. C. (1989). Impact of television news reports. *Suicide Research Digest, 3,* 1–2.

Clark, D. C., & Gibbons, R. D. (1987). Does one nonlethal suicide attempt increase the risk for a subsequent nonlethal attempt? *Medical Care, 25*(Suppl.), S87–S88.

Clark, S., & Goldney, R. D. (1995). Grief reactions and recovery in a support group for people bereaved by suicide. *Crisis, 16,* 27–33.

Clarke, G. N., Rohde, P., Lewinsohn, P. M., Hops, H., & Seeley, J. R. (1999). Cognitive-behavioral treatment of adolescent depression: Efficacy of acute group treatment and booster sessions. *Journal of the American Academy of Child and Adolescent Psychiatry, 38,* 272–279.

Clarke, R. V., & Lester, D. (1987). Toxicity of car exhausts and opportunity for suicide. *Journal of Epidemiology and Community Health, 41,* 114–120.

Cleiren, M., & Diekstra, R. (1995). After the loss: Bereavement after suicide and other types of death. In B. Mishara (Ed.), *The impact of suicide* (pp. 7–39). New York: Springer.

Clements, C. D., Sider, R. C., & Perlmutter, R. (1983). Suicide: Bad act or good intervention. *Suicide and Life-Threatening Behavior, 13,* 28–41.

Coccaro, E. F., & Kavoussi, R. J. (1997). Fluoxetine and impulsive aggressive behavior in personality-disordered subjects. *Archives of General Psychiatry, 54*, 1081–1088.

Cohen, J. (1986). Statistical approaches to suicidal risk factor analysis. *Annals of the New York Academy of Sciences, 487*, 34–41.

Cohen, Y., Spirito, A., Sterling, C., Donaldson, D., Seifer, R., Plummer, B., et al. (1996). Physical and sexual abuse and their relation to psychiatric disorder and suicidal behavior among adolescents who are psychiatrically hospitalized. *Journal of Child Psychology and Psychiatry, 37*, 989–993.

Cohen-Sandler, R., Berman, A. L., & King, R. (1982a). Life stress and symptomatology: Determinants of suicidal behavior in children. *Journal of the American Academy of Child Psychiatry, 21*, 178–186.

Cohen-Sandler, R., Berman, A. L., & King, R. (1982b). A follow-up study of hospitalized suicidal children. *Journal of the American Academy of Child Psychiatry, 21*, 398–403.

Colt, G. W. (1987). The history of the suicide survivor: The mark of Cain. In E. J. Dunne, J. L. McIntosh, & K. Dunne-Maxim (Eds.), *Suicide and its aftermath*. New York: Norton.

Comstock, B. S. (1977). Suicide events and indications for hospitalization. In P. Cantor (Ed.), *Proceedings of the Tenth Annual Meeting of the American Association of Suicidology* (pp. 75–77). Denver, CO: American Association of Suicidology.

Consensus Statement on Youth Suicide by Firearms. (1998). *Archives of Suicide Research, 4*, 89–94.

Corder, B. F., Schorr, W., & Corder, R. F. (1974). A study of social and psychological characteristics of adolescent suicide attempters in an urban disadvantaged area. *Adolescence, 9*, 1–6.

Cotgrove, A. J., Zirinsky, L., Black, D., & Weston, D. (1995). Secondary prevention of attempted suicide in adolescents. *Journal of Adolescence, 18*, 569–577.

Cotton, C. R., & Range, L. M. (1996). Suicidality, hopelessness, and attitudes toward life and death in clinical and nonclinical adolescents. *Death Studies, 20*, 601–610.

Cowen, E. L. (1983). Primary prevention in mental health: Past, present, and future. In R. D. Felner, L. A. Jason, J. N. Morisugu, & S. S. Farber (Eds.), *Preventive psychology: Theory, research and practice* (pp. 11–25). New York: Pergamon Press.

Cross, C. K., & Hirschfield, R. M. A. (1985, September). *Role of life stressors and attributes in suicide*. Paper presented at New York Academy of Sciences Conference on Psychobiology of Suicidal Behavior, New York.

Crumley, F. E. (1979). Adolescent suicide attempts. *Journal of the American Medical Association, 241*, 2404–2407.

Davidson, L., & Gould, M. S. (1989). Contagion as a risk factor for youth suicide. In *Alcohol, Drug Abuse, and Mental Health Administration, Report of the Secretary's*

Task Force on Youth Suicide: Vol. 2. Risk factors for youth suicide (DHHS Publication No. ADM 89-1622, pp. 88–109). Washington, DC: U.S. Government Printing Office.

Davidson, L., & Marshall, M. (2003). *School-based suicide prevention.* Decatur, GA: The Task Force for Child Survival and Development.

Davidson, L. E., Rosenberg, M. L., Mercy, J. A., Franklin, J., & Simmons, J. T. (1989). An epidemiologic study of risk factors in two teenage suicide clusters. *Journal of the American Medical Association, 17,* 2687–2692.

Davis, J. M., & Sandoval, J. (1991). *Suicidal youth: School-based intervention and prevention.* San Francisco: Jossey-Bass.

Davis, N. J. (1999). *Resiliency: Status of the research and research based programs* (Working Paper Draft). Washington, DC: Substance Abuse and Mental Health Services Administration, Center for Mental Health Services.

De Rosis, L. E. (1961). Suicide: The Horney point of view. In N. L. Farberow & E. S. Shneidman (Eds.), *The cry for help* (pp. 236–254). New York: McGraw-Hill.

de Wilde, E. L., Kienhorst, I., Diekstra, R., & Wolters, W. (1993). The specificity of psychological characteristics of adolescent suicide attempters. *Journal of the American Academy of Child and Adolescent Psychiatry, 32,* 51–59.

Delhaise, T., Andriessen, K., & Forceville, G. (2001). Who takes care for the bereaved by suicide? In O. Grad (Ed.), *Suicide risk and protective factors in the next millennium.* Ljubljana, Cankarjev dom.

DeMartino, R. E., Crosby, A. E., Echo Hawk, M., Litts, D. A., Pearson, J., Reed, G., & West, M. (2003). A call to collaboration: The federal commitment to suicide prevention. *Suicide and Life-Threatening Behavior, 33,* 101–110.

Denning, D. G., Conwell, Y., King, D., & Cox, C. (2000). Method, choice, intent, and gender in completed suicide. *Suicide and Life-Threatening Behavior, 30,* 282–288.

Department of Health and Human Services. (1992). *The Third National Injury Control Conference.* (DHHS Publication No. 1992-634-666). Washington, DC: U.S. Government Printing Office.

DePaulo, J. R. (2002). *Understanding depression.* New York: Wiley.

DePaulo, J. R. (2003, May). *The genetics of suicide for suicide survivors.* Presentation at NIMH/NIH Office of Rare Diseases and the American Foundation for Suicide Prevention's Survivors of Suicide Research Workshop, Washington, DC.

Deutsch, C. J. (1984). Self-report sources of stress among psychotherapists. *Professional Psychology: Research and Practice, 15,* 833–845.

Dew, M. A., Bromet, E. J., Brent, D., & Greenhouse, J. B. (1987). A quantitative literature review of the effectiveness of suicide prevention centers. *Journal of Consulting and Clinical Psychology, 55,* 239–244.

Dexter-Mazza, E. T., & Freeman, K. A. (2003). Graduate training and the treatment of suicidal clients: The students' perspective. *Suicide and Life-Threatening Behavior, 33,* 211–218.

Diegmuller, K. (1987, August 10). The violent killing of youths: Adolescent fact of death. *Insight, The Washington Times,* pp. 18–20.

Diekstra, R. F. W. (1989). Suicidal behavior in adolescents and young adults: An international picture. *Crisis, 10,* 16–35.

Diekstra, R. F. W. (1996). The epidemiology of suicide and parasuicide. *Archives of Suicide Research, 2,* 1–29.

Domino, G. (1980). Altering attitudes towards suicide in an abnormal psychology course. *Teaching of Psychology, 7,* 239–240.

Domino, G. (1981). Attitudes towards suicide among Mexican-American and Anglo youth. *Hispanic Journal of Behavioral Sciences, 3,* 385–395.

Domino, G. (1985). Clergy's attitudes toward suicide and recognition of suicide lethality. *Death Studies, 9,* 187–199.

Domino, G., & Leenaars, A. A. (1989). Attitudes toward suicide: A comparison of Canadian and U.S. college students. *Suicide and Life-Threatening Behavior, 19,* 160–171.

Douglas, J. D. (1967). *The social meaning of suicide.* Princeton, NJ: Princeton University Press.

Drozd, J. F., Jobes, D. A., & Luoma, J. B. (2000). The collaborative assessment and management of suicidality in air force mental health clinics. *The Air Force Psychologist, 18,* 6–11.

Dryfoos, J. (1990). Adolescents at risk: Prevalence and prevention. New York: Oxford University Press.

Dublin, L. I., & Bunzel, B. (1933). *To be or not to be: A study of suicide.* New York: Smith & Haas.

Dubow, E. F., Blum, M. C., & Reed, J. (1988, April). *Adolescent life stress, social support, and suicidal ideation.* Paper presented at the annual meeting of the American Association of Suicidology, Atlanta, GA.

Dunn, R. G., & Morrish-Vidners, D. (1987–1988). The psychological and social experience of suicide survivors. *Omega, 18,* 175–215.

Dunne, E. J. (1987). Special needs of survivors in therapy. In E. J. Dunne, J. L. McIntosh, & K. Dunne-Maxim (Eds.), *The aftermath of suicide* (pp. 142–148). New York: Norton.

Dunner, D. L. (2004). Correlates of suicidal behavior and lithium treatment in bipolar disorder. *Journal of Clinical Psychiatry, 65*(Suppl. 10), 5–10.

Durkheim, E. (1951). *Suicide: A study in sociology.* New York: Free Press. (Original work published 1897)

Dwyer, M. S., Levy, R. A., & Meander, K. B. (1986). Improving medication compliance through the use of modern dosage forms. *Journal of Pharmacy Technology, 2,* 166–170.

Earle, J. (2003, May). *Responses of police.* Presentation at NIMH/NIH Office of Rare Diseases and the American Foundation for Suicide Prevention's Survivors of Suicide Research Workshop, Washington, DC.

Easterlin, R. (1978). What will 1984 be like? Socioeconomic implications of recent twists in age structure. *Demography, 15,* 397–432.

Easterlin, R. (1980). *Birth and fortune.* New York: Basic Books.

Eastgard, S. (2000). *Youth suicide prevention program toolkit.* Seattle, WA: Youth Suicide Prevention Program.

Eddleston, M., & Phillips, M. R. (2004). Self poisoning with pesticides. *British Medical Journal, 328,* 42–44.

Eddy, D. M., Wolpert, R. L., & Rosenberg, M. L. (1989). Estimating the effectiveness of interventions to prevent youth suicides: A report to the Secretary's Task Force on Youth Suicide. In *Alcohol, Drug Abuse, and Mental Health Administration, Report of the Secretary's Task Force on Youth Suicide: Vol. 4. Strategies for the prevention of youth suicide* (DHHS Publication No. ADM 89-1624, pp. 37–81). Washington, DC: U.S. Government Printing Office.

Egan, M. P., Rivera, S. G., Robillard, R. R., & Hanson, A. (1997). The "no suicide contract": Helpful or harmful? *Journal of Psychosocial Nursing Mental Health Services, 35,* 31–33.

Egeland, J., & Sussex, J. (1985). Suicide and family loading for affective disorders. *Journal of the American Medical Association, 254,* 915–918.

Eggert, L. L., Karovsky, P. P., & Pike, K. C. (1999). *School-based public education campaign. Washington State Youth Suicide Prevention Program: Pathways to enhancing community capacity in preventing youth suicidal behaviors. Final Report.* Seattle: University of Washington.

Eggert, L. L., Thompson, E. A., Herting, J. R., & Nicholas, L. J. (1995). Reducing suicide potential among high-risk youth: Tests of a school-based prevention program. *Suicide and Life-Threatening Behavior, 25,* 276–296.

Elias, M. J., Gara, M. A., Schuyler, T. F., Branden-Muller, L. R., & Sayette, M. A. (1991). The promotion of social competence: Longitudinal study of a preventive school-based program. *American Journal of Orthopsychiatry, 61,* 409–417.

Elkind, D. (1980). Egocentrism in adolescence. In R. E. Muuss (Ed.), *Adolescent behavior and society: A book of readings* (pp. 79–88). New York: Random House. (Original work published 1967)

Ellenbogen, S., & Gratton, F. (2001). Do they suffer more? Reflections on research comparing suicide survivors with other survivors. *Suicide and Life-Threatening Behavior, 31,* 83–90.

Emery, P. E. (1983). Adolescent depression and suicide. *Adolescence, 18,* 245–258.

Erikson, E. (1959). *Identity and the life cycle.* New York: International Universities Press.

Erikson, E. (1968). *Identity: Youth in crisis.* New York: Norton.

Esposito, C., Johnson, B., Wolfsdorf, B. A., & Spirito, A. (2003). Cognitive factors: Hopelessness, coping, and problem-solving. In A. Spirito & J. C. Overholser (Eds.), *Evaluating and treating adolescent suicide attempters: From research to practice* (pp. 89–112). San Diego, CA: Academic Press.

Esposito, C., Spirito, A., & Overholser, J. (2003). Behavioral factors: Impulsive and aggressive behavior. In A. Spirito & J. C. Overholser (Eds.), *Evaluating and treating adolescent suicide attempters: From research to practice* (pp. 147–159). San Diego, CA: Academic Press.

Esposito-Smythers, C., Jobes, D. A., Lester, D., & Spirito, A. (2004). Case of adolescent suicide: Tim. *Archives of Suicide Research, 8,* 187–197.

Evans, W., Smith, M., Hill, G., Albers, E., & Neufeld, J. (1996). Rural adolescent views of risk and protective factors associated with suicide. *Crisis Intervention, 3,* 1–12.

Eyman, J., & Smith, K. (1986). Lethality trends in multiple suicide attempts. In R. Cohen-Sandler (Ed.), *Proceedings of the Nineteenth Annual Meeting of the American Association of Suicidology* (pp. 75–77). Denver, CO: American Association of Suicidology.

Fairbairn, W. R. D. (1952). *Psychoanalytic studies of personality.* London: Routledge & Kegan Paul.

Farber, M. L. (1968). *Theory of suicide.* New York: Funk & Wagnalls.

Farberow, N. L. (1989). Preparatory and prior suicidal behavior factors. In *Alcohol, Drug Abuse, and Mental Health Administration, Report of the Secretary's Task Force on Youth Suicide: Vol. 2. Risk factors for youth suicide.* (DHHS Publication No. ADM 89-1622, pp. 34–55). Washington, DC: U.S. Government Printing Office.

Farberow, N. L. (1993). Bereavement after suicide. In A. A. Leenaars (Ed.), *Suicidology: Essays in honor of Edwin S. Shneidman* (pp. 337–345). Northvale, NJ: Jason Aronson.

Farberow, N. L. (2001). Helping suicide survivors. In D. Lester (Ed.), *Suicide prevention: Resources for the millennium.* Series in death, dying, and bereavement. (pp. 189–212). New York: Brunner-Routledge.

Favazza, A. R. (1989). Why patients mutilate themselves. *Hospital and Community Psychiatry, 40,* 137–145.

Fawcett, J. (1988). Predictors of early suicide: Identification and appropriate intervention. *Journal of Clinical Psychiatry, 49*(Suppl. 10), 7–8.

Fawcett, J. (2001). The anxiety disorders, anxiety symptoms and suicide. In D. Wasserman (Ed.), *Suicide: An unnecessary death* (pp. 59–63). London: Martin Dunitz.

Fawcett, J., Busch, K. A., Jacobs, D., Kravitz, H. M., & Fogg, L. (1997). Suicide: A four-pathway clinical-biochemical model. *New York Academy of Sciences, 836,* 288–301.

Fawcett, J., Scheftner, W., & Fogg, L. (1990). Time-related predictors of suicide in major affective disorders. *American Journal of Psychiatry, 147,* 1189–1194.

Fekete, S., & Schmidtke, A. (1996). Suicidal models: Their frequency and role in suicide attempters, non-suicidal psychiatric patients, and normal control cases: A comparative German-Hungarian study. *Omega, 33,* 233–241.

Feldman, B. (2004, April). *Suicide assessment and intervention for social workers: Current standards of care.* Workshop presented at the 37th annual meeting of the American Association of Suicidology, Miami, FL.

Felner, R. D., Felner, T. Y., & Silverman, M. M. (2000). Prevention in mental health and social intervention: Conceptual and methodological issues in the evolution of the science and practice of prevention. In J. Rappaport & E. Seidman (Eds.), *Handbook of community psychology* (pp. 10–55). New York: Plenum Press.

Felner, R. D., & Silverman, M. M. (1989). Primary prevention: A consideration of general principles and findings for the prevention of youth suicide. In *Alcohol, Drug Abuse, and Mental Health Administration. Report of the Secretary's Task Force on Youth Suicide: Vol. 3. Prevention and interventions in youth suicide* (DHHS Publication No. ADM 89-1623, pp. 23–30). Washington, DC: U.S. Government Printing Office.

Felts, W. M., Chenier, T., & Barnes, R. (1992). Drug use and suicide ideation and behavior among North Carolina public school students. *American Journal of Public Health, 82,* 870–872.

Fergusson, D. M., Horwood, L. J., & Lynskey, M. T. (1995). Maternal depressive symptoms and depressive symptoms in adolescents. *Journal of Child Psychology and Psychiatry, 36(7),* 1161–1168.

Fergusson, D. M., & Lynskey, M. T. (1995). Suicide attempts and suicide ideation in a birth cohort of 16-year old New Zealanders. *Journal of the American Academy of Child and Adolescent Psychiatry, 34,* 1308–1317.

Fergusson, D. M., Woodward, L. J., & Horwood, L. J. (2000). Risk factors and life processes associated with the onset of suicidal behavior during adolescence and early adulthood. *Psychological Medicine, 30,* 23–39.

Ferster, C. B. (1973). A functional analysis of depression. *American Psychologist, 28,* 857–870.

Fingerhut, L. (2003, April). *Suicide: Trends and current status, 1980–2000.* Paper presented at the 36th Annual Meeting of the American Association of Suicidology, Santa Fe, NM.

Fishman, H. C. (1988). *Treating troubled adolescents.* New York: Basic Books.

Frances, A., & Blumenthal, S. J. (1989). Personality as a predictor of youth suicide. In *Alcohol, Drug Abuse, and Mental Health Administration, Report of the Secretary's Task Force on Youth Suicide: Vol. 2. Risk factors for youth suicide* (DHHS Publication No. ADM 89-1622, pp. 160–171). Washington, DC: U.S. Government Printing Office.

Franklin, J. L., Comstock, B. S., Simmons, J. T., & Mason, M. (1989). Characteristics of suicide prevention/intervention programs: Analysis of a survey. In *Alcohol, Drug Abuse, and Mental Health Administration, Report of the Secretary's Task Force on Youth Suicide: Vol. 3. Prevention and interventions in youth suicide* (DHHS Publication No. ADM 89-1623, pp. 93–102). Washington, DC: U.S. Government Printing Office.

Frederick, D. J., & Resnik, H. L. P. (1971). How suicidal behaviors are learned. *American Journal of Psychotherapy, 25,* 37–55.

Freud, A. (1958). Adolescence. *The Psychoanalytic Study of the Child, 13,* 261–277.

Freud, S. (1905/1957). *Three essays on the theory of sexuality.* Standard Edition (Vol. 7). London: Hogarth Press.

Freud, S. (1920). *Beyond the pleasure principle.* Standard Edition (Vol. 18). London: Hogarth Press.

Freud, S. (1957). Mourning and melancholia. In J. Strachey (Ed.), *The standard edition of the complete works of Sigmund Freud* (Vol. 14, pp. 237–260). London: Hogarth Press. (Original work published in 1917)

Friedman, P. (Ed.). (1967). *On suicide: With particular reference to suicide among young students.* New York: International Universities Press.

Friedman, R. C., Clarkin, J. F., Corn, R., Aronoff, M. S., Hurt, S. W., & Murphy, M. C. (1982). DSM-III and affective pathology in hospitalized adolescents. *Journal of Nervous and Mental Disease, 170,* 511–521.

Friend, T. (2003, October 13). Letters from California—Jumpers: The fatal grandeur of the Golden Gate Bridge. *The New Yorker,* 48–59.

Galen, R., & Gambino, S. (1975). *Beyond normality: The predictive value and efficiency of medical diagnoses.* New York: Wiley.

Garfield, S. (1996). Some problems associated with "validated" forms of psychotherapy. *Clinical Psychology: Science and Practice, 3,* 218–229.

Garfinkel, B. D., Froese, A., & Hood, J. (1982). Suicide attempts in children and adolescents. *American Journal of Psychiatry, 139,* 1257–1261.

Garmezy, N., & Masten, A. S. (1986). Stress, competence, and resilience: Common factors for therapist and psychologist. *Behavior Therapy, 17,* 500–521.

Garrison, C. Z., McKeown, R. E., Valois, R. F., & Vincent, M. L. (1993). Aggression, substance use, and suicidal behaviors in high school students. *American Journal of Public Health, 83,* 179–184.

Geller, J., Brown, K. E., Zaitsoff, S. L., Goodrich, S., & Hastings, F. (2003). Collaborative versus directive interventions in the treatment of eating disorders: Implications for care providers. *Professional Psychology: Research and Practice, 34,* 406–413.

Gessner, B. D. (1997). Temporal trends and geographic patterns of teen suicide in Alaska, 1979-1993. *Suicide and Life-Threatening Behavior, 27,* 264–273.

Gibbs, J., & Martin, W. T. (1964). *Status integration and suicide.* Eugene, OR: University of Oregon Press.

Glaser, K. (1978). The treatment of depressed and suicidal adolescents. *American Journal of Psychotherapy, 32,* 252–269.

Goldacre, M., & Hawton, K. (1985). Repetition of self-poisoning and subsequent death in adolescents who take overdoses. *British Journal of Psychiatry, 146,* 395–398.

Goldfried, M. R. (Ed.). (1980). Some views on effective principles of psychotherapy. *Cognitive Therapy and Research, 4,* 269–306.

Goldsmith, S. K., Pellmar, T. C., Kleinman, A. M., & Bunney, W. E. (2002). *Reducing suicide: A national imperative.* Washington, DC: National Academy Press.

Goldstein, L. S., & Buongiorno, P. A. (1984). Psychotherapists as suicide survivors. *American Journal of Psychotherapy, 38,* 392–398.

Goldston, D. (2003). *Measuring suicidal behaviors and risk among children and adolescents.* Washington, DC: American Psychological Association.

Goldston, D., Daniel, S., Melton, B., Reboussin, D., Kelley, A., & Frazier, P. (1998). Psychiatric disorders among previous suicide attempters, first-time, and repeat attempters on a adolescent inpatient psychiatric unit. *Journal of the American Academy of Child and Adolescent Psychiatry, 37*, 924–932.

Goldston, D., Daniel, S., Reboussin, D., Keeley, A., Ievers, C., & Brunstetter, R. (1996). First-time suicide attempters, repeat attempters, and previous attempters on an adolescent inpatient unit. *Journal of the American Academy of Child and Adolescent Psychiatry, 35*, 631–639.

Goldston, D., Daniel, S., Reboussin, D., Reboussin, E., Frazier, P., & Kelley, A. (1999). Suicide attempts and formerly hospitalized adolescents: A prospective naturalistic study of risk during the first 5 years after discharge. *Journal of the American Academy of Child and Adolescent Psychiatry, 38*, 660–671.

Goldston, D., Daniel, S., Reboussin, B., Reboussin, D., Frazier, P., & Kelley, A. (2001). Cognitive risk factors and suicide attempts among formerly hospitalized adolescents: A prospective naturalistic study. *Journal of the American Academy of Child and Adolescent Psychiatry, 40*, 91–99.

Goldston, D. B. (2000). *Measuring suicidal behavior and risk in children and adolescents.* Washington, DC: American Psychological Association.

Goodin, J., & Hanzlick, R. (1997). Mind your manners. Part II: General results from the National Association of Medical Examiners Manner of Death Questionnaire, 1995. *American Journal of Forensic Medical Pathology, 18*, 224–227.

Goodman, L. A., Mack, J. E., Beardslee, W. R., & Snow, R. (1983). The threat of nuclear war and the nuclear arms race: Adolescent experience and perceptions. *Political Psychology, 4*, 501–530.

Goodwin, R., Gould M. S., Blanco, C., & Olfson, M. (2001). Prescription of psychotropic medications to youths in office-based practice. *Psychiatric Services, 52*, 1081–1087.

Gordon, A. K. (1986). The tattered cloak of immortality. In C. A. Corr & J. M. McNeil (Eds.), *Adolescence and death.* New York: Springer Publishing Company.

Gould, M. S., Fisher, P., Parides, M., Flory, M., & Shaffer, D. (1996). Psychosocial risk factors of child and adolescent completed suicides. *Archives of General Psychiatry, 53*, 1155–1162.

Gould, M. S., Greenberg, T., Belting, D. M., & Shaffer, D. (2003). Youth suicide risk and preventive interventions: A review of the past 10 years. *Journal of the American Academy of Adolescent Psychiatry, 42*, 386–405.

Gould, M., Jamieson, P., & Romer, D. (2003). Media contagion and suicide among youth. *American Behavioral Scientist, 46*, 1269–1284.

Gould, M. S., & Kramer, R. A. (2001). Youth suicide prevention. *Suicide and Life-Threatening Behavior, 31*(Suppl.), 6–31.

Gould, M. S., & Shaffer, D. (1986). The impact of suicide in television movies: Evidence of imitation. *New England Journal of Medicine, 315*, 690–694.

Gould, M. S., Shaffer, D., Fisher, P., & Garfinkel, R. (1998). Separation/divorce and child and adolescent completed suicide. *Journal of the American Academy of Child and Adolescent Psychiatry, 37*, 155–162.

Gould, M. S., Wallenstein, S., & Davidson, L. (1989). Suicide clusters: a critical review. *Suicide and Life-Threatening Behavior, 19,* 17–29.

Grad, O. T. (2003). Surviving the suicide of somebody. In L. Vijayakumar (Ed.), *Suicide prevention: Meeting the challenge together* (pp. 123–135). Himayatnagar, Hyderabad, India: Orient Longman.

Grad, O., & Zavasnik, A. (1996). Similarities and differences in the process of bereavement after suicide and after traffic fatalities in Slovenia. *Omega, 33,* 243–251.

Greany, S. (1995). *Psychologists' behaviors and attitudes when working with the non-hospitalized suicidal patient.* Unpublished doctoral dissertation, Pacific Graduate School of Psychology, Palo Alto, CA.

Green, M. R. (1961). Suicide: The Sullivanian point of view. In N. L. Farberow & E. S. Shneidman (Eds.), *The cry for help* (pp. 220–235). New York: McGraw-Hill.

Groholt, B., Ekeberg, O., Wichstrom, L., & Haldersen, T. (2000). Young suicide attempters: A comparison between a clinical and an epidemiological sample. *Journal of American Academy of Child and Adolescent Psychiatry, 39,* 868–875.

Gross, A. M., & Levin, R. B. (1987). Learning. In V. B. Van Hasselt & M. Hersen (Eds.), *Handbook of adolescent psychology* (pp. 77–90). New York: Pergamon Press.

Grossman, D. C., Reay, D. T., & Baker, S. (1999). Self-inflicted and unintentional firearm injuries among children and adolescents: The source of the firearm. *Archives of Pediatric Adolescent Medicine, 153,* 875–878.

Grossman, J. A., & Kruesi, M. J. P. (2000). Innovative approaches to youth suicide prevention: An update of issues and research findings. In R.W. Maris, S. S. Canetto, J. L. McIntosh, & M. M. Silverman (Eds.), *Review of suicidology 2000* (pp. 170–201). New York: Guilford Press.

Group for the Advancement of Psychiatry (GAP). (1989). *Suicide and ethnicity in the United States. Report No. 128.* New York: Brunner/Mazel.

Gunnell, D., & Ashby, D. (2004). Antidepressants and suicide: What is the balance of benefit and harm? *British Medical Journal, 329,* 34–38.

Gunnell, D., Middleton, N., Whitely, E., Dorling, D., & Frankel, S. (2003). Influence of cohort effects on patterns of suicide in England and Wales, 1950–1999. *British Journal of Psychiatry, 182,* 164–170.

Guntrip, H. (1968). *Schizoid phenomena, object relations, and the self.* Madison, CT: International Universities Press.

Guo, B., & Harstall, C. (2002). *Efficacy of suicide prevention programs for children and youth.* Edmonton, Alberta, Canada: Alberta Heritage Foundation for Medical Research.

Gutheil, T. G. (1989, October). Physician liability in suicide. In R. S. Brown (Chair), *Forensic issues in suicide.* Symposium conducted at the meeting of the American Academy of Psychiatry and the Law, Washington, DC.

Gutheil, T. G. (1999). Liability issues and liability prevention in suicide. In D. Jacobs (Ed.), *The Harvard Medical School guide to suicide assessment and intervention* (pp. 561–578). San Francisco: Jossey-Bass.

Gutierrez, P. M., Osman, A., Kopper, B. A., & Barrios, F. X. (2000). Why young people do not kill themselves: The Reasons for Living Inventory for Adolescents. *Journal of Clinical Child Psychology, 29*(2), 177–187.

Hall, B. L., & Epp, H. L. (2001). Can professionals and nonprofessionals work together following a suicide? *Crisis, 22,* 74–78.

Hall, G. S. (1904). *Adolescence: Its psychology and its relation to physiology, anthropology, sociology, sex, crime, religion, and education.* (Vols. 1–2). Englewood Cliffs, NJ: Prentice-Hall.

Hamilton, J. D., Decker, N., & Rumbaut, R. D. (1986). The manipulative patient. *American Journal of Psychotherapy, 40,* 189–200.

Hansen, D. J., Watson-Perczel, M., & Christopher, J. S. (1989). Clinical issues in social-skills training with adolescents. *Clinical Psychology Review, 9,* 365–391.

Hanzlick, R., & Goodin, J. (1997). Mind your manners. Part III: Individual scenario results and discussion of the National Association of Medical Examiners Manner of Death Questionnaire, 1995. *American Journal of Forensic Medical Pathology, 18*(3), 228–245.

Harkavy-Friedman, J., Asnis, G., Boeck, M., & DiFiore, J. (1987). Prevalence of specific suicidal behaviors in a high school sample. *American Journal of Psychiatry, 144,* 1203–1206.

Harkavy-Friedman, J. M., Nelson, E. A., Venarde, D. F., & Mann, J. J. (2004). Suicidal behavior in schizophrenia and schizoaffective disorder: Examining the role of depression. *Suicide and Life-Threatening Behavior, 34,* 66–76.

Harrington, R., Kerfoot, M., Dyer, E., McNiven, F., Gill, J., Harrington, V., et al. (1998). Randomized trial of a home-based family intervention for children who have deliberately poisoned themselves. *Journal of the American Academy of Child and Adolescent Psychiatry, 37,* 512–518.

Harrington, R., & Saleem, Y. (2003). Cognitive behavioral therapy after deliberate self-harm. In R. A. King & A. Apter (Eds.), *Suicide in children and adolescents* (pp. 251–270). Cambridge, England: Cambridge University Press.

Harrington, R., Whittaker, J., Shoebridge, P., & Campbell, F. (1998). Systematic review of efficacy of cognitive behaviour therapies in childhood and adolescent depressive disorders. *British Medical Journal, 316,* 1559–1563.

Harris, H. E., & Myers, W. C. (1997). Adolescents' misperceptions of the dangerousness of acetaminophen in overdose. *Suicide and Life-Threatening Behavior, 27,* 274–277.

Hauser, M. J. (1983). Bereavement outcomes for widows. *Journal of Psychosocial Nursing and Mental Health Services, 21,* 22–31.

Hauser, M. J. (1987). Special aspects of grief after suicide. In E. J. Dunne, J. L. McIntosh, & K. Dunne-Maxim (Eds.), *Suicide and its aftermath* (pp. 57–70). New York: Norton.

Havik, O., & VandenBos, G. (1996). Limitations of manualized psychotherapy for everyday clinical practice. *Clinical Psychology: Science and Practice, 3*, 264–267.

Hawkins, J. D., Catalano, R. F., Kosterman, R., Abbott, R., & Hill, K. G. (1999). Preventing adolescent risk behaviors by strengthening protection during childhood. *Archives of Pediatric Adolescent Behavior, 153*, 226–234.

Hawton, K. (1986). *Suicide and attempted suicide among children and adolescents*. Beverly Hills, CA: Sage.

Hawton, K. (1987). *Attempted suicide*. New York: Oxford.

Hawton, K. (1998). Why has suicide increased in young males? *Crisis, 19*, 119–124.

Hawton, K. (2002). United Kingdom legislation on pack sizes of analgesics: Background, rationale, and effects on suicide and deliberate self-harm. *Suicide and Life-Threatening Behavior, 32*, 223–229.

Hawton, K. A., Arensman, E., Townsend, E., Bremner, S., Feldman, E., & Goldney, R. (1998). Deliberate self harm: Systematic review of efficacy of psychosocial and pharmacological treatments in preventing repetition. *British Medical Journal, 31*, 441–447.

Hawton, K., Cole, D., O'Grady, J., & Osborn, M. (1982). Motivational aspects of deliberate self-poisoning in adolescents. *British Journal of Psychiatry, 14*, 286–291.

Hawton, K., Fagg, J., & Simkin, S. (1996). Deliberate self-poisoning and self-injury in children and adolescents under 16 years of age in Oxford, 1976–1993. *British Journal of Psychiatry, 169*, 202–208.

Hawton, K., Simkin, S., Deeks, J. H., O'Connor, S., Keen, A., Altman, D. G., Philo, G., & Bulstrode, C. (1999). Effects of a drug overdose in a television drama on presentations to hospital for self poisoning: Time series and questionnaire study. *British Medical Journal, 318*, 972–977.

Hawton, K., & van Heeringen, K. (2000). *The international handbook of suicide and attempted suicide*. New York: Wiley.

Haynes, R. B., McKibbon, K. A., & Kanani, R. (1996). Key issues and suggestions for patient compliance assessment: Sources of information, focus of measures, and nature of response options. *Journal of Compliance in Health Care, 2*, 37–53.

Heilig, S. M. (1985, April). Survey of 41 survivor groups; Abstract. In R. Cohen-Sandler (Ed.), *Proceedings of the Eighteenth Annual Meeting of the American Association of Suicidology* (pp. 110–113). Denver, CO: American Association of Suicidology.

Hendin, H. (1987). Youth suicide: A psychosocial perspective. *Suicide and Life-Threatening Behavior, 17*, 151–165.

Hendin, H., Haas, A. P., Maltsberger, J. T., Szanto, K., & Rabinowicz, H. (2004). Factors contributing to therapists' distress after the suicide of a patient. *American Journal of Psychiatry, 161*, 1442–1446.

Hendin, H., & Mann, J. J. (Eds.). (2001). The clinical science of suicide prevention. *Annals of the New York Academy of Sciences, 392*, 1–241.

Hengeveld, M. W., Jonker, D. J., & Rooijmans, H. G. (1996). A pilot study of a short cognitive-behavioral group treatment for female recurrent suicide attempters. *International Journal of Psychiatry and Medicine, 26*, 83–91.

Henriques, G., Beck, A. T., & Brown, G. K. (2003). Cognitive therapy for adolescent and young adult suicide attempters. *American Behavioral Scientist, 46,* 1258–1268.

Henry, A., & Short, J. (1954). *Suicide and homicide.* Glencoe, IL: Free Press.

Hersch, L. (1995). Adapting to health care reform and managed care: Three strategies for survival and growth. *Professional Psychology: Research and Practice, 26,* 16–26.

Hjelmeland, H., Hawton, K., Nordvik, H., Bille-Brahe, U., DeLeo, D., Fekete, S., et al. (2002). Why people engage in parasuicide: A cross-cultural study of intentions. *Suicide and Life-Threatening Behavior, 32,* 380–393.

Hlady, W. G., & Middaugh, J. P. (1988). The underreporting of suicides in state and national records, Alaska, 1983–1984. *Suicide and Life-Threatening Behavior, 18,* 237–244.

Ho, T. P. (2003). The suicide risk of discharged psychiatric patients. *Journal of Clinical Psychiatry, 64,* 702–707.

Hoberman, H. M., & Garfinkel, B. D. (1988a). Completed suicide in children and adolescents. *Journal of the American Academy of Child and Adolescent Psychiatry, 27,* 689–695.

Hoberman, H. M., & Garfinkel, B. D. (1988b). Completed suicide in youth. *Canadian Journal of Psychiatry, 33,* 494–502.

Hoff, L. A. (1994). *People in crisis: Understanding and helping.* Menlo Park, CA: Addison Wesley.

Holinger, P. C. (1979). Violent death among the young: Recent trends in suicide, homicide, and accident. *American Journal of Psychiatry, 142,* 1144–1147.

Holinger, P. C. (1984). Suicide prevention and intervention. In *The Carter Center, Closing the Gap Project.* Atlanta, GA: Centers for Disease Control.

Holinger, P. C., & Offer, D. (1981). Perspectives on suicide in adolescence. *Research in Community and Mental Health, 2,* 139–157.

Holinger, P. C., & Offer, D. (1982). Prediction of adolescent suicide: A population model. *American Journal of Psychiatry, 139,* 302–307.

Holinger, P. C., Offer, D., & Zola, M. A. (1988). A prediction model of suicide among youth. *Journal of Nervous and Mental Disease, 176,* 275–279.

Horgas, P. (2003). *Emergency room/EMS responses.* Presentation at NIMH/NIH Office of Rare Diseases and the American Foundation for Suicide Prevention's Survivors of Suicide Research Workshop, Washington, DC.

Horowitz, R. I., & Horowitz, S. M. (1993). Adherence to treatment and health outcomes. *Archives of Internal Medicine, 153,* 1863–1868.

Houston, K., Hawton, K., & Shepperd, R. (2001). Suicide in young people aged 15–24: A psychological autopsy study. *Journal of Affective Disorders, 63,* 159–170.

Hovey, J. D. (2000). Acculturative stress, depression, and suicidal ideation among Central American immigrants. *Suicide and Life-Threatening Behavior, 30,* 125–139.

Hsiung, R. C. (2002). *E-therapy: Case studies, guiding principles, and the clinical potential of the Internet.* New York: Norton.

Huff, C. (1999). Source, recency, and degree of stress in adolescence and suicide ideation. *Adolescence, 34,* 81–89.

Hynes, P. (1989, April). *Principles of long-term psychotherapy with chronically suicidal patients.* Paper presented at the annual meeting of the American Association of Suicidology, San Diego, CA.

Iowa cops fear teen suicide pact. (2003, October 8). *CBS News.* Retrieved June 20, 2005, from http://www.cbsnews.com/stories/2003/10/08/national/main577148.shtml

Isacsson, G., Bergman, U., & Rich, C. L. (1996). Epidemiological data suggest antidepressants reduce suicide risk among depressives. *Journal of Affective Disorders, 41,* 1–8.

Isometsa, E. T., Heikkinen, M. E., Marttunen, M. J., Henriksson, M. M., Aro, H. M., & Lonnqvist, J. K. (1995).The last appointment before suicide: is suicide intent communicated? *American Journal of Psychiatry, 152,* 919–922.

Jacobs, D. (1999). *The Harvard Medical School guide to suicide assessment and intervention.* San Francisco: Jossey-Bass.

Jacobson, G. (1999). The inpatient management of suicidality. In D. G. Jacobs (Ed.), *The Harvard Medical School guide to suicide assessment and intervention* (pp. 383–405). San Francisco: Jossey-Bass.

Jacobziner, H. (1965). Attempted suicide in adolescence. *Journal of the American Medical Association, 10,* 22–36.

Jan-Tausch, J. (1963). *Suicide of children 1960-1963, New Jersey public school studies.* Trenton: New Jersey Public Schools, Department of Education.

Jensen, E. (1993). When "hired guns" backfire: The witness immunity doctrine and the negligent expert witness. *University of Missouri at Kansas City Law Review, 62,* 185–207.

Jick, H., Kaye, J. A., & Jick, S. S. (2004). Antidepressants and the risk of suicidal behaviors. *Journal of the American Medical Association, 292,* 338–343.

Jobes, D. A. (1995a). The challenge and the promise of clinical suicidology. *Suicide and Life-Threatening Behavior, 25,* 437–449.

Jobes, D. A. (1995b). Psychodynamic treatment of adolescent suicide attempters. In J. K. Zimmerman & G. M. Asnis (Eds.), *Treatment approaches with suicidal adolescents* (pp. 137–154). New York: Wiley.

Jobes, D. A. (2000). Collaborating to prevent suicide: A clinical-research perspective. *Suicide and Life-Threatening Behavior, 30,* 8–17.

Jobes, D. A. (2001, June). *Contemporary trends in clinical suicidology: Implications for research and practice.* Psychiatry Grand Rounds presented at the Mayo Clinic, Rochester, MN.

Jobes, D. A. (2003a). *Manual for the collaborative assessment and management of suicidality—revised (CAMS–R).* Unpublished manuscript.

Jobes, D. A. (2003b). Understanding suicide in the 21st century. *Preventing Suicide: The National Journal, 2,* 2–4.

Jobes, D. A. (2004a). CAMS: *The Collaborative Assessment and Management of Suicidality.* Contracted book manuscript in preparation.

Jobes, D. A. (2004b, October). *The psychology of suicide: Research on what suicidal patients have to say.* Keynote address at the 3rd Annual Military Suicide Prevention Conference, Crystal City, VA.

Jobes, D. A., & Berman, A. L. (1984). *Response biases and the impact of psychological autopsies on medical examiners' determination of mode of death.* Paper presented at the annual meeting of the American Association of Suicidology, Anchorage, AK.

Jobes, D. A., & Berman, A. L. (1993). Suicide and malpractice liability: Assessing and revising policies, procedures, and practice in outpatient settings. *Professional Psychology: Research and Practice, 24,* 91–99.

Jobes, D. A., Berman, A. L., & Josselson, A. R. (1986). The impact of psychological autopsies on medical examiners' determination of manner of death. *Journal of Forensic Sciences, 31,* 177–189.

Jobes, D. A., Berman, A. L., & Josselson, A. R. (1987). Improving the validity and reliability of medical-legal certifications of suicide. *Suicide and Life-Threatening Behavior, 17,* 310–325.

Jobes, D. A., Berman, A. L., & Martin, C. E. (2000). Adolescent suicidality and crisis intervention. In A. R. Roberts (Ed.), *Crisis intervention handbook* (2nd ed., pp. 131–151). New York: Oxford University Press.

Jobes, D. A., Berman, A. L., O'Carroll, P. W., Eastgard, S., & Knickmeyer, S. (1996). The Kurt Cobain suicide crisis: Research, public health, and news media perspectives. *Suicide and Life-Threatening Behavior, 26,* 260–271.

Jobes, D. A., Casey, J. O., Berman, A. L., & Wright, D. G. (1991). Empirical criteria for the determination of suicide. *Journal of Forensic Sciences, 36,* 244–256.

Jobes, D. A., & Drozd, J. F. (2004). The CAMS approach to working with suicidal patients. *Journal of Contemporary Psychotherapy, 34,* 73–85.

Jobes, D. A., Drozd, J. F., Neal-Walden, T., Wong, S. A., & Kiernan, A. (2003, April). *Clinical research in the U.S. Air Force 10th medical group: The impact of CAMS vs. treatment as usual on suicidal outpatients.* Paper presented at the annual conference of the American Association of Suicidology, Santa Fe, NM.

Jobes, D. A., Eyman, J. R., & Yufit, R. I. (1995). How clinicians assess suicide risk in adolescents and adults. *Crisis Intervention and Time-Limited Treatment, 2,* 1–12.

Jobes, D. A., Jacoby, A. M., Cimbolic, P., & Hustead, L. A. T. (1997). The assessment and treatment of suicidal clients in a university counseling center. *Journal of Counseling Psychology, 44,* 368–377.

Jobes, D. A., & Karmel, M. P. (1996): Case consultation with a suicidal adolescent. In A. Leenaars & D. Lester (Eds.), *Suicide and the unconscious.* Northvale, NJ: Aronson.

Jobes, D. A., Luoma, J. B., Hustead, L. A. T., & Mann, R. (2000). In the wake of suicide: Survivorship and postvention. In R. Maris (Ed.), *Textbook of suicidology and suicide prevention* (pp. 536–561). New York: Guilford Press.

Jobes, D. A., Luoma, J. B., Jacoby, A. M., & Mann, R. E. (1998). *Manual for the Collaborative Assessment and Management of Suicidality (CAMS)*. Unpublished manuscript.

Jobes, D. A., & Maltsberger, J. T. (1995). The hazards of treating suicidal patients. In M. Sussman (Ed.), *A perilous calling: The hazards of psychotherapy practice* (pp. 200–214). New York: Wiley.

Jobes, D. A., & Mann, R. E. (1999). Reasons for living versus reasons for dying: Examining the internal debate of suicide. *Suicide and Life-Threatening Behavior, 29*, 97–104.

Jobes, D. A., & Mann, R. E. (2000). Letters to the editor—Reply. *Suicide and Life-Threatening Behavior, 30*, 182.

Jobes, D. A., Nelson, K. N, Peterson, E. M., Pentiuc, D., Downing, V., Francini, K., et al. (2004). Describing suicidality: An investigation of qualitative SSF responses. *Suicide and Life-Threatening Behavior, 34*, 99–112.

Jobes, D. A., Small, J., Peterson, R., Rustad, R., & Safer, M. (2000, April). *Suicide-suggestive themes in rock music and videos*. Panel presented at the meeting of the American Association of Suicidology, Los Angeles, CA.

Jobes, D. A., Wong, S. A., Conrad, A., Drozd, J. F., & Neal-Walden, T. (in press). The Collaborative Assessment and Management of Suicidality vs. treatment as usual: An ex post facto study with suicidal outpatients. *Suicide and Life-Threatening Behavior*.

Joffe, P. (2003, February). *An empirically supported program to prevent suicide among a college population*. Paper presented at Stetson College of Law National Conference on Law and Education, Clearwater, FL.

Johnson, G. R., Krug, E., & Potter, L. B. (2000). Suicide among adolescents and young adults: A cross-national comparison of 34 countries. *Suicide and Life-Threatening Behavior, 30*, 74–82.

Johnson, W. B., Lall, R., Bongar, B., & Nordlung, M. D. (1999) The role of objective personality inventories in suicide risk assessment: An evaluation and proposal. *Suicide and Life-Threatening Behavior, 29*, 165–185.

Joiner, T. (2003a). *Supplementary application, part 3: Statement of plans*. Unpublished portion of J. S. Guggenheim Memorial Foundation award application.

Joiner, T. (2003b). *An interpersonal-psychological theory of attempted and completed suicide*. Unpublished manuscript.

Joiner, T. (2004, April). *The three components of completed suicide*. Keynote address at the Annual Conference of the American Association of Suicidology, Miami, FL.

Joiner, T. E., Johnson, F., & Soderstrom, K. (2002). Association between serotonin transporter gene polymorphism and family history of completed and attempted suicide. *Suicide and Life-Threatening Behavior, 32*, 33–41.

Joiner, T. E., Lewinsohn, P. M., & Seeley, J. R. (2002). The core of loneliness: Lack of pleasurable engagement—more so than painful disconnection—predicts social impairment, depression onset, and recovery from depressive disorders among adolescents. *Journal of Personality Assessment, 79*, 472–491.

Joiner, T. E., & Rudd, M. D. (2000). Intensity and duration of suicidal crises vary as a function of previous suicide attempts and negative life events. *Journal of Consulting and Clinical Psychology, 68,* 909–916.

Joiner, T. E, Voelz, Z. R., & Rudd, M. D. (2001). For suicidal adults with comorbid depressive and anxiety disorders, problem-solving treatment may be better than treatment as usual. *Professional Psychology: Research and Practice, 32,* 403–411.

Jones, F. A. (1987). Therapists as survivors of client suicide. In E. J. Dunne, J. L. McIntosh, & K. Dunne-Maxim (Eds.), *Suicide and its aftermath* (pp. 126–141). New York: Norton.

Jordan, J. R. (2001). Is suicide bereavement different? A reassessment of the literature. *Suicide and Life-Threatening Behavior, 31,* 91–102.

Jung, C. G. (1959). The soul and death. In H. Feifel (Ed.), *The meaning of death.* New York: McGraw-Hill.

Kalafat, J. (2001, May). *A systems approach to youth suicide prevention.* Paper presented at the Institute of Medicine, The National Academies Committee on Pathophysiology and Prevention of Adolescent and Adult Suicide Workshop on Suicide Prevention, Washington, DC.

Kalafat, J. (2003). School approaches to youth suicide prevention. *American Behavioral Scientist, 46,* 1211–1223.

Kalafat, J., & Elias, M. (1992). Adolescents' experience with and response to suicidal peers. *Suicide and Life-Threatening Behavior, 22,* 315–321.

Kalafat, J., Ryerson, D., & Underwood, M. (2001). *Lifelines ASAP: Adolescent suicide awareness & response program.* Piscataway, NJ: Rutgers Graduate School of Applied and Professional Psychology.

Kalafat, J., & Underwood, M. (1989). *Lifelines: A school-based adolescent suicide response program.* Dubuque, IA: Kendall/Hunt.

Kalediene, R. (1999). Time trends in suicide mortality in Lithuania. *Acta Psychiatrica Scandinavica, 99,* 397–398.

Kallman, F. J., & Anastasia, M. M. (1947). Twin studies on the psychopathology of suicide. *Journal of Nervous and Mental Diseases, 105,* 40–50.

Kaltiala-Heino, R., Rimpela, M., Marttunen, M., Rimpela, A., & Rantanen, P. (1999). Bullying, depression, and suicidal ideation in Finnish adolescents: School survey. *British Medical Journal, 319,* 330–331.

Kamali, M., Oquendo, M. A., & Mann, J. J. (2001). Understanding the neurobiology of suicidal behavior. *Depression and Anxiety, 14,* 164–176.

Kaplan, M. L., Asnis, G. M., Sanderson, W. L., Keswani, L., DeLecuona, J. M., & Joseph, S. (1994). Suicide assessment: Clinical interviews vs. self-report. *Journal of Clinical Psychology, 50,* 294–298.

Kaplan, R. D., Kottler, D. B., & Frances, A. J. (1982). Reliability and rationality in the prediction of suicide. *Hospital and Community Psychiatry, 33,* 212–215.

Kastenbaum, R. (1986). Death in the world of adolescence. In C. A. Corr & J. N. McNeil (Eds.), *Adolescence and death* (pp. 4–15). New York: Springer.

Katz, P. (1995). The psychotherapeutic treatment of suicidal adolescents. *Adolescent Psychiatry, 20*, 325–341.

Kellermann, A. L., Rivara, F. P., Rushforth, N. B., Banton, J. G., Reay, D. T., Francisco, J. T., et al. (1993). Gun ownership as a risk factor for homicide in the home. *The New England Journal of Medicine, 329*, 1084–1091.

Kellermann, A. L., Rivara, F. P., Somes, G., Reay, D. T., Francisco, J., Banton, J. G., et al. (1992). Suicide in the home in relationship to gun ownership. *The New England Journal of Medicine, 327*, 467–472.

Kerfoot, M., Dyer, E., Harrington, V., Woodham, A., & Harrington, R. (1996). Correlates and short-term course of self-poisoning in adolescents. *British Journal of Psychiatry, 168*, 38–42.

Kernberg, P. (1994). Psychological interventions for the suicidal adolescent. *American Journal of Psychotherapy, 48*, 52–63.

Kessler, R. C., Downey, G. D., Milavsky, J. R., & Stipp, H. (1988). Clustering of teenage suicides after television news stories about suicides: A reconsideration. *American Journal of Psychiatry, 145*, 1379–1383.

Kestenberg, J. (1968). Phases of adolescence with suggestions for a correlation of psychic and hormonal organization: Part III. Puberty growth, differentiation, and consolidation. *Journal of American Academy of Child Psychiatry, 7*, 108–151.

Khan, A., Khan, S., Kolts, R., & Brown, W. A. (2003). Suicide rates in clinical trials of SSRIs, other antidepressants, and placebo: Analysis of FDA reports. *American Journal of Psychiatry, 160*, 790–792.

Kienhorst, I. C. W. M., Wilde, E. J., Diekstra, R. F. W., & Wolters, W. H. G. (1995). Adolescents' image of their suicide attempt. *Journal of the American Academy of Child and Adolescent Psychiatry, 34*, 623–628.

King, C. A. (1997). Suicidal behavior in adolescence. In R. W. Maris, M. M. Silverman, & S. S. Canetto (Eds.), *Review of suicidology, 1997* (pp. 61–95). New York: Guilford Press.

King, C. A., Segal, H., Kaminski, K., Naylor, M. W., Ghaziuddin, N., & Radpour, L. (1995). A prospective study of adolescent suicidal behavior. *Suicide and Life-Threatening Behavior, 25*, 327–338.

King, R. A. (2003). Psychodynamic approaches to youth suicide. In R. A. King & A. Apter (Eds.), *Suicide in children and adolescents* (pp. 150–169). Cambridge, England: Cambridge University Press.

King, R. A., & Apter, A. (Eds.). (2003). *Suicide in children and adolescents.* Cambridge, England: Cambridge University Press.

King, S. R., Hampton, Jr., W. R., Bernstein, B., & Schichor, A. (1996). College students' views on suicide. *Journal of American College Health, 44*, 283–287.

Kleck G. (1988). Miscounting suicides. *Suicide and Life-Threatening Behavior, 18*, 219–236.

Kleespies, P. M., Penk, W., & Forsyth, J. (1993). The stress of patient suicidal behavior during clinical training: Incidence, impact, and recovery. *Professional Psychology: Research and Practice, 24*, 293–303.

Kleespies, P. M., Smith, M. R., & Becker, B. R. (1990). Psychology interns as patient-suicide survivors: Incidence, impact, and recovery. *Professional Psychology: Research and Practice, 21*, 257–263.

Klerman, G. L. (1987). Clinical epidemiology of suicide. *Journal of Clinical Psychiatry, 48*, 33–38.

Klerman, G. L., & Weissman, M. M. (1989). *Interpersonal psychotherapy of depression*. New York: Basic Books.

Klimes-Dougan, B., Free, K., Ronsaville, D., Stilwell, J., Welsh, C. J., & Radke-Yarrow, M. (1999). Suicide ideation and attempts: A longitudinal investigation of children of depressed and well mothers. *Journal of the American Academy of Child and Adolescent Psychiatry, 38*, 651–659.

Kohut, H. (1971). *The analysis of the self*. New York: International Universities Press.

Kohut, H. (1977). *The restoration of the self*. New York: International Universities Press.

Kohut, H., & Wolf, E. (1978). Disorders of the self and their treatment: An outline. *International Journal of Psychoanalysis, 59*, 413–425.

Koons, C. R., Robins, C. J., Bishop, G. K., Morse, J. Q., Tweed, J. L., Lynch, T. R., & Gonzalez, A. M. (1998, November). *Efficacy of dialectical behavior therapy with borderline women veterans. A randomized controlled trial*. Paper presented at the annual meeting of the Association for the Advancement of Behavior Therapy, Washington, DC.

Kosky, R. J., Eshkevari, H. S., Goldney, R. D., & Hassan, R. (1998). *Suicide prevention: The global context*. New York: Plenum Press.

Kosky, R., Silburn, S., & Zubrick, S. (1986). Symptomatic depression and suicidal ideation: A comparative study with children. *Journal of Nervous and Mental Disease, 174*, 523–528.

Kosky, R., Silburn, S., & Zubrick, S. R. (1990). Are children and adolescents who have suicidal thoughts different from those who attempt suicide? *Jounal of Nervous and Mental Diseases, 178(1)*, 38–43.

Kotila, L., & Lonnqvist, J. (1987). Adolescents who make suicide attempts repeatedly. *Acta Psychiatrica Scandinavia, 76*, 386–393.

Kraemer, H. C., Kazdin, A. E., Offord, D. R., Kessler, R. C., Jensen, P. S., & Kupfer, D. J. (1997). Coming to terms with terms of risk. *Archives of General Psychiatry, 54*, 337–343.

Kreitman, N. (1977). *Parasuicide*. New York: Wiley.

Kreitman, N. (1988). The two traditions in suicide research (the Dublin lecture). *Suicide and Life-Threatening Behavior, 18*, 66–72.

Kroll, L., Harrington, R., Jayson, D., Fraser, J., & Gowers, S. (1996). Pilot study of continuation cognitive-behavioral therapy for major depression in adolescent psychiatric patients. *Journal of the American Academy of Child and Adolescent Psychiatry, 35*, 1156–1161.

Kruesi, M. J., Grossman, J., Pennington, J. M., Woodward, P. J., Duda, D., & Hirsch, J. G. (1999). Suicide and violence prevention: Parent education in the emergency department. *Journal of the American Academy of Child and Adolescent Psychiatry, 38*, 250–255.

Kubin, M. (1994). *The study of suicide in marriage and family therapists training curriculum.* Palo Alto, CA: Pacific Graduate School of Psychology.

Kubler-Ross, E. (1969). *On death and dying.* New York: Macmillan.

Kuhn, T. S. (1970). *The structure of scientific revolutions.* Chicago: University of Chicago Press.

Landau-Stanton, J. L., & Stanton, M. D. (1985). Treating suicidal adolescents and their families. In M. P. Mirkin & S. L. Koman (Eds.), *Handbook of adolescents and family therapy* (pp. 309–328). New York: Gardner Press.

Leenaars, A. A. (1988). *Suicide notes: Predictive clues and patterns.* New York: Human Sciences Library.

Leenaars, A. A. (1989). Are young adults' suicides psychologically different from those of other adults? *Suicide and Life-Threatening Behavior, 19*, 249–263.

Leenaars, A. A., & Balance, W. (1984). A predictive approach to Freud's formulations regarding suicide. *Suicide and Life-Threatening Behavior, 14*, 275–283.

Leenaars, A. A., Connolly, J., Gailiene, D., Goldney, R., Schlebusch, L., Bosch, B., et al. (2003). Ethical and legal issues: A workshop. In L. Vijayakumar (Ed.), *Suicide prevention: Meeting the challenge together.* Himayatnagar, Hyderabad, India: Orient Longman.

Leenaars, A. A., Maltsberger, J. T., & Neimeyer, R. A. (Eds.). (1994). *Treatment of suicidal people.* Washington, DC: Taylor & Frances.

Leonard, C. V. (1967). *Understanding and preventing suicide.* Springfield, IL: Charles C Thomas.

Lerner, M. S., & Clum, G. A. (1990). Treatment of suicide ideators: A problem-solving approach. *Behavior Therapy, 21*, 403–411.

Lerner, S., & Lerner, H. E. (1983). A systematic approach to resistance: Theoretical and technical considerations. *American Journal of Psychotherapy, 37*, 387–399.

Lester, D. (1979). Temporal variation in suicide and homicide. *American Journal of Epidemiology, 109*, 517–520.

Lester, D. (1984). The quality of life and suicide. *Journal of Social Psychology, 125*, 279–280.

Lester, D. (1987). A subcultural theory of teenage suicide. *Adolescence, 22*, 317–320.

Lester, D. (1988a). Youth suicide: A cross-cultural perspective. *Adolescence, 23*, 955–958.

Lester, D. (1988b). One theory of teen-age suicide. *Journal of School Health, 58*, 193–194.

Lester, D. (1989). Restricting methods of suicide as a means of preventing suicide: The case of drugs. *Perceptual and Motor Skills, 68,* 273–274.

Lester, D. (1994). A comparison of 15 theories of suicide. *Suicide and Life-Threatening Behavior, 24,* 80–88.

Lester, D. (2001). *Suicide prevention: Resources for the millennium.* Philadelphia: Brunner-Rutledge.

Levenson, M., & Neuringer, C. (1971). Problem-solving behavior in suicidal adolescents. *Journal of Consulting and Clinical Psychology, 37,* 433–436.

Levin, C. (1994). *Graduate training in clinical social work and suicide.* Palo Alto, CA: Pacific Graduate School of Psychology.

Lewinsohn, P. M., Clarke, G. N., Hops, H., & Andrews, J. P. (1990). Behavioral treatment for depressed adolescents. *Behavior Therapy, 21,* 385–401.

Lewinsohn, P. M., Garrison, C. Z., Langhinrichsen, J., & Marsteller, F. (1989). *The assessment of suicidal behavior in adolescents: A review of scales suitable for epidemiologic and clinical research* (Contract Nos. 316774 and 316776). Rockville, MD: National Institute of Mental Health.

Lewinsohn, P. M., Rohde, P., & Seeley, J. R. (1993). Psychosocial characteristics of adolescents with a history of suicide attempt. *Journal of American Academy of Child and Adolescent Psychiatry, 32,* 60–68.

Lewinsohn, P. M., Rohde, P., & Seeley, J. R. (1994). Psychosocial risk factors for future adolescent suicide attempts. *Journal of Consulting and Clinical Psychology, 62,* 297–305.

Lewinsohn, P. M., Rohde, P., & Seeley, J. R. (1996). Adolescent suicide ideation and attempts: Prevalence, risk factors, and clinical implications. *Clinical Psychology: Science and Practice, 3,* 25–46.

Linehan, M. M. (1985, September). *Descriptive studies of suicidal acts.* Paper presented at New York Academy of Sciences Conference on Psychobiology of Suicidal Behavior.

Linehan, M. M. (1986). Suicidal people: One population or two? *Annals of the New York Academy of Sciences, 487,* 16–33.

Linehan, M. M. (1993a). *Cognitive behavioral therapy of borderline personality disorder.* New York: Guilford Press.

Linehan, M. M. (1993b). *Skills training manual for treating borderline personality disorder.* New York: Guilford Press.

Linehan, M. M. (1997). Behavioral treatments of suicidal behaviors: Definitional obfuscation and treatment outcomes. In D. M. Stoff & J. J. Mann (Eds.), *The neurobiology of suicidal behavior* (pp. 302–328). New York: Annals of the New York Academy of Sciences.

Linehan, M. M. (1998, April). *Is anything effective for reducing suicidal behavior?* Paper presented at the annual meeting of the American Association of Suicidology, Bethesda, MD.

Linehan, M. M. (2004, April). *Suicidal behavior: Dialectical behavior therapy.* Keynote address at the annual conference of the American Association of Suicidology, Miami, FL.

Linehan, M. M., Armstrong, H. E., Suarez, A., Allmon, D., & Heard, H. L. (1991). Cognitive-behavioral treatment of chronically parasuicidal borderline patients. *Archives of General Psychiatry, 48,* 1060–1064.

Linehan, M. M., Comtois, K. A., Koerner, K., Bown, M., Dimeff, L. A., Tutek, D., et al. (1998, November). *University of Washington study of dialectical behavior therapy: A preliminary report.* Paper presented at the annual meeting of the Association for the Advancement of Behavior Therapy, Washington, DC.

Linehan, M. M., Goodstein, J. L., Nielsen, S. L., & Chiles, J. A. (1983). Reasons for staying alive when you are thinking of killing yourself: The reasons for living inventory. *Journal of Consulting and Clinical Psychology, 51,* 276–286.

Litman, R. (1965). When patients commit suicide. *American Journal of Psychotherapy, 19,* 570–576.

Litman, R. E. (1982). Hospital suicides: Lawsuits and standards. *Suicide and Life-Threatening Behavior, 12,* 212–220.

Litman, R. E. (1987, May). *Responsibility and liability for suicide.* Paper presented at the annual meeting of the American Association of Suicidology, San Francisco, CA.

Litman, R. E. (1990a). Suicides: What do they have in mind? In D. Jacobs & H. Brown (Eds.), *Suicide: Understanding and responding* (pp. 143–156). Madison, CT: International Universities Press.

Litman, R. E. (1990b). Suicides: What do they have in mind? In D. Jacobs & H. Brown (Eds.), *Suicidology: Contemporary developments* (pp. 528–546). New York: Grune & Stratton.

Litman, R. E., Curphey, T., Shneidman, E. S., Farberow, N. L., & Tabachnick, M. D. (1963). Investigations of equivocal suicides. *Journal of the American Medical Association, 184,* 924–929.

Litt, I. F., Cuskey, W. R., & Rudd, S. (1983). Emergency room evaluation of the adolescent who attempts suicide: Compliance with follow-up. *Journal of Adolescent Health Care, 4,* 106–108.

Lively, P. (1987). *Moon tiger.* New York: Harper & Row.

Lonczak, H. S., Abbott, R. D., Hawkins, J. D., Kosterman, R., & Catalano, R. F. (2002). Effects of the Seattle social development project on sexual behavior, pregnancy, birth, and sexually transmitted disease outcomes by age 21 years. *Archives of Pediatric Adolescent Medicine, 156,* 438–447.

Lonnqvist, J. K., Henriksson, M. M., Isometsa, E. T., Marttunen, M. J., Heikkinen, M. E., Aro, H. M., et al. (1995). Mental disorders and suicide prevention. *Psychiatry Clinics of Neuroscience, 49*(Suppl. 1), S111–116.

Luoma, J. B., Martin, K. E., & Pearson, J. L. (2002). Contact with mental health and primary care providers before suicide: A review of the evidence. *American Journal of Psychiatry, 159,* 909–916.

Maltsberger, J. T. (1986). *Suicide risk: The formulation of clinical judgment.* New York: New York University Press.

Maltsberger, J. T. (1988). Suicide danger: Clinical estimation and decision. *Suicide and Life-Threatening Behavior, 18,* 47–54.

Maltsberger, J. T. (1993). Problems in the care of suicidal patients. *American Association of Suicidology Newslink, 19,* 3–5.

Maltsberger, J. T. (1994). Calculated risk-taking in the treatment of suicidal patients: Ethical and legal problems. In A. Leenaars, J. Maltsberger, & R. Neimeyer (Eds.), *Treatment of suicidal people* (pp. 195–205). Washington, DC: Taylor & Francis.

Maltsberger, J. T., & Buie, E. H. (1974). Countertransference hate in the treatment of suicidal patients. *Archives of General Psychiatry, 30,* 625–633.

Maltsberger, J. T., Hendin, H., Haas, A. P., & Lipschitz, A. (2003). Determination of precipitating events in the suicide of psychiatric patients. *Suicide and Life-Threatening Behavior, 33,* 111–119.

Mann, J. J. (1998). The neurobiology of suicide. *Nature Medicine, 4,* 25–30.

Mann, J. J. (2003). Neurobiology of suicidal behavior. *Nature Reviews/Neuroscience, 4,* 813–828.

Mann, J. J., & Arango, V. (1992). Integration of neurobiology and psychopathology in a unified model of suicidal behavior. *Journal of Clinical Psychopharmacology, 12,* 2–6.

Mann, J. J., & Arango, V. (2001). Neurobiology of suicide and attempted suicide. In D. Wasserman (Ed.), *Suicide: An unnecessary death* (pp. 29–34). London: Martin Dunitz.

Mann, J. J., & Kapur, S. (1991). The emergence of suicidal ideation and behavior during antidepressant pharmacotherapy. *Archives of General Psychiatry, 48,* 1027–1033.

Mann, J. J., Malone, K. M., Nielson, D. A., Goldman, D., Erdos, J., & Glertner, J. (1997). Possible association of a polymorphism of the tryptophan hydroxylase gene with suicide behavior in depressed patients. *American Journal of Psychiatry, 154,* 1451–1453.

Mann, J. J., Waternaux, C., Haas, G. L., & Malone, K. M. (1999). Toward a clinical model of suicidal behavior in psychiatric patients. *American Journal of Psychiatry, 156,* 181–189.

Mann, R. (2002). *Reasons for living vs. reasons for dying: The development of suicidal typologies for predicting treatment outcomes.* Unpublished dissertation. The Catholic University of America, Washington, DC.

Marion, M. S., & Range, L. M. (2003). Do extenuating circumstances influence African American women's attitudes toward suicide? *Suicide and Life-Threatening Behavior, 33,* 44–51.

Maris, R. W. (1981). *Pathways to suicide: A survey of self-destructive behaviors.* Baltimore: Johns Hopkins University Press.

Maris, R. W., Berman, A. L., & Maltsberger, J. T. (1992). Summary and conclusions: What have we learned about suicide assessment and prediction? In R. W. Maris, A. L. Berman, J. T. Maltsberger, & R. I. Yufit (Eds.), *Assessment and prediction of suicide* (pp. 640–672). New York: Guilford Press.

Maris, R. W., Berman, A. L., & Silverman, M. M. (2000). *Comprehensive textbook of suicidology.* New York: Guilford Press.

Marks, P. A., & Haller, D. L. (1977). Now I lay me down for keeps: A study of adolescent suicide attempts. *Journal of Clinical Psychology, 33,* 390–400.

Marsella, A. J., & Yamada, A. (2000). Culture and mental health: An introduction and overview of foundations, concepts, and issues. In I. Cuellar & F. A. Paniagua (Eds.), *Handbook of multicultural mental health: Assessment and treatment of diverse populations* (pp. 3–24). San Diego, CA: Academic Press.

Marshall, K. (1980). When a patient commits suicide. *Suicide and Life-Threatening Behavior, 10,* 29–40.

Martin, G., & Koo, L. (1996). Celebrity suicide: Did the death of Kurt Cobain influence young suicides in Australia? *Archives of Suicide Research, 3,* 187–198.

Martunnen, M., Aro, H., Henrikksson, M., & Lonnqvist, J. (1991). Mental disorders in adolescent suicide: *DSM III–R* axes I and II diagnoses in suicides among 13–19 year olds in Finland. *Archives of General Psychiatry, 48,* 834–839.

Martz, L. (1987, March 23). The copycat suicides. *Newsweek,* 28–29.

Marzuk, P. M., Tardiff, K., & Hirsch, C. S. (1992). The epidemiology of murder-suicide. *Journal of American Medical Association, 267,* 3179–3183.

Mattison, R. E. (1988). Suicide and other consequences of childhood and adolescent anxiety disorders. *Journal of Clinical Psychiatry, 49*(Suppl. 10), 9–11.

Maxim, K., & Brooks, C. (1985, April). Multi-impact family therapy: A therapeutic approach following a client's suicide (Abstract). In R. Cohen-Sandler (Ed.), *Proceedings of the Eighteenth Annual Meeting of the American Association of Suicidology* (pp. 106–109). Denver, CO: American Association of Suicidology.

May, P., Van Winkle, N. W., Williams, M. B., McFeeley, P. J., DeBruyn, L. M., & Serna, P. (2002). Alcohol and suicide death among American Indians of New Mexico: 1980–1998. *Suicide and Life-Threatening Behavior, 32,* 240–255.

Mazza, J. J., & Eggert, L. L. (2001). Activity involvement among suicidal and non-suicidal high-risk and typical adolescents. *Suicide and Life-Threatening Behavior, 31,* 265–281.

McAdams, C. R., & Foster, V. A. (2000). Client suicide: Its frequency and impact on counselors. *Journal of Mental Health Counseling, 22,* 107–122.

McBride, C. M., Curry, S. J., Cheadle, A., Anderman, C., Wanger, E. H., Diehr, P., et al. (1995). School-level application of a social bonding model to adolescent risk-taking behavior. *Journal of School Health, 65,* 63–68.

McCaffery, M., & Pasero, C. (1999). *Pain clinical manual.* New York: Mosby, Inc.

McCarthy, B. W., Wasserman, C. W., & Ferree, F. H. (1975). The growth and development of a university companion program. *Journal of Counseling Psychology, 22,* 66–69.

McIntosh, J. L. (1987). Suicide as a mental health problem: Epidemiologic aspects. In E. K. Dunne, J. L. McIntosh, & K. Dunne-Maxim (Eds.), *Suicide and its aftermath* (pp. 19–30). New York: Norton.

McIntosh, J. L. (1993). Control group studies of suicide survivors: A review and critique. *Suicide and Life-Threatening Behavior, 23,* 146–160.

McIntosh, J. L. (1996). Survivors of suicide: A comprehensive bibliography update, 1986–1995. *Omega, 33,* 147–175.

McIntosh, J. L., Albright, S., & Jones, F. A. (2002, April). *Therapist survivors: An AAS survey.* Poster presented at the annual conference of the American Association of Suicidology, Bethesda, MD.

McKenry, P. C., Tishler, C. L., & Kelly, C. (1983). The role of drugs in adolescent suicide attempts. *Suicide and Life-Threatening Behavior, 13,* 166–175.

McKeown, R. E., Garrison, C. Z., Cuffe, S. P., Waller, J. L., Jackson, K. L., & Addy, C. L. (1998). Incidence and predictors of suicidal behaviors in a longitudinal sample of young adolescents. *Journal of the American Academy of Child and Adolescent Psychiatry, 37,* 612–619.

McLeavey, B. C., Daly, J. D., Ludgate, J. W., & Murray, C. M. (1994). Interpersonal problem-solving skills training in the treatment of self-poisoning patients. *Suicide and Life-Threatening Behavior, 24,* 382–394.

McManus, B. L., Krues, M. J., Dontes, A. E., Defazio, C. R., Piotrowski, J. T., & Woodward, P. J. (1997). Child and adolescent suicide attempts: An opportunity for emergency departments to provide injury prevention education. *American Journal of Emergency Medicine, 15,* 357–360.

Meltzer, H. Y. (1999). Suicide in schizophrenia: Risk factors and clozapine treatment. *Journal of Clinical Psychiatry, 60*(Suppl. 12), 47–50.

Meltzer, H. Y., & Okayli, G. (1995). Reduction of suicidality during clozapine treatment of neuroleptic-resistant schizophrenia: Impact on risk-benefit assessment. *American Journal of Psychiatry, 152,* 183–190.

Menninger, K. (1938). *Man against himself.* New York: Harcourt Brace.

Mercy, J. A., Kresnow, M. J., O'Carroll, P. W., Lee, R. K., Powell, K. E., Potter, L. B., et al. (2001). Is suicide contagious? A study of the relation between exposure to the suicidal behavior of others and nearly lethal suicide attempts. *American Journal of Epidemiology, 154,* 120–127.

Middlebrook, D. L., LeMaster, P. L., Beals, J., Novins, D. K., & Manson, S. (2001). Suicide prevention in American Indian and Alaska Native communities: A critical review of programs. *Suicide and Life-Threatening Behavior, 31*(Suppl.), 132–149.

Miller, A. L. (1999). Dialectic behavior therapy: A new treatment approach for suicidal adolescents. *American Journal of Psychotherapy, 53,* 413–417.

Miller, A. L., Rathus, J. H., Linehan, M. M., Wetzler, S., & Leigh, E. (1997). Dialectical behavior therapy adapted for suicidal adolescents. *Journal of Practical Psychiatry and Behavioral Health, 3,* 78–86.

Miller, K. E., King, C. A., Shain, B. N., & Naylor, M. W. (1992). Suicidal adolescents' perceptions of their family environment. *Suicide and Life-Threatening Behavior, 22,* 226–239.

Miller, M. C. (1999). Suicide-prevention contracts: Advantages, disadvantages, and an alternative approach. In D. Jacobs (Ed.), *The Harvard Medical School guide to suicide assessment and intervention* (pp. 463–481). San Francisco: Jossey-Bass.

Miller, M. C., & Hemenway, D. (1999). The relationship between firearms and suicide: A review of the literature. *Aggression and Violent Behavior, 4*, 59–75.

Miller, M. C., Jacobs, D., & Gutheil, T. G. (1998). Talisman or taboo: The controversy of the suicide-prevention contract. *Harvard Review of Psychiatry, 6*, 78–87.

Miner, J. R. (1922). Suicide and its relation to climatic and other factors. *American Journal of Hygiene Monographs* (Series No. 2).

Minuchin, S. (1974). *Families and family therapy.* Cambridge, MA: Harvard University Press.

Mitchell, P. (2000). *Valuing young lives: Evaluation of the national youth suicide prevention strategy.* Melbourne, Commonwealth of Australia: Australian Institute of Family Studies.

Modestin, J. (1987). Counter-transference reactions contributing to completed suicide. *British Journal of Medical Psychology, 60*, 379–385.

Mohler, B., & Earls, F. (2001). Trends in adolescent suicide: Misclassification bias? *American Journal of Public Health, 91*, 150–153.

Molock, S. D. (2003). *Role of first responders: Responses of African American churches to suicide survivors.* Presentation at NIMH/NIH Office of Rare Diseases and the American Foundation for Suicide Prevention's Survivors of Suicide Research Workshop, Washington, DC.

Montgomery, S. A. (1997). Suicide and antidepressants. *Annals of New York Academy of Science, 836*, 329–338.

Montgomery, S. A., Dunner, D. L., & Dunbar, G. C. (1995). Reduction of suicidal thoughts with patoxetine in comparison with reference antidepressants and placebo. *European Neuropsychopharmacology, 5*, 5–13.

Morrell, S., Page, A., & Taylor, R. (2003). Birth cohort effects in New South Wales suicide, 1865–1998. *Acta Psychiatrica Scandinavica, 107*, 160.

Morris, W. (1973). *The American heritage dictionary of the English language.* Boston: Houghton Mifflin.

Moscicki, E. K. (1995). Suicide in childhood and adolescence. In F. C. Verhulst & H. M. Kult (Eds.), *The epidemiology of childhood and adolescent psychopathology* (pp. 291–308). New York: Oxford University Press.

Motto, J. A. (1983). Clinical implications of moral theory regarding suicide. *Suicide and Life-Threatening Behavior, 13*, 304–312.

Motto, J. A. (1984). Suicide in male adolescents. In H. S. Sudak, A. B. Ford, & N. B. Rushforth (Eds.), *Suicide in the young* (pp. 227–244). Boston: John Wright-PSG Inc..

Mufson, L., Moreau, D., Weissman, M. M., & Klerman, G. L. (1993). *Interpersonal psychotherapy for depressed adolescents.* New York: Guilford Press.

Mufson, L., Moreau, D., Weissman, M. M., Wickramaratne, P., Martin, J., & Samoilov, A. (1994). Modification of interpersonal psychotherapy with depressed adolescents (IPT-A): Phase I and Phase II studies. *Journal of the American Academy of Child and Adolescent Psychiatry, 33,* 695–705.

Mufson, L., Weissman, M. M., Moreau, D., & Garfinkel, R. (1999). Efficacy of interpersonal psychotherapy for depressed adolescents. *Archives of General Psychiatry, 56,* 573–579.

Müller-Oerlinghausen, B., Müser-Causemann, B., & Volk, J. (1992). Suicides and parasuicides in a high risk patient group on and off lithium long-term medication. *Journal of Affective Disorders, 25,* 261–270.

Murphy, G. E. (1983). On suicide prediction and prevention. *Archives of General Psychiatry, 40,* 343–344.

Murphy, G. E., & Wetzel, R. (1982). Family history of suicidal behaviour among suicide attempters. *Journal of Nervous and Mental Diseases, 170,* 86–90.

Murray, H. A. (1938). *Explorations in personality.* New York: Oxford University Press.

Nathan, P. (1998). Practice guidelines: Not yet ideal. *American Psychologist, 53,* 290–299.

National Association of Social Workers. (1999). *Code of ethics of the National Association of Social Workers.* Washington, DC: Author.

National Center for Chronic Disease Prevention and Health Promotion. (2004). *YRBSS: Youth risk behavior surveillance system.* Retrieved June 16, 2005, from http://www.cdc.gov/HealthyYouth/YRBS/

National Center for Health Statistics. (2001). *DHHS, Mortality Statistics Branch. Annual summary.* Hyattsville, MD: U.S. Public Health Service.

National Center for Injury Prevention and Control. (2005). *WISQARS fatal injuries: Mortality reports.* Retrieved June 16, 2005, from http://webapp.cdc.gov/sasweb/ncipc/mortrate.html

Negron, R., Piacentini, J., Graae, F., Davies, M., & Shaffer, D. (1997). Microanalysis of adolescent suicide attempters and ideators during the acute suicidal episode. *Journal of the American Academy of Child and Adolescent Psychiatry, 36,* 1512–1519.

Nelson, F. L., Farberow, N. L., & MacKinnon, D. R. (1978). The certification of suicide in eleven western states. *Suicide and Life-Threatening Behavior, 8,* 75–88.

Ness, D. E., & Pfeffer, C. R. (1990). Sequelae of bereavement resulting from suicide. *American Journal of Psychiatry, 147,* 279–285.

Neuringer, C. (1964). Rigid thinking in suicidal individuals. *Journal of Consulting and Clinical Psychology, 76,* 91–100.

Neuringer, C. (1976). Current developments in the study of suicidal thinking. In E. S. Shneidman (Ed.), *Suicidology: Contemporary developments* (pp. 229–252). New York: Grune & Stratton.

New Freedom Commission on Mental Health. (2003). *Achievinig the promise: Transforming mental health care in America. Final report.* DHHS Pub. No. SMA-03-3832, Rockville, MD.

Newman, S. C., & Dyck, R. J. (1988, May). *Age, period, cohort analyses of suicide rates.* Paper presented at the annual meeting of the American Association of Suicidology, San Francisco, CA.

Nielson, D. A., Goldman, D., Virkkunen, M., Tokola, R., Rawlings, R., & Linnoila, M. (1994). Suicidality and 5-hydroxindoleactic acid concentration associate with a tryptophan hydroxylase polymorphism. *Archives of General Psychiatry, 51,* 34–38.

NMHA/Jed Foundation. (2002). *Safeguarding your students against suicide. Expanding the safety net.* Alexandria, VA: NMHA.

Norton, E. M., Durlak, J. A., & Richards, M. H. (1989). Peer knowledge of and reactions to adolescent suicide. *Journal of Youth and Adolescence, 18,* 427–437.

Novaco, R. (1979). The cognitive-behavioral regulation of anger. In P. C. Kendall & S. D. Hollon (Eds.), *Cognitive-behavioral interventions: Theory, research and procedures* (pp. 241–286). New York: Academic Press.

Nunno, K. M., Jobes, D. A., Peterson, E. M., Pentiuc, D., & Kiernan, A. (2002, April). *A qualitative examination of suicide status form variables.* Paper presented at the annual conference of the American Association of Suicidology, Washington, DC.

NYU shaken by suicide jumpers at Bobst Library. (2003, October 20). *American Libraries online.* Retrieved June 20, 2005, from http://www.ala.org/al_onlineTemplate.cfm?Section=aloct03&Template=/ContentManagement/ContentDisplay.cfm&ContentID=46918

O'Carroll, P. W. (1989). A consideration of the validity and reliability of suicide mortality data. *Suicide and Life-Threatening Behavior, 19,* 1–16.

O'Carroll, P. W., Berman, A. L., Maris, R. W., Moscicki, E. K., Tanney, B. L., & Silverman, M. (1996). Beyond the tower of Babel: A nomenclature for suicidology. *Suicide and Life-Threatening Behavior, 26,* 237–252.

O'Carroll, P. W., & Potter, L. B. (1994) Suicide contagion and the reporting of suicide: Recommendations from a national workshop. *Morbidity and Mortality Weekly Report, 43,* 9–18.

O'Connor, R. C., O'Connor, D. B, O'Connor, S. M., Smallwood, J., & Miles, J. (2004). Hopelessness, stress, and perfectionism: The moderating effects of future thinking. *Cognitions and Emotion, 18,* 1099–1120.

Offer, D. (1987). In defense of adolescents. *Journal of the American Medical Association, 257,* 3407–3408.

Offer, D., & Schonert-Reichel, K. A. (1992). Debunking the myths of adolescence: Findings from recent research. *American Journal of Child and Adolescent Psychiatry, 31,* 1003–1014.

Ohring, R., Apter, A., Ratzoni, G., Weizman, R., Tyano, S., & Plutchik, R. (1996). State and trait anxiety in adolescent suicide attempters. *Journal of the American Academy of Child and Adolescent Psychiatry, 35,* 154–157.

Olfson, M., Marcus, S. C., Druss, B., Elinson, L., Tanielian, T., & Pincus, H. A. (2002). National trends in the outpatient treatment of depression. *Journal of the American Medical Association, 287,* 203–209.

Olfson, M., Marcus, S. C., Druss, B., & Pincus, H. A. (2002). National trends in the use of outpatient psychotherapy. *American Journal of Psychiatry, 159,* 1914–1920.

Olfson, M., Marcus, S. C., Druss, B., Pincus, A. H., & Weissman, M. M. (2003). Parental depression, child mental health problems, and health care utilization. *Medical Care, 41,* 716–721.

Olfson, M., Marcus, S. C., Pincus, H. A., Zito, J. M., Thompson, J. W., & Zarin, D. A. (1998). Antidepressant prescribing practices of outpatient psychiatrists. *Archives of General Psychiatry, 55,* 310–316.

Olfson, M., Marcus, S. C., Weissman, M. M., & Jensen, P. S. (2002). National trends in the use of psychotropic medications by children. *Journal of American Academy of Child and Adolescent Psychiatry, 41,* 514–521.

Olfson, M., Shaffer, D., Marcus, S. C., Greenberg, T. (2003). Relationship between antidepressant medication treatment and suicide in adolescents. *Archives of General Psychiatry, 60,* 978–982.

Orbach, I., Kedem, P., Gorchover, O., Apter, A., & Tyano, S. (1993). Fears of death in suicidal and nonsuicidal adolescents. *Journal of Abnormal Psychology, 102,* 553–558.

Orbach, I., Mikulincer, M., Sirota, P., & Gilboa-Schechtman, E. (2003). Mental pain: A multidimensional operationalization and definition. *Suicide and Life-Threatening Behavior, 33,* 219–230.

Orbach, I., Rosenheim, E., & Hary, E. (1987). Some aspects of cognitive functioning in suicidal children. *Journal of the American Academy of Child and Adolescent Psychiatry, 26,* 181–185.

Oregon State Health Division, Center for Health Statistics. (2000). *Oregon vital statistics report* (Vol. 2). Portland, OR: Author.

Osman, A., Kópper, B., Barrios, F., Osman, J., Besett, T., & Linehan, M. (1996). The Brief Reasons for Living Inventory for Adolescents (BRFL-A). *Journal of Abnormal Child Psychology, 24,* 433–443.

Ostroff, R., Giller, E., Bonese, K., Ebersole, E., Harkness, L., & Mason, J. (1982). Neuroendocrine risk factors of suicidal behavior. *American Journal of Psychiatry, 139,* 1323–1325.

Overholser, J. (2003). Predisposing factors in suicide attempts: Life stressors. In A. Spirito & J. C. Overholser (Eds.), *Evaluating and treating adolescent suicide attempters: From research to practice* (pp. 41–52). San Diego, CA: Academic Press.

Overholser, J., Freheit, S. R., & DiFilippo, J. M. (1997). Emotional distress and substance abuse as risk factors for suicide attempts. *Canadian Journal of Psychiatry, 42,* 402–408.

Overholser, J., & Spirito, J. (2003). Precursors to adolescent suicide attempts. In A. Spirito & J. C. Overholser (Eds.), *Evaluating and treating adolescent suicide attempters: From research to practice* (pp. 19–40). San Diego, CA: Academic Press.

Papadimitriou, G., Linkowski, P., Delabre, C., & Medeleuicz, J. (1991). Suicide on the paternal and maternal sides of depressed patients with a lifetime history of suicide. *Acta Psychiatrica Scandinavica, 83*, 417–419.

Peck, D. L. (1986). Completed suicides: Correlates of choice of method. *Omega, 16*, 309–323.

Peck, M. L. (1985). Crisis intervention treatment with chronically and acutely suicidal adolescents. In M. L. Peck, N. L. Farberow, & R. E. Litman (Eds.), *Youth suicide* (pp. 112–122). New York: Springer.

Perry, C. L., Williams, C. L., Komro, K. A., Veblen-Mortenson, S., Forster, J. L., Bernstein-Lachter, R., et al. (2000). Project northland high school interventions: Community action to reduce adolescent alcohol use. *Health Education Behavior, 27*, 29–49.

Peruzzi, N., & Bongar, B. (1999). Assessing risk for completed suicide in patients with major depression: Psychologists' views of critical factors. *Professional Psychology: Research and Practice, 30*, 576–580.

Pescosolido, B. A., & Mendelsohn, R. (1986). Social causation or social construction of suicide? An investigation into the social organization of official rates. *American Sociological Review, 51*, pp. 81–100.

Peterson, A. C., & Taylor, B. (1980). The biological approach to adolescence: Biological change and psychological adaptation. In J. Adelson (Ed.), *Handbook of adolescent psychology* (pp. 117–155). New York: Wiley.

Peterson, E. M., Luoma, J. B., & Dunne, E. (2002). Suicide survivors' perceptions of the treating clinician. *Suicide and Life-Threatening Behavior, 32*, 158–166.

Petzel, S. V., & Riddle, M. (1981). Adolescent suicide: Psychosocial and cognitive aspects. *Adolescent Psychiatry, 9*, 342–398.

Pfeffer, C. R. (1986). *The suicidal child.* New York: Guilford Press.

Pfeffer, C. R. (1989). Studies of suicidal preadolescent and adolescent inpatients: A critique of research methods. *Suicide and Life-Threatening Behavior, 19*, 58–77.

Pfeffer, C. R. (1990). Clinical perspectives on treatment of suicidal behavior among children and adolescents. *Psychiatric Annals, 20*, 143–150.

Pfeffer, C. R., Conte, H. R., Plutchik, R., & Jerrett, I. (1980). Suicide behavior in latency-age children: An outpatient population. *Journal of the American Academy of Child and Adolescent Psychiatry, 19*, 703–710.

Pfeffer, C. R., Plutchik, R., & Mizruchi, M. S. (1983). Suicidal and assaultive behavior in children: Classification, measurement, and interrelations. *American Journal of Psychiatry, 140*, 154–157.

Phillips, D. P. (1985). The Werther effect. *The Sciences, 25*, 33–39.

Phillips, D. P., & Feldman, K. (1973). A dip in deaths before ceremonial occasions. *American Sociological Review, 38*, 678–696.

Phillips, D., & Paight, D. J. (1987). The impact of televised movies about suicide: A replicative study. *New England Journal of Medicine, 317*, 809–811.

Phillips, D. P., & Ruth, T. E. (1993). Adequacy of official suicide statistics for scientific research and public policy. *Suicide and Life-Threatening Behavior, 23*, 307–319.

Piacentini, J., Rotheram-Borus, M. J., Gillis, J. R., Graae, F., Trautman, P., Cantwell, C., et al. (1995). Demographic predictors of treatment attendance among adolescent suicide attempters. *Journal of Consulting and Clinical Psychology, 63,* 469–473.

Plutchik, R., van Praag, H. M., & Conte, H. R. (1989). Correlates of suicide and violence risk: III. A two stage model of countervailing forces. *Psychiatry Research, 28,* 215–225.

Pokorny, A. D. (1983). Prediction of suicide in psychiatric patients. *Archives of General Psychiatry, 40,* 249–257.

Pope, K. S. (1989). Malpractice suits, licensing disciplinary actions, and ethics cases: Frequencies, causes, and costs. *The Independent Practitioner, 9,* 22–26.

Poteet, D. J. (1987). Adolescent suicide: A review of 87 cases of completed suicide in Shelby County, TN. *American Journal of Forensic Medicine and Pathology, 8,* 12–17.

Potter, L., Powell, K. E., & Kachur, P. S. (1995). Suicide prevention from a public health perspective. *Suicide and Life-Threatening Behavior, 25,* 82–91.

Qin, P., Agerbo, E., & Mortenson, P. B. (2003). Suicide risk in relation to socioeconomic, demographic, psychiatric, and familial risk factors: A national register-based study of all suicides in Denmark, 1981–1997. *American Journal of Psychiatry, 160,* 765–772.

Quinn, J. (1999). Where need meets opportunity: Youth development programs for early teens. *Future of Children, 9,* 96–116.

Rachlin, S. (1984). Double jeopardy: Suicide and malpractice. *General Hospital Psychiatry, 6,* 302–307.

Randell, B. P., Eggert, L. L., & Pike, K. C. (2001). Immediate post intervention effects of two brief youth suicide prevention interventions. *Suicide and Life-Threatening Behavior, 31,* 41–61.

Range, L. (1998). When a loss is due to suicide: Unique aspects of bereavement. In J. H. Harvey (Ed.), *Perspectives on loss: A sourcebook on death, dying, and bereavement* (pp. 213–220). Philadelphia: Brunner/Mazel.

Range, L. M., & Knott, E. C. (1997). Twenty suicide assessment instruments: evaluation and recommendations. *Death Studies, 21,* 25–58.

Rathus, J. H., & Miller, A. L. (2002). Dialectical behavior therapy adapted for suicidal adolescents. *Suicidal and Life-Threatening Behavior, 32,* 146–157.

Reed, M. D. (1998). Predicting grief symptomatology among the suddenly bereaved. *Suicide and Life-Threatening Behavior, 28,* 285–300.

Rehm, L. (1987). Approaches to the prevention of depression with children: A self-management perspective. In R. F. Munoz (Ed.), *Depression prevention: Research directions* (pp. 79–91). Washington, DC: Hemisphere Publication Services.

Reid, W. H. (1998): Promises, promises: Don't rely on patients' no-suicide/no-violence "contract." *Journal of Practical Psychiatry and Behavioral Health, 4,* 316–318.

Reinherz, H. Z., Giaconia, R. M., Silverman, A. B., Friedman, A., Pakiz, B., Frost, A. K., et al. (1995). Early psychosocial risks for adolescent suicidal ideation and attempts. *Journal of the American Academy of Child and Adolescent Psychiatry, 34,* 599–611.

Remafedi, G. (1998). The University of Minnesota Youth and AIDS Projects' Adolescent Early Intervention Program: a model to link HIV-seropositive youth with care. *Journal of Adolescent Health, 23,* 115–121.

Renberg, E. S., & Jacobsson, L. (2003). Development of a questionnaire on attitudes towards suicide (ATTS) and its application in a Swedish population. *Suicide and Life-Threatening Behavior, 33,* 52–64.

Resnick, M. D. (2000). Protective factors, resiliency, and healthy youth development. *Adolescent Medicine: State of the Art Reviews, 11,* 157–164.

Resnick, M. D., Bearman, P. S., Blum, W. R., Bauman, K. E., Harris, K. M., Jones, J., et al. (1997). Protecting adolescents from harm: Findings from the national longitudinal study on adolescent health. *Journal of the American Medical Association, 278,* 823–832.

Reynolds, F. M. T., & Cimbolic, P. (1988–1989). Attitudes toward suicide survivors as a function of survivors' relationship to the victim. *Omega, 19,* 125–133.

Reynolds, P., & Eaton, P. (1986). Multiple attempters of suicide presenting at an emergency department. *Canadian Journal of Psychiatry, 31,* 328–330.

Reynolds, W. M., & Coats, K. I. (1986). A comparison of cognitive-behavioral therapy and relaxation training for the treatment of depression. *Journal of Consulting and Clinical Psychology, 54,* 653–660.

Reynolds, W. M., & Mazza, J. J. (1994). Suicide and suicidal behaviors in children and adolescents. In W. W. Reynolds & H. F. Johnston (Eds.), *Handbook of depression in children and adolescents* (pp. 525–580). New York: Plenum Press.

Rich, C. L. (1986). Endocrinology and suicide. *Suicide and Life-Threatening Behavior, 16,* 219–229.

Rich, C. L., Young, D., & Fowler, R. C. (1986). San Diego suicide study I: Young vs. old subjects. *Archives of General Psychiatry, 43,* 577–582.

Rich, C. L., Young, D., Fowler, R. C., & Rosenfeld, S. K. S. (1984, May). *The difference between data of suicide act and recorded death certificate date in 204 consecutive suicides.* Paper presented at the annual meeting of the American Association of Suicidology, Anchorage, AK.

Richman, J. (1984). The family therapy of suicidal adolescents: Promises and pitfalls. In H. S. Sudak, A. B. Ford, & N. B. Rushforth (Eds.), *Suicide in the young* (pp. 393–406). Boston: John Wright-PSG Inc.

Richman, J. (1986). *Family therapy for suicidal people.* New York: Springer.

Robbins, D., & Conroy, R. (1983). A cluster of adolescent suicide attempts: Is suicide contagious? *Journal of Adolescent Health Care, 3,* 253–255.

Roberts, A. (1991). *Contemporary perspectives on crisis intervention and prevention.* Englewood Cliffs, NJ: Prentice-Hall.

Robins, E. (1981). *The final months.* New York: Oxford University Press.

Robins, L. N., & Kulbok, P. A. (1986). Methodological strategies in suicide. *New York Academy of Sciences, 487,* 1–15.

Robins, L. N., & Kulbok, P. A. (1988). Epidemiological studies in suicide. *Psychiatric Annals, 18,* 619–627.

Robins, S., & Novaco, R. W. (1999). Systems conceptualization and treatment of anger. *Journal of Clinical Psychology, 55,* 325–337.

Rogers, J. R. (2001). Theoretical grounding: The "missing link" in suicide research. *Journal of Counseling and Development, 79,* 16–25.

Rosen, A. (1959). Detection of suicidal patients: An example of some limitations in the prediction of infrequent events. *Journal of Consulting Psychology, 18,* 397–405.

Rosenberg, M. (1999, April). *Toward the year 2000: Suicide prevention—a public health perspective.* Keynote address at the annual conference of the American Association of Suicidology, Houston, TX.

Rosenberg, M. L., Mercy, J. A., & Houk, V. N. (1991). Guns and adolescent suicides. *Journal of the American Medical Association, 266,* 2989–2995.

Rosenberg, M. L., Smith, J. C., Davidson, L. E., & Conn, J. M. (1987). The emergence of youth suicide: An epidemiologic analysis and public health perspective. *Annual Review of Public Health, 8,* 417–440.

Rosenblatt, P. C., Jackson, D. A., & Walsh, R. P. (1972). Coping with anger and aggression in mourning. *Omega, 3,* 271–284.

Rosenstock, H. A. (1985). The first 900: A 9 year longitudinal analysis of consecutive adolescent inpatients. *Adolescent, 20,* 959–973.

Ross, C. P., & Motto, J. A. (1984). Group counseling for suicidal adolescents. In H. S. Sudak, A. B. Ford, & N. B. Rushforth (Eds.), *Suicide in the young* (pp. 367–392). Boston: John Wright-PSG Inc.

Rotheram, M. J. (1987). Evaluation of imminent danger for suicide among youth. *American Journal of Orthopsychiatry, 57,* 102–110.

Rotherham-Borus, M. J. (1993). Suicidal behavior and risk factors among runaway youths. *American Journal of Psychiatry, 150,* 103–107.

Rotheram-Borus, M. J., Piacentini, J., Cantwell, C., Belin, T. R., & Juwon, S. (2000). The 18-month impact of an emergency room intervention for adolescent female suicide attempters. *Journal of Consulting and Clinical Psychology, 68,* 1081–1093.

Rotheram-Borus, M. J., Piacentini, J., Miller, S., Graee, F., & Castro-Blanco, D. (1994). Brief cognitive-behavioral treatment for adolescent suicide attempters and their families. *Journal of the American Academy of Child and Adolescent Psychiatry, 33,* 508–517.

Rotheram-Borus, M. J., Piacentini, J., Miller, S., Graae, F., & Castro-Blanco, D. (1996). Toward improving treatment adherence among adolescent suicide attempters. *Clinical Child Psychology and Psychiatry, 1,* 99–108.

Rotheram-Borus, M. J., Piacentini, J., Van Rossem, R., Graee, F., Cantwell, C., Castro-Blanco, et al. (1996). Enhancing treatment adherence with a specialized emergency room program for adolescent suicide attempters. *Journal of the American Academy of Child and Adolescent Psychiatry, 35,* 654–663.

Rotheram-Borus, M. J., & Trautman, P. D. (1988). Hopelessness, depression and suicidal intent among adolescent suicide attempters. *Journal of the American Academy of Child and Adolescent Psychiatry, 27,* 700–704.

Roy, A. (1983). Family history of suicide. *Archives of General Psychiatry, 40,* 971–974.

Roy, A., & Seigel, N. (2001). Suicidal behavior in twins: A replication. *Journal of Affective Disorders, 66,* 71–74.

Rubenstein, J. L., Heeren, T., Housman, D., Rubin, C., & Stechler, G. (1989). Suicidal behavior in "normal" adolescents: Risk and protective factors. *American Journal of Orthopsychiatry, 59,* 59–71.

Rudd, M. D. (1989). The prevalence of suicidal ideation among college students. *Suicide and Life-Threatening Behavior, 19,* 173–183.

Rudd, M. D. (1998). An integrative conceptual and organizational framework for treating suicidal behavior. *Psychotherapy: Theory, Research, Practice, Training, 35,* 346–360.

Rudd, M. D. (2000). Integrating science into the practice of clinical suicidology: A review of the psychotherapy literature and a research agenda for the future. In R. W. Maris, S. S. Canetto, J. McIntosh, & M. M. Silverman (Eds.), *Review of Suicidology 2000* (pp. 47–67). New York: Guilford Press.

Rudd, M. D. (2003). *Rethinking hopelessness: The suicide cognitions scale.* Unpublished manuscript.

Rudd, M. D., Dahm, P., & Rajab, H. (1993). Diagnostic comorbidity in persons with suicidal ideation and behavior. *American Journal of Psychiatry, 150,* 928–934.

Rudd, M. D., & Joiner, T. E. (1998): The assessment, management, and treatment of suicidality: Towards clinically informed and balanced standards of care. *Clinical Psychology: Science and Practice, 5,* 135–150.

Rudd, M. D., Joiner, T. E., Jobes, D. A., & King, C. A. (1999). The outpatient treatment of suicidality. An integration of science and recognition of its limitations. *Professional Psychology: Research and Practice, 30,* 437–446.

Rudd, M. D., Joiner, T. E., & Rajab, H. (1996). Relationships among suicide ideators, attempters, and multiple attempters in a young adult sample. *Journal of Abnormal Psychology, 105,* 541–550.

Rudd, M. D., Joiner, T. E., & Rajab, H. (2001). *Treating suicidal behavior: An effective time-limited approach.* New York: Guilford Press.

Rudd, M. D., Rajab, H., Orman, D. T., Stulman, D. A., Joiner, T. E., & Dixon, W. (1996). Effectiveness of outpatient problem-solving intervention targeting suicidal young adults: Preliminary results. *Journal of Consulting and Clinical Psychology, 64,* 179–190.

Runeson, B. (1989). Mental disorder in youth suicide. *Acta Psychiatrica Scandinavica, 79,* 490–497.

Rush, A. J., & Beck, A. T. (1978). Cognitive therapy of depression and suicide. *American Journal of Psychotherapy, 32*, 201–219.

Russel, S. T., & Joyner, K. (2001). Adolescent sexual orientation and suicide risk: Evidence from a national study. *American Journal of Public Health, 91*, 1276–1281.

Rustad, R. A., Small, J. E., Jobes, D. A., Safer, M. A., & Peterson, R. J. (2003). The impact of rock music videos and music with suicidal content on thoughts and attitudes about suicide. *Suicide and Life-Threatening Behavior, 33*, 120–131.

Ryerson, D. (1990). Suicide awareness education in schools: The development of a core program and subsequent modifications for special populations or institutions. *Death Studies, 14*, 371–390.

Sabbath, J. C. (1969). The suicidal adolescent—the expendable child. *Journal of American Academy of Child Psychiatry, 8*, 272–289.

Sager, M. (2003, October 1). The man of tomorrow goes to the prom. *Esquire, 140*, 140–148.

Sainsbury, P. (1955). *Suicide in London*. London: Chapman & Hall.

Sainsbury, P., & Jenkins, J. S. (1982). The accuracy of officially reported suicide statistics for purposes of epidemiological research. *Journal of Epidemiological and Community Health, 36*, 43–48.

Salkovskis, P. M. (1996). *Frontiers of cognitive therapy*. New York: Guilford Press.

Salkovskis, P. M. (2001). Psychological treatment of suicidal patients. In D. Wasserman (Ed.), *Suicide: An unnecessary death* (pp. 161–172). London: Martin Dunitz.

Salzman, C., Wolfson, A. N., Schatzberg, A., Looper, J., Henke, R., Albanese, M., et al. (1995). Effect of fluoxetine on anger in symptomatic volunteers with borderline personality disorder. *Journal of Clinical Psychopharmacology 15*, 23–29.

Sanchez, L. E., & Le, L. T. (2001). Suicide in mood disorders. *Depression and Anxiety, 14*, 177–182.

Sanddal, N. D., Sanddal, T. L., Berman, A. L., & Silverman, M. M. (2003). General systems approach to suicide prevention: Lessons from cardiac prevention and control. *Suicide and Life-Threatening Behavior, 33*, 341–352.

Sartre, J. P. (1956). *Being and nothingness*. New York: Pocket Books.

Schein, H. M. (1976). Suicide care: Obstacles in the education of psychiatric residents. *Omega, 7*, 75–82.

Schmid, C. F. (1928). *Suicide in Seattle, 1914 to 1925*. Seattle: University of Washington Publications in the Social Sciences.

Schmidtke, A., & Schaller, S. (2000). The role of mass media in suicide prevention. In K. Hawton & K. van Heeringen (Eds.), *The international handbook of suicidology and attempted suicide* (pp. 675–697). Chichester, England: Wiley.

Schou, M. (1999). Perspectives on lithium treatment of bipolar disorder: Action, efficacy, effect on suicidal behavior. *Bipolar Disorder, 9*, 5–10.

Segal, Z. V., Williams, J. M. G., & Teasdale, J. D. (2002). *Mindfulness-based cognitive therapy for depression*. New York: Guilford Press.

Seguin, M., Lesage, A., & Kiely, M. C. (1995). Parental bereavement after suicide and accident: A comparative study. *Suicide and Life-Threatening Behavior, 25*, 489–499.

Seiden, R. H. (1969). *Suicide among youth: A review of the literature, 1900–1967* [Suppl. to the Bulletin of Suicidology]. Washington, DC: U.S. Government Printing Office.

Seiden, R. H. (1983). Death in the West: A spatial analysis of the youthful suicide rate. *Western Journal of Medicine, 139*, 783–795.

Shaffer, D., & Bacon, K. (1989). A critical review of preventive efforts in suicide, with particular reference to youth suicide. In *Alcohol, Drug Abuse, and Mental Health Administration, Report of the Secretary's Task Force on Youth Suicide: Vol. 3. Prevention and interventions in youth suicide* (DHHS Publication No. ADM 89-1623, pp. 31–61). Washington, DC: U.S. Government Printing Office.

Shaffer, D., & Croft, L. (1999). Methods of adolescent suicide prevention. *Journal of Clinical Psychiatry, 60*, 70–74.

Shaffer, D., Garland, A., Gould, M., Fisher, P., & Trautman, P. (1988). Preventing teenage suicide: A critical review. *Journal of the American Academy of Child and Adolescent Psychiatry, 27*, 675–687.

Shaffer, D., Garland, A., Vieland, V., Underwood, M. M., & Busner, C. (1991). The impact of a curriculum-based suicide prevention program for teenagers. *Journal of American Academy of Child and Adolescent Psychiatry, 27*, 675–687.

Shaffer, D., Garland, A., & Whittle, B. (1988, March). *An evaluation of youth suicide prevention programs. New Jersey adolescent suicide prevention project.* Final project report, New Jersey Division of Mental Health and Hospitals, Trenton, NJ.

Shaffer, D., & Gould, M. (1987). *A study of completed and attempted suicide in adolescents* (Progress report, Grant No. MH 38198). Rockville, MD: National Institute of Mental Health.

Shaffer, D., Gould, M. S., Fisher, P., Trautman, P., Moreau, D., Kleinman, M., et al. (1996). Psychiatric diagnosis in child and adolescent suicide. *Archives of General Psychiatry, 53*, 339–348.

Shaffer, D., & Pfeffer, C. R. (2001). Practice parameter for the assessment and treatment of children and adolescents with suicidal behavior. *Journal of the American Academy of Child and Adolescent Psychiatry, 40*(Suppl.), 4S–23S.

Shaffer, D., Wilcox, H., Lucas, C., Hicks, R., Busner, C., & Parides, M. (1996, October). *The development of a screening instrument for teens at risk for suicide.* Poster presented at the meeting of the American Academy of Child and Adolescent Psychiatry, NY.

Shafii, M., Carrigan, S., Whittinghill, J. R., & Derrick, A. (1985). Psychological autopsy of completed suicide in children and adolescents. *American Journal of Psychiatry, 142*, 1061–1064.

Shafii, M., & Shafii, S. L. (1982). Self-destructive, suicidal behavior, and completed suicide. In M. Shafii & S. L. Shafii (Eds.), *Pathways of human development: Normal growth and emotional disorders in infancy, childhood and adolescence* (pp. 164–180). New York: Thieme-Stratton.

Shafii, M., Steltz-Lenarsky, J., Derrick, A. M., Beckner, C., & Whittinghill, J. R. (1988). Co-morbidity of mental disorders in the post-mortem diagnosis of completed suicide in children and adolescents. *Journal of Affective Disorders, 15*, 227–233.

Shapiro, E. R., & Freedman, J. (1987). Family dynamics of adolescent suicide. *Adolescent Psychiatry, 14*, 271–290.

Shea, S. C. (1999). *The practical art of suicide assessment.* New York: Wiley.

Shenassa, E. D., Catlin, S. N., & Buka, S. L. (2003). Lethality of firearms relative to other suicide methods: A population based study. *Journal of Epidemiology and Community Health, 57*, 120–124.

Sherman, M., & Thelen, M. (1998). Distress and professional impairment among psychologists in clinical practice. *Professional Psychology: Research and Practice, 29*, 79–85.

Shiang, J. (2000). Considering cultural beliefs and behaviors in the study of suicide. In R. W. Maris, S. S. Canetto, J. L. McIntosh, & M. M. Silverman (Eds.), *Review of suicidology 2000* (pp. 226–241). New York: Guilford Press.

Shneidman, E. S. (1967). *Bulletin of suicidology (No. 1).* Rockville, MD: The National Institute of Mental Health Center for Studies of Suicide Prevention.

Shneidman, E. S. (1980). Suicide. In E. S. Shneidman (Ed.), *Death: Current perspectives* (pp. 416–434). Palo Alto, CA: Mayfield Publishing.

Shneidman, E. S. (1985). *Definition of suicide.* New York: Wiley.

Shneidman, E. S. (1988). Some reflections of a founder. *Suicide and Life-Threatening Behavior, 18*, 1–12.

Shneidman, E. S. (1992). A conspectus of the suicidal scenario. In R. W. Maris, A. L. Berman, J. T. Maltsberger, & R. I. Yufit (Eds.), *The assessment and prediction of suicide* (pp. 50–64). New York: Guilford Press.

Shneidman, E. S. (1993). *Suicide as psychache: A clinical approach to self-destructive behavior.* Northvale, NJ: Aronson.

Shneidman, E. S. (1996). *The suicidal mind.* New York: Oxford University Press.

Shneidman, E. S. (1995). *Definition of suicide.* New York: Wiley.

Shneidman, E. S. (1999). The psychological pain assessment scale. *Suicide and Life-Threatening Behavior, 29*, 287–294.

Shneidman, E. S. (2001). *Comprehending suicide: Landmarks in 20th-century suicidology.* Washington, DC: American Psychological Association.

Shneidman, E. S., & Farberow, N. L. (1957). Some comparisons between genuine and simulated suicide notes in terms of Mower's concepts of discomfort and relief. *Journal of General Psychology, 56*, 251–256.

Shneidman, E. S., & Farberow, N. L. (1961). Suicide—The problem and its magnitude. *Medical Bulletin of the Veterans Administration, 7*, 11.

Silk, K. R., & Yager, J. (2003). Suggested guidelines for e-mail communication in psychiatric practice. *Journal of Clinical Psychiatry, 64*, 799–806.

Silverman, E., Range, L., & Overholser, J. (1994–1995). Bereavement from suicide as compared to other forms of bereavement. *Omega, 30*, 41–51.

Silverman, M. M. (1996). Approaches to suicide prevention: A focus on models. In R. F. Ramsay & B. L. Tanney (Eds.), *Global trends in suicide prevention: Toward the development of national strategies for suicide prevention* (pp. 25–94). Mumbai, India: Tata Institute of Social Sciences.

Silverman, M. M., Davidson, L., & Potter, L. (2001). National suicide prevention conference background papers. *Suicide and Life-Threatening Behavior, 31,* 1–149.

Silverman, M. M., & Felner, R. D. (1995). Suicide prevention programs: Issues of design, implementation, feasibility, and developmental appropriateness. *Suicide and Life-Threatening Behavior, 25,* 92–104.

Silverman, M. M., & Koretz, D. S. (1989). Preventing mental health problems. In R. E. Stein (Ed.), *Caring for children with chronic illness: Issues and strategies* (pp. 213–229). New York: Springer Publishing Company.

Silverman, M. M., & Maris, R. W. (1995). The prevention of suicidal behaviors: An overview. In M. M. Silverman & R. W. Maris (Eds.), *Suicide prevention: Toward the year 2000* (pp. 10–21). New York: Guilford Press.

Silverman, M. M., Meyer, P. M., Sloan, F., Raffel, M., & Pratt, D. M. (1997). The big ten student suicide study: A 10-year study of suicides on Midwestern university campuses. *Suicide and Life-Threatening Behavior, 27,* 285–303.

Silverman, M. M., Tanney, B. L., Berman, A. L., Jobes, D. A., & Sanddal, N. D. (2005). *Revisiting the tower of babel: A revised nomenclature for suicidology.*

Silverman, P. R. (1978). *Mutual help groups: A guide for mental health workers.* National Institute of Mental Health Monograph (DHEW Publication No. ADM 78-646). Washington, DC: U.S. Government Printing Office.

Simon, R. I. (1991). The suicide-prevention pact: Clinical and legal considerations. In R. I. Simon (Ed.), *American Psychiatric Press review of clinical psychiatry and the law II* (pp. 441–451). Washington, DC: American Psychiatric Press.

Simon, R. I. (1999): The suicide prevention contract: Clinical, legal, and risk management issues. *Journal of the American Academy of Psychiatry Law, 27,* 445–450.

Simon, R. I. (2004). *Assessing and managing suicide risk: Guidelines for clinically based risk management.* Washington, DC: American Psychiatric Publishing, Inc.

Simon, T. R., Swann, A. C., Powell, K. E., Potter, L. B., Kresnow, M., & O'Carroll, P. W. (2001). Characteristics of impulsive suicide attempts and attempters. *Suicide and Life-Threatening Behavior, 32*(Suppl.), 49–59.

Slaikeu, K. (1990). *Crisis intervention* (2nd ed.). Boston: Allyn & Bacon.

Slap, G. B., Vorters, D. F., Chaudhuri, S., & Centor, R. M. (1989). Risk factors for attempted suicide during adolescence. *Pediatrics, 84,* 762–772.

Sloan, J. H., Rivara, F. P., Reay, D. T., Ferris, J. A., & Kellerman, A. L. (1990). Firearm regulations and rates of suicide: A comparison of two metropolitan areas. *New England Journal of Medicine, 322,* 369–373.

Small, J. E., Jobes, D. A., & Peterson, R. J. (2003). *Reactions to rock music with suicide-suggestive lyrical content: An empirical inquiry.* Unpublished manuscript.

Smart, R., & Ogborne, A. (1994). Street youth in substance abuse treatment: Characteristics and treatment compliance. *Adolescence, 29,* 733–745.

Smith, J. (1998). *Suicide postvention guidelines: Suggestions for dealing with the aftermath of suicide in the schools* (2nd ed.). Unpublished manuscript developed by the American Association of Suicidology School Suicide Prevention Programs Committee, Washington, DC.

Smith, K. (1985). Suicide assessment: An ego vulnerabilities approach. *The Bulletin of the Menninger Clinic, 49,* 489–499.

Smith, K., & Crawford, S. (1986). Suicidal behavior among normal high school students. *Suicide and Life-Threatening Behavior, 16,* 313–325.

Smith, K., Conroy, R. W., & Ehler, B. D. (1984). Lethality of suicide attempt rating scale. *Suicide and Life-Threatening Behavior, 14,* 215–242.

Snow, R. (1984). Decision making for a nuclear age. *Boston University Journal of Education, 166,* 103–107.

Snowden, J., & Hunt, G. E. (2002). Age, period, and cohort effects on suicide rates in Australia, 1919–1999. *Acta Psychiatrica Scandinavica, 105,* 265–270.

Somers-Flanagan, J., & Somers-Flanagan, R. (1995). Intake interviewing with suicidal patients: A systematic approach. *Professional Psychology: Research and Practice, 26,* 41–47.

Spicer, R. S., & Miller, T. T. (2000). Suicide acts in 8 states: Incidence and case fatality rates by demographics and method. *American Journal of Public Health, 90,* 1885–1891.

Spirito, A. (1997). Individual therapy techniques with adolescent suicide attempters. *Crisis, 18,* 62–64.

Spirito, A. (2003). Understanding attempted suicide in adolescence. In A. Spirito & J. C. Overholser (Eds.), *Evaluating and treating adolescent suicide attempters: From research to practice* (pp. 1–18). San Diego, CA: Academic Press.

Spirito, A., Brown, L., Overholser, J., & Fritz, G. (1989). Attempted suicide in adolescence: A review and critique of the literature. *Clinical Psychology Review, 9,* 335–363.

Spirito, A., Francis, G., Overholser, J., & Frank, N. (1996). Coping, depression, and adolescent suicide attempts. *Journal of Clinical Child Psychology, 25,* 147–183.

Spirito, A., & Overholser, J. C. (Eds.). (2003). *Evaluating and treating adolescent suicide attempters: From research to practice.* San Diego, CA: Academic Press.

Spirito, A., Plummer, B., Gispert, M., Levy, S., Kurkjian, J., Lewander, W., Hagberg, S., & Devost, L. (1992). Adolescent suicide attempts: Outcomes at follow-up. *American Journal of Orthopsychiatry, 62,* 464–468.

Spirito, A., Stark, L. J., Fristad, M., Hart, K., & Owens-Stively, J. (1987). Adolescent suicide attempters hospitalized on a general pediatrics floor. *Journal of Pediatric Psychology, 12,* 171–189.

Stack, S. (1987a). The sociological study of suicide: Methodological aspects. *Suicide and Life-Threatening Behavior, 17,* 133–150.

Stack, S. (1987b, May). *The impact of relative cohort size on national suicide trends, 1950–1980: A comparative analysis.* Paper presented at the annual meeting of the American Association of Suicidology, San Francisco, CA.

Stack, S., Gundlach, J., & Reeves, J. L. (1994). The heavy metal subculture and suicide. *Suicide and Life-Threatening Behavior, 24,* 15–23.

Stanley, M., Mann, J., & Cohen, L. (1986). Serotonin and serotonergic receptors in suicide. *Annals of the New York Academy of Sciences, 487,* 122–127.

Stein, D., Brom, D., Elizur, A., & Witztum, E. (1998). The association between attitudes toward suicide and suicide ideation in adolescents. *Acta Psychiatrica Scandinavica, 97,* 195–201.

Stiffman, A. R. (1989). Suicide attempts in runaway youth. *Suicide and Life-Threatening Behavior, 19,* 147–159.

Stoelb, M., & Chiriboga, J. (1998). A process model for assessing adolescent risk for suicide. *Journal of Adolescence, 21,* 359–370.

Stromberg, C., and colleagues from the law firm of Hogan & Hartson in Washington, DC. (1993). Privacy, confidentiality, and privilege. *The Psychologist's Legal Update, 1,* 1–15.

Suicide of a 12-year-old. (2003, October 29). *CBS News.* Retrieved June 20, 2005, from http://www.cbsnews.com/stories/2003/10/28/60II/main580507.shtml

Suyemoto, K. L. (1998). The functions of self-mutilation. *Clinical Psychology Review, 18,* 531–554.

Swedo, S. E., Rettew, D. C., Kuppenheimer, M., Lum, D., Dolan, S., & Goldberger, E. (1991). Can adolescent suicide attempters be distinguished from at-risk adolescents? *Pediatrics, 88,* 620–629.

Tabachnick, N. (1971). Theories of self-destruction. *American Journal of Psychoanalysis, 32,* 53–61.

TADS Team. (2004). Fluoxetine, cognitive-behavioral therapy, and their combination for adolescents with depression. Treatment for Adolescents with Depression Study (TADS) randomized controlled trial. *Journal of the American Medical Association, 292,* 807–820.

Taffel, R. (2001). The wall of silence. *Psychotherapy Networker, 25,* 52–64.

Taylor, L., & Adelman, H. S. (1989). Reframing the confidentiality dilemma to work in children's best interests. *Professional Psychology: Research and Practice, 20,* 79–83.

Thompson, R. (1990). *Post-traumatic loss debriefing: Providing immediate support for survivors of suicide or sudden loss. Highlights: An ERIC/CAPS Digest.* (Report No. ED315708). Ann Arbor, MI: ERIC Clearinghouse on Counseling and Personnel Services.

Tishler, C. L., McKenry, P. C., & Morgan, K. C. (1981). Adolescent suicide attempts: Some significant factors. *Suicide and Life-Threatening Behavior, 11,* 86–92.

Tondo, L., Jamison, K. R., & Baldessarini, R. J. (1997). Effect of lithium maintenance on suicidal behavior in major mood disorders. *Annals of the New York Academy of Science, 836,* 340–351.

Topol, P., & Reznikoff, M. (1982). Perceived peer and family relationships, hopelessness, and locus of control as factors in adolescent suicide attempts. *Suicide and Life-Threatening Behavior, 12,* 141–150.

Townsend, E., Hawton, K., Harriss, L., Bale, E., & Bond, A. (2001). Substances used in deliberate self-poisoning 1985–1997: Trends and associations with age, gender, repetition, and suicide intent. *Social Psychiatry and Psychiatric Epidemiology, 36,* 228–234.

Trautman, P. D. (1995). Cognitive behavior therapy for adolescent suicide attempters. In J. K. Zimmerman & G. M. Asnis (Eds.), *Treatment approaches with suicidal adolescents* (pp. 155–173). New York: Wiley.

Trautman, P. D. (1989). Specific treatment modalities for adolescent suicide attempters. In *Alcohol, Drug Abuse, and Mental Health Administration, Report of the Secretary's Task Force on Youth Suicide: Vol. 3. Prevention and interventions in youth suicide* (DHHS Publication No. ADM 89-1623, pp. 253–263). Washington, DC: U.S. Government Printing Office.

Trautman, P. D., & Shaffer, D. (1984). Treatment of child and adolescent suicide attempters. In H. S. Sudak, A. B. Ford, & N. B. Rushforth (Eds.), *Suicide in the young* (pp. 307–323). Boston: John Wright.

Trautman, P., Stewart, N., & Morishima, A. (1993). Are adolescent suicide attempters non-compliant with outpatient care? *Journal of the American Academy of Child and Adolescent Psychiatry, 32,* 89–94.

Tseng, W. (2001). *Handbook of cultural psychiatry.* San Diego, CA: Academic Press.

Unger, J., Kipke, M., Simon, T., Montgomery, S., & Johnson, C. (1977). Homeless youths and young adults in Los Angeles: Prevalence of mental health problems and the relationship between mental health and substance abuse disorders. *American Journal of Community Psychology, 25,* 371–394.

United Nations. (1996). *Prevention of suicide: Guidelines for the formulation and implementation of national strategies.* New York: Author.

Upanne, M. (2001). *Professional paradigms of suicide prevention: Evolving a conceptual model* (Research Report 121). Finland: National Research and Development Centre for Welfare and Health.

U.S. Department of Health and Human Services. (1999). *Mental health: A report of the Surgeon General.* Rockville, MD: Author.

U.S. Department of Health and Human Services. (2000). *Healthy people 2010: With understanding and improving health objectives for improving health* (2nd ed.). Washington, DC: U.S. Government Printing Office.

U.S. Food and Drug Administration. (2004). *Antidepressant use in children, adolescents, and adults.* Retrieved June 20, 2005, from http://www.fda.gov/cder/drug/antidepressants/

U.S. Public Health Service. (1999): *The Surgeon General's call to action to prevent suicide.* Washington, DC: USPHS/DHHS.

U.S. Public Health Service. (2000). *Report of the Surgeon General's conference on children's mental health: A national action agenda.* (DHHS/USPHS/NIH Publication No. NIH 00-4919).Washington, DC: U.S. Government Printing Office.

U.S. Public Health Service. (2001). *National strategy for suicide prevention: Goals and objectives for action*. Rockville, MD: U.S. Department of Health and Human Services.

Van der Wal, J. (1989–1990). The aftermath of suicide: A review of empirical evidence. *Omega, 20*, 149–171.

Van Dongen, C. J. (1993). Social context of postsuicide bereavement. *Death Studies, 17*, 125–141.

van Heeringen, C. (2001). Suicide in adolescents. *International clinical psychopharmacology, 16*(Suppl. 2), S1–S5.

van Heeringen, C., & Vincke, J. (2000). Suicidal acts and ideation in homosexual and bisexual young people: A study of prevalence and risk factors. *Social Psychiatry and Psychiatric Epidemiology, 35*, 494–499.

Velez, C. N., & Cohen, P. (1988). Suicidal behavior and ideation in a community sample of children: Maternal and youth reports. *Journal of the American Academy of Child and Adolescent Psychiatry, 27*, 349–356.

Velting, D. M., Rathnus, J. H., & Asnis, G. M. (1998). Asking adolescents to explain discrepancies in self-reported suicidality. *Suicide and Life-Threatening Behavior, 28*, 187–196.

Verkes, R. J., & Cowen, P. J. (2000). Pharmacotherapy of suicidal ideation and behavior. In K. Hawton & K. van Heeringen (Eds.), *The international handbook of suicide and attempted suicide* (pp. 487–502). New York: Wiley.

Verkes, R. J., Van der Mast, R. C., Hengeveld, M. W., Tuyl, J. P., Zwinderman, A. H., & Van Kempen, G. (1998). Reduction of paroxetine of suicidal behavior in patients with repeated suicide attempts but not major depression. *American Journal of Psychiatry, 155*, 543–546.

Vijayakumar, L. (2003). *Suicide prevention: Meeting the challenge together*. Himayatnagar, Hyderabad, India: Orient Longman.

Vlasek, G. J. (1975). Medical sociology. In S. Perlin (Ed.), *A handbook for the study of suicide* (pp. 131–146). New York: Oxford Press.

Wade, N. L. (1987). Suicide as a resolution of separation-individuation among adolescent girls. *Adolescence, 22*, 169–177.

Wagner, B. M. (1997). Family risk factors for child and adolescent suicidal behavior. *Psychological Bulletin, 121*, 246–298.

Wagner, B. M., Cole, R. E., & Schwartzman, P. (1995). Psychosocial correlates of suicide attempts among junior and senior high school youth. *Suicide and Life-Threatening Behavior, 25*, 358–372.

Wagner, B. M., Silverman, M. A. C., & Martin, C. E. (2003). Family factors in youth suicidal behaviors. *American Behavioral Scientist, 46*, 1171–1191.

Wagner, B. M., Wong, S. A., & Jobes, D. A. (2002). Mental health professionals' determinations of adolescent suicide attempts. *Suicide and Life-Threatening Behavior, 32*, 284–300.

Wahl, C. W. (1957). Suicide as a magical act. In E. S. Shneidman & N. L. Farberow (Eds.), *Clues to suicide* (pp. 22–30). New York: McGraw-Hill.

Walsh, B. W., & Rosen, P. (1985). Self-mutilation and contagion: An empirical test. *American Journal of Psychiatry, 142,* 119–120.

Watson, D., Goldney, R., Fisher, L., & Merritt, M. (2001). The measurement of suicide ideation. *Crisis, 22,* 12–14.

Weisman, A., & Worden, J. W. (1972). Risk-rescue rating in suicide assessment. In A. T. Beck, H. L. P. Resnick, & D. J. Lettieri (Eds.), *The prediction of suicide.* Bowie, MD: Charles Press.

Weissberg, R. P., & Elias, M. J. (1993). Enhancing young peoples' social competence and health behavior: An important challenge for educators, scientists, policymakers, and funders. *Applied and Preventive Psychology, 2,* 179–190.

Weissman, M. M., Paykel, E. S., & Klerman, G. L. (1972). The depressed woman as a mother. *Social Psychiatry, 7,* 89–108.

Werenko, D. D., Olson, L. M., Fullerton-Gleason, A. W., Zumwalt, R. E., & Sklar, D. P. (2000). Child and adolescent suicide deaths in New Mexico, 1990–1994. *Crisis, 21,* 36–44.

West, M. L., Spreng, S. W., Rose, S. M., & Adam, K. S. (1999). Relationship between attachment-felt security and history of suicidal behaviours in clinical adolescents. *Canadian Journal of Psychiatry, 44,* 578.

Wetzler, S., Asnis, G. M., Hyman, R. B., Virtue, C., Zimmerman, J., & Rathus, J. H. (1996). Characteristics of suicidality among adolescents. *Suicide and Life-Threatening Behavior, 26,* 37–45.

Williams, M. (2001). *Suicide and attempted suicide.* London: Penguin Books

Winnicott, D. (1965). *The maturational processes and the facilitating environment.* London: Hogarth Press.

Winslow, F. (1840). *The anatomy of suicide.* London: Renshaw.

Wong, S. A. (2003). *Effectiveness of an assessment and treatment protocol for suicidal outpatients.* Unpublished doctoral dissertation. The Catholic University of America, Washington, DC.

Wood, A., Harrington, R., & Moore, A. (1996): Controlled trial of a brief cognitive-behavioral intervention in adolescent patients with depressive disorders. *Journal of Child Psychology and Psychiatry, 37,* 737–746.

Working Group on the Classification and Reporting of Suicide. (1984). *Minutes of the Las Vegas meeting.* Atlanta, GA: Centers for Disease Control.

World Health Organization, Department of Mental Health. (2000). *Preventing suicide: A resource for teachers and other school staff.* Geneva, Switzerland: Author.

World Health Organization. (2002). *World report on violence and health.* Geneva, Switzerland: Author.

www.demographia.com. (2004). *USA state index.* Retreived June 16, 2005, from http://demographia.com/db-landstatepop.htm

Yang, B., & Clum, G. (1994). Life stress, social support, and problem-solving skills predictive of depressive symptoms, hopelessness, and suicide ideation in an Asian student population: A test of a model. *Suicide and Life-Threatening Behavior, 24,* 127–139.

Yoder, K. A. (1999). Comparing suicide attempters, suicide ideators, and non-suicidal homeless and runaway adolescents. *Suicide and Life-Threatening Behavior, 29,* 25–36.

Young, J. E. (1982). Loneliness, depression and cognitive therapy: Theory and application. In L. A. Peplau & D. Perlman (Eds.), *Loneliness: A sourcebook of current theory, research and therapy* (pp. 379–405). New York: Wiley.

Zahn-Waxler, C., Klimes-Dougan, B., & Kendziora, K. (1998). The study of emotion socialization: Conceptual, methodological, and developmental considerations. *Psychological Inquiry, 9,* 313–316.

Zenere, F. J., & Lazarus, P. J. (1997). The decline of youth suicidal behavior in an urban, multicultural public school system following the introduction of a suicide prevention and intervention program. *Suicide and Life-Threatening Behavior, 4,* 387–403.

Zilboorg, G. (1936). Suicide among civilized and primitive races. *American Journal of Psychiatry, 92,* 362.

Zimmerman, J. K., & Asnis, G. M. (Eds.). (1995). *Treatment approaches with suicidal adolescents.* New York: Wiley.

Zinner, E. S. (1985). Group survivorship: A model and case study application. In E. S. Zinner (Ed.), *Coping with death on campus* (pp. 51–68). San Francisco: Jossey-Bass.

Zlotnick, C., Donaldson, D., Spirito, A., & Pearlstein, T. (1997). Affect regulation and suicide attempts in adolescent inpatients. *Journal of the American Academy of Child and Adolescent Psychiatry, 36,* 793–798.

Zung, W. K. W., & Green, R. L. (1974). Seasonal variation of suicide and depression. *Archives General Psychiatry, 30,* 89–91.

AUTHOR INDEX

Aaronson, S. L., 211
Abbott, R., 317
Achte, K., 54, 86
Adam, K. S., 108
Adams, D., 78, 109
Adams, J., 185
Adams, M., 185
Adelman, H. S., 280
Adler, A., 53
Agerbo, E., 31
Ahrens, B., 201
Albers, E., 317
Albright, S., 360
Alessi, N. E., 105
Allen, B. G., 342
Allen, B. P., 72
Allman, C., 78, 84, 91, 99, 129, 307
Allmon, D., 61, 175
Anastasia, M. M., 338
Andrews, J. A., 104
Andrews, J. P., 176
Andriessen, K., 354
Appel, Y. H., 350
Appleby, L., 226
Apter, A., 72, 104, 131, 207
Arango, V., 66, 109, 200
Armstrong, H. E., 61, 175
Arnett, J. J., 69
Aro, H., 129
Asaranow, J. R., 105, 109
Asberg, M., 65
Aseltine, R., 312
Ashby, D., 203
Ashworth, J., 174, 244
Asnis, G., 38, 89, 178
Attig, T., 71
Averill, J. R., 340
Azrael, D., 38

Bacon, K., 103, 124
Bailey, W. B., 22
Bailley, S. E., 342–343
Baker, S., 33
Balance, W., 54
Baldessarini, R. J., 205, 264
Bale, E., 42

Barbe, R. P., 180
Barber, C., 35
Barlow, C. A., 348
Barnes, R., 38
Baron, R., 72
Bauer, G. B., 6
Bauer, M. N., 86
Baugher, M., 78, 84, 103, 107–109, 114, 162
Baume, P. J. M., 28, 34
Baumeister, R. F., 54
Beals, J., 24
Beardslee, W. R., 71
Beautrais, A. L., 104–105, 109, 115, 131
Beck, A. T., 57, 59, 105, 109, 136, 153, 172, 184, 194
Beck, J. S., 239
Becker, B. R., 6
Beckner, C., 129
Bedrosian, R. C., 184
Beery, L., 84
Belin, T. R., 178, 212
Belting, D. M., 293
Berglund, M., 33
Bergman, U., 203
Berman, A. L., 6, 7, 13, 18–19, 22, 25, 34, 46, 48, 55, 66, 74, 77, 81–83, 85, 87, 89, 100, 102, 104, 106–107, 112–113, 121, 147, 199, 220, 221, 224–245, 272, 291, 293–294, 307–308, 314, 321, 345
Bernstein, B. 73
Bernstein, G. A., 105
Beutler, L. E., 228, 348
Bille-Brahe, U., 42
Billow, C. J., 350
Binder, R., 360
Birmaher, B., 180, 185
Blachly, P. H., 32
Black, D., 178
Blair-West, G. W., 15
Blanco, C., 202
Bleich, A., 104
Bloodworth, R., 322
Blum, M. C., 100

Blum, R. W., 38, 115
Blumenthal, S. J., 66–67, 105, 116, 124
Boeck, M., 38, 89
Boergers, J., 81
Boggiano, W. E., 151
Boldt, M., 72
Bolton, I., 345
Bonanno, G. A., 341
Bond, A., 42, 95
Bongar, B., 6–7, 120, 153, 265, 272, 280
Bonner, R. L., 89
Borowsky, I. W., 38, 115
Bostock, T., 73
Bowlby, J., 55, 341
Boyd, J. H., 37
Brådvik, L., 33
Brand, E. F., 89
Branden-Muller, L. R., 317
Brener, N. D., 39
Brent, D. A., 33, 37–38, 42, 65, 78, 84–85,
         91, 96, 99, 102–103, 107–108,
         114, 121–122, 129, 132–133,
         139, 148, 151, 162, 176, 180,
         185, 224, 242, 307, 311, 321,
         343
Brickman, A., 105
Brickmayer, J., 38
Bridge, J., 84, 108, 180, 343
Brinkman-Sull, D. C., 105
Brom, D., 73
Bromet, E. J., 311
Brooks, C., 350
Brown, G., 57
Brown, G. K., 172
Brown, G. L., 86
Brown, H. N., 6
Brown, J., 108
Brown, K. E., 251
Brown, L., 103, 176
Brown, S., 196, 249
Brown, W. A., 203
Buchanan, C. M., 69
Budenz, D., 184
Buie, E. H., 219, 264
Buka, S. L., 38
Bunney, W. E., 173, 291
Bunzel, B., 22
Buongiorno, P. A., 360
Burns, B. H., 303
Busch, K. A., 226, 263, 362
Busner, C., 312
Byrne, D., 72

Cairns, R. B., 139
Caitlin, S. N., 38
Calhoun, L. G., 342
Callahan, J., 346
Canetto, S. S., 95
Cann, A., 342
Canobbio, R., 343
Cantor, C. H., 15, 28, 34
Cantor, P. C., 292, 307–308
Cantwell, C., 178, 212
Cantwell, D. P., 105, 124
Caplan, G., 293
Carlson, G. A., 105, 124
Carrigan, S., 85, 127, 222
Carroll, T., 6, 81, 106
Casey, J. O., 85
Castro-Blanco, D., 90, 178, 212
Catalano, R. F., 317
Cavan, R. S., 48
Centor, R. M., 107
Chaudhuri, S., 107
Chemtob, C. M., 6
Chen, J., 84
Chenier, T., 38
Chiles, J. A., 61, 150, 239
Chiriboga, J., 132
Christopher, J. S., 247
Cichetti, D, 71
Cimbolic, P., 45, 89, 175, 221
Clark, S., 101, 342
Clarke, G. N., 176, 184
Clarke, R. V., 307
Clarkin, J. F., 105
Cleiren, M., 342
Clements, C. D., 270
Clum, G., 110
Clum, G. A., 90, 175
Coats, K. I., 186
Coccaro, E. F., 206
Cohen, L., 66
Cohen, P., 103, 108
Cohen, Y., 83, 89
Cohen-Sandler, R., 7, 74, 89, 102,
         106–107, 109, 220
Cole, D., 97
Cole, R. E., 89, 105, 107
Colt, G. W., 337, 338
Comstock, B. S., 165, 309
Conn, J. M., 19
Connolly, J., 65, 108
Conrad, A., 157, 192, 251
Conroy, R. W., 74, 87, 147

Conte, H. R., 104, 107
Conwell, Y., 321
Corder, B. F., 110
Corder, R. F., 110
Corn, R., 105
Cotgrove, A. J., 178
Cotton, C. R., 72
Cowen, E. L., 296
Cowen, P. J., 201
Cox, C., 321
Crawford, S., 38, 89, 99, 110
Croft, L., 312
Cross, C. K., 95
Crumley, F. E., 105
Curphey, T., 85
Cuskey, W. R., 214

Dahm, P., 174
Daly, J. D., 185
Davidson, L., 19, 83, 111, 301, 302, 318,
    325, 346–347
Davies, J. R., 105
Davis, J. M., 115, 317
Decker, N., 221
Delabre, C., 109
Delhaise, T., 354
DeMartino, R. E., 291, 312
Denning, D. G., 321
DePaulo, J. R., 338
De Rosis, L . E., 54
Derrick, A. M., 85, 127, 129, 222
Deutsch, C. J., 6
Dew, M. A., 311
de Wilde, E. L., 133
Dexter-Mazza, E. T., 6
Diegmuller, K., 292
Diekstra, R. F. W., 28, 133, 211, 342
DiFilippo, J. M., 103
DiFiore, J., 38, 89
Diller, J., 34
Domino, G., 72
Donaldson, D., 81, 92
Dorling, D., 31
Douglas, J. D., 48, 82
Downey, G. D., 112
Drozd, J. F., 157, 192–193, 195, 244
Druss, B., 170, 176
Dryfoos, J., 334
Dublin, L. I., 22
Dubow, E. F., 100
Dunbar, G. C., 203
Dunham, K., 342

Dunn, R. G., 343
Dunne, E. J., 271, 348–349, 358
Dunner, D. L., 203, 205
Durkheim, E., 46–48, 82–83
Durlak, J. A., 332
Dwyer, M. S., 176
Dyck, R. J., 31
Dyer, E., 103, 133

Earle, J., 352
Earls, F., 18
Easterlin, R., 31, 32
Eastgard, S., 83, 293, 324
Eaton, P., 98
Eddleston, M., 35
Eddy, D. M., 124, 308
Egan, M. P., 243
Egeland, J., 108
Eggert, L. L., 106, 314, 324–325
Ehler, B. D., 87, 147
Ekeberg, O., 106
Elias, M. J., 317, 332
Elizur, A., 73
Elkind, D., 211
Ellenbogen, S., 341
Emery, G., 109, 184, 185
Emery, P. E., 55
Epp, H. L., 350
Erikson, E., 55, 70
Eshkevari, H. S., 291
Esposito, C., 105, 110
Esposito-Smythers, C., 353
Evans, W., 317
Eyeson-Annan, M. L., 15
Eyman, J., 98, 152

Fagg, J., 106
Fairbarin, W. R. D., 182
Fairley, N., 32
Farber, M. L., 61
Farberow, N. L., 30, 85, 93, 101, 106,
    349–351
Favazza, A., 92
Fawcett, J., 205–206, 210, 226, 263, 362
Fekete, S., 343
Feldman, B., 6
Feldman, K., 33
Felner, R. D., 133, 293, 295–296, 306
Felner, T. Y., 295
Felts, W. M., 38
Feree, F. H., 246
Fergusson, D. M., 108, 133, 243

Ferris, J. A., 37
Ferster, C. B., 57
Fingerhut, L., 30
Fisher, L., 39
Fisher, P., 78, 85, 91, 102, 104–105, 108, 129, 307
Fishman, H. C., 196
Flory, M., 78
Fogg, L., 210
Forceville, G., 354
Forsyth, J., 6, 272
Foster, V.A., 6
Fowler, R. C., 33, 85, 127
Frances, A., 79, 105
Francis, G., 78
Frank, N., 78
Frankl, S., 31
Franklin, J. L., 111, 309
Fraser, J., 176
Frederick, D. J., 57
Freedman, J., 55–56, 214
Freeman, K. A., 6
Freheit, S. R., 103
Freud, A., 69, 70
Freud, S., 52, 182
Fridstad, M., 42
Friedman, P., 22
Friedman, R. C., 105
Friend, A., 84
Fritz, G., 95, 103, 176
Froese, A., 104
Fullerton-Gleason, A. W., 31

Gaffney, D., 211
Galen, R., 79
Gambino, S., 79
Gara, M. A., 317
Garfield, S., 174
Garfinkel, B. D., 33, 41, 84, 104–106, 110, 129, 133, 314
Garfinkel, R., 108, 191
Garland, A., 105–106, 129, 307, 311–312, 314
Garmezy, N., 150
Garrison, B., 57, 105, 187
Garrison, C. Z., 38, 153
Geller, J., 251
Gessner, B. D., 31
Ghaziuddin, N., 89
Gibbons, R. D., 101
Gibbs, J., 48
Gilboa-Schechtman, E., 100

Glaser, K., 199
Goldacre, M., 96
Goldfried, M. R., 215
Goldney, R., 39, 291, 342
Goldsmith, S. K., 173–175, 182, 197, 199, 291, 314
Goldstein, C., 103, 121–122, 129, 133
Goldstein, L. S., 360
Goldston, D., 80–81, 89, 95, 99, 148, 152, 153
Goodin, J., 18
Goodman, L. A., 71
Goodrich, S., 251
Goodstein, J. L., 150
Goodwin, R., 202
Gorchover, O., 72
Gordon, A. K., 71
Gordon, R. S., 299
Gould, M. S., 24, 29, 78, 83, 85, 91, 102, 104–106, 108–112, 127, 129, 132–133, 146, 202, 293, 306–307, 311–312, 314, 317, 334
Gowers, S., 176
Graae, F., 105, 178
Grad, O. T., 342, 353–355
Grapentine, L., 105
Gratton, F., 341
Greany, S., 6
Green, M. R., 54
Green, R. L., 32
Greenberg, T., 293, 334
Greenhouse, J. B., 311
Grisham, J. R., 57
Groholt, B., 106
Grossman, D. C., 33
Grossman, J. A., 323
Grunbaum, 39–41
Gundlach, J., 83
Gunnell, D., 31, 203
Guntrip, H., 70, 182, 217
Guo, B., 326
Gutheil, T. G., 243, 272
Guthrie, D., 105
Gutierrez, P. M., 150

Haas, A., 271, 360
Haas, G. L., 200
Haldorsen, T., 106
Hall, B. L., 350
Hall, G. S., 69
Haller, D. L., 101

Hamada, R. S., 6
Hamilton, J. D., 221
Hampton, W. R., 73
Hangeveld, M. W., 199
Hansen, D. J., 247
Hanson, A., 243
Hanzlick, R., 18
Harkavy-Friedman, J., 38, 89, 110, 205
Harmantz, M., 6, 7
Harrington, R., 90, 103, 133, 176, 178, 185, 197
Harrington, V., 133
Harris, H. E., 96, 321
Harriss, L., 42
Harstall, C., 326
Hart, K., 42
Hary, E., 110
Hassan, R., 291
Hastings, F., 251
Hauser, M. J., 340
Havik, D., 174
Hawkins, J. D., 317
Hawton, K., 28, 42, 45, 95–97, 100, 106, 109, 127, 137, 177, 257, 291, 293, 308
Haynes, R. B., 176
Heard, H. L., 61, 175
Heeren, T., 150
Heilig, S. M., 350
Hemenway, D., 37, 38
Hendin, H., 49, 271, 291, 360
Henrikksson, M., 129
Henriques, G., 57, 172, 184, 186
Henry, A., 48–49
Herting, J. R., 324
Hill, G., 317
Hill, K. G., 317
Hillbomi, E., 86
Hirsch, C. S., 307
Hirschfield, R. M. A., 95
Hjelmeland, H., 138
Hlady, W. G., 82
Ho, T. P., 226
Hoberman, H. M., 33, 84, 104, 106, 129, 133, 314
Hoff, L. A., 222
Holen, A., 341
Holinger, P. C., 22, 307, 308
Hollon, S. D., 184, 186
Hood, J., 104
Hops, H., 176, 184

Horgas, P., 352
Horney, K., 54
Horowitz, M. J., 341
Horowitz, R. I., 176
Horowitz, S. M., 176
Horwood, L. J., 108
Houk, V. N., 33
Housman, D., 150
Houston, K., 127, 129, 131–133
Hovey, J. D., 174
Hsiung, R. C., 240
Huff, C., 109
Hunt, G. E., 31
Hustead, L. A. T., 45, 175, 343
Hynes, P., 219

Ireland, M., 38, 115
Isacsson, G., 203
Isometsa, E. T., 263

Jackson, D. A., 340
Jacobs, D. G., 226, 243, 263, 291, 345, 362
Jacobson, G., 281
Jacobsson, L., 73
Jacoby, A. M., 45, 175, 192
Jacobziner, H., 41
Jamieson, P., 111, 112
Jamison, K. R., 205, 264
Jan-Tausch, J., 54
Jayson, D., 176
Jenkins, J. S., 29, 82
Jensen, E., 260
Jensen, P. S., 201
Jerrett, I., 107
Jick, H., 203
Jick, S. S., 203
Jobes, D. A., 18–19, 45, 48–49, 54, 61, 63, 74, 77–78, 82–85, 90, 100, 112–113, 121, 150, 152–154, 157, 172–176, 181–182, 192–193, 195, 219–221, 224, 230, 239, 241, 244, 251, 270, 272, 293–294, 311, 343–345, 352–353
Joffe, P., 331
Johnson, B. A., 65, 108, 110, 139
Johnson, C., 107
Johnson, F., 65
Johnson, G. R., 37
Johnson, J. G., 108
Johnson, W. B., 153

Joiner, T. E., 50–51, 57, 65, 90, 95, 98, 121, 132, 173–174, 176, 188, 197, 239, 247
Jones, F. A., 358, 360
Jonker, D. J., 199
Jordan, J. R., 342–343
Josselson, A. R., 18, 82, 85
Joyce, P. R., 104–105, 109, 131
Joyner, K., 106
Jung, C., 54
Juwon, S., 178, 212

Kaarovsky, P. P., 314
Kachur, P. S., 37, 291, 332
Kalafat, J., 312, 317, 324, 326, 332
Kalediene, R., 31
Kallman, F. J., 338
Kaltiala-Heino, R., 106–107
Kamali, M., 86
Kanani, R., 176
Kann, L., 39
Kaplan, M. L., 153
Kaplan, R. D., 79, 133
Kapur, S., 203
Karmel, M. P., 181, 220
Kastenbaum, R., 71
Katz, P., 217
Kavousi, R. J., 206
Kaye, J. A., 203
Kedem, P., 72
Kellerman, A. L., 38–39, 162
Kelly, C., 107
Keltner, D., 341
Kendziora, K., 71
Kerfoot, M., 90, 103, 133, 136, 178, 197
Kerkhof, 42
Kernberg, P., 212
Kessler, R. C., 112
Kestenberg, J., 71
Khan, A., 203
Khan, S., 203
Kiely, M. C., 342
Kienhorst, I. C. W. M., 133, 211
Kiernan, A., 192–193, 251
King, C. A., 89–90, 108, 173–174, 182, 196, 207
King, D., 321
King, R. A., 40–41, 89, 107, 109
King, S. R., 73
Kinney, B., 6
Kipke, M., 107
Kleck, G., 18

Kleespies, P. M., 6, 272
Kleinman, A. M., 173, 291
Klerman, G. L., 14, 56, 191
Klimes-Dougan, B., 71, 81, 108, 110
Knickmeyer, S., 83, 293
Knott, E. C., 152
Kohut, H., 70, 182
Kolko, D. J., 85, 108, 180
Kolts, R., 203
Koo, L., 83, 112
Koons, C. R., 190
Koretz, D. S., 295–296
Kosky, R. J., 103, 133, 291
Kosterman, R., 317
Kotila, L., 98
Kottler, D. B., 79
Kovacs, M., 57, 105, 187
Kraemer, H. C., 14
Kral, M. J., 342
Kramer, R. A., 24, 29, 132, 306, 312, 317
Kreitman, N., 82, 95
Kroll, L., 176
Kruesi, M. J. P., 223, 323
Krug, E., 37, 39
Kubin, M., 6
Kubler-Ross, E., 341
Kulbok, P. A., 29, 81–82
Kupfer, D. J., 66–67, 116, 124

Lall, R., 153
Landau-Stanton, J. L., 165
Langhinrichsen, J., 153
Lazarus, P. J., 314, 324
Le, L. T., 103
Leenaars, A. A., 45, 54, 85, 178, 272
Leigh, E., 90, 190
LeMaster, P. L., 24
Leonard, C. V., 54
Lerner, H. E., 220
Lerner, M. S., 90, 175
Lerner, S., 220
Lesage, A., 342
Lester, D., 28, 32, 46, 49, 95, 244, 307, 353
Levenson, M., 109
Levin, C., 6
Levy, K. B., 176
Lewinsohn, P. M., 42, 95, 99, 103–104, 109, 137, 153, 176, 184, 247
Linden, M., 201

Linehan, M. M., 61, 78–79, 90, 95, 150, 174–175, 177–178, 180, 189–190, 194, 270
Linkowski, P., 109
Lipschitz, A., 360
Litman, R. E., 34, 58, 85, 91, 160, 271, 358
Litt, I. F., 214
Lively, P., 68
Lonczak, H. S., 317
Lonnqvist, J. K., 86, 98, 103, 129
Lucas, C., 80
Ludgate, J. W., 185
Luoma, J. B., 15, 127, 192–193, 271, 343–344, 352
Lynskey, M. T., 243

Mack, J. E., 71
MacKinnon, D. R., 30
Malone, K. M., 200
Maltsberger, J. T., 54, 66, 149, 174, 178, 219, 224, 233, 264, 271, 360
Mann, J. J., 66, 86, 109, 200, 203, 205, 291
Mann, R. E., 100, 150, 154, 192, 343
Manson, S., 24
Marcus, S. C., 170–171, 176, 201
Marion, M. S., 72
Maris, R. W., 13, 18, 48, 65–66, 83, 87, 101, 199, 291, 297
Marks, P. A., 101
Marsella, A. J., 175
Marshall, K., 360
Marshall, M., 318, 325, 346–347
Marsteller, F., 153
Martin, C. E., 107, 121, 215
Martin, G., 83, 112
Martin, K. E., 15, 127
Martin, W. T., 48
Martunnen, M., 107
Martz, L., 292
Marzuk, P. M., 307
Mason, M., 309
Masten, A. S., 150
Mattison, R. E., 105, 129
Maxim, K., 350
Mazza, J. J., 42, 106
McAdams, C. R., 6
McBride, C. M., 317
McCaffery, M., 134
McCarthy, B. W., 246
McIntosh, J. L., 340, 344, 360
McKenry, P. C., 107, 110
McKeown, R. E., 38, 108

McKibbon, K. A., 176
McLeavey, B. C., 185
McManus, B. L., 223
McManus, M., 105
Meander, K. B., 176
Medeleuicz, J., 109
Mellsop, G. W., 15
Meltzer, H. Y., 205, 264
Mendelsohn, R., 18, 82
Mendelsohn, S., 104
Menninger, K., 53
Mercy, J. A., 33, 111–112
Merritt, M., 39
Meyer, P. M., 329
Middaugh, J. P., 82
Middlebrook, D. L., 24
Middleton, N., 31
Mikulincer, M., 100
Milavsky, J. R., 112
Miller, A. L., 90, 176, 178, 196
Miller, M. C., 37, 38, 61, 172, 190, 242, 243, 244
Miller, S., 90, 212, 223
Miller, T. T., 41
Miner, J. R., 22
Minuchin, S., 55
Mitchell, P., 326
Mitchell, R., 228
Mizruchi, M. S., 104
Modestin, J., 219
Mohler, B., 18
Molock, S. D., 352
Montgomery, S. A., 107, 203, 206
Moore, A., 176
Moreau, D., 191
Morgan, K. C., 110
Morishima, A., 172
Moritz, G., 78, 84, 91, 99, 107–108, 114, 129, 162, 343
Morrell, S., 31
Morris, W., 221
Morrish-Vidners, D., 343
Morrison, H., 348
Mortenson, P. B., 31
Mortiz, G., 103
Moscicki, E. K., 14, 37, 87
Motto, J. A., 78, 96, 124, 146, 151, 198, 270
Mufson, L., 176, 191
Mulder, R. T., 104–105, 109, 131
Müller-Oerlinghausen, B., 205
Murphy, G. E., 79–80, 110

Murray, C. M., 185
Murray, H., 63
Müser-Causemann, B., 205
Myers, W. C., 96, 321

Naylor, M. W., 196
Naylor, O., 89
Neal-Walden, T., 157, 192, 193, 251
Neckerman, H., 139
Negron, R., 105
Neimeyer, R. A., 178
Nelson, E. A., 205
Nelson, F. L., 30
Ness, D. E., 343
Neufeld, J., 317
Neuringer, C., 57, 109
Newman, S. C., 31
Nicholas, L. J., 324
Nielsen, S. L., 150
Nielson, D. A., 65
Nordlung, M. D., 153
Norton, E. M., 332
Novaco, R., 247
Novins, D. K., 24
Nunno, K. M., 192

O'Carroll, P. W., 18, 38, 82–83, 86–87, 95,
    113, 255, 293, 306, 347
O'Connor, J. M., 100
Offer, D., 22, 69
Ogborne, A., 107
O'Grady, J., 97
Ohring, R., 211
Okayli, G., 205
Olfson, M., 170–171, 176, 201–203
Olson, E., 89
Olson, L. M., 31
O'Neill, K., 341
Oquendo, M. A., 86
Orbach, I., 72, 100, 109
Osborn, M., 97
Osman, A., 150
Ostroff, R., 86
Overholser, J., 78, 95, 98, 103, 105, 109,
    176, 178, 212, 342
Owens-Stively, J., 42

Page, A., 31
Paight, D. J., 112
Papa, A., 341
Papadimitriou, G., 109
Parides, M., 78

Pasero, C., 134
Paykel, E. S., 56
Pearlstein, T., 92
Pearson, J. L., 15, 127
Peck, M. L., 95
Pell, T. C., 291
Pellmar, T. C., 173
Penk, W., 6, 272
Pentiuc, D., 192
Perlmutter, R., 270
Perper, J. A., 78, 84–85, 91, 99, 103,
    107–108, 114, 121–122, 129,
    133, 162, 224, 307, 343
Perry, C. L., 317
Peruzzi, N., 7
Pescosolido, B. A., 18, 82
Peterson, A. C., 71
Peterson, E. M., 192, 271, 282, 358
Peterson, G., 139
Peterson, R. J., 83–84
Petzel, S. V., 48
Pfeffer, C. R., 107, 174, 185, 196, 200,
    217, 223–224, 228, 243,
    333, 343
Phillips, D. P., 18, 33, 82–83, 112
Phillips, M. R., 35
Piacentini, J., 90, 105, 178, 212, 223, 224
Piaget, J., 70
Pike, K. C., 314, 325
Pincus, A. H., 176
Pincus, H. A., 170
Plutchik, R., 104, 107
Pokorny, A. D., 79
Poling, D., 185
Pope, K. S., 272
Poteet, D. J., 104
Potter, L. B., 37, 291, 301–302, 332, 347
Powell, K. E., 37, 291, 332
Pratt, D. M., 329

Qin, P., 31
Quinn, J., 115

Rabinowicz, H., 271
Raffel, M., 329
Rajab, H., 57, 90, 95, 98, 121, 132,
    174–176, 188, 197, 239
Randell, B. P., 325
Range, L. M., 72, 152–153, 342
Rantanen, P., 107
Rathus, J. H., 38, 90, 176, 178, 190
Reay, D. T., 33, 37

Reed, J., 100
Reed, M. D., 342
Reeves, J. L., 83
Rehm, L., 186
Reid, W. H., 242
Reinherz, H. Z., 133
Remafedi, G., 106
Renberg, E. S., 73
Resnick, H. L. P., 57
Resnick, M. D., 38, 115
Reynolds, F. M. T., 89
Reynolds, P., 98
Reynolds, W. M., 42, 186
Reznikoff, M., 74
Rich, A. R., 89
Rich, C. L., 33, 85–86, 91, 127, 203
Richards, M. H., 332
Richman, J., 55, 74, 163, 197, 249
Riddle, M., 48
Riggs, S., 95
Rimpela, A., 107
Rimpela, M., 106
Rivara, F. P., 37
Rivera, S. G., 243
Robbins, D., 74
Roberts, A., 222–223
Robillard, R. R., 243
Robins, E., 348
Robins, L. N., 29, 81–82
Robins, S., 247
Rogers, J. R., 63
Rohde, P., 42, 95, 99, 103, 137, 184
Romer, D., 111–112
Rooijmans, H. G., 199
Rose, S. M., 108
Rosen, A., 80
Rosen, P., 92
Rosenberg, M. L., 19, 22, 33, 37, 100,
    111, 124
Rosenblatt, P. C., 340
Rosenfeld, S. K. S., 33
Rosenheim, E., 109
Rosenstock, H. A., 104
Ross, C. P., 198
Roth, C., 91, 103, 114
Rotheram, M. J., 242
Rotherham-Borus, M. J., 90, 105, 107, 161,
    178, 211–212, 223
Roy, A., 109, 111
Rubenstein, J. L., 150
Rubin, C., 150
Rudd, D. A., 175

Rudd, M. D., 57, 59, 89–90, 95, 98, 100,
    121, 132, 136, 159, 160,
    173–177, 180, 184, 188, 197,
    222, 239, 243, 252, 256
Rudd, S., 214
Rumbaut, R. D., 221
Rush, A. J., 57, 109, 184, 185
Russell, S. T., 106
Rustad, R. A., 83, 84
Ruth, T. E., 18, 82
Ryerson, D., 324

Sabbath, J. C., 74, 196, 214
Safer, M. A., 83
Sainsbury, P., 29, 48, 82
Saleem, Y., 185
Salkovskis, P. M., 172, 175, 183, 191–192,
    257
Salzman, C., 206
Sanchez, L. E., 103
Sanddal, N. D., 77, 291
Sandoval, J., 317
Sartre, J. P., 45
Sayette, M. A., 317
Schaller, S., 293
Scheftner, W., 210
Schein, H. M., 6, 222
Schichor, A., 73
Schmid, C. F., 48
Schmidtke, A., 293, 343
Schonert-Reichel, K. A., 69
Schorr, W., 110
Schou, M., 205
Schuyler, T. F., 317
Schwartz, R., 100, 104
Schwartzman, P., 89, 105, 107
Schweers, J., 91, 103, 114, 162
Seeley, J. R., 42, 95, 99, 103, 137, 184, 247
Segal, Z. V., 61
Seguin, M., 342
Seiden, R. H., 29, 35
Shaffer, D., 56, 78, 80, 84–85, 91,
    102–106, 108, 124, 127, 129,
    132, 146, 174, 185, 200, 203,
    223–224, 228, 243, 293, 307,
    311–312, 314, 332–333
Shafii, M., 33, 85, 91, 96, 101, 104, 106,
    110, 127, 129, 222
Shafii, S. L., 33
Shain, B. N., 196
Shapiro, E. R., 55–56, 214
Shaw, B., 109, 184–185

Shea, S. C., 136
Shenassa, E. D., 38, 321
Shepherd, G., 147, 245, 321
Shepperd, R., 127
Shiang, J., 175
Shneidman, E. S., 46, 52–53, 57, 62–63,
        85, 134, 172, 209, 222, 237,
        338, 363
Short, J., 48–49
Sider, R. C., 270
Siegel, N., 109
Silburn, S., 103
Silk, K. R., 240
Silverman, E., 105, 342
Silverman, M. A. C., 107, 215
Silverman, M. M., 13, 48, 77, 87, 133, 147,
        199, 245, 291, 293, 295–297,
        301–302, 306, 321, 329, 342
Silverman, P. R., 350
Simkin, S., 106
Simmons, J. T., 111, 309
Simon, R. I., 241, 243, 260, 265
Simon, T. R., 39, 107, 139
Sirota, P., 100
Sklar, D. P., 31
Slaikeu, K., 222
Slap, G. B., 107
Sloan, F., 329
Sloan, J. H., 37
Smailes, E. M., 108
Small, J. E., 83–84
Smart, R., 107
Smith, J., 19, 346
Smith, K., 38, 54, 87, 89, 98–99, 110, 147,
        148
Smith, M., 317
Smith, M. R., 6
Snow, R., 71
Snowden, J., 31
Soderstrom, K., 65
Somers-Flanagan, J., 160
Speechley, 18
Spicer, R. S., 41
Spirito, A., 78, 92, 95, 102–106, 110, 176,
        178, 212, 353
Spirito, J., 95, 98
Spreng, S. W., 108
Stack, S., 32, 81, 83
Stanley, M., 66
Stanton, M. D., 165
Stark, L. J., 42
Stavraky, 19

Stechler, G., 150
Steer, R. A., 57, 105, 136, 153, 187
Stein, D., 73
Steltz-Lenarsky, J., 129
Stewart, N., 172
Stiffman, A. R., 107
Stipp, H., 112
Stoelb, M., 132
Stromberg, C., 282
Strosahl, K. D., 61, 239
Suarez, A., 61, 175
Sullivan, H. S., 54
Sussex, J., 109
Suyemoto, K. L., 92
Swedo, S. E., 105
Szanto, K., 271

Tabachnick, M. D., 85
Tabachnick, N., 52–53
Tadeschi, R. G., 342
Taffel, R., 70
Tanney, B. L., 77
Tardiff, K., 307
Taylor, L., 280
Taylor, R., 31
Teasdale, J. D., 61
Thompson, E. A., 324
Thompson, R., 347
Tishler, C. L., 107, 110
Tondo, L., 205, 264
Topol, P., 74
Torigoe, R. Y., 6
Toth, S. L., 71
Townsend, E., 42
Trautman, P. D., 56, 90, 105, 129, 161,
        172, 176, 199, 230, 307
Tseng, W., 174
Tyano, S., 72, 104

Underwood, M. M., 109, 211, 312, 324
Unger, J., 107
Upanne, M., 291

Valois, R. F., 38
VandenBos, G., 174
van der Wal, J., 341
Van Dongen, C. J., 342
van Heeringen, C., 106
van Heeringen, K., 95, 291
van Praag, H. M., 104
Van Rossem, R., 178, 212, 223
Velez, C. N., 103

Velting, D. M., 38
Venarde, D. F., 205
Verkes, R. J., 201, 206
Vieland, V., 312
Vijayakumar, L., 291
Vincent, M. L., 38
Vincke, J., 106
Vlasek, G. J., 222
Voelz, Z. R., 90, 197
Volk, J., 205
Vorters, D. F., 107

Wade, N. L., 54
Wagner, B. M., 56, 74, 77, 81, 86–87, 89,
　　　　95, 98, 105, 107–108, 114, 198,
　　　　215, 281
Wahl, C. W., 54
Wallenstein, S., 83
Walsh, B. W., 92
Walsh, R. P., 340
Wasserman, C. W., 28, 246
Waternaux, C., 200
Watson, D., 39
Watson-Perczel, M., 247
Weisman, A., 87
Weissberg, R. P., 317
Weissman, M. M., 56, 191, 201
Werenko, D. D., 31
West, M. L., 108
Weston, D., 178
Wetzel, R., 110
Wetzler, S., 90, 190
Whitely, E., 31
Whittinghill, J. R., 85, 127, 129, 222
Whittle, B., 314
Wichstrom, L., 106
Wilcox, H., 80
Wilde, E. J., 211
Williams, C. L., 73

Williams, J. M., 100
Williams, M., 59–61
Winnicott, D., 70
Winslow, F., 338
Witztum, E., 73
Wolf, E., 182
Wolfsdorf, B. A., 110
Wolpert, R. L., 124
Wolters, W. H. G., 133, 211
Wong, F., 251
Wong, S. A., 77, 157, 192–193, 251
Wood, A., 176
Woodham, A., 103, 133
Woodward, L. J., 108
Worden, J. W., 87
Wright, D. G., 85
Wrobleski, A., 350

Yager, J., 240
Yamada, A., 175
Yang, B., 110
Young, D., 33, 85, 127
Young, J. E., 184, 247
Yufit, R. F., 152

Zahn-Waxler, C., 71
Zaitsoff, S. L., 251
Zavasnik, A., 342
Zelenak, J. P., 85
Zenere, F. J., 314, 324
Zilboorg, G., 53
Zimmerman, J. K., 178
Zinner, E. S., 344
Zirinsky, L., 178
Zlotnick, C., 92
Zola, M. A., 22
Zubrick, S., 103
Zumwalt, R. E., 31
Zung, W. K. W., 32

SUBJECT INDEX

Abandonment, feelings of, 55
Acute risk, 159
Adler, A., 53
Adolescent
    death and, 71
    development and, 68–75
    knowledge of lethality of poisons,
        321
    perceptions of suicide, 71–73, 293
    psychology of, 69–72
Adolescent suicide
    how of: methods, 34–38
    statistics, 19–32
    when of, 32–33
    where of, 33
Adolescent Suicide Awareness Program
    (ASAP), 324
Affective disorder, 91, 111, 129, 206.
        See also Depression
Affective system, evaluation, 134–136
AFSP. See American Foundation for
        Suicide Prevention
Age
    confidentiality and, 279–282
    prevalence rates and, 26–28
Age effects, 27
Aggression, 31, 91, 104, 105, 127, 139,
        206, 218, 247, 248
AIDS, 314
AIM. See Awareness, intervention, and
        methodology
Air Force Suicide Prevention Initiatives,
        327–328
Alaska Natives
    attempted suicides, 38
    suicide rates, 24, 30
Alcoholics Anonymous (AA), 248
Alcohol use or abuse, 24, 25, 26, 29, 30,
        92, 120, 146, 233, 248, 250,
        274, 284, 291, 292, 299, 327
Alice in Chains, 84
Alienation, feelings of, 106, 116, 135, 162
Alliance, therapeutic, 173, 208–211, 269
    confidentiality, 281, 282
    countertransference, 218–221, 255
    enhancing, 216–217
    importance in assessment, 263

initial contact, 217–218
    pitfalls, 250–252
    quality, 215
    transference, 218, 220
Alternative high schools, suicide attempting
        behaviors, 40
Altruistic suicide, 47
AMA. See American Medical Association
Ambivalence, feelings of, 150, 251
American Academy of Child and
        Adolescent Psychiatry, 224,
        262, 281, 333
American Association of Suicidology
        (AAS), 86, 113, 142, 225,
        226–227, 290, 307
    Clinician Survivor Task Force, 358
    Web site, 359
    guidelines, 346–347
    Survivor Committee, 352
American Foundation for Suicide
        Prevention (AFSP), 113,
        352, 360
American Indians. See Native Americans
American Medical Association (AMA),
        240
American Medical Informatics
        Association (AMIA), 240
American Psychiatric Association, Ethical
        Code, 278
American Psychological Association,
        Ethics Code, 278
AMIA. See American Medical
        Informatics Association
Amphetamines, 268
Anger, 119, 336, 348
    assessment and, 268
    screening, 312
    survivors, 270, 271
    treatment and, 190, 191, 210, 211,
        218, 247
Annenberg Public Policy Center, 113
Anomic suicide, 47, 48
Anorexia, 92
Antidepressants, 171, 199, 201, 202–204,
        206, 308
    black box warnings, 180, 203
    tricyclic, 186

Antisocial personality. *See* Personality
    characteristics, antisocial
Anxiety, 105, 120, 200, 211, 249, 268
    assessment of, 129
    treatment of, 189, 201, 205–206, 221,
        236, 237
ASAP. *See* Adolescent Suicide Awareness
    Program
ASIST (Applied Suicide Intervention
    Skills Training), 223
Assertiveness, 246
Assessment of risk, 81, 119–167, 283, 356
    214
    AAS recommendations, 226–227*ex*
    biological markers, 158
    of communication, 135, 140–146
    compliance, 151
    confidentiality, 279
    contraindications, 149–151
    of coping skills, 149–151
    demographic risk variables, 158
    developmental trauma, 133
    early detection, 293
    family history, 132
    hospitalization, 165–166
    intake assessment, 262–263
    lethality and intent, 138–139,
        147–148
    liability issues, 260, 261
    malpractice, 269, 274, 275
    mental status evaluation, 134
    multifocal, 293–294
    by paraprofessionals, 158–159
    past attempts, 132
    patient functioning and history, 124
    personality traits, 131–132
    predisposing vulnerabilities, 125–126
    prevention and, 296, 299, 311,
        326–328, 334
    psychometric, 152–157
    of psychopathology, 127–131
    referral context, 122–123
    referral source, 121–122
    screening, 159–164
    significance of, 120
    treatment, linkage with, 203–204,
        205–206, 222, 253, 265
    triggers, 133
Attachment, 249, 257
Attempted suicide, 283, 291, 292
    assessment and, 132–133, 138–139
    empirical evidence and, 86–89, 95–97

epidemiology of, 38–42
inpatient samples, 89
"normal" samples, 89
prevention and, 223, 245, 297
repeat, 98–99, 146, 159, 232, 234,
    235, 251, 252
threateners, 99
treatment and, 170, 186, 198, 206,
    209–210, 212, 214, 225,
    229, 251
Attention deficit disorder, 91, 92, 164
Australia
    hangings in, 34
    postvention developments, 353
Australian Institute of Family Studies,
    326
Autonomy, issues of, 55, 212, 215, 229,
    251, 270
Autopsies, psychological. *See* Psychological
    autopsies
Avoidant personality. *See* Personality
    characteristics, avoidant
Awareness, intervention, and methodology
    (AIM), 302

Baby boomers, cohort effects and, 31
Beck, Aaron T., 59
Behavioral Health Survey (U.S. Air
    Force), 328
Behavioral theory, 56–61
Behavioral therapy, 175
Belgium, postvention developments, 354
Benzodiazepines, 206
Bereavement, 340–343, 349, 357
    evolving perspectives, 340–341
    suicide, 341–343
Beyond the Pleasure Principle (Freud), 53
Big 10 Universities Student Suicide Study,
    329
Binging and purging, 94, 250
Biological markers, 157–158
Bipolar disorder. *See* Depression,
    bipolar disorder
Black adolescents, violent deaths, 24
"Blue Monday," 33
Bolton, Iris, 344, 345
Borderline personality. *See* Personality
    characteristics, borderline
Bowlby, John, 340
Bridge barriers, 309*f*, 310*f*
British Medicines and Healthcare, 179
Bullying, 106–107

Call to Action to Prevent Suicide
(Satcher), 302
Campus, suicide, 33, 329, 330ex
CAMS. See Collaborative Assessment and
Management of Suicidality
Cancellations, 217
Case-control research, 17
Case study method, 84
Causal risk factor, 14
CBT. See Cognitive–behavioral therapy
CDC. See Centers for Disease Control
Celebrity suicides, 112
Centers for Disease Control (CDC), 17,
32, 39, 111, 291, 293, 300, 311,
315, 332, 345
Cerebrospinal fluid (CSF), 65, 86, 158
Child-driven profile, 65
Children's Depression Rating
Scale–Revised, 179
"Children's Mental Health: Developing a
National Action Agenda," 304
Child survivors, 350–351
Chronic risk, 159, 160
Chronic suicide, 65
CISD. See Critical Incident Stress
Debriefing
Clear and imminent danger, hospitalization
and, 224
Clinical care, impact of changes in, 169,
170
Clinical treatment research, 90
Clozapine, 205
Clusters, suicide, 111–113, 291, 292, 293,
311
Cobain, Kurt, 112, 293, 311
suicide crisis, 113f, 114f
Cobain Effect, 311
Cocaine, 233, 234
Cognitive–behavioral therapy (CBT), 175,
176, 179, 184–189, 191–192,
253, 256, 257
model of suicidality, 60f
Cognitive characteristics
assessment and, 136–139, 149
cognitive triad, 185
treatment concerning, 172, 175, 183,
185–189, 210, 247, 248
Cognitive system, evaluation, 136–139
Cognitive theory, 56–61, 187
Cognitive therapy, 57
Cognitive triad, 57
Cohort effects, 31

Collaborative Assessment and
Management of Suicidality
(CAMS), 154, 192–195, 194f
Collaborative Assessment and
Management of Suicidality—
Problem-Solving Treatment
(CAMS–PST), 195
Collaborative empiricism, 184–185
College students
Safeguarding Against Suicide
checklist, 331ex
suicide prevention, 329–332
Columbine High School shootings, 74,
135
Communication. See also Diary/journal
assessment, 140–146
behavioral, 146
campaigns, 323
clinical guidelines, 217
family, 108
skills building, 332
teaching of
in prevention and postvention,
241–244, 314
in treatment, 198, 237–241, 263,
264
Community
role in prevention and postvention,
223–224, 298, 299, 300, 313,
316, 318, 319, 322, 327,
328–329, 333
treatment and, 332
Comorbidity, 23
Comparative rates, 17
Completed suicide, 252
behavior, 90–92
empirical treatment literature, 178
prevention and postvention and,
245, 348
psychopathology, 127, 128
Completed suicide research
case study, 84
ecological methods, 82–83
medical examiner and coroner data,
84–85
postmortem studies, 86
psychological autopsies, 85
social correlate, 83–84
suicide notes, 85–86
Compliance, assessment of, 151–152
Conduct disorder, 91, 103, 104, 128, 129,
170, 272

Confidentiality, 216, 217, 240, 241,
    254, 275
    minors, 279–282
Conflict resolution training, 332
Contagion. *See* Clusters, suicide
Contraindications, 149–151
Control, issues of, 105
    in assessment, 139
    in treatment, 199
Coping strategies
    assessment of, 149–151
    coping card approach, 239–240
    prevention and, 327
Copycat suicides, 292, 311
Coroner, 292, 351
    data, 84–85
    role of, 17, 18, 28, 78
Countertransference, 202, 218–221, 255,
    264, 348
Crime, 334
Crisis
    hotlines, 332
    intervention, 221–228, 281, 306,
        309–312, 325
    prevention and postvention, 333
    response plan, 242
Critical Incident Stress Debriefing
    (CISD), 348
CSF. *See* Cerebrospinal fluid
Cubic model of suicide, 62*f*
Culture, 174–175, 181

Day of the week of suicide, 33
Day treatment, 227–228
DBT. *See* Dialectical behavior therapy
Death, 10 leading causes of (U.S.), by age
    group, 16*f*
Death certificate, 15, 17
Death instinct, 53
Defenses, 209, 220
Demographics, 19–32
    race, 24, 27
    risk variables, 158
Denial, 213–214
Dependability, 262
Depression, 91, 96, 283
    assessment of, 123, 127, 128, 131,
        166, 268, 356
    bipolar disorder, 103, 199, 205
    empirical evidence of, 106
    screening, 312
    substance abuse, 103–104

suicide rates and, 31
theories of suicide and, 57
treatment and, 171, 179, 184, 185,
    189, 198, 201, 202–205, 211,
    232, 247, 254, 284
unipolar, 66, 100, 103, 283
Descriptive epidemiology, focus of, 15
Desensitization effect, 72
Desire for suicide, 51*f*
Developmental context
    adolescent psychology, 69–71
    adolescents, death, and suicide, 71–73
        adolescent perceptions of suicide,
        71–73
Developmental theory, 55
Developmental trauma, 125, 133
Diagnosis, 231, 254, 262, 264, 272, 274,
    275, 312
*Diagnostic and Statistical Manual of
    Mental Disorders, Third
    Edition (DSM–III)*, 105
Dialectical behavior therapy (DBT),
    61, 189–190, 191–192, 194,
    256, 257
Diary/journal, 134, 140, 141, 142, 143*f*,
    144*f*, 145, 185, 233, 241
Diet, 248
Direct causation, 273
Discharge, emergency planning checklist,
    282*t*
Dissociative states, 94
Distal risk factors, 14
Divorce, impact of, 3, 140, 334
Documentation, 265, 283
    legal issues, 261
    malpractice, 274
Drug abuse. *See* Substance use or abuse
Duck Valley Indian Reservation,
    suicide rate and violent deaths
    at, 25
Durkheim, Emile, 46, 47, 48, 82, 83
Duty of care, 259–260
Dysphoria, 116, 134, 186

Eating disorders, 94, 250, 272
Ecological fallacy, 83
Ecological methods of research, 82–83
Economic strain, theory of, 22
Education, professional, 319
Egoistic suicide, 47
E-mail, 238
    strategic use of, 240–241

Emergency Medical Services for Children
    grants, 324
Emergency medical technicians, 351
Emergency room personnel, 351
Emery, P. E., 55
Empirical findings, 56, 72–73
    challenges, 77–81
    descriptive, 80–81
    methodology: review and critique,
        81–90
    statistical approach, 79–80
    suicide statistics
        reliability of, 79–80
        validity of, 78, 82
    survivorship, 338
    workable prevention strategies,
        321
Empirical treatment literature, 175
Empowerment, 189
Entrapment, 59, 61
Epidemiology, 13–42, 293
    attempted suicide, 38–42
    defined, 14
    demographics, 19–32
    historical trends, 21–23
    statistics: constraints and limitations,
        17–19
Epstein, Jesse, 5
Erikson, E., 70
Ethical issues, 81, 265, 270, 275, 278, 280
Ethnicity, 174–175
Etiology, 295, 296, 306
Europe, nonfatal suicide attempts, 42
Exercise, 248
Expert witnesses, 260

Failure, feelings of, 3, 26
Family
    adolescent problems with, 55, 56,
        74, 93, 95, 96, 129, 251,
        273–274, 292
    confidentiality, 279, 281
    denial and, 213–214
    dysfunctional, 51–52, 55–56, 98, 104,
        125, 126–127, 334
    factors, 108–109, 110
    history of, 132, 160–161, 165
    impact of suicide, 342–343
    intake assessment, 262
    malpractice, 269
    prevention, 304
    psychopathology, 108
    role in treatment, 173, 181,
        196–198, 213–215, 256,
        283, 299, 332
    runaways, 107, 148, 164
    suicide history, 110, 111
    as survivors, 348–349
Family psychotherapy, 196–198
Family systems theory, 55–56
Family therapy, 249, 277
Fantasies about suicide, 362
Farber, M. L., 61
Fatalistic suicide, 47, 48
Fear, 50
Federal Steering Group (FSG), 291, 302
Females, leading causes of suicide among,
    36f
Firearms. See Methods
First responders, training, 351–352
5-hydroxyindoleacetic acid (5-HIAA), 65,
    66, 158, 201
Fluoxetine, 179, 180, 204
Focal suicide, 53
Food and Drug Administration, 180, 203,
    204
Forensic suicidology, 9
Forseeability, and liability, 260
Fraud, 276
Frederick, D. J., 57
Freud, Anna, 69, 70
Freud, Sigmund, 52, 53, 181
Friends, role of. See also Peer relationships
    prevention/postvention and, 293,
        311, 312
    treatment and, 198, 229
FSG. See Federal Steering Group
Funding issues, 324

GAF. See Global Assessment of
    Functioning
Gatekeeper training, 223–224, 306,
    312, 323
Gender differences, 26, 27
    females, 26, 35, 42, 72, 85, 95, 112,
        113, 127, 158, 161, 178
    males, 26, 35, 85, 113, 127
    world suicide rates, 27
Generational challenges, clinical alliance,
    215
Genetics and suicide, 65–66, 181, 200, 201
Geography of suicide, 28–30
Georgia, youth suicide prevention plans,
    322

Global Assessment of Functioning (GAF), 164
Goals and Objectives for Action, 302
Goethe, 112
Gothic scene, 313
Grief, 340, 341, 345, 348
Group psychotherapy, 198–199
Group therapy, 235
Guns. *See* Methods

Hall, G. Stanley, 69
Hallucinations, 93, 94, 99, 163, 268, 362
Hanging. *See* Methods
Harris, Eric, 74, 135, 136
Healing, survivors, 343–353
Health care, access to, 332
Health Information and Portability and Accountability Act (HIPAA), 261, 278, 279
Health Resources and Services Administration, 301
Healthy People 2010, 302
Help-seeking, 318, 319
Hendin, H., 49
HIPAA. *See* Health Information and Portability and Accountability Act
Historical trends, study of, 21–23
Holidays, 32
Homelessness, 334
Homosexuality. *See* Sexual issues
Hope, 61
    absence of, 334
Hope Kit, 187–188
Hopelessness, feeling of, 31
    in assessment (prediction), 120, 130, 136, 161, 214
    empirical evidence for, 57, 105, 116
    theories and, 72, 74
    treatment and, 172, 183, 187, 211, 254
Horney, Karen, 54
Hospitalization, 41, 42, 45, 74, 81, 88, 89, 93, 98, 99, 104, 125, 127, 128, 129, 130, 131, 165–166, 169, 170, 172, 205, 218, 221, 224–228, 235, 237, 253, 257, 267, 268, 276, 361
    partial, 227–228
Hostility, 52, 53
Humiliation, 134
Humor, 150, 217, 248

Hypothesis testing, 210–211

IASP. *See* International Association for Suicide Prevention
Ideation, suicide, 267, 321
    assessment of, 120, 123, 136–137, 138, 160, 212, 263, 274
    empirical evidence and, 86–89
    empirical studies of, 99–102, 100, 101, 103, 104, 106–107
    journal drawings, 143*f*, 144*f*
    prevention, 313
    screening, 312
    theories and, 39, 59
    treatment and, 193, 197, 208, 226, 254
Identity crisis, 70
Imitation, 111–113
Imminent risk, 163–164
Impulsive–aggressive type, 132
Impulsivity, 33, 105, 211
    assessment of, 139, 161, 222, 276
    treatment and, 172, 188, 206, 247, 253, 257
Inadequacy, feelings of, 31
Incidence of suicide, 15
Indian Health Service, 301
Individuation, 249
Informed consent, 254, 279
Ingestion. *See* Methods
Insight-oriented therapies, 236
Insomnia, 131, 146, 237, 274
Instinct, 53, 70
Institute of Medicine, of National Academy of Sciences, 353
Institutional survivors, 360–361
Instrumental suicide-related behavior (ISRB), 95
Intake assessment, 262–263
Integrated models, 71
Integrative–eclectic treatment approach, 207–257
    clinical alliance, 215–221
    crisis intervention, 221–228
    family role, 213–215
    ongoing clinical treatment, 248–249
    outpatient treatment, 228–248
    pitfalls, 250–252
    practice recommendations, 252–256
    pragmatic problem-solving orientation, 208–211

termination, 249–250
therapeutic encounter, 211–212
Integrative psychological models, 61–63
Intent, suicidal, 91, 92, 95, 96, 97, 251,
        361
    assessment of, 90–91, 137, 138
    method and, 33
    prevention and, 321
Interactive journaling, 241
International Association for Suicide
        Prevention (IASP), 290
International prevention strategies, 326
International rates, for youth suicides,
        28–29
International Suicide Prevention Trial,
        205
Internet, 238
Interpersonal functioning
    assessment of, 139, 222
    empirical studies of, 95, 97, 104, 116
    theories of, 73–75
    treatment and, 189, 190–191, 234
"Interpersonal-Psychological Theory of
        Attempted and Completed
        Suicide" (Joiner), 50
Interpersonal psychotherapy (IPT),
        190–192
Interpsychic orientation, to suicide,
        48, 49
Intervention. See also Treatment
    developing and testing, 299
    evaluating, 300
    implementing, 300
Intrapsychic orientation, to suicide,
        48, 49
Intuitive models, 43–46
IPT. See Interpersonal psychotherapy
IPT for Adolescents (IPT-A), 191
Isolation, 29, 94, 116, 162, 327
    decreasing, 245–247
    social, 29, 245–247, 327
    survivors, 342
ISRB. See Instrumental suicide-related
        behavior (ISRB)

JASON Foundation, 352
JCAHO. See Joint Commission on the
        Accreditation of Healthcare
        Organizations
Jed Foundation, 329, 332, 352
Jobes, D. A., 63
Joiner, Thomas, 50, 51

Joint Commission on the Accreditation of
        Healthcare Organizations
        (JCAHO), 361

Klebold, Dylan, 74, 135, 136
Kraepelinian model, 193f
Kristin Brooks Hope Center, 352
K–SADS (Kiddie Schedule for Affective
        Disorders and Schizophrenia),
        104
Kubler-Ross, Elizabeth, 340

Law, 271, 272–273, 283, 329
Learning disability, 92
Legal issues, 104, 133, 164, 259–260,
        270–278, 283, 334
Leonard, C. V., 54
Lester, David, 49
Lethality, 42
    access, 244–245, 307–308, 334
    assessment of, 81, 88–89, 147–149,
        164, 223, 251, 252
    decreasing, 237
    means restriction, 323
    prevention and, 321
    ratings, 126, 147, 148
    studies regarding, 50, 95, 97, 98, 104
    treatment and, 225, 232
Lethality of Suicide Attempt Rating Scale,
        148
Liability, 260
Life events, 109
    precipitating, 116, 133
Lifetime prevalence, 15
Likert pain scale, 134f, 154
Linehan, Marsha, 61
Link's National Resource Center, The, 352
Listening, 314
Lithium, 205
Lively, P., 68
Loneliness
    feelings of, 134
    treatment and, 247
Los Angeles Medical Examiner's Office,
        338
Los Angeles Suicide Prevention Center,
        338
Loss, prevention and postvention, 250
LSD, 233, 274

Maine, youth suicide prevention plans,
        322

Males
    firearm suicide rates, *37*
    leading causes of suicide among, *35f*
Malpractice, 242, 261, 264, 269, 277–278,
        281, 283, 285, 361
    litigation, 169
    script, 270–278
Man Against Himself (Menninger), 53
Managed care, malpractice, 271
Managed mental health care, 169, 171,
        173
Mann, J. John, 200
Marijuana, use of, 233, 268, 274, 284
Marital discord, 334
Mastery, 186
Maternal and Child Health Block Grant,
        324
Means restriction, 307–308, 323
    bridge barriers, 309*ex*, 310*ex*
MedGuides, 203, 204
Media
    influence of, 83, 84
    suicide reporting guidelines, 347, 353
Medical examiners, 18, 28, 78, 84–85
Medical records, 78, 278
Medication, 96, 169, 170, 171, 173, 176,
        179, 199–206, 210, 248, 264,
        277, 284
    means restriction, 307–308
Medicines and Healthcare Products
        Regulatory Authority
        (MHRA), 203
Menninger, Karl, 53
Mental disorder–hopelessness type, 132
Mental Health: A Report of the Surgeon
        General, 302
Mental health system (U.S.), transformed,
        goals in, 305–306*ex*
Mental status evaluation, 134–146
    affective system, 134–136
    behavioral activation, 139–140
    behavioral communications, 146
    cognitive system, 136–139
    communications, 140–146
Methods, 33–38
    among females, 36*f*
    among males, 35*f*, 36*f*
    availability and accessibility of, 117,
        162, 223, 244–245, 263, 274,
        323, 334
    carbon monoxide poisoning, 34, 291,
        292, 307

    choosing, 34
    drug ingestion, 35, 42
    explosives, 47, 113
    firearms, 30, 33, 35, 36, 37*t*, 162, 274
    gas explosion, 269
    guns, 4, 37, 38, 44, 52, 112, 114, 147,
        245, 336
    hanging, 34, 35, 46, 47, 91, 114, 120,
        149, 277, 283, 284, 357, 362
    jumping from heights, 4, 308
    means restriction, 307–308
    overdose, 34, 96, 97, 98, 110, 114,
        125, 126, 129, 130, 131, 147,
        148, 198, 212, 213, 214, 228,
        234, 235, 308, 361
    poisoning, 35, 321
    suffocation, 35, 36
    wrist slashing, 34, 44, 231, 252
MHRA. *See* Medicines and Healthcare
        Products Regulatory Authority
Mindfulness, 61, 189
Minnesota Multiphasic Personality
        Inventory (MMPI), 152, 153
Minority. *See* Race
Minors, confidentiality, 279–282
Mirroring, 208
MMPI. *See* Minnesota Multiphasic
        Personality Inventory
Modeling, 111–113
Molecular genetics research, 109
Mondays, suicide rates, 33
Monitoring suicidality, 254–255
Monroe, Marilyn, 112
Mood, 103, 127, 128, 129, 136, 164, 200,
        312
Mood spectrum disorders, treatment of,
        202–205
Mourning, 340, 351
Mourning and Melancholia (Freud), 52
Murray, Henry, 63
Music, 71, 84
    heavy metal, 162, 292

NA. *See* Narcotics Anonymous
Narcissistic–perfectionist type, 131–132
Narcotics Anonymous (NA), 248
National Academy of Sciences/Institute of
        Medicine (NAS/IOM), 291
National Ambulatory Medical Care
        Survey, 201, 202
National Association of Social Workers,
        Code of Ethics, 278

National Center for Health Statistics
(NCHS), 18, 23
National Institutes of Health (NIH), 301
National Institute of Mental Health
(NIMH), 78, 86, 152, 180
National Medical Expenditure Survey,
170, 171
National Mental Health Association,
329
National Registry of Effective Programs
(NREP), 326
National Strategy for Suicide Prevention,
41, 42
    aims, 303*ex*
    goals, 303*ex*
National Strategy for Suicide Prevention:
    Goals and Objective for
    Action, 303, 338
National Suicide Prevention Conference
    (1988), 301–302
National Suicide Prevention Technical
    Resource Center, 291
National Violent Death Reporting System
    (NVDRS), 15, 17, 18
National Youth Suicide Prevention
    Strategy, 326
Native Americans, 29
    attempted suicides, 38
    suicide rates, 24, 25
NCHS. *See* National Center of Health
    Statistics
Negligence, 264, 269, 277
    four elements of proof (4D), 260
Neurobiological theories, of suicide,
    65–66
Neurocognitive development, 71
Neurotransmitters, 65, 200
New Mexico, suicide rates, 30*ex*
New Zealand, hangings in, 34
NIH. *See* National Institutes of Health
NIMH. *See* National Institute of Mental
    Health
Nirvana, 293
Nomenclature, 86, 87*f*
Noncompliance, 212, 213, 214, 224, 269
    documenting, 262
Nondirective supportive therapy (NST),
    176
Nonfatal suicide behaviors
    empirical treatment literature, 178
    YRBS survey, 39, 40, 41
Norway, postvention developments, 354

No-suicide agreements and contracts, 152,
    241–244
Notes, suicide, 85–86, 163, 357
NREP. *See* National Registry of Effective
    Programs
NST. *See* Nondirective supportive therapy
NVDRS. *See* National Violent Death
    Reporting System

OASSIS. *See* Organization for
    Attempters and Survivors
    of Suicide in Interfaith
    Services
Obesity, 267
Obsessive–compulsive disorder, 203
Office of the Surgeon General, 291, 301
Oregon
    surveillance of nonfatal suicidal
        behaviors, 26*n*
    youth suicide prevention plans, 322*ex*
Organization for Attempters and
    Survivors of Suicide in
    Interfaith Services (OASSIS),
    352
Outpatient treatment, 228–230
Overlap model, 66, 67*f*

Pain
    psychological, 62, 63, 100, 126, 134,
        154, 172, 209
    theories and, 45, 59
    treatment and, 232
Panic, 164, 205
Paranoia, 268
Paraprofessionals, role of, 158–159
Parasuicide, 95, 189
Parent
    assessment and, 125, 126, 127
    confidentiality, 279, 280
    education, 319–320
    malpractice issues, 269, 270–271, 272,
        277
    noncompliance, 214
    prevention/postvention and, 324
    relationship to adolescent, 93–94, 96,
        99, 107
    suicide, 350
    survivors, 336
    treatment and, 170, 171, 191, 197,
        198, 200, 229, 256, 264, 277,
        284
Parent-driven profile, 56

Passivity, 218
Pathogenesis, 295
PCP, 233
Pearl Jam, 84
Pediatric Drugs Advisory Committee, 203
Peer relationships, 92
    assessment of, 127, 251
    empirical findings and, 110
    prevention/postvention and, 314, 321, 324
    theories concerning, 49–50, 73, 74
    treatment and, 173, 181, 198, 229, 247
Perfectionism, feelings of, 105
Period effects, 27
Personal fable, 211
Personality characteristics, 131–132
    antisocial, 91, 128, 161
    avoidant, 166
    borderline, 61, 93, 100, 105, 128, 161, 186, 189, 190, 199, 206
Perturbation
    decreasing, 237
    feelings of, 62, 63
Pharmacotherapies, 128
Physical illness, 334
Piaget, Jean, 70
Pleasure, 186
Poisons. See Methods
Police officers, 351, 352
Population density, 29
    suicide rates and, 30t
Postmortem findings, 66, 86
Posttraumatic loss debriefing, 347–348
Posttraumatic stress, treatment of, 189, 205
Postvention, 8, 312, 323, 335–363
    groups and systems, 345–348
    school-based, 320
Poverty, 334
Precursors, 50
Prediction. See Assessment of risk
Pregnancies, 317
President's New Freedom Commission on Mental Health, 304
Press, 62, 63
Prevalence, 15
Prevention, 8, 241–244, 244–245, 289–334
    approaches, 306–321

    community, 307–308
    crisis hotlines, 309–312
    school-based, 312–321, 324–326
    assessment and, 221–224
    assumptions about, 297ex
    bridge barriers, 309ex, 310ex
    conceptual model of strategies, 295ex
    decision points, 298ex
    developments in, 290–293
    direct, 333
    epidemiological definitions, 293, 294ex
    federal and public health initiatives, 300–304
    means restriction, 307–308, 323
    models, 294–296
    practice considerations, 321
    primary, 293, 294, 320, 326, 333
    public health approach, 298–300
    secondary, 293, 294
    suicidal behaviors and models, 296–297
    tertiary, 293, 294
    theory, 293–294
    unworkable strategies, 332
    workable strategies, 321–332
Prevention of Suicide: Guidelines for the Formulation and Implementation of National Strategies (UN/WHO), 301
Primary prevention, 293, 294, 320, 326, 333
Prinze, Freddie, 112
Privacy, 240
Problem solving, 149–150, 191
    approaches, 183–184
    deficits in, 108, 109, 172, 183, 222, 224
    exploration phase, 208
    suicide as, 109
    training in, 195, 196, 210, 246, 314, 317
Professional education, 319
Professional Military Education (PME) curricula, 327
"Progression/regression ratio," 55
Protective factors, 115, 136, 299, 306
Proximal risk factors, 14
Proximate causation, 273
Psychoanalysis, 182
Psychoanalytically oriented theory, 52–55

Psychodynamic (or insight-oriented) therapies, 175
Psychodynamic psychotherapy, 181–183
Psychological autopsies, 85, 91t, 102, 127, 349, 361
Psychological theories, of suicide, 51–64
Psychologist, 6
    malpractice issues, 272
    role of, 355
Psychometric risk assessment, 152–157
    qualitative, 154–156
    quantitative, 152–154
Psychopathology, 314
    as predisposing factor, 127–131
    theories and, 70
Psychopharmaceuticals, clinical use of, 202–206
    anxiety disorders, 205–206
    bipolar disorders, 205
    mood spectrum disorders, 202–205
    personality disorders, 206
    psychotic disorders, 205
Psychopharmacologic Drugs Advisory Committee, 203
Psychopharmacology, 173, 248
    general considerations, 199–202
Psychotherapist
    prevention and, 327
    role of, 271
    survivorship issues, 357
Psychotherapy, 170–171, 173, 174, 175, 177, 314
    family, 196–198, 229
    group, 198–199, 233
    individual, 181–190, 233, 248–249
    interpersonal, 190–192
    outpatient, 228–230
    survivors, 348–349
Psychotic disorders, 205
Psychotropic medications, 201
Public awareness, 291, 292
Public health, 293
Public Health Service Regional Health Administrators, 301–302

QPR. See Question, Persuade, and Refer
Qualitative risk assessment, 154–156
Quantitative risk assessment, 152–154
Question, Persuade, and Refer (QPR), 223

Race, prevalence by, 24, 27, 174–175

Black, 24, 27, 37, 72, 158, 326
    minorities, 161
    White, 24, 27, 35, 37, 326
Rage, feelings of, 31, 52, 55, 74, 105, 135
    assessment of, 139, 149, 213, 214, 273
    treatment and, 198
Randomized clinical trials (RCTs), 177, 178, 257
Rate of suicide, 15
RCA. See Root cause analysis
RCTs. See Randomized clinical trials
Reasonable care, 260
Reasons for Living (RFL) Inventory, 150, 153ex
Reciprocal profile, 56
"Reconnecting Youth" program, 324, 325
Record keeping, 265
    legal issues, 261
    malpractice, 273, 274
Referral issues, 121–124
    context, 122–123
    source, 121–122
Rehearsal behaviors, 97
Relapse prevention task (RPT), 188
Relatedness, 257
Relationship. See Alliance, therapeutic
Relative cohort size, 31
Religion, as support, 73, 174–175, 306
Reporting of death statistics, 19
Research. See Empirical findings
Resistance, 74, 220
Resources
    availability and accessibility of, 149, 246
    identifying, 319
Richman, Joseph, 55
Rigidity, 109, 110, 128, 197, 222
Risk. See also Prevention; Treatment
    assessment of, 124–133, 356
    early detection, 319
Risk factors, 102–117
    behavior, 106–107
    cognitive strategies, 109–110
    common themes, 115–117
    family and parental characteristics, 107–109
    imitation and suggestibility, 110–111
    means of death, 113–115
    protective factors, 115
    psychiatric diagnoses, 103–106
    psychopathology and personality characteristics, 102–103

sexual orientation, 106
stress, 109
suicide clusters and media influence,
111–113
types of, 14
Rock music videos, 84
Rogers, J. R., 63, 64
Root cause analysis (RCA), 361,
362–363
Rorschach Inkblot Test, 152
RPT. *See* Relapse prevention task
Rudd, M. D., 57, 188
Runaways, 107, 148, 162, 164, 274
RY. *See* Reconnecting Youth program

Safe and Drug-Free Schools and
Communities Act, 324
Safety contracts, 172, 241–244
Satanic cults, 313
Satcher, David, 302, 304, 338
SAVE. *See* Suicide Awareness Voices of
Education
Scale for Suicide Ideation, 153*ex*
Scapegoating, 108
Schizoaffective disorder, 186
Schizophrenia, 99, 125, 199, 200, 205
School
alienation, 106
awareness, 306
School-based prevention/postvention,
312–321, 324–326, 346
School-Based Suicide Prevention Guide,
325
School-based suicide prevention plan,
components, 318*ex*,
319–320
"School Health Guidelines to Prevent
Unintentional Injuries and
Violence" (CDC), 315,
316*ex*
Screening, 80, 159–164
programs, 312
risk assessment categorization,
159–160
severity of risk, 160–164
imminent risk, 163–164
Level 1 risk, 160–161
Level 2 risk, 161–162
Level 3 risk, 162–163
Season of suicide, 33
Seattle Crisis Center, 311
Secondary prevention, 293, 294

Secretary's Task Force on Youth Suicide,
290, 300–301
Secret sharing, 314
Selective serotonin reuptake inhibitors
(SSRIs), 96, 120, 179, 199,
201, 203, 204, 205, 206, 264
Self-care, 196
Self-control
feelings of, 229, 234, 248
training, 186
Self-esteem, 150, 162, 199, 249, 254
Self-harm, protection from, 237
Self-mutilation, 92–94, 232, 268
Self-preservation instincts, 306
Sensitivity, 79*n*
Separation, feelings of, 196, 249, 250
September 11 terrorist attacks (U.S.), 70
Serotonin, 66
Sexual issues, 92, 93, 94, 148, 229,
232–233, 234, 272, 334
abuse, 278
fantasies, 161
homosexuality, 106, 235, 355, 356
Shame, 134
Shneidman, Edwin, 62, 63
Shoplifting, 119, 274
Signs of Suicide (SOS), 312, 326
Sleep regulation, 248
Slovenia, postvention developments,
354–355
Smith, K., 54
SNAP. *See* Successful Negotiation/Acting
Positively
Social correlate approaches, 83–84
Social isolation, 29, 327
decreasing, 245–247
Social issues, treatment and, 187, 189, 191
Social-psychological approaches, to suicide,
48–50
Social-skills training, 246–247
Sociocultural influences, prevalence rates
and, 28–30
Socioeconomic status, 31–32
Sociological theories, of suicide, 46–48
Sorrows of Young Werther, The (Goethe),
112
SOS. *See* Signs of Suicide
Specificity, 79*n*
Spiritual considerations, 173
SSF. *See* Suicide Status Form
SSF reasons for living vs. reasons for dying,
101*t*

SSRIs. *See* Selective serotonin reuptake inhibitors
Stabbing Westward, 84
Standard of care, 260, 262
 breaches in, 267–269, 273–278, 285
 commonly alleged failures in meeting of, 265–267t
State suicide prevention plans, 322–324
Statistics
 adolescent suicide, 19–32
 constraints and limitations, 17–19
Stigmatization, 337, 338, 342, 363
Stress, 31, 116, 133. *See also* Life events
 management, 314, 327
 treatment strategies and, 199, 209
Stress-diathesis model of suicide, 200
Sturm and Drang, 69
Subcultures, 49, 50, 74
Substance Abuse and Mental Health Services Administration (SAMHSA), 291, 301
Substance Abuse Prevention and Treatment Block Grant, 324
Substance use or abuse, 35, 49, 92, 94, 103–104, 120, 128, 129, 162, 164, 170, 200, 268, 272, 274, 283, 291, 299
 assessment and, 88, 251
 impact on suicide, 334
 prevention and, 314, 327
 screening, 312
 treatment and, 233, 234, 248
Successful Negotiation/Acting Positively (SNAP), 178
Suicidal behaviors, general model of, 68f
Suicidal careers, 48
Suicidal cube, 62
Suicidality
 cognitive–behavioral approach to, 57–59
 Cognitive–Behavioral Therapy model of, 60
 phenomenological model of, 64f
Suicide. *See also* Adolescent suicide
 altruistic, 47
 anomic, 47
 bereavement, 341–343
 constructive pathways leading to, 64f
 egoistic, 47
 fatalistic, 47
 incidence of, 15

phenomenology of, 172
rate of, 15
Suicide: A Study in Sociology (Durkheim), 47
Suicide and Life-Threatening Behavior, 86, 90
Suicide attempting behaviors, 38–42
Suicide Awareness Voices of Education (SAVE), 352
Suicide notes, 54, 78, 85–86, 163, 357
Suicide pacts, 4, 18, 291, 292, 293, 313
Suicide Prevention Advocacy Network (SPAN USA), 113, 290, 301, 338, 352
Suicide Prevention Research Center, 291
Suicide rates
 by age, 1950–2000, 21f
 age and, 26–28
 ages 10–24, 1994–1995 vs. 1999–2000, 23f
 ages 15–24, 1900–2000, 20f
 ages 15–19 vs. 20–24, 1980–2000, 21f
 at Duck Valley Indian Reservation, 25
 firearms, males, 37t
 gender, 26
 by gender and race, 1960-2000, 24t
 geography and sociocultural influences, 28–30
 socioeconomic status, 31–32
 U.S., ages 15–19, 1994–1998, 29f
 world, ages 15–24, by gender and male–female ratio, 27t
Suicide Status Form (SSF), 154, 155f, 192
 coding categories and example responses, 156–157t
Suicide watch, 262
Suicidology, 147, 290, 316, 336
 clinical, 172, 180
 survivor movement, 338–339, 353, 354
 training in, 6–7
Support. *See* Resources
Support groups, 350, 360
Supportive therapy, 175
Surveillance, 298, 328
Survivor movement, 344
 chronology, 339ex
Survivors, 270–271, 272–273, 282, 323, 335–363
 activism, 344–345, 352–353

child, 350–351
  helping, 345–352
  history of survivorship, 337–339
  identifying, 343–345
  institutional, 360–361
  international perspective, 353–355
  social processes, 342
  support groups, 350

Task Force for Child Survival and
        Development, 346
Telephone
  hotline services, 309–312
  treatment use of, 238, 239, 253
Temporal linkages, 236–237
Termination, 146, 217, 249–250, 265
Tertiary prevention, 293, 294
Theories of suicide, 43–75
  neurobiological and genetic,
        65–66
  overview of, 46
  psychological, 51–64
    cognitive–behavioral, 56–61
    developmental, 55
    family systems, 55–56
    integrative, 61–63
    psychoanalytically oriented,
        52–55
  social–psychological, 48–50
  sociological, 46–48
  summary of, 66–67
Theory of economic strain, 22
Therapeutic contracts, 241–244
Therapist, 285
  assessment by, 208–211
  availability and accessibility of,
        236, 237–239, 244, 253,
        264, 284
  duty of care, 259–260
  encounter, 211–213
  malpractice, 270–278
  reactions to suicide, 359ex
  role in prevention/postvention,
        289, 320
  role in treatment, 228–230, 257,
        263–165
  standard of care, 260, 262
  surviving suicide of, 349–350
  survivors and, 348–349, 357–360
  termination, 249–250
Threateners, 99
"Tower of Babel Nomenclature," 86

TPH gene. See Tryptophan hydroxylase
        (TPH) gene
Transference, 182, 202, 218, 220, 236
Trauma, developmental, 125, 133
Treating Suicidal Behavior: An Effective
        Time-Limited Approach (Rudd
        et al.), 57, 188
Treatment, 169–206, 257, 263, 275, 276,
        282
  confidentiality, 280
  culture, race, ethnicity, and religion,
        174–175
  duration, 255
  empirical literature, 175–180
  integrative–eclectic approach,
        207–257
  major approaches, 180–206
  outcome monitoring, 255–256
  overview, 169–174
  plan for, 230–235
  providing, 263–265, 267–269
  temporal linkages, 236–237
Treatment for Adolescents with Depression
        Study (TADS), 179, 180
Trends in youth suicide. See Epidemiology
Tryptophan hydroxylase (TPH) gene, 65

Underachievement, issues of, 106, 334
Unipolar depression. See Depression,
        unipolar
United States, suicide rates, ages 15–19,
        1994–1998, 29
Universal, indicated, and selected
        interventions, 299
Universal programs, 325ex
Urban-rural differences, 29–30
U. S. Air Force Suicide Prevention
        Program, 326–329
U. S. Department of Education, 32
U. S. Department of Health and Human
        Services, 13, 290, 301
U. S. Department of Justice, 32
USSR (former), suicide rates, 29
Utah, suicide prevention in, 323

Validation, 189
Validity of suicide statistics. See Empirical
        findings
Vandalism, 272
Variable risk factor, 14
Violence, prevention/postvention and,
        317, 334

Violent deaths
    Native Americans, 24, 25
    race and, 24, 25
Vulnerability, 124

Wade, N. L., 54
Wagner, B. M., 56
Washington, youth suicide prevention
       plans, 322, 323*ex*
Werther Effect, 83, 112
Weyrauch, Elsie, 338
Weyrauch, Jerry, 338
White House Conference on Mental
       Health (1999), 303
WHO. *See* World Health Organization

Williams, Mark, 59, 60–61
World Health Organization (WHO),
    290
World Psychiatric Association (WPA),
    290
World Suicide Prevention Day, 290
WPA. *See* World Psychiatric Association

Yellow Ribbon Campaign, 352
Youth Risk Behavior Survey (YRBS),
    15, 296
    suicide attempting behaviors, 39*f*,
      40*f*, 41*f*

Zilboorg, Gregory, 53

ABOUT THE AUTHORS

Alan L. Berman, PhD, is executive director of the American Association of Suicidology (AAS), a past president of the AAS, and a recipient, as was Dr. Jobes, of the AAS's Shneidman Award (for Outstanding Contributions in Research in Suicidology). He formerly was a tenured, full professor (1969–1991) at the American University and director (1991–1995) of the National Center for the Study and Prevention of Suicide at the Washington School of Psychiatry.

He has published over 100 professional articles and book chapters and 7 books on suicidology. A fellow of the American Psychological Association and the International Academy of Suicide Research, Dr. Berman, an American Board of Professional Psychology diplomate, maintains a practice of psychotherapy and forensic consultation in Washington, DC.

David A. Jobes, PhD, is professor of psychology at Catholic University of America and codirector of training of the PhD clinical psychology program. With expertise in clinical suicidology, Dr. Jobes publishes and trains extensively. He consults to the U.S. Air Force Suicide Prevention Program and the Washington, DC, VA Medical Center. Dr. Jobes is an associate editor (Treatment) of the journal *Suicide and Life-Threatening Behavior* and was a past president, treasurer, and board member of the American Association of Suicidology. As a board-certified clinical psychologist (American Board of Professional Psychology), Dr. Jobes has a private clinical and forensic practice at the Washington Psychological Center.

Morton M. Silverman, MD, is senior advisor to the National Suicide Prevention Resource Center. Dr. Silverman was the first associate administrator for Prevention in the Alcohol, Drug Abuse, and Mental Health

Administration (1985–1987). From 1987 to 2002, he was an associate professor of psychiatry and director of the Student Counseling and Resource Service at the University of Chicago, where he currently is a clinical associate professor of psychiatry. Since 1996, he has been the editor-in-chief of *Suicide and Life-Threatening Behavior*. A distinguished fellow of the American Psychological Association, he has coauthored or authored more than 40 professional articles and chapters and 4 books related to suicidology.